THE DYNAMICS
OF DIPLOMACY

THE DYNAMICS

OF DIPLOMACY

Jean-Robert Leguey-Feilleux

Viva Books

New Delhi | Mumbai | Chennai | Kolkata | Bangalore | Hyderabad | Kochi | Guwahati

First Indian Edition 2010

VIVA BOOKS PRIVATE LIMITED

- 4737/23 Ansari Road, Daryaganj, New Delhi 110 002
  E-mail: vivadelhi@vivagroupindia.net, Tel. 42242200

- Plot No. 76, Service Industries, Shirvane, Sector 1, Nerul, Navi Mumbai 400 706
  E-mail: vivamumbai@vivagroupindia.net, Tel. 27721273, 27721274

- Jamals Fazal Chambers, 26 Greams Road, Chennai 600 006
  E-mail: vivachennai@vivagroupindia.net, Tel. 28290304, 28294241

- B-103, Jindal Towers, 21/1A/3 Darga Road, Kolkata 700 017
  E-mail: vivakolkata@vivagroupindia.net, Tel. 22836381, 22816713

- 7, Sovereign Park Apartments, 56-58, K. R. Road, Basavanagudi, Bangalore 560 004
  E-mail: vivabangalore@vivagroupindia.net, Tel. 26607409, 26607410

- 101-102 Mughal Marc Aptt., 3-4-637 to 641, Narayanguda, Hyderabad 500 029
  E-mail: vivahyderabad@vivagroupindia.net, Tel. 27564481, 27564482

- First Floor, Beevi Towers, SRM Road, Kaloor, Kochi 682 018, Kerala
  E-mail: vivakochi@vivagroupindia.net, Tel: 0484-2403055, 2403056

- 232, GNB Road, Beside UCO Bank, Silpukhuri, Guwahati 781 003
  E-mail: vivaguwahati@vivagroupindia.net, Tel: 0361-2666386

Published by arrangement with

Lynne Rienner Publishers Inc.
1800 30th Street, Boulder,
Colorado 80301
USA

ISBN 978-81-309-1218-9

Published by Vinod Vasishtha for Viva Books Private Limited, 4737/23, Ansari Road, New Delhi - 110 002. Printed and bound by Anand Sons, Delhi - 110 092.

To the memory of my mother

To my wife, Virginia

To my children,
Michèle
Monique and Joe
Suzanne
Christy and Ken

Contents

Tables

Acknowledgments

I owe so much to my wife, Virginia. I thank her particularly for her patience and understanding as I worked on this book. I am grateful for the research grant received from St. Louis University (SLU) and for the generous help of my research assistant, Patrick Lynd. I want to express my gratitude to Timothy J. Lomperis, who read parts of the manuscript; I am thankful for his wise suggestions and enthusiastic encouragement. And I gratefully acknowledge the gracious and always timely assistance of Phyllis Forchee, Political Science Department secretary, and John R. Montre, SLU librarian.

—*Jean-Robert Leguey-Feilleux*

1 Introduction

This book analyzes the changing character of diplomacy—the changing ways in which states and other international actors communicate, negotiate, and otherwise interact. The world has undergone dramatic change, and some traditional forms of diplomacy are losing their prominence. Our complex global society has turned to new means of interaction to address international problems, and some scholars argue that diplomacy, a critical instrument of international relations, has been discarded, subverted, or supplanted. Hans Morgenthau, a prominent political scientist, repeated for more than thirty years that "diplomacy has lost its vitality, and its functions have withered away to such an extent as is without precedent in the history of the modern state system."[1] Is it truly the end of diplomacy? But what is diplomacy?

■ The Meaning of Diplomacy as an Issue

"Diplomacy" is a term that is often used rather loosely. A number of books on "the diplomacy" of certain countries are really about their foreign policy or, more generally, the course of their foreign relations.[2] Other works, on the subject of *diplomatic history,* are really about the history of foreign relations.[3] And then there are books on the practice of diplomacy—that is, diplomacy as a *method* of political interaction at the international level—and the techniques used to carry out political relations across international boundaries (e.g., representation and communication). This is the sense in which "diplomacy" will be used here.[4]

At the core of the concept of diplomacy is the idea of communicating, interacting, maintaining contact, and negotiating with states and other international actors. Diplomacy, too, is an institution.[5] Many of its practices, perhaps initially the result of expediency or simple practicality, were institutionalized

1

over the years. and became part of customary international law. They were codified in the 1961 Vienna Convention on Diplomatic Relations[6] and in the 1963 Vienna Convention on Consular Relations.[7]

Diplomacy also implies a mode of behavior, a way of doing business, a certain professional style. Diplomats need to act with tact and circumspection in approaching foreign governments; they deal with matters of state that are frequently delicate. Discretion is essential. They need to work with officials who frequently have enormous egos, an acute sense of their importance, and exaggerated expectations of deference.[8]

Finesse is required to handle complex international issues in a foreign cultural environment, using a different language and dealing with very different modes of behavior. One needs to be cautious and highly perceptive, as misunderstandings can so easily arise and complicate further interaction.[9] By analogy, this type of behavior is occasionally called "diplomatic" when encountered in other walks of life or professions ("The matter was handled so diplomatically!"). As international relations change, "diplomacy" is used to refer to a larger variety of interactions, such as the international dialogue or negotiations carried out by heads of state in summit meetings (see Chapter 10).

The subject matter of diplomacy, too, has vastly expanded. For centuries, diplomacy was primarily concerned with matters of war and peace—the use of force—encompassing high politics and strategic interests. These matters are of course still prominent, and now include questions of international security, but a vast variety of other matters have been added to the diplomatic agenda, pertaining to the economy, technology, scientific developments, education, the arts, law, and so much more. There is virtually no aspect of life in society that has not, at one time or another, been on the diplomatic agenda. Interdependence and globalization have greatly contributed to this development. Many issues that once were primarily domestic, such as human rights, are now of international concern and of relevance to diplomacy.[10]

Diplomats need to be versatile; but in highly technical transactions (e.g., dealing with scientific issues or arms control), experts who are not members of the foreign service of their government must be brought in. The roles assigned to them secure their diplomatic status (even when their skills are less than diplomatic; but then again, the skills of diplomats have always varied considerably). It may also be noted that international relations are no longer the exclusive preserve of foreign ministries. A large variety of government departments are involved in foreign relations,[11] even to the point of sending their own personnel on diplomatic missions—a matter that complicates the task of coordinating a nation's foreign relations. Diplomacy is thus increasingly carried out by a variety of people who are not foreign service officers.[12] Though many nations, including the United States, have long resorted to political appointments (i.e., outside the foreign service career) in selecting their ambassadors—people who need to acquire diplomatic proficiency on the job—they are not necessarily unprepared for their assignments (although some are). Many have extensive international experience and knowledge of international affairs.[13]

A number of contemporary participants in diplomacy are not even "agents" or "intermediaries" in the traditional diplomatic sense of carrying out orders and implementing policy. Heads of state engage in negotiations and other forms of diplomacy in summit meetings. Granted, they *represent* their states; but they are chief decisionmakers. Similarly, directors of international agencies (e.g., the UN Development Programme [UNDP]), who are chief executive officers and top administrators, practice diplomacy in the fulfillment of their mandates. All of these are rather different from the typical diplomatic representative, although we must remember that a typical ambassador needs administrative skill, having an embassy to run.[14] Career diplomats are still important, but contemporary diplomacy is now carried out by many diverse people. Their work needs to be included in the concept of diplomacy. They are instruments in the conduct of international relations; they are the essential means of international transactions of the most diverse nature.

The functions served by diplomacy are expanding, and this, too, helps to explain the broadening of the concept.[15] Aside from representation, communication, negotiation, observation of the political situation abroad, and reporting (functions to be discussed in Chapter 7), diplomatic personnel in our age of mass communication must engage in a good deal of public relations. On the other hand, a greater portion of international relations is bureaucratized, which creates a greater amount of administrative work for members of diplomatic missions. Embassies must serve the needs of an expanding contingent of their fellow citizens traveling and working abroad. There is also a growing amount of legal work in the interpretation and application of international regulations, the processing of legal claims, and much more. The diplomatic process in international organizations has created even more functions to be served by diplomats. Some of these functions are somewhat unconventional, such as serving in non-national capacities in certain international offices, as will be seen later.[16] All of these developments have brought diplomacy far from the confines of traditional embassies in national capitals. Diplomacy retains many of its basic characteristics, but it has undergone significant changes.

Resort to different forms of diplomacy has contributed to the expansion of diplomatic functions. As the global environment has changed, new forms of interaction have evolved. The resident embassy in a national capital remains a very important element in the conduct of diplomacy, although its mission and structure are changing (see Chapter 7). Multilateral diplomacy is now an essential tool of international affairs;[17] increasing numbers of large international conferences and elaborate international organizations have required the opening of permanent delegations at the sites of organization—a new form of resident representation (see Chapter 8).

Multilateral diplomacy entails a variety of new techniques: the formation of national blocs, diplomatic caucusing, debating, elaborate decisionmaking processes, extensive committee work, and the use of parliamentary procedures. This is a very different diplomatic environment, generating greater interaction and new modes and styles of diplomatic work (see Chapters 8–10).[18] International actors, including national governments, accept all of this as diplomacy. They handle it as part and parcel of their diplomatic routine: the boundaries of the concept of diplomacy are thus expanding—hardly surprising given the changing nature of our global system and the need to address new problems. Under the pressure of necessity, international actors devise new ways of working together, supplementing or modifying older diplomatic techniques. Diplomacy is likely to continue evolving, with its essential characteristics probably retained, but other modes of interaction are coming into use.

The fact that states are no longer the only actors in the international political process is diversifying diplomacy and broadening the concept. International organizations are now significant participants in international relations. Their agents are diplomats who work with the representatives of nation-states and other organizations. The Secretary-General of the United Nations and his envoys are examples of this new category of diplomats.[19] They do not serve the interests of any particular nation-state; they are international public servants subject only to their own organization's chain of command. Some engage in specialized lines of work—for example, many representatives of the World Bank are financial professionals, and many agents of the World Health Organization are physicians or public health administrators. It is interesting to note that the directors of these organizations are chief executive officers who participate in a considerable amount of diplomatic work.

The expanding realm of transnational relations is adding a new layer of diplomacy to international transactions.[20] The international actors involved are primarily nongovernmental organizations (NGOs) and multinational corporations (MNCs), also called transnational corporations. Some NGOs, such as the International Committee of the Red Cross (ICRC), and a number of environmental organizations are extremely active in international relations. They want to influence the decisions of other international actors, and thus send representatives of their own to engage those actors (see Chapter 5).

Recently, a number of international organizations (the Office of the UN High Commissioner for Refugees [UNHCR], the World Health Organization [WHO], the UN Children's Fund [UNICEF]) have found it effective to work with NGOs to implement some of their programs without having to work through governmental bureaucracies (and thus avoid red tape and corruption). NGO representatives are invited to participate in project planning, supervision of project implementation in the field, and various forms of consultation and cooperative missions. This amounts to significant institutional interaction. Some governments work with NGOs in similar fashion.[21]

Many multinational corporations seek to influence the governments of the countries in which they operate in order to obtain a variety of concessions (tax breaks, permissive legislation, exemptions from sundry environmental or other restrictions) to enhance their earning capacity, and to this end use some of their officers to maintain contact with government officials who may serve their purposes. Some MNC agents are posted in national capitals just for this purpose. In some countries, these MNC agents compete with the diplomatic representation of foreign governments (e.g., to obtain multimillion-dollar contracts—defense procurement is a huge field for this kind of activity). These can be very high-stakes negotiations.[22]

Thus the concept of diplomacy is now much broader. Later chapters will examine how this expansion is affecting international relations. But it must be understood here that it is the international actors themselves—the entities involved in international politics—that have caused this definitional broadening, by accepting the new modes of interaction as diplomacy. The advantages and limitations of these new modes will be discussed later in this volume.[23]

■ Negotiation

Negotiation is widely regarded as one of the major functions of diplomacy. In fact, diplomacy is frequently equated with negotiation.[24] It must be observed, however, that many diplomats are rarely called upon to negotiate anything; their work (e.g., in an embassy) simply entails other duties.[25] Diplomacy serves a large variety of functions, and negotiation, albeit important, is only one of them. It is nonetheless true that global society today is generating an increasingly large volume of negotiation, in part the result of complex interdependence. Each form of diplomacy examined in Part 2 of this volume brings its own method to the process, and must be studied separately. A substantial amount of negotiation is multilateral, taking place within a growing number of international conferences and international organizations (see Chapters 8 and 9). Resident missions in national capitals are now frequently asked to take up with their host governments certain aspects of multilateral negotiations presently conducted elsewhere. For example, through its embassy in a particular country, a government may seek to obtain greater cooperation from that state's representative who is currently involved in multilateral negotiations in a UN conference (i.e., the embassy will try to persuade the host government to issue instructions to its representative to be more cooperative). This embassy's intervention with the foreign government supplements the negotiations taking place in the multilateral forum. This is called "parallel diplomacy."

Some of these negotiations are used to conclude an increasingly larger number of treaties.[26] An even more extensive volume of negotiations, although less structured, takes place in the day-to-day decisionmaking process of the many organizations involved in today's international relations (the Food and Agriculture Organization [FAO], the International Labour Organization [ILO], the UN Security Council, and the North Atlantic Treaty Organization [NATO], to mention a few). State interaction aimed at coordinating their efforts, or seeking joint activities, is in fact negotiation of a sort, taking the form of consultation.[27]

The process of negotiation[28] is made more elaborate by the number of participants, their diverse negotiating styles,[29] and the complexity of the issues facing global society: for example, the Law of the Sea Conference took nine years to produce its new treaty.[30] And, as interdependence increases, more diverse issues are brought to the international agenda. Preparation for formal negotiations is often as important as the official phase itself.[31] For negotiations among a very large number of states, a preparatory committee (often made up of all invitees) is frequently given the task of laying the groundwork over a period of several years, which means that the negotiations actually start long before the official process. Furthermore, the participants engage in side-negotiations to harmonize regional or "bloc" interests, and pairs of countries try, in periodic exchanges of their own, to harmonize their strategies for the main event.[32] Large multilateral negotiation efforts therefore lead to extensive diplomatic activity. Summit meetings, although usually small, or even bilateral, also require elaborate preparation, because the participants do not want their meetings to end in failure. Furthermore, they cannot meet for extended periods of time. Prior negotiations must therefore clear the way for rapid settlement when they do meet.[33]

Contemporary negotiations, particularly in large multilateral settings, are often made more difficult by the ideological stance of many of the participants. This tends to reduce the ability or even the desire to look for a common ground and to compromise. Ideology tends to foster rigidity among the negotiating parties. Self-righteousness, zeal for one's cause, conviction that fundamental principles are at stake—all of these make negotiations difficult. Compromise is viewed as a breach of faith, a betrayal of one's ideals. A crusading stance can easily block the search for a practical solution, as ideology often blurs one's perception of reality.[34] A related problem is the infusion into the negotiating process of extraneous issues, such as when a conference on healthcare is used to condemn Israel for its oppression of the Palestinian people.[35]

The diplomatic process is thus made more complex. It requires the involvement of more seasoned multilateral negotiators—people who are able to navigate through the turbulent waters of these proceedings. But many countries seem unwilling to face reality in this connection. Global society remains more proficient at approaching technology than human relations, and international actors do not attach enough importance to the selection of the people who act for them. Narrow political, monetary, or social considerations overshadow the requirements of cross-border interaction. Insufficient attention is paid to preparing delegates for multilateral work. Too many nations still treat bilateral and multilateral appointments interchangeably: a few tours of duty in national capitals alternating with multilateral work. This issue requires greater attention.[36]

NGOs are a factor in some international negotiations, especially in world conferences, such as the UN Conference on the Environment and Development (Rio de Janeiro, 1992) and the International Conference on Population and Development (Cairo, 1994). Many NGO representatives try to influence the negotiation process. They attempt to reach government delegates wherever they may be accessible—outside conference halls, in the streets, or in their hotels. Conference organizers must now bear in mind this NGO drive to be heard. Special programs for NGO delegates may be held during conferences. Some NGO representatives are even occasionally invited to make presentations in the course of the official proceedings. Chapter 5 will discuss the role of the private sector in the diplomatic process.

The media constitute another factor of growing importance in international negotiations.[37] The media play a role in determining what receives public attention, of course, but they have a more direct effect on the negotiation process.[38] It is a well-accepted proposition that effective negotiations require a high level of confidentiality and secrecy. Offers and counteroffers are often too tentative to publicize; they would create a false impression of what the countries involved are trying to accomplish.[39] The media can have a negative effect on the negotiations when speculation and inaccurate information are taken as factual reporting, particularly when highly controversial or emotional issues are at stake.[40]

Dag Hammarskjöld, UN Secretary-General at the time of the 1956 Suez crisis, recalled how harmful erroneous media reports were during the extremely difficult efforts to restore peace in the region:

> The role of the press during delicate negotiations is indeed of incalculable importance. . . . The fact was that Egypt had made concessions which, if published, might create a serious problem for Nasser [the Egyptian president], but as long as the arrangements were not published some important segments of the world press would continue to proclaim that Hammarskjold had surrendered to Nasser. . . .
>
> In such circumstances it is extremely difficult, if not impossible for the Secretary-General to set the record straight without destroying his position of confidence with the governments with which he is dealing, and he must usually suffer in silence the criticism aroused by false accounts of his own activities.[41]

It is impossible to keep the media from discussing the issues or from speculating; but to reduce this tendency, it is wise to provide plenty of material that they can use for their reports. For this purpose, important negotiation meetings are equipped with effective public information staffs, who provide ample background material, position papers, and public transcripts, and hold press conferences at regular intervals. This, of course, does not put an end to speculation and erroneous reporting. Neither can it prevent intentional leaks, but professional negotiators know that this method of embarrassing or pressuring the other side creates distrust and hampers the negotiation process. Those who are interested in reaching an agreement may hesitate to break confidentiality.

The media can be used constructively. They provide a means of testing ideas and policy alternatives. They can be used to generate public support for the negotiations, and perhaps also to sustain momentum in the bargaining process, by publicizing what has already been accomplished and playing up the successful dimensions of the talks.[42] In any case, the media remain a fact of life. Organizers of high-visibility negotiations need to prepare for their onslaught and protect the negotiators from massive interference. This adds to the complexity of organizing large-scale negotiation events and increases the cost of the proceedings.

▉ Foreign Policy

States usually follow established foreign policy in instructing their diplomats.[43] Of course, there are times when, on a given issue, a state may not have formulated its foreign policy, perhaps because the issue has just arisen and the matter is still under review, or possibly out of neglect or lack of foresight. In this case, the foreign ministry's instructions will simply be an ad hoc response to the situation in light of the circumstances and the preferences of whoever makes those decisions in the government (the foreign minister, cabinet, etc., depending upon the importance of the matter and the way the government's decisionmaking process is structured).

In any case, diplomacy is generally perceived as the implementation of foreign policy.[44] Diplomats are usually expected to make the best of the instructions they receive (although there will be times when they are directed to use their own judgment and act as they see fit). Diplomats do not make foreign policy, though their reports on what is happening in their host countries and recommendations as to what should be done may be factors in its formulation. But many other elements usually shape a nation's foreign policy: national priorities, the chief executive's leadership, advisers' recommendations, position papers from various sources, bureaucratic politics and the interaction of many other departments, intelligence reports, legal considerations, electoral politics, public opinion, the media, and much more.[45]

It is not surprising, then, that diplomats frequently feel ignored in the formulation of national policy.[46] Information overload can be a problem. With the phenomenal increase in the volume of communication between diplomatic posts and national capitals, some messages are not reaching policymakers. Communication gaps may also be the result of ineffective bureaucratic structures. When serious international problems arise, the chief of mission is usually brought home for consultation with decisionmakers to explore possible responses. The give and take in such conversations may better inform the diplomat on all the factors and often-conflicting interests involved.[47] Foreign offices, of course, are supposed to keep their diplomats informed about political trends at home. Periodically, a tour of duty at the foreign ministry helps to keep them in touch with the larger context of domestic politics. Still, there is often a substantial difference of perspective between the field and the home office, with diplomats feeling ignored when they receive their instructions.

All of this pertains only to the diplomacy of nation-states, still the prime movers in global affairs and the relevant entities to examine when discussing foreign policy. Other actors have their own decisionmaking processes.[48] Their representatives, too, have their own instructions to contend with and their own problems in communicating with those who direct their efforts. Even the UN Secretary-General must report to the Security Council or the General Assembly and justify his diplomacy—and he occasionally becomes embroiled in intense political controversy.[49] The Secretary-General's own envoys must carry out his instructions. Transnational relations are very different (see Chapter 5), but even here, someone (or a committee, or a board of directors) is providing direction, more or less.

▓ The Art of Diplomacy

People involved in international fieldwork, particularly in the area of political relations, must be able to bridge many differences—cultural, geopolitical, and ideological—as well as conflicting state interests of all kinds, including strategic concerns. Career diplomats are prepared to be posted abroad; they are trained for it and, over the years, learn from experience. It must of course be acknowledged that the diplomatic career varies enormously from one state to the next.[50] Even within a specific foreign service bureaucracy, there will be significant differences in the proficiency of individual officers.[51] This is inevitable. People have different skills, different potentials; they respond differently to training programs. Political appointees have diverse backgrounds.[52] Some may be appointed for the worst of reasons—for example, as a reward for campaign contributions, or, in unstable systems, posted outside the national capital if they are perceived as a threat to the ruling faction.[53]

Beyond the regular foreign service, one now finds a growing category of government officials who end up in international posts as a result of circumstances, job specifications, or whatever moves people around in a government bureaucracy—for example, a labor department official in Washington being sent as a delegate to an annual meeting of the International Labour Organization in Geneva. Many will be challenged by a foreign assignment; others will see a long-standing ambition fulfilled. But can they be effective in the task of bridging the international differences mentioned earlier? To be sure, there will be some low-risk assignments of a primarily bureaucratic nature in which deskwork is the main part of the job, and where the greatest extent of intercultural relations occurs after work in their apartment building or at the grocery store. But what about truly diplomatic placements? What qualities are needed for effective performance?

The most useful attributes are probably interpersonal skills (particularly communication) adapted to a milieu involving people of different cultures representing different political systems.[54] Good verbal skills are an asset, especially when assorted with a good working knowledge of foreign languages. Important multilateral meetings may be equipped for simultaneous translation. But there is always a good deal of consultation and communication to be undertaken outside from formal meetings and without the benefit of an interpreter.[55] Patience is insufficiently appreciated in modern societies.[56] It may be true that some international issues require fast action, But hasty decisions can be counterproductive. Diplomats often have a hard time convincing their superiors back home that they must wait for a more propitious moment to approach delicate questions. Also, many cultures do not attach the same importance to the clock as do industrial societies. For a person in the field, these questions are often a matter of common sense; but having to explain them to someone back home, thousands of miles away, who has little knowledge of local circumstances, is more difficult.

Tact and circumspection are useful in approaching important (and proud?) foreign officials. Formality and concern for protocol, too, remain characteristic of official relations, although the trend is toward fewer rigors, particularly in international organizations.[57] Adaptability is helpful.[58] Negotiations may be demanding.[59] Self-control and an ability to size up a situation or one's counterpart are important, although the stakes will not always be high. There is no substitute for experience. Imagination is of great value to creating alternatives to conflicting positions and finding common ground. Compromise may be the essence of diplomacy, but one's superiors back home frequently control what negotiators can do in this respect. Ideological stances foster rigidity.[60]

In most situations (and not just in negotiations), the development of trust with one's counterparts is a valuable asset.[61] But friendship, respect, and trust cannot be achieved overnight. Enmity or friction between international actors will complicate interpersonal relationships. Periods of tension can create polarization, making interpersonal relations more difficult. In conference work and other temporary assignments, diplomats hope to find people with whom they have already had constructive relations in earlier assignments. International networking is useful and frequently sought. But one problem in the development of lasting relations is the relatively frequent rotation of diplomatic personnel that many governments favor, which means moving to a new post every three years or so. And with every move comes the need to build a new set of contacts and relationships. To be effective and knowledgeable about the host country and its politics implies that considerable time be spent in that country.[62]

Many countries justify the practice of frequent rotation as an effort to keep diplomatic officers from becoming too attached to the host country and, presumably, from developing a bias toward it ("localitis," as they call it).[63] This belief implies a remarkable lack of trust in the ability of foreign service personnel to remain committed to the defense of the interests of their own nation even when they appreciate what the host country has to offer. Keeping foreign service officers familiar with the priorities and needs of their own nation can be achieved by periodic visits to their own capital, with briefings by relevant policymakers. This would seem far less disruptive than frequent rotation.

Multilateral diplomacy (see Chapter 8) is substantially different from the kind of work done in the normal resident mission (it involves, among other things, a multicultural environment, the use of parliamentary procedures, and extensive public speaking or debating). Allowing diplomatic officers to acquire experience in this multilateral environment and develop the necessary skills enhances their effectiveness.[64] Many countries, however, rotate their diplomatic personnel between bilateral and multilateral posts as if the functions were readily interchangeable. The skills needed in the diplomatic profession vary substantially with the functions and role of the individual officer. Many nonstate actors do not have the benefit of institutionalized "career diplomats."[65] In practice, nonstate agents have demonstrated diplomatic proficiency, learning as they go and making a career of it.[66] Experience will always be a critical element in this profession.

▨ Analytical Framework.

Despite the considerable advances made by the social sciences and by political science in particular, there is no general theory of diplomacy or theoretical framework to facilitate systematic analysis.[67] The significant changes taking place in contemporary diplomatic practice are probably making the development of a general theory more difficult. It is nevertheless possible to devise an analytic framework to help this examination of what is happening in diplomacy.

A number of political scientists have followed the lead provided in 1961 by J. David Singer, who used two levels of analysis (domestic and international) in his study of international relations.[68] Singer pointed out: "In any area of scholarly inquiry, there are always several ways in which the phenomena under study may be sorted and arranged for purposes of systemic analysis."[69] Other analysts refashioned this approach to serve their own purposes and to focus on those aspects of the phenomenon they wanted to examine. The units of analysis do not have to be identified as "levels." The matter to be researched may be arranged differently. Kenneth Waltz, seeking to determine the major causes of war, ordered his investigation under three headings: people, the structure of the separate states, and the global system. He called these three categories "images of international relations"—his units of analysis—and organized his book around them.[70] It is to be observed that not only does each level (however identified) provide the boundaries for the analysis undertaken, but it also gives a different perspective for an examination of the material concerned—that is, a perspective pertaining specially to the level selected. For example, a political phenomenon examined from a global perspective is likely to look different when seen from a national vantage point.

James Rosenau distinguished five levels in building a "pre-theory of foreign policy."[71] Others have designed categories to meet the specific needs of their projects—for example, by adding a regional level of analysis.[72] Bruce Russett and Harvey Starr made very successful use of six levels in their introduction to world politics.[73] Numerous writers of international politics textbooks are also using this organizing device.[74] A similar approach can be used to explore the transformation of diplomatic method, with a number of adjustments to meet the special needs of this study. The focus here is of course much narrower. The transformation of diplomatic method involves far fewer variables than the study of the entire structure of international politics or the making of foreign policy. It must furthermore be noted that many of the changes occurring at any one level do not modify diplomatic *method*,[75] even when the *substance*[76] of foreign relations is transformed: the same diplomatic procedures can be used over the years for very different diplomatic objectives or courses of action. Thus the analysis is more circumscribed. Five levels of inquiry are of particular importance here.[77]

First, a useful point of departure is an examination of the changes taking place at the *global level* that are leading to new avenues of diplomatic interaction. Chapters 3 and 4 examine developments at this level, the former focusing on the impact of complex interdependence,[78] and the latter taking up the changes produced by technological advancements.

Second, the *national level,* too, generates changes contributing to the transformation of diplomatic method.[79] Changes here are rooted in the way domestic societies and governments operate. The world remains essentially divided into nation-states, each one tending to embody a national culture and distinct political system. To be sure, states are no longer the only international actors, but they have a major impact on diplomatic method. Some of the ways in which states approach diplomacy tend to converge and may lead to new, and generally accepted, diplomatic methodologies. Other state practices diverge, thus producing greater diversity and, occasionally, problems.[80] This level of analysis provides material for a number of chapters in this volume where national influence is identified more particularly, Chapters 6, 7, 9, and 10.[81]

Third, the *transnational level* is of relatively recent vintage. It represents a growing phenomenon fostered by technological developments, a greater awareness of international civil society, and a growing trend toward globalization.[82] It amounts to the private sector of society interacting across international boundaries beyond the reach of state authorities. Interaction at this level bypasses intergovernmental activity, but does not hesitate to work with the public sector whenever it serves its purpose (particularly to modify its agenda).[83] Conversely, the public sector is increasingly finding it useful to work with the transnational order.[84]

Transnational phenomena are undoubtedly less momentous for the transformation of diplomacy than what is happening at the preceding levels. Nevertheless, transnational forces are growing and have an impact on diplomacy. Transnational actors, such as nongovernmental organizations and multinational corporations, are playing an increasingly larger role in international society (particularly in the massive process of economic globalization) and affect diplomatic methodology. Chapter 5 examines the extent of its contribution (see in particular the case study on the diplomacy of the landmine treaty).

Fourth, changes are also generated at the *professional level*—that is, the level of individual participants in diplomacy, which is no longer limited to members of the foreign service. The practitioners themselves in their day-to-day interaction initiate new ways of doing their work. Chapter 6 deals with the changes introduced by the people who actually carry out diplomatic relations and who, to a significant extent, give diplomacy its special character. In this analysis, the roles of the individual players are considered (some analysts consider roles as a separate level).[85] Each role, or position, carries with it responsibilities (professional, social, and psychological demands and expectations) that influence behavior.[86]

Roles have a conservative tendency that inhibits novel behavior. In diplomacy, some roles are steeped in tradition and are a factor of continuity. But it must be remembered that superiors will redefine the roles of their agents. Changed circumstances will lead to collective pressures to perform differently. This has been very noticeable in the case of heads of international agencies.[87] The chapters in Part 2 of this volume, in their examination of diplomatic modes, consider the effect of roles.

Fifth and finally is the *functional level,* to which Part 2 of this volume is devoted. "Functional" is used in a broad sense, not at all limited to function, but including other elements such as structure and modus operandi in examining the various modes of diplomacy currently in use.[88]

Some of the diplomatic modes are well established, but evolving.[89] They are adjusting to changed circumstances, and it is important to examine how useful they remain and their prospects for further change. Other diplomatic modes are new and very different. They represent attempts by international actors to meet changing needs.[90] It is not certain whether they may all qualify as "diplomacy," and this needs to be examined. It is also important to inquire into their actual contribution to the international process and to see how they interact with the more traditional procedures.

Five chapters deal with this functional level of inquiry. Chapter 7 examines the current status of permanent representation in national capitals, the "classic" mode of diplomacy. It has lost much of its luster but remains useful.[91] It still has many of its traditional functions, but has acquired new roles[92] and is still adjusting to the new diplomatic environment.

Chapter 8 focuses on the rapidly expanding mode of international organization diplomacy, which has introduced a number of new practices—for example, diplomacy by international officials, such as heads of international agencies speaking for their organizations rather than a specific nation-state. It is doubtless the most diverse of diplomatic modes.[93]

Chapter 9 examines the use of temporary missions for a variety of purposes, two in particular: mediation (an analysis of its interaction with other diplomatic modes, especially resident representation—see the Yemen case study) and representation at international conferences, a proliferating mode of diplomatic interaction.[94]

Chapter 10 turns to summit diplomacy, which has become a standard way of conducting international business and seems to be acquiring greater popularity. Does it deserve the place it now holds in international affairs? This will be looked into as well as the specific ways in which it is carried out, requiring a good deal of diplomacy by other professionals. The chapter also presents another form of diplomacy, now extensively used: interaction between heads of executive departments across international boundaries, not only foreign ministers but other division heads as well (e.g., ministers of agriculture negotiating food issues). This can be viewed as "near-summit" diplomacy. It is widely called "ministerial" diplomacy, and serves a role that needs to be carefully reviewed. It is a new diplomatic trend that will likely expand.

Chapter 11 covers novel forms of interaction, some of them unconventional enough to be seen as reaching the edge of diplomacy. "Track II diplomacy" involves private citizens in the diplomatic affairs of states, although this form of transaction remains of limited scope and frequency.

Chapter 12 concludes the volume by examining trends, drawing lessons, and pondering the future of diplomacy in its complex and diverse manifestations. Throughout the volume, text boxes illustrate aspects of the diplomatic methods examined here, and case studies provide practical applications of modern diplomacy in their historical context.

▧ Study Questions and Discussion Topics

1. What is diplomacy? Why is its definition an object of disagreement?

2. Who can be called a diplomat? Why is the issue debatable?

3. What is the role of negotiations in diplomacy? Why fear negotiations?

4. What distinction can be made between foreign policy and diplomacy? To what extent is it wise to make such a distinction?

5. What is the role of diplomacy in the formulation of foreign policy?

6. How is foreign policy formulated? What are the factors that contribute to its formulation?

■ Suggested Reading

Barston, R. P. *Modern Diplomacy.* New York: Longman, 1988.

Berridge, G. R. *Diplomacy: Theory and Practice.* 3d ed. New York: Palgrave, 2005.

Cohen, Raymond. *Theater of Power: The Art of Diplomatic Signalling.* New York: Longman, 1987.

Hamilton, Keith, and Richard Langhorne. *The Practice of Diplomacy: Its Evolution, Theory, and Administration.* New York: Routledge, 1995.

Jönsson, Christer, and Richard Langhorne, eds. *Diplomacy.* 3 vols. (vol. 1, *Theory of Diplomacy;* vol. 2, *History of Diplomacy;* vol. 3, *Problems and Issues in Contemporary Diplomacy*). London: Sage, 2004.

Kremenyuk, Victor A. *International Negotiation: Analysis, Approaches, Issues.* San Francisco: Jossey-Bass, 1991.

Nicolson, Harold. *Diplomacy.* 3d ed. New York: Oxford University Press, 1964.

Plischke, Elmer. *Modern Diplomacy: The Art and the Artisans.* Washington, DC: American Enterprise Institute, 1979.

Rana, Kishan S. *Inside Diplomacy.* 2d ed. New Delhi: Manas, 2002.

Watson, Adam. *Diplomacy: The Dialogue Between States.* New York: Routledge, 2004.

Wittkopf, Eugene R., Charles W. Kegley Jr., and James M. Scott. *American Foreign Policy: Pattern and Process.* 6th ed. Belmont, CA: Wadsworth, 2003.

Zartman, I. William, and Maureen R. Berman. *The Practical Negotiator.* New Haven: Yale University Press, 1982.

■ Notes

1. Hans J. Morgenthau, *Politics Among Nations: The Struggle for Power and Peace,* revised by Kenneth W. Thompson (New York: McGraw-Hill, 1993), p. 367. See also Barbara Gamarekian, "Has Diplomacy Become Out of Date?" in *The Modern Ambassador,* edited by Martin F. Herz (Washington, DC: Institute for the Study of Diplomacy, School of Foreign Service, Georgetown University, 1983), pp. 16–18. For additional criticism of diplomacy, see Adam Watson, *Diplomacy: The Dialogue Between States* (New York: Routledge, 2004), chap. 10, "Criticisms of Contemporary Diplomacy," pp. 132–157. The diverse arguments will be discussed later, in the chapters pertaining to the diverse forms of diplomacy.

2. For example, Robert L. Hutchings, *American Diplomacy and the End of the Cold War: An Insider's Account of U.S. Policy in Europe, 1989–1992* (Washington, DC: Woodrow Wilson Center, 1997); Vernon McKay, ed., *African Diplomacy: Studies in the Determinants of Foreign Policy* (New York: Praeger, 1966).

3. For example, Robert H. Ferrell, *American Diplomacy: The Twentieth Century,* 4th ed. (New York: Norton, 1988); Robert D. Schulzinger, *American Diplomacy in the Twentieth Century* (New York: Oxford University Press, 1984); George F. Kennan, *American Diplomacy,* expanded ed. (Chicago: University of Chicago Press, 1984); Gaddis Smith, *American Diplomacy During the Second World War, 1941–1945,* 2d ed. (New York: Knopf, 1985).

4. Elmer Plischke, "Diplomacy: Search for Its Meaning," in *Modern Diplomacy: The Art and the Artisans,* edited by Elmer Plischke (Washington, DC: American Enterprise Institute for Public Policy Research, 1979), pp. 27–40.

5. Christer Jönsson and Martin Hall, *Essence of Diplomacy* (New York: Palgrave Macmillan, 2005), pp. 25–30.

6. Lori F. Damrosch, Louis Henkin, Richard Crawford Pugh, Oscar Schachter, and Hans Smit, eds., *International Law: Basic Documents Supplement,* 4th ed. (St. Paul, MN: West Group, 2001), pp. 574–583.

7. Ibid., pp. 583–593. Other international conventions have codified the practice of diplomacy—for example, the 1946 Convention on the Privileges and Immunities of the United Nations; ibid., pp. 605–610. Like other institutions, however, diplomacy changes over time. The 1946 convention is an illustration of this evolution, as it formalized the application of diplomacy within the new framework of the United Nations.

8. Harold Nicolson, *Diplomacy,* 3d ed. (New York: Oxford University Press, 1964), pp. 55–67.

9. Ibid. See also François de Callières, *On the Manner of Negotiating with Princes,* translated by A. F. Whyte (Washington, DC: University Press of America, 1963 [1716]), pp. 103–132.

10. Robert O. Keohane and Joseph S. Nye, *Power and Interdependence,* 2d ed. (Glenview, IL: Scott Foresman, 1989), pp. 26–27.

11. Strobe Talbott, "Globalization and Diplomacy: A Practitioner's Perspective," in *Diplomacy,* edited by Christer Jönsson and Richard Langhorne (London: Sage, 2004), vol. 3, *Problems and Issues in Contemporary Diplomacy,* pp. 368–370.

12. George F. Kennan, "Diplomacy Without Diplomats," *Foreign Affairs* 76, no. 5 (September–October 1997), pp. 198–212.

13. See Herz, *Modern Ambassador,* pp. 117–143, 167–176.

14. Which means having extensive administrative duties.

15. Hedley Bull, "Diplomacy and International Order," in Jönsson and Langhorne, *Diplomacy,* vol. 1, pp. 81–91.

16. For example, when elected to chair certain UN committees, national delegates are usually expected to help these committees carry out their work programs rather than act in partisan fashion to protect their own national interests. See Chadwick F. Alger, "Decision-Making and Human Conflict," in *The Nature of Human Conflict,* edited by Elton B. McNeil (Englewood Cliffs, NJ: Prentice-Hall, 1965), pp. 283–285. See also Chapter 8 in this volume.

17. Inis L. Claude Jr., "Multilateralism—Diplomatic and Otherwise," in Jönsson and Langhorne, *Diplomacy,* vol. 1, pp. 367–377.

18. See also ibid.; Volker Rittberger, "Global Conference Diplomacy and International Policy-Making: The Case of UN-Sponsored World Conferences," in Jönsson and Langhorne, *Diplomacy,* vol. 1, pp. 378–395.

19. A. LeRoy Bennett and James K. Oliver, *International Organizations: Principles and Issues,* 7th ed. (Upper Saddle River, NJ: Prentice-Hall, 2002), pp. 412–438. See also Robert W. Cox, Harold K. Jacobson, et al., *The Anatomy of Influence: Decision Making in International Organization* (New Haven: Yale University Press, 1974).

20. Transnational relations are relations across national boundaries *without* significant, direct participation or control by high-level governmental actors. Bruce Russett, Harvey Starr, and David Kinsella, *World Politics: The Menu for Choice,* 6th ed. (Boston: Bedford, 2000), p. 400.

21. Andrew F. Cooper and Brian Hocking, "Governments, Non-Governmental Organizations, and the Re-calibration of Diplomacy," in Jönsson and Langhorne, *Diplomacy,* vol. 3, pp. 79–95.

22. Susan Strange, "States, Firms, and Diplomacy," in Jönsson and Langhorne, *Diplomacy,* vol. 1, pp. 352–366.

23. See also Rik Coolsaet, "The Transformation of Diplomacy at the Threshold of the New Millennium," in Jönsson and Langhorne, *Diplomacy,* vol. 3, pp. 1–24.

24. G. R. Berridge, *Diplomacy: Theory and Practice,* 2d ed. (New York: Palgrave, 2002), p. 1.

25. R. P. Barston, *Modern Diplomacy,* 2d ed. (New York: Longman, 1997); Shawn Dorman, ed., *Inside a U.S. Embassy: How the Foreign Service Works for America,* rev. ed. (Washington, DC: American Foreign Service Association, 2005).

26. In the period between 1946 and 1996, the United States concluded more than 6,900 treaties (6,303 bilateral and 599 multilateral). Elmer Plischke, *U.S. Department of State: A Reference History* (Westport: Greenwood, 1999), p. 528; see tables of bilateral treaties, pp. 545–548, and multilateral treaties, pp. 559–560.

27. See Fred Charles Iklé, *How Nations Negotiate* (New York: Harper and Row, 1964), pp. 26–42.

28. See I. William Zartman and Maureen R. Berman, *The Practical Negotiator* (New Haven: Yale University Press, 1982). See also Dennis Ross, *Statecraft: And How to Restore America's Standing in the World* (New York: Farrar, Straus and Giroux, 2007), "Negotiations: Twelve Rules to Follow," pp. 187–215.

29. See the series of studies sponsored and published by the US Institute of Peace—for example, Nigel Quinney, *U.S. Negotiating Behavior,* Special Report no. 94 (October 2002); Charles Cogan, *French Negotiating Behavior: Dealing with La Grande Nation* (2003); W. R. Smyser, *How Germans Negotiate: Logical Goals, Practical Solutions* (2003). See also Raymond Cohen, *Negotiating Across Cultures: International Communication in an Interdependent World,* rev. ed. (Washington, DC: US Institute of Peace, 1997); Lawrence E. Harrison and Samuel P. Huntington, *Culture Matters: How Values Shape Human Progress* (New York: Basic, 2001).

30. See James K. Sebenius, *Negotiating the Law of the Sea* (Cambridge: Harvard University Press, 1984).

31. Ibid., pp. 42–146. See also Berridge, *Diplomacy,* pp. 29–44.

32. That is, at the opening of the multilateral conference or the beginning of the international organization meeting that the membership is·to attend.

33. See Erik Goldstein, "The Politics of the State Visit," Jönsson and Langhorne, *Diplomacy,* vol. 2, pp. 357–380.

34. Richard W. Sterling, *Macropolitics: International Relations in a Global Society* (New York: Knopf, 1974), pp. 156–178. See also Watson, *Diplomacy,* pp. 69–81.

35. This has been referred to as the "politicization" of conference proceedings. See Chapter 9.

36. James P. Muldoon Jr., JoAnn Fagot Aviel, Richard Reitano, and Earl Sullivan, eds., *Multilateral Diplomacy and the United Nations Today* (Boulder: Westview, 1999).

37. Berridge, *Diplomacy,* pp. 67–68. See also Chapter 6 in this volume.

38. Nicolson, *Diplomacy,* pp. 50–53.

39. Zartman and Berman, *Practical Negotiator,* pp. 215–219. See also W. Philips Davison, "News Media and International Negotiation," *Public Opinion Quarterly* 38 (1974), pp. 174–193.

40. Michele J. Gelfand and Jeanne M. Brett, eds., *The Handbook of Negotiation and Culture* (Stanford: Stanford Business Books, 2004).

41. Brian Urquhart, *Hammarskjold* (New York: Norton, 1972), pp. 216, 221.

42. Berridge, *Diplomacy,* pp. 67–68.

43. Barston, *Modern Diplomacy,* pp. 9–28.

44. It is to be noted that within the framework of broad foreign ministry guidelines, diplomats may be given enough room for initiatives of their own. But this varies with the political system and its leadership. Some ministries are addicted (to their own detriment) to micromanagement.

45. Steven W. Hook, *U.S. Foreign Policy: The Paradox of World Power* (Washington, DC: Congressional Quarterly, 2005), pp. 153–188. See also Eugene R. Wittkopf, Charles W. Kegley Jr., and James M. Scott, *American Foreign Policy: Pattern and Process,* 6th ed. (Belmont, CA: Wadsworth, 2003), pp. 147–514.

46. J. Robert Schaetzel, "Modernizing the Role of the Ambassador," in Plischke, *Modern Diplomacy,* pp. 266–276.

47. Wittkopf, Kegley, and Scott, *American Foreign Policy,* pp. 147–514.

48. See Paul F. Diehl, ed., *The Politics of International Organizations: Patterns and Insights* (Chicago: Dorsey, 1989). See also Cox et al., *Anatomy of Influence,* for various forms of decisionmaking in international organizations.

49. See, for instance, Urquhart, *Hammarskjold;* or C. V. Narasimhan, *The United Nations: An Inside View* (New Delhi: Vikas, 1988).

50. See, for instance, David Armstrong, "Revolutionary Diplomacy," Jönsson and Langhorne, *Diplomacy,* vol. 2, pp. 381–394.

51. George F. Kennan, speaking of the US foreign service, noted: "The Service is, in the human sense, a very mixed bag." *Foreign Affairs* 76, no. 5 (September–October 1997), p. 209.

52. Clare Boothe Luce, "The Ambassadorial Issue: Professionals or Amateurs?" in Herz, *Modern Ambassador,* pp. 128–136, also pp. 117–127, 137–176.

53. Martin F. Herz, "Maxwell Gluck and All That," in Herz, *Modern Ambassador,* pp. 96–104; "Ambassadorships: Findings of the Watergate Committee," in Herz, *Modern Ambassador,* pp. 105–109.

54. Christer Jönsson and Martin Hall, "Communication: An Essential Aspect of Diplomacy," Jönsson and Langhorne, *Diplomacy,* vol. 1, pp. 396–415.

55. See Ambassador Melissa Foelsch Wells in Ann Miller Morin, *Her Excellency: An Oral History of American Women Ambassadors* (New York: Twayne, 1995), pp. 212, 214–215.

56. Nicolson, *Diplomacy,* pp. 62–63.

57. (Lord) Gore-Booth, ed., *Satow's Guide to Diplomatic Practice,* 5th ed. (New York: Longman, 1979), pp. 20ff.

58. Karl Gruber, "Common Denominators of Good Ambassadors," in Herz, *Modern Ambassador,* pp. 62–66.

59. Fred Charles Iklé, "Negotiating Effectively," in Plischke, *Modern Diplomacy,* pp. 364–372.

60. Sterling, *Macropolitics,* pp. 156–178; Watson, *Diplomacy,* pp. 69–81.

61. Zartman and Berman, *Practical Negotiator,* pp. 27–41.

62. It seems that governments would benefit from longer tenure in the same post. See Schaetzel, "Modernizing the Role," p. 275.

63. François de Laboulaye and Jean Laloy, "Qualifications of an Ambassador," in Herz, *Modern Ambassador,* pp. 67–71. See also Thomas A. Bailey, "Advice for Diplomats," in Plischke, *Modern Diplomacy,* pp. 230–231.

64. See Seymour Maxwell Finger, *American Ambassadors at the UN: People, Politics, and Bureaucracy in Making Foreign Policy,* 2d ed. (New York: Holmes and Meier, 1988).

65. However, some organizations are creating their own diplomatic service (e.g., the European Union).

66. Like their colleagues in the foreign service, some do well and others have more to learn.

67. See, for example, James E. Dougherty and Robert L. Pfaltzgraff Jr., *Contending Theories of International Relations: A Comprehensive Survey,* 4th ed. (New York: Longman, 1997); Ernst-Otto Czempiel and James N. Rosenau, eds., *Global Changes and Theoretical Challenges: Approaches to World Politics for the 1990s* (Lexington, MA: Lexington Books, 1989); Joseph Kruzel and James N. Rosenau, eds., *Journeys Through World Politics: Autobiographical Reflections of Thirty-four Academic Travelers* (Lexington, MA: Lexington Books, 1988). For more on a general theory, see James N. Rosenau and Mary Durfee, *Thinking Theory Thoroughly: Coherent Approaches to an Incoherent World* (Boulder: Westview, 1995); Jönsson and Langhorne, *Diplomacy,* vol. 1, *Theory of Diplomacy.* See also Berridge, *Diplomacy.*

68. J. David Singer, "The Level-of-Analysis Problem in International Relations," in *The International System: Theoretical Essays,* edited by Klaus Knorr and Sidney Verba (Princeton: Princeton University Press, 1961), pp. 77–92. See also James N. Rosenau, ed., *International Politics and Foreign Policy,* 2d ed. (New York: Free Press, 1969), pp. 20–29; see critique by William B. Moul, "The Level of Analysis Problem Revisited," *Canadian Journal of Political Science* 6 (1973), pp. 494–513.

69. Singer, "Level-of-Analysis Problem," p. 77. He reasoned that an observer may always choose to focus on the parts or on the whole, the micro or the macro level of analysis. In the operation of general systems theory, however, he saw potential difficulty in the way in which the researcher would select the subsystems (the component parts of the whole system), and his study was intended to address this problem.

70. Kenneth N. Waltz, *Man, the State, and War: A Theoretical Analysis* (New York: Columbia University Press, 1959), p. 12.

71. These are the individual, role, governmental, societal, and systemic sets of variables. He did not call them "levels" of analysis but rather "philosophies" of analysis. James N. Rosenau, *The Scientific Study of Foreign Policy: Essays on the Analysis of World Politics,* rev. ed. (New York: Nichols, 1980), pp. 128–129.

72. See, for example, James N. Rosenau, with Kenneth W. Thompson and Gavin Boyd, *World Politics: An Introduction* (New York: Free Press, 1976), pp. 8–10. Here, Rosenau uses three levels of analysis—the national, regional, and global—as a framework to organize the book. Note that other levels, especially those that involve subnational actors, are also analyzed in a number of Rosenau's chapters, thus illustrating the flexibility of this method. See also Timothy J. Lomperis, *Flawed Realism: Hans Morgenthau and Kenneth Waltz on Vietnam—The Case for a Regional Level of Analysis* (unpublished, St. Louis University, 2005).

73. World system, international relations, characteristics of the society, governmental structure, roles of decisionmakers, and individual decisionmakers. Russett, Starr, and Kinsella, *World Politics,* pp. 12–16.

74. For example, Charles W. Kegley Jr. and Eugene R. Wittkopf, *World Politics: Trends and Transformations,* 9th ed. (Belmont, CA: Wadsworth, 2004), p. 17; John T. Rourke, *International Politics on the World Stage,* 10th ed. (New York: McGraw-Hill,

2005), pp. 57–96; Steven L. Spiegel, Jennifer Morrison Taw, Fred L. Wehling, and Kristen P. Williams, *World Politics in a New Era,* 3d ed. (Belmont, CA: Wadsworth, 2004), pp. 33–95.

75. Understood in a broad sense—that is, form, procedure, means, modes of interaction, channels utilized, and all the other elements that will be studied in Part 2.

76. For example, when the states concerned decide to go to war.

77. Other levels of analysis could be chosen. The phenomena to be studied could be approached differently, and other researchers may choose to do so. But it seems that these levels are the most pertinent in examining the transformation taking place in diplomatic method and its consequences.

78. For example, the vast expansion and diversification of the subject matter of diplomacy. Many diplomats need new skills. Experts without diplomatic skill find themselves involved in diplomatic negotiations. See, for instance, Chapter 6. The question is now raised: "Diplomacy without diplomats?" See article of this title, by career diplomat George F. Kennan, in *Foreign Affairs* 76, no. 5 (September–October 1997), pp. 198–212.

79. It is acknowledged that what is done at the national level is often a consequence of transformation at the global level. Units of analysis do not operate in airtight compartments. This needs to be taken into account in one's research work.

80. To a considerable extent, states control what their envoys do abroad—even if counterproductive. And the world has had its share of "exotic" systems (e.g., Muammar Qadaffi's or the Taliban's).

81. In Chapter 6, the personal level is emphasized, but national governments have a large impact on the methods used by their own diplomats. Chapter 7 is focused on the changes taking place in resident missions—the traditional embassies in foreign capitals. Chapter 9, particularly the segment on special missions, shows the bulk of them are still sent by national governments. Chapter 10 focuses on summit and ministerial diplomacy, in which the national element is important, although summitry is heavily propelled by developments at the global level.

82. Hence much influence from the global level, and what is discussed in Chapter 3. See also Sterling, *Macropolitics,* pp. 492–514; Keohane and Nye, *Power and Interdependence,* pp. 33–34.

83. Many nongovernmental organizations distrust the governmental sector.

84. See also Strange, "States, Firms, and Diplomacy," pp. 352–366.

85. For example, Russett, Harvey, and Starr apply this tool of analysis to the larger category of "decisionmakers": *World Politics,* pp. 14–15.

86. These tend to shape the individual's perception of how he or she should perform. Wittkopf, Kegley, and Scott, *American Foreign Policy,* pp. 448–449.

87. For example, new expectations have developed in the diplomatic roles of UN Secretaries-General. See Urquhart, *Hammarskjold.* See also Cox et al., *Anatomy of Influence,* for other high international officials.

88. It is acknowledged that in political science, "functional analysis" is an ambiguous label. William Flanigan and Edwin Fogelman identify several kinds of functional analysis. The broad type used here is presented as "eclectic functionalism"; it is the least developed theoretically. "Empirical functionalism" was given its impetus by Robert K. Merton in *Social Theory and Social Structure* (New York: Free Press, 1957). "Structural-functional analysis," the most ambitious, was developed by Talcott Parsons in *The Social System* (New York: Free Press, 1951), and by Parson with Edward Shils. eds., in *Toward a General Theory of Action* (Cambridge: Harvard University Press, 1951), and by Marion Levy in *The Structure of Society* (Princeton: Princeton University Press, 1951). See Flanigan and Fogelman, "Functional Analysis," in *Contemporary*

Political Analysis, edited by James C. Charlesworth (New York: Free Press, 1967), pp. 72–85. Functionalists are also found in international organization theory, where they focus on the rational administration of technical activities toward a higher degree of integration of global society. See Bennett and Oliver, *International Organizations,* pp. 11–13; Kegley and Wittkopf, *World Politics,* pp. 598–600. See also Ernst B. Haas, *Beyond the Nation-State: Functionalism and International Organization* (Stanford: Stanford University Press, 1964).

89. For example, permanent representation in foreign capitals—the traditional embassies. See Chapter 7.

90. For example, direct interaction between executive departments of different countries (other than foreign ministries)—transgovernmental relations. See Chapter 3.

91. More than half of the countries of the world maintain only a limited number of embassies abroad. See Chapter 7.

92. For example, helping with the multilateral transactions carried out elsewhere. See Chapter 7.

93. The latest innovations are found in the European Union, which remains a grouping of independent states with their own diplomatic establishments. See Brian Hocking and David Spence, eds., *Foreign Ministries in the European Union: Integrating Diplomats* (New York: Palgrave Macmillan, 2006).

94. Many of the diplomatic procedures used in international conferences are comparable to what is done in international organizations (which have occasionally been called "permanent conferences"). The temporary nature of these conference missions, nevertheless, is a major difference in the conduct of diplomacy.

2 Diplomacy in Historical Context

Diplomacy is as old as civilization. But international society keeps changing and diplomacy keeps evolving as a matter of course to serve its purpose and facilitate the interaction of its members. The changes are normally a reflection of what international society has become, for better or worse. Moreover, perspectives on the role of the state and the function of its government continue evolving. Thus it is not surprising that different notions of diplomacy would arise over time.[1]

■ Prologue

The leaders of the earliest empires and city-states maintained international contact using their own kinds of agents for that purpose. Diplomatic interaction was a matter of practicality.[2] They sent messages in cuneiform inscriptions on clay tablets,[3] sought information on what their neighbors were up to, exchanged gifts, and negotiated trade agreements, alliances, and peace treaties. Some sovereigns provided mediation in the disputes of their neighbors. All of this amounted to a good deal of "diplomacy."[4] But the information we have on how it was conducted, its style, and its methods remains very limited. We have the evidence that it took place; but the records, more often than not, do not amount to comprehensive archives, and the information is unevenly distributed. The most important for the study of diplomacy are the tablets found at El Amarna.[5] This documentation is especially useful, as it is extensively focused on international relations and covers most of the Middle East (although not consistently), from Egypt to Babylonia, Upper Mesopotamia, and Anatolia.[6] Other sources provide more documents: the Hittite archives found at Boğazköy,[7] the Mari tablets,[8] the Ugarit archives,[9] and more recently discovered, the Ebla documents (see Table 2.1).[10] These

Table 2.1   Important Archival Discoveries

	Period	Place	First Deciphering
El Amarna	1600–1200 B.C.E.	Egypt	1887
Boğazköy	1300–1200 B.C.E.	Turkey	1906–1907
Mari (Tell Hariri)	1700–1600 B.C.E.	Syria	1933–1939
Ugarit	pre-1180 B.C.E.	Northern Syrian coast	1951–1957
Ebla (Tell Mardikh)	2300 B.C.E.	Northern Syria	1975

sources are of great value, of course, but we are concerned with a large portion of civilization over a period of some three thousand years. Thus, in the end, we are still frequently groping in the dark.

Diplomatic customs were created, some dating back to the third millennium B.C.E.[11] Rules of procedure and appropriate ceremonial became established, governing international relations,[12] most particularly in the making of treaties along strikingly similar patterns.[13] Representatives were sent abroad—some were simple messengers, others were men of importance, experienced in affairs of state. They were given some latitude in negotiating the details of important agreements with heads of state. Although some representatives were referred to as resident envoys, available documents seem to indicate that their appointments were for specific missions and terminated upon their completion. But they may well have resided abroad for considerable durations, as travel was difficult and often dangerous. Many titles were used for them and for other types of agents. The titles were often used interchangeably, despite the fact that the functions of these agents were very different. There was no accepted typology, which hinders us in identifying the roles of the people concerned as we review this part of history today. Some historians use terms familiar to us in a generic sense, such as "ambassador," despite the fact that the title would not be invented for another couple of millennia.[14]

As diplomatic representatives, they often enjoyed special treatment (but there were exceptions). For example, on their return journey, the rulers of some host states provided for their needs—food, clothing, and other travel necessities, as well as fresh supplies at various stages along the way. When the journey was hazardous, as was frequently the case, envoys of friendly states often traveled together in a group. They were sometimes also given military protection.[15] Codes of international conduct became established in western Asia throughout the second and first millennia B.C.E. and provided a foundation for the diplomacy of future civilizations (see Table 2.2).

Table 2.2 Diplomacy in the Ancient World

Period	Early Practitioners
3000–2370 B.C.E.	Sumer
2600–2240 B.C.E.	Ebla
2370–2200 B.C.E.	Akkad
2150–2000 B.C.E.	Sumerian revival and Third Dynasty of Ur
1894–1600 B.C.E.	Babylon and Amorite kings
1570–1085 B.C.E.	Egyptian empire (eighteenth dynasty)
1460–1200 B.C.E.	Hittite empire
1122–256 B.C.E.	China: Zhou dynasty
1100–600 B.C.E.	Assyria
553–530 B.C.E.	Persia: Cyrus, king of Medes and Persians
522–486 B.C.E.	Persia: Darius brings empire to apex of territorial possessions
520–327 B.C.E.	Persian presence in India
500–100 B.C.E.	Greece
322–231 B.C.E.	India: Mauryan empire

■ Sumer

Sumer was the site of the first independent urban communities, around 3000 B.C.E., with complex social, economic, and political structures in southern Mesopotamia,[16] where the Euphrates and the Tigris reached the northern end of what is now the Persian Gulf.[17] Among the main city-states were Ur, Lagash, Uruk, and Kish. They were independent and each of them was ruled by a king in the name of a separate god or goddess. The king was the vicar of the deity. Diplomacy was perceived as the instrument of the relevant gods or goddesses. Sumerian city-states collectively chose one (more powerful) city to regulate or oversee their interstate relations, but the nature of the diplomatic process remains uncertain for lack of documentation. This chosen city would also mediate the many conflicts of the other cities in the name of a great god who was seen as the overlord of the other individual gods or goddesses. Much diplomatic work of course resulted from this supervisory function, although the process has not been identified.[18]

The cities were trading far up the Euphrates and controlled the eastern end of the Fertile Crescent.[19] They were in constant dispute about water rights, boundaries, and trade relations, which occasioned much mediation and arbitration. Sumerian tablets make reference to messengers sent on foreign missions for the exchange of letters and gifts, and to more important envoys for the negotiation of international agreements (with oaths before deities and for malization by sacrifices and ritual ceremonies).[20] Considering that this form of diplomacy continued for six or seven centuries, it can be assumed that the procedures involved would achieve a high degree of institutionalization. But the established political order and its international relations came to an end when Sumer was conquered by Sargon of Akkad (c. 2370 B.C.E.).[21]

▓ Ebla

When Sumer was flourishing, another source of thriving diplomacy was the city-state of Ebla in the northern part of Syria.[22] At the height of its power (c. 2600–2240 B.C.E.) Ebla dominated northern Syria, Lebanon, southeastern Turkey, and parts of northern Mesopotamia. It maintained trade and diplomatic relations with Egypt, what is now Iran, and Sumer. Ebla controlled a group of seventeen city-states, probably in Lebanon and southeastern Turkey, among which much interaction took place. Diplomacy as well as limited warfare protected Ebla's influence and trade. For example, Ebla had a diplomatic ally in what is now Iran. Trade treaties were negotiated with other cities as well.[23] But following Sargon's conquest of Sumer, Ebla was destroyed by the Akkadians around 2240 B.C.E.[24]

▓ Akkad

Sargon established the first military empire in history (c. 2370 B.C.E.) in central Mesopotamia, and was considered the founder of the Mesopotamian military tradition.[25] He conquered all Sumerian city-states and later pushed into northern Syria. He created Akkad as his capital (the city has not yet been found).[26] The Sumerian cities, however, did not readily give up their autonomy. Sargon retained control by means of troops and representatives in the conquered areas. The kind of relations maintained by these officials with the local governments is unclear. More attention has been given to Sargon's military pursuits, although an elaborate myth was built around his persona and place in society. At least for commercial relations and to meet the needs of the country (the economy was highly planned), some diplomatic relations must have been maintained.

The Akkadian language acquired literary prestige comparable to that of Sumer and eventually replaced it. Its use spread from Syria to Elam in the east, and Akkadian texts found their way to far-off regions, from Egypt, in the Amarna period, and Anatolia to Persia. There is no evidence that this was the result of Akkadian diplomatic activity, although it appears that Akkadian became a diplomatic language. The empire, however, quickly declined. Within a hundred years or so, it collapsed from the invasion of barbarians, the Gutians (c. 2200 B.C.E.), who came from the hills east of the Tigris and conquered all the former city-states, ushering in a dark age.[27]

■ Sumerian Revival and the Third Dynasty of Ur

The Sumerians despised the Gutians about as much as they did the Akkadians and eventually rose against their domination (c. 2150 B.C.E.) and pushed them out of the region. But about 2113 B.C.E., ambitious Ur-Nammu, a social and political reformer, established the Third Dynasty of Ur, claimed universal kingship, and tried to unify all Sumerians and Akkadians.[28] It is reported that agents of the central government were sent on missions to the four corners of the empire. And there was much coming and going of messengers between Mesopotamia and Iran, far beyond Elam. But there is no evidence of any relations with Egypt.[29] And in any case the empire soon collapsed, invaded by the Amorites, who conquered Mesopotamia about 2000 B.C.E.[30]

■ Babylon

The Amorites were troublesome nomads, invaders from the desert (possibly Arabia). They eventually dominated the history of Mesopotamia and Syria. Almost all the kings of Babylonia were Amorites. Babylon itself was a city of southern Mesopotamia that became the nucleus of a small kingdom established about 1894 B.C.E. by the Amorite king Sumuabum.[31] The sixth and best-known member of the dynasty was Hammurabi (c. 1792–1750 B.C.E.). This period, as revealed by the rich Mari archives,[32] was a time of intense diplomatic activity.[33] No state enjoyed superiority. The more ambitious rulers sought to attain their international objectives by negotiating alliances, but these often proved unreliable; political alignments changed and more coalition agreements needed to be negotiated.[34]

Hammurabi made skillful use of diplomacy to increase his power. After spending the first twenty-nine years of his reign developing his famous code of law, he turned to the conquest of all the city-states of southern Mesopotamia. However, as was often the case in Mesopotamia, the life span of the empire was cut short by foreign invasions involving the Hittites, coming from Anatolia (where they had migrated beginning about 2000 B.C.E.), and the Kassites (of unknown origins). Babylon was destroyed around 1600 B.C.E.[35] The reign of Hammurabi was in many ways the apex and the end of Mesopotamian political eminence.[36]

■ Egypt and the Hittites

For the longest time, the two major centers of civilization in the Middle East, Egypt and Mesopotamia, maintained little diplomatic contact. But things changed with the New Kingdom and the eighteenth dynasty (c. 1570 B.C.E.).[37] Militarism and imperialism characterized the new orientation, and diplomacy became an important instrument in Egyptian foreign relations. Economic and military expansion brought the pharaohs into contact with other states (and Akkadian was the language of diplomacy).[38] Surviving records indicate that when these states were too strong to be conquered or too dangerous to be ignored, Egypt engaged in diplomatic dialogue.[39] Diplomatic contact was helped by the protection given internationally to messengers even between enemy armies as battle was approaching—perhaps to determine whether an easier way of prevailing was possible without fighting.

The most significant diplomatic relations were with the Hittite empire (c. 1460–1200 B.C.E.—the height of the Hittite expansion was around 1350 B.C.E.).[40] Included in this diplomatic dialogue were the regulation of trade, the determination of boundaries, the negotiation of alliances, averting war, bringing conflict to an end, and strengthening friendly relations. Relations between the Egyptian and Hittite empires were not just a casual matter. They represented an elaborate system of interaction that also involved neighboring communities in a network of strategic and economic relations. Egyptians and Hittites belonged to very different civilizations and their rapports required elaborate conventions and procedures—very different from what happened in Sumerian and Mesopotamian societies, which shared a common culture and religion. Egypt and the Hittites became involved in a profound struggle for power. Egypt lost ground; the Hittites gained the upper hand, culminating in their victory at the Battle of Kadesh (1287 B.C.E.)—the apex of their destiny. Ironically, Egypt survived; the barbarian onslaught of 1200 B.C.E. wiped out the Hittite empire.[41]

Assyria

Assyria did not become an independent state until about 1400 B.C.E. Ashur, the city of the sun-god, was on the upper reaches of the Tigris (160 miles north-northwest of modern Baghdad), in the northern region of the Fertile Crescent. The Assyrians were conquered several times and subjected for a long time to rule by Babylon, but they reasserted their independence.[42] They were the first to use iron weapons and armor on a large scale.[43] Surrounded by states that were very different from one another, the Assyrians, very early, depended upon diplomacy to remain in contact with their neighbors and find out as much as they could about their intentions, their armies, and their politics—always trying to negotiate some kinds of alliance. Their resources being limited, the Assyrians used diplomacy to attain their foreign relations objectives. They were aware of the dangers of war and tried to let others fight for them, which required skillful diplomacy and the wielding of promises and threats.[44]

The Assyrians grew in power and formed a large empire that lasted some 500 years (c. 1100–600 B.C.E.). But they could not govern it all by themselves. They organized a political system of vassals—native governments requiring regular diplomatic intervention (Assyrian authority was thus looser than the term "empire" suggests). Moreover, beyond the reach of Assyrian power were fully independent states involved with the empire through trade and diplomacy.[45] In the end, after several centuries, the rulers of the subordinate states, like Egypt, had in practice enough freedom of action to use their own diplomatic contacts to negotiate anti-Assyrian coalitions with external enemies of the empire such as the Medes.[46] About 612 B.C.E., the new kingdoms of the Medes and the Chaldeans (neo-Babylonians), having agreed to join forces, obliterated Nineveh, and within two years the Assyrian empire disappeared.[47]

▨ Persia

The Medes and the Persians were originally nomadic horsemen from the steppes north of the Black Sea and the Caspian. They migrated slowly at first, but by 1000 B.C.E. their southward progress reached massive proportions. They flooded the hills east of Assyria and united to resist the advance of the Assyrians. They settled in what is now Iran. About 625 B.C.E., the Medes established an independent kingdom over Iran, Upper Mesopotamia, and Syria.[48] The Persians intermarried with the rulers of Media. About 553 B.C.E., Cyrus overthrew his grandfather, the Median monarch, and became recognized as king of the Medes and the Persians.[49] Restrained in victory, he encouraged the Medes to take a personal stake in the empire and placed Medes in high offices. From 522 to 486 B.C.E., Darius brought the Persian empire to its most extensive territorial dominion, a political system twice the size of the Assyrian empire—all conquered in a remarkably short time.[50]

The size and diversity of the empire led to the adoption of a very decentralized political system relying on persuasion and consent and much diplomacy,[51] reminiscent of the way Assyria approached its own governance problem. For two centuries, the Persians ventured into the Indus Valley, interacting with Indian city-states beyond their borders that had diplomatic traditions of their own. Persia also maintained very active diplomatic relations with the independent city-states of Greece, supporting a number of Greek leagues in their own efforts to maintain their independence against the strongest Greek polis of the day, even providing ships and money to that end. Persia even served as mediator in a number of disputes among these city-states.[52] Leading Greek states also became associated with Persia for commercial purposes, and the Persian connection stimulated Egypt's external trade.[53] In fact, the whole eastern Mediterranean area maintained a high level of interdependence, generating diplomatic contacts in which Persia was an active participant.

▨ Ancient India

The peoples of the Indian subcontinent (about two-fifths the size of Europe) came into contact with their neighbors in lands to the northwest in the third millennium B.C.E., and early patterns of civilization began to appear in the Indus Valley. Still, well-defined advances in culture and social organization became visible only during the first half of the first millennium, and seem to have had little effect on the Middle East. Vast barbarian migrations from the northwest overwhelmed India around 1500 B.C.E., as a consequence of which organized political life, writing, and all forms of artistic expression vanished. The sixth century B.C.E. seems to have been the time when civilization reappeared. Through the fifth and fourth centuries B.C.E., independent states developed in the river plains, some as kingdoms, others as republics.[54] Trade expanded, relations between neighbors flourished, treaties were negotiated, and diplomacy was employed to make alliances, ensure protection against the more powerful states, and maintain peace.[55]

On the northwest fringe, Persia expanded its dominion through Afghanistan, to the edge of the Indus Valley. After two centuries of Persian presence (c. 520–327 B.C.E.), Alexander the Great, king of Macedonia, came to India in 327 B.C.E. and conquered most of the Indus Valley. Immediately after Alexander's death in 323 B.C.E., the notable Mauryan dynasty of India became established in the north. Its founder, Chandragupta (322–298 B.C.E.), conquered the basins of the Indus and the Ganges as well as Afghanistan.[56] Simultaneously, a man of great learning, Kautilya, wrote an unusual body of doctrine on politics and diplomacy. His thought was articulated in his famous treatise *Arthashastras* (The Science of Politics and Administration), ahead of its time by almost two millennia. It was a pragmatic, amoral set of guidelines and directions for the establishment of an empire and the wielding of political power—just as the Mauryan dynasty was in the process of doing—and has been compared to Machiavelli's *Prince*.[57]

Kautilya saw conflict as the normal relationship between states, but stressed the importance of diplomacy in international relations—although not necessarily to be preferred to war: the powerful would gain more by outright conquest. Relations between states were to be established and carried out by means of diplomatic representation, which he perceived as falling into three categories: plenipotentiary (i.e., fully empowered to represent the sovereign), then a lesser category of envoys with limited negotiating authority, and last the simple messengers. Remarkably, Kautilya recommended that a diplomatic mission be stationed in all foreign states on a permanent basis (some 1,800 years before this very thing became established international practice, around C.E. 1450). All these diplomats were to enjoy special international protection. However, Kautilya expected representatives to spy, engage in acts of sabotage, and attempt to secure defections from the enemy's army.[58]

Treaties were to be an important element in the maintenance of peace, detailing the terms and conditions on which it rested. He identified many kinds of treaties, laying down a variety of stipulations, temporary and long-term instruments, and sincere and dishonest commitments, but always attempting to outsmart the adversary. Kautilya also envisioned the possibility of a neutral state, totally uninvolved in the conflicts of other states. In war, diplomacy remained essential, in order to win allies, delay military operations when experiencing vulnerability, and of course, make postwar arrangements for a new international order.[59]

The Mauryan empire did not amount to an implementation of Kautilya's teachings. Its story was not too different from that of other empires. It was strong enough to defeat Seleucus's attempt to reconquer Persian India in 305 B.C.E., and came to a friendly understanding cemented by a marriage alliance. Chandragupta's grandson Asoka (272–231 B.C.E.) expanded the empire, but at his death, it was fragmented and India quickly returned to the diverse mix of independent and warring states that had preceded the Mauryan era.[60]

■ Ancient China

The history of ancient China was essentially characterized by its relative isolation. Chinese tradition remembers three dynasties at the dawn of civilization: Hsia (c. 2205–1766 B.C.E.); Shang (c. 1766–1122 B.C.E.); and Chou, now Zhou (c. 1122–256 B.C.E.).[61] Little is known of the first. The second, when it fell, was a fairly small district in the plains of northern China. The main qualities of historical Chinese civilization were, at the time, not yet fixed. The third dynasty was a different story. The Zhou kings were at first able to hold their nobles in check, but when defeated by the barbarians (c. 771 B.C.E.), the lords became virtually independent. Some 200 states have been identified as existing around 700 B.C.E.[62] These states developed diplomatic practices of their own.

They maintained contact by means of messengers and other representatives. Members of the nobility were employed for more important missions, particularly to arrange marriages between royal houses. Diplomatic representatives were customarily granted safe passage; harming them was seen as a grave international offense. Interestingly, some of the envoys were also used to make preparations for court visits, some of them matters of courtesy; but there is evidence that some of these summit meetings were convened to strengthen relations or to address some international disputes. Conferences, too, were held, such as for planning war campaigns, some of which were attended by a large number of states. Weaker states created a league to achieve protection from powerful neighbors. In 679 B.C.E., a conference of league members recognized the need for a single leader to wage war and conduct diplomacy. The league lasted some seventy years.[63]

Numerous treaties were concluded to reaffirm friendships, create alliances, or bring wars to an end. Some of these covenants were multilateral, involving oath rituals and the sacrifice of animals. Important officials or members of the nobility were, on occasion, given asylum in neighboring states as an established custom. Mediation among states was customary, an extension of a practice deeply embedded in Chinese life. The mediator might be a prince or a minister of state. Mediation was used not only to settle disputes, but also to facilitate relations or even to conclude economic transactions.

Thus, extensive diplomatic relations flourished for almost 500 years among these numerous states until the state of Ch'in (now Qin) radically terminated their independence, crushing them in a series of wars lasting until 221 B.C.E. and creating a new empire, starkly authoritarian and determined to obliterate the very memory of the old system.[64]

▓ Ancient Greece: Bridge to the West

Beginning about 500 B.C.E., Greece played a more important role in the evolution of diplomacy than any of the systems preceding it—undoubtedly because of the enormous influence it exercised on the development of Western civilization.[65] It was the result of the interaction of small city-states in close proximity, sufficiently interdependent, sharing a common culture, language, and religious traditions, but acutely quarrelsome[66] and critically anxious to defend their own policies. This situation of course led to a profusion of international activity, changing alignments, and conflicts.[67] This was an environment that invited intense diplomatic interaction.[68] The Greek city-states thus contributed their own special character to the evolution of diplomacy,[69] but it must be acknowledged that the diplomatic traditions developed earlier in the ancient Middle East were a foundation for what the Greeks did in the field.

The protection of diplomatic envoys among Greek city-states was inherited from the practice of the states preceding them. In Greece, however, diplomatic representatives were regarded as possessing special sanctity conferred upon them by Zeus himself.[70] But there were no resident representatives. From the sixth century B.C.E. onward, the popular assemblies of these city-states routinely sent agents on temporary, ad hoc missions. Their method, however, departed sharply from earlier practice. They pleaded their cause publicly before the assemblies of other city-states and engaged in fierce debates on the policies of their government. These envoys were therefore chosen for their oratorical skills, usually by the city assembly.[71]

A surprising peculiarity of Greek practice was the number of representatives sent on a given mission (as many as ten), representing different political parties and points of view. An important reason for this odd procedure was the profound distrust of assembly members sending the missions; each party wanted to ensure that its own slant would be presented, which led to the spectacle of a diplomatic mission conveying conflicting messages. On occasion, animosity in a mission was so pronounced that the diplomatic representatives wanted no association with one another, even refusing to sit at the same table or sleep in the same house. These envoys were often noted for their indiscretion, tactlessness, and garrulousness, leading Harold Nicolson to observe: "It seems curious to us that intelligent people should have permitted so bad a diplomatic method to survive."[72]

City-state governments were also distrustful of the agents they sent abroad to negotiate treaties. Rarely were envoys given full powers. Their instructions were usually detailed and restrictive. When agreement could not be reached, they had to return home for new instructions—a difficult approach to treaty-making, particularly in an age of slow, difficult travel. Regardless of the nature of the mission, home assemblies tended to be harsh with delegates who did not achieve success in their foreign transactions. The practice of conducting all proceedings in the open was also an enormous handicap.[73]

Nevertheless, the Greek city-states contributed to the development of diplomacy. Their resort to international arbitration reached unprecedented levels, demonstrating the practicality of peaceful settlement. They also created the extremely useful institution of the resident consul—still in use today. Interestingly, this official was a local citizen serving the interests of a foreign state. The position was held in great respect, widely perceived as a distinction or an honor. The function tended to become hereditary. Consuls not only served merchants in their foreign endeavors; they were also used to facilitate diplomatic relations, help visiting envoys, and foster a friendly outlook toward the state employing them—a function that we would now call public relations.[74] In the final analysis, by the fifth century B.C.E., the Greeks had developed an elaborate apparatus of foreign relations together with a substantial body of diplomatic practice, which, despite its flaws, endured for several centuries.

Rome

The Romans were the next civilization to add to this legacy. From its early and uncertain beginnings in the sixth century B.C.E., Rome rose to prominence and remained significant until the fifth century of the common era, but contributed much less to diplomacy than its remarkable accomplishments elsewhere would have led one to expect.[75]

Under the Roman republic,[76] diplomatic relations continued to be conducted, as previously, by means of temporary missions; but representatives were of much greater stature—prominent citizens appointed and instructed by the prestigious Roman senate. Some were of senatorial rank. They were worthy representatives of the imposing power of Rome.[77] One vastly significant contribution to diplomatic practice was Roman pride in good faith,[78] particularly significant in the conclusion of treaties. These international agreements were highly valued and carefully negotiated and recorded. Showing the respect in which they were held, their terms were usually carved onto bronze or stone tablets, which were then kept in a place of great political or religious significance, such as a temple, or on public display, where anyone could read them.[79] Rome made extensive use of agreements and alliance treaties to extend its influence, particularly in the early consolidation of its power. By 264 B.C.E., more than 150 separate treaties had been concluded, often inducing neighboring communities to become allies, some of whom eventually demonstrated impressive loyalty.[80] Provincial governors used diplomacy to maintain peaceful relations with their neighbors.

Foreign delegations were received in Rome and given hospitality. Their domestic requirements were provided by the host state. Immunity granted by ancient tradition was expanded beyond customary practice to include their staffs, but does not seem to have applied to their diplomatic correspondence or to their residences or their servants. Members of a diplomatic delegation who committed some offense or broke the law were sent back to their own country instead of being tried locally, thus expanding the scope of diplomatic immunity. Envoys would normally be received by the senate, or by smaller groups of senior magistrates. In the early republic, there was little formal procedure. If it happened that the senate refused to receive a visiting diplomatic mission, as in the case of the Carthaginian delegation in 205 B.C.E., the representatives were denied diplomatic immunity and expelled.[81]

Under the Roman Empire (end of the first century B.C.E.),[82] the practice of diplomacy changed substantially, particularly with the personal involvement of the emperor—for example, in receiving foreign missions with appropriate solemnity. It is recorded that when he was absent, foreign envoys were required to pay homage to his statue and military standards, thus emphasizing who was in charge. Augustus set the pattern for the emperor's personal control of the diplomatic process.[83] But he was distracted by imperial affairs and military concerns, and there was no central machinery or institution in Rome to oversee the conduct of foreign relations (although the senate retained its ceremonial importance). The emperor came to negotiate international agreements in person beginning in the second century of the common era, thus reducing his interest in Rome's representation abroad.[84] Diplomacy was not effectively used as a means of maintaining Rome's supremacy. It was used in international business transactions and legal relations, and in these areas broke new ground for orderly international relations under the rule of law.[85] Rome also innovated in the practice of arbitration with the creation of commissions made up of two arbitrators, one representing each party, with a neutral umpire presiding for the adjudication of international claims.[86]

Less worthy was the Roman peacetime practice of inserting into treaties the delivery of hostages as guarantors of their execution. Articles specified the numbers, qualities, ages, and types of hostages to be delivered, and whether they could be replaced by others after a certain number of years. So long as the terms of the treaty were respected, the hostages were well treated during their enforced residence in Rome (it seems that they were given a good deal of freedom while living there). But if the terms were broken, the hostages were immediately arrested and treated as prisoners of war.[87] The practice was of course unjust. But it became widespread, particularly in time of war, until finally outlawed in the modern law of war,[88] and in the UN's 1979 Hostages Convention.[89]

■ Byzantine Empire

The Eastern Roman Empire at Byzantium, or Byzantine Empire (c. C.E. 330–1453), drastically changed the use of diplomacy.[90] The Byzantines made it an important instrument—at times, the main instrument—of their foreign relations. Diplomacy is still regarded as one of the Byzantines' foremost skills. They used it more continuously and more assiduously than had other governments before them. They also changed its character because of their deviousness. In the process they tarnished its image. As a result of their close relations with Venice, this new style of diplomacy was brought to the Italian city-states, and eventually to France, Spain, and eventually Europe.

The Byzantine Empire was the first to create a special branch of government to deal with foreign relations and to train professionals to serve as diplomats.[91] To a certain extent it was a forerunner of the modern diplomatic system. Missions, however, remained ad hoc and temporary. The Byzantines faced the threat of invasion across virtually all of their borders, but did not have the military capability to resist. They had to use diplomacy to avoid disaster.[92] Their alignment with the Church of Rome gave them an aura that served them well. They staged elaborate, costly, glittering ceremonies and rituals, beyond the means or capabilities of the "barbarians" on their borders, and with great regularity, evoking envy and admiration.[93]

Of greater consequence, new techniques were added to the art of diplomacy.[94] Deception was advocated by the emperors—and came to characterize the diplomatic profession for several centuries.[95] The Byzantines continuously sought to disseminate false information. Duplicity in foreign relations, opportunism, faithlessness, dishonesty, and all kinds of unscrupulous dealings such as bribery, subversion, and even stealing came to be symptomatic of diplomatic practice—in other words, truly "Byzantine."

The other method extensively used by Byzantine diplomats was to divide enemies and embroil them with each other. Gathering information about the internal politics and external relationships of other nations thus became a major function of diplomatic missions. Merchants, frontier officials, and other citizens abroad were also expected to collect intelligence. In fact, it was assumed in Byzantium that it was a universal endeavor, explaining why foreigners in Constantinople, including visiting envoys, were viewed with suspicion and kept under surveillance (visiting envoys were confined to special residences).[96]

Giving new meaning to the Roman hostage-taking practice,[97] the Byzantines took hostages from their northern allies, literally for public relations purposes. Each year, imperial agents collected hostages in these underdeveloped territories, and entertained them in Constantinople. They were treated lavishly and given all the honors that the emperor could bestow, and were even invited to court ceremonies as friends. Upon return to their northern steppes, presumably impressed with the splendor of the imperial capital, they dazzled their compatriots with what they had seen, inspiring awe and respect.[98] Byzantium innovated, pushing diplomacy to the next level even though discrediting it by its unscrupulous practices.

■ Medieval Europe

Medieval Europe stood in stark contrast to happenings in the east.[99] Its political structure virtually disintegrated. The church, rather than kings, had the allegiance of the people. The effective power of governments, in spite of large local variations, did not extend far beyond the walls of their capitals. Feudal "states" (almost a misnomer) were fragmented. Lords governed the land around their castles, and lawlessness prevailed in between. The growth of effective central governments was impeded by a variety of obstacles, including primitive economic conditions, sparsity of population, difficulties of communication, and dangerous, woefully slow, and arduous travel. These conditions endured from about the ninth to the thirteenth century.[100] Diplomatic contacts were intermittent and infrequent, although political marriages, alliances, truces, and peace treaties were negotiated. Political intrigue and plots still required interaction. The church maintained contact and political issues were easily intertwined with religious concerns. Ad hoc diplomatic missions were sent. Envoys were primarily messengers working from narrow, inflexible instructions, which protracted negotiations. Back-and-forth envoy travel took inordinate amounts of time. Rare summit meetings took place between neighbors, but language and cultural difficulties often made them counterproductive.[101]

As feudal societies changed in the later Middle Ages, and as relations became more complex over greater distances, envoys were given more important functions to avoid the interminable succession of messages exchanged back and forth. They were empowered to negotiate and conclude agreements. This procedure became increasingly common in the latter part of the twelfth century.

Historians have tended to refer to representatives who enjoyed this kind of authority as "procurators"; but in the Middle Ages, the names given to envoys were still broad, nontechnical terms, often used interchangeably—among others, "orator," "nuncius," "legatus," "procurator," and "ambassador." The papal chancery did apply special meaning to "nuncius" and "legatus," and Venetian officials reserved the term "ambassador" for diplomats belonging to the nobility. The consensus of historical opinion is that the use of "ambassador" in diplomacy stems from thirteenth-century Italy; but for a long time, state practice was not uniform and a variety of titles continued to be used.[102]

Full powers to bind one's ruler—plenipotentiary diplomacy—became more common in the thirteenth century. But as diplomatic activity intensified in the fourteenth and fifteenth centuries, and communications improved, full powers were prudently controlled to give heads of state the latitude to review what had been negotiated.[103] Ceremony acquired unprecedented importance in the conduct of diplomacy toward the end of the Middle Ages. The arrival of a new envoy and the conclusion of a treaty were occasions for glittering receptions involving large numbers of diplomatic representatives with substantial retinues, sumptuous garments, and solemn oratory. Extravagant gifts were commonly presented. Protocol was critically important and the order of precedence of diplomatic envoys was taken very seriously and occasionally generated international disputes.[104]

Diplomatic personnel remained entitled to special protection and privileges. This was now well established in international law. Violations occurred, but they led to protest, compensation, or retaliation. Diplomats were exempt from all taxes and customs on goods or property necessary for their missions. Such immunities applied to the members of their retinues as well. Similar protection applied when diplomats were traveling through neighboring states en route to their posts. The scope of diplomatic immunity, however, was more limited than it is today. Misconduct in the host state exposed them to the judicial process and the penalties of the law. They could be sued for certain debts incurred during the mission, and their property seized. Their status gave them no immunity from punishment for crimes committed in the host country.[105]

■ The Renaissance

The Renaissance marked only the beginning of modern diplomacy—another two centuries would be needed to reach this level. The many states of the Italian peninsula were perpetually engaged in fierce power struggles, rivalries, and intrigue. Diplomacy was of critical importance in this intense, bitterly competitive environment. In the process, the Italian states made a number of significant diplomatic innovations that were adopted throughout the peninsula in the fifteenth and sixteenth centuries, and eventually in the rest of Europe.

The most important was the establishment of permanent diplomatic missions in foreign capitals. While the Pope had maintained a permanent representative at the court of Byzantium beginning in C.E. 453 and the Archbishop of Ravenna had long maintained an envoy at the Curia in Rome,[106] it must also be remembered that resident consuls had long engaged in diplomatic activity.[107] Toward the end of the Middle Ages, too, envoys on temporary missions could remain in foreign capitals for extended periods. As the intelligence function became more important, states tended to keep their diplomatic agents longer in foreign capitals without making them permanent residents. As a result, the distinction between ad hoc diplomats and permanent residents became blurred. The first true resident embassy in the modern sense was opened in Italy in the mid–fifteenth century, and the practice was quickly adopted by the major states of the peninsula.[108]

The use of permanent representatives led to new diplomatic practices. Anxious to maintain a continuous flow of communication, governments increased their use of couriers, who carried instructions to representatives abroad and returned with the latest intelligence. Couriers were provided with special travel documents. In the sixteenth century, ciphers and codes began to be used and the practice spread throughout Europe.[109] Permanent representatives became the foremost source of information. The Venetians were the first to create an organized system of diplomacy.[110] By the 1460s, they were providing secretaries for some of their resident diplomats; they even adopted the sensible practice of temporarily retaining the secretary after a diplomat was replaced, so that the new envoy could benefit from the secretary's experience.[111]

The Venetians were also the first to preserve their state archives in a systematic fashion.[112] By the mid–fifteenth century, all the major Italian states had established chanceries that required written reports from their diplomats and kept extensive records. This was a profound improvement over the casual attitude of their predecessors toward state papers and their storage. When diplomats employed their own secretaries who were not public servants, the tendency for archives to disappear was widespread.[113] The new chanceries became the center of a network of permanent embassies providing a constant flow of communication with their important neighbors.[114] The Venetians were the first to inform their permanent representatives abroad of events and political developments at home by means of regular reports.[115]

Despite the growing importance attached to permanent representation, special envoys continued to be used for the negotiation of even minor agreements. Important ceremonies or celebrations also called for special missions, so that the sending state could be represented by high officials, a sign of greater respect—and a practice still in use today. Another legacy of this era is the enormous importance attached to pomp and ceremony. Upon reaching his post, an ambassador often had to negotiate, for weeks, every detail of his official reception.[116] Resident and special representatives received full diplomatic status.

Occasionally, princes were their own diplomatic links, and for these occasions there were no rules.[117] Face-to-face meetings between sovereigns in the fifteenth century required extensive security precautions, as an attack was always feared. Language difficulties could hamper the exchange. Some of these encounters in fact became acrimonious, thus complicating future relations. Philippe de Comines, a diplomat from this period, was led to observe: "Two great Princes, who wish to establish good personal relations, should never meet each other face to face, but ought to communicate through good and wise ambassadors."[118] In their ceaseless power struggles and diplomatic intrigue, it is not surprising that the small states of the Italian peninsula inherited from Byzantium the attitude that the interests of the state—raison d'état—took precedence over all ethical considerations. Machiavelli's works, too, had a profound influence on the conduct of politics in the region, and colored diplomatic practice. For example, in the sixteenth century, and even beyond, it was not considered disgraceful to receive monetary gifts from foreign powers. Italian governments encouraged this way of influencing official behavior.[119]

In the mid–fifteenth century, the major focal point of the Italian diplomatic system was the papal court. The popes increasingly intervened in politics and Rome became the center of high political intrigue. Its influence in the establishment of permanent diplomacy both in Italy and in Europe was enormous. No other court in Europe would bring together so many distinguished diplomats. Consequently, Rome became the main center for the diffusion of Italian diplomatic practice to the rest of Europe. And it was the birthplace of another diplomatic institution: the first signs of an organized diplomatic corps. The popes developed the practice of bringing all foreign representatives together to make important announcements. They would also assign them a special place at all ceremonies, and occasionally issued regulations applicable to all envoys. These diplomats eventually developed a sense of professional solidarity, communicating their collective needs to the popes and acting together as the occasion arose, particularly in times of crisis. New customs thus emerged, leading to the modern institution of the diplomatic corps in major capitals.[120]

The diplomatic method of the Italian Renaissance became established in continental Europe along with a pervasive distrust—a universal assumption that no state would keep a promise longer than served its purpose—and diplomats remained essentially suspect throughout Europe.[121] But there were significant variations between different parts of the continent. The weaker states through the sixteenth century in eastern and northern Europe were slow to adopt the new system of the resident embassy. They remained attached to ad hoc temporary representation. Missions of several ambassadors, especially for ceremonial purposes, were still in use, even in the west.[122]

Throughout the fifteenth and sixteenth centuries, none of the main states of western or central Europe had anything that could be called a diplomatic service. A number of rulers sent foreigners to represent them abroad. Most diplomats were poorly or irregularly paid, leaving them with insufficient resources to meet their normal expenses. Travel was difficult and even dangerous. At the end of the sixteenth century, papal couriers normally needed fifteen days to travel from Rome to Paris. The weather and hazards of the road were important factors. The lack of roads in eastern Europe made it even more difficult. The journey from Vienna to the Russian capital could take four months. A Jesuit sent by the Pope in 1582 to mediate between Russia and Poland wrote that a traveler must have a tent to sleep in when there was no lodging available or he might have to share a room with several other travelers, together with their horses for the sake of warmth in winter.[123]

Danger compounded the problem. In the fifteenth and sixteenth centuries, diplomats in Europe were sometimes captured for ransom. Others were taken prisoner while passing through the territory of one state en route to another if the captors deemed the diplomats' activities as a threat to their interests. In 1509, the Florentine government instructed its envoy to Emperor Maximilian to take the precaution of returning home disguised as a merchant.[124] Because of all the hardships involved in the profession, diplomats were inclined to accept a post as a stepping-stone to a better appointment at home. Europe was slowly entering the modern world, but unevenly. At the end of the sixteenth century, there was no common language in diplomacy.[125]

▇   The Age of Richelieu

The Age of Richelieu ushered in modern diplomacy—not overnight, but building on the innovations of the Italian Renaissance and reforming what had been received from Byzantium.[126] This new era was to span three centuries, the seventeenth through the nineteenth. It was seen as the age of French diplomacy, which many see as "classical diplomacy," and which a few, even today, would like to resurrect. But the clocks cannot be turned back. The world keeps changing— faster than ever. And diplomacy must keep changing with it.

Cardinal Richelieu, prime minister of Louis XIII of France from 1624 to 1642, was a decisive force in restoring the integrity of diplomacy and creating a profession to carry it out. In his eighteen years at the helm, he transformed the French foreign service into an effective tool of his ambitious foreign relations. He perceived diplomacy as an instrument of power to be used continuously, rather than occasionally as events required. With him, diplomacy became a permanent process, a systematic endeavor instead of the result of improvisation.[127] He set out to strengthen the quality of diplomatic representation. Honesty, integrity, and trustworthiness became mandatory as he rooted out the pernicious Byzantine ways of the Italian era. Treaties were seen to be critically important. They were to be scrupulously observed; hence they were to be negotiated with utmost caution. The formulation and execution of foreign policy, as well as the control of foreign service officers, were therefore to be concentrated in a single ministry (achieved on March 11, 1626, under Richelieu's constant supervision). Dispersal of responsibility was seen as an element of confusion. Coherence was an important objective of the new order, and great importance was attached to written instructions. Under no circumstances were diplomats to exceed them.

The French diplomatic service became more extensive than that of any other power, with envoys sent systematically to all centers of political activity. Diplomatic officers were classified under the categories of ambassadors extraordinary, ambassadors ordinary (eventually dropped), envoys, and residents.[128] Richelieu's reforms had a profound influence on the practice of diplomacy in Europe. They generated an enormous growth in professionalism throughout the continent in the seventeenth and eighteenth centuries.[129] France's stature and unprecedented power gave greater weight to its diplomatic work. The magnificence of its next sovereign, Louis XIV, who reigned for seventy-two years (1643–1715), did even more to establish the new diplomatic order. It set the tone for European diplomacy until World War I, and French became the language of diplomacy for the next two centuries.[130] A French diplomat, François de Callières, contributed to the international transformation of diplomatic practice by writing a treatise, first published in 1716, based on his own experience of the new system. This volume became a classic manual of diplomatic procedure throughout Europe. It is still in print today.[131]

Italian Renaissance diplomacy developed many of the practices that underlie the modern system. But the French reform set a totally different tone based on the conviction that sound diplomacy requires the creation of confidence, possible only with a foundation of good faith.[132] Furthermore, the new professionalism attached great importance to knowledge and experience. Style, too, was emphasized as a significant factor of effective diplomacy. Across Europe, a diplomatic community developed. The major powers gave their envoys fairly similar training; they understood the importance of confidentiality in negotiations.[133] The diplomatic profession became better organized; different ranks characterized the importance of diplomatic office. Professional bonds developed among diplomats of different countries; most of them shared the same professional standards, all of which facilitated diplomacy even between countries engaged in intense power struggles.

However, in the seventeenth century, travel remained difficult, especially to the more remote capitals of eastern and northern Europe, hampering communication. Intense sensitivity over diplomatic ceremony created problems, particularly with regard to precedence—a result of the presence of permanent embassies in the same capital. It took more than a hundred years for consensus on the subject to develop (codified at the Congress of Vienna in 1815).

Endless battles took place over the shape of the table, seating arrangements, and whether a delegate should be near a mirror, window, or door. In fact, adding mirrors, windows, and doors to the grand halls became necessary to reach agreement.[134] Crises of precedence declined as the nineteenth century approached, but did not disappear.[135]

The Congress of Vienna formed a committee to examine ranks in the diplomatic community. After two months of negotiations, it was decided that three categories of diplomats should be acknowledged "in order to prevent the embarrassment which has frequently resulted . . . from claims of precedence among the various diplomatic agents": (1) ambassadors, nuncios, and legates; (2) envoys, ministers, and other agents accredited to a sovereign; (3) chargés d'affaires accredited to ministers of foreign affairs.[136] It was also decided that precedence among diplomats of the same rank should depend upon the seniority of their residence in a particular capital. The Congress of Vienna further decided who was entitled to be dean of the diplomatic corps in a given capital.[137]

All of this helped, but did not completely resolve the problem. Even when precedence was not perceived as a matter of national honor, diplomatic representatives were interested in how their state was treated in comparison with all other states, in a wide variety of circumstances, from official dinners to presentations at international gatherings. Eventually, foreign ministries individually addressed issues of protocol for their own capitals, taking into account international law, local traditions, and cultural idiosyncrasies.

The Nineteenth Century

The nineteenth century saw a significant increase in the number of states involved in the diplomatic process and an expansion of ambassadorial conferences. For example, in 1815, Britain had nineteen resident diplomatic missions, only two of which were not in Europe (the Ottoman Empire and the United States). By 1914, representation had grown to forty-one British missions, nineteen of them outside Europe. Other major powers also expanded their foreign representation. Interestingly, the British consulates in Greece, Serbia, Romania, and Bulgaria served as diplomatic posts when these countries were still under Ottoman sovereignty. Similarly, between 1827 and 1842, France, aside from its legations to Argentina, Brazil, Colombia, and Mexico, used its consulates-general in the other former Spanish colonies as diplomatic missions, in some cases giving the rank of chargé d'affaires to its consular officers. Gradually, all these posts were upgraded. France also opened one legation in Guatemala City covering all five Central American republics.[138]

The United States, by 1854, had twenty-eight diplomatic missions abroad. A similar pattern of diplomatic expansion occurred elsewhere in the Americas. Brazil, for instance, had twenty-two missions abroad by 1860, including four in Europe. Japan was forced by the arrival of Commodore Matthew Perry and a small squadron of US warships in 1853 to accept Western consuls, ending two centuries of isolation.[139] By the 1870s, Japan was sending its own diplomatic missions abroad. China refused to take part in the new diplomacy until it was militarily compelled to accept representation in Peking from Britain, France, the United States, and Russia in 1860, Prussia in 1864, and Japan a decade later.[140]

In the East, the Ottoman Empire long maintained diplomatic relations with European states. It established an embassy in Tehran in 1849, probably the first among Muslim states. Persia, itself long isolated, received a British resident mission in 1809 (and subsequently from France and Russia), but did not open permanent missions in Europe until 1862–1863.[141] Europe had diplomatic ties with Morocco and maintained missions in Algiers, Tunis, and Tripoli when they were still nominally under Ottoman sovereignty.[142]

The growth of diplomatic relations in the nineteenth century is probably best illustrated by the nature of international participation in the Hague Peace Conferences of 1899 and 1907. In 1899, in the context of a worsening power struggle in Europe, twenty-six nations met at The Hague, in the Netherlands, to devise a framework to prevent the oncoming war. They failed, but decided to try again in 1907. This time, forty-four states were represented. Diplomacy was no longer so exclusively European.[143]

The nineteenth century witnessed another development in the field: a new trend in multilateral diplomacy. Multilateral work was not unprecedented, as the major wars of the past had brought heads of state and their key ministers together to pick up the pieces and share the spoils. The Congress of Vienna was given the challenge of repairing the monumental disruption wrought by Napoleon, and diplomats began to warm up to multilateral work. Conferences were convened to address international issues other than the termination of war.[144] Technology was changing the nation-state system, resulting in greater interdependence and easier communication. And the world was experiencing more problems that transcended the boundaries of nation-states, problems that required collective work.

Following the Congress of Vienna was the question of whether France would become a problem again (or if not France, then the revolutionary ideal of 1789). This led to the Concert of Europe, a series of occasional meetings intended to review how stable the European situation was. Four of these took place between 1818 and 1822.[145] But as the political situation settled, these meetings were discontinued.[146] Other conferences, however, were convened, usually to deal with specific issues, such as the intricacies of the Schleswig-Holstein question or the Middle East.[147] Between 1822 and 1914, twenty-six conferences were held at which all the great powers were represented. Other conferences brought only three or four of them together. Smaller powers participated when their interests were involved. Two more end-of-war congresses of the classic type were convened: in Paris in 1856, at the end of the Crimean War; and in Berlin in 1878, at the end of the Russo-Turkish conflict.[148] Diplomacy had to adjust to the multilateral environment, which was very different from that of resident representation in national capitals. New techniques were developed, such as a committee structure to address the conference agenda (these issues of multilateral diplomacy are discussed in Chapters 8 and 9). Many of these conferences, however, remained small and uncomplicated in contrast to those of the post–World War II era.

The nineteenth century saw the birth of small intergovernmental organizations designed to administer fairly technical or specialized international tasks—for example, the navigation of European rivers to facilitate international trade, and the operation of the international postal system.[149] National representatives would ensure the cooperation of member states, make policy, and see to the effective functioning of the administrative body that they created. Quite naturally, a good deal of diplomacy was required to keep the participating states working together. Many of these organizations were performing international tasks under their own international corporate personalities, and this was the beginning of a new category of international actors. As industry spread and commerce expanded, more organizations were created, mostly in the last third of the nineteenth century. By 1909, thirty-seven were in operation.[150]

The Interwar Period

World War I brought significant transformation in diplomatic method. First, the victors created new international structures for diplomatic interaction in an attempt to prevent the outbreak of another devastating war. The League of Nations was unprecedented. The Hague Peace Conferences of 1899 and 1907 could not bring themselves to establish anything so unconventional. The League system led to new diplomatic procedures, for better or worse: multilateral consultation, public debates, international parliamentary procedures, and collective decisionmaking.[151] The main purpose of the League was to keep states from rushing to war in a crisis. But an enduring nineteenth-century fixation on sovereignty and reluctance to engage in collective efforts limited what multilateral diplomacy could accomplish here.[152]

The most radical departure from nineteenth-century diplomatic procedure was negotiated at Versailles: the creation of the International Labour Organization (ILO). In the wake of abusive labor practices in many industrialized nations, which led to widespread labor unrest, as well as the Russian Revolution, the ILO was established to create international labor standards. This was unconventional enough when the world was not yet thinking of universal human rights. But even more innovative, in terms of procedure, was the system of national representation in the organization. Each member state was to send four delegates: two representing the government, one representing labor, and one representing management. Labor and management were allowed to participate, negotiate, and vote *independently* from their government. Labor and management could form their own multinational coalitions.[153] This system was ahead of its time, to say the least, and is still operating today, now in association with the United Nations. In 1969, upon its fiftieth anniversary, the ILO was awarded the Nobel Peace Prize.

League of Nations diplomacy did not reduce the importance of resident diplomacy in national capitals, but it opened new channels of international relationship. Growing interdependence led states to turn (slowly, at first) to multilateral efforts to address economic, social, and cultural issues. The diplomatic agenda was expanding. Issues that formerly had been exclusively domestic now needed to be addressed internationally. Though international organizations did not accomplish much to solve the Great Depression, the League of Nations was confronted with many more economic and social issues than had been contemplated in 1919, and it responded as problems arose, piecemeal. Finally, the time came to take stock of what had been done in fits and starts. In May 1939, the League created the Bruce Committee to suggest a reorganization of its machinery that would better enable it to deal with the many economic and social activities that the architects of the League Covenant had not foreseen.[154] The committee's report was published in August 1939 and recommended the creation of a "Central Committee for Economic and Social Questions" to supervise and coordinate all League activities in this area,[155] but World War II began in Europe on September 3. Time had run out, but this effort was not lost; it helped the United Nations move in a new direction.

▓ World War II and the Postwar Era

World War II generated an enormous amount of diplomacy, foremost to organize a collective effort in the face of devastating aggression.[156] After the United States entered the war, a large array of multinational bodies created joint strategies, coordinated military operations, and distributed staggering amounts of supplies and matériel in the global war effort. Simultaneously, and long before victory was in sight, the Allies began negotiating the creation of new institutions for postwar restructuring. First came the establishment of the United Nations Relief and Rehabilitation Administration (UNRRA) and the Food and Agriculture Organization,[157] to address matters that had not been among the concerns of the post–World War I negotiators. Diplomacy was following a different course. Priorities were broader. Then came the 1944 Bretton Woods negotiations for the creation of the first global banking institutions and the Chicago conference of the same year, which led to the creation of the first global civil aviation organization. Simultaneously, negotiations were taking place to establish an organization of unprecedented dimensions and authority,[158] the United Nations.

The architects of the future peace were convinced that international organization was of critical importance for postwar stability in a large variety of fields. After the war, international structures, a number of them regional, multiplied. Today, a larger amount of diplomacy is now conducted in international organizations than ever before. And now the European Union is providing its own special type of interaction—not a federation, but so much more than an international organization of the twentieth-century type.[159] It is in many respects supranational, but its twenty-seven members are still sovereign states that must employ diplomacy within the organization to keep it operating—and the process is elaborate.

The twentieth century also witnessed a vast expansion of conference diplomacy (despite the large-scale operations of all the international organizations). Today, thousands of conferences, large and small, are convened annually, overtaxing the personnel capacity of even well-endowed foreign ministries. Diplomats travel more than ever before—and not only diplomats, but also chief executives, foreign ministers, and even heads of executive departments in national governments, all engaging in diplomatic negotiations of their own. Some government departments conduct their own foreign relations in their fields of specialization without using the diplomatic facilities of their governments' foreign ministries. This is now called "transgovernmental relations"—convenient in day-to-day, businesslike relations, and usually bilateral, although multilateral conferences of this type of specialized personnel (e.g., conferences of health ministers) take place, often initiated by international organizations.

Technological development contributes significantly to the evolution of diplomatic method, particularly in the field of communication—and there is much more to come (virtual diplomacy?). Chief decisionmakers are able to interact directly and almost instantly when the need arises. Early-warning systems may permit more timely diplomatic responses. Unprecedented also are the number and diversity of international actors—giant powerful states and micro states, perhaps weak but participating in international affairs. Coalition diplomacy gives them greater influence. And a multiplicity of nonsovereign entities play an expanding role in diplomatic circles. International organizations have become significant international actors (even though representing the collective will of their members). Some organization executives play major diplomatic roles, sending their own diplomats on special missions, intervening in international crises, and affecting the course of events—roles that are in fact more potent than those of many national decisionmakers.

Diplomacy today is made even more complex also by the advent of transnational actors, whose intervention potential is magnified by communication technology, which mobilizes support around the world and wields political power itself. Many NGOs intervene in the diplomatic process in international conferences or as mediators in international conflicts. Some are invited to participate in the decisionmaking of international organizations such as the World Bank. Even if their intervention is less than decisive, they have become part of international politics and the diplomatic process.

In the midst of all this transformation, is diplomacy recognizable? Is it still serving its purpose? The remainder of the volume addresses these important questions.

■ Study Questions and Discussion Topics

1. Why study the history of diplomacy?

2. To what extent was Greek diplomacy less proficient than Italian Renaissance diplomacy?

3. What distinguishes post-Richelieu diplomacy from Italian Renaissance diplomacy?

4. What characterizes modern diplomacy? When did it start?

5. What is special about the diplomacy of the post–World War II era?

6. What factors led to the use of international organizations for the conduct of diplomacy?

7. What difference does it make if some of the new modes of interaction are not officially recognized as "diplomacy"?

■ Suggested Reading

Anderson, Matthew S. *The Rise of Modern Diplomacy, 1450–1919*. New York: Longman, 1993.

Barston, R. P. *Modern Diplomacy*. 2d ed. New York: Longman, 1997.

Hamilton, Keith, and Richard Langhorne. *The Practice of Diplomacy: Its Evolution, Theory, and Administration*. New York: Routledge, 1995.

Jönsson, Christer, and Richard Langhorne, eds. *Diplomacy*. Vol. 2, *History of Diplomacy*. London: Sage, 2004.

Mattingly, Garrett. *Renaissance Diplomacy*. Boston: Houghton Mifflin, 1955.

Nicolson, Harold. *The Evolution of Diplomatic Method*. London: Constable, 1954.

Plischke, Elmer, ed. *Modern Diplomacy: The Art and the Artisans*. Washington, DC: American Enterprise Institute for Public Policy Research, 1979.

Queller, Donald E. *The Office of Ambassador in the Middle Ages*. Princeton: Princeton University Press, 1967.

■ Notes

1. This explains comments on the contingent nature of diplomacy and the changing boundaries of the field, as will be seen in subsequent chapters of this book.

2. Adam Watson, *The Evolution of International Society* (New York: Routledge, 1992), pp. 19–46. Pierre Jouguet et al., *Les Premières Civilisations*, 2d ed. (Paris: Presses Universitaires de France, 1950), pp. 705–711. See also Raymond Cohen, "The Great Tradition: The Spread of Diplomacy in the Ancient World," in *Diplomacy*, edited by Christer Jönsson and Richard Langhorne (London: Sage, 2004), vol. 2, *History of Diplomacy*, pp. 44–46, 49–51; Ragmar Numelin, *The Beginnings of Diplomacy* (New York: Philosophical Library, 1950).

3. Inscriptions in wedge-shaped characters used at the time—for example, in Assyria, Babylonia, and Persia. See Chester G. Starr, *A History of the Ancient World*, 4th ed. (New York: Oxford University Press, 1991), pp. 27ff.

4. Cohen, "Great Tradition," pp. 44–50.

5. Found in 1887 at El Amarna, on the east bank of the Nile, some 190 miles south of modern Cairo. They cover the Late Bronze Period (c. 1600–1200 B.C.E.).

6. Mario Liverani, *International Relations in the Ancient Near East, 1600–1100 B.C.* (New York: Palgrave, 2001), p. 2. See also Mario Liverani, *Three Amarna Essays* (Malibu, CA: Undena, 1979).

7. Found in 1906–1907 at Hattusa, the Hittite capital (modern Boğazköy is in northern central Turkey, some ninety-five miles east of Ankara). These documents date back to the thirteenth and fourteenth centuries B.C.E., with only a few of the tablets originating earlier than the seventeenth century B.C.E. See http://www.britannica.com/eb.

8. Found in 1933–1939 at Tell Hariri, on the western bank of the Euphrates, some seventy-five miles southeast of Deir ez-Zor, in modern Syria. It was an important relay point between Sumerian cities of lower Mesopotamia and the cities of northern Syria. They pertain to the eighteenth to seventeenth centuries B.C.E. Liverani, *International Relations*, p. 2.

9. Found in 1951–1957 at Ugarit, the capital city of an ancient principality in what is today on the northern part of the Syrian coast, just north of modern Latakia. Ugarit was destroyed in 1180 B.C.E. See http://lexicorient.com/e.o/ugarit.

10. Found in 1975, pushing back in time the documentation of international relations to the twenty-fourth century B.C.E. It is located in northern Syria about thirty miles southwest of Aleppo. The site is known today as Tell Mardikh. Cyrus H. Gordon, *Forgotten Scripts: Their Ongoing Discovery and Decipherment* (New York: Basic, 1982), p. 155; Paolo Matthiae, *Ebla in the Period of the Amorite Dynasties and the Dynasty of Akkad: Recent Archaeological Discoveries at Tell Mardikh (1975)* (Malibu, CA: Undena, 1979).

11. Cohen, "Great Tradition," pp. 44–50.

12. See Joan M. Munn-Rankin, "Diplomacy in Western Asia in the Early Second Millennium B.C.," in Jönsson and Langhorne, *Diplomacy*, vol. 2, pp. 1–2, 13–32, 34, which points to diplomatic records of several empires of this period.

13. Moshe Weinfeld, "Covenant Terminology in the Ancient Near East and Its Influence on the West," *Journal of the American Oriental Society* 93 (1973), pp. 190–199; Moshe Weinfeld, "The Common Heritage of Covenantal Traditions in the Ancient World," in *I Trattati nel Mondo Antico: Forma, Ideologia, Funzione*, edited by Luciano Canfora, Mario Liverani, and Carlo Zaccagnini (Rome: L'Erma di Bretschneider, 1990), pp. 175–191; Moshe Weinfeld, "Covenant Making in Anatolia and Mesopotamia," *Journal of the Ancient Near Eastern Society of Columbia University* 22 (1993), pp. 135–139. The Mari archives spell out the procedures and ritual acts required for the conclusion of international agreements.

14. Munn-Rankin, "Diplomacy in Western Asia," pp. 25–32; Liverani, *International Relations*, pp. 71–76.

15. Munn-Rankin, "Diplomacy in Western Asia," pp. 29–31.

16. *Cambridge Ancient History,* 3d ed. (London: Cambridge University Press, 1970), vol. 1, *Early History of the Middle East;* S. N. Kramer, *History Begins at Sumer* (Philadelphia: University of Pennsylvania Press, 1981); Rushton Coulborn, *Origin of Civilized Societies* (Princeton: Princeton University Press, 1969); Hans Jörg Niesen, *The Early History of the Ancient Near East, 9000–2000 B.C.* (Chicago: University of Chicago Press, 1988).

17. It was one of the earliest civilizations. The Persian Gulf at the time penetrated farther inland and the two rivers reached the Gulf separately. Eventually, sedimentation filled this end of the Gulf, and the two rivers merged. Thomas W. Africa, *The Ancient World* (Boston: Houghton Mifflin, 1969), p. 4. The earliest records that have survived and could be deciphered came from Sumer. Starr, *History of the Ancient World,* pp. 34–45.

18. Watson, *Evolution of International Society,* pp. 24–2⁵.

19. Ibid. The Fertile Crescent covered Mesopotamia and Syria, then turned south again through Palestine along the Mediterranean.

20. Munn-Rankin, "Diplomacy in Western Asia," pp. 13–32. See also Starr, *History of the Ancient World,* pp. 35–50.

21. Africa, *Ancient World,* pp. 7–9.

22. About thirty miles southwest of Aleppo in the northern part of modern Syria.

23. The script of the Ebla tablets is Sumerian.

24. "Ebla," *Encyclopaedia Britannica Online,* http://search.eb.com/eb/article-9031862.

25. *Encyclopaedia Britannica Online,* http://search.eb.com/eb/article-9065776.

26. The city was probably situated on the west bank of the Euphrates, in present-day Iraq, about thirty miles southwest of Baghdad. Africa, *Ancient World,* pp. 7–8. See also Jouguet et al., *Les Premières Civilisations,* pp. 116–120.

27. Africa, *Ancient World,* pp. 7–8. Jouguet et al., *Les Premières Civilisations,* pp. 121–125.

28. Africa, *Ancient World,* pp. 8–9; Michael Cheilik and Anthony Inguanzo, *Ancient History,* 2d ed. (New York: HarperCollins, 1991), pp. 17–18. Jouguet et al., *Les Premières Civilisations,* pp. 125–129.

29. Neither is there any evidence of relations between Egypt and Babylon (in the Old Babylonian Period at the end of the third millennium). *Encyclopaedia Britannica Online,* http://search.eb.com/eb/article-55479.

30. The Amorites probably originated in Arabia. They not only caused the downfall of the empire, but were also important in the history of Mesopotamia, Syria, and Palestine from about 2000 to 1600 B.C.E. *Encyclopaedia Britannica Online,* http://search.eb.com/eb/article-9007224.

31. Joan Oates, *Babylon,* 2d ed. (New York: Thames and Hudson, 1986).

32. See note 8.

33. Africa, *Ancient World,* p. 9.

34. Munn-Rankin, "Diplomacy in Western Asia," p. 34, also pp. 23–32.

35. Cheilik and Inguanzo, *Ancient History,* p. 19.

36. Starr, *History of the Ancient World,* pp. 46–48; A. Leo Oppenheim, *Ancient Mesopotamia* (Chicago: University of Chicago Press, 1977).

37. First and second dynasties (c. 3200–2700 B.C.E.); the Old Kingdom—third and fourth dynasties (c. 2700–2185 B.C.E.); first Intermediate Period (c. 2200–2050 B.C.E.); Middle Kingdom—eleventh and twelfth dynasties (c. 2050–1800 B.C.E.); second Intermediate Period (c. 1800–1570 B.C.E.); New Kingdom—eighteenth dynasty (c. 1570–1085 B.C.E.). Cheilik and Inguanzo, *Ancient History,* p. 21; Watson, *Evolution of International Society,* pp. 30–31; Alan Gardiner, *Egypt of the Pharaohs* (New York:

Oxford University Press, 1964); J. R. Harris, ed., *Legacy of Egypt,* 2d ed. (Oxford University Press, 1971). Egyptians began to call their kings pharaohs in the eighteenth dynasty. Africa, *Ancient World,* p. 20.

38. For example, with the Hittites in Anatolia, the Kassites in Babylon, or the kingdom of Mitanni in northeastern Syria. Africa, *Ancient World,* pp. 20–21.

39. Watson, *Evolution of International Society,* pp. 30–31.

40. Oliver Robert Gurney, *The Hittites,* 2d ed. (New York: Penguin, 1990). See also Liverani, *International Relations,* pts. 1–3.

41. Cheilik and Inguanzo, *Ancient History,* pp. 31, 37; Watson, *Evolution of International Society,* pp. 31–32.

42. Albert T. Olmstead, *History of Assyria* (Chicago: University of Chicago Press, 1975).

43. End of the Bronze Age, beginning of the Iron Age. Starr, *History of the Ancient World,* pp. 129–130. See also Theodore A. Wertime and James D. Muhly, eds., *The Coming of the Age of Iron* (New Haven: Yale University Press, 1980).

44. Watson, *Evolution of International Society,* pp. 33–34. See also Leroy Waterman, *Royal Correspondence of the Assyrian Empire,* 4 vols. (Ann Arbor: University of Michigan Press, 1930–1936).

45. Starr, *History of the Ancient World,* pp. 130–137; Watson, *Evolution of International Society,* p. 38; Waterman, *Royal Correspondence.*

46. Africa, *Ancient World,* pp. 46–48; Starr, *History of the Ancient World,* pp. 137–140.

47. Cheilik and Inguanzo, *Ancient History,* p. 42.

48. See *The Cambridge History of Iran,* 7 vols. (New York: Cambridge University Press, 1968–1991), vol. 2, edited by Ilya Gerschevitch; Richard N. Frye, *The History of Ancient Iran* (Munich: Beck'sche, 1984).

49. Africa, *Ancient World,* p. 53; Cheilik and Inguanzo, *Ancient History,* p. 32. See also John M. Cook, *The Persian Empire* (New York: Barnes and Noble, 1993).

50. Cheilik and Inguanzo, *Ancient History,* p. 32; Watson, *Evolution of International Society,* p. 41; Africa, *Ancient World,* pp. 52–54.

51. Watson, *Evolution of International Society,* pp. 41–42. See also *Cambridge Ancient History,* 2d ed., vol. 4, *Persia, Greece, and the Western Mediterranean, c. 525 to 479 B.C.*

52. Starr, *History of the Ancient World,* pp. 360–364. See also Andrew R. Burn, *Persia and the Greeks: The Defense of the West, c. 546–478 B.C.,* 2d ed. (London: Duckworth, 1984); *Cambridge Ancient History,* 2d ed., vol. 4.

53. Watson, *Evolution of International Society,* p. 45.

54. Starr, *History of the Ancient World,* pp. 111, 164–165, 171–172; Watson, *Evolution of International Society,* pp. 77–78. See also Ramesh Chandra Majumdar, H. C. Raychaudhuri, and Kalikinkar Datta, eds., *An Advanced History of India,* 4th ed. (Delhi: Macmillan India, 1978); A. L. Basham, *The Wonder That Was India,* 3d ed. (London: Sidgwick and Jackson, 1967).

55. Giri Deshingkar, "Strategic Thinking in Ancient India and China: Kautilya and Sunzi," in Jönsson and Langhorne, *Diplomacy,* vol. 2, p. 81.

56. Starr, *History of the Ancient World,* p. 632.

57. Understanding of course that it was written in the context of Indian civilization and its state system almost 2,000 years earlier—undoubtedly remarkable. See G. R. Berridge, "Machiavelli," in G. R. Berridge, Maurice Keens-Soper, and T. G. Otte, *Diplomatic Theory from Machiavelli to Kissinger* (London: Palgrave, 2001), pp. 7–32.

58. Deshingkar, "Strategic Thinking " pp. 84–87.

59. Deshingkar, "Strategic Thinking," pp. 84–87. See also Watson, *Evolution of International Society*, pp. 77–84.

60. Watson, *Evolution of International Society*, pp. 83–84.

61. Starr, *History of the Ancient World*, pp. 114–115, 164, 172; Watson, *Evolution of International Society*, pp. 85–93.

62. Roswell Britton, "Chinese Interstate Intercourse Before 700 B.C.," in Jönsson and Langhorne, *Diplomacy*, vol. 2, p. 92. See also Henri Maspero, *China in Antiquity* (Amherst: University of Massachusetts Press, 1978); Hsu Cho-yun, *Ancient China in Transition* (Stanford: Stanford University Press, 1968).

63. Watson, *Evolution of International Society*, pp. 86–88. See also Deshingkar, "Strategic Thinking," pp. 87–90.

64. Watson, *Evolution of International Society*, pp. 92–93.

65. Greek diplomatic tradition was just one of the (lesser) elements that came with the monumental contribution of Greek civilization, culture, and politics.

66. They were afflicted by what has been called "that ancient malady of the Greeks, the love of discord," quoted by Harold Nicolson in *The Evolution of Diplomatic Method* (London: Constable, 1954), p. 10, who adds, "their jealousy was so poisonous that it stung and paralysed their instinct for self-preservation."

67. *Cambridge Ancient History*, 2d ed.: vol. 5, *The Fifth Century B.C.;* vol. 6, *The Fourth Century B.C.;* vol. 7, pt. 1, *The Hellenistic World*.

68. Frank Adcock and D. J. Mosley, *Diplomacy in Ancient Greece* (London: Thames and Hudson, 1975).

69. Christer Jönsson and Martin Hall, *Essence of Diplomacy* (New York: Palgrave Macmillan, 2005), pp. 136–143.

70. Nicolson, *Evolution*, p. 3.

71. Keith Hamilton and Richard Langhorne, *The Practice of Diplomacy: Its Evolution, Theory, and Administration* (New York: Routledge, 1995), pp. 8–9; Martin Wight, "The States-System of Hellas," in Jönsson and Langhorne, *Diplomacy*, vol. 2, pp. 62–64.

72. Nicolson, *Evolution*, p. 7.

73. Ibid., pp. 6, 10.

74. Cohen, "Great Tradition," p. 50; Nicolson, *Evolution*, p. 8; Hamilton and Langhorne, *Practice of Diplomacy*, pp. 10–11.

75. Brian Campbell, "Diplomacy in the Roman World (c. 500 B.C.–A.D. 235)," in Jönsson and Langhorne, *Diplomacy*, vol. 2, pp. 175–192. See also *Cambridge Ancient History*, 2d ed., vol. 7, pt. 2, *The Rise of Rome to 220 B.C.*

76. *Cambridge Ancient History*, 2d ed.: vol. 8, *Rome and the Mediterranean to 113 B.C.;* vol. 9, *The Last Age of the Roman Republic, 146–43 B.C.*

77. Campbell, "Diplomacy," pp. 175–192.

78. Nicolson, *Evolution*, p. 17.

79. Campbell, "Diplomacy," p. 182.

80. Ibid., pp. 177–178.

81. Nicolson, *Evolution*, pp. 18–19.

82. *Cambridge Ancient History:* new ed., vol. 10, *The Augustan Empire, 43 B.C.–A.D. 69;* new ed. (change in volume sequence), vol. 11, *The Imperial Peace;* 2d ed., vol. 11, *The High Empire, A.D. 70–192;* 2d ed., vol. 12, *The Crisis of Empire, A.D. 193–337.*

83. Campbell, "Diplomacy," pp. 182–183.

84. Hamilton and Langhorne, *Practice of Diplomacy*, pp. 12–13.

85. Ibid.

86. Nicolson, *Evolution,* p. 20.

87. Ibid., pp. 20–21.

88. The 1949 Geneva Convention Relative to the Protection of Civilian Persons in Time of War, art. 34; also art. 3 common to all four 1949 Geneva Conventions. See Lori F. Damrosch, Louis Henkin, Richard Crawford Pugh, Oscar Schachter, and Hans Smit, *Basic Documents Supplement to International Law Cases and Materials,* 4th ed. (St. Paul, MN: West Group, 2001), pp. 427, 431.

89. International Convention Against the Taking of Hostages, adopted by the UN General Assembly on December 17, 1979. See Cindy C. Combs, *Terrorism in the Twenty-First Century* (Upper Saddle River, NJ: Prentice-Hall, 1997), pp. 162–163.

90. *Cambridge Ancient History,* 2d ed.: vol. 13, *The Late Empire,* A.D. *337–425;* vol. 14, *Late Antiquity Empire and Successors,* A.D. *425–600.*

91. Nicolson, *Evolution,* pp. 24–25.

92. Dimitri Obolensky, "The Principles and Methods of Byzantine Diplomacy," in Jönsson and Langhorne, *Diplomacy,* vol. 2, pp. 112–119.

93. Jonathan Shepard, "Information, Disinformation, and Delay in Byzantine Diplomacy," in Jönsson and Langhorne, *Diplomacy,* vol. 2, p. 133.

94. Obolensky, "Principles and Methods," vol. 2, pp. 112–128.

95. Emperor Anastasios wrote in 515: "There is a law that orders the Emperor to lie and to violate his oath if it is necessary for the well being of the empire." Hamilton and Langhorne, *Practice of Diplomacy,* p. 17. Many modern leaders seem to agree.

96. Hamilton and Langhorne, *Practice of Diplomacy,* pp. 18–20. See also Shepard, "Information, Disinformation, and Delay," pp. 130–174.

97. See Thomas F. Madden, "Venice's Hostage Crisis: Diplomatic Efforts to Secure Peace with Byzantium Between 1171 **and** 1184," in *Medieval and Renaissance Venice,* edited by Ellen E. Kittel and Thomas F. Madden (Urbana: University of Illinois Press, 1999), pp. 96–108.

98. Shepard, "Information, Disinformation, and Delay," p. 152.

99. Jönsson and Hall, *Essence of Diplomacy,* pp. 143–149.

100. J. L. Brierly, *The Law of Nations,* 5th ed. (Oxford: Clarendon, 1955), pp. 2–5.

101. Hamilton and Langhorne, *Practice of Diplomacy,* pp. 24–26.

102. Donald E. Queller, *The Office of Ambassador in the Middle Ages* (Princeton: Princeton University Press, 1967), pp. 26–27, 37, 61. See also Donald E. Queller, "Medieval Diplomacy," in Jönsson and Langhorne, *Diplomacy,* vol. 2, pp. 193–213, reprinted from *Dictionary of the Middle Ages* (New York: Scribner, 1984), vol. 4, pp. 201–214.

103. Queller, *Office of Ambassador,* p. 37.

104. Queller, "Medieval Diplomacy," pp. 209–211.

105. Garrett Mattingly, *Renaissance Diplomacy* (Boston: Houghton Mifflin, 1955), pp. 46–47. See also Queller, "Medieval Diplomacy," pp. 208–209.

106. Nicolson, *Evolution,* p. 33.

107. Dating back to classical Greece, as discussed earlier in this chapter.

108. Nicolson, *Evolution,* p. 33. Historians, however, disagree as to what state must be given credit for opening the first permanent embassy. See Garrett Mattingly's detailed presentation in his article "The First Resident Embassies: Medieval Italian Origins of Modern Diplomacy," in Jönsson and Langhorne, *Diplomacy,* vol. 2, pp. 214–231. See also Mattingly, *Renaissance Diplomacy.*

109. Matthew S. Anderson, *The Rise of Modern Diplomacy, 1450–1919* (New York: Longman, 1993), pp. 22–23.

110. See Donald E. Queller, *Early Venetian Legislation on Ambassadors* (Geneva: Librairie Droz, 1966).

111. Mattingly, *Renaissance Diplomacy,* p. 104.
112. Nicolson, *Evolution,* p. 27.
113. Hamilton and Langhorne, *Practice of Diplomacy,* pp. 60–61.
114. Mattingly, *Renaissance Diplomacy,* p. 101.
115. Nicolson, *Evolution, pp.* 27–28.
116. See, for example, Nicolson, *Evolution,* pp. 43–44. Protocol remains important, but it is now codified in each capital.
117. Mattingly, *Renaissance Diplomacy,* pp. 88, 102.
118. Quoted in Nicolson, *Evolution,* p. 43.
119. Hamilton and Langhorne, *Practice of Diplomacy,* p. 61. See also Nicolson, *Evolution,* p. 37.
120. Mattingly, *Resident Embassies,* pp. 106–107; Mattingly, *Renaissance Diplomacy,* pp. 224–225.
121. See Mattingly, *Renaissance Diplomacy,* chap. 24, "Men Sent to Lie Abroad," pp. 233–239.
122. Anderson, *Rise of Modern Diplomacy,* pp. 31–36.
123. Ibid., pp. 32–38.
124. Ibid., pp. 38–40.
125. Mattingly, *Renaissance Diplomacy,* p. 237.
126. See Charles H. Carter, "The Ambassadors of the Early Modern Europe: Patterns of Diplomatic Representation in the Early Seventeenth Century," in Jönsson and Langhorne, *Diplomacy,* vol. 2, pp. 232–250.
127. G. R. Berridge, "Richelieu," in Berridge, Keens-Soper, and Otte, *Diplomatic Theory,* pp. 71–87. See also G. R. Berridge, *Diplomatic Classics: Selected Texts from Commynes to Vattel* (New York: Palgrave Macmillan, 2004).
128. Nicolson, *Evolution,* pp. 52–53, 55.
129. Anderson, *Rise of Modern Diplomacy,* pp. 69–96.
130. Matthew Anderson commented that it was the immense prestige of French culture and the status of the French monarchy as a model for much of Europe that gave the language its dominant position in diplomacy; ibid., p. 102. Bismarck refused to receive notes in Russian from the tsar's representative in Berlin, but they agreed that their written communications would henceforth be in French. Hamilton and Langhorne, *Practice of Diplomacy,* p. 106.
131. François de Callières, *On the Manner of Negotiating with Princes,* translated by A. F. Whyte (Washington, DC: University Press of America, 1963 [1716]). See Maurice Keens-Soper, "François de Callières and Diplomatic Theory," Jönsson and Langhorne, *Diplomacy,* vol. 1, pp. 1–24.
132. Nicolson, *Evolution,* pp. 52–53; de Callières, *Negotiating with Princes,* pp. xii, 31–32, 129–130.
133. Nicolson, *Evolution,* pp. 76–77.
134. Hamilton and Langhorne, *Practice of Diplomacy,* pp. 64–67.
135. Anderson, *Rise of Modern Diplomacy,* pp. 56–68.
136. Congress of Vienna regulations. (Lord) Gore-Booth, ed., *Satow's Guide to Diplomatic Practice,* 5th ed. (New York: Longman, 1979), p. 82. These categories are now found in the 1961 Vienna Convention on Diplomatic Relations, art. 14. Ibid., p. 83.
137. Except in those capitals where the papal nuncio was automatically dean of the diplomatic corps, the position would be held by the longest-serving ambassador or minister.
138. Hamilton and Langhorne, *Practice of Diplomacy,* p. 110.
139. Ibid., pp. 111–114.

140. J. C. Hurewitz, "Ottoman Diplomacy and the European State System," in Jönsson and Langhorne, *Diplomacy,* vol. 2, p. 307. See also Hamilton and Langhorne, *Practice of Diplomacy,* pp. 110–111.

141. Hurewitz, "Ottoman Diplomacy," pp. 305–309. See also Hamilton and Langhorne, *Practice of Diplomacy,* p. 112.

142. Hamilton and Langhorne, *Practice of Diplomacy,* p. 112.

143. Anderson, *Rise of Modern Diplomacy,* pp. 257–265.

144. Richard Langhorne, "The Development of International Conferences, 1648–1830," in Jönsson and Langhorne, *Diplomacy,* vol. 2, p. 284.

145. Aix-la-Chapelle, 1818; Troppau, 1820; Laibach, 1821; and Verona, 1822.

146. Some historians claim that a number of subsequent nineteenth-century conferences represented a continuation of the Concert of Europe.

147. Hamilton and Langhorne, *Practice of Diplomacy,* pp. 90–98.

148. Ibid., pp. 94–95.

149. The European Danube Commission (1856) and the Universal Postal Union (1875). See other examples in Daniel S. Cheever and H. Field Haviland Jr., *Organizing for Peace: International Organization in World Affairs* (Boston: Houghton Mifflin, 1954), pp. 36–37, 41ff.

150. Union of International Associations, *Yearbook of International Organizations 1909/1999,* http://www.uia.org/uiastats.

151. A. LeRoy Bennett and James K. Oliver, *International Organizations: Principles and Issues,* 7th ed. (Upper Saddle River, NJ: Prentice-Hall, 2002), pp. 27–45. President Woodrow Wilson attempted to lead his colleagues to abandon secrecy in their negotiations ("open treaties openly arrived at"). Predictably, this did not work.

152. See F. P. Walters, *A History of the League of Nations,* 2 vols. (New York: Oxford University Press, 1952).

153. Cheever and Haviland, *Organizing for Peace,* pp. 172–177.

154. The committee was headed by Stanley Bruce of Australia. Bennett and Oliver, *International Organizations,* p. 42.

155. Bennett and Oliver, *International Organizations,* p. 42.

156. Smith Gaddis, *American Diplomacy During the Second World War, 1941–1945,* 2d ed. (New York: Knopf, 1985).

157. Started respectively in 1942 and 1943. Cheever and Haviland, *Organizing for Peace,* pp. 227–236.

158. Particularly with the Security Council, a political chief executive (the Secretary-General), an unprecedented Economic and Social Council, and much more. See Bennett and Oliver, *International Organizations,* pp. 46–79.

159. Jönsson and Hall, *Essence of Diplomacy,* pp. 150–162.

PART 1

The Forces of Change

Change is a basic feature of the international system. International actors naturally adjust to changing circumstances in their modes of interaction; they try new ways of dealing with one another and of approaching the problems that confront them. It is a matter of practical adaptation. However, not all changes taking place in our global environment require changes in established methods of diplomatic interaction. As long as diplomatic procedures remain effective, there is no reason to change them. It is important to remember also that much of diplomacy is rooted in long-established tradition, which creates inertia and fosters continuity.

The chapters in Part 1 of this volume are concerned only with the kinds of change that lead international actors to modify their diplomatic practices (and a good deal of international transformation has not had this effect). Many diplomatic techniques have proved versatile and quite capable of handling a wide variety of situations. This inquiry is thus not intended to produce an inventory of all the changes found in contemporary international relations. The evolution of diplomatic procedure remains the main focus.

3 The Consequences of Interdependence

Interdependence means mutual dependence, a form of inter-connectedness made more extensive by spectacular advances in technology and the integration of the global economy (see Box 3.1). Interdependence is a condition fostered by the complex interaction of a wide variety of factors: more effective means of transportation, the communication revolution, material need, and a host of other reasons. Governments may be driven by power considerations, strategic interests, and economic gain, but also by cultural and scientific objectives, perceptions of mutual benefits, and other factors. These factors of course lead to greater interaction across international boundaries.[1] Another cause of interdependence is the proliferation of problems that no one nation, however powerful, can solve through simple self-reliance. Nation-states are increasingly vulnerable to a variety of phenomena that escape their control.[2]

Environmental destruction can, to some extent, be fought by means of more responsible national practices. Ultimately, however, ecosystems do not respect national boundaries. Global warming, destruction of the ozone layer of our atmosphere, and pollution of the oceans can only be remedied by collective means. The maintenance of economic stability, however complex a task, needs to be addressed internationally: a crisis anywhere can threaten the most prosperous countries. Drug traffic, organized crime, the migration of people in search of a decent existence, the flow of refugees, the spread of contagious disease, and many more scourges cannot be contained without concerted efforts on the part of a large number of states, and not just the rich and powerful, although, doubtless, they have more to contribute. This interdependence calls for diplomatic efforts on an unprecedented scale (see Box 3.2).

Global interdependence, however, is really not a new phenomenon. It developed slowly, gaining momentum with the industrial revolution,[3] and is now growing faster. There are more states and even more nonstate international actors, such as international organizations, involved in international affairs.

Box 3.1   Interdependence in the News

On August 20, 2001, a *New York Times* headline read: "World Economy
Slows in Rare Lockstep—Big Surprise in Europe, Which Had Thought It
Could Avoid a Downturn as in U.S." As the article explained: "[The] widespread malaise is the flip side of the record-setting United States–led expansion of the 1990's. Greater world integration in trade, finance and technology fueled the expansion. But increased interdependence—trade now
accounts for about a quarter of world output, double its share 25 years ago—
means that much of the world can move down in tandem, just as it moved
up in tandem." In 2002 another headline read: "Stocks Tumble, and the Fall-
out Is Going Global—Fears of a Slowdown in the World's Economy." And
in 2004: "Around the Clock, Around the World, Markets Down"; as the article explained: "Stock markets worldwide fell sharply yesterday as the
prospect of higher interest rates in the United States, high oil prices and the
war in Iraq unnerved investors."

*   *   *

In 2007, the International Monetary Fund reported: "Recent turmoil in the
world's financial markets, sparked by concerns about subprime mortgage
lending in the United States, seems to have hit Europe particularly hard."

*   *   *

On November 24, 2007, the *New York Times* reported: "The American mortgage crisis continues to infect Europe's financial system in new and unexpected places."

   Sources: New York Times, August 20, 2001, pp. A1, A8; *New York Times,* July
23, 2002. pp. A1, C11; *New York Times,* May 11, 2004, p. C1; *International Monetary Fund (IMF) Survey Magazine,* November 1, 2007, http://www.imf.org/
external/pubs/ft/survey; *New York Times,* November 24, 2007, pp. B1, B4.

Transnational relations are rapidly increasing—that is, interaction across national boundaries between nongovernmental organizations (NGOs), multinational corporations (MNCs), other institutions of civil society, and even private individuals—without significant participation by national governments,
or even against their occasional efforts to bring some transnational activities
under control.[4] Already in 1975, Alex Inkeles could write: "Recent decades reveal a general tendency for many forms of human interconnectedness across
national boundaries *to be doubling every ten years*."[5] In 2007, the International Monetary Fund (IMF) reported that "since 1995, global capital flows
have tripled to $6.4 trillion, reaching about 14.5 percent of world GDP."[6] More
and more formal as well as informal links are created around the world by

---

Box 3.2   Pressure for International Efforts

As the Earth Warms Up, Virus from the Tropics Moves to Italy in 2007

CASTIGLIONE DI CERVIA. DECEMBER 2007. Panic was spreading this August through this tidy village of 2,000 as one person after another fell ill. No doctor could figure out what was wrong. "We were terrified." After a month of investigation, Italian public officials discovered that it was a tropical disease, chikungunya, a relative of dengue fever, normally found in the Indian Ocean region. "This is the first case of an epidemic of a tropical disease in a developed, European country," said Dr. Roberto Bertollini, director of the World Health Organization's Health and Environment program; "climate change . . . opens the door to diseases that did not exist here previously."

*   *   *

WHO Urges Effort to Fight Fast-Spreading New Diseases

New infectious diseases are emerging at an "unprecedented rate," and have the potential to spread rapidly across the globe. The new watchwords are diplomacy, cooperation, transparency and preparedness. As an example of increased international efforts, a new UN plan commits $2.15 billion to fight drug-resistant tuberculosis. It is estimated that up to 1.2 million lives may be saved by 2015 through this program.

Sources: New York Times, December 23, 2007, p. 21; *New York Times,* August 27, 2007, p. A9.

---

means of a multiplicity of channels, and our consciousness of interdependence is growing.[7]

The very same factors that progressively generated interdependence are leading to the globalization of human endeavor. The expansion of knowledge of what is available elsewhere in the world fosters globalization. Technology makes it more accessible, and globalization generates more interdependence. More and more human activity is affected by this globalization tendency: corporate business, trade, manufacturing, technology, communication, popular culture, sports and entertainment, tourism, the spread of disease, and criminal activity. Democratization, generating greater freedom, undoubtedly contributes to this phenomenon, and it is probable that one of the most significant factors in the rapid growth of globalization is that it can be very lucrative. However, there are costs.

Massive flights of capital[8] produce severe economic disruption; industrial relocation and outsourcing generate unemployment; competition in open markets can lead to a costly disregard of environmental constraints; and human migrations threaten to destabilize entire societies. Some forms of international control are increasingly seen as necessary, but states are not anxious to surrender any of their freedom of action and reforms tend to lag. Independent states remain the foremost components of international society—very diversely (often woefully) governed, frequently self-centered, and always protective of their independence. This is far from helpful in a world becoming more and more interdependent. Changes in methods of interaction tend to be slow, piecemeal, and often simply incremental. It should be noted also that interdependence is not uniform around the world. If it is true that no nation is self-sufficient, some are better sheltered from certain international upheavals—geography, the distribution of natural resources, and elements of national culture are factors that create differences in the interdependence of societies, some of which experience greater need for protection from events beyond national control, which complicates international cooperation in addressing the effects of interdependence and globalization.[9]

▓ Diplomatic Effects

Not only does state foreign policy tend to affect more states around the world, but vastly expanding human interconnectedness also frequently leads to domestic situations in a given society affecting the domestic order of other societies (discussed further in Chapter 5). States are thus more vulnerable to domestic developments elsewhere. Domestic issues become matters of foreign policy.[10] For example, a festering management problem at the huge state-controlled Venezuelan oil company led to a general strike in early April 2002 that sent oil prices in the United States into wild gyrations. US industry experts warned that if these disruptions were prolonged and oil prices continued to rise, US economic recovery could be impeded.[11] Many governments, when faced with such domestic disruptions, resort to some form of diplomatic intervention or international action if such may alleviate the situation. The realm of governmental interaction is thus vastly expanded.

Expanded Diplomatic Agenda

Diplomats are now called upon to deal with a large variety of issues that have rarely appeared on the traditional diplomatic agenda. In 1975, Secretary of State Henry Kissinger observed: "[D]ealing with the traditional agenda is no longer enough. A new and unprecedented kind of issue has emerged. The problems of energy, resources, environment, population, the uses of space and the seas now rank with questions of military security, ideology and territorial rivalry which have traditionally made up the diplomatic agenda."[12]

The range of issues dealt with internationally keeps growing (see Box 3.3). Transnational organizations, such as NGOs, play a role in this expansion of the subject matter of diplomacy by pressing governments to address the problems they are concerned with, such as population, the environment, or human rights. Thus the line between domestic and international matters tends to become blurred. To put it differently, domestic and international politics are more difficult to keep apart. Another consequence of this phenomenon is that the volume of diplomatic interaction is correspondingly increasing. Other factors, discussed later, add to the diplomatic workload.

More Government Agencies Dealing with International Issues

Interestingly, as might be expected from the preceding discussion, many governmental agencies (besides foreign ministries and their foreign service personnel)

Box 3.3   Global Battle Against HIV/AIDS: The 2008 Offensive

The United Nations has been fighting HIV/AIDS for decades, and the United States has been part of the global effort. But in early January 2003 something happened. Jean W. Pape departed Haiti, where he was treating AIDS patients, and flew to Washington, D.C., for a secret meeting with President George W. Bush, who was considering the creation of a global program of unprecedented size and scope to combat HIV/AIDS (the President's Emergency Plan for AIDS Relief, known as "Pepfar"). A five-year program was announced in the 2003 State of the Union address, calling for $15 billion for HIV/AIDS prevention, treatment, and care, concentrating on fifteen hard-hit nations in Africa and the Caribbean. This was a radical change, since Bush, when running for the White House in 2000, talked of letting "Africa solve Africa's problems."

In 2002, the president had called Tommy G. Thompson, the new administration's health and human services secretary, and Anthony S. Fauci, a prominent HIV/AIDS expert, and sent them as special envoys to Africa to examine what could be done about the AIDS situation. In their report, they proposed a $500 million program to prevent mother-to-child transmission of the disease. Bush approved it. But he wanted to embark upon a much larger foreign mission. Healthcare was no longer simply a national concern. The program received large bipartisan support.

On the global front, a coalition of ten UN agencies, under the banner of UNAIDS, is now cosponsoring an HIV/AIDS campaign with larger resources.

Source: New York Times, January 5, 2008, pp. A1, A6.

are now involved in international relations. The US Department of Justice, for example, works with its counterparts in other countries with regard to the arrest and prosecution of terrorists. The US Labor Department sends its own representatives to attend the annual meeting of the International Labour Conference in Geneva, the policymaking body of the International Labour Organization (ILO), which is a specialized agency of the United Nations. Drug enforcement officials want to remain in contact with the countries involved in the international drug trade, such as Colombia and Pakistan. Dozens of agencies are similarly involved in international affairs, each in its own area of specialization.[13]

A foreign relations division is usually found in these bureaucracies. For example, the US Department of Agriculture has a division on farm and foreign agriculture services, headed by an undersecretary, with sections on foreign agricultural affairs, international cooperation and development, and international trade policy.[14] The department also maintains a "world agricultural outlook" board.[15] The Department of the Treasury has an international affairs division, headed by an undersecretary, with regional sections headed by deputy assistant secretaries and country desks, reminiscent of the State Department's internal structure.[16] Other Treasury subdivisions are focused on international development, debt and environment policy, international monetary and financial policy, technical assistance policy, and trade and investment policy.[17]

These agencies normally post some of their own officials in US embassies in foreign capitals for the fulfillment of their mission. Such officials are formally under the authority of the embassy chief of mission. However, they are not taking their orders from the US secretary of state, since they are in the service of the executive agency that posts them abroad. In some embassies, these non–foreign service officials constitute some 60 or even 70 percent of the personnel,[18] a situation that greatly complicates the coordinating efforts of the chief of mission. Working in unison is not always easy, since agencies have very diverse (and occasionally divergent) interests.

Transgovernmental Relations

Some of these executive departments, in fact, maintain direct contact with their counterparts abroad by written communications, telephone, and now electronic means.[19] This has been given the name "transgovernmental relations." They also send their own representatives to meet with their foreign colleagues in the executive agencies concerned, or in international conferences, bypassing altogether the foreign ministries of their governments. The heads of these departments (i.e., "ministries" in most governments) even hold their own bilateral or multilateral international meetings. The UN encourages ministerial diplomacy. Because heads of ministries are chief executives in their own areas of concern, they can more readily commit resources for joint international projects. Effectively, many ministries now maintain their own foreign relations in their fields of specialization—separately from the ministry of foreign affairs.

Some observers of contemporary diplomacy believe that, in the Western world, such direct international contacts between ministries tend to supersede relations through the regular channels provided by foreign ministries and embassies.[20] In any case, this form of interaction does not facilitate the overall coordination of a nation's diplomacy, although this kind of department-to-department direct cooperation often takes place at the technical level (rather than at the higher levels of state policy).

Transgovernmental interaction is particularly developed among the armed forces of allied nations, in planning joint operations and battle plans, providing logistical support, and coordinating force deployment.[21] This is *military diplomacy*—even if the terms make traditional diplomats wince—although foreign service officers have long been familiar with military attachés. A good deal of this military diplomacy is now carried out in peacetime—for example, in the military organs of the North Atlantic Treaty Organization (NATO). However, the high politics of alliance are negotiated in diplomatic conferences or in the political organs of defense organizations, such as the NATO Council.

An example of extensive transgovernmental work is provided in the area of international drug control. The Drug Enforcement Administration (DEA) of the US Department of Justice maintains extensive relations with foreign law enforcement authorities and other government agencies in countries involved in this traffic, and participates in a large number of multilateral enforcement programs. In Washington, the DEA has an international operations office within the US Department of Justice, which itself maintains seventy-nine offices in fifty-eight countries. The main components of the DEA's international operations are its twenty-nine Sensitive Investigative Units (SIUs), which operate in nine countries and investigate major drug-trafficking organizations and money-laundering operations in cooperation with foreign law enforcement agencies. For example, the SIU in Thailand carried out a multinational investigation involving the DEA and law enforcement agencies in Thailand, China, and Hong Kong that culminated in April 2002 with the seizure of 354 kilograms of heroin and the arrest of thirteen traffickers with ties to an international insurgent organization.[22]

The DEA takes on a variety of international initiatives, such as counternarcotics training, using mobile training teams. It offers both in-country and regional training programs, and organizes international operations. For example, in February 2002, the DEA brought together representatives of twenty-five countries in Ankara, Turkey, to develop a coordinated, post-Taliban counter-drug strategy to deprive international terrorist groups of the financial resources for their operations. This project also targeted weapons, ammunition, and currency. The participants agreed on joint efforts of law enforcement and customs authorities in Central Asia, the Caucasus, Europe, and Russia, in operations to be coordinated by the Southeast European Cooperative Initiative (SECI) Regional Center for Combating Transborder Crime in Bucharest, Romania, and the Bishkek Command Center in Bishkek, Kyrgyzstan.[23]

So many government departments are now involved in international matters that it is hardly surprising to find an enormous amount of transgovernmental interaction in the day-to-day conduct of foreign relations. The nature of the political relations maintained by specific countries (friendly versus hostile) makes a great deal of difference in the extent of their transgovernmental relations. Countries in a state of mutual tension are less likely to engage in much of the latter. The nature of the political systems of the countries concerned is also likely to make a difference: highly centralized or authoritarian systems will probably impose restrictions on the freedom of their government ministries to engage in their own transgovernmental operations. The level of interdependence between states is another significant factor in the volume and intensity of transgovernmental relations.[24] Geographical proximity often increases interdependence. Neighboring countries normally engage in a great deal of routine transactions that lend themselves to direct interaction between many segments of their governmental bureaucracies. The United States and Canada provide a good example of this phenomenon.

It is usually difficult to quantify transgovernmental relations, as they tend to be routine and informal, often transacted over the telephone or by e-mail. Kal Holsti and Thomas Levy, however, cited figures obtained from a Canadian House of Commons document that revealed a large amount of business transacted by direct visits of officials of both countries. In 1968, Canadian heads of agencies and other officials made 4,687 visits to the United States (i.e., 90 visits per week, or about 13 visits a day). US counterparts made 1,843 visits to Canada (i.e., 35 visits per week, or about 5 visits a day).[25] One can assume that the number of telephone communications made directly between officials of bureaucratic units and their foreign counterparts must be much greater.

In addition, direct transborder contacts are made between Canadian provinces and Washington, D.C., on the one hand, and between US states and Ottawa on the other, as well as between Canadian provincial and US state governments, even if, at times, these contacts are made without explicit authority. Transgovernmental cooperation is very practical—for example, cooperation between Canadian provinces and US states in setting highway load limits, license fees, and other regulations; border-area forest fire prevention; and cross-border hydroelectric power production and distribution. Cooperation may be facilitated by joint membership of subnational units of intergovernmental organizations.[26]

Foreign ministries and their diplomats of course retain their significance. Major matters of foreign relations will continue to be discussed through conventional channels. But with the continued growth of interdependence, direct interaction between most governmental departments across international boundaries will account for an even greater volume of international transactions. Direct interaction between these departments and international organization bureaucracies will also increase. One can see this evolution as a mark of integration in global society.[27]

Multiplicity of Diplomatic Channels

Traditional embassies in foreign capitals, the classic form of diplomatic representation, remain important, but their functions are changing. *Special missions* sent by foreign ministries are used more extensively for a wide variety of purposes, including the important function of mediation. *International conferences* permit a multiplicity of specialized issues to be addressed, and this mode of diplomacy is still expanding. *International organizations* provide increasingly important diplomatic channels. Heads of state or government now meet with greater frequency, engaging in *summit diplomacy*—another channel of interaction (see Box 3.4). Many diplomats, however, are also involved in summit diplomacy, preparing for the meetings and actually participating in summit negotiations.

The ease of transportation and communication, as well as the proliferation of international issues that must be addressed by chief executives, has led to a substantial increase in summit diplomacy. Foreign ministers, too, are now engaged in a great deal of interaction with their counterparts abroad. Heads of other ministries (e.g., agriculture, commerce) are increasingly meeting internationally and negotiating issues pertaining to their areas of specialization. This is *ministerial diplomacy*, another level of interaction whereby executive departments may bypass the traditional channels of foreign ministries and their embassies. As discussed previously, *transgovernmental relations* are not restricted to heads of agencies, and they are becoming more extensive.[28]

Transnational channels are very different, and play an increasing role in connecting societies. Various institutions of civil society, NGOs, multinational corporations, and nongovernmental elites interact across international borders (see Chapter 5).[29] They enter the intergovernmental process when trying to alter the course of international events (e.g., during international conferences or meetings of international organizations).[30] Doubtless, governments play a dominant role in shaping the course of international affairs; nevertheless, transnational agents are now active participants. Some governments, in fact, find it useful to work with transnational institutions in attaining some of their international objectives.

International organizations have shown even greater interest in working with NGOs. The UN Charter (1945) made provision for the Economic and Social Council (ECOSOC) to enter into consultative arrangements with NGOs.[31] In 2002, 2,143 NGOs were participating in this program. Virtually all of the UN's specialized agencies have entered into consultative agreements with

Box 3.4   Economic Interdependence and Diplomacy: The G-8

Most states are fiercely protective of their sovereignty and right to act as they please. Interdependence, however, pushes them to work together.

A serious economic recession somewhere in the world tends to spread. The 2001 US downturn did spread to Europe, even though for a while the European Union was buoyant and confident it would remain unaffected. Thus the eight major industrialized free-market economies meet annually at the summit level to discuss economic policy and avoid working at cross-purposes. It all started in 1975 when an overvalued US currency was threatening economic growth. The United States, Japan, Germany, France, and Britain succeeded in coordinating their efforts to address the problem. Pleased with the results, they decided to meet annually at the summit level, inviting Canada and Italy to join their conversations, and so was born the G-7 summit.

In 1997, they decided to invite Russia to join their efforts and the G-7 became the G-8. Discussions have not remained limited to economic issues. Interdependence affects other matters of international relations, such as democratization and combating international terrorism. Though these summit conversations and efforts to achieve voluntary coordination on economic and global monetary policy may be insufficient to cope with the highly complex problems of interdependence, they are useful in conjunction with other efforts, such as those of the International Monetary Fund, the World Bank, and the World Trade Organization. Representatives of the European Union are now invited to attend G-8 summits. States may not like to curtail their freedom of action, but the growing interconnectedness of global society leads them to work together to avoid downturn epidemics.

Sources: John T. Rourke, *International Politics on the World Stage,* 10th ed. (New York: McGraw-Hill, 2005), pp. 443–444; Andrew C. Sobel, *Political Economy and Global Affairs* (Washington, DC: Congressional Quarterly, 2006), pp. 279–280.

NGOs. Some of them involve NGOs in the implementation of their projects (see Box 3.5).[32] Conferences organized by the UN have long worked with NGOs, finding ways to involve them in an observer capacity. Secretary-General Kofi Annan himself actively promoted expanded UN partnership with civil society.[33]

Interorganization channels offer another mode of interaction in global society. As international organizations were created by nation-states to address the many problems facing them—for example, the UN and its affiliated agencies, such as the International Civil Aviation Organization (ICAO), ensuring the safety of global air transportation—these institutions became players on

---

Box 3.5   World Bank Partnership in Rio

In September 1997, World Bank director James Wolfensohn attended the completion ceremony of a project that had been undertaken in one of the hillside slums of Rio de Janeiro, Brazil. The World Bank had worked with a number of social welfare NGOs, the city government, the local water company, and slum residents themselves to install a simple sewer system and provide running water. Thousands of women in the community now had the luxury of obtaining their water by simply opening a tap, instead of having to drag buckets up to their homes from the bottom of the hill.

Source: New York Times, September 14, 1997, sec. 3, pp. 1, 13.

---

the global chessboard, with corporate identities of their own. Their actions are controlled by their state membership; but once given a mandate or a mission, they have the task of fulfilling that mandate, and it is quite natural for these institutions to cooperate for this purpose. For example, the World Bank, the UN Development Programme (UNDP), and the World Health Organization (WHO) work with the UN Children's Fund (UNICEF) to reduce infant mortality in underdeveloped areas of the world. Representatives of these organizations work together diplomatically to attain their common objectives, devising joint projects and working out means of transborder implementation.[34] Representatives of organizations attend meetings of other organizations, consult, and negotiate just as state representatives consult and negotiate. Our interdependent global society relies on this interorganization diplomacy to address international problems.

As international society changes and faces new challenges, one must anticipate that new methods of interacting will develop. *Novel channels of interaction* are thus created. Some of the new channels, in fact, may be so different as not to qualify as "diplomacy." The European Union is sufficiently unconventional to lead to such developments. The European Parliament is a good example: member countries are represented, but their delegates are elected by the citizenry of each member state, on the basis of party affiliation.[35] In the Parliament, representatives of similar political orientation (but from different countries) tend to vote together, transcending national allegiances. State "representation" is thus a misnomer. International issues may not be automatically debated along national lines.[36] Members of the European Parliament do not take orders from EU governments. National diplomats lobby elected representatives to influence parliamentary action that affects foreign policy.

To some extent, representation in the International Labour Organization, one of the UN's specialized agencies, also tends to blur national distinctions. As discussed in Chapter 2, each member state is represented by four persons:

two government delegates, one employer delegate, and one worker delegate. In selecting the employer and worker delegates, governments are obligated to consult "with the industrial organizations, if such organizations exist, which are the most representative of employers or workpeople, as the case may be, in their respective countries."[37] These representatives do not vote as a national unit: employer and worker delegates take part in the work of the organization, having equal status with government delegates. Thus, when workers' interests diverge from those of the other groups, they tend to unite their efforts across national lines, with labor representatives, for example, voting against the representatives of their own government. Employer and worker groups act somewhat like political parties in the annual International Labour Conference, the main deliberative and quasi-legislative organ of the ILO.

Track II channels are different in that people who do not formally represent governments negotiate international issues, occasionally at the secret invitation of the governments concerned. This happens when the issues are too controversial for governmental intervention, or when the situation is too polarized for open conversation (see Chapter 11's case studies on the Dominican crisis and the Oslo negotiations). Some forms of track II negotiation have been identified as *back-channel diplomacy*.[38] The growing multiplicity of international channels increases the ability of societies to interact. The diplomatic process has thus become more diverse, and will likely keep changing.

Greater Diplomatic Participation of Specialized Personnel

Another significant transformation in diplomatic practice is rooted in the more diversified and often more technical subject matter of diplomacy, leading to the use of more specialized personnel in the conduct of international relations (discussed further in Chapter 6). For example, concerted international efforts to combat HIV/AIDS require the participation of delegates with medical and public health expertise. The agenda of the World Health Assembly, the annual meeting of the World Health Organization in Geneva, includes such items as the following:

- Global strategy for infant and young child feeding
- Health promotion
- Strengthening health services delivery
- Tobacco control
- Combating HIV/AIDS
- Smallpox eradication
- Revised drug strategy
- International classification of disability
- Health effects of depleted uranium
- Global health security: epidemic alert and response, control of schisto-

To address these issues, in 2002 the US delegation was headed by the secretary of health and human services and included nine representatives from his department, six members of the US Permanent Mission in Geneva (presumably foreign service officers), three officers from the US Department of State (Bureau of International Organization Affairs and US Agency for International Development), and five experts and healthcare specialists.[40] This composition of the US delegation and its resort to technical personnel are typical for this kind of assembly, although other delegations trend to be smaller.

Other specialized agencies of the United Nations show the same preponderance of specialized personnel (i.e., from ministries other than foreign affairs) in the composition of national delegations to their annual meetings. Member states, however, maintain a permanent mission at organization headquarters that is normally composed of foreign service delegates, including a chief of mission of ambassadorial rank. It is interesting to note that, today, foreign ministries, in their organization and personnel, reflect the enormous diversification in the subject matter of diplomacy and the need for expertise in the conduct of foreign relations. For example, the US Department of State has an undersecretary for global affairs in charge of the following bureaus and offices:

- Bureau of Democracy, Human Rights, and Labor
- Bureau for International Narcotics and Law Enforcement Affairs
- Bureau of Oceans and International Environmental and Scientific Affairs
- Bureau of Population, Refugees, and Migration
- International Women's Issues
- Office of the Science and Technology Adviser
- Office to Monitor and Combat Trafficking in Persons[41]

The diversity of issues for which specialized preparation is deemed necessary is further illustrated by the structure of the US Bureau of Oceans and International Environmental and Scientific Affairs (another State Department bureau headed by an assistant secretary):

- Environment and Conservation
- Oceans
- Science and Technology Cooperation
- Space and Advanced Technology
- Global Climate Change
- International Health Affairs
- Sustainable Development
- Invasive Species
- Regional Hub Program[42]

This structure is of course modified as the international situation warrants (and

Madeleine Albright led a department wide initiative titled "Science and Diplomacy: Strengthening State for the 21st Century." This was the result of a study prepared by a senior State Department task force.[43]

Interestingly, the opening paragraph of this study emphasized:

> Science-based issues are increasingly prominent on the foreign affairs agenda, from nonproliferation and arms control to global environmental threats, such as ozone layer depletion and global climate change, to HIV/AIDS, to international science and technology (S&T) cooperation agreements. The Department of State is responsible for assuring that science and technology considerations are taken into account and integrated into US foreign policy, and that opportunities for fruitful international cooperation involving the US science community are identified and exploited.[44]

Secretary Albright acknowledged the department's deficiencies in this respect and stressed, "What I envision is not a one-shot quick fix, but a multi-year, multi-administration, bipartisan mission."[45] She endorsed the study's call for "developing better-equipped personnel to handle [science-based] issues," and for "targeted recruitment, expanded training opportunities, and enhanced rewards for S&T work."[46] The objective here was to "broaden and deepen . . . in-house science and technology expertise."[47] She also supported the study's recommendation to establish an active, long-term "partnership with the science community in academia, the private sector, and other agencies dealing with science and technology issues within the US Government."[48] On September 19, 2000, she appointed a science and technology adviser to the secretary of state to implement her policy and integrate science into US diplomacy.[49]

Even with greater expertise (here in the area of science and technology), the diplomatic service must still enlist the help of professionals in many fields to address such highly specialized and complex issues as included in the annual World Health Assembly agenda (not to mention the ongoing activities of the World Health Organization's executive board, also composed of member state representatives who must be "technically qualified in the field of health."[50] It must be pointed out that such issues are not exceptionally part of the diplomatic agenda. They have become a routine component of global relations. Inevitably, a larger share of diplomatic work must involve scientific personnel with limited or no foreign service experience. Insofar as they are employed in an agency that is regularly involved in multinational interaction, they can, like traditional diplomatic personnel, acquire the intercultural skills to facilitate work across international boundaries. Some, however, are only occasionally appointed to serve on international missions, particularly when it comes to staffing delegations to occasional international meetings. In such cases, it is important to include professional foreign service officers to facilitate the intercultural and political dimensions of the function.

Though some individuals are naturally attuned to this type of interaction been noted, and I have personally observed such situations, that professionals without diplomatic background or international experience may focus too exclusively on the technical aspects of the mission—for example, the medical aspects of disease prevention—and become impatient with the cultural or political impediments in devising a "solution" for the medical problem at hand (not to mention the possible difficulties and irritation involved in communicating with an imperfect knowledge of foreign languages—"Why can't *they* speak better English?").

Multilateral Relations

Even more important for the evolution of diplomacy, interdependence has magnified resort to *multilateral interaction.* The classic model of diplomacy—resident representation in foreign capitals—is too slow and piecemeal to manage the problems of global interdependence. In the history of diplomacy, some form of multilateral interaction was achieved through multilateral conferences (e.g., peace conferences: Westphalia, 1648; Utrecht, 1713; Vienna, 1815). *Multilateral conferences,* many of a global nature, are now proliferating, to the point of overtaxing the diplomatic facilities of many foreign ministries (see Chapter 9).

Conferences are useful because they permit a multilateral approach focused on a specific problem or a limited set of issues. Participation can be restricted according to political need (invitation to attend can be as selective as desired). These diplomatic gatherings, however, are normally of limited duration—a serious shortcoming when problems require more continuous and sustained attention. International organizations therefore serve a critical function in international affairs and have generated new forms of diplomacy (see Chapter 8). Nation-states, however, were long reluctant to create such international institutions. In the last third of the nineteenth century, a limited number of organizations were established to address certain problems of a technical or economic nature (e.g., telecommunications, postal services, weights and measures).[51] But in the realm of international politics, not even the approach of World War I, the risk of which was clearly perceived (witness the convening of the two Hague Peace Conferences in 1899 and 1907), succeeded in getting states to experiment with new forms of international organization. Edward Grey, British foreign minister, acknowledged in July 1914 that his fondest hope, an organized concert of nations, was still "too utopian to form the subject of definite proposals."[52] The devastating world conflict overcame some of the resistance and the League of Nations provided a hesitant beginning. World War II marked the opening of the floodgates.

Giving an idea of the current scope of the multilateral environment of diplomacy is difficult because of its diversity. There is no easy way to count international organizations. The 2006–2007 *Yearbook of International Organizations* uses fourteen categories. The categories most relevant here include

244 "conventional international bodies," such as the UN and the Organization of American States (OAS); 1,593 "other international bodies," such as inter-governmental banks; and 499 "subsidiary and internal bodies" (many of which function autonomously), like the UN Children's Fund—for a total of 2,336.[53] These institutions do not all have the same diplomatic significance, of course; but even in an international bank, such as the World Bank, a great deal of important diplomacy, however specialized, takes place daily.

Other organizations are the result of cooperation among intergovernmental organizations, nation-states, and private sector institutions or NGOs. Interdependence and the growth of transnational activities are fostering this kind of relationship, which in turn affects the conduct of diplomacy. An example of this type of international organization is the Consultative Group on International Agricultural Research (CGIAR), created in 1971, whose membership is open to international organizations, governments, and private foundations. It includes twenty-two developing countries, twenty-one industrialized countries, twelve regional and international organizations, and three private foundations. The Food and Agriculture Organization (FAO), the International Fund for Agricultural Development (IFAD), the UNDP, and the World Bank (all UN institutions) are the cosponsors of CGIAR.[54] Another example is the Consultative Group to Assist the Poorest (a consortium of forty-two state and multilateral donor agencies as well as private institutions that support microfinancing). Its members include twenty-four bilateral donor agencies and state institutions, twelve multilateral donor agencies, four international financial institutions, and two private institutions.[55]

▒ The Changing Significance of Sovereign States

States remain the most significant players in international politics and in the diplomatic process. It is important to realize, however, that in specific international situations, the role of nonstate actors may acquire special importance. Nation-states still emphasize their formal sovereignty,[56] but complex interdependence, in practice, is eroding their freedom of action. Since the end of World War II, the number of sovereign states has increased in spectacular fashion from about 70, or perhaps 75, to about 200, depending upon how one counts.[57] From a different perspective, the United Nations had 51 members in 1945 (enemy states were initially excluded), and 192 in 2008. This enormous increase in the number of independent states is due to the dismantling of colonial empires as well as the rise of ethnic and national identity, which has led to the partition of a number of states, such as the former Soviet Union and Yugoslavia. Given global interdependence, this transformation in the structure of the international system is having a profound influence on the course of international relations and the practice of diplomacy.

More sovereign states are likely to emerge in the future. In the 1990–1995 period, there were 268 active ethnopolitical groups spread over 115 states, with 112 in open rebellion.[58] Ethnic loyalty is increasing globally. Many of the new states that emerged from the dismantling of colonial empires are multiethnic, with boundaries drawn by colonial powers according to the fortunes of war and conquest, or for administrative reasons, without regard for the profound divisions found in these populations—precolonial social and political divisions (tribes, chieftaincies, kingdoms), as well as divisions based on language, religion, and sometimes mode of subsistence. Some of these groups had a long history of mutual hostility. But the boundaries endured when these colonies became independent.

To this day, many of the different ethnic or tribal groups have failed to develop any sense of loyalty to the people governing them or to the states in which they live. Their growing desire for independence is most likely to lead to a further restructuring of the political system. There are no fewer than 1,000 distinct ethnic groups among the more than 50 countries of the African continent.[59] In India, more than 500 languages are in use. Decolonization added to the disparity found among independent states. St. Kitts and Nevis, in the Caribbean, for example, has a population of 41,000 and a national territory of 116 square miles; Nauru, in the Pacific, has a population of 10,000 and a national territory of 8 square miles. Forty-six states show similar limitations.[60] The World Bank lists 65 states having a gross national income (GNI) per capita of $745 or less (which compares with 52 countries in the high-income category of $9,206 or more).[61]

Conditions of extreme underdevelopment (in addition to the internal divisions just noted) have contributed to political instability in many parts of the world.[62] This situation has a profound effect on the foreign relations of the countries concerned, even creating instability in entire regions, another consequence of interdependence. Since 1948, the UN has deployed some twenty-two peacekeeping forces and almost forty observer missions.[63] In a few of these countries, such as Somalia, the public order has completely disintegrated. Political scientists refer to them as "failed states," a new category;[64] they are the object of great humanitarian concern and have led to a variety of diplomatic initiatives.

In the nineteenth century (and to some extent even in the early twentieth century), small, weak states were not active participants in world affairs; the great powers tended to ignore them, except for geopolitical or strategic reasons. This situation has drastically changed. During the Cold War, East and West competed for their support. These third world nations quickly saw themselves as pawns in great power struggles, and they began to work together to protect their interests. In fact, they became very active and assertive. In 1955, twenty-nine Asian and African countries met in Bandung, Indonesia, to devise a strategy to combat colonialism. In 1961, leaders of twenty-five countries, mostly former colonies, met in Belgrade, Yugoslavia, where they founded the Nonaligned Movement, whose membership eventually grew to more than a hundred countries. The UN gave these underdeveloped countries an effective forum to play a greater role in world affairs. Bloc voting gave them considerable significance in the UN General Assembly, in which they could muster majorities of some 130. They were also able to dominate the deliberations of ECOSOC, a smaller body.[65] But it takes a great deal of diplomacy to act in unison. .

In their struggle for economic development, third world countries formed another coalition, the Group of 77 (G-77), which now numbers more than 120 nations. This took place in 1964 at the inaugural meeting of the UN Conference on Trade and Development (UNCTAD), which became a permanent organization with its own secretariat, a "lobby" or action group for the underdeveloped, adding to their diplomatic influence. Small, weak states are no longer simply standing on the sidelines. They fight to be heard. Their diplomacy has given them a place in the sun, not the commanding position enjoyed by the industrialized world, but a place of considerable significance. Great and medium powers as well as international organizations maintain diplomatic contact with these blocs.

A new dimension in the role of underdeveloped states is that a small number of them are developing weapons of mass destruction (chemical, biological, radiological), thereby becoming an uncommon threat even to large powers, particularly when they choose to network with terrorist groups. The possession of nuclear weapons greatly magnifies the importance of such states as North Korea or Pakistan. Other states are likely to choose this road to significance (e.g., Iran). Even without chemical, biological, and radiological weapons, some small states in various parts of the world have become a threat because they help terrorists (training, financing, or arming them, as Libya and Sudan did in the 1990s). Other small states acquire significance because of geopolitical or strategic considerations, or because of their involvement in a number of regional conflicts. All of these considerations have made the large increase in the number of poor, underdeveloped states a significant transformation in the global diplomatic framework.

The sheer number of participants in multilateral diplomacy is another consequence of the proliferation of international actors. More than 150 delegations, each with at least two or three officials in attendance (assistants, counselors, experts on the topic at hand), attend the meetings of global organizations. Of course, smaller groups also conduct a good deal of diplomatic business. Simultaneously with, or in the margin of, large group meetings is the constant interaction in twos and threes (representatives negotiating, consulting, maintaining contact, comparing notes, etc.). Multilateral diplomacy has a beehive quality to which diplomats must accustom themselves.[66] Another consequence of large numbers of participants is the imposing volume of documentation. Delegates forever need to circulate drafts of documents to be discussed or considered, which amount to hundreds and hundreds of pages to be translated, printed, and distributed (presumably read, too, although a good deal of the reading is usually very selective).

■ Case Study: Interdependence and the Diplomacy of the Suez Crisis

At the root of the problem was President Gamal Abdel Nasser of Egypt, an ambitious and charismatic leader who aspired to liberate Egypt from colonial influence, lead the Arab world toward modernity, and prepare for the next war with Israel.[67] His dreams, however, impinged upon Cold War politics, great power interests, and the stability of the Middle East—all essentially interdependent.

In an effort to keep Nasser from embracing the Eastern bloc, the United States agreed to help him finance his monumental Aswan Dam project. Nasser, however, tried to obtain more arms from Prague and Moscow. This was too much for Secretary of State John Foster Dulles.[68] The United States rescinded the Aswan Dam offer. Infuriated, Nasser sought a way to strike back. There was not much that he could do to the United States. On the other hand, the very lucrative Suez Canal Company was owned by British and French stockholders. On July 26, 1956, seven days after the US policy reversal, Nasser nationalized the Suez Canal Company, thus humiliating two close US allies and prominent colonial powers. Nasser also boasted that canal revenues would make up for lost Western funding.[69] The Egyptian masses were jubilant and Nasser got all the praise.[70] Thus, US Cold War policy with regard to Egypt impacted Britain and France—another dimension of interdependence (even when we simply speak of "ripple effects").

The United States did not want an aggravation of the confrontation and pushed for a negotiated solution in which the stockholders would receive some compensation and international access to the canal would be guaranteed. The matter was taken to the UN and negotiations started. Britain and France, however, secretly decided to retake the canal by force and enlisted the support of Israel. The latter enthusiastically supported the venture (another unanticipated development in this chain of events—and there was more to come). Egypt had long organized Fedayeen raids across the border and Israel was anxious to strike back. Furthermore, Egypt continuously advertised that it was at war with Israel and denied Suez Canal access to Israeli shipping.

The game plan was that Israel would attack Egypt and head for the Suez Canal across the Sinai. At this point, Britain and France would launch their operation and move in to "protect" the canal and restore it to the canal company. But, in this very interdependent environment, things did not quite work out this way. The United States, probably aware of what was happening, warned its allies not to do anything foolish.

With the negotiations still in progress at the UN, Israel launched its attack as planned, on October 29, 1956. The UN Security Council was immediately brought into session. On October 30, Britain and France issued an ultimatum to stop the fighting within twelve hours. On October 31, they vetoed Security Council efforts to avoid an escalation of the conflict, whereupon the matter was taken to the General Assembly, which discussed the matter until 4:20 A.M. on November 2, nothing particularly unusual at the UN in times of crisis: the diplomatic situation becomes very fluid, and changes rapidly as alternatives are sought; the pace becomes hectic and exhausting.[71]

Before the emergency meeting of the Assembly, Canadian delegate Lester Pearson suggested to his close friend UN Secretary-General Dag Hammarskjöld that a UN force might become necessary. The Secretary-General was initially doubtful of the feasibility of this idea. Pearson himself was not sure how to formulate such a proposal. However, in the early hours of November 2, he did suggest to the General Assembly that the Secretary-General be authorized "to begin to make arrangements with Member States for a United Nations Force large enough to keep these borders at peace while a political settlement is being worked out . . . a truly international peace and police force."[72]

This was not yet a formal proposal for a resolution, and the General Assembly began by ordering a cease-fire. Egypt accepted it on condition that the attacking armies did not continue their aggression. Israel followed suit: it had reached its objective on the Suez Canal and was awaiting the arrival of its allies.[73] Britain and France held to their contention that their military intervention was necessary to protect the canal, and their invasion continued. The African-Asian group in the General Assembly wanted to involve the Secretary-General in the negotiations. They prepared a resolution to this effect, which was adopted, specifying that the General Assembly authorize the Secretary-General and General Burns (working for Hammarskjöld) to obtain the withdrawal of the British, French, and Israeli forces.[74] This amounted to giving international organization officials a diplomatic mission, a practice soon to become fairly routine.

In the meantime, Hammarskjöld had prolonged discussions with Pearson about the creation of a UN force, but remained skeptical. Still, the two men began to see how the many difficulties involved could be circumvented. Pearson wrote a draft resolution suggesting the creation of an Assembly committee to study the possible establishment of such a force. The US delegate, however, proposed that, to save time, Hammarskjöld himself should do the necessary exploration instead of an Assembly committee, and Pearson proceeded accordingly. He introduced his resolution and the Assembly adopted it in the early morning hours of November 4. No one was sleeping much. Hammarskjöld himself, in times of crisis, would sleep for a couple of hours in his office, and be ready to put in another twenty hours of negotiations. His stamina was astounding. The resolution read in part: "The General Assembly . . .

requests, as a matter of priority, the Secretary-General to submit to it within forty-eight hours a plan for the setting up, *with the consent of the nations concerned,* of an emergency international United Nations Force (UNEF) to secure and supervise the cessation of hostilities."[75] Note the requirement that all concerned give their *consent.* It would take a good deal of diplomacy to achieve that. On the same day, Hammarskjöld asked the Assembly for an immediate decision on the establishment of a UN command, with General Burns as commander. The Assembly endorsed it. The Egyptian representative at the UN telephoned Cairo and received Nasser's agreement, in principle, to the idea of a UN force. Things were beginning to look better. The British and the French, too, gave indications that they saw the possible usefulness of such a force. But this did not amount to a firm agreement.

On November 5, an ominous development occurred: the Soviet Union requested a meeting of the Security Council to hear its proposal that the British, French, and Israeli forces withdraw within three days and that the Soviet Union, the United States, and other member states having the capability give armed assistance to Egypt, unless Britain, France, and Israel complied with the Assembly cease-fire resolution.[76] This was a bombshell.

In notes to Britain, France, and Israel, Nikita Khrushchev threatened to intervene while Premier Nikolai Bulganin announced that the Red Army was prepared to crush the aggressors and restore peace in the East.[77] The United States would never have accepted a Soviet military intervention in the area and would probably have considered a military response of its own if the Soviets had entered the fray—and who knows where this might have led. It is possible—and even probable—that this brief episode of Soviet saber-rattling was only a political maneuver, but it added urgency to the negotiations. The Soviets gained enormous popularity in the Arab world.

The Security Council refused to adopt the Soviet agenda item because the United States pointed out that it "embodied an unthinkable suggestion" that would "convert Egypt into a still larger battlefield."[78] The Soviets, however, might still come to the assistance of Egypt without UN endorsement. It was important to bring the conflict to an end—fast.

By 2:00 A.M. on November 6, Hammarskjöld's plan for a UN force was ready and was immediately communicated to Britain and France, which, before lunch that same day, announced that a cease-fire by their forces would come into operation at midnight. Their original scheme had failed and the UN force offered a way out. Both countries were alarmed by the widespread international opposition to their invasion, and the Soviet move made the whole venture so much more dangerous. Now Hammarskjöld had to produce a force, manage to deploy it in Egypt without delay, and secure the departure of all invasion forces, a formidable test of his diplomatic skill.

In a matter of a few days, some twenty-one countries offered to contribute troops. Ralph Bunche, a member of Hammarskjöld's team, quipped: "This is the most popular army in history, an army which everyone fights to get into."[79] But it was not popular in Egypt. The stationing of a UN force on the territory of a member state had never been attempted before, and it could be perceived as an infringement of sovereignty, another form of foreign occupation. Nasser was very uncomfortable with this proposition. To make things more difficult, Israel absolutely refused to allow any stationing of the force in its territory. To protect Egypt's sovereignty, Nasser sought numerous clarifications and guarantees. He insisted that every national contingent be subject to his approval.

The United States volunteered to fly national contingents from their home bases to a staging area near Naples, Italy. US planes were not allowed in Egypt, as the permanent members of the Security Council were barred from participating in the operation. Swissair planes were used to ferry the troops to Cairo.

Hammarskjöld was aware of the vital importance of a rapid deployment before the belligerents changed their minds and the hostilities escalated. Nasser, however, kept postponing his authorization. He wanted agreement on how long the force would stay in Egypt, what it would be allowed to do, and where it would be stationed. Hammarskjöld finally succeeded in convincing him to let the first elements enter on November 14, leaving all other questions for later specification. Hammarskjöld himself left New York on the evening of November 14 for three days of negotiations with the Egyptian foreign minister and with Nasser in Cairo, but these never produced formal agreement on all aspects of UNEF. Hammarskjöld admitted that ambiguity was necessary if the force was to be deployed at all.[80]

"In order to gain the necessary time," he told the UN, "I accepted a certain lack of clarity."[81] He did not like the lack of specificity on the UNEF mission and on the question of what circumstances would allow Nasser to order its departure, but greater efforts to obtain formal clarification could have killed the peacekeeping operation. Nations frequently agree to do more in fact than they will, if they have to specify it formally in a written document. In the end, the international force became a reality even if, more than once, everything threatened to unravel.[82] The conflict did not escalate and Hammarskjöld was able to say that "the operation has simply succeeded."[83] The British and French forces withdrew by December 22, 1956. Israeli forces took longer. Delicate negotiations, international pressure, and ambiguous understandings were needed to bring this about.

Interdependence in a bitterly divided world had led from the financing of a dam to a war that nearly brought in the superpowers. Skillful diplomacy at the UN and a peacekeeping force saved the day. The use of such a force was an important innovation and a model for future crisis management. At the end of 2007, there were seventeen peacekeeping operations under way throughout the world (see Table 3.1).[84]

Table 3.1   UN Peacekeeping Operations in 2007

Current peacekeeping operations	17
Special political and peacebuilding missions directed and supported by the UN Department of Peacekeeping Operations	3
Peacekeeping operations since 1948	63
Total personnel in seventeen current peacekeeping operations	100,484
Countries contributing uniformed personnel	119
Estimated cost of operations, July 1, 2007–June 30, 2008	$7.0 billion
Outstanding contributions to peacekeeping, August 31, 2007	$2.5 billion

Source: http://www.un.org/depts/dpko/dpko/bnote.

▓ Study Questions and Discussion Topics

1. What are the limitations of the state system? What are its benefits?

2. What is interdependence? How does it affect diplomacy?

3. In what ways does the Suez case study illustrate interdependence?

4. What forces are changing the structure of our global political system?

5. What are the diplomatic consequences of interdependence?

6. What is the future of the sovereign state?

7. In what respects is globalization a challenge to diplomacy? What contradictions are built into globalization?

8. In what ways has diplomacy become diverse?

▓ Suggested Reading

Axworthy, Lloyd. "Toward a New Multilateralism." In *To Walk Without Fear: The Global Movement to Ban Landmines,* edited by Maxwell A. Cameron, Robert J. Lawson, and Brian M. Tomlin. New York: Oxford University Press, 1998.

Center for Strategic and International Studies, Advisory Panel on Diplomacy in the Information Age. *Reinventing Diplomacy in the Information Age.* Washington, DC, 1998.

Dizard, Wilson, Jr. *Digital Diplomacy: US Foreign Policy in the Information Age.* Westport: Praeger, 2001.

Florini, Ann M., ed. *The Third Force: The Rise of Transnational Civil Society.* Washington, DC: Carnegie Endowment for International Peace, 2000.

Higgott, Richard A., Geoffrey R. D. Underhill, and Andreas Bieler, eds. *Non-State Actors and Authority in the Global System.* New York: Routledge, 2000.

Hopkins, Raymond. "The International Role of 'Domestic' Bureaucracy." *International Organization* 30, no. 3 (Summer 1976), pp. 405–432.

Kennan, George F. "Diplomacy Without Diplomats?" *Foreign Affairs* 76, no. 5 (September–October 1997), pp. 198–212.

Keohane, Robert O., and Joseph S. Nye. *Power and Interdependence.* 2d ed. Glenview, IL: Scott Foresman, 1989.

Rosenau, James N., and J. P. Singh, eds. *Information Technologies and Global Politics: The Changing Scope of Power and Governance.* Albany: State University of New York Press, 2002.

Simmons, P. J., and Chantal de Jonge Oudraat, eds. *Managing Global Issues: Lessons Learned.* Washington, DC: Carnegie Endowment for International Peace, 2001.

Smith, Gordon S. *Reinventing Diplomacy: A Virtual Necessity.* Washington, DC: US Institute of Peace, 1999. http://www.usip.org/virtualdiplomacy/publications/reports/gsmithisa99.

Starr, Harvey. *Anarchy, Order, and Integration: How to Manage Interdependence.* Ann Arbor: University of Michigan Press, 1997.

World Bank. *World Bank–Civil Society Collaboration: Progress Report for Fiscal Years 2000 and 2001.* Washington, DC, 2002. http://www.worldbank.org; http://web.worldbank.org/wbsite/external/topics/cso.

World Health Organization. *Collaboration Within the United Nations System and with Other Intergovernmental Organizations.* Report by the Secretariat A54/32, April 18, 2001, and A54/32 Add. 1. Geneva, 2001. http://www.who.int/ and http://www.who.int/civilsociety/en/.

Wriston, Walter B. "Bits, Bytes and Diplomacy." *Foreign Affairs* 76, no. 5 (September–October 1997), pp. 172–182.

▨ Notes

1. Harvey Starr, *Anarchy, Order, and Integration: How to Manage Interdependence* (Ann Arbor: University of Michigan Press, 1997).

2. P. J. Simmons and Chantal de Jonge Oudraat, eds., *Managing Global Issues: Lessons Learned* (Washington, DC: Carnegie Endowment for International Peace, 2001).

3. See Robert K. Schaeffer, *Understanding Globalization: The Social Consequences of Political, Economic, and Environmental Change* (New York: Rowman and Littlefield, 1997). See also Jackie Smith and Hank Johnston, eds., *Globalization and Resistance: Transnational Dimensions of Social Movements* (New York: Rowman and Littlefield, 2002).

4. Ann M. Florini, ed., *The Third Force: The Rise of Transnational Civil Society* (Washington, DC: Carnegie Endowment for International Peace, 2000); John Boli and George M. Thomas, "World Culture in the World Polity: A Century of International Non-Governmental Organization," in *The Globalization Reader,* edited by Frank J. Lechner and John Boli (Walden, MA: Blackwell, 2000), pp. 262–268.

5. Alex Inkeles, "The Emerging Social Structure of the World," *World Politics* 27 (July 1975), p. 479, emphasis added.

6. See http://www.imf.org/external/pubs/ft/survey/so/home.

7. Robert O. Keohane and Joseph S. Nye, *Power and Interdependence,* 2d ed. (Glenview, IL: Scott Foresman, 1989), chaps. 1, 2, 8. See also Loyd Axworthy, "Toward a New Multilateralism," in *To Walk Without Fear: The Global Movement to Ban Landmines,* edited by Maxwell A. Cameron, Robert J. Lawson, and Brian M. Tomlin (New York: Oxford University Press, 1998), pp. 448–459.

8. In 1998, $1.5 trillion worth of global currencies were traded every day, up from less than $200 billion in 1986. Bruce Russett, Harvey Starr, and David Kinsella, *World Politics: The Menu for Choice,* 6th ed. (Boston: Bedford, 2000), p. 403.

9. James N. Rosenau, *The Study of Global Interdependence* (New York: Nichols, 1980). Keohane and Nye, *Power and Interdependence,* pt. 1, "Understanding Interdependence," pp. 1–60.

10. Keohane and Nye, *Power and Interdependence,* "The Characteristics of Complex Interdependence," pp. 24–29.

11. *New York Times:* April 8, 2002, p. A4; April 9, 2002, p. A1; April 13, 2002, pp. A9, B1.

12. Henry A. Kissinger, "A New National Partnership," *Department of State Bulletin* (February 17, 1975), p. 199, quoted in Keohane and Nye, *Power and Interdependence,* p. 26.

13. Francis O. Wilcox acknowledged that some fifty-five US government agencies are interested in international affairs. Linda M. Fasulo, *Representing America: Experiences of U.S. Diplomats at the UN* (New York: Praeger, 1984), p. 46.

14. *2001 Government Phone Book USA: A Comprehensive Guide to Federal, State, County, and Local Government in the United States* (Detroit: Omnigraphics, 2001), p. 28.

15. Ibid., p. 25.

16. Ibid., pp. 223–224.

17. Ibid. See also *The United States Government Manual 2001–2002* (Washington, DC: US Government Printing Office, 2001); Raymond Hopkins, "The International Role of 'Domestic' Bureaucracy," *International Organization* 30, no. 3 (Summer 1976), pp. 405–432.

18. George F. Kennan, "Diplomacy Without Diplomats?" *Foreign Affairs* 76, no. 5 (September–October 1997), p. 206.

19. Keohane and Nye, *Power and Interdependence,* p. 26.

20. Adam Watson, *Diplomacy: The Dialogue Between States* (New York: Routledge, 2004), p. 147.

21. Much has been said about General Dwight D. Eisenhower's diplomatic skill in getting his Allied commanders to work together for the 1944 landing in Normandy and invasion of Europe.

22. See http://www.dea.gov/pubs/cngrtest. See also A. LeRoy Bennett and James K. Oliver, *International Organizations: Principles and Issues,* 7th ed. (Upper Saddle River, NJ: Prentice-Hall, 2002), pp. 376–379.

23. See http://www.dea.gov/pubs/cngrtest.

24. A large amount of work was done during the ministers' meeting in the Council of the European Union. See David M. Wood and Birol A. Yeşilada, *The Emerging European Union,* 3d ed. (New York: Pearson, 2004), pp. 91–100.

25. The total number of Canadian visits given in the document is actually 12,900, but this number includes 8,313 visits by staff from the Department of National Defense, a large proportion of which (estimated at all but 100) are Canadian armed forces personnel sent to the United States for special training; those visits of course do not qualify as contacts between government officials. Kal J. Holsti and Thomas Allen Levy, "Bilateral Institutions and Transgovernmental Relations Between Canada and the United States," in *Canada and the United States: Transnational and Transgovernmental Relations,* edited by Annette Baker Fox, Alfred O. Hero Jr., and Joseph S. Nye Jr. (New York: Columbia University Press, 1976), pp. 289–290.

26. Holsti and Levy, "Bilateral Institutions," pp. 295–304.

27. See Philip E. Jacob and James V. Toscano, eds., *The Integration of Political Communities* (Philadelphia: Lippincott, 1964).

28. Keohane and Nye, *Power and Interdependence,* p. 26.

29. Florini, *Third Force.*

30. Axworthy, "Toward a New Multilateralism," pp. 448–459. See also Richard A. Higgott, Geoffrey R. D. Underhill, and Andreas Bieler, eds., *Non-State Actors and Authority in the Global System* (New York: Routledge, 2000).

31. UN Charter, art. 71.

32. Bennett and Oliver, *International Organizations,* p. 291; United Nations, "Consultative Relations Between ECOSOC and NGOs," http://www.un.org/esa/coordination/ngo.faq.htm.

33. See website of the UN Fund for Global Partnership, http://www.un.org/unfip. See also http://www.un.org/issues/civilsociety; United Nations, Report of the Secretary-General, *Cooperation Between the UN and All Relevant Partners, in Particular the Private Sector,* UN Doc. A/56/323, October 9, 2001, http://www.un.org/unfip/flash/partnershipreport; United Nations, Address by Deputy Secretary-General Louise Fréchette to the 2004 UN General Assembly, *Civil Society Partnership,* Press Release DSG/SM/233 GA/10269 NGO/550, http://www.un.org/news/press/docs/2004.

34. World Health Organization, *Collaboration Within the United Nations System and with Other Intergovernmental Organizations,* fifty-fourth World Health Assembly, A54/32, April 18, 2001, and A54/32 Add.1, May 8, 2001, http://www.who.int/gb.

35. James Hanlon, *European Law,* 3d ed. (London: Sweet and Maxwell, 2003), pp. 30–34.

36. Charlotte Bretherton and John Vogler, *The European Union as a Global Actor* (New York: Routledge, 1999).

37. ILO constitution, art. 3, sec. 5.

38. Back-channel transactions may also involve other forms of secret contacts while official negotiations are under way. See G. R. Berridge, *Diplomacy: Theory and Practice,* 3d ed. (New York: Palgrave, 2005), pp. 69–70.

39. World Health Organization, *Provisional Agenda,* fifty-fourth World Health Assembly, A54/1 Rev. 1, May 14–22, 2001, Committee A, http://www.who.int/gb. Schistosomiasis is a disease caused by infestation of the blood with parasites belonging to a class of flatworms (trematode). Certain snails, in which part of the life cycle of the schistosome takes place, act as intermediate hosts in the transmission of the disease, http://www.nlm.nih.gov/medlineplus/ency/article/001321.

40. Ibid., List of Delegates, A54/DIV/1 Rev. 1, http://www.who.int/gb.

41. See http://www.state.gov.

42. Ibid.

43. See http://www.state.gov/www/global/oes/science.

44. Ibid.

45. Secretary of State Madeleine K. Albright, "Science and Diplomacy: Strengthening State for the 21st Century," report (March 8, 2000) and policy statement (May 12, 2000), http://www.state.gov/www/statements/2000/0005.

46. Ibid.

47. Ibid.

48. Ibid.

49. See http://www.state.gov/g/stas.

50. See http://www.who.int/m/topicgroups/governance/en/index.

51. International Telegraphic Union (1865), Universal Postal Union (1874), and Metric Union (1875). Other organizations of this type can be found in D. W. Bowett, *The Law of International Institutions* (New York: Praeger, 1963), pp. 5–8. See also Daniel S. Cheever and H. Field Haviland Jr., *Organizing for Peace: International Organization in World Affairs* (Boston: Houghton Mifflin, 1954), pp. 40–42.

52. Quoted in Cheever and Haviland, *Organizing for Peace,* p. 46.

53. *Yearbook of International Organizations, 2006–2007,* 43d ed. (Munich: Saur, 2006), vol. 1B, p. 3024.

54. See http://www.cgiar.org.

55. See list at http://www.cgap.org/about/donors. Additional information on this consortium is available at this website.

56. Jo-Anne Pemberton, *Interpreting Sovereignty* (New York: Palgrave Macmillan, 2006).

57. The World Bank provides data for 207 economies with populations of more than 30,000. See http://www.worldbank.org/data.

58. Russett, Starr, and Kinsella, *World Politics,* pp. 202–203.

59. Herbert S. Lewis, "Ethnic Loyalties Are on the Rise Globally," in *Africa,* edited by F. Jeffress Ramsay, 6th ed. (Guilford, CT: Dushkin, 1995), pp. 181–182; Ali A. Mazrui, "The Bondage of Boundaries: Why Africa's Maps Will Be Redrawn," in Ramsay, *Africa,* pp. 182–185.

60. Russett, Starr, and Kinsella, *World Politics,* app. B table (n.p.).

61. Gross national income (GNI) is a new statistical criterion used by the World Bank, instead of gross national product (GNP). See http://www.worldbank.org/data.

62. Woeful public administration, corruption, and poor leadership have also contributed to the problem.

63. Bennett and Oliver, *International Organizations,* pp. 157–160. See also http://www.un.org/depts.dpko/dpko/bnote.

64. Defined as "States that are internationally recognized, but whose governments (if they exist) cannot provide their citizens with even the minimum level of security and well-being expected of sovereign states." Bruce Russett, Harvey Starr, and David Kinsella, *World Politics: The Menu for Choice,* 7th ed. (Belmont, CA: Wadsworth, 2004), p. 216.

65. Eighteen members in 1945, enlarged to twenty-seven in 1965, and fifty-four in 1973. Bennett and Oliver, *International Organizations,* 6th ed., p. 70.

66. See Jo Ann Fagot Aviel, "The Evolution of Multilateral Diplomacy," in James P. Muldoon Jr., JoAnn Fagot Aviel, Richard Reitano, and Earl Sullivan, eds., *Multilateral Diplomacy and the United Nations Today* (Boulder: Westview, 1999), pp. 11–12.

67. William L. Cleveland, *A History of the Modern Middle East,* 2d ed. (Boulder: Westview, 2000), pp. 295–304.

68. Townsend Hooper, *The Devil and John Foster Dulles* (Boston: Little, Brown, 1973).

69. As it turned out, the Soviets offered to pay for the dam—another toehold for them in the Middle East.

70. Sydney Nettleton Fisher and William Ochsenwald, *The Middle East: A History,* 4th ed. (New York: McGraw-Hill, 1990), pp. 695–705.

71. The days and nights are filled with endless contacts, meetings, maneuvers, tentative proposals, arrangements, telephone calls, exchanges of cables, and formal speeches. The diplomatic situation becomes convoluted, and even confusing, as more proposals are made, discussed, and reformulated. See Brian Urquhart, *Hammarskjold* (New York: Norton, 1972), pp. 175–179.

72. Urquhart, *Hammarskjold,* p. 176.

73. Gerard Clarfield, *United States Diplomatic History: The Age of Ascendancy* (Englewood Cliffs, NJ: Prentice Hall, 1992), vol. 2, *Since 1900,* p. 567.

74. Urquhart, *Hammarskjold,* p. 178.

75. Ibid., pp. 178–179, emphasis added.

76. Urquhart, *Hammarskjold,* p. 180.

77. Clarfield, *US Diplomatic History,* p. 568.

78. Ibid., p. 180.

79. Urquhart, *Hammarskjold,* p. 190.

80. United Nations, *The Blue Helmets: A Review of UN Peace-Keeping,* 2d ed. (New York: UN Department of Public Information, 1990), pp. 51–59.

81. Urquhart, *Hammarskjold,* p. 189.

82. Eventually, some 6,000 troops from ten countries were deployed. United Nations, *Blue Helmets,* pp. 56–57.

83. Urquhart, *Hammarskjold,* p. 227.

84. United Nations, "UN Peacekeeping Operations," background note, http://www .un.org/depts/dpko/dpko/bnote. In its count, the Department of Peace Keeping Operations includes a few political missions that are under its jurisdiction, in addition to the primarily military missions. In some cases the distinction between political mission and peacekeeping mission is not hard and fast, which hinders count accuracy.

4 The Impact of Technology

Technology is a factor of interdependence and contributes to the many changes in diplomacy examined in this volume. The twenty-first-century pace of life is fast, and so is the tempo of diplomacy. There is less patience with formality, although it must be admitted that the diplomatic world is still addicted to the ceremonial (the legacy of earlier centuries and a by-product of national pride). Nations and peoples are more interconnected than ever before, which in turn has led to a large expansion of diplomatic activity. International problems affect more nations, and governments find it more difficult to remain aloof and uninvolved.

Rapid intercontinental transportation contributes to a vast increase in diplomatic travel. Multilateral conferences, many of them global, are proliferating. Heads of state, heads of government, foreign ministers, and other important officials and heads of departments now routinely leave their national capitals to engage in high-level diplomacy. Not only can they get there fast (with a contingent of support staff), but they can also remain in touch with the nerve centers of their own governments. This is also the age of "shuttle diplomacy" and the use of special missions for international troubleshooting and mediation, with diplomats traveling back and forth between conflicting parties who refuse to meet face to face. Even heads of permanent missions find themselves traveling more (e.g., returning to their own national capitals for consultation and participation in policy conversations). Participants in global interaction (and this includes many international organization officials) are thus increasingly on the move (discussed further in Chapters 9 and 10).

Technology makes it possible to cope with the awesome logistics of global conferences: wiring for sound and simultaneous translation (and now, when meeting halls are not adequately equipped, pocket receivers and head phones as wireless substitutes); fast transcription of proceedings with copies almost instantly available; fast duplication and circulation of documents; and equally important, electronic voting, without which decisionmaking in large meetings becomes inordinately time-consuming.[1] At the United Nations, in fact, meetings are occasionally postponed when rooms wired for this purpose are not available.[2]

The revolution in communication technology is changing the relationship between diplomats and their national governments. Foreign ministries are able to maintain tighter control over their diplomats abroad. The latter, however, often complain that their instructions show a lack of understanding of the situation in the host capital, and that excessive control hampers them in the fulfillment of their mission. Micromanagement can be a handicap in many professions. On the other hand, diplomats in the field can more easily contribute to the decisionmaking process back home by means of their reports and policy recommendations. They can also more easily se ̇x new instructions or documentation from their ministry as the need arises.

In the mid-1980s, the US Department of State was reporting that message traffic with the field had been increasing by 100,000 communications a year since 1980, and had reached 1.8 million communications in 1986.[3] By the turn of the century, it was electronically processing over 140,000 official records and 90,000 data messages each day, supporting more than 250 diplomatic posts around the world. Over 20 million electronic messages were posted annually by department personnel, representing a huge transformation in communication patterns.[4] The Center for Strategic and International Studies (CSIS) in Washington, D.C., predicted that the Internet would become "the central nervous system of international relations."[5]

It must be noted, however, that the vast communication expansion can result in information overload—messages never reaching the person to whom they are sent or otherwise getting lost in the shuffle. Decisionmakers may need to be "protected" from the onslaught of communication. And it is clear that the usefulness of communication technology greatly depends upon the effectiveness of administrative adjustments. The human element must not be forgotten in assessing the effects of technological transformation. Controversy in the United States over the failure to share information prior to September 11, 2001, and in the struggle against international terrorism generally, is an example of the kind of bureaucratic complications that many governments have to cope with. It may be argued that as technology changes, administrative structures (the bureaucracy) eventually adjust to the new reality. However, experience shows that adjustments are seldom automatic or timely. Inertia is a factor. It may take a discerning person to see what needs to be done differently to take advantage of technological advancements. And money is usually a factor in administrative restructuring and in having access to the new technology.

■ The CNN Factor

Another consequence of the information revolution is that unfolding events become known almost instantly around the world: "the CNN factor" (see Box 4.1).[6] In a crisis, governments will hear from the media the latest developments (along with wider and wider audiences), all of which creates pressure for faster response. Thus crises tend to escalate more rapidly and diplomatic response time is shorter.[7] There is less time for deliberation, and less time to create alternative strategies. Crises are likely to be discussed simultaneously in a number of capitals and international organizations, and decisions may be made with insufficient consultation. Crisis decisionmaking is thus more problematic and more dangerous.[8] Even beyond crisis situations, the pace of diplomacy is becoming faster.

The hot line established between Washington and Moscow in the early 1960s was an effort to cope with this problem under exceptional circumstances: technology was used to bypass the dangerously slow traditional channels. The 1962 Cuban missile crisis was a direct military confrontation between the United States and the Soviet Union. President John F. Kennedy demanded the removal of the Soviet nuclear missiles being deployed in Cuba and ordered a blockade of the island. The US Navy would stop Soviet vessels on their way to Cuba. The United States might even attack the Soviet missile sites in Cuba. If neither side backed down, a military clash between the superpowers might ensue. Would it trigger a nuclear exchange?

Chairman Nikita Khrushchev eventually made a conciliatory move, but retracted it within hours (apparently under pressure from his hard-liners in Moscow). The next day (Sunday, October 28), another message reached Washington: Khrushchev's position had changed again—he agreed to remove all

---

Box 4.1 The Media for Instant Diplomatic Communication

During the 1991 Gulf War, Saddam Hussein proposed what was viewed in Washington as a worthless peace settlement. President George H. W. Bush was anxious to communicate his conclusion to all members of the coalition. Marlin Fitzwater, former White House press secretary, recalls that the "quickest and most effective way was CNN, because all countries in the world had it and were watching it on a real-time basis . . . and 20 minutes after we got the proposal . . . I went on national television . . . to tell the 26 members [of the coalition] . . . that the war was continuing."

Source: Walter B. Wriston, "Bits, Bytes, and Diplomacy, " *Foreign Affairs* 76, no. 5 (September–October 1997), p. 174.

missiles. President Kennedy wanted to signal his acceptance immediately, before the Russian position changed again. Kennedy wanted Khrushchev to know that his latest decision was seen as marking the end of the crisis. Several hours later, however, Kennedy's message, to be communicated by conventional diplomatic channels, had not arrived. Timing was so critical that Kennedy used a press conference to broadcast his acceptance of Khrushchev's latest offer.[9] It worked, and the crisis came to an end. But the antagonists decided to remedy the communication problem by creating a hot line between Washington and Moscow.

Initially, the hot line was a wire connection backed up by radio, with teleprinter terminals at both ends, but no voice capability. In 1971, the hot line was upgraded with a satellite connection. In 1985, it was given fax capacity. In 1999, a parallel hot line was established between the US secretary of state and her Russian counterpart.[10] Other pairs of countries have established their own hot lines (mostly secure telephone connections).[11] Regular telephone communication, however, is used extensively in diplomacy (see Box 4.2).

Chief executives call each other (independently of any hot line arrangements) on a variety of occasions. The telephone has become important for immediate contact, clarification, and consultation. This occurs primarily between leaders who seek to maintain friendly relations, on routine matters as well as on serious issues. Such conversations also take place outside friendly circles. When situations become tense, some chief executives spend hours calling their counterparts, back and forth. The telephone may not be the main way of maintaining official contacts between international actors, but it is used extensively. In fact, officials at a lower level (e.g., foreign ministers and other heads of executive departments) also routinely communicate by telephone. When Hamas defeated Fatah in Gaza, creating an unexpected crisis in this part of the Middle East, the so-called quartet of peace brokers (the United States, the European Union, Russia, and the United Nations) held an emergency teleconference on June 15, 2007, to review the grim realities of the new situation.[12]

It is readily acknowledged that telephone negotiations are less effective than face-to-face interaction. Facial expressions and body language—important elements of physical presence—are missing from electronic communication. Video conferencing, though still lacking elements of personal presence, also brings decisionmakers quickly together at minimal cost; and with more bandwidth available, it will be increasingly feasible to make such "virtual meetings" secure.[13] The UN is already using video conferencing on occasion to bring officials together—a profound advantage given the physical separation of its headquarters in New York, Geneva, and Vienna.[14] In fact, Gordon Smith reported in 2000 that the military in many countries had been holding virtual meetings using secure video links "for some time."[15]

Box 4.2 Mediation by Telephone in the Israeli-Palestinian Conflict

In September 1995, after a year of delicate negotiations between the Israelis and Palestinians to carry out the Oslo peace process and expand Palestinian control over segments of the West Bank beyond Gaza and Jericho, Dennis Ross, Middle East negotiator for the US State Department, was on the phone three or four times a day for two weeks, talking to the chief Israeli negotiator, and then to his Palestinian counterpart. He explained to each of them the terms that the other side was insisting upon in the agreement to win the support of his domestic constituency. Each party was obsessed by the likely public reaction to the terms of the agreement they were working on.

On September 24, Yasir Arafat stormed out of the negotiations in Taba, Egypt, screaming that Israel was trying to shove down his throat totally unfair territorial terms. At 3:00 A.M., Ross received a call at his home in the Washington, D.C., area from Israel's top negotiator, who was alarmed at this turn of events and needed help in calming Arafat.

From 3:15 to 6:00 A.M., Ross spoke with Arafat, Shimon Peres (Israel's foreign minister), Ahmed Qurei (chief Palestinian negotiator), and Uri Savir (chief Israeli negotiator), trying to convince them that they were just a few steps away from an agreement, and that they should not throw away a year of hard work. After some frantic brainstorming about security arrangements and which side should control which pieces of real estate, the two sides agreed to make concessions.

At 7:00 A.M., Arafat and Peres called U.S. secretary of state Warren Christopher and announced that agreement had been reached. Then came President Bill Clinton's turn to get on the phone: he called Prime Minister Yitzhak Rabin and Arafat to congratulate them and invite them to the signing ceremony, which would take place a few days later in Washington. He also called King Hussein of Jordan, King Hassan II of Morocco, and President Hosni Mubarak of Egypt and invited them to attend the ceremony.

Sources: Steven Greenhouse, "Mideast Shuttle's New Twist: U.S. Aid Mediated by Phone," *New York Times*, September 25, 1995, pp. A1, A4; Dennis Ross, *The Missing Peace: The Inside Story of the Fight for Middle East Peace* (New York: Farrar, Straus and Giroux, 2004).

■ Virtual Diplomacy

The US Institute of Peace sees the growing use of information and communication technology in the conduct of foreign affairs as generating "virtual diplomacy," thus dramatizing the changes taking place in the field.[16] Others speak of "digital diplomacy."[17] And undoubtedly, the new means of communication and remarkable access to information are changing the way diplomacy is conducted—even if diplomacy is not really being "reinvented."[18]

As early as 1979, digital technology gave US negotiators a remarkable advantage in the course of the World Administrative Radio Conference held in Geneva by the International Telecommunication Union, a specialized agency of the UN that deals with radio channel allocations. Among the 150 national delegations, the US mission alone had the advantage of knowing the status of each of the thousands of proposals generated each day on the conference agenda. As each item was negotiated, changes were recorded on a desktop computer at the US delegation office, thus permitting a fast and effective way of sorting out and accessing a vast array of data. Having a timely and accurate record of any progress made in the negotiations gave the US delegates a critical advantage in developing their negotiating strategy.[19]

It is useful to note, however, that many governmental bureaucracies are slow in adjusting to the new modes of communication. Many countries cannot afford to invest in and develop these expensive systems. Even the US Congress took years to fund the State Department's communication modernization. Diplomacy, too, remains attached to well-established traditions long after they have outlived their usefulness. It took decades for the profession to warm up just to the use of the telephone in official transactions. Often, a cultural change is needed before diplomacy can make effective use of the new technology. Change is taking place, obviously but unevenly, around the world.

Satellite Imagery

Satellite imagery and geographic information systems are now used to facilitate international negotiations as well as coordination of joint fieldwork between governments, international organizations, and nongovernmental organizations. The technology involves computer systems capable of storing, processing, and displaying data according to their geographical location, using various types of imagery acquired by orbiting satellites.[20]

An example of the benefits provided by this type of technology can be seen in the 1995 Bosnia peace negotiations in Dayton, Ohio. The US State Department's new digital resources provided access to global positioning satellite facilities and information systems that had special relevance to what was being negotiated, particularly detailed map displays and three-dimensional terrain imagery, in ways that facilitated the task of establishing boundary lines between the contending parties, a key factor in arriving at a final agreement.[21]

Complex diplomatic work involved in the deployment and control of multinational peacekeeping forces can be immeasurably facilitated by this type of technology.[22] The success of such operations is heavily dependent upon negotiations to win the consent and cooperation of highly antagonistic and distrustful parties in situations fraught with uncertainty. Geographical details are usually of the utmost importance in informing the contending parties about the requirements and limitations of given situations on the ground, or in deciding who is to be allowed in specific locations and the resultant implications for the maintenance of cease-fires or disengagement of military units. This technology can also be useful in negotiating many other types of international monitoring and supervision[23]—matters of critical significance in today's age of ethnic conflict.

Satellite imagery and geographic information technology have been put to good use in large-scale humanitarian operations involving agencies of multiple governments, international organizations, and civil society personnel (particularly nongovernmental organizations [NGOs]) that have widely different information needs. Satellite images are processed and analyzed according to the specific needs of the organizations concerned, and are distributed to users in the field and to decisionmakers in regional offices and headquarters. Geographically organized information can include details on infrastructure, food and medical resources availability, population distribution, and climatic conditions.[24] Some relief operations take place in underdeveloped and unfamiliar areas—for example, refugees streaming across mountainous regions in eastern Afghanistan, or victims of earthquakes in remote and isolated villages. The many entities trying to provide assistance have an acute need for accurate geographical information about safe relocation areas.

Virtual On-Site Coordination

The UN is involved in disaster relief and to this end endeavors to achieve global coordination of relief efforts. For that purpose, its Office for the Coordination of Humanitarian Affairs (OCHA) in Geneva has created the Virtual Operations on Site Coordination Center (Virtual OSOCC), whose main object, through the ReliefWeb site, is to facilitate decisionmaking for a widespread response to major disasters across international borders by means of real-time information exchange among all international actors involved in such operations, including a variety of international organizations, governments, and NGOs.[25] All agencies and field staff have access to the information pertaining to specific operations and can provide comments on existing information and thereby discuss issues of concern with other participants. Disaster information can be exchanged continuously and simultaneously from anywhere in the world.

ReliefWeb was launched in October 1996. It maintains three offices (New York, Geneva, and Kobe, Japan) to update the website around the clock and has seen a steady growth. In 2002, ReliefWeb received 1.5 million hits per week; in 2004, it received 1 million hits per day. Shortly after the December 2004 tsunami disaster in southern Asia, it received an average of 3 million hits per day. In addition, ReliefWeb services over 70,000 subscribers, providing resources specifically targeted to relief professionals.[26] The website even includes a regularly updated list of vacancies in humanitarian relief posts around the world (primarily available in international organizations and NGOs).

Early Warning and Crisis Management

Rapid communication technology offers the possibility of better early warning for crisis management and preventive diplomacy. International problems are easier to manage before they reach the crisis stage.[27] As the work of crisis response organizations becomes more complex, a number of institutions are seeking to develop more effective techniques. For example, the Crisis Management Initiative[28] and the US Institute of Peace[29] cohosted a conference on information and communications technology and crisis management in Helsinki, Finland, in September 2003, focused on creating conditions that enable separate organizational structures (governmental and nongovernmental) to communicate and share information. They define this capability as "interoperability."[30] The conference was attended by government and international organization representatives, communication technology experts, crisis management NGOs, business enterprises, and academics. Representatives of the United Nations, the North Atlantic Treaty Organization (NATO), the European Union, and the Organization for Security and Cooperation in Europe (OSCE) spoke about the need to achieve such interoperability in crisis management.[31]

Though diplomatic efforts can be facilitated by better means of communication and access to information, states often hesitate to intervene diplomatically when the situation does not seem serious enough—that is, when real danger is uncertain or too remote. International organizations and NGOs show fewer inhibitions, but effective prevention is more problematic without the support of influential states. Frequent warnings of terrorist attacks after September 11, 2001, have engendered lassitude (the old problem of crying wolf too often). Early warning needs to achieve credibility. Information and communication technology can make a difference by providing more specificity to the warning, and greater reliability in sources of information.

Cybersecurity

Expanding use of information and communication technology in international affairs raises the issue of communication security. In a 2003 study of computer security, more than half of the twenty-four US federal agencies surveyed received a grade of D or F.[32] The Department of Homeland Security, which has a division devoted to monitoring cybersecurity, received the lowest overall score. Also earning an F was the Justice Department, the agency charged with investigating and prosecuting cases of hacking and other forms of cybercrime.[33] In international affairs, maintaining confidentiality is of course of particular importance, aside from protection from disruption and incapacitation of electronic systems. And cybersecurity will remain a continuing quest: as soon as a new defensive system is in place, hackers, assorted code-breakers, and perhaps even would-be terrorists will be at work to bypass it or find new ways to attain their objectives. This is an old form of interaction. The infusion of technology into the diplomatic process has added a new dimension to the classic relationship.[34]

Cyberterrorism

Cyberterrorism is widely discussed among information technology professionals, who stress that its risk has increased since the September 11, 2001, attacks. Although it is pointed out that no single instance of cyberterrorism has been recorded, computer attacks by hackers give an idea of the damage that can be done (by means of computer break-ins, swarming [bombarding targets with thousands of messages at once], and computer viruses and worms, among other techniques).[35] During the NATO operations to evict Serbian forces from Kosovo, for example, businesses, public entities, and academic institutions in NATO countries received virus-laden e-mails from a range of Eastern European nations.[36]

▓ Network Power

The remarkable development of information and communication technology is dramatically magnifying the role of civil society in global affairs. Mass access to radio and television, even in the developing world, has increased political consciousness and has undoubtedly contributed to the growth of an activist global civil society.[37] NGOs have also been a major factor in this phenomenon. They mobilize opinion, play a leadership role, and, thanks to digital technology, are able to network around the world. NGOs are becoming more politically aggressive and resorting to their own diplomatic outreach to achieve their objectives, especially in international organizations.

All connected groups can instantly receive the latest information and instructions on what needs to be done. Massive responses to international events, conferences, meetings of international organizations, and governmental action can be coordinated. The most impressive example of network power in action is provided by the International Campaign to Ban Landmines (ICBL), a network of more than 1,200 organizations around the world that, under the leadership of Jody Williams, influenced governments and their diplomatic processes to the point that NGO representatives actually participated in the negotiations that led to concluding the 1997 landmine treaty (see case study in Chapter 5). Networking is one of the hallmarks of the transnational phenomenon, and it has significant political consequences and diplomatic ramifications. International

organizations and their officials are increasingly and more extensively networking among themselves and with NGOs. Even governments and their diplomats
are now routinely doing the same.[38] Information and communication technology is literally transforming the international political process—and this transformation has only just begun.[39]

Electronic Spying

A related effect of communication technology is electronic eavesdropping or
spying. Because diplomacy involves the exchange of politically sensitive information, states naturally sought to develop international rules to protect confidentiality (legal inviolability of the means of diplomatic communication,
couriers, the diplomatic pouch, legal immunities for diplomatic premises, and
much more). But the harsh realities of international politics have led the same
states to find ways to obtain the privileged information—and technology has
made it easier (see case study on the US embassy in Moscow at the end of this
chapter).[40] What is interesting is that illegal access efforts are not restricted to
states engaged in conflict.

British spying on UN Secretary-General Kofi Annan was revealed in late
February 2004 in an interview with Clare Short, an outspoken former member of the Tony Blair cabinet who resigned in the summer of 2003 and who
has called on Blair to do the same.[41] She said that Britain had regularly spied
on the Secretary-General and that transcripts of conversations with him had
circulated freely in the cabinet. It is widely understood that this is a long-
established practice. In a BBC interview one day after the Clare Short revela-
tions, former UN Secretary-General Boutros Boutros-Ghali said: "From the
first day I entered my office, they told me, 'Beware, your office is bugged,
your residence is bugged.' It is the tradition that member states that have the
technical capacity to bug will do it without hesitation."[42] Richard Butler, former Iraq weapons inspector, interviewed in the same BBC program, added:
"There was abundant evidence that we were being constantly monitored." He
said that if he had something sensitive to discuss, "I had to go to the basement
café in the UN where there was heaps of noise or I'd go and take a walk in
Central Park."[43]

Equally interesting, Stephen C. Schlesinger, author of a recent book on
the creation of the UN,[44] in a *New York Times* interview also occasioned by the
British uproar, said that there were three US intelligence agencies at work in
San Francisco in 1945 during the international conference in the course of
which the UN Charter was negotiated: "The Army Signal Corps was intercept-
ing all the cable traffic among the diplomats, so we knew in advance the negotiating strategies of practically all the 46 countries coming to San Francisco.
Second was the F.B.I. which was tapping the phones of many of the American

visitors and observers at the conference, and there was some belief that they were also tapping the calls of the members of the U.S. delegation itself. The third intelligence agency was the Office of Strategic Services, the O.S.S., and they were supplying all sorts of technical equipment to the U.S. delegation to track . . . the papers being passed around."[45]

In 2003, Katharine Gun, a linguist working for one of Britain's intelligence agencies, reported that "she had seen an American request for British help in bugging the diplomats of six Security Council members whose votes were being courted for the resolution" that the United States sought to authorize the war against Iraq.[46] Shortly thereafter, the European Union uncovered a bugging operation directed at five of its members. Listening devices were found late in February 2003 in the offices of the French, German, British, Austrian, and Spanish delegations at a sprawling glass-and-marble EU headquarters building in central Brussels, used for EU summit meetings. This discovery occurred during a tense time when EU leaders, particularly from France and Germany, were vehemently criticizing the George W. Bush administration's decision to use force against Iraq.[47] Electronic spying seriously complicates the task of the diplomatic profession. Confidentiality is essential for many of the delicate negotiations that diplomats engage in. While espionage has always been a factor in the conduct of foreign relations, advanced technology has made the problem more ubiquitous—and the problem will become worse as new technological breakthroughs occur.

Case Study: The US Embassy in Moscow

The US embassy in Moscow had long been considered inadequate for the maintenance of diplomatic relations with the Soviet government. A larger, more modern facility was needed. After seven years of protracted negotiations, the Soviet authorities finally authorized the project and construction on a massive new building began. In 1985, after a further seven years, when the building was nearing completion, the whole project came to a shuddering halt: US security experts discovered tens of thousands of microscopic listening devices embedded in the concrete walls of the eight-story structure. The United States had bowed to the Soviet demand that most of the workers and building materials be provided by the Soviet Union—and the Kremlin had used this golden opportunity to apply its technology.

US counterintelligence experts analyzed the situation—better late than never—and tested and retested the structure after diverse corrective efforts had been attempted. But the technology defied remedial action, and for more than a decade the building remained empty and useless, the victim of modern technology and lax counterintelligence supervision. The US government considered razing the structure and building a new one in its place, but this solution was deemed too expensive. In 1991, President Bill Clinton finally persuaded Congress to spend $240 million to do something with the building.

Three hundred US construction workers were flown in (after thorough security screening) for the task. All permanent building materials were shipped from the United States. To avoid contact with the outside world, the construction crews were housed in a temporary, prefabricated village on embassy property. They had their own cafeteria, infirmary, barbershop, and gymnasium. Two floors of the embassy were demolished, and four new stories, hopefully free from listening devices, were added to the remaining structure.

Today, confidential embassy work is restricted to the newer, upper floors, while unclassified work is conducted below, in the areas still replete with listening devices.[48] Perhaps the United States regrets that it was not given the opportunity to do the same (perhaps more subtly) to the Soviet embassy in Washington. The only thing that is predictable is that they will all try to get classified information and that technology will provide new opportunities.

■ Study Questions and Discussion Topics

1. How has technology changed the diplomatic process? Has it affected the character and effectiveness of diplomacy?

2. What is "virtual diplomacy"? Is it appropriately labeled? Is it likely to replace conventional diplomacy?

3. Is instant communication detrimental to diplomacy? Is it helpful? What are its diplomatic consequences?

4. In what respects is modern technology complicating the conduct of diplomacy? In what respects is it facilitating the diplomatic process?

5. What diplomatic developments can we expect in the near future as a result of modern technology?

■ Suggested Reading

Bjorgo, Einar. *Space Aid: Current and Potential Uses of Satellite Imagery in Humanitarian Organizations.* Virtual Diplomacy Report no. 12. Washington, DC: US Institute of Peace, 2002. http://www.usip.org/virtualdiplomacy/publications/reports/12.

Center for Strategic and International Studies, Advisory Panel on Diplomacy in the Information Age. *Reinventing Diplomacy in the Information Age.* Washington, DC, 1998.

Dizard, Wilson, Jr. *Digital Diplomacy: U.S. Foreign Policy in the Information Age.* Westport: Praeger, 2001.

Kitfin, Karen T. "Public Eyes: Satellite Imagery, the Globalization of Transparency, and New Networks of Surveillance." In *Information Technologies and Global Politics: The Changing Scope of Power and Governance,* edited by James N. Rosenau and J. P. Singh. Albany: State University of New York Press, 2002.

Lund, Michael S. "Early Warning and Preventive Diplomacy." In *Managing Global Chaos: Sources of, and Responses to, International Conflict,* edited by Chester A. Crocker and Fen Osler Hampson, with Pamela Aall. Washington, DC: US Institute of Peace, 1996.

Ramcharan, B. G. *The International Law and Practice of Early Warning and Preventive Diplomacy: The Emerging Global Watch.* Dordrecht: Nijhoff, 1991.

Rosenau, James N., and J. P. Singh, eds. *Information Technologies and Global Politics: The Changing Scope of Power and Governance.* Albany: State University of New York Press, 2002.

Smith, Gordon S. *Reinventing Diplomacy: A Virtual Necessity.* Washington, DC: US Institute of Peace, 1999. http://www.usip.org/virtualdiplomacy/publications/reports/gsmithisa99.

Solomon, Richard, and Sheryl J. Brown. *Creating a Common Communications Culture: Interoperability in Crisis Management.* Virtual Diplomacy Report no. 17. Washington, DC: US Institute of Peace, 2004. http://www.usip.org/virtualdiplomacy/publications/reports/17.

Weimann, Gabriel. *Cyberterrorism: How Real Is the Threat?* Special Report no. 119. Washington, DC: US Institute of Peace, 2004.

———. *http://www.terror.net: How Modern Terrorism Uses the Internet.* Special Report no. 116. Washington, DC: US Institute of Peace, 2004.

Wriston, Walter B. "Bits, Bytes, and Diplomacy." *Foreign Affairs* 76, no. 5 (September–October, 1997), pp. 172–182.

▓ Notes

1. In the UN's major halls and meeting rooms, each desk is equipped with voting buttons (green = yes, red = no, orange = abstain). Large panels on the wall near the president's chair show how each member state is voting—which helps nations that are anxious to coordinate their decisions (as many do). Before a vote comes to an end and the voting machines are locked, the presiding officer usually invites the delegates to verify their votes and correct them as needed.

2. So many meetings are to be held simultaneously (particularly during sessions of the General Assembly) that the proper meeting room cannot be reserved when it is needed.

3. Eric Schmitt, "Of Diplomacy and Software," *New York Times,* April 18, 1986, p. 12.

4. Wilson Dizard Jr., *Digital Diplomacy: U.S. Foreign Policy in the Information Age* (Westport: Praeger, 2001), p. 100.

5. In 1998, the Internet had 100 million users; it was expected to reach one billion people by 2005. By 2010, half the world's population is expected to have Internet access. A new website is created every four seconds. Center for Strategic and International Studies (CSIS), Advisory Panel on Diplomacy in the Information Age, *Reinventing Diplomacy in the Information Age* (Washington, DC, 1998), pp. x–xi.

6. Warren P. Strobel, "The Media and U.S. Policies Toward Intervention: A Closer Look at the 'CNN Effect,'" in *Managing Global Chaos: Sources of, and Responses to, International Conflict,* edited by Chester A. Crocker and Fen Osler Hampson, with Pamela Aall (Washington, DC: US Institute of Peace, 1996), pp. 357–376; Christer Jönsson, "Diplomatic Signaling in the Television Age," in *Diplomacy,* edited by Christer

Jönsson and Richard Langhorne (London: Sage, 2004), vol. 3, *Problems and Issues in Contemporary Diplomacy*, pp. 120–138.

7. "There's no way to get around the need for more rapid response, really almost immediate response to most events." CSIS, *Reinventing Diplomacy*, p. 94.

8. Charles W. Kegley Jr. and Eugene R. Wittkopf, *World Politics: Trends and Transformations*, 8th ed. (Boston: Bedford, 2001), pp. 527–529.

9. See David L. Larson, *The "Cuban Crisis" of 1962: Selected Documents and Chronology* (Boston: Houghton Mifflin, 1963), pp. 240–243. Nikita Khrushchev himself had his Sunday morning concession letter broadcast over Radio Moscow "because events in the Cuban Crisis seemed to be running ahead of diplomacy." Ibid., p. 319.

10. G. R. Berridge, *Diplomacy: Theory and Practice*, 2d ed. (New York: Palgrave, 2002), p. 96.

11. Ibid., p. 91, also pp. 97–98.

12. *New York Times*, June 16, 2007, p. A7.

13. Gordon S. Smith, *Reinventing Diplomacy: A Virtual Necessity* (Washington, DC: US Institute of Peace, 1999), p. 8, http://www.usip.org/virtualdiplomacy/publications/reports/gsmithisa99.

14. Berridge, *Diplomacy*, p. 101.

15. Smith, *Reinventing Diplomacy*, p. 8.

16. The US Institute of Peace sponsors research in this area. Its Virtual Diplomacy Initiative explores the role of information and communication technology in the conduct of foreign affairs, particularly its effects upon international conflict management and resolution. Since 1995, it has sponsored workshops, conferences, and symposia, and published reports and essays on virtual diplomacy. See Einar Bjorgo, *Space Aid: Current and Potential Uses of Satellite Imagery in Humanitarian Organizations*, Virtual Diplomacy Report no. 12 (Washington, DC: US Institute of Peace, 2002), http://www.usip.org/virtualdiplomacy/publications/reports/12; Smith, *Reinventing Diplomacy;* Richard Solomon and Sheryl J. Brown, *Creating a Common Communications Culture: Interoperability in Crisis Management*, Virtual Diplomacy Report no. 17 (Washington, DC: US Institute of Peace, 2004), http://www.usip.org/virtualdiplomacy/publications/reports/17. An entire series of articles can be found under the title *Net Diplomacy*, edited by Barry Fulton: Virtual Diplomacy Reports 14–16 (Washington, DC: US Institute of Peace, 2002), http://www.usip.org/virtualdiplomacy/publications/reports.

17. See, for example, Dizard, *Digital Diplomacy*.

18. See, for example, Smith, *Reinventing Diplomacy*.

19. Dizard, *Digital Diplomacy*, p. 107.

20. See Bjorgo, *Space Aid*, pp. 1–2.

21. Dizard, *Digital Diplomacy*, p. 109.

22. See, for example, Chapter 3's case study on the Suez crisis, which involved deployment of a UN peacekeeping force. In 1956, of course, none of this technology was available. "Today Apache helicopters flying over Bosnia upload detailed pictures of action on the ground to a satellite, record them with a video camera, or beam them directly to local headquarters." Walter B. Wriston, "Bits, Bytes, and Diplomacy," *Foreign Affairs* 76, no. 5 (September–October 1997), p. 178.

23. Karen T. Litfin, "Public Eyes: Satellite Imagery, the Globalization of Transparency, and New Networks of Surveillance," in *Information Technologies and Global Politics: The Changing Scope of Power and Governance*, edited by James N. Rosenau and J. P. Singh (Albany: State University of New York Press, 2002), pp. 65–89.

24. Bjorgo, *Space Aid*, pp. 1ff.

25. See http://www.reliefweb.int/virtualosocc.

26. See ibid. See also http://ocha.unog.ch/virtualosocc.

27. Michael S. Lund, "Early Warning and Preventive Diplomacy," in Crocker, Hampson, and Aall, *Managing Global Chaos*, pp. 379–402; B. G. Ramcharan, *The International Law and Practice of Early Warning and Preventive Diplomacy: The Emerging Global Watch* (Dordrecht: Nijhoff, 1991).

28. "The Information Technology and Crisis Management (ITCM) project is a joint venture of governmental, non-governmental, private and academic actors developing a decision-making support and knowledge management system for the use of international crisis management operations." See http://www.itcm.org.

29. An independent, federally funded institution, established in Washington, D.C., by Congress in 1984. The board of directors is appointed by the president of the United States and confirmed by the Senate. See http://www.usip.org.

30. See Solomon and Brown, *Creating a Common Communications Culture.*

31. Conference on Crisis Management and Information Technology, "Toward Interoperability in Crisis Management" (Helsinki, 2003), http://www.itcm.org/pdf/itcm_conference_report_2003.

32. Conducted by the US House of Representatives, Government Reform Subcommittee on Technology.

33. Gabriel Weimann, *Cyberterrorism: How Real Is the Threat?* Special Report no. 119 (Washington, DC: US Institute of Peace, 2004), p. 8. See also Gabriel Weimann, *How Modern Terrorism Uses the Internet*, Special Report no. 116 (Washington, DC: US Institute of Peace, 2004); Gabriel Weimann, *The Diplomacy of Counterterrorism: Lessons Learned, Ignored, and Disputed,* Special Report no. 80 (Washington, DC: US Institute of Diplomacy, 2002).

34. See, for example, Dean A. Minix and Sandra M. Hawley, *Global Politics* (St. Paul, MN: West Group, 1998), "The Game of Nations: Intelligence and the Making of Policy," pp. 320–364, and bibliography on the subject, pp. 362–364.

35. Weimann, *Cyberterrorism.*

36. Ibid., p. 5.

37. See Wriston, *Foreign Affairs*, p. 175.

38. Technology is creating conditions that enable separate organizational structures, governmental and nongovernmental, to communicate and share information (interoperability).

39. See Smith, *Reinventing Diplomacy.*

40. See also James Bamford, *Body of Secrets: Anatomy of the Ultra-Secret National Security Agency: From the Cold War Through the Dawn of a New Century* (New York: Doubleday, 2003).

41. Warren Hoge, "On Bugging News, Annan Had Low-Key Reaction to Old Practice," *New York Times*, February 28, 2004, p. A6.

42. Ibid.

43. Ibid.

44. Stephen C. Schlesinger, *Act of Creation: The Founding of the United Nations— Story of Superpowers, Secret Agents, Wartime Allies and Enemies, and Their Quest for Peaceful World* (Boulder: Westview, 2003).

45. Hoge, "On Bugging News," p. A6.

46. "Tony Blair's Iraq Hangover," *New York Times*, February 28, 2004, p. A26.

47. *New York Times*, March 20, 2003, p. A7. The listening devices were found in the Justus Lipsius building, inaugurated in 1995.

48. Alessandra Stanley, "In Moscow, Rebuilding Without Bugs," *New York Times*, May 4, 1997, p. 10.

5 The Role of Nonstate Actors

One important structural change affecting the conduct of diplomacy is the emergence of new actors in world affairs.[1] The world used to be known as the "nation-state" system. This notion was so well established that the term is still in use today, and many nation-states remain critical players in world affairs. Day in, day out, however, they interact with a large variety of potent actors that are not nation-states—the events of September 11, 2001, will long be remembered, especially in the United States, the mightiest of nation-states. And even if nonstate actors do not compare with nation-states in shaping world events, they increase the complexity of diplomacy and diversify the way in which it is carried out.

International Organizations

In the nineteenth century, states created a number of international organizations to do specialized tasks or administer international projects (see Chapter 2). For example, they created the European Danube Commission in 1856 to develop that river as a major trade artery. Following World War I, states experimented with more complex international structures, such as the League of Nations and the International Labour Organization. But it was not until World War II that international organizations proliferated and became major players in world affairs. The World Court gave formal recognition to their status in 1949. In the Court's own words:

> The Organization was intended to exercise and enjoy, and is in fact exercising and enjoying, functions and rights which can only be explained on the basis of the possession of a large measure of international personality and the capacity to operate upon an international plane.

Accordingly, the Court has come to the conclusion that the Organization is an international person. That is not the same thing as saying that it is a State, which it certainly is not, or that its legal personality and rights and duties are the same as those of a State. Still less is it the same thing as saying that it is a "super-State," whatever that expression may mean. It does not even imply that all its rights and duties must be upon the international plane, any more than all the rights and duties of a State must be on that plane. What it does mean is that it is a subject of international law and capable of possessing international rights and duties, and that it has capacity to maintain its rights by bringing international claims.[2]

International institutions were endowed with international authority, rights, and duties a long time before such status was officially acknowledged. This landmark decision, however, clearly identifies their international status. These organizational actors do not all have the same roles and powers, but neither do states. They, too, engage in diplomacy, at times with critically important consequences (the kind of diplomacy they conduct, which is substantially different from that of the nineteenth century, is discussed in Chapter 8). The number of international organizations increased considerably following World War II (see Table 5.1).

It is difficult to provide an accurate count of international organizations because of their diversity. The 244 "conventional" organizations cited in Table 5.1 for 2006 include universal as well as regional organizations. However, also provided in 2006 statistics are "other international bodies" such as intergovernmental banks and funds. They add another 1,593 organizations that are de-

Table 5.1   Conventional International Organizations, 1909–2006

	Number of Organizations
1909	37
1951	123
1964	179
1972	280
1978	289
1985	378
1991	297
1995	266
1999	251
2001	243
2006	244

Sources: Union of International Associations, *Yearbook of International Organizations* (Munich: Saur, various years), http://www.uia.org/uiastats.
Note: These are organizations whose members are national governments (otherwise called intergovernmental organizations).

pendent upon the diplomatic process for their operations. "Subsidiary and internal bodies," many of which function autonomously, provide another 499.[3]

These institutions have a considerable impact on the conduct of diplomacy, making it more complex, and adding to the burden of interaction. On the positive side, of course, international organizations help to cope with interdependence and the problems facing international society. Though some of these organizations are very specialized and regionally circumscribed, diplomatic representation in all of them presents personnel issues hardly experienced fifty years ago. Diplomacy is conducted on a vaster scale. Many of the poorer countries cannot afford to maintain delegations large enough for effective participation in the more complex organizations, such as the United Nations; even affluent states are occasionally constrained.

Not only is the international process affected by the larger number of actors, but a number of these actors have unprecedented roles as well—for example, the deployment of peacekeeping forces—thus requiring much more extensive diplomatic involvement. The European Union, an organization of sovereign states rather than a federation, enjoys some supranational powers in speaking for its twenty-seven members. This, in itself, requires an unusual amount of diplomacy on the part of its member states *within* the Union, in addition to the diplomatic work of each of the twenty-seven outside the Union. International organizations thus create new layers of diplomatic interaction, making the global political process much more complex.[4]

▒ Transnational Innovations

Transnational relations occur between private individuals, associations, and organizations of the private sector working together across national boundaries without involvement on the part of national governments or the intervention of public authorities.[5] Transnational relations can be traced as far back as records of human activity can be found. People have always moved about the world, however politically organized their domestic societies. Even before classical antiquity, merchants were sending their goods as far as their boats or caravans could carry them, establishing thriving business relationships. Explorers and adventurers were establishing contacts with people around the globe. Artists worked for patrons outside their home borders. Philosophers were maintaining lively dialogues in foreign lands, and so were the scientists of the day.

Cross-border relations of this kind were so natural that they were taken for granted. No one was surprised that exotic products would reach local markets and that merchants would provide this kind of valuable service. And as technology made it easier to move about, transnational relations expanded.[6] What is different today is the scale on which it is taking place.[7] The real revolution is that of instant, cheap communication by means of computers and the development of the Internet. The world is only beginning to see the consequences of this incredible breakthrough—although it is already taken for granted. Transnational relations clearly impact society, even if the public is still primarily focused on the actions of states and their governments, which is natural enough given how these institutions can mobilize support and resources and use them on a scale beyond the capacity of the institutions of civil society, even global civil society.

For the purpose of this volume, it is important to examine the ways in which the transnational phenomenon affects diplomacy. An initial response might well be that diplomacy is a state instrument, an official means of interaction for states and their governments. Transnational activities take place in the margin of governmental activity, but within the fram.· work of governmentally structured society, under rule of law and protection of the state rather than under conditions of anarchy. It could even be argued that transnational relations are facilitated by the public order provided by state institutions (both domestically and internationally). Civil society needs the framework and institutions of a political system. But transnational relations take place without the necessary intervention of the public authorities. A passport is needed to travel abroad (but then again, a piece of identity is needed to cash a check domestically). The private order and the public order work together in the normal functioning of society.[8] A transnational initiative is not caused by an act of the public authorities. So, how is diplomacy affected by wnat the private order undertakes?

Nongovernmental Organizations

Nongovernmental organizations (NGOs) are components of civil society. They are particularly active in open societies, and cover a broad spectrum of human activity.[9] Many have nothing to do with the political process (e.g., garden clubs). Others are lobbies (i.e., special interest groups that try to influence the political system to protect and promote their causes). Some have a broad purpose, such as improving the democratic process, and are interested in a multiplicity of issues (e.g., Common Cause); others have a narrow focus (e.g., the National Rifle Association). Some have a limited constituency, no financial resources, and rely exclusively on volunteers. Others are large, affluent, and powerful. In the United States, the enormous impact of their financial contributions on political institutions has been a barely disguised form of corruption undermining democratic governance.

Some NGOs do not limit their endeavors to domestic societies.[10] They network across international boundaries but remain uninterested in politics, domestic or international (e.g., scientific networks). Others want to affect the course of international affairs, and their causes are just as diverse (e.g., from protection of the environment to protection of Israel).[11] The communication revolution has greatly increased the transnational activity of NGOs and the number of transnationally active groups has vastly expanded (see Table 5.2). The effect of NGO activity on the diplomatic process varies enormously with the issues at hand, the NGOs involved, their leadership, their networking proficiency, and the forums in which decisions are made.[12] Nation-states and international organizations remain the major players in the diplomatic process, but the role of NGOs has greatly expanded.[13]

Hallway diplomacy. Often presented as a sign of NGOs being kept on the margin of the diplomatic process, "hallway diplomacy" implies NGO representatives trying to communicate with diplomats wherever they can be reached, between rounds of diplomatic negotiations, when these NGO agents are refused access to the diplomatic forum, which used to be the case in most diplomatic gatherings. Here, NGO representatives try to find out how the diplomatic interaction is proceeding, hoping for leaks that they can use to apply pressure on governments. They also try to win the support of individual diplomats to defend their causes at the diplomatic table. But diplomats normally work within the policy guidelines articulated by their governments. They have their own instructions to carry out, and when new developments occur, they seek instructions about what is to be done. So, unless the sending state is favorable to an NGO's cause, NGO lobbying with individual diplomats may not seem too promising a method to affect the course of diplomatic events.

Diplomats, however, participate in the conduct of international relations in a vast variety of ways depending upon their rank, importance, their own personal influence with their own government, foreign colleagues, and their specific role

Table 5.2 Nongovernmental Organizations, 1909–2006

	Number of NGOs
1909	176
1951	832
1964	1,718
1972	2,795
1978	8,347
1985	13,768
1991	16,113
1995	14,274
1999	17,077
2001	18,323
2006	21,026

Source: Union of International Associations, *Yearbook of International Organizations* (Munich: Saur, various years), http://www.uia.org/uiastats.

Notes: For the years 1909–1978, beyond the main body of nongovernmental organizations, secondary "other bodies" were irregularly included in these figures.

or function in the current mission. In their reporting and recommendations, diplomats (particularly heads of mission) may influence the policymaking process. And some instructions leave a good deal of leeway for matters of implementation. Thus, developing a good working relationship with diplomats is not necessarily a marginal endeavor. It is to be noted also that some diplomats value contacts with NGOs, which can be valuable sources of information on various aspects of the host society. Interaction is thus profitable to both diplomats and NGOs in specific contexts and circumstances. This is not an approach that works casually. But conditions of trust can be created between NGO representatives and diplomats. This is the business of political influence, which goes far beyond buttonholing diplomats in the hallway of an international organization or during a conversation at a diplomatic reception, although buttonholing does have its uses.[14]

Mobilizing public support or opposition. NGOs may affect the diplomatic process when they succeed in rallying public support behind diplomatic initiatives or, contrariwise, in generating massive opposition.[15] Diplomats or their superiors may encourage or even seek this outcome. Key elements in NGO effectiveness are skill in creating coalitions,[16] networking, and framing issues in the public discourse in such a way that they will "ring true."[17]

The international campaign in the mid-1990s to ban landmines shows how NGO mobilization of support led to the historic landmine treaty, against the opposition of major states, including the United States (see the case study at the end of this chapter). Massive NGO coalitions have also been formed in opposition to international projects—for example, in 1997–1998 negotiations undertaken by the twenty-nine members of the Organization for Economic Cooperation and Development (OECD) to conclude an agreement intended to provide greater enforceable protection to international investors.[18] A protest movement of more than 600 very diverse NGOs in seventy countries (showing the same concerns as the antiglobalization movement)[19] associated itself with the resistance generated by developing nations during an initial attempt to achieve the same results within the World Trade Organization. The projected treaty was vehemently denounced on the Internet and through letter-writing campaigns, petitions, and public demonstrations. The OECD negotiations foundered and were eventually discontinued.[20]

Establishing relationships with states. States have been ambivalent toward NGOs. As a rule, they prefer not to see them get in the way. In turn, many NGOs distrust governments and do not want to be associated with them.[21] However, on some issues of international relations, states have worked with NGOs. In the negotiations of the global climate treaty, which culminated at the Earth Summit in Rio de Janeiro in 1992, more NGO members served on government delegations than ever before and actively participated in official decisionmaking. The tiny nation of Vanuatu, in the Pacific, actually turned its delegation over to an NGO that had expertise in international law, a group based in London and funded by a US foundation, thereby making itself a key player in the fight to control global warming (an extremely important issue to an island state likely to be flooded by the melting of polar ice).[22]

The NGO representatives serving on government delegations, whether from developing or developed countries, were tightly organized in global and regional "climate action" networks. These were able to bridge the North-South differences among governments (which had been expected to prevent an agreement). NGOs would fight out contentious issues among themselves, united as they were in their passionate pursuit of a treaty. They could then take an agreed position to their respective national delegations. When NGOs could not reach an agreement, they served as invaluable back channels, letting both sides know where the problems lay and where a compromise might be found.[23]

In the campaign to ban landmines, an NGO representative was actually invited to join the French diplomatic delegation to the 1996 Ottawa strategy conference. Other NGO representatives were invited by Canada to sit at the conference table and participate in strategy discussions.[24] US senator Patrick Leahy stated: "Never before have representatives of civil society collaborated with governments so closely, and so effectively, to produce a treaty to outlaw a weapon."[25] Bringing to the conference table sensitivity toward civil society may be important in a variety of negotiations.[26]

Consultative role in the UN Economic and Social Council. In 1945, Article 71 of the UN Charter specified that the Economic and Social Council (ECOSOC) "may make suitable arrangements for consultation with non-governmental organizations"—an early recognition of their significance. Accordingly, the council created a standing committee on nongovernmental organizations and offered consultative status with ECOSOC to three categories of organizations according to the scope of their activities. It was a beginning, and interested organizations pressed for greater participation. Three major revisions of NGO status were carried out, in 1950, 1968, and 1996, and the number of accepted organizations grew to 2,143 in 2002,[27] and to 2,719 in 2005,[28] up from 692 in 1976.[29] In addition, some 400 NGOs are currently accredited to the Commission on Sustainable Development, a subsidiary body of ECOSOC.[30]

Three groups of NGOs are still distinguished. The "general" category is composed of organizations concerned with most of the activities of ECOSOC and its subsidiary bodies. They tend to be fairly large, well-established international NGOs with a broad geographical reach. The "special" category is made up of organizations that have a special competence in only a few fields of concern to ECOSOC. These tend to be smaller and more recently established. The third category, the "roster," includes organizations that can make occasional contributions to the work of ECOSOC or its subsidiary bodies.

These organizations tend to have a rather narrow or technical focus.[31] The scope of the functions of these NGOs associated with the UN has greatly expanded beyond simple consultation (see Table 5.3).[32] ECOSOC currently has some sixty-five subsidiary bodies accessible to NGOs.

Participation in the work of other international organizations. Virtually all of the UN's specialized agencies[33] have entered into working agreements with NGOs, ranging from 15 for the World Meteorological Organization, to 580 for the UN Educational, Scientific, and Cultural Organization (UNESCO).[34] Each agency cooperates with NGOs according to its own needs. One significant expansion of the role of NGOs pertains to the implementation of the programs of some of these agencies at the grassroots level, particularly in the developing nations.[35] Local NGOs have an intimate knowledge of the communities in which these programs are to be carried out, and provide invaluable services—for example, in implementing the HIV/AIDS program of the World Health Organization (WHO). A consequence of these developments was the introduction of a significant number of grassroots organizations to a direct relationship with the UN system. In the last revision of its NGO policy, ECOSOC encouraged national NGOs, particularly from developing countries, to apply for official consultative status.[36]

Table 5.3   NGO Privileges at the UN

Privilege	General NGOs	Special NGOs	Roster NGOs
Invited to UN conferences	yes	yes	yes
Authorized to propose items for ECOSOC agenda	yes	no	no
Authorized to attend UN meetings	yes	yes	yes
Authorized to speak at ECOSOC meetings	yes	no	no
Authorized to speak at meetings of ECOSOC subsidiary bodies	yes	yes	no
Authorized to circulate statements at ECOSOC meetings	2,000 words	500 words	no
Authorized to circulate statements at meetings of ECOSOC subsidiary bodies	2,000 words	1,500 words	no

Source: http://www.un.org/esa/coordination/ngo/faq.
Notes: General NGOs tend to be large, well established, and international. Special NGOs have a special competence in only a few fields of concern to ECOSOC. Roster NGOs can make occasional contributions to the work of ECOSOC.

A current trend is for international agencies, especially multilateral development banks, to involve NGOs in their decisionmaking process, quite significantly for the planning of their field projects.[37] The World Bank, in response to the widespread criticism that it has failed to be sensitive to social needs and human suffering in the developing nations, has involved NGOs as partners in various facets of its policymaking and in the implementation of development projects.[38] For example, in the mid-1990s, it secured the cooperation of the World Wildlife Fund to develop an approach to forest management. A coalition of more than 500 NGOs agreed to join an eighteen-month program to assess the effectiveness of the Bank's policies in seven nations (see Box 5.1). The success of such cooperative endeavors is reinforcing the trend toward a much wider international role for NGOs.[39]

NGOs have sought to participate in the work of the UN General Assembly, a body widely perceived as more important than ECOSOC. A substantial number of member states, however, have shown their opposition. Nevertheless, select NGOs have been invited to participate in special General Assembly functions. Since the 1970s, NGOs have taken part in the committee work of special sessions of the General Assembly concerned with disarmament, economic and social development, drugs, and apartheid.[40] Significantly also, NGOs have participated in the work of a number of subsidiary bodies of the General Assembly. This was the case beginning in the early 1960s with the Special Committee on Decolonization, the Special Committee Against Apartheid, and the Committee on Palestinian Rights. Such participation has been common with a number of UN programs and funds.[41]

For example, in 1994, the Office of the UN High Commissioner for Refugees (UNHCR) (an agency that now employs more than 5,000 staff and operates in 120 countries, helping some 20 million uprooted people)[42] created the Partnership in Action program to facilitate its relationship with more than

---

Box 5.1   NGOs at the 2006 Annual Meeting of the World Bank and IMF

About 500 nongovernmental groups came to Singapore to take part in some of the sessions of the September 2006 annual meeting of the World Bank and IMF, to issue reports critical of the policies of the host institutions. Concerned over the protests at past annual meetings, Singapore, at the last minute, denied visas to some of the leaders of civil society groups who had been invited to participate in the meeting. Western government leaders protested this action and the government of Singapore relented, allowing twenty-two of the twenty-seven banned representatives to enter the country.

Source: New York Times, September 16, 2006, p. B9.

800 NGOs involved in its humanitarian mission around the world. UNHCR acknowledges that this is a huge undertaking that has at times proved difficult to manage. From the outset, the perceptions of NGOs and UNHCR often differed, and there were communication problems even between the NGOs themselves. There were also difficulties in achieving effective cooperation between local governments, NGOs, and UNHCR.

UNHCR and its NGO partners have worked together to improve their relationship. For example, they jointly produced a field guide for NGOs to facilitate the protection of refugees. In the end, the Partnership in Action program succeeded in increasing cooperation with local and national NGOs. The number of partnerships has tripled since 1994. National and international NGOs have been brought together and have raised the capability of local organizations.[43] Other agencies have extensive cooperation programs with NGOs, among them the UN Children's Fund (UNICEF), the UN Conference on Trade and Development (UNCTAD), the UN Development Programme (UNDP), and the UN Environment Programme (UNEP). After the International Conference on Population and Development in Cairo in September 1994, the UN Population Fund (UNFPA) established a new NGO advisory committee to facilitate operational relationships with NGOs and, significantly, to monitor progress in the implementation of the Cairo action program agreed upon at the 1994 conference.[44]

Participation in UN conferences.[45] Before the 1970s, NGOs had considerably fewer rights in conferences than in ECOSOC. Participation in the debates was often limited to a single NGO speaker on the last day to represent the whole NGO community.[46] With the convening of high-visibility global conferences such as the 1972 Stockholm Conference on the Environment,[47] the UN was faced with the problem of accommodating huge numbers of NGO representatives converging on the conference site. This led to the organization of "parallel forums" at the site of the conference but separate from the diplomatic proceedings. In these large NGO forums, NGO representatives make presentations and hear accounts of the diplomatic proceedings. Daily newsletters help the process of communication. None of this, of course, amounts to *participation* in the diplomatic process, although some state delegations remain attentive to the NGO deliberations.

In some fields, such as population, the environment, and human rights, NGOs have been active participants in a number of committees, particularly in small working groups where the more difficult issues are negotiated.[48] These have tended to be ad hoc arrangements, leading to some extensive diplomatic involvement, for example in the second UN Conference on Human Settlements (Habitat II, 1996), where approaches to contemporary urban problems were discussed.[49] In the intercessional drafting groups of the preparatory committee (on the importance of the diplomatic role of preparatory committees, see Chapter 8), NGOs sat with government representatives and provided amendments to the text of documents being prepared for the conference, because the participating governments and their delegates acknowledged the importance of groups having an intimate knowledge of urban problems in the drafting of international policy guidelines.

An interesting arrangement was worked out to receive the contribution of civil society to its proceedings. While government representatives negotiated in "Conference Committee I," representatives of local authorities, businesses, foundations, parliamentarians, academics, trade unions, other NGOs, and UN secretariats gave a series of presentations. Instead of these presentations being made part of the unofficial parallel NGO forum, they were recognized as constituting "Conference Committee II," an integral part of the official proceedings. In addition, NGO suggestions for changes in the draft of the final document of the conference were accepted and seen as further evidence of participation in the proceedings. Although greater NGO participation tends to be conference-specific, it is nevertheless much more extensive than in the early days of the UN, and experience shows that it can make a positive contribution to the proceedings.

NGO mediation diplomacy and peacemaking. NGOs have for several decades practiced mediation in international and revolutionary conflicts, taking diplomatic initiatives of their own. Their effectiveness in this pursuit has given them prominence as international actors.[50] More than once, NGOs have been the first international actors to attempt bringing belligerents to the conference table.[51] Their efforts often parallel the mediation efforts of states.[52] However, NGO intervention may complicate the task of state mediators. Even so, NGO efforts can be more credible than those of states, because they are seen as more impartial and more genuinely committed to a fair settlement. Much depends, of course, on the NGOs involved—they are indeed very diverse. In revolutionary situations, they find it easier to establish a dialogue with underground forces or outlawed groups.[53] States often hesitate to maintain contact with such groups, fearing to give them a degree of legitimacy or to bolster their international status.

Some NGOs have been extensively involved in conflict resolution—for example, the Carter Center in Atlanta or the International Committee of the Red Cross (ICRC), which has a long history of humanitarian mediation.[54] Some of these civil society organizations have developed sophisticated methods of conflict resolution. With the proliferation of ethnic strife and wars of national liberation since the end of the Cold War,[55] there is increasing demand for NGO efforts. Their negotiations are easily comparable to the mediation work of state diplomats, although some states may be able to offer guarantees, instruments of verification, and occasionally, positive inducements (i.e., material rewards) beyond the means of most NGOs. Nongovernmental organizations can be expected to remain extensively involved in the diplomacy of peacemaking. One of their contributions is the implementation of conflict resolution agreements—for example, in monitoring what is happening in the field, such as the disarming of militias, and publicly reporting such developments. They also promote reconciliation and the restoration of "normalcy," including the return of refugees.[56]

NGO assistance in preventive diplomacy. In addition to mediation and conflict resolution diplomacy, NGOs have intervened with political groups to avert looming crises and the onset of violence.[57] This diplomatic function is often difficult for states. Governments are frequently reluctant to intervene before problems become dangerous, as official intervention is easily perceived as unwarranted meddling.[58] Yet history shows that conflicts stand a better chance of being peacefully resolved in their early stages.

NGOs can be less intrusive and less objectionable than states in their efforts to prevent conflict. Their representatives are often among the few people who can be trusted by both sides in a growing conflict.[59] And when the parties to a confrontation are not responsive, NGO failure is less likely to complicate the international situation, as NGO attempts tend to have a low profile. One favorite method has been that of seminars in which conflicting parties are invited to explore alternative courses of action and possible solutions to the problems at hand.[60] These sessions invite the contestants to work together in some sort of "interactive problem-solving."[61] This may alter the way antagonists perceive one another and reduce mistrust.[62] (See other examples in Chapter 11.)

Related to preventive diplomacy efforts, NGOs can play a useful role in early warning. Because of their ties to the grassroots in conflicting societies, they are often in a position to identify, at a very early stage, danger signs and factors that can lead to violence. With the help of their local constituencies, they can press governments and international organizations to respond to the problems they have detected,[63] although it is usually difficult to generate a sense of urgency toward future threats.[64] Early response is rarely attractive to people who have more than enough to do in coping with what is happening in the present.

Other NGO diplomatic functions. NGOs are now finding more occasions to work with government representatives at the international level[65] and acquire new international functions.[66] One example is provided by the Commission on Sustainable Development, a functional commission of the UN Economic and Social Council created in December 1992 to ensure effective follow-up to the UN Conference on the Environment and Development (UNCED, the Earth Summit, Rio, 1992), as well as to monitor and report on the implementation of Earth Summit agreements at the local, regional, national, and international levels.[67] Its annual meetings bring together government representatives—some fifty ministers attend each year—and NGO members. Government and NGO representatives thus interact on a multiplicity of issues.[68] The increasing participation of NGOs in UN activities is reflected in their being frequently referred to as "nongovernmental partners" in various UN documents.[69]

The Joint UN Programme on HIV/AIDS (UNAIDS), an interagency body set up to oversee all AIDS activities in the UN system, has five NGOs taking part in the work of its program coordination board. These NGO representatives are board members rather than observers. NGOs are also providing input to the development, implementation, and evaluation of the work program of the Habitat Center, the UN secretariat section that deals with human settlements as part of the UN Environment Programme.[70] And in a different type of activity, NGOs play a role in monitoring the implementation of the Convention on the Rights of the Child: The convention requires governments to report regularly to the committee overseeing its application. In many countries, coalitions of NGOs prepare alternative reports for the working groups in Geneva. In fact, the convention itself provides that "other competent bodies" (which of course includes some NGOs) are to provide expert advice on its implementation.[71]

The involvement of civil society, particularly NGOs, is thus extensive in an extremely wide variety of international activities and the UN system is a major factor in this proliferating role. UN Secretary-General Kofi Annan acknowledged that "non-governmental organizations are now seen as essential partners of the United Nations, not only in mobilizing public opinion, but also in the process of deliberation and policy formulation and—even more important—in the execution of policies, in work on the ground."[72]

Diplomacy is affected because government representatives have more and more occasions to work with NGO agents.[73] They are often full participants in joint diplomatic pursuits. But the perspective of NGOs can be substantially different from that of government or international organization authorities, as UNHCR has found in its extensive work with civil society agencies.[74] NGOs have their own difficulties in agreeing on a common position, particularly with regard to complex issues, and they occasionally need to find ways of controlling the disrupting effects of their more radical representatives.[75]

Some observers have commented that increased NGO participation in international affairs is a form of democratization of the international process; civil society is now participating in what used to be almost exclusively state business. But it is not without its own kind of problem. Many NGOs, perhaps most NGOs, represent special interests. Although many serve the global common good, as in the promotion of human rights and economic and social development, some are more controversial in their perspective, such as groups defending euthanasia or the right to carry firearms.

More problematic, these groups are often one-issue constituencies (important as they may be). Society must cope with a multiplicity of issues, and governments and their diplomatic agents have the difficult task of balancing those diverse and often conflicting interests. NGOs are fighting for their own causes. The task of maintaining a balance is not theirs. In a pluralistic society (and this is the enormous advantage of democracies), it is important to have all those conflicting interests defended, so long as the final decisions are not in the hands of groups who are not concerned about interests other than their own. Many NGOs are pluralistic and democratic in orientation, but not all, and not on every issue.[76]

The diplomatic task has thus become more intricate, as it must contend with influences that did not exist a mere fifty years ago.[77] States retain the upper hand—but the policies of far too many states are not designed to serve the international common good. By and large, national pursuits remain, as in the past, exceedingly self-centered.[78] NGOs, for all their limitations, add pluralism and global concern to the business of diplomacy, even if this addition must complicate the lives of national representatives.[79]

Multinational Corporations

Multinational corporations (MNCs) constitute another growing category of transnational actors, also called "transnational corporations," particularly at the UN. They are a potent force in the process of economic globalization.[80] The number of multinational corporations has grown enormously in recent years. The UN reports that the number of firms that have become multinational has risen exponentially over the past three decades. In the case of fifteen developed countries, that number increased from 7,000 at the end of the 1960s to some 40,000 in the second half of the 1990s. The number of parent firms worldwide was about 63,000 in 1999—a sixfold increase since the early 1990s—with an estimated 690,000 affiliates.[81] The parent firms are very diverse and span all countries and industries, and include a large and growing number of small and medium-sized enterprises. The global marketplace has expanded from manufacturing to virtually all economic fields, including services and retail.

The multinationals of the 1960s were mostly US corporations,[82] but more and more corporations from around the world are now taking part. In 1995, the European Union was home to thirty-nine of the largest hundred MNCs (most of these British, French, or German), the United States to thirty, and Japan to eighteen.[83] The developing countries themselves were home to a number of significant MNCs.[84] The UN estimated that, at the close of the twentieth century, the global assets of MNCs exceeded $13 trillion, and global sales were in excess of $9.5 trillion. This volume of investments and sales accounted for more than one-fifth of the global economy and one-third of the world's exports.[85] The expansion of MNCs has been facilitated by transnational banks, which themselves contributed to the globalization process. At the start of 1999, the combined assets of the world's twenty largest banks exceeded $425 trillion,[86] and the process of cross-border mergers and acquisitions is continuing at a rapid pace.[87]

Enterprises today seek to become more international, and the rapid growth, geographical spread, and international integration of MNC activities make it increasingly difficult to draw traditional distinctions between domestic and foreign firms or between production in different locations.[88] Inevitably, the foreign relations of states are affected by this kind of economic relationship. Charles Kegley and Eugene Wittkopf note that General Electric, for example, "one of the most 'American' of all US MNCs, has co-production agreements with Nuovo Pignone of Italy, Mitsubishi and Hitachi of Japan and Mannessmann and AEG Telefunken of Germany." They observe further that "joint production and strategic corporate alliances to create temporary phantom 'virtual corporations' complicate the problem of identity."[89] About one-third of the $6 trillion global trade in goods and services recorded in 1996 occurred within multinationals from one branch to another. Trade between different multinationals accounted for another third of world trade.[90]

A number of MNCs have greater earning capacity and financial resources than states, including some developed industrialized countries.[91] This equates to enormous political influence. Ranking states and MNCs by size of earnings in 2005–2006, the top nineteen were states. Immediately following Sweden (ranked nineteenth, $321.4 billion) came Wal-Mart Stores ($288 billion), British Petroleum ($285.1 billion), Exxon Mobil ($270.8 billion), then Turkey (twenty-third, $268.7 billion), Royal Dutch/Shell Group (twenty-fourth, $268.7 billion), and Austria (twenty-fifth, $262.1 billion). Among the top fifty, thirty-six were states and fourteen were MNCs. In the next fifty, only fourteen were states; the remaining thirty-six were MNCs. Russia (ranked sixteenth, $487.3 billion) was only four places above Wal-Mart.[92]

In the countries in which they operate, MNCs provide new technology. They cover patent costs and underwrite research and development. Some of the technology, however, is ill-suited to an underdeveloped environment. MNCs also provide jobs: they employ more than 73 million people. Each MNC job generates additional jobs. For example, the Nike Footwear Company employed about 9,000 people in its core staff, but another 75,000 through subcontracting.[93] MNCs also provide valuable job training. In their countries of origin, jobs are often lost when MNCs relocate some of their operations abroad (hence labor opposition to globalization). MNCs are a source of investment, although the strategies vary,[94] and they generate a considerable amount of related economic activity. Nevertheless, their profits tend to be sent out of the host country. Sales of foreign affiliates worldwide in 1999, a broad measure of the revenue generated by international production, amounted to $14 trillion (compared to $3 trillion in 1980), and are twice as high as global exports.[95]

MNCs have engaged in diplomacy of their own, aside from their lobbying and other political activities in their countries of origin.[96] Their diplomacy has been different from the diplomatic efforts of NGOs, and their public purpose more problematic. Primarily bilateral, MNC diplomacy aims at enhancing profitability in the host country, gaining protection from regulation, and gaining preferential treatment in the host society. In government-MNC negotiations, many developing nations have often complained of the weakness of their position and their difficulty in defending the national interest, to the point that UNCTAD has been conducting training seminars to enhance government negotiating capacity in dealing with MNCs.

Some MNCs maintain permanent representation in the capitals of their host states, to remain in contact with key decisionmakers, remain abreast of political developments likely to affect their economic potential, and negotiate business arrangements with the government. Some MNC representatives find themselves in competition with the diplomatic missions of foreign states on certain commercial transactions, and occasionally with the diplomats of their own state, when the policies of the latter do not coincide with the commercial interests of the multinational (e.g., in arms transactions). Some US missions, in fact, have complained that they are at a disadvantage in dealing with their host governments because competing MNCs have larger resources and more personnel.

MNCs negotiate with governments to protect their business interests. A good deal of diplomatic action is often needed to maintain good relations with governments that may be under popular pressure to control their activities. This diplomatic work is fully comparabl∂ to that of foreign governments. Some MNCs have more political clout than nation-states. A number of governments negotiate with their own MNCs abroad to ensure their support in some aspects of national policy (e.g., on the distribution of sensitive technology). Or they may have to contend with the competing interests of foreign MNCs. For example, when mail-disseminated anthrax hit US media and government offices in September and October 2001, the German pharmaceutical MNC Bayer AG faced intense pressure from the US government to reduce the price of its antibiotic Cipro. It did.[97]

MNCs are also involved in the multilateral diplomatic environment. Some international organizations, such as the UN Development Programme, work with them in a variety of joint projects. For this purpose, UNDP maintains a "Division of Business Partnerships."[98] MNCs participate in advisory panels and business councils created by international organizations in their efforts to work with the private sector, and they provide input in the development of standards of conduct (e.g., with the OECD).[99] But they also use their diplomatic resources to fight international projects that hurt their interests. For example, in October 2002, Gro Harlem Brundtland, head of the World Health Organization, alerted the members of a negotiating session in Geneva that tobacco companies were trying to undermine efforts to draft a treaty aimed at controlling the sale and use of tobacco and contemplating a ban on advertising.[100] MNCs are significant international actors. Huge economic interests are at stake, and their involvement in the diplomatic process will expand as globalization increases.

Not surprisingly, MNCs have also generated serious concerns among governments, particularly in developing countries and among a variety of civil society institutions. MNCs are ultimately concerned about maximizing their profitability rather than improving the social conditions in their host societies—and the problem is that the microeconomic interests of MNCs and the development objectives of host countries do not necessarily coincide. Initially, it was feared that MNCs could be used as instruments of political intervention on the part of their home countries. This happened in Chile in the early 1970s, where the International Telephone and Telegraph Company tried to prevent the election of Marxist-oriented Salvador Allende as president, and later, working with the US Central Intelligence Agency, disrupted the Chilean economy and sought his overthrow.[101] MNCs tend to escape control and may have detrimental effects on host societies.[102]

MNCs foster monopolistic practices and inhibit the growth of infant industries. They take advantage of substandard labor conditions, exploit underpaid workers, and use child labor. Their methods of production aggravate environmental degradation. Their elaborate structure, blurred nationality, and manipulation of offshore banking permit widespread tax evasion.[103] They send their profits out of the country. They are able to internalize cross-border transactions and elude national control and scrutiny.[104] They have even used their enormous economic power to coerce host governments.

Many become disconnected from the national interests of their countries of origin, moving production and jobs abroad as serves their needs. One may wonder where this leaves state economic "sovereignty." Moreover, the globalization of financial markets places private currency traders outside governmental control. In 1997, more than $1 trillion changed hands daily, an amount that exceeded the total foreign exchange reserves of all governments.[105] The economic impact of this phenomenon can be staggering. It is widely admitted that some form of international accountability is necessary,[106] but the diplomatic process has not yet succeeded in creating the necessary modes of regulation.

Developing nations have sought international assistance in controlling the activities of MNCs and turned to the UN for the development of standards of conduct applicable to the multinationals.[107] This generated a great deal of diplomatic activity in the tumultuous 1970s, when acrimony over MNCs reached its apex. But the matter became enmeshed with the East-West struggle as well as the North-South tug-of-war. The Soviet Union stressed the exploitive dimensions of this form of capitalism and the United States resisted control measures in the name of free enterprise.

In 1974, the UN's Economic and Social Council created its Commission on Transnational Corporations, consisting of forty-eight UN members and a secretariat, the Center on Transnational Corporations. The main task was to produce a code of conduct for MNCs. As expected, it was extremely difficult to reach a consensus on the subject. Agreement was eventually reached within the commission in 1990 on a draft code of conduct. But agreement was achieved only by couching disputed issues in language abstract enough to accommodate competing positions without resolving underlying differences.

The president of the UN General Assembly initiated a round of informal consultations on the code of conduct in July 1992, but the only conclusion reached was that no consensus was possible. Industrialized nations want international law to apply to both MNCs and host states, most particularly to protect investments from expropriation. Developing nations stress the exercise of sovereignty within their boundaries and the application of national law.[108] The diplomatic battle has also been fought in UNCTAD, a forum for developing-nation issues, with a current focus on corporate social responsibility and the matter of addressing such problems as child labor, dangerous and unhealthy work environments, abusive conditions, excessively long workdays, and unfair wages. In light of the impossibility of developing an internationally enforceable legal code, diplomacy endeavored to develop nonbinding codes of corporate conduct, the type of conduct expected of "good corporate citizens." These have been called "soft law codes."

In 1976 the Organization for Economic Cooperation and Development developed a set of guidelines for multinational enterprises, and in 1977 the International Labour Organization (ILO) produced a tripartite declaration of principles concerning multinational enterprises and social policy. UNCTAD drafted a code on restrictive business practices, which was adopted by the UN General Assembly in 1980.[109] A more focused approach was used by other UN agencies, such as the World Health Organization, which developed an international code on marketing of breast-milk substitutes; and the Food and Agriculture Organization (FAO), which developed an international code of conduct on distribution and use of pesticides.[110]

A good deal of diplomacy has thus been focused on MNC activities. Civil society institutions are increasingly voicing their concerns and attempting to apply pressure on MNCs to accept norms of social responsibility.[111] A long series of corporate scandals are adding to the pressure for transparency and accountability,[112] and corporations are beginning to respond. UN Secretary-General Kofi Annan challenged world business leaders at the World Economic Forum in Davos, Switzerland, on January 31, 1999, to demonstrate good global citizenship by "embracing and enacting" in their individual corporate practices the values and principles of the Global Compact, developed in cooperation with five UN organizations.[113] The Global Compact is not a regulatory instrument. Its implementation relies on public accountability, transparency, the self-interest of companies, and the pressure exercised by organized labor, civil society, and the sponsoring UN institutions.[114] But more needs to be done. The continued growth of MNCs and current globalization trends will make this category of transnational actors even more important in years to come. More interaction will take place between international organization officials, government delegates, MNC officers, and NGOs concerned with social and corporate responsibility. Difficult negotiations can be anticipated; it may take an outrageous scandal or crisis to achieve results.

Churches and Religious Movements

Many churches and religious movements are involved in international affairs. A number of them participate in diplomatic activities, such as mediation of international conflicts.[115] Their international transactions tend to match those of NGOs, leading to a wide variety of diplomatic interaction. Church groups, as international actors, are themselves extremely diverse. For example, the World Council of Churches is a fellowship of 347 churches in more than 120 countries, from virtually all Christian traditions.[116] The Community of Sant'Egidio, a church lay association established in Rome in 1968, counts some 50,000 members in more than 70 countries.[117] Even more different are radical Islamic groups such as Gamaat al-Islamyya, based in Egypt,[118] and Al-Qaida (more frequently listed as a terrorist organization), a loose association of Islamic fundamentalist movements.[119]

The Organization of the Islamic Conference, on the other hand, is an organization of Islamic states. It is an intergovernmental organization. Participants are state diplomats. The one entity that tends to be categorized uniquely is the Catholic Church, internationally referred to as the Holy See, and occasionally as the Vatican. Its complex history complicates the task of assigning a place to it in the transnational sphere.[120] The first person recorded as maintaining permanent diplomatic representation with a sovereign, in the fifth century, was a pope.[121] From 755 to the final unification of Italy in 1870, the popes also ruled a temporal domain actively involved in international affairs, a sovereign state called the Papal States. Their diplomatic representation was viewed in international law as sovereign representation. Between 1870 and 1929, however, the Holy See was no longer a sovereign territorial entity (having lost all of its territory), but it continued participating in international affairs, engaging in diplomatic negotiations, concluding international treaties, and maintaining extensive diplomatic relations. In 1929, according to the terms of the Lateran Treaty concluded with the Italian government, the Holy See was given sovereignty over Vatican City in Rome. Once again, the Holy See was a sovereign territorial entity.

Papal diplomatic representatives of the first class are nuncios; they hold a rank equivalent to that of ambassador. Representatives of the second class are internuncios, corresponding to the rank of envoy or minister.[122] Nuncios and internuncios are recognized in the 1961 Vienna Convention on Diplomatic Relations.[123] In countries that do not select the papal representative as dean of the diplomatic corps, such a person of ambassadorial rank will be known as pro-nuncio. However, an apostolic delegate is a papal official responsible to the Holy See for the supervision of ecclesiastical matters and has no diplomatic status. States maintain permanent representatives at the Vatican and a breakdown of the states represented there reveals no political or religious homogeneity.[124] A significant number of the envoys at the Vatican represent countries that cannot be called Catholic even remotely. There is no inherent confessional note in maintaining diplomatic relations with the Holy See; it is a purely diplomatic and political act.[125]

The Holy See maintains an observer mission at the United Nations, participates in meetings of other international organizations and in international diplomatic conferences, and negotiates treaties with states.[126] Its international involvement is guided by the social teaching of the Catholic Church. It is therefore particularly active in matters pertaining to human rights, third world development, poverty, the environment, social justice, and the maintenance of peace. But a Holy See delegation also attended the Law of the Sea Conference (1973–1982).[127] In the diplomatic process, the Vatican does not shy away from international controversy.[128] For example, it has defended the right of the Palestinian people to a state of their own, and has fought abortion at world population conferences. This type of diplomatic work is comparable to official governmental activity rather than transnational interaction. The Catholic Church, as well as other churches, operates also through a large variety of church-related civil society organizations, some of which are very involved in international affairs. They are very diverse, ranging from pluralist to fundamentalist, liberal to ultra-conservative, and function very much like NGOs.

Transnational Terrorists and Revolutionaries

International terrorism is a growing phenomenon that is becoming more lethal and disruptive with the evolution of technology. The boundaries of terrorism are slippery, since it is an instrument of revolution.[129] With the growth of interdependence and transnational interaction, it is now common for revolutionaries and terrorists to network across national boundaries[130]—and as pointed out earlier, there are now more than 110 groups engaged in active rebellion around the world.[131] Some of the terrorism experienced in Europe since 1968 is rooted in Middle East conflicts. The 1972 Lod Airport massacre in Israel was carried out by a group of Japanese terrorists who were initially trained in arms and explosives in Japan and North Korea, given further training under the auspices of the Palestinian Front for the Liberation of Palestine, obtained forged passports in West Germany, and provided with weapons in Rome. The 1977 attack against a Lufthansa airliner hijacked en route from Mallorca to Mogadishu, Somalia, was carried out by a team of Palestinians and West Germans.[132]

Some terrorists are transnational from their inception, either because of their universal goals (e.g., transforming the entire world) or because they are fighting for the oppressed, whatever the cause of their oppression, and no matter where. Terrorist and revolutionary networks are now a more frequent phenomenon. For example, Al-Qaida is a large, more extreme movement that brings together terrorists from various parts of the world. Some terrorists become practitioners of diplomacy, anomalous as this may seem. Beyond the violence, revolution is a political endeavor, and the leadership usually seeks international support and political recognition, implying negotiations and diplomatic interaction. Revolutionary and terrorist groups thus become international actors.

These movements are very diverse. Many, particularly at the beginning of their struggles, are not organized to use diplomacy in the service of their causes. But as their campaigns gain momentum, they seek support abroad. Some have been remarkably successful in their diplomatic endeavors—for example, the Palestine Liberation Organization,[133] under the politically astute leadership of Yasir Arafat, gained special status in the United Nations and maintained a diplomatic mission in New York. International organizations—especially regional organizations—have frequently given representatives of revolutionary movements many occasions to present their views on international issues. States supporting them go so far as to give their missions full diplomatic status. Even states opposing them often end up negotiating with their representatives in order to contain the conflict or to find a political solution to the problem.

Private Individuals

Private individuals—people who come together to advance the interests they hold in common—are at the heart of transnational activity.[134] They contribute to the growth of international civil society. Most of the individuals who become involved in the diplomatic process do so as a result of their work in NGOs.[135] Some, however, play an international role independently as a result of their stature, such as Nobel laureates; their personal association with political leaders, as was the case with business magnate Armand Hammer; or their wealth and high visibility, such as Ted Turner, who donated $1 billion to the United Nations to help the destitute in the third world. International affairs scholars, too, have become involved as a result of their professional work, as in the case of Terje Rød Larsen in the Oslo peace process. Others play a role because of their political background, such as Jimmy Carter and Henry Kissinger, although the organizations they create may contribute to their continued involvement in international affairs.

This category of international players is likely to remain small, even with the continued expansion of transnational relations and the communication revolution. Circumstances play an important role in their diplomatic involvement, but their contributions can be significant, even if only under exceptional circumstances. This type of diplomatic work is more widely acknowledged today as one form of "Track II diplomacy" (see Chapter 11).

■ **Case Study: The Role of NGOs in the Diplomacy of the Landmine Treaty**

NGOs started the mass movement that ultimately led to the treaty banning antipersonnel mines,[136] a monumental enterprise recognized with the award of the 1997 Nobel Peace Prize jointly to the International Campaign to Ban Landmines (ICBL) and its remarkable coordinator, Jody Williams. This case study shows what imaginative strategies led NGOs to play a significant role in the attainment of this humanitarian objective.[137]

In October 1992, six NGOs (three based in the United States, one in France, one in Germany, and one in Britain) met in New York and agreed to work together for a comprehensive ban on antipersonnel mines and for the creation of a fund to support mine clearance and assistance to mine victims. To this end, they created the International Campaign to Ban Landmines. The first task was to raise public awareness of the inhumane nature of antipersonnel mines: their low cost,[138] their use by the millions in conflicts around the world,[139] and their residual presence after hostilities end. Landmines indiscriminately kill and maim an estimated 40,000 civilians a year, mostly farmers, women, and children.[140] In seeking to expand its NGO network, ICBL asked a wide variety of groups to add the banning of landmines to their other pursuits (such as human rights, children, social welfare, and disarmament).[141] Throughout the campaign, all these NGOs were to maintain contact by phone, fax, and newsletter, but also, and most importantly, through face-to-face meetings.[142]

ICBL's first conference was convened in London in May 1993. More than fifty NGOs attended. Jody Williams was appointed ICBL coordinator. Each national group was to develop its own campaign strategy to fit the local political culture, with an emphasis on media work and keeping the message simple.[143] The new organization also decided to enlist the support of the International Committee of the Red Cross, which had long been involved in the struggle against landmines, and to involve national Red Cross societies in the campaign.

In December 1993, the UN General Assembly agreed to convene a diplomatic conference (September 1995 in Vienna) to strengthen a 1980 treaty that placed certain restrictions on the use of landmines. ICBL seized this opportunity to recruit more NGOs and mobilize the media in support of the UN's effort. By the opening of the 1995 negotiations, the number of NGOs associated with ICBL reached 350 (in thirty-two countries); over 60 of them gathered in Vienna. For the first time, ICBL lobbied government representatives who were participating in the negotiations. ICBL was even allowed to address a plenary session of the Vienna Conference. More than twenty speakers representing mine victims and relief, humanitarian, human rights, and religious organizations demanded an immediate ban on antipersonnel mines. ICBL held regular media briefings, published a newsletter providing information on what was happening at the conference, and published testimonies and stories from the field.[144]

ICBL also circulated a list that it called "The Good, the Bad, and the Ugly," classifying governments according to their landmines policies, with appropriate documentation. The list was update regularly as the negotiations progressed. This was intended to pressure governments to bring their public statements in line with the realities of their negotiating positions, or vice versa. As expected, this profoundly irked some governments; others even lobbied ICBL to get into the "Good" listing.[145]

Three weeks of diplomatic negotiations, however, failed to produce any revision toward a mine ban.[146] Though a handful of states supported a total ban, there was significant contention. The biggest stumbling block proved to be how to define antipersonnel mines, as there was enormous diversity in design.[147] The conference adjourned without progress, but agreed to reconvene in 1996. However, support for a total ban was generated elsewhere. UN Secretary-General Boutros Boutros-Ghali, in his September 1994 report concerning the creation of a UN fund for mine-clearing operations, stated: "The best and most effective way to solve the global landmine problem is a complete ban on the use, production, and transfer of all landmines."[148]

In May 1995, Pope John Paul II appealed for an end to the production and use of antipersonnel mines. A month later, the Council of the Organization of African Unity adopted a resolution calling on member states to support a total landmine ban, and in July Sadako Ogata of the Office of the UN High Commissioner for Refugees called for a total ban, announced that his organization would not purchase anything from companies that sold or manufactured antipersonnel mines or their components, and suggested that they should be considered "criminals against humanity"[149]—powerful language from prominent people and respected leaders, which helped ICBL in its drive. More highly visible people would soon lend their prestige and support to the global campaign. The mobilization of public opinion was gaining momentum.

The 1996 Dutch NGO Initiative: Governments Join the NGO Campaign

A new strategy was suggested in January 1996 by the Dutch Campaign to Ban Landmines: ICBL should bring together those governments that had officially announced support for a total ban. Since the Vienna Conference, their number had increased to over twenty. Most ICBL members opposed the idea. NGOs did not usually convene conferences of government representatives. If the invited states refused to attend, the momentum might be lost. But in the decentralized practice of the coalition, each national campaign could take its own initiatives, and the Dutch campaign went ahead and organized a meeting of pro-ban states.

Twenty-two countries were invited to send delegations. Seven did,[150] as well as Canada, which had not been invited, as its government had not yet endorsed a total ban. The meeting endeavored to overcome the reluctance of NGOs and states to work together. They exchanged ideas and explored possible strategies. Some of the delegates felt that pro-ban countries were beginning to experience a sense of solidarity. A Canadian delegate, upon his return to Ottawa, wrote a memorandum to the newly appointed foreign minister, Lloyd Axworthy, proposing to explore Canadian initiative on the ban issue. The foreign minister supported the idea. This marked the beginning of active governmental involvement in the global campaign.[151]

A second joint NGO-government meeting took place in April 1996 in Geneva, during the resumed UN landmine conference. This time, fourteen countries participated. Canada proposed convening a small strategy conference for pro-ban countries in the fall, bringing together experts, state officials, and NGOs. Most of the participating countries supported this proposal.[152] On May 3, 1996, the resumed UN landmine conference came to an end but did not achieve a total ban. The UN Secretary-General voiced his regret, saying that by the next review conference, estimated to take place in 2001, "an additional 50,000 human beings will have been killed, and a further 80,000 injured by landmines. Furthermore, 10 to 25 million landmines will have been added to the 110 million [still] uncleared . . . the world cannot wait for the eventual elimination of landmines. They must be eliminated now."[153]

Beginning the Ottawa Process

The Canadian government, as planned, extended an invitation to participate in a strategy conference in Ottawa on October 3–5, 1996, toward a global ban on antipersonnel mines. It was a self-selecting invitation. Any government interested in this objective could participate. A draft plan of action was distributed in advance. Between May and October 1996, members of the Canadian government and ICBL consulted frequently on nearly every aspect of the conference, including how to ensure maximum attendance by governments. It was indeed a partnership.[154]

Fifty states attended as full participants, twenty-four as observers, as did a wide range of NGOs. The Canadian government initially proposed that states and NGOs would be equal participants in all discussions. Bitter rejection of this formula by some officials prevented adoption of this plan. However, NGO delegates were allowed to participate if they were members of government delegations. To encourage governments to involve NGOs, Canada decided to increase the number of delegates that could be accredited to the conference by one, if the national delegation included an NGO representative.[155] About fifteen countries brought NGO leaders in their official missions.[156] The Canadian government went further and gave ICBL a seat at the conference table as a full participant, while those governments unwilling to declare themselves in favor of banning antipersonnel mines had to sit in the back as observers.[157]

NGO campaigners were actively involved in drafting the precise language of both the final declaration and the action plan. This extraordinary level of co-operation between NGOs and governments would become a defining feature of what came to be known as the Ottawa Process.[158] In a process described as an exercise in unconventional diplomacy by design, state officials and government ministers shared plenary meetings and workshop sessions with parliamentary delegates, mine victims, and NGO representatives, advocating a comprehensive ban, large-scale mine clearance, and victim assistance.[159] Speaker after speaker, infused with the passion of ICBL, called for action, and Jody Williams repeatedly spoke of the need for governments to step forward and offer leadership.[160]

Axworthy's Challenge

Most government representatives indicated their support for an eventual ban. However, Lloyd Axworthy, the Canadian foreign minister, on the last day of the conference, took everyone by surprise with a dramatic announcement: Canada would host a signing ceremony in December 1997 for a treaty instituting a total ban on antipersonnel mines. Challenging the world to do it in barely one year was audacious—many state representatives thought it foolhardy.[161]

Axworthy clearly stated that Canada planned to work in open partnership with ICBL to achieve his goal.[162] The NGOs gave him a standing ovation, an honor not often bestowed on foreign ministers by the NGO community.[163] The International Committee of the Red Cross was firmly supportive.[164] His challenge received the immediate endorsement of the UN Secretary-General,[165] and on December 19, 1996, the UN General Assembly passed a resolution urging states "to pursue vigorously an effective, legally binding international agreement to ban the use, stockpiling, production, and transfer of anti-personnel landmines with a view to completing the negotiation as soon as possible."[166] The final vote was 155 to 0 in favor, with 10 abstentions and 20 states absent.

The eight states that met in early 1996 were now joined by South Africa, the Philippines, Germany, and the Netherlands to constitute the core group of states in the Ottawa Process. This group, eventually enlarged as the process gained momentum, would take the lead in supporting Canada and ICBL. At their first formal meeting with ICBL and the ICRC, they agreed that they needed to involve a greater number of states, particularly from the third world, to avoid a North-South split in the negotiations, and they volunteered to bring into the process the states with which they maintained close relations.[167] Much traditional diplomacy was used to generate support. Diplomats and political leaders of the core group, including the Canadian prime minister and foreign minister, traveled the globe seeking allies. Each key diplomatic meeting of the Ottawa Process was preceded by intense telephone and fax diplomacy through which common policy objectives were established and tactical moves were planned.

ICBL, with the help of its own legal experts, attempted to draft the kind of landmine treaty that would achieve its objectives. The ban needed to be comprehensive and exception-free to avoid dividing the anti-mine coalition. This effort helped ICBL to understand the complexity of the task and prepared it to engage later in legal interaction during the treaty negotiations undertaken by state representatives in Oslo.[168] The ICBL treaty team pressed hard throughout the Ottawa Process to ensure that the official mine convention would incorporate as much of the ICBL draft as possible. ICBL's views on treaty language were sought by diplomats throughout the process, and ICBL was an active participant in each of the government conferences.[169]

Preparatory Conferences and Networking

In early 1997, extensive discussions between Austria and Canada produced a draft plan to energize the diplomatic process. Austria agreed to host a meeting in Vienna in February to review a draft convention to serve as a working text for the diplomatic negotiations (to be held in Oslo in September). It was a first test following the Ottawa meeting (October 1996) to see how many countries were genuinely interested in banning antipersonnel mines.[170] To the surprise of the sponsors, 111 countries attended the meeting.[171] A second meeting on the draft convention was hosted by Germany in April 1997, and a third by Belgium in June, remarkably attended by 155 states, 97 of which signed a declaration to ban antipersonnel mines. ICBL and ICRC contributed to the review of the draft convention.[172] Jody Williams gave one of the three keynote addresses at the opening of the Brussels conference, along with the Belgian foreign minister and the head of the Canadian delegation—unusual prominence given to the NGO coordinator. During her talk, she coined the refrain that ICBL would use in all meetings leading to the Oslo negotiations: "no exceptions, no reservations, no loopholes."[173]

Canadian officials engaged in a series of consultations with their partners in the global private sector on how to generate concrete support for a ban from key governments and how to bring together the vast number of ICBL-, ICRC-, and government-sponsored events into a coherent campaign. By March 1997, more than 800 NGOs had pledged their full support to the Ottawa Process. Canadian consultations with the Organization of African Unity produced an agreement that the latter would work with Canada, South Africa, ICBL, and ICRC to host an Africa-wide landmine conference in South Africa in late May 1997.[174]

Much of the preparation for the Oslo conference (rules of procedure, voting formula, etc.) was undertaken by the core group of nations supporting a total ban.[175] Members of this group remained in constant contact. In the eleven months preceding the Oslo negotiations, ten global, regional, and subregional NGO-government conferences took place. All these events generated massive media efforts. Prominent personalities, among them Princess Diana, Archbishop Desmond Tutu, Jimmy Carter, and the new UN Secretary-General, Kofi Annan, used their international stature to alert the public to the importance of the forthcoming negotiations. The Canadian prime minister and foreign minister, in a carefully timed series of letters and phone calls, reached their counterparts around the world. An unusual synergy developed among the political, bureaucratic, and civil society supporters of the ban,[176] which helped to generate the momentum behind the Ottawa Process.[177]

The Oslo Diplomatic Conference, September 1997

Eighty-seven participating countries and thirty-three observer states met in Oslo to negotiate the mine-ban convention. Two days before the opening ceremony, Princess Diana, one of the ardent supporters of the ban, died in her tragic accident in Paris. This added drama to the Oslo proceedings.

During the conference, the intermingling of state diplomats and NGO representatives that had characterized the entire Ottawa Process continued. NGO representatives were accommodated on a grand scale.[178] The ICBL and ICRC delegations sat along with the government missions in the hall itself and, throughout the conference, pressed the delegates to incorporate into the convention what they deemed essential.[179] Everywhere, NGOs kept up the pressure on the negotiators. They divided the assembled delegates among themselves for lobbying purposes. They had detailed information on the progress of the negotiations from the NGO representatives who were members of national delegations, and used it to interact with other government delegates, helping some and pressuring others.[180]

The greatest challenge was presented by a package of amendments submitted by the United States, which proposed a number of exceptions in the application of the convention.[181] There was great desire to persuade the United States to become a party to the treaty, hence the risk to compromise, allow exceptions, and destroy the integrity of the ban. Ironically, the United States kept this from happening by insisting on having its entire package of amendments and exceptions accepted. The proposal was non-negotiable; it was all or nothing. And it proved unacceptable to the conference. The prevailing attitude was for no delay, no exception, no reformulation.

On September 17, 1997, the US team announced that it was abandoning its effort to modify the draft. The following day, the conference adopted the convention, and the conference was brought to an end, with the delegates jumping to their feet for a prolonged standing ovation. A clear, unambiguous convention that totally banned antipersonnel mines had been completed, a remarkable achievement.[182]

At this point, the campaign orchestrated by ICBL, ICRC, and the core group of states geared up to persuade the less committed states to sign the convention at the formal Ottawa ceremony scheduled for early December 1997. Intensive lobbying took place during the UN General Assembly that fall. A wide range of governments conducted public diplomacy campaigns, and all the NGOs involved in ICBL—by then, more than 1,200 of them—carried out yet another letter, fax, and poster offensive and vast media outreach. This effort was given a fitting grand finale when, on December 10, the Nobel Committee announced that Jody Williams and ICBL were to be awarded the 1997 Nobel Peace Prize.

The Ottawa Signature Conference

On December 2–4, 1997, the concluding conference brought together some 2,400 participants, including more than 500 members of the international media, representatives from 157 countries (122 of which signed the convention), and 400–500 delegates from NGOs and international organizations.[183] Over half a billion dollars was pledged during the conference for mine removal and assistance to mine victims.[184] The Ottawa conference was also used to launch the Ottawa Process II—the implementation phase. An additional two-day seminar for members of the NGO community took place on December 6–7 for consultation and planning focused on what civil society could do to carry out the convention and maintain NGO momentum.[185] It was a remarkable achievement for civil society intervention in the diplomatic process, an example of partnership with governmental institutions.

▓ Study Questions and Discussion Topics

1. Who are the nonstate actors today?
2. How do nonstate actors enter the diplomatic process?
3. Are all nonstate actors playing a comparable role in the diplomatic process?
4. What have nongovernmental organizations accomplished by means of diplomacy?
5. Will nongovernmental organizations be given a larger role in the diplomatic process? How? Is this desirable?
6. Are nongovernmental organizations likely to force their way into the diplomatic process? How?
7. Are multinational corporations truly involved in diplomacy?
8. Can multinational corporations be effectively regulated?

▨ Suggested Reading

Aall, Pamela. "Nongovernmental Organizations and Peacemaking." In *Managing Global Chaos: Sources of, and Responses to, International Conflicts,* edited by Chester A. Crocker and Fen Osler Hampson, with Pamela Aall. Washington, DC: US Institute of Peace, 1996.

Boli, John, and George M. Thomas. "World Culture in the World Polity: A Century of International Non-Governmental Organizations." In *The Globalization Reader,* edited by Frank J. Lechner and John Boli. Malden, MA: Blackwell, 2000.

Edwards, Michael, and John Gaventa, eds. *Global Citizen Action.* Boulder: Lynne Rienner, 2001.

Fatemi, Khosrow, ed. *The New World Order: Internationalism, Regionalism, and the Multinational Corporations.* New York: Pergamon, 2000.

Florini, Ann M. "Transnational Civil Society." In *Global Citizen Action,* edited by Michael Edward and John Gaventa. Boulder: Lynne Rienner, 2001.

Haley, Usha C. V. *Multinational Corporations in Political Environment: Ethics, Values, and Strategies.* River Edge, NJ: World Scientific, 2001.

Korten, David C. *Getting to the Twenty First Century Voluntary Action and the Global Agenda.* West Hartford, CT: Kumarian, 1990.

Rotberg, Robert I., ed. *Vigilance and Vengeance: NGOs Preventing Ethnic Conflict in Divided Societies.* Washington, DC: Brookings Institution, 1996.

Simmons, P. J. "Learning to Live with NGOs." *Foreign Policy* no. 112 (Fall 1998), pp. 82–96.

Tussie, Diana, ed. *Civil Society and Multilateral Development Banks: Global Governance* (special issue) 6 (October–December 2000), pp. 399–517.

Warkentin, Craig, and Karen Mingst. "International Institutions, the State, and Global Civil Society in the Age of the World Wide Web." *Global Governance* 6, no. 2 (April–June 2000), pp. 237–257.

▨ Notes

1. Geoffrey Wiseman, "'Polylateralism' and New Modes of Global Dialogue," in *Diplomacy,* edited by Christer Jönsson and Richard Langhorne (London: Sage, 2004), vol. 3, *Problems and Issues in Contemporary Diplomacy,* pp. 36–57.

2. "Reparations for Injuries Suffered in the Service of the United Nations." Louis Henkin, Richard Crawford Pugh, Oscar Schachter, and Hans Smit, *International Law: Cases and Materials,* 3d ed. (St. Paul, MN: West Group, 1993), p. 350.

3. This provides a grand total of 2,336. *Yearbook of International Organizations, 2006–2007,* 43d ed. (Munich: Saur, 2006), vol. 1B, pp. 3017–3025.

4. An entire array of diplomatic techniques has resulted from this interaction (see Chapter 8).

5. Ann M. Florini, "Transnational Civil Society," in *Global Citizen Action,* edited by Michael Edwards and John Gaventa (Boulder: Lynne Rienner, 2001), pp. 29–40, and bibliography, pp. 293–306. See also Ann M. Florini, ed., *The Third Force: The Rise of Transnational Civil Society* (Washington, DC: Carnegie Endowment for International Peace, 2000); James N. Rosenau, *The Study of Global Interdependence: Essays on the Transnationalisation of World Affairs* (New York: Nichols, 1980).

6. John Boli and George Thomas, "World Culture in the World Polity: A Century of International Non-Governmental Organizations," in *The Globalization Reader*, edited by Frank J. Lechner and John Boli (Oxford: Blackwell, 2000), pp. 262–268.

7. John D. Clark, "Ethical Globalization: The Dilemmas and Challenges of Internationalizing Civil Society," in Edwards and Gaventa, *Global Citizen Action*, p. 20.

8. Horst Mendershausen, *The Diplomat as a National and Transnational Agent: Dilemmas and Opportunities* (Santa Monica: Rand, 1969); Bruce Cronin, "The Two Faces of the United Nations: The Tension Between Intergovernmentalism and Transnationalism," *Global Governance* 8, no. 1 (January–March 2002), pp. 53–71.

9. Anthony Judge, "NGOs and Civil Society: Some Realities and Distortions: The Challenge of 'Necessary-to-Governance Organizations' (NGOs)," *Transnational Associations* 47, no. 3 (1995), pp. 156–180, http://www.uia.org.

10. JoAnn Fagot Aviel, "NGOs and International Affairs: A New Dimension of Diplomacy," in *Multilateral Diplomacy and the United Nations Today*, edited by James P. Muldoon Jr., JoAnn Fagot Aviel, Richard Reitano, and Earl Sullivan (Boulder: Westview, 1999), pp. 156–164.

11. Jackie Smith, Charles Chatfield, and Ron Pagnucco, eds., *Transnational Social Movements and Global Politics: Solidarity Beyond the State* (Syracuse, NY: Syracuse University Press, 1997); David C. Korten, *Getting to the 21st Century: Voluntary Action and the Global Agenda* (West Hartford, CT: Kumarian, 1990).

12. Peter Willetts, ed., *Pressure Groups in the Global System: The Transnational Relations of Issue-Oriented Non-Governmental Organizations* (New York: St. Martin's, 1982); P. J. Spiro, "New Global Communities: Nongovernmental Organizations in International Decision-Making Institutions," *Washington Quarterly* 18, no. 1 (1995), pp. 45–56.

13. Peter Willetts, "From 'Consultative Arrangements' to 'Partnership': The Changing Status of NGOs in Diplomacy at the UN," *Global Governance* 6, no. 2 (April–June 2000), pp. 191–212. See also A.-M. Clark, "Non-Governmental Organizations and Their Influence on International Society," *Journal of International Affairs* 48, no. 2 (1995), pp. 507–525.

14. A.-M. Clark, E. J. Friedman, and K. Hochstetler, "The Sovereign Limits of Global Civil Society: A Comparison of NGO Participation in UN World Conferences on the Environment, Human Rights, and Women," *World Politics* 51, no. 1 (1998), pp. 1ff.

15. Elizabeth Smythe, "State Authority and Investment Security: Non-State Actors and the Negotiation of the Multilateral Agreement on Investment at the OECD," in *Non-State Actors and Authority in the Global System*, edited by Richard A. Higgott, Geoffrey R. D. Underhill, and Andreas Bieler (New York: Routledge, 2000), pp. 74–90.

16. The International Campaign to Ban Landmines brought together more than 1,200 NGOs from about sixty countries. See case study at the end of this chapter.

17. See Craig Warkentin and Karen Mingst, "International Institutions, the State, and Global Civil Society in the Age of the World Wide Web," *Global Governance* 6, no. 2 (April–June 2000), pp. 237–257.

18. Perceived as, once again, protecting the rich.

19. Among these concerns were loss of jobs, lack of human rights protection for the workers in enterprises affected by international investments, lack of provisions for environmental protection, fear of third world exploitation by rich nations, that governments would lower living standards to attract capital, and frustration over the matter that the projected agreement attempted to protect investors but did not look after the interests of the host state and its citizens. Warkentin and Mingst, "International Institutions," pp. 240–242.

20. Warkentin and Mingst, "International Institutions," pp. 242–246.

21. See also R. Tandon, *NGO-Government Relations: A Source of Life or the Kiss of Death?* (New Delhi: Society for Participatory Research in Asia, 1989).

22. Jessica T. Mathews, "Power Shift," *Foreign Affairs* 76, no. 1 (January–February 1997), p. 55.

23. Ibid.

24. Warkentin and Mingst, "International Institutions," pp. 247–248.

25. Ibid.

26. Leon Gordenker and Thomas G. Weiss, "NGO Participation in the International Policy Process," in *NGOs, the UN, and Global Governance*, edited by Thomas G. Weiss and Leon Gordenker (Boulder: Lynne Rienner, 1996), pp. 209–222.

27. See http://www.un.org/esa/coordination/ngo/faq.

28. See http://www.un.org/esa/coordination/ngo.

29. Moshe Y. Sachs, ed., *The United Nations: A Handbook on the United Nations, Its Structure, History, Purposes, Activities, and Agencies* (New York: Wiley, 1977), p. 29.

30. See http://www.un.org/esa/coordination/ngo.

31. Ibid.

32. Chadwick Alger, "The Emerging Roles of NGOs in the UN System: From Article 71 to a People's Millennium Assembly," *Global Governance* 8, no. 1 (January–March 2002), pp. 93–117.

33. The UN's specialized agencies are independent organizations, some of them older than the UN. Each agency has its own separate membership and is linked to the UN by an agreement of association and works within the UN system, cooperating with all the other UN bodies.

34. A. LeRoy Bennett and James K. Oliver, *International Organizations: Principles and Issues,* 7th ed. (Upper Saddle River, NJ: Prentice-Hall, 2002), p. 291.

35. World Bank, *Involving Non-Governmental Organizations in Bank-Supported Activities* (Washington, DC: World Bank, 1998).

36. See http://www.un.org/esa/coordination/ngo.

37. Diana Tussie and Maria Fernanda Tuozzo, "Opportunities and Constraints for Civil Society Participation in Multilateral Lending Operations: Lessons from Latin America," in Edwards and Gaventa, *Global Citizen Action*, pp. 105–117. Willetts, "From 'Consultative Arrangements' to 'Partnership,'" pp. 191–212.

38. Paul Nelson, *The World Bank and NGOs: The Limits of Apolitical Development* (London: Macmillan, 1995). See also the six articles in Diana Tussie, ed., *Civil Society and Multilateral Development Banks: Global Governance* (special issue) 6 (October–December 2000), pp. 399–517.

39. See World Bank, *World Bank–Civil Society Collaboration: Progress Report for Fiscal Years 2000 and 2001* (Washington, DC), http://www.worldbank.org.

40. Willetts, "From 'Consultative Arrangements' to 'Partnership,'" p. 196.

41. UN programs and funds are bodies under the control of the General Assembly and included in the regular UN budget) to run certain field activities (e.g., UNICEF). These twenty-five to thirty bodies vary in size and scope.

42. UNHCR is a UN program.

43. See Office of the UN High Commissioner for Refugees, "Our Partners" and "Strategy for Enhancing National NGO Partner Effectiveness," http://www.unhcr.ch.

44. Willetts, "From 'Consultative Arrangements' to 'Partnership,'" p. 194.

45. NGO participation in conferences convened outside the UN framework depends upon the decisions of convening governments or organizations and varies widely.

46. Willetts, "From 'Consultative Arrangements' to 'Partnership,'" pp. 193–194.

47. Global conferences are now regular instruments in the UN work program, focusing on such issues as human rights, the status of women, economic and social development, and the population problem. In particular, see Martha Alter Chen, "Engendering World Conferences: The International Women's Movement and the UN," in Weiss and Gordenker, *NGOs*, pp. 139–158.

48. Willetts, "From 'Consultative Arrangements' to 'Partnership,'" p. 194; Matthias Finger, "Environmental NGOs in the UNCED Process," in *Environmental NGOs in World Politics*, edited by Thomas Princen and Matthias Finger (London: Routledge, 1994), pp. 186–216.

49. Clark, Friedman, and Hochstetler, "Sovereign Limits," pp. 1ff.

50. Andrew S. Natsios, "An NGO Perspective," in *Peacemaking in International Conflict: Methods and Techniques*, edited by I. William Zartman and J. Lewis Rasmussen (Washington, DC: US Institute of Peace, 1997), p. 338. See also Chapter 11 in this volume.

51. J. Lewis Rasmussen, "Peacemaking in the Twenty-First Century: New Rules, New Roles, New Actors," in Zartman and Rasmussen, *Peacemaking*, pp. 23–50. See reviews of efforts in Sri Lanka, the Horn of Africa, and Latin America in "Mobilizing Transnational Resources in National Conflicts," pt. 2 of *Transnational Social Movements and Global Politics: Solidarity Beyond the State*, edited by Jackie Smith, Charles Chatfield, and Ron Pagnucco (Syracuse, NY: Syracuse University Press, 1997), pp. 81–140. See also Pamela Aall, "Nongovernmental Organizations and Peacemaking," in Crocker, Hampson, and Aall, *Managing Global Chaos*, pp. 433–443.

52. See, for instance, Fabienne Hara, "Burundi: A Case of Parallel Diplomacy," in Chester A. Crocker and Fen Osler Hampson, with Pamela Aall, eds., *Herding Cats: Multiparty Mediation in a Complex World* (Washington, DC: US Institute of Peace, 1999), pp. 135–158.

53. Nadim N. Rouhana, "Unofficial Intervention: Potential Contributions to Resolving Ethno-National Conflicts," in *Innovation in Diplomatic Practice*, edited by Jan Melissen (New York: St. Martin's, 1999), pp. 111–132. See also I. William Zartman and Saadia Touval, "International Mediation in the Post–Cold War Era," in Crocker, Hampson, and Aall, *Managing Global Chaos*, p. 450.

54. David P. Forsythe, "Humanitarian Mediation by the International Committee of the Red Cross," in *International Mediation in Theory and Practice*, edited by Saadia Touval and I. William Zartman (Boulder: Westview, 1985), pp. 233–250.

55. David A. Lake and Donald Rothchild, eds., *The International Spread of Ethnic Conflict: Fear, Diffusion, and Escalation* (Princeton: Princeton University Press, 1998).

56. Natsios, "An NGO Perspective," p. 342.

57. See nine case studies of NGO involvement in preventive diplomacy in Robert I. Rotberg, ed., *Vigilance and Vengeance: NGOs Preventing Ethnic Conflict in Divided Societies* (Washington, DC: Brookings Institution, 1996).

58. Michael S. Lund, *Preventing Violent Conflicts: A Strategy for Preventive Diplomacy* (Washington, DC: US Institute of Peace, 1996), "Lessons from Experience," pp. 51–105. Kevin M. Cahill, ed., *Preventive Diplomacy: Stopping Wars Before They Start* (New York: Basic, 1996).

59. Judy Mayotte, "NGOs and Diplomacy," in Muldoon et al., *Multilateral Diplomacy*, p. 170.

60. See discussion of problem-solving workshops in Chapter 11. Beyond diplomacy, many NGOs engage in a multiplicity of activities to foster peace, such as other kinds of seminars for opinion leaders and other civil society persons, as well as justice-

oriented initiatives, reconciliation work, and relief programs. See Kenneth Hackett, "The Role of International NGOs in Preventing Conflict," in Cahill, *Preventive Diplomacy,* pp. 269–284.

61. Herbert C. Kelman, "Informal Mediation by the Scholar/Practitioner," in Jacob Bercovitch and Jeffrey Z. Rubin, eds., *Mediation in International Relations: Multiple Approaches to Conflict Management* (New York: St. Martin's, 1992), pp. 64–96.

62. Mayotte, "NGOs and Diplomacy," p. 167.

63. Hackett, "Role of International NGOs," pp. 269–284.

64. Aall, "Nongovernmental Organizations and Peacemaking," p. 437. On the practical difficulties involved in securing action upon early warning and achieving effective prevention, see Robert I. Rotberg, "Conclusions: NGOs, Early Warning, Early Action, and Preventive Diplomacy," in Rotberg, *Vigilance and Vengeance,* pp. 263–268.

65. Many NGOs remain suspicious of governments and want nothing to do with them.

66. Mayotte, "NGOs and Diplomacy," pp. 167–176; Hackett, "Role of International NGOs," pp. 269–284.

67. Felix Dodds, "From the Corridors of Power to the Global Negotiating Table: The NGO Steering Committee of the Commission on Sustainable Development," in Edwards and Gaventa, *Global Citizen Action,* pp. 203–213.

68. See http://www.un.org/esa/sustdev/csdgen. More than a thousand NGOs are accredited to participate in the commission's work.

69. For example, the Office of the UN High Commissioner for Refugees; see http://www.unhcr.ch.

70. Willetts, "From 'Consultative Arrangements' to 'Partnership,'" pp. 204–205.

71. Ibid., p. 204.

72. Quoted in Aviel, "NGOs and International Affairs," p. 152.

73. At the 1997 UN General Assembly special session (Earth Summit II) to review Agenda 21, approved by the 1992 Rio Conference on Environment and Development (Earth Summit), ten representatives of major NGOs were allowed to address the Assembly meeting at the head-of-state or head-of-government level. Dodds, "From the Corridors of Power," pp. 208–209.

74. See http://www.unhcr.ch.

75. See Dodds, "From the Corridors of Power," pp. 205–206.

76. John Gaventa, "Global Citizen Action: Lessons and Challenges," in Edwards and Gaventa, *Global Citizen Action,* pp. 275–287.

77. P. J. Simmons, "Learning to Live with NGOs," *Foreign Policy* no. 112 (Fall 1998), pp. 82–96.

78. Witness the slow responses to the crises in Rwanda, Bosnia, and Darfur, among others.

79. Andrew F. Cooper and Brian Hocking, "Governments, Non-Governmental Organizations, and the Re-calibration of Diplomacy," in *Diplomacy,* edited by Christer Jönsson and Richard Langhorne (London: Sage, 2004), vol. 3, *Problems and Issues in Contemporary Diplomacy,* pp. 79–95.

80. Alice Landau, *Redrawing the Global Economy: Elements of Integration and Fragmentation* (New York: Palgrave, 2001), pp. 137–160. See also Khosrow Fatemi, ed., *The New World Order: Internationalism, Regionalism, and the Multinational Corporations* (New York: Pergamon, 2000); A. Claire Cutler, Virginia Haufler, and Tony Porter, eds., *Private Authority and International Affairs* (Albany: State University of New York Press, 1999).

81. UN Conference on Trade and Development (UNCTAD), *World Investment Report 2000* (New York, 2001), pp. 8–9.

82. Mathews, "Power Shift," p. 56.

83. Bruce Russett, Harvey Starr, and David Kinsella, *World Politics: The Menu for Choice*, 6th ed. (Boston: Bedford, 2000), p. 63.

84. See list of the top fifty in UNCTAD, *World Investment Report 2000*, pp. 82–83.

85. Charles W. Kegley Jr. and Eugene R. Wittkopf, *World Politics: Trends and Transformations*, 8th ed. (Boston: Bedford, 2001), p. 226. See also UNCTAD, *World Investment Report 1998*.

86. Kegley and Wittkopf, *World Politics*, p. 227.

87. See UNCTAD, *World Investment Report 2000*, pp. 99–158.

88. Ibid., pp. 8–13.

89. Kegley and Wittkopf, *World Politics*, p. 235.

90. Ibid.

91. Richard J. Barnet and Ronald E. Müller, *Global Reach: The Power of the Multinational Corporation* (New York: Simon and Schuster, 1974).

92. Charles W. Kegley Jr., *World Politics: Trends and Transformations*, 11th ed. (Boston: Wadsworth, 2008), p. 207. For updated data on MNC sales, see http://www .fortune.com. For updated data on country gross domestic products, see International Monetary Fund, "World Economic Outlook Database," http://www.imf.org/external/ pubs/ft/weo. This comparison is of course very imperfect. UNCTAD achieves different rankings by using value-added measurements for MNCs, defined as the sum of salaries, pre-tax profits, and depreciation and amortization. The results still demonstrate the economic power of MNCs. See UNCTAD, *World Investment Report 2002*, chap. 4, http://www.unctad.org/en/docs/wir.

93. Kegley and Wittkopf, *World Politics*, pp. 226–227.

94. UNCTAD, *World Investment Report 1999*, pp. 158–160.

95. UNCTAD, *World Investment Report 2000*, pp. xv–xvi.

96. James P. Muldoon Jr., "The Challenges of the Global Economy for Post–Cold War Diplomacy," in Muldoon et al., *Multilateral Diplomacy*, pp. 80–86; Jeremy Taylor, "Private-Sector Diplomats in the Global Economy," in Muldoon et al., *Multilateral Diplomacy*, pp. 102–110.

97. Christopher O'Leary, "Economic Affairs," *2002 Britannica Book of the Year* (Chicago: Encyclopaedia Britannica, 2002), p. 205.

98. See UNDP, "UNDP and the Business Sector," http://www.undp org/ business/buse9dec02.pdf.

99. UNCTAD, *World Investment Report 1999*, p. 366.

100. Among other things, she accused the industry of encouraging young people to start smoking. *New York Times*, October 16, 2002, p. A6.

101. Richard J. Barnet and Ronald E. Müller, "Corporate Diplomacy and National Loyalty," in Barnet and Müller, *Global Reach*, pp. 72–104.

102. Kenneth A. Rodman, *Sanctions Beyond Borders: Multinational Corporations and U.S. Economic Statecraft* (Lanham: Rowman and Littlefield, 2001).

103. Mathews, "Power Shift," pp. 56–57.

104. UNCTAD, *World Investment Report 2000*, p. xvi.

105. Mathews, "Power Shift," p. 57.

106. UNCTAD, *World Investment Report 1999*, "Social Responsibility," pp. 345ff.

107. Bennett and Oliver, *International Organizations*, pp. 280–282.

108. Lori F. Damrosch, Louis Henkin, Richard Crawford Pugh, Oscar Schachter, and Hans Smit, *International Law Cases and Materials*, 4th ed. (St. Paul, MN: West Group, 2001), pp. 1623–1625.

109. UNCTAD, *World Investment Report 1999,* pp. 349–350; International Labour Organization, *Codes of Conduct for Multinational Enterprises,* CD-ROM (Geneva, 2002); Virginia Haufler, "Industry Regulation and Self-Regulation: The Case of Labor Standards," in *Enhancing Global Governance: Toward a New Diplomacy?* edited by Andrew F. Cooper, John English, and Ramesh Thakur (Tokyo: UN University Press, 2002), pp. 162–186.

110. UNCTAD, *World Investment Report 1999,* p. 350. See also "Multilateral Companies and the Establishment of International Rules," six studies in Higgott, Underhill, and Bieler, *Non-State Actors,* pp. 49–154.

111. Usha C. V. Haley, *Multinational Corporations in Political Environments: Ethics, Values, and Strategies* (River Edge, NJ: Word Scientific, 2001).

112. Including the spectacular case of Enron. In 2003–2005, Jordan Goodman's weekly report on the economy (NBC) included a "Rogues Gallery" segment citing the business executives who have been caught, week by week, for their involvement in corporate scandals.

113. UNCTAD, *World Investment Report 1999,* p. 353. The UN Global Compact was launched on July 26, 2000, at UN headquarters in New York. See http://www.unglobalcompact.org.

114. Office of the UN High Commissioner for Human Rights, UN Environment Program, International Labour Organization, UN Development Programme, and UN Industrial Organization. See http://www.unglobalcompact.org.

115. See, for example, Thomas Princen, "Mediation by a Transnational Organization: The Case of the Vatican," in *Mediation in International Relations: Multiple Approaches to Conflict Management,* edited by Jacob Bercovitch and Jeffrey Z. Rubin (New York: St. Martin's, 1992), pp. 149–175; Thomas Princen, *Intermediaries in International Conflict,* chap. 9, "Biafra: The OAU, the British, and the Quakers Mediate the Nigerian Civil War, 1967–1970" (Princeton: Princeton University Press, 1992), pp. 186–213; Andrea Bartoli, "Mediating Peace in Mozambique: The Role of the Community of Sant'Egidio," in Crocker, Hampson, and Aall, *Herding Cats,* pp. 245–277.

116. See http://wcc.coe.org. See also Bartoli, "Mediating Peace."

117. See http://www.santegidio.org.

118. *The Middle East,* 10th ed. (Washington, DC: Congressional Quarterly, 2005), pp. 235–237.

119. Benjamin Orbach, "Usama bin Laden and al-Qa'ida: Origins and Doctrines," *Middle East Review of International Affairs* 54 (December 2001), pp. 58–61; Mark Sedgwick, "Al-Qaeda and the Nature of Religious Terrorism," in *Terrorism and Counterterrorism: Understanding the New Security Environment,* 2d ed., edited by Russell D. Howard and Reid L. Sawyer (Dubuque, IA: McGraw-Hill, 2006), pp. 187–206; Quintan Wiktorowicz, "A Genealogy of Radical Islam," in Howard and Sawyer, *Terrorism and Counterterrorism,* pp. 207–229. See also Jessica Stern, *Terror in the Name of God: Why Religious Militants Kill* (New York: HarperCollins, 2003).

120. See Robert A. Graham, *Vatican Diplomacy: A Study of Church and State on the International Plane* (Princeton: Princeton University Press, 1959).

121. Harold Nicolson, *Diplomacy* (New York: Oxford University Press, 1964), p. 13. It was not until 1455 that the first permanent mission was established between two states, when the Duke of Milan sent a representative to Genoa. Ibid. See also Chapter 2 in this volume.

122. Often given the double title of envoy extraordinary and minister plenipotentiary. (Lord) Gore-Booth, ed., *Satow's Guide to Diplomatic Practice,* 5th ed. (New York: Longman, 1979), pp. 86–87.

123. Article 14.

124. In 1984, 108 nations maintained diplomatic relations with the Holy See. *Origins* 13, no. 33 (January 25, 1984), p. 557.

125. Graham, *Vatican Diplomacy,* pp. 17–18.

126. André Dupuy, *La Diplomatie du Saint-Siège Après le IIe Concile du Vatican: Le Pontificat de Paul VI, 1963–1978* (Paris: TEQUI, 1980), pp. 301–307.

127. Ibid., pp. 301–315.

128. See Robert Bosc, *La Société Internationale et l'Eglise* (Paris: Bibliothèque de la Recherche Sociale, 1968), vol. 2, pp. 1132–1137.

129. Russell D. Howard and Reid L. Sawyer, eds., *Terrorism and Counterterrorism: Understanding the New Security Environment,* rev. ed. (Guilford, CT: McGraw-Hill, 2002), pp. 2–52; Charles W. Kegley Jr., *The New Global Terrorism: Characteristics, Causes, Controls* (Upper Saddle River, NJ: Prentice-Hall, 2003), pp. 1–91.

130. John Arquilla and David Ronfeldt, eds., *Networks and Netwars: The Future of Terror, Crime, and Militancy* (Santa Monica: Rand, 2001), pp. 29–60.

131. Russett, Starr, and Kinsella, *World Politics,* p. 203. See discussion of the terrorist theaters around the world presented in Clifford E. Simonsen and Jeremy R. Spindlove, *Terrorism Today: The Past, the Players, the Future* (Upper Saddle River, NJ: Prentice-Hall, 2000), pp. 75–296.

132. Paul Wilkinson, *Terrorism and the Liberal State,* 2d ed. (New York: New York University Press, 1986), pp. 246–247.

133. Kemal Kirisci, *The PLO and World Politics: A Study of the Mobilization of Support for the Palestinian Cause* (New York: St. Martin's, 1986). An example of PLO diplomatic endeavors can be seen in its efforts to gain membership in the World Health Organization. See, for example, US Congress, House Committee on Foreign Affairs, Subcommittee on International Operations, *PLO Application for Membership in WHO: Hearing,* 101st Congress, 1st sess., on H.R. 2145, May 9, 1989 (Washington, DC: US Government Printing Office, 1989).

134. Edwards and Gaventa, *Global Citizen Action,* p. 2; Gaventa, "Global Citizen Action," in Edwards and Gaventa, *Global Citizen Action,* pp. 275–287.

135. Harold H. Saunders, *Politics Is About Relationship: A Blueprint for the Citizens' Century* (New York: Palgrave Macmillan, 2005).

136. Convention on the Prohibition of the Use, Stockpiling, Production, and Transfer of Anti-Personnel Mines and on Their Destruction, signed in Ottawa, December 3, 1997, by 122 states, and eventually by 150 (the "Ottawa Convention"). Entered into force on March 1, 1999. Metoko Mekata, "Building Partnerships Toward a Common Goal: Experiences of the International Campaign to Ban Landmines," in Florini, *The Third Force,* p. 166. Ratified by 141 states as of September 20, 2003. See text of the convention in Maxwell A. Cameron, Robert J. Lawson, and Brian W. Tomlin, eds., *To Walk Without Fear: The Global Movement to Ban Landmines* (New York: Oxford University Press, 1998), app. B, pp. 464–478. Also available at http://www.mines actioncanada.com.

137. Governments and the International Committee of the Red Cross had been working to strengthen a 1980 treaty placing some restrictions on the use of landmines.

138. Costing as little as $3 apiece. Mekata, "Building Partnerships," p. 156.

139. See http://www.icrc.org.

140. See Stuart Maslen, "The Role of the International Committee of the Red Cross," in Cameron, Lawson, and Tomlin, *To Walk Without Fear,* pp. 80–98.

141. Warkentin and Mingst, "International Institutions," p. 247.

142. Jody Williams and Stephen Goose, "The International Campaign to Ban Land Mines," in Cameron, Lawson, and Tomlin, *To Walk Without Fear,* pp. 23–25.

143. Ibid., pp. 22–23.

144. Mekata, "Building Partnerships," p. 155.

145. Maxwell A. Cameron, "Global Civil Society and the Ottawa Process: Lessons from the Movement to Ban Anti-Personnel Mines," in Cooper, English, and Thakur, *Enhancing Global Governance,* p. 76.

146. See Williams and Goose, "International Campaign," pp. 31–33.

147. The United States wanted to continue using "smart mines" equipped with self-destructing or neutralizing devices that led to their incapacitation after a set period. But China, India, and Russia objected, because they could not afford to spend as much as the United States on their production (the least expensive mine, at the time, could be produced for $3, while smart mines cost as much as $300 apiece). Mekata, "Building Partnerships," p. 156.

148. Mekata, "Building Partnerships," p. 153.

149. Ibid., p. 154.

150. Austria, Belgium, Denmark, Ireland, Mexico, Norway, and Switzerland.

151. See Robert J. Lawson, Mark Gwozdecky, Jill Sinclair, and Ralph Lysyshyn, "The Ottawa Process and the International Movement to Ban Anti-Personnel Mines," in Cameron, Lawson, and Tomlin, *To Walk Without Fear,* pp. 160–184; Brian W. Tomlin, "On a Fast Track to a Ban: The Canadian Policy Process," in Cameron, Lawson, and Tomlin, *To Walk Without Fear,* 194–198.

152. See Valerie Warmington and Celina Tuttle, "The Canadian Campaign," in Cameron, Lawson, and Tomlin, *To Walk Without Fear,* pp. 48–59. See also Mekata, "Building Partnerships," p. 158; Williams and Goose, "International Campaign," pp. 34–35.

153. Mekata, "Building Partnerships," pp. 158–159.

154. Williams and Goose, "International Campaign," p. 35.

155. Tomlin, "On a Fast Track," p. 198.

156. Cameron, "Global Civil Society," p. 77.

157. Williams and Goose, "International Campaign," p. 35. See Tomlin, "On a Fast Track," pp. 198–199.

158. Williams and Goose, "International Campaign," p. 35.

159. Some meetings were exclusively for government missions to satisfy governments that could not accept the scrutiny of NGOs. Tomlin, "On a Fast Track," p. 198.

160. Lawson et al., "Ottawa Process," pp. 161–162.

161. See Tomlin, "On a Fast Track," pp. 185–211.

162. Williams and Goose, "International Campaign," p. 34; Mekata, "Building Partnerships," p. 159.

163. Lawson et al., "Ottawa Process," p. 162; Mekata, "Building Partnerships," p. 161.

164. Maslen, "Role of the International Committee of the Red Cross," p. 91.

165. Lawson et al., "Ottawa Process," p. 162.

166. Mekata, "Building Partnerships," p. 162.

167. Lawson et al., "Ottawa Process," p. 167.

168. Mekata, "Building Partnerships," pp. 161–162.

169. Williams and Goose, "International Campaign," p. 36.

170. Lawson et al., "Ottawa Process," p. 170.

171. Michael Dolan and Chris Hunt, "Negotiating in the Ottawa Process: The New Multilateralism," in Cameron, Lawson, and Tomlin, *To Walk Without Fear,* p. 406; Lawson et al., "Ottawa Process," p. 170.

172. Dolan and Hunt, "Negotiating," p. 406; Maslen, "Role of the International Committee of the Red Cross," p. 92.

173. Williams and Goose, "International Campaign," p. 36.

174. Lawson et al., "Ottawa Process," p. 172. See Noel Scott, "The South African Campaign," in Cameron, Lawson, and Tomlin, *To Walk Without Fear,* pp. 68–75.

175. Lawson et al., "Ottawa Process," p. 171.

176. "Partnership does not mean that you agree on everything or are in the government's pockets. You have the same goals and bring comparative advantages to the achievement of these goals." Cameron, "Global Civil Society," p. 78, citing a dominant view in ICBL. Or as a senior Canadian official put it, "The role of governments and NGOs is different. NGOs don't want to be public servants. There will always be some mistrust and competition for ideas and leadership." Yet in the Ottawa Process, there was cooperation between governments and NGOs. Ibid., p. 79.

177. Lawson et al., "Ottawa Process," pp. 173–174.

178. Iver B. Neumann, "Harnessing Social Power: State Diplomacy and the Land Mine Issue," in Cooper, English, and Thakur, *Enhancing Global Governance,* p. 124.

179. Maslen, "Role of the International Committee of the Red Cross," p. 93.

180. Neumann, "Harnessing Social Power," p. 124.

181. Mekata, "Building Partnerships," pp. 163–166. See also Mary Wareham, "Rhetoric and Policy Realities in the United States," in Cameron, Lawson, and Tomlin, *To Walk Without Fear,* pp. 212–243; Dolan and Hunt, "Negotiating," pp. 409–415.

182. Lawson et al., "Ottawa Process," p. 180.

183. Cameron, Lawson, and Tomlin, *To Walk Without Fear,* p. 7. The convention came into force on September 23, 1998. Mekata, "Building Partnerships," p. 166. As of August 15, 2007, 155 states are parties to the convention. See http://www.icbl.org/treaty/members.

184. Lawson et al., "Ottawa Process," p. 181.

185. See Mekata, "Building Partnerships," pp. 166–167. Civil society is thus maintaining the pressure on states, just as it has done in other human rights issues with the help of such organizations as Amnesty International.

6 Changes in the Diplomatic Profession

As international actors adjust to global change and turn to new kinds of diplomatic relations, a good deal of role redefinition is taking place among the professionals involved in the field. New ways of conducting diplomacy are devised and the profession evolves. New types of practitioners and new kinds of professionals are entering the field and contribute to the changes taking place in the profession.[1] But diplomacy has long been influenced by tradition, so it should therefore not be surprising to find that some practices endure even beyond their usefulness. An examination of the diplomatic profession will thus reveal both continuity and change.

▓ Structural Causes of Professional Transformation

A major factor of professional transformation resides in the substantial changes that have taken place in the international system.[2] Other actors have emerged and are interacting with states, although as a rule they do not have the same impact on the course of events—then again, nation-states do not all have the same impact on the course of events either. Many of the new actors, sovereign or not sovereign, make a considerable difference in what is happening in the world. Inevitably, the new international actors have generated new professional techniques. Their functions are different (e.g., the World Health Organization [WHO]). The work conditions vary widely, as, for example, in the case of representatives of nongovernmental organizations (NGOs) working with state diplomats in the decisionmaking bodies of a number of international organizations (further discussed in Chapter 5). And some of the issues to be dealt with can be very technical (e.g., the eradication of malaria).

International law has been slow in acknowledging nonsovereign actors, although some UN officials have diplomatic immunity under several international agreements.[3] This recognition has been slower to materialize in the case of transnational actors, but there are some exceptions—for example, the International Committee of the Red Cross (ICRC), an NGO, given functions under the international law of war. It will happen sooner or later with regard to multinational corporations (if only for the sake of international accountability). Already, under the rules of the International Center for the Settlement of Investment Disputes (ICSID) and of the Multilateral Investment Guarantee Agency (MIGA), both subsidiary organs of the World Bank, business corporations are given international protection.[4] Agents of these corporations act on their behalf before these international agencies. Under the headquarters agreement between the World Bank and the United States, a procedure is available for such agents to travel to the Bank (located in Washington, D.C.), facilitating their entry into the United States. Representatives, agents, and delegates of NGOs and MNCs carry out their international duties, such as in negotiations with states or international organizations, without the benefit of diplomatic status, unless so granted for the purpose at hand, such as to serve as official members of a state or UN mission. But even foreign service personnel on special missions (see Chapter 9) do not automatically enjoy diplomatic immunities.[5]

The large increase in the number of international actors leads to more numerous diplomatic links and more extensive diplomatic activity. Thus a much larger number of diplomatic representatives are needed, and the cost of foreign relations is increasing. Many underdeveloped states can ill afford this expense. Other states, ironically including the United States, are unwilling to spend what it takes to maintain this extensive international network.[6] As a result, many international delegations are understaffed, lack the facilities to carry out their diplomatic relations, or cannot afford to pay for the normal cost of diplomatic representation. All of this affects the diplomatic process. Too many countries are inadequately represented at important diplomatic meetings (e.g., one delegate has to cover the activities of several committees when the delegation cannot have one representative on each). And, of course, this situation greatly increases the workload of individual agents. A similar problem is found in many international organizations, as states have been reluctant to fund the international agencies they have created. International organization officials are thus frequently hampered in the performance of their functions for lack of resources.

▓ Professional Diversity

The large increase in the number of independent states (close to 200 in 2008, up from about 70 in the mid–twentieth century)[7] has created a more heterogeneous diplomatic environment. Cultural diversity among the practitioners of diplomacy has vastly increased, and with it, diversity of behavior and perspective. Many of the new states did not share the diplomatic traditions of the well-established countries. Some of the newly independent states were anxious to shed their colonial heritage. These new groups brought with them their different cultures, work habits, and negotiating styles.[8] Diversity is the hallmark of global conferences and international organization meetings. The UN has to contend with six official languages.[9] However, as the years go by, diplomats, diverse as they are, learn to work together, and a new diplomatic culture tends to emerge. It does not obliterate diversity, but diplomats can handle the cultural differences; they learn how to deal with them so that these differences do not constitute an obstacle to productivity. This has always been a characteristic of diplomacy: the ability to maintain contact and to build bridges across national and cultural differences. Experience is the best road to proficiency in this respect (although some never learn). Diversity is also found in the professional backgrounds of the people engaged in diplomatic work, and there is a tendency for this phenomenon to become more pronounced as international actors find new ways of working together, involving different types of personnel (as in transnational work).

Foreign Service: Career Officers and Political Appointees

It is often assumed that nations rely on the services of trained career officers for their representation abroad.[10] Through most of history, however, heads of state have sent people close to their immediate entourage to represent them abroad, people they deemed trustworthy—we would call them today "political appointees" (some were sent to another court simply to get them out of the way, but that is another story). The French monarchy, in the seventeenth century, began the practice of systematic professional representation. Training and experience resulting from career continuity were found most effective, and the practice spread (see Chapter 2).[11]

Nevertheless, many states always included political appointees in their foreign service. New states initially did not have much of a choice. Many authoritarian systems found political security in selecting people from the ranks of the ruling elite. Today, even states with a well-established professional foreign service include appointees outside the profession. The United States has a long tradition of recruiting about one-third of its chiefs of mission outside the foreign service,[17] a number of them among people who made large financial contributions to presidential campaigns.[13] Ambassadorial appointments have to be approved by the US Senate, but past practice shows that few candidates are turned away for incompetence (even when plainly revealed during confirmation hearings). And since these appointments are intended as rewards, they are for the more glamorous, or at least more "interesting," capitals of the developed world (e.g., London or Paris). This practice creates morale problems in the career, since it deprives some meritorious officers of the ultimate reward of reaching the rank of ambassador.[14]

The issue has long been hotly debated in the professional literature, but there is no indication that it will soon change.[15] There is agreement that the incompetent should be kept out. And it is acknowledged that appointing seasoned non–foreign service professionals with political experience, knowledge of international affairs, and a record of public service or relevant expertise has produced excellent results.[16] A person of prominence who has close contact with the US president has been useful to head the US mission at the United Nations—for example, Henry Cabot Lodge Jr., Adlai Stevenson, and Arthur Goldberg.[17] Such appointments have also been successful in other embassies, as with Averell Harriman and Walter Mondale. Such individuals can bring fresh ideas to the job, and can act without having to worry about the furtherance of their career. Routinely using them to fill one-third of the posts, however, is excessive.

Another Kind of Non–Foreign Service Personnel

The foreign relations of states are no longer conducted exclusively by foreign ministries (State Department in the United States). Many other agencies of national governments are involved—up to several dozen.[18] Among them are defense, agriculture, commerce, labor, treasury, justice, energy, and transportation. Some departments cooperate in selecting their foreign relations personnel (e.g., commerce and state in the United States); others do it on their own. Some of the foreign work of these departments is done from offices in the national capital. Some departments communicate and interact directly with their foreign counterparts, bypassing altogether the state department and its diplomatic apparatus—transgovernmental relations—and an increasing amount of work is done in this fashion, with departments preferring to conduct their own foreign relations, particularly in technical fields, in which they feel more qualified (see Chapter 3). Some of this work is done by posting their own agents in their state's embassies (see Box 7.1). The foreign service now provides less than half of the US personnel at US embassies.[19] These people officially work under the authority of the embassy's chief of mission, but in practice they follow the agenda of the appointing agency.

Some staff members of these government departments do their international work from their home offices, while others are given diplomatic assignments abroad, unconnected with their embassy. For example, the US Department of Labor maintains a Bureau of International Labor Affairs, under the direction of a deputy undersecretary for international labor affairs. This bureau is composed of five divisions: the International Child Labor Program; the National Administrative Office, created by the North American Agreement on Labor Cooperation in supplement to the North American Free Trade Agreement (NAFTA); the Office of Foreign Relations; the Office of International Economic Affairs; and the Office of International Organizations. Department of Labor officers represent the United States (over a period of several months each year, working closely with the Departments of Commerce and State) at the annual meeting of the International Labour Organization (ILO) in Geneva. They also represent the United States in the Employment, Labor, and Social Affairs Committee of the Organization for Economic Cooperation and Development (OECD) in Paris.[20]

Many agencies are so organized that personnel in their international affairs divisions can make a career of their international relations work in the specialized area of their agency. These people acquire years of experience representing their country in international circles, negotiating international agreements, and cooperating with other agencies in implementing the foreign relations of their country, particularly when they are posted in embassies and are working in close contact with foreign service officers.[21] Some of these people can be said to be doing "diplomatic" work, although they are not members of the foreign service.

International Organization Personnel

The personnel of nonsovereign actors are to be distinguished from the representatives of the member states who are national delegates conducting the diplomacy of their country in the organizations concerned. Intergovernmental organizations, commonly referred to as international organizations, carry out their activities by means of their bureaucracies (i.e., secretariat personnel). In most organizations, these officials fall into two categories: the general staff and the so-called professional staff, including administrators in charge of agencies and their subdivisions.[22]

At the highest levels (e.g., secretary-general, director-general, undersecretaries, assistant secretaries), these officers are not only executives (the UN Secretary-General is the head of the entire UN bureaucracy and chief administrator of the organization), but are also recognized to be of diplomatic grade.[23] They are entitled to diplomatic immunities. Officers in this diplomatic category are selected under the authority of the chief administrative officer of the organization (e.g., the UN Secretary-General).

Some appointments are for limited-term contracts; others are for long-term service. Personnel in this category are the equivalent of career diplomats. Although international organizations usually do not have a foreign service,[24] this could be viewed as an equivalent function, but with some important differences: secretariat diplomats represent *the organization,* carry out its policies, and interact with the diplomats of the member states; but, in addition, many of them are executives in charge of an entire division of the bureaucracy.

Program directors of international organizations are usually seen as administrators, but the programs are multinational. They are run by boards of directors composed of state representatives (the diplomats representing their states at the seat of the organization). Program directors deal with states in administering their programs; they need to be good diplomats to succeed in their executive functions: states give them their mandates, provide their funds, and review their performance. This implies *political* in addition to functional effectiveness. Thus we have here a special category of administrator-diplomat.[25] Some of these officers may not have diplomatic immunity, but their work still entails a large amount of diplomacy.

Transnational Agents

Transnational agents—a very different category—comprise, for example, representatives of NGOs and multinational corporations (MNC) working with foreign state officials and diplomats as well as international bureaucracies.[26] The bulk of international issues are of course handled by diplomatic agents working for nation-states and, in a growing number of significant cases, by international organization diplomats. Nevertheless, NGOs and MNCs exert a growing influence in international diplomacy and their representatives interact with state diplomats. A number of countries and international organizations in fact invite the participation of NGO representatives, and occasionally even MNC agents, in their diplomatic interaction and in the development of policy.[27] The NGO and MNC officers involved in those interactions are usually not characterized as diplomats. Nonetheless, they need diplomatic skill to engage in these international activities. Diplomats work with them and acknowledge the need to adjust to this new reality (see the case study on the diplomacy of the landmine treaty in Chapter 5). NGO and MNC agents play important roles in a growing number of international transactions, hence adding to the diversity of the diplomatic environment.

NGO and MNC agents are themselves extremely diverse in culture as well as in professional preparation. MNCs are usually represented by high-level business executives wielding the influence of the considerable resources of their firms. They are taken very seriously by their counterparts in the public sector. Some state officials, particularly in developing nations, are intimidated by their power.[28] NGO personnel are more diverse. Some of them have impressive credentials, having had long careers in public service. Others have come from the ranks of international NGOs and have learned from practical experience (as diplomats do). Professional diversity in contemporary diplomacy is thus extensive and likely to increase, adding to the complexity of the diplomatic field.

▓ Greater Need for Specialized Skills

The diplomatic agenda now covers the full range of human endeavors (see Chapter 3). Diplomatic work thus requires greater specialized skill than before. The need for specialization is particularly visible in the work of international organizations and in the growing number of international conferences on highly specialized or technical topics such as global warming, arms control, population, crime prevention, and drug abuse.[29] More and more non–foreign service experts need to be included in national delegations, thus adding to the diversity of personnel assembled in these international gatherings.[30]

This situation has been one of the causes for involving the full spectrum of government ministries in the conduct of foreign relations.[31] For example, an agriculture ministry will provide a large contingent for a conference delegation to discuss hunger in East Africa; a health ministry will send delegates for a discussion of HIV/AIDS or the development of new pharmaceutical standards. The involvement of highly specialized personnel in international negotiations has an impact on the conduct of diplomacy. Specialists are likely to focus on the technical issues and to become impatient with the political complications that are frequently infused into the dialogue. They become impatient also with delegation members who have to take into account the political aspects of the situation.[32]

Specialists have less opportunity to develop diplomatic or negotiating skills over long involvement in the international process, as their professional pursuits may keep them from participating regularly in international exchanges. Indeed, their professional pursuits have nothing to do with diplomacy and perhaps not even with international relations. Many enter the diplomatic process as advisers, although if a technical issue becomes an enduring feature of some international situation, some experts can be invited to serve for an indefinite period of time. This is the case, for example, in continuous arms control negotiations.[33] In these circumstances, experts can develop diplomatic skills. Still, some experts or specialized personnel may already have diplomatic skills of their own, perhaps because of their multicultural background, upbringing, or foreign experience, rather than as a result of their professional pursuits.

▨ Evolving Diplomatic Culture

Until fairly recently, diplomats were widely perceived as an elite group. The aristocracy in many countries were fond of the diplomatic profession and eager to serve. The ornate setting of diplomatic functions, eleborate ceremonies, and regular contacts with important figures contributed to the special aura of diplomacy.[34]

In the eyes of many, diplomats are still an exclusive and elitist group.[35] An emphasis on secrecy in diplomatic work, certainly confirmed by the perpetual reluctance of diplomats to talk about their work, probably contributes to this impression. And in some countries, diplomats still come from the upper classes. Current trends, however, indicate substantial changes in the diplomatic culture.[36] Elitism has been attacked in many democracies, and governments are under pressure to hire people from all walks of life. In these societies, foreign service posts are no longer the exclusive preserve of the upper class. Ironically, in the United States, budgetary constraints are such that in expensive capitals (for example London, Paris, and Rome), a US ambassador cannot run the embassy without independent means. What the State Department provides is simply inadequate. Hence these prestigious posts have often been given to better-endowed persons, which is not the best way of addressing the problem (see Box 6.1).[37]

Many developing countries, of course, experience serious financial constraints in carrying out their diplomatic relations, and this affects their style of representation. Some embassies are less than glamorous—just a few rooms in a nondescript office building. Today, diplomatic work involves more humdrum, bureaucratic routine. Contemporary need for more rapid action in an age of fast communication fosters impatience with cumbersome pomp. Diplomatic jobs are less prestigious as presented by the mass media. Those who have to live on their foreign service salaries can ill afford an exclusive lifestyle. The greater importance of competence has also tended to open the ranks of the profession. Performance is more credible than lineage, and class considerations are becoming less important. Another factor of change is related to gender issues, and it operates at two levels: women are entering the diplomatic profession in greater numbers, and diplomatic wives are more insistent on their independence, both of which are substantially affecting the diplomatic profession.

Box 6.1   Defense Secretary Urges More Spending for US Diplomacy, November 2007

Defense secretary Robert M. Gates forcefully advocated a larger budget for the State Department. He called for "a dramatic increase in spending on the civilian instruments of national security—[specifically] diplomacy, strategic communications . . . and development." He stressed that the US government must improve its skills in the field of public diplomacy, going so far as to say: "We are miserable at communicating to the rest of the world what we are about as a society and culture."

Source: New York Times, November 27, 2007, p. A6.

▓ Gender Issues

The diplomatic profession has long been dominated by men, as a result of which a variety of traditions, rules of procedure, and protocol simply assume that diplomatic agents are men and provisions are made for the roles to be played by their wives.[38] For example, upon arrival, the wife of a new ambassador must visit the wives of the other ambassadors in the capital. Customary practices have a tendency to endure. Nevertheless, a good deal of change is now taking place, however unevenly. The diplomatic profession is in the process of adjusting to the changing role of women in modern society.

Women in the Diplomatic Profession

Some nations were ahead of the times. Myrtha Tavares-Liz de Grossman, minister-counselor of the permanent mission of the Dominican Republic to the United Nations, stated in a symposium organized at the UN and recorded especially for the UN Institute for Training and Research (UNITAR)[39] that since the birth of her country in 1844, women have played an important role in Dominican politics and diplomatic service. The delegate who signed the UN Charter in 1945 on behalf of the Dominican Republic was a woman. Interestingly, by 1974, Latin American countries had fifty-three women in their permanent missions at the UN, more than any other regional group.[40] In many countries, however, the conditions of service were initially draconian. Arundhati Ghose, first secretary of India's permanent mission to the United Nations, reported that when she was interviewed by the Indian foreign service eleven years earlier (1963–1964), she was informed that upon getting married, women officers had to submit their resignations. These resignations were not accepted immediately, but could become effective at any time if the Indian government felt that the officer's domestic life was interfering with the effective discharge of her duties. This rule was later rescinded.[41]

Elinor Constable, a US foreign service officer, married and was asked to resign, but she challenged the system in 1958. She questioned the legality of this practice and demanded to be shown the rule. There was no rule. The entire practice rested on tradition and there were no legal grounds for it. She left the service, but eventually came back and rose to become an ambassador and later an assistant secretary of state.[42] (See also the case study on Melissa Wells at the end of this chapter.). In the US foreign service, no woman served as chief of a diplomatic mission until 1933, and no woman attained the rank of ambassador until 1949. Both women were noncareer officers. The first US foreign service career woman to attain ambassador rank was sent to Switzerland in 1953. Until 1984, forty-four women served as US ambassadors.[43] Of these, only 37 percent were career foreign service women. The pool of career candidates available for promotion to the rank of ambassador was then very small. Prior to the 1980s, no woman had ever been placed in charge of any of the State Department's five major geographic bureaus, the Office of International Organizations, or the Economic and Business Affairs offices.

For the period 1975–1980, the State Department assigned 16.9 percent more women to its consular section and 17.6 percent fewer women to its political section (more prestigious and more conducive to promotion to the higher ranks) than regular hiring practices should have generated. In 1986, 34.4 percent of women generalists were assigned to the consular section and 26.6 percent to the political section. At the same time, only 16.4 percent of male generalists were assigned to the consular section while 43.2 percent were placed in the political section. Additional data indicate that 40.4 percent of the women originally assigned to the political section were transferred into the consular section, compared to only 15.5 percent of the men.[44] In 1970, to counter discrimination, a handful of US foreign service women formed the Women's Action Organization to lobby for changes in the State Department. In 1976, nine members filed a sex discrimination suit that challenged virtually all the hiring, assignment, evaluation, and promotion practices of the US foreign service.[45] The suit took nine years to come to trial. But in a landmark decision (*Palmer et al. v. Baker,* 1987),[46] the court found a purposive pattern of discrimination against women. Under pressure, the Department of State began to make adjustments. Table 6.1 compares the number of women in the US foreign service in 1970 and 1989.

For the period 1990–1993, 38 percent of the 676 entering officers were women. At the upper end of the spectrum, in 1993, about 10 percent of the US chiefs of mission were women, and about one-third of all the candidates on the 1993 list of nominations for promotion to the senior foreign service were women.[47] In August 2002, out of 160 ambassadors on the State Department list (including both career officers and political appointees), 29 were women

Table 6.1   Women in the US Foreign Service, 1970 and 1989

	December 1970		December 1989	
Rank	Number of Women Foreign Service Officers	Women as Percentage of Total	Number of Women Foreign Service Officers	Women as Percentage of Total
Senior (SFS)	23	2.1	54	6.9
Middle (FS 1–3)	261	8.2	777	20.4
Junior (FS 4–6)	1,409	37.9	1,231	34.7

Source: Nancy E. McGlen and Meredith Reid Sarkees, *Women in Foreign Policy* (New York: Routledge, 1993), p. 76.

(18.13 percent).[48] In December 2007, out of 182 chiefs of mission (again including both career officers and political appointees), 45 were women (24.73 percent).[49]

It must be taken into account that life at post can be difficult for women diplomats with young families—and this does not help to enlarge the pool of available women candidates. Indeed, it is hard for mothers to combine diplomatic duties and family responsibilities. It is difficult for all career mothers to meet professional and family obligations, but it is much more difficult in some foreign locations: 60 percent of US embassies and consulates are designated "hardship posts." Initially, the United States sent its women ambassadors exclusively to European locations. In the 1960s, however, women began to be posted wherever needed, even where they faced political turmoil, guerrilla warfare, poor hospitals, substandard schools, and oppressive weather.[50]

Furthermore, children must make new friends with each relocation, and the differences in language and culture make the transition even more difficult. Relocation may be especially difficult for teenagers. Some in fact are left back home—but is it "home" for them? Wendy Chamberlin, US ambassador to Pakistan, resigned her post in May 2002 to rejoin her two teenage daughters, who had been separated from her because of security concerns.[51] Many women are nevertheless accepting the challenge, and they are succeeding in their diplomatic roles. Even countries that refuse to let women enter careers usually held by men have worked with foreign women diplomats in their capitals. The United States, for example, regularly assigns women ambassadors to countries in the Middle East. Many of these women, in fact, believe that being women gives them an advantage, principally in allowing them to speak bluntly to male officials, as their words are not perceived as threats.[52]

They have found it easier than men to ask men for advice and information. They can more freely speak and consult with local women and thus achieve a better understanding of the social conditions and all manner of humanitarian issues. Ann Miller Morin, in her extensive study of women ambassadors, concluded that they "have been viewed as more caring, more interested, more approachable, more believable," and noted that "it is not uncommon for a woman ambassador to be fondly remembered by the people years after she has left the country."[53] It seems that diplomacy worldwide is adjusting to the gender transformation. Discrimination is still widespread, but women are increasing their presence in the diplomatic field.[54] Their example is helping women in more restrictive societies to achieve greater freedom.

Foreign service officers who marry within the foreign service may experience serious complications. The United States now has a policy of trying to keep the spouses in the same location, which helps. But if both rise in rank and are in the same line of work, being posted in the same embassy becomes difficult. For example Carol Laise was US ambassador in Katmandu, Nepal. In

1967, her new husband, Ambassador Ellsworth Bunker, was assigned to Saigon, where wives were not allowed because of the war in Vietnam—and the war determined his schedule. They saw each other occasionally.[55]

Diplomatic Wives

For women, marrying a diplomat used to mean marrying the foreign service as well. In the United States this was perceived as "two for the price of one." Diplomatic wives were expected to host dinners and parties, undertake public diplomacy in the host capital, involve themselves in the local community, visit orphanages, and do other charitable work.[56] Some wives of diplomats of higher rank used their status to lord it over the wives of diplomats of lower rank. The diplomatic lore is full of tales of "dragon ladies" making other wives miserable. In the US foreign service, the performance of the diplomatic wife was officially evaluated and taken into account when her husband was up for promotion.

The gender revolution of the 1960s significantly changed the outlook of Western wives, and eventually spread, although not evenly, to the East among other diplomatic wives. But even in Western nations, different perspectives can be observed. Some wives retain the traditional outlook, finding fulfillment in working with their husbands in all the established diplomatic functions. It is teamwork, sharing life at post. It is also a matter of pride in serving one's country. Others accept the obligations but resent having to serve without being paid for their considerable efforts or given compensation for such items as the new dresses required to remain socially respectable. One ambassador's wife, Betty Atherton, in Cairo, Egypt, insisted on having an office in the embassy, where she took care of her own responsibilities and coordinated the various receptions and dinners that she and her husband hosted, programs for entertaining the spouses of official visitors, and coordinating duties with the family liaison officer. She kept track of all the hours she spent "on the job," just for the record. She also attended embassy staff meetings (for which she had to obtain security clearance). She was unpaid, of course. "What I do," she said, "more than anything else, is consciousness raising."[57]

Other wives, perhaps younger and closer to the "now generation," assert their independence at post and cut off all ties with the embassy and their husbands' jobs. They aggressively seek their freedom. Some have their own professions and want to continue with their own pursuits. But even this attitude has various forms of expression. Some are willing to attend certain functions, if they fit into their own professional schedule or suit their lifestyle; but they do not want to be controlled by the embassy.[58]

In 1972 the State Department officially changed the rules. Henceforth, wives were on their own. They would no longer be treated as unpaid department employees, and their performance would no longer be mentioned in their husbands' personnel files or efficiency reports.[59] The new policy was initially hailed as an important first step in eliminating many of the injustices of the past, but eventually there was a backlash. Formal independence would not change the continuing demands of foreign service life. Much of the work still had to be done, if only for the sake of their husbands,[60] but it would no longer be acknowledged by the State Department. The official partnership (essentially exploitive) was terminated. There is no easy remedy for the hardships inherent in the foreign service lifestyle. A number of diplomatic wives want to support their husbands' careers, they want to remain involved, they find meaning in serving their country—but they want their services and hard work to be recognized, and continue their efforts to obtain better status from the State Department.[61]

In 1993, US senator Joseph Biden told the Senate Foreign Relations Committee: "One of the things we vastly underestimate in this government is the sacrifices that spouses, male or female, make, allowing career diplomats to pursue their careers. I am of the view, and I am in a distinct minority, that . . . an ambassador's spouse should be paid, because they are required, as a matter of course, to provide certain duties and functions on behalf of the United States government. In short, their entire life is consumed by the job."[62] Interestingly, also in 1993, a federal appeals court declared First Lady Hillary Rodham Clinton a "*de facto* officer or employee" of the government; and Jewell Fenzi commented that this was "the first time the judiciary extended official recognition to the role of the spouse."[63] More and more women are trying to continue their own professional pursuits abroad. But the periodic changes imposed by relocation, and the different social, cultural, and economic settings, sometimes hinder professional continuity. The foreign environment tends to add to the challenge, particularly in the less developed countries.

Each foreign service has addressed the problems of the diplomatic wife in its own way according to its own culture.[64] In the United States, the Association of American Foreign Service Women has long worked with the US government to provide assistance; its efforts led to the creation, within the State Department, of the Family Liaison Office in 1978, which provided counseling on such matters as employment abroad, schools, divorce, and medical and mental health.[65] The Foreign Service Institute in Washington, D.C., has made its resources available to spouses, including language training, area studies, career workshops, and seminars on the impact on family life of overseas assignments and reentry into the United States.[66] Indeed, some American children, raised at various posts abroad, feel like immigrants when they finally arrive in their own country.

But even when foreign ministries are accommodating, non–foreign service husbands may experience problems as well. Most have a career of their own, which may not travel so readily. Some host states freely permit diplomatic spouses to practice their careers, but eventually, diplomats are sent to a different country and the working spouses, male or female, must relocate and find a new way to maintain their professional status. Some states (including the United States) rotate diplomatic assignments every three to four years. In the end, many spouses remain separated for extended periods. Some, however, find imaginative ways to cope with relocation. For example, a young South African consul posted in Chicago told me that her husband was having a wonderful time. He loved golf. Eventually, perhaps without giving up the golf course, he decided to earn a master's degree in business administration during his wife's tenure, and they both enjoyed what life had brought them. Non–foreign service husbands, being a relatively new species, are not included in the tradition of "spousal service" at post.

▓ Changing Style of Interaction

Since the end of World War II, the international system has changed drastically. It was inevitable that the style of diplomatic interaction would evolve, pushed by events and necessity, different perceptions, and changing lifestyles. Tradition is still acting as a brake, a moderating force. But the profession cannot be held to its old ways. More nations interact, and newcomers bring to the table their different ways.[67] In the end, the diplomatic profession has proved rather versatile.

Diplomatic style is changing. While the diplomatic profession remains addicted to a good deal of pomp and formality, a combination of factors— including modern culture, practicality, and time pressures—is fostering change. Much streamlining is occurring in the way things are done.[68] Economic constraints, too, are playing a part. The traditional lavishness of diplomatic functions has been considerably toned down, although some missions still feel the need to outshine others. Many countries, even the very affluent, are trying to spend less, and the United States is one of them. Max Finger, a member of the US permanent delegation at the UN, recalled that in the mid-1960s, "except for the Russians, there was no other large country on as tight an entertainment budget as the United States. . . . We had to resort to various stratagems. . . . For two successive years, we entertained delegates to the Fourth (Decolonization) Committee by having a wine-tasting party, with free wine and cheese provided by the California Wine Growers Association."[69] A reduction in the volume of social functions would undoubtedly help (and few diplomats would miss them).[70]

Many diplomatic meetings are more businesslike, with a minimum of formality. International organizations, the UN in particular, contribute their own style of parliamentary diplomacy, essentially pragmatic. While issues are being debated, some representatives may be seen negotiating in the aisles in small groups of four or five, or huddled at another delegate's desk and planning their voting strategy. Moments of levity by the chair are not infrequent and may bring laughter among the large number of assembled delegates. The atmosphere is often reminiscent of large academic meetings. The diplomats may refer to each other as "the distinguished delegate from such and such country," but otherwise the style is very laid-back. The language today is often more blunt than in the past, particularly in open forums, even occasionally angry and aggressive—hardly what used to be called "diplomatic."[71]

Diplomacy becomes even less formal and unstructured when the presiding officer, seeing that the assembled delegates are not reaching agreement in the business at hand, resorts to a period of "informal consultation" (perhaps thirty to forty-five minutes), right then and there, in the assembly hall, with the delegates moving about and negotiating with their colleagues to find a solution. Multilateral diplomacy (see Chapter 8) is fostering a new style involving debates and votes, numerous deadlines on specific items of business, and a very fluid process. For example, it is not unusual that some issue may be put to a vote much sooner than expected, leaving no time to obtain new instructions from one's home office.[72]

A multilateral setting also invites diplomatic interaction across diplomatic ranks. In a given committee, an ambassador may interact with a junior diplomat, since each diplomatic delegation decides how to deploy its diplomats. There is a greater division of labor among the members of a delegation, hence a greater need to coordinate the efforts of these diplomats so that a country may speak with the same voice, more or less. Diplomacy here is more conspicuously teamwork, and the participants need to learn new roles. What is done in multilateral forums ultimately influences diplomacy elsewhere, particularly when streamlined procedures prove effective. Multilateral work is expanding and more diplomats are being exposed to its style.[73]

▧ Ideology

Ideology affects the diplomatic profession.[74] However, much depends on the values held and the extent to which decisionmakers are intent on their promotion.[75] Shared ideology may facilitate international agreement (although we know how people of the same political persuasion can often find occasion to disagree). Ideological *conflict,* on the other hand, can lead to profound polarization, as was seen during the Cold War. The normal task of diplomats is to permit communication, to maintain a dialogue across political, cultural, and ideological boundaries. This implies an ability to work with people of different persuasions, to compromise, and to seek common ground, which in turn implies a good deal of pragmatism. Polarization implies the opposite. Polarization emphasizes differences. Ideological polarization tends to make diplomatic work more difficult.

When governments give ideologically rigid instructions, diplomats experience greater difficulty reconciling international differences. There are times when the diplomats themselves are swayed by ideology and become less capable of maintaining any form of dialogue with their counterparts. Ideology has pernicious tendencies. In the name of dedication to a value system, it may encourage intolerance and parochialism.[76] Ideology creates barriers. Diplomats are of course entitled to their own value preferences, but they have to be able to work with people who may not share these values. Ideology may foster tunnel vision—an inability to perceive what is not encompassed by the ideology. In more extreme cases, the international situation is seen exclusively through the distorted lens of the ideology. Moreover, ideological zeal often infuses an emotional dimension into political situations, complicating the diplomatic dialogue and negotiation process.[77]

Since the end of the Cold War, the role of ideology in international affairs has diminished. Though we no longer have a bipolar system, many facets of international relations remain affected by other ideological elements, such as various forms of nationalism and conservatism, or by other political values raised to the level of ideology, such as democratic versus undemocratic, North versus South, globalization versus antiglobalization (as manifest during the riots in Seattle), and religious fundamentalism versus secularism.[78] Thus diplomats are still confronted by ideological stances in their work, which makes dealing with the problems at hand more difficult. Ideologically oriented governments are likely to seek representatives to defend (with appropriate conviction) their rigid positions in international forums.

Ideology can derail negotiations by forcing the participants to confront issues totally foreign to the subject matter of the meeting. This is what political science calls "politicization." Some delegations push their ideological agenda and envenom the proceedings, to the point that the focus of the discussion is altogether changed. Cold War and North-South conflict, for example, have prevented discussion of important questions that had nothing to do with those ideological issues. But occasions are taken to give one more hearing to the same old arguments. Diplomatic work is indeed more difficult in a polarized ideological setting.

▓ Public Diplomacy

Public diplomacy (i.e., public relations) is now an extension of the diplomatic mission (see Chapter 7 in this volume). Governments expect their diplomats to reach out to the public, speak before local organizations and universities, and remain in contact with opinion leaders.[79] Public diplomacy is thus making diplomats more accessible.[80] Of course, the extent to which public diplomacy can be carried out varies with the nature of the host country. In closed societies, very little is feasible. Attempts to bypass state controls lead to official protests and strain diplomatic relations. In open societies, many embassies have media specialists on their own staffs. They maintain professional media sections whose task it is to develop intimate knowledge of communication in the host country and good media contacts.[81] Major powers obviously have a significant advantage in getting their story to the public because of their prominence and impact on the course of events. Smaller powers need to be more imaginative and work harder to interest the media.

Ambassador Allan Gotlieb of Canada noted that "the new diplomacy, as I call it, is, to a large extent, public diplomacy and requires different skills, techniques, and attitudes than those found in traditional diplomacy."[82] The growing diplomatic interest in public opinion is demonstrated also by the manner in which consulates are used to reach out beyond the national capital. Many countries have consulates in the major commercial centers of the host country. All of them engage in a regional form of public relations, which is easier to carry out because of their knowledge of the area and the contacts they have developed in the local communities.[83]

Diplomats in international organizations, particularly the United Nations, are doing some public diplomacy of their own, although seldom comparable to the outreach functions of the regular embassies in national capitals. The media cover the activities of these organizations as well as the open debates in which diplomats discuss international issues and the policies of their governments. Reporters remain in contact with many delegates, often as part of a mutually beneficial relationship.[84] With the increasing significance of public opinion and of civil society, with its NGOs and transnational ties, it is to be expected that public diplomacy will increase in importance, probably changing the diplomatic profession still further.

▓ Diplomatic Immunities

Diplomatic immunity is one of the oldest diplomatic institutions. Often misunderstood by the public, diplomatic immunities are important because diplomats are called upon to maintain contacts between international actors that are frequently at odds with one another. They have to deal with political issues that are often delicate, to say the least. Moreover, diplomats in resident missions need to live for extended periods of time in foreign societies that operate under very different legal systems and political institutions. They need special protection. Governments understand the basic usefulness of these immunities and reciprocity has ensured their observance.[85] International law adds to their legitimacy.

In 1961, a UN treaty, the Vienna Convention on Diplomatic Relations, codified existing international law on the subject.[86] Diplomats cannot be arrested or prosecuted, no matter what their offenses may be; they cannot be forced to testify in court proceedings, unless their home state waives their immunities. The host state may expel them (declaring them *persona non grata*).[87] However, this is generally perceived as drastic action, and the sending state is usually offended by the measure. Under normal relations, states simply ask for the recall of the offending diplomat, but they tend to be cautious and do it sparingly, anxious as they are to protect their diplomatic relations.

Diplomats are exempt from host state taxation as well as from import duties on what they bring into the country.[88] Diplomatic premises are immune, and cannot be entered by the public authorities without permission (contrary to popular belief, diplomatic premises remain part of the sovereign domain of the host state). Diplomatic documents, correspondence, and means of communication cannot be tampered with. Couriers are protected. Diplomatic residences are equally immune, and so is the property of diplomatic personnel, including their automobiles. Members of the families of diplomatic agents forming part of their households enjoy the same privileges and immunities. Administrative personnel enjoy almost the full extent of these immunities (but service personnel—e.g., chauffeurs and servants—are immune only for actions undertaken in the performance of their duties). Diplomatic immunities are thus extensive.[89]

However, as the international system changes, some of the rules will eventually need to be revised. A number of international conventions have been negotiated covering the special needs of international organizations and their personnel, most particularly headquarters agreements regulating the elaborate relationship between the main offices and the host states. As well, the number of persons entitled to diplomatic immunities has vastly increased, as there are more states and even more international organizations employing diplomatic agents today than in the past.

One problem has been that some diplomats are abusing their privileges and immunities. It is clearly and formally acknowledged in international law that diplomats must respect the laws and regulations of the host state.[90] However, because they are immune from any type of local enforcement action or judicial process in the host country (unless their immunities are waived by the sending state), some diplomats choose to act irresponsibly, often outside the exercise of their official functions. It is the responsibility of the sending state to take corrective measures or appropriate disciplinary action. Some states, however, turn a blind eye to the misdeeds of their diplomatic agents. Receiving states, in practice, tend to show a great deal of tolerance, preferring to avoid friction in their diplomatic relations over what they consider minor issues (i.e., in the context of world affairs).[91] Local authorities and the public, however, take a dimmer view of the matter and are quick to vent their outrage and frustration (see Box 6.2).

Abuses are not limited to parking violations. Unpaid rent. damaged living quarters, drunken driving and related accidents, sexual assaults, repeated acts

---

**Box 6.2   New York City vs. UN Diplomats
(and the US Department of State)**

New York City is the scene of a continuing battle between City Hall (supported by the irate public) and the United Nations. Parking in Manhattan is typically a nightmare. Diplomats make it worse: they leave their cars wherever it serves their purpose—in loading zones, in driveways, double parked in traffic lanes, and worse, in total disregard of the chaos they create. In 1996, New York City reported 116,345 unpaid parking tickets. The judicial system, of course, cannot touch them, as diplomatic cars enjoy diplomatic immunity (signaled by "DPL" license plates).

In March 1997, in a public ceremony, New York City signed an agreement with the US Department of State. The city promised to provide 111 more parking spaces to UN missions, and the State Department pledged to rescind the license plates of diplomatic cars whose tickets were not paid within the year. This caused much public rejoicing.

Within days of the agreement, however, diplomats were in an uproar and a storm of protest was coming from the United Nations. The UN's Office of the Legal Adviser issued an opinion that the agreement violated international law, and the UN Secretary-General appealed to the US government to consider the concerns of the diplomatic corps. The State Department backed down and Mayor Rudolph W. Giuliani angrily denounced this breach of faith and accused the US government of cowering before the UN. The mayor acknowledged that the city had no way to force the State Department to honor the agreement. The battle continues.

Sources: U.S. News & World Report, April 14, 1997, p. 44; David Firestone, "For Now, Peace Has No Chance: Parking Ticket Uproar at the UN," *New York Times,* April 11, 1997, pp. A1, A16.

---

of vandalism by teenage children of diplomats, drug traffic, and rarely even murder all of these are shielded from host state law enforcement because of diplomatic immunity.[92] Such a situation generates angry and widespread attacks against this form of diplomatic protection.[93] These abuses are in fact harmful to the diplomatic profession and occasionally cause a backlash. A number of parliaments,[94] responding to public resentment and outcry on the occasion of the more dramatic incidents (particularly resulting in the death of innocents),[95] have taken steps to restrict diplomatic immunities or have adopted countermeasures of their own. For example, in 1995, in the wake of persistent public complaints, the US Congress passed a law to withhold foreign aid from countries that failed to pay their court fines.[96]

Foreign ministries and (not surprisingly) the diplomatic profession have been staunch supporters of diplomatic immunities. They have repeatedly warned that strong unilateral measures of redress will lead to retaliation and a reduction of diplomatic protection for their own diplomats. For example, in the wake of an investigation of diplomatic abuses by the Foreign Affairs Committee of the British House of Commons in 1984,[97] the British government responded: "Alleged cases of serious offences should be kept in perspective. As the Committee noted, they are comparatively small in percentage terms. For instance in 1983 . . . the 15,000 or so persons entitled to diplomatic immunity for acts of a personal nature were allegedly responsible between them for 59 serious offences."[98]

This is fairly typical of government responses. Foreign ministries tend to see diplomatic abuses as a small price to pay for immunities they consider indispensable. However, comparatively few as they may be, these incidents cause a great deal of resentment and anger (even on a national scale in the more outrageous cases) in the receiving states, and they give a bad image to the profession. Laxity in enforcing proper standards of behavior encourages delinquent diplomats to flout the system more blithely. Without resorting to drastic measures in the margin of international law, foreign ministries can do much more to enlist the support and cooperation of sending states. No government can derive any benefit from being represented by individuals who make a nuisance of themselves at post.

A problem that foreign ministries take more seriously pertains to abuses of diplomatic-bag privileges—that is, making use of diplomatic protection (exemption from inspection) to engage in illicit traffic in narcotics, firearms, rare antiquities, and assorted prohibited items.[99] In 1984, the Nigerian embassy in London even stuffed a man into a diplomatic crate—he had been kidnapped by Nigerian agents and was to be returned to Nigeria.[100] The UN International Law Commission was given the task to study changes in the status of the diplomatic courier and diplomatic bag, to be introduced as revisions to the 1961 Vienna Convention on Diplomatic Relations. But no agreement was achieved.[101] Most governments readily concede that they are not prepared to revise the convention or reduce existing immunities.[102]

However, governments are now showing caution when invited to expand diplomatic immunities. In the late 1960s, considering that nations were making more extensive use of special missions, the UN International Law Commission examined what immunities these diplomats could be entitled to, following which, in 1969, the Convention on Special Missions (the New York Convention) was negotiated.[103] Few governments, however, ratified it.[104]

Governments remain under pressure to correct diplomatic abuses, which regrettably are still widespread.[105] There is a trend to interpret the 1961 Vienna Convention more restrictively[106] and to enforce its provisions more effectively, consistently, and in nondiscriminatory fashion (see, for instance, discussion of the Abisinito incident in Box 6.3). The functional approach to immunities (explicitly endorsed by the Vienna Convention) is sound: namely, immunities "to ensure the efficient performance of the functions of diplomatic missions."[107] Many of the immunities that need tightening have no bearing on the efficient performance of diplomatic duties. Should a diplomat's dependent be allowed to use a car with diplomatic plates (and a full set of immunities) to run personal errands and double-park with impunity in traffic lanes, or worse? Under the 1961 convention, some restrictions have been formulated. For example, a diplomat will not enjoy immunity with regard to any commercial activity in the receiving state outside his or her official functions.[108] More restrictions of this nature are needed.

Some countries have devised remedies for victims of diplomatic abuses, such as government funds to compensate landlords for thousands of dollars in unpaid (and otherwise unrecoverable) rent. The United States requires diplo-

---

Box 6.3   The Abisinito Incident: Prosecution of Ambassador for Unofficial Acts

About fifteen minutes past midnight, on Friday, February 13, 1987, Ambassador Kiatro Abisinito of Papua New Guinea was driving his car in Washington, D.C., on Wisconsin Avenue. As the police report stated, he was "obviously drunk"—in fact so drunk that he crashed into the rear of a parked car in which two people were sitting. The ambassador was traveling so fast that his car then caromed off two empty cars on the opposite side of the avenue, jumped a sidewalk, hit another car waiting at an intersection, and bounced back across the avenue, until it was stopped by a small brick wall. The two people in the parked car were injured—one of them, Stephen Hagan, critically. Abisinito was also injured and released from the hospital the following day.

The police charged him for his reckless driving, and agreed with State Department officials that Abisinito could not be prosecuted because of his diplomatic immunity. Instead, the chief of the Office of Foreign Missions at the State Department immediately revoked Abisinito's driving permit. But interestingly, the State Department did not stop there. On the same day, it requested the district attorney to prepare a criminal case against Ambassador Abisinito, "the first time the State Department had ever made such a request" (foreign offices have, as a rule, shied away from meaningful action; the response, in this case, was unusual). Though the ambassador could not be prosecuted at that time because of his immunity, he could be prosecuted later if he decided to return to the United States in a private capacity. The government's action was intended to serve as a warning to the members of the diplomatic community: when appropriate, others would be charged.

continues

Box 6.3   Cont.

Abisinito was recalled by his government, and he announced that he would leave by February 24. The Papuan embassy, however, referring to the 1961 Vienna Convention regarding a diplomat's immunity from criminal jurisdiction, conveyed its government's request for assurances that any criminal investigation or indictment of the former ambassador would be quashed. The State Department rejected the embassy's requests, stating (in a long-overdue conclusion) that "the Vienna Convention . . . makes clear that the immunities of former diplomats do not subsist in respect of acts that, during the period of performance of diplomatic functions, were not performed in the exercise of functions as a member of the mission." Eventually, Hagan recovered and, seventeen months after the incident, he and the Papua New Guinean government reached a negotiated, out-of-court settlement reported to be in excess of $200,000.

While this kind of response remains exceptional, if consistently applied, it would probably reduce indefensible behavior by diplomatic agents. One may wonder, however, whether this welcome kind of toughness would be applied to diplomats from countries deemed more important to the United States.

Sources: Grant V. McClanahan, *Diplomatic Immunity: Principles, Practices, Problems* (New York: St. Martin's, 1989), pp. 132–136; *Washington Post,* February 14, 1987; *Washington Post,* February 15, 1987; *American Journal of International Law* 81, no. 3 (October 1987), pp. 937–939; *Washington Post,* July 30, 1988.

mats who drive to carry liability insurance, so that victims of accidents caused by diplomatic personnel will be able to gain compensation. Britain imposes a similar rule.[109] In fact, in a memorandum to diplomatic missions in London, the British government specified that "a failure by a diplomat to hold third-party insurance for himself or any member of his family who drives a car is likely to lead to a request for his transfer from the United Kingdom."[110]

Such measures, of course, are only palliatives—to compensate victims of diplomatic abuses. What is needed, if the 1961 convention cannot be revised, or if better rules cannot be included in a new convention, is a greater sense of responsibility on the part of the foreign ministries of *both* sending states and receiving states. In the sending states, greater effort is needed to recruit and train more professional foreign service officers who will represent their government abroad with greater pride and responsibility and refrain from the demeaning behavior that leads them to abuse immunity. A foreign service that tolerates even a minority of officers who commit such acts displays a strange sense of national service or duty, considering the kind of impression these individuals leave abroad (witness the anger and resentment reported regularly by the media in national capitals). In the receiving states, greater diligence is needed in enforcing the law, using the means provided in the international conventions. Diplomacy can only benefit from a greater effort to curb irresponsible behavior (see Box 6.4).

Box 6.4   UN Withdrew Immunity of Four in 2004 Shooting

The United Nations withdrew the immunity of four Jordanians working for the international organization in Kosovo, thus making them subject to the local judicial process. This occurred when another Jordanian opened fire on a group of Americans in April 2004. Two were killed and ten were wounded. Prior to UN action, detectives had been unable to speak to the four Jordanian detainees because of their immunity.

Source: New York Times, April 20, 2004, p. A4.

■ **Security Consequences of
Political Unrest and Terrorism**

Diplomats face greater physical danger today because of the widespread political instability found in so many parts of the world. Depending upon how widespread the violence is in a given country and the political character of the rebellion, embassies and diplomats experience great risk. It is often a matter of being caught in the crossfire of the contending parties (rather than being targeted)—being in the wrong place at the wrong time, as happened to Ambassador Melissa Wells, who faced death several times in the chaos following the 1979 removal of dictator Idi Amin in Uganda (see case study at the end of this chapter).

An important source of insecurity is the widespread use of terrorism, often as an instrument of revolutionary warfare.[111] Embassies and diplomats have been targeted with substantial frequency in the past four decades. The reasons for such attacks vary widely: to make the headlines and publicize a cause, to embarrass the host government (since it is the host government's responsibility to protect diplomatic facilities), or to retaliate for certain actions of the sending state. The embassies and diplomats of some countries (e.g., Israel and the United States) are more frequently attacked than those of others.[112] Nevertheless, between 1968 and 1983, diplomats from 113 countries were attacked; among them, 23 ambassadors from thirteen countries were assassinated.[113] Diplomats are at risk even when their own embassy is not targeted (see Box 6.5).

Diplomatic facilities may be attacked even in countries in which there is no conflict. Terrorists and revolutionaries network and travel with considerable ease.[114] A target may be chosen simply because it is more vulnerable (e.g.,

---

Box 6.5   Diplomats as Hostages in Lima, Peru

December 17, 1996. Fourteen Tupac Amaru guerrillas forced their way into the Japanese ambassador's residence and captured the guests at a diplomatic reception in Lima, and demanded that the Peruvian government release 400 guerrillas captured in previous confrontations. President Alberto Fujimori was determined not to make any concessions, but opened negotiations. Gradually, the guerrillas, to simplify their task, released hundreds of hostages, retaining only seventy-two, including senior Peruvian officials, Fujimori's brother, foreign diplomats, and the Japanese ambassador.

Britain, Germany, Israel, and the United States all offered to help in a rescue attempt. Fujimori was under intense pressure to resolve the matter, but he refused to act hastily and started preparing methodically for a rescue operation by Peru's own special forces as the negotiations dragged on for 126 days. The hostages were confined to the second floor of the residence. Humanitarian agencies and the Red Cross were allowed to meet some of their needs.

The government brought professional miners to dig tunnels and provide as many as six different points of access for a rescue attempt. To prevent the terrorists from hearing the construction work, the Peruvian forces played martial music at full volume day and night outside the residence. This was also intended to keep the captors from sleeping and to undermine their resolve. During the standoff, listening devices were smuggled into the building, some hidden in a guitar and a thermos bottle that Red Cross workers were allowed to deliver; others were placed in buttons in clothing brought to the hostages.

continues

---

the US embassy in Nairobi, Kenya, a country with no history of terrorism).[115] The world is now faced with a growing phenomenon of transnational terrorism.[116] The birth of Al-Qaida in the early 1990s, with its global struggle against secular states, vastly increases the risks.[117] However, the popularity of diplomatic targets varies over time. Although terrorism statistics are unreliable (because there is no certainty as to what is counted as an act of terrorism), the number of international terrorist incidents involving diplomats from all countries increased dramatically in the early 1980s compared to the prior decade, according to the US Department of State (see Table 6.2). The worst year of the 1970s was 1979, with 180 attacks. In 1980 the total jumped to 273. In the early 1980s, about 54 percent of all terrorist attacks were directed against diplomats.[118] Incidents involving diplomats are now less frequent, but the numbers remain quite substantial (see Table 6.3).

Box 6.5   Cont.

The devices enabled the authorities to monitor all the movements of terrorists and hostages, and to note patterns of behavior. It was determined that each afternoon at about 3:00 P.M., the rebels played soccer in the huge ground-floor living room and stacked their weapons in a corner of the room. Meanwhile, the government's special forces were training for the rescue operation in mockups of the building. During the final four days, intelligence agents posing as doctors brought in miniature two-way radios that permitted communication with the military and police commanders who were hostages.

At 3:10 P.M. on the day of the rescue operation, the listening devices indicated that at least eight of the captors were playing soccer. The hostages were alerted by the miniature radios to take cover. Explosives were set off in the tunnel directly under the room where the terrorists were playing, killing four of them and opening a hole through which the troops could pour in. Other members of the special forces entered from the upper floor after scaling the walls with the help of the hostages, and shot all the guerrillas who were climbing the stairs to kill the hostages. Only one of the hostages died, reportedly of a heart attack. All the terrorists died in the assault.

It was one of the most precisely executed rescue operations on record, and a huge success for President Fujimori. But it was a trying experience for the hostages throughout the four months of this episode—something that diplomats everywhere unfortunately run the risk of facing.

Sources: Cindy C. Combs, *Terrorism in the Twenty-First Century,* 3d ed. (Upper Saddle River, NJ: Prentice-Hall, 2003), pp. 232–234; Martin F. Herz, ed., *Diplomats and Terrorists: What Works, What Doesn't* (Washington, DC: Institute for the Study of Diplomacy, School of Foreign Service, Georgetown University, 1982).

The 1961 Vienna Convention on Diplomatic Relations specifies that the host state "shall take all appropriate steps to prevent any attack on [the diplomat's] person, freedom, or dignity."[119] But history demonstrates that protecting *anyone* or *anything* from terrorist attacks is a very difficult task (see Box 6.6). Most capitals are hosts to a multiplicity of embassies located in the heart of the city; diplomats move about and attend public functions; and diplomats' residences are widely dispersed.[120]

In the wake of the second destruction of the US embassy in Beirut in a car bomb attack (September 1984),[121] members of Congress called for greater US embassy security. The State Department appointed an eight-member special advisory panel on overseas security, which in June 1985 judged almost half of the 262 US embassies and consulates around the world as being too vulnerable to espionage or terrorist attack and recommended their renovation or replacement. The report recommended that over the successive seven years, 75

Table 6.2   Attacks and Threats Against Diplomats, 1968–1982

	Number of Attacks	Number of Threats
1968	69	11
1969	69	10
1970	162	42
1971	109	36
1972	139	61
1973	106	68
1974	119	17
1975	116	15
1976	133	41
1977	127	28
1978	179	86
1979	180	61
1980	273	136
1981	239	128
1982	215	189

Source: US Department of State, Office for Combating Terrorism, reported in Natalie Kaufman Hevener, ed., *Diplomacy in a Dangerous World: Protection for Diplomats Under International Law* (Boulder: Westview, 1986), p. 69.

embassies and consulates should be abandoned and rebuilt at new locations. Another 50 were to be substantially improved or rebuilt on-site. In addition, 210 offices of other US agencies (e.g., Foreign Commercial Services, and US Agency for International Development) were to be restructured or replaced. The cost would be a minimum of $3.5 billion (in 1985 dollars) to be spread over at least five budget years.[122]

Over the years the State Department was given less than one-third of the money needed and the security measures were carried out piecemeal. On August

Table 6.3   Attacks Against Diplomats, 1995–2003

	Number of Attacks
1995	22
1996	24
1997	30
1998	35
1999	69
2000	30
2001	18
2002	14
2003	15

Sources: US Department of State, *Patterns of Global Terrorism* (Washington, DC, various years), http://www.state.gov/s/ct/rls/crt, "Chronology of Significant International Terrorist Incidents." *Note:* Threats were not included in the Department of State's tabulations.

**Box 6.6   US Diplomat and Driver Shot Dead in Sudan
on January 1, 2008**

John Granville, thirty-three, a US diplomat in Sudan, and his driver were
shot to death around 2:30 A.M. Granville was being driven home in an up-
scale neighborhood in central Khartoum, the capital, after attending a New
Year's Eve party at the British embassy. Gun crime is rare in Khartoum,
considered one of the safest cities in Africa.

A Sudanese government official said that the attack appeared well
planned. The assailants' car sped in front of the diplomat's car shortly before
he reached his home, cutting it off. Two gunmen got out of their car; one of
them shot Granville and the other shot the driver. Seventeen shots were
fired.

The United Nations had recently warned its staff in Sudan that there
was credible evidence of a terrorist cell in the country that was planning to
attack foreigners. Granville had been serving in Sudan as well as in Nairobi,
Kenya, for about ten years and took great pleasure in his work.

Source: New York Times, January 2, 2008, p. A8.

7, 1998, the US embassies in Nairobi, Kenya, and Dar es Salaam, Tanzania,
were destroyed in coordinated attacks. Intelligence reports of impending attacks
led to the temporary closing of the US embassies in Albania, Kuwait, Ghana,
Togo, and Malaysia. Twice in the months before the bombing and total destruction of the embassy in Nairobi, Ambassador Prudence Bushnell had requested a
relocation of the embassy. She had pointed out that the embassy was located on
a major thoroughfare in the heart of the capital and was so vulnerable that it was
impossible to protect. Her request was denied for budget reasons.[123]

Once again, the State Department sent a commission of counterterrorism
specialists to inspect US embassies and consulates around the world to determine which were most vulnerable. "Once upon a time, you wouldn't worry so
much about embassy security in a nation like Kenya, which has no history of
terrorism," one of the officials observed.[124] Embassies may now be targeted
anywhere in the world. The State Department recommended that the government spend $14 billion over the next decade. President Bill Clinton asked for
$568 million for the first year. In July 1999, the House of Representatives ap-
proved $1.4 billion for embassy security; the Senate approved $300 million. It
will be a while before overseas posts can be more secure.[125] Many countries
will undoubtedly make do with a high degree of vulnerability.

States can provide special training for their diplomatic personnel who are
scheduled to work in regions particularly threatened. Terrorism specialists out-
line strategies to avoid being taken hostage. They recommend vigilance and

suggest various steps to achieve greater personal protection. They also teach techniques for survival after being captured.[126] Moorehead Kennedy, who was held in the US embassy in Iran in 1979–1980, complained that the State Department's training program in this respect was inadequate.[127] In short, diplomats today are much more exposed and at risk than in the past. States have frequently made sweeping pronouncements against terrorists in hopes of deterring future action (and probably also to pacify public opinion). Practitioners have cautioned governments against making threats or announcing policies that they may be unable to implement. The United States, for example, has over the years repeated that the first element of its antiterrorist policy is that it "will make no concessions to individuals or groups holding official or private U.S. citizens hostage. . . . It is U.S. Government policy to deny hostage takers the benefits of ransom, prisoner releases, policy changes, or other acts of concessions."[128] But concessions have occasionally been made (e.g., return of Iran's frozen assets for the release of the US hostages), and then explained away or rationalized. In any case, terrorists are rarely deterred by threats.

States need to achieve greater international cooperation to combat terrorism. However, international efforts were initially controversial, as many nations, particularly in the third world, sympathized with the national liberation movements that frequently resorted to this form of violence. Widespread attacks against diplomats and foreign businesspeople in Latin America, however, led the Organization of American States (OAS) in 1971 to implement the Convention to Prevent and Punish the Acts of Terrorism Taking the Form of Crimes Against Persons That Are of International Significance.[129] Importantly, this convention specified that these crimes "shall be considered common crimes of international significance, regardless of motive," which made it possible for the contracting parties to extradite or punish the alleged perpetrators.[130] Most extradition treaties exclude crimes committed for a political end, which usually means that terrorists cannot be extradited.[131]

The 1972 effort by the United States to negotiate a generic convention in the UN General Assembly for the prevention and punishment of terrorism failed, but revealed that a large number of states were concerned about the protection of their diplomats. In response, in 1973, the Assembly endorsed the Convention on the Prevention and Punishment of Crimes Against Internationally Protected Persons, Including Diplomatic Agents. The important element in this convention is Article 7, in which, as in the 1971 OAS convention, the parties pledged either to extradite alleged offenders or to punish them: "The State Party in whose territory the alleged offender is present shall, if it does not extradite him, submit *without exception whatsoever* and without undue delay, the case to its competent authorities for the purpose of prosecution, through proceedings in accordance with the laws of the State."[132]

Also relevant are the European Convention on the Suppression of Terrorism (1977),[133] the International Convention Against the Taking of Hostages (1979),[134] the Convention on the Safety of United Nations and Associated Personnel

(1994),[135] and the International Convention for the Suppression of Terrorist Bombings (1997).[136] Unfortunately, a country's desire to enforce the law can be selective.[137] Failure to apply a treaty to which it is a party is a breach of obligation. But countries are accustomed to finding excuses. Legal sanctions can be sought, but political considerations frequently intervene and application of the law is less than guaranteed. This is one of the problems of international society. Moreover, better enforcement will not eliminate terrorist attacks against diplomats. Terrorism is easy to carry out. It disrupts and makes an impact on target governments. The diplomatic profession will thus remain at risk for the foreseeable future and be compelled to find new ways to carry out its mission.

▧ Case Study: The Story of Ambassador Melissa Wells

This is the story of a woman in the US foreign service; the problems she encountered as the service was changing; the hurdles that made her life a challenge; the hardships, even the dangers, inherent in this type of work; and the courage and stamina needed to proceed with her assignments while raising two young children and fighting a painful parasitic disease picked up during one of her overseas assignments.[138] Her career is a clear demonstration of the contribution that women have made—and are now making in much larger numbers as the US foreign service evolves and adjusts to changed circumstances. Other countries are slowly making similar adjustments.

She was born Meliza Foelsch in Estonia in 1932, the daughter of a physicist and a professional singer.[139] Her mother took the whole family to Hollywood in the 1930s to star in MGM films, showing an inclination for adventure, or at least the unconventional, which Melissa herself would show later in her foreign service career. Melissa was raised in California and Mexico, and completed two years at a Catholic women's college. Six feet tall and strikingly beautiful, she entered show business as a showgirl and synchronized swimmer in a traveling troupe. She was interested in the foreign service and when the troupe went broke in Europe, she was admitted by the School of Foreign Service at Georgetown University in Washington, D.C., working her way through as a secretary. She graduated *cum laude* in 1956. After passing the proverbially challenging exam, she entered the foreign service in 1958. Within two years, she married a foreign service officer, Alfred Wells. Unexplainably, she was not asked to resign. The matter was being challenged and it may well be that the State Department was ready to abandon this tradition (as discussed previously concerning Elinor Constable's 1958 challenge of the legality of this practice). Nor did Melissa volunteer to resign.

Her marriage deteriorated and her husband was transferred to London. With an infant dependent, she was retained in the service and sent to Trinidad, which her biographer reported as a post suitable for a single-parent family, an

Trinidad she was sent to Paris, and on to London, where she and her ex-husband were reconciled. She gave birth to a second son and became the first woman officer to have a baby at post, although this was not considered to be so unusual a situation in the private sector. Her husband retired from the foreign service to study architecture, which reduced their family housing and other allowances from his class 2 level to that of her class 5.[141] To complicate matters, she discovered that there were no family allowances for a woman officer. Women, at the time, were far from established in the system. But she fought that battle and won.

US Ambassador to Guinea-Bissau, Cape Verde, and the United Nations

After five years in the service, she was promoted to class 3 and arranged for her transfer to Brazil as commercial counselor, where she learned to speak Portuguese—eventually an important factor in her being chosen to become, in 1976, the first US ambassador to Guinea-Bissau, a small country of about half a million people in West Africa that had become independent from Portugal in 1974. Simultaneously, she was appointed ambassador to Cape Verde, an island state of some 200,000 people, 300 miles offshore, that had also received its independence from Portugal, in 1975.[142]

It is not unusual for an ambassador to be accredited simultaneously to two or three countries, usually small, so long as the receiving states raise no objection.[143] This sort of representation means more careful juggling of one's timetable and more traveling. She opened both posts under difficult conditions, not altogether surprising in countries recently independent after long political struggles and wars of national liberation with former colonial powers. Ambassador Wells quipped that her first office in Cape Verde was a park bench.[144] While in this post she met Andrew Young, President Jimmy Carter's new permanent representative at the UN, and a strong advocate for African nations, who stopped in Bissau for a visit. Soon after his return to New York, he offered Melissa Wells the post of US delegate to the Economic and Social Council (ECOSOC), with the rank of ambassador (ECOSOC is one of the six main organs of the United Nations).[145] She left Africa in 1977 and found her new assignment in New York very demanding as she confronted the enormous pressure to address issues that multiplied with incredible speed (see Chapter 8).[146] She found the work useful, but she liked to joke that this was the only assignment she had ever had in trench warfare (because it felt like somebody was always shooting at her).[147] There was indeed a great deal of North-South confrontation at the time, especially in the economic and social development field.

The pace was dizzying and very different from the well-focused bilateral work of an embassy. There was never enough time. The work was more complex, as the diplomats were required to deal with many different players, including the very influential UN Secretariat. The pace was even more hectic during the three months of the annual meeting of the General Assembly, when everyone operated on tight deadlines. Importantly, Melissa Wells found her knowledge of foreign languages always helpful. She knew French, German, Italian, Spanish, and Portuguese. She noted that most of her foreign counterparts preferred to speak English, until they discovered that she had lived or worked in their country and could speak their language. She found that it created a little bond. They would go back to using English, but her effort at communicating in their language showed care and appreciation. It was a human touch. And she certainly made good use of all her language skills.

At this point in her career, Melissa was suffering from a parasite infection she had picked up during her assignment in Brazil: cysticercosis. The parasite migrated to her brain, causing a serious inflammation and excruciating headaches. She was in and out of hospitals, undergoing one test after another, for a year (cysticercosis is an extremely rare occurrence in New York). When the disease was finally diagnosed, she found that no cure was available for it. But as she put it, she learned to live with it.

Senior UN Representative in Uganda

After two and a half years at UN headquarters, Melissa needed a change. Now, however, she had the problem of obtaining her medical clearance. Bradford Morse, director of the UN Development Programme (UNDP) at the time, offered her the post of senior UN representative in Uganda, East Africa. In this post she would no longer be working for the US State Department. She therefore needed a secondment, meaning that she would be, so to speak, "on loan" to the UN and could eventually return to State once her UN assignment was over (in her previous post at ECOSOC, she had served as US representative). She could not obtain her medical clearance until a parasitologist was called in by the State Department. She was eager to go to Uganda and convinced him that she must get on with her life—and he let her go. The pain did not disappear, but she was determined not to let it control her existence.

Uganda was dangerous. It was her most difficult assignment. She arrived after the notorious President Idi Amin had been ousted. The country had fallen into a state of total anarchy. The police had all been eliminated. The Uganda Liberation Army and the Tanzanian Army, which removed Amin from power, were in charge, more or less. But there were no resources—no money or food—to support an army. The soldiers had their weapons and lived off the land. No one controlled them.[148] Melissa Wells was the senior UN official in Uganda monitoring UNDP activities. She also became Special Representative of the Secretary-General (SRSG) and was in personal danger.[149] Once while she was being driven home to Entebbe from Kampala, the capital, a car moved alongside hers. Men were at the windows with pistols and ordered her driver to stop. They dragged him

out and beat him and then ordered her out of the car. (Two weeks earlier, a Canadian priest had been killed on the same road.) But they did not shoot her. They
jumped into the car and drove away. It was dark, and it was a long time before
anyone stopped to give her and her driver assistance. But they were both alive.[150]

Another time, while being driven to Kenya, a soldier ordered her driver to
stop the car. There was a man bleeding on the side of the road. The driver
stopped and gunfire started. The soldier jumped into the front seat and ordered
the driver to pull away. People were shooting at the car. An ambush had taken
place just as Melissa's car arrived; the soldier wanted to flee as fast as he
could. Again, she and her driver were not harmed.[151] The UN was trying to
help Uganda, and Melissa was involved in relief operations. The situation was
so dangerous that her family had to live in the neighboring country of Kenya,
in Nairobi. It was of course difficult for them, knowing that she was exposed
to danger. Her job required traveling in Uganda. There were roadblocks everywhere, and at every roadblock she literally had to negotiate her way through,
giving the liberation handshake, trying to convince the armed men that she
was on their side and that she presented no threat to the new regime. A difficult time indeed. From all this experience, Melissa concluded that women can
often deal with stress better than men in such situations.[152]

She found the UN to be very helpful in reviving Uganda, in fact more so
than national governments in taking the needed initiatives, such as a police-
training program she started. National governments were uncooperative; the
UN opened doors and provided the needed facilities. When her Uganda assignment was over, she transferred to Geneva to work on a new UN program.
However, in early 1985, a whole new set of symptoms emerged, and she had
to return to her doctors in New York. A new experimental drug had been developed, but it was a risky treatment. She was an outpatient at the National Institute of Health, in Bethesda, Maryland, for six or seven months—but the results were spectacular: she did not have headaches anymore.

The State Department was interested in reviewing her secondment status.
She had served at the UN for seven years and was interested in getting back to
diplomatic work for the United States. But she told her review committee that
she wanted "an interesting post"—in other words, a post with a lot of action.
And the committee obliged. In 1986, she was nominated by the secretary of
state to the post of ambassador to Mozambique. She was delighted, as Africa
had long fascinated her.

US Ambassador to Mozambique and Zaire

Her confirmation, however, got caught in the crossfire of Washington politics.
Senator Jesse Helms was strongly opposed to the State Department's policy in
Mozambique and he held up her confirmation in an attempt to force the United

States to recognize a rebel group, Renamo, that was fighting to topple the current regime. Secretary George Schultz, however, supported her. The standoff lasted eleven months, until September 1987, setting a new record for the longest confirmation. Melissa was excited about her new job. Mozambique was among the least-developed nations, with the world's lowest per capita gross national product,[153] a failing Marxist-Leninist regime, and a destructive fifteen-year civil war in which some 100,000 Mozambicans had been killed. Children were being abducted to become soldiers, and 1,200,000 people had become refugees.[154] Her friends could not understand why she wanted to go there. But the challenge of the situation appealed to her.

She was helped in this difficult assignment by her confirmation problems. By the time she arrived in Mozambique, she was well-known. Jesse Helms, the supporter of Renamo, had lost. She was a hero. She was admired. Parents were naming their daughters after her. All this publicity opened doors for her, and her performance on the job increased her popularity. She spoke Portuguese and was experienced in Africa, knowledgeable about Mozambique, and endlessly energetic. The government was ready to abandon its Marxist-Leninist trappings and had started a new economic policy determined by market forces. Melissa helped this transition. The peace talks remained disappointing, but a new commitment to political pluralism was created.

In 1991 she left her post in Mozambique to become ambassador to Zaire (eventually renamed the Congo), another destabilized country, another challenge to her energy and ingenuity. The situation continued to deteriorate. Against a background of rapid inflation and ever more strident political criticism at home and abroad, President Mobutu Sese Seko maneuvered steadily to hold on to power. In September 1991, soldiers went on a rampage in Kinshasa, the capital, demanding higher pay. French and Belgian troops were flown in to protect foreign nationals. The United States suspended aid to Zaire.[155] A national conference convened to study constitutional change elected Mobutu's most prominent opponent as prime minister. In 1993, Mobutu appointed a different prime minister. The country now had two prime ministers and was headed for chaos, with unpaid troops rioting and extorting money from businesspeople. Many lives were lost, including that of the French ambassador. Unending political turmoil had a disastrous impact on the economy,[156] and Melissa was brought home in 1993.[157]

No doubt Melissa could have sought easier posts, but she wanted the challenge. Deep down, she probably liked the excitement, although there were times when these posts provided too much of it. Melissa Wells is a marvelous example of what women can contribute to the foreign service. Worldwide, diplomacy is being transformed. Though it is still an uphill battle in many countries, women are taking their place in the profession—accepting the adventures and the hardships—and establishing their presence in international relations.

▧ Study Questions and Discussion Topics

1. What are the causes of transformation in the diplomatic profession?
2. What is the meaning of "diplomacy by nondiplomats"? Is this an appropriate characterization?
3. What is the role of women in diplomacy today? How does it affect the diplomatic process?
4. What are the benefits of noncareer political appointments? What are the pitfalls?
5. Why is there now talk about "professional diversity" in the field of diplomacy? What does it mean? How does it affect the conduct of diplomacy?
6. Is the increasing need for experts and nonpolitical specialists hampering the diplomatic process?
7. In what ways can diplomats exercise leadership?
8. Is it likely that abuse of diplomatic immunities will decline?
9. Are the media a blessing or a curse for contemporary diplomacy?

▧ Suggested Reading

Barker, J. Craig. *The Abuse of Diplomatic Privileges and Immunities: A Necessary Evil?* Brookfield, VT: Dartmouth, 1996.

Center for Strategic and International Studies, Advisory Panel on Diplomacy in the Information Age. *Reinventing Diplomacy in the Information Age.* Washington, DC, 1998.

Fasulo, Linda M. *Representing America: Experiences of U.S. Diplomats at the UN.* New York: Praeger, 1984.

Finger, Seymour Maxwell. *American Ambassadors at the UN: People, Politics, and Bureaucracy in Making Foreign Policy.* 2d ed. New York: Holmes and Meier, 1988.

————. *Inside the World of Diplomacy: The U.S. Foreign Service in a Changing World.* Westport: Praeger, 2002.

Frey, Linda S., and Martha L. Frey. *The History of Diplomatic Immunity.* Columbus: Ohio State University Press, 1999.

Herz, Martin F., ed. *Diplomacy: The Role of the Wife. A Symposium.* Washington, DC: Institute for the Study of Diplomacy, Edmund A. Walsh School of Foreign Service, Georgetown University, 1981.

Kennan, George F. "Diplomacy Without Diplomats?" *Foreign Affairs* 76, no. 5 (September–October 1997), pp. 198–212.

McGlen, Nancy E., and Meredith Reed Sarkees. *Women in Foreign Policy.* New York: Routledge, 1993.

Morin, Ann Miller. *Her Excellency: An Oral History of American Women Ambassadors.* New York: Twayne, 1995.

Smith, Gerard C. *Disarming Diplomat: The Memoirs of Gerard C. Smith, Arms Control Negotiator.* New York: Madison, 1996.

Stearns, Monteagle. *Talking to Strangers: Improving American Diplomacy at Home and Abroad.* Princeton: Princeton University Press, 1996.

▓ Notes

1. George F. Kennan, "Diplomacy Without Diplomats?" *Foreign Affairs* 76, no. 5 (September–October 1997), pp. 198–212.

2. Paul Sharp, "Who Needs Diplomats? The Problem of Diplomatic Representation," in *Diplomacy,* edited by Christer Jönsson and Richard Langhorne (London: Sage, 2004), vol. 3, *Problems and Issues in Contemporary Diplomacy,* pp. 58–78; Brian Hocking and David Spence, eds., *Foreign Ministries in the European Union: Integrating Diplomats* (New York: Palgrave Macmillan, 2006).

3. For example, the Convention on the Privileges and Immunities of the United Nations (1946), the Agreement Between the United Nations and the United States of America Regarding the Headquarters of the United Nations (1947). Lori F. Damrosch, Louis Henkin, Richard Crawford Pugh, Oscar Schachter, and Hans Smit, *International Law: Basic Documents Supplement,* 4th ed. (St. Paul, MN: West Group, 2001), pp. 605–615; and other headquarters agreements.

4. Damrosch et al., *International Law,* pp. 1628–1637.

5. (Lord) Gore-Booth, ed., *Satow's Guide to Diplomatic Practice,* 5th ed. (New York: Longman, 1979), pp. 76–160, esp. chap. 19, "Special Missions," pp. 158–160. The Convention on Special Missions, usually known as the New York Convention on Special Missions, was adopted by the UN General Assembly on December 8, 1969. But the major powers, including the United States, have refused to ratify it, as they fear that its application would cause too many administrative difficulties. Ibid., p. 157. The convention entered into force on June 21, 1985; but as of December 31, 2006, only thirty-eight states were parties to it. Louis Henkin, Richard Crawford Pugh, Oscar Schachter, and Hans Smit, *International Law: Cases and Materials,* 3d ed. (St. Paul, MN: West Group, 1993), pp. 1210–1211; and United Nations, *Multilateral Treaties Deposited with the Secretary-General of the United Nations* (New York: United Nations, 2008).

6. Hans Binnendijk, "Tin Cup Diplomacy," in *The Future of American Foreign Policy,* edited by Eugene R. Wittkopf and Christopher M. Jones, 3d ed. (New York: St. Martin's, 1999), pp. 279–282.

7. Bruce Russett, Harvey Starr, and David Kinsella, *World Politics: The Menu for Choice,* 7th ed. (Belmont, CA: Wadsworth, 2004), app. B. One hundred twenty-four states were created after World War II.

8. See research done by the US Institute of Peace for its series on negotiating styles: for example, Scott Snyder, *Negotiating on the Edge: North Korean Negotiating Behavior* (Washington, DC: US Institute of Peace, 1999), http://www.usip.org.

9. Arabic, Chinese, English, French, Russian, and Spanish. See World Health Organization, *Use of Languages in WHO,* fifty-fourth annual World Health Assembly, A54/INF.DOC/2, April 2001, http://www.who.int/gb. Translation costs become a major consideration.

10. See Monteagle Stearns, *Talking to Strangers: Improving American Diplomacy at Home and Abroad* (Princeton: Princeton University Press, 1996), pp. 72–85.

11. See also Harold Nicolson, *The Evolution of Diplomatic Method* (London: Constable, 1954), pp. 52–53.

12. Elmer Plischke, "Career Status of United States Diplomats," in *Modern Diplomacy: The Art and the Artisans,* edited by Elmer Plischke (Washington, DC: American Enterprise Institute for Public Policy Research, 1979), pp. 297–304. See also Elmer Plischke, *U.S. Department of State: A Reference History* (Westport: Greenwood, 1999), pp. 393–654.

13. Martin F. Herz, "Maxwell Gluck and All That," in *The Modern Ambassador: The Challenge and the Search*, edited by Martin F. Herz (Washington, DC: Institute for the Study of Diplomacy, School of Foreign Service, Georgetown University, 1983), pp. 96–104. See also "Ambassadorships: Findings of the Watergate Committee" (US Senate, Select Committee on Presidential Campaign Activities, final report, 1974), in Herz, *Modern Ambassador*, pp. 105–109.

14. Ellis O. Briggs, "This Is a Professional Game," in Herz, *Modern Ambassador*, pp. 146–153. See also Malcolm Toon, "In Defense of the Foreign Service," in Herz, *Modern Ambassador*, pp. 154–162.

15. Martin F. Herz, "Who Should Be an American Ambassador?" in Herz, *Modern Ambassador*, pp. 163–166.

16. Clare Boothe Luce, "The Ambassadorial Issue: Professionals or Amateurs?" in Herz, *Modern Ambassador*, pp. 128–136; Gerald C. Smith, "Non-Professional Diplomats: Do We Need Them?" in Herz, *Modern Ambassador*, pp. 168–170; and Martin F. Herz, "Some Principles Regarding Appointments," in Herz, *Modern Ambassador*, pp. 171–176.

17. See Ivor Richard, "The Council President as a Politician," in *Paths to Peace: The UN Security Council and Its Presidency*, edited by Davidson Nicol (New York: Pergamon, 1981), pp. 242–254.

18. Depending on the political system. Francis O. Wilcox, assistant secretary of state for international organization affairs, once counted fifty-five US government agencies involved in international affairs. Linda M. Fasulo, *Representing America: Experiences of U.S. Diplomats at the UN* (New York: Praeger, 1984), p. 46. Governmental structures vary over time.

19. Center for Strategic and International Studies, Advisory Panel on Diplomacy in the Information Age, *Reinventing Diplomacy in the Information Age* (Washington, DC, 1998), p. 31.

20. See http://www.dol.gov/ilab.

21. R. P. Barston, *Modern Diplomacy*, 2d ed. (New York: Longman, 1997), pp. 173–175.

22. A. LeRoy Bennett and James K. Oliver, *International Organizations: Principles and Issues*, 7th ed. (Upper Saddle River, NJ: Prentice-Hall, 2002), pp. 416–424; Lawrence Ziring, Robert Riggs, and Jack Plano, *The United Nations: International Organization and World Politics*, 4th ed. (Belmont, CA: Wadsworth, 2005), pp. 138–145.

23. Bennett and Oliver, *International Organizations*, pp. 424–438; Ziring, Riggs, and Plano, *United Nations*, pp. 145–156.

24. The European Union now does.

25. Robert W. Cox, Harold K. Jacobson, et al., *The Anatomy of Influence: Decision Making in International Organization* (New Haven: Yale University Press, 1974). See also Ziring, Riggs, and Plano, *United Nations*, pp. 145–159; Robert S. Jordan, ed., *International Administration: Its Evolution and Contemporary Applications* (New York: Oxford University Press, 1971).

26. See Michael Edwards and John Gaventa, *Global Citizen Action* (Boulder: Lynne Rienner, 2001); and Chapter 5 in this volume. See also Ann M. Florini, "Lessons Learned," in Ann M. Florini, ed., *The Third Force: The Rise of Transnational Civil Society* (Washington, DC: Carnegie Endowment for International Peace, 2000), pp. 211–240.

27. See, for example, Richard W. Stevenson, "The Chief Banker for the Nations at the Bottom of the Heap," *New York Times*, September 14, 1997, sec. 3, pp. 1, 13.

28. Jessica T. Mathews, "Power Shift," *Foreign Affairs* 76, no. 1 (January–February 1997), pp. 56–58, 63–66. Richard J. Barnet and Ronald E. Müller, "Corporate Diplomacy and National Loyalty," in Richard J. Barnet and Ronald E. Müller, *Global Reach: The Power of the Multinational Corporation* (New York: Simon and Schuster, 1974), pp. 72–104.

29. In the UN General Assembly, each diplomatic representative (when there are enough of them) specializes in one of the six main committees: disarmament and international security; politics and decolonization; economics and finance; social, humanitarian, and cultural affairs; administrative and budgetary affairs; and legal affairs. See http://www.unsystem.org/ga/56/index.

30. See, for instance, the composition of the US delegation to the World Food Conference (Rome, 1974) in Edwin M. C. Martin, *Conference Diplomacy: A Case Study—The World Food Conference, Rome, 1974* (Washington, DC: Institute for the Study of Diplomacy, School of Foreign Service, Georgetown University, n.d.), pp. 31–33.

31. Adam Watson, *Diplomacy: The Dialogue Between States* (New York: Routledge, 1982), p. 121.

32. I observed this phenomenon while working with a group of US industrial experts on a mission to France dealing with the French shoe industry.

33. See Gerard C. Smith, *Disarming Diplomat: The Memoirs of Gerard C. Smith, Arms Control Negotiator* (New York: Madison, 1996).

34. Harold Nicolson, *Diplomacy,* 3d ed. (New York: Oxford University Press, 1964), pp. 28–40. See also François de Callières, *On the Manner of Negotiating with Princes,* translated by A. F. Whyte (Washington, DC: University Press of America, 1963 [1716]).

35. See, for example, CSIS, *Reinventing Diplomacy:* "The culture of diplomacy must be overhauled to make it more accessible and participatory" (p. xii); "Reform the culture of diplomacy by discouraging secrecy and exclusivity" (p. xiii).

36. Geoffrey Wiseman, "Pax Americana: Bumping into Diplomatic Culture," *International Studies Perspectives* 6, no. 4 (November 2005), pp. 409–430. See also Lawrence E. Harrison and Samuel P. Huntington, *Culture Matters: How Values Shape Human Progress* (New York: Basic, 2001).

37. Robert L. Borosage, "Money Talks: The Implications of U.S. Budget Priorities," in *Global Focus: U.S. Foreign Policy at the Turn of the Millennium,* edited by Martha Honey and Tom Barry (New York: St. Martin's, 2000), pp. 5–9. For an example of financial constraints in the field, see Arthur Goldberg's problem as US permanent representative at the UN, reported in Seymour Maxwell Finger, *Your Man at the UN: People, Politics, and Bureaucracy in Making Foreign Policy* (New York: New York University Press, 1980), p. 166. See also Warren Christopher, "Obtaining the Resources to Lead," *In the Stream of History: Shaping Foreign Policy for a New Era* (Stanford: Stanford University Press, 1998), pp. 316–317.

38. See, for example, Gore-Booth, *Satow's Guide,* sec. 20.8, pp. 162–163.

39. Published as "The Woman Diplomat," *UNITAR News* (1975), pp. 37–42.

40. Ibid., p. 37.

41. Ibid.

42. Ann Miller Morin, *Her Excellency: An Oral History of American Women Ambassadors* (New York: Twayne, 1995), p. 291, n. 2.

43. Larger numbers were found in the lower ranks. Ibid., pp. xi, 1. See also J. Workman, "Gender Norming," *New Republic* 205, no. 1 (July 1, 1991).

44. James M. Scott and Elizabeth A. Rexford, "Finding a Place for Women in the World of Diplomacy: Evidence of Progress Toward Gender Equity and Speculation on Policy Outcomes," *Review of Public Personnel Administration* 17, no. 2 (Spring 1997), pp. 31–56.

45. Workman, "Gender Norming."

46. *Palmer et al v. Baker,* 662 E. Supp. 1551 (D.C. Cir. 1987), and *Palmer et al v. Baker,* remedial order (D.C. Cir. 1989), cited in Scott and Rexford, "Finding a Place," n. 10. Discussed in Nancy E. McGlen and Meredith Reid Sarkees, *Women in Foreign Policy: The Insiders* (New York: Routledge, 1993), pp. 65–66.

47. Morin, *Her Excellency,* pp. 271, 276. See also Workman, "Gender Norming."

48. See http://www.state.gov/r/pa/ei/biog.

49. Ibid. The difference in the total number of officers is unexplained. The data for 2002 refer to "ambassadors," compared to "chiefs of mission" for 2007. Not all chiefs of mission are ambassadors. In both cases, some posts were vacant. The total number of vacancies was not the same for 2002 and 2007, but this would account only for a small discrepancy between the two periods.

50. *New York Times,* July 22, 2002, pp. A1, A7. See also the case study on Melissa Wells in the revolutionary environment of Uganda, at the end of this chapter. Morin, *Her Excellency,* pp. 217–220.

51. In the months that followed the war in Afghanistan, Al-Qaida and Taliban fighters remained a threat. A *Wall Street Journal* reporter was murdered, and there was a growing threat of war between India and Pakistan *New York Times,* July 22, 2002, pp. A1, A7.

52. Morin, *Her Excellency,* pp. 272–273.

53. Ibid., p. 273.

54. Phyllis E. Oakley. "Paving the Way for Women: Department of State 2002," in *Inside a U.S. Embassy: How the Foreign Service Works for America,* edited by Shawn Dorman, rev. ed. (Washington, DC: American Foreign Service Association, 2005), pp. 129–130.

55. "Dedicated Public Servant: Caroline Clendening Laise (1917–1991) (Nepal, 1966–1973)," in Morin, *Her Excellency,* pp. 71–72.

56. See, for example, comments by Wendelgard von Staden, wife of a German foreign service officer, and by Mariko Kitahara, wife of a Japanese diplomat, in Martin F. Herz, ed., *Diplomacy: The Role of the Wife—A Symposium* (Washington, DC: Institute for the Study of Diplomacy, School of Foreign Service, Georgetown University, 1981), pp. 5–8, 32–36.

57. Herz, *Diplomacy,* pp. 13–14.

58. See, for instance, ibid., pp. 5–8, 18–22, 24–30, 54–56. See also Edward P. Lazear et al., "Women in the Labor Market," *Journal of Economic Perspectives* 3, no. 1 (Winter 1989), pp. 3–75.

59. Herz, *Diplomacy,* p. 1.

60. See comments by Penelope B. Laingen, in Herz, *Diplomacy,* p. 71.

61. Jewell Fenzi, *Married to the Foreign Service: An Oral History of the American Diplomatic Spouse* (New York: Twayne, 1994), "A Future for the Foreign Service Spouse?" pp. 231–234.

62. Ibid., pp. 261–262.

63. Ibid., p. 262.

64. "Diplomacy would be foolish, I thought, not to take advantage of the new role that wives could play. Diplomacy, this great art of interpretation across frontiers, between different mentalities . . . would simply have to adapt to the new age of technology that has created a new species of wives," said Wendelgard von Staden, wife of a

German foreign service officer, herself a former member of the German foreign service. Herz, *Diplomacy,* p. 8.

65. Herz, *Diplomacy,* p. 4. See also Joan Pryce's experience as the employment program coordinator in the family liaison office, discussed in Fenzi, *Married to the Foreign Service,* pp. 259–260.

66. Herz, *Diplomacy,* p. 37.

67. See research done by the US Institute of Peace for its series on negotiating styles: for example, Snyder, *Negotiating on the Edge.*

68. See, for example, Herz, *Modern Ambassador,* pp. 32–59.

69. Finger, *Your Man at the UN,* p. 166.

70. Diplomats call these activities "representational duties."

71. See Grant V. McClanahan, *Diplomatic Immunity: Principles, Practices, Problems* (New York: St. Martin's, 1989), "Blurring Diplomatic Traditions and Declining Standards of Diplomatic Courtesy," pp. 142–146.

72. Diplomatic representatives need to adjust to this different environment, and even develop new skills. See Finger, *Your Man at the UN,* esp. pp. 306–310. See also Linda M. Fasulo, *Representing America: Experiences of U.S. Diplomats at the UN* (New York: Praeger, 1994).

73. See Bennett and Oliver, *International Organizations.* See also Chapter 8 in this volume.

74. Watson, *Diplomacy,* pp. 69–81.

75. Sterling, *Macropolitics,* pp. 156–202. See also Hans Kohn, *Nationalism* (New York: Van Nostrand, 1955), and Crane Brinton, *The Shaping of Modern Thought* (Englewood Cliffs, NJ: Prentice-Hall, 1963).

76. Sterling, *Macropolitics,* pp. 161–171.

77. Watson, *Diplomacy,* pp. 78–79.

78. Juergen Kleiner, "Diplomacy with Fundamentalists: The United States and the Taliban," *The Hague Journal of Diplomacy* 1, no. 3 (November 2006), pp. 209–234.

79. Jarol B. Manheim, *Strategic Public Diplomacy and American Foreign Policy: The Evolution of Influence* (New York: Oxford University Press, 1994), pp. 3–35.

80. Jan Melissen, ed., *The New Public Diplomacy: Soft Power in International Relations* (New York: Palgrave Macmillan, 2006); Kathy R. Fitzpatrick, "Advancing the New Public Diplomacy: A Public Relations Perspective," *The Hague Journal of Diplomacy* 2, no. 3 (October 2007): 187–211.

81. R. S. Zaharna, "The Soft Power Differential: Network Communication and Mass Communication in Public Diplomacy," *The Hague Journal of Diplomacy* 2, no. 3 (October 2007), pp. 213–228.

82. CSIS, *Reinventing Diplomacy in the Information Age,* p. 35.

83. Martin F. Herz, ed., *The Consular Dimension of Diplomacy* (Washington, DC: Institute for the Study of Diplomacy, School of Foreign Service, Georgetown University, 1983), pp. 17–19. See discussion on creation of "American Presence Posts," and "The Consular Function," in Chapter 7; see also Box 7.1.

84. Thomas G. Weiss, David P. Forsythe, and Roger A. Coates, *The United Nations and Changing World Politics,* 2d ed. (Boulder: Westview, 1997), p. 88.

85. Linda S. Frey and Marsha L. Frey, *The History of Diplomatic Immunity* (Columbus: Ohio State University Press, 1999).

86. Damrosch et al., *International Law,* pp. 574–583. A companion treaty, the 1963 Vienna Convention on Consular Relations, codified this part of international law.

87. It can do so at any time, without having to provide any explanation.

88. Some restrictions apply to taxation. See Article 34 of the 1961 convention.

89. The rules of application are, in many respects, detailed. The 1961 convention has forty-seven articles, many with elaborate sections and subsections.

90. Article 1 of the 1961 Vienna Convention. Barry E. Carter and Phillip R. Trimble, eds., *International Law: Selected Documents* (Boston: Little, Brown, 1991), p. 283.

91. In 1986, the British government reported 71 minor offenses and 22,331 unpaid parking fines. It also reported 41 serious offenses, including 24 cases of drunken driving and related serious accidents. Its foreign office requested the recall of 17 diplomats. J. Craig Barker, *The Abuse of Diplomatic Immunities: A Necessary Evil?* (Brookfield, VT: Dartmouth, 1996), p. 151. Local citizens often complain that their government is much too tolerant of the misbehavior of diplomats as they are the ones who suffer the consequences (e.g., damage to private property and nonpayment of personal debts).

92. A great deal has been published on such abusive behavior. See, for example, McClanahan, *Diplomatic Immunity,* tabs. 1–2, pp. 170–171. See also Dror Ben-Asher, *Human Rights Meet Diplomatic Immunities: Problems and Possible Solutions* (Cambridge: Harvard Law School, November 2000), p. 3, and nn. 75, 168, 176, 180, 183; Charles B. (Chuck) Ashman and Pamela Trescott, *Diplomatic Crime: Drugs, Killings, Thefts, Rapes, Slavery, and Other Outrageous Crimes* (Washington, DC: Acropolis, 1987).

93. McClanahan, *Diplomatic Immunity,* pp. 165ff.; Ben-Asher, *Human Rights,* n. 297; John Shaw, "Privilege of Diplomatic Immunity Facing Challenges from All Sides," *Washington Diplomat* (March 2002), p. 1, http://www.washingtondiplomat.com; Frey and Frey, *History of Diplomatic Immunity,* chap. 12, "Diplomacy and the New Barbarism," pp. 479–538.

94. For example, in the United Kingdom, Germany, the Netherlands, the United States, Canada, Japan, and Australia. Ben-Asher, *Human Rights,* n. 310.

95. For example, a shooting at a crowd of protesters from the Libyan embassy in London in 1984 during which a policewoman (Yvonne Fletcher) was killed. McClanahan, *Diplomatic Immunity,* pp. 5–6.

96. *Insight on the News* 13, no. 4 (February 3, 1997), p. 42.

97. Barker, *Abuse of Diplomatic Privileges;* Ben-Asher, *Human Rights,* n. 63.

98. Barker, *Abuse of Diplomatic Privileges,* p. 147. See also Rosalyn Higgins, "UK Foreign Affairs Committee Report on the Abuse of Diplomatic Immunities and Privileges: Government Response and Report," *American Journal of International Law* 80 (1985), p. 135.

99. See, for instance, William R. Slomanson, *Fundamental Perspectives on International Law,* 4th ed. (Belmont, CA: Wadsworth, 2003), pp. 333–334.

100. Umaru Dikko, an outspoken Nigerian dissenter in exile in London, was wanted by the Nigerian government. He was drugged and packed into a crate with appropriate diplomatic identification (the "diplomatic bag" for the purpose at hand). At the airport, however, the crate was heard to moan and some diplomats had a lot of explaining to do. McClanahan, *Diplomatic Immunity,* p. 159.

101. Ben-Asher, *Human Rights,* n. 307. See also Stephan C. McCaffrey, "Current Development: The Thirty-Eighth Session of the International Law Commission," *American Journal of International Law* 81 (1987), p. 677.

102. See, for example, the 1985 British government report in Barker, *Abuse of Diplomatic Privileges:* "Given the difficulties in the way of achieving any restrictive amendment to the Convention, and the doubtful net benefit to the UK of so doing, it would be wrong to regard amendment of the Vienna Convention as the solution to the problem of abuse of diplomatic immunities" (p. 136).

103. Gore-Booth, *Satow's Guide,* pp. 156–160.

104. As of 2006, only thirty-eight states were parties to (i.e., bound by) this convention. United Nations, *Multilateral Treaties*. See Chapter 9 in this volume for more discussion on special missions. See also McClanahan, *Diplomatic Immunity*, p. 142; Gore-Booth, *Satow's Guide*, pp. 157–158; Frey and Frey, *History of Diplomatic Immunity*, pp. 499–501.

105. McClanahan, *Diplomatic Immunity*, pp. 160–161.

106. Frey and Frey, *History of Diplomatic Immunity*, pp. 481–486, 501; McClanahan, *Diplomatic Immunity*, pp. 3–4, 142.

107. Preamble to the 1961 Vienna Convention. See Eileen Denza, *Diplomatic Law: A Commentary on the Vienna Convention on Diplomatic Relations*, 2d ed. (Oxford: Clarendon, 1998); James Parkhill, "Diplomacy in the Modern World: A Reconsideration of the Bases for Diplomatic Immunity in the Era of High-Tech Communications," *Hastings International and Comparative Law Review* 21 (1988), pp. 565–596.

108. Article 31 of the 1961 Vienna Convention.

109. Leslie Shirin Farhangi, "Insuring Against Abuse of Diplomatic Immunity," *Stanford Law Review* 38, no. 6 (July 1986), pp. 1517–1547. See also *Dickinson v. Del Solar* (1930), 1 K.B. 376, in which the court held that an insurance company cannot rely on the immunities of a diplomat in order to escape a legal liability for which the insurance company has agreed to provide indemnification or compensation. William W. Bishop Jr., *International Law: Cases and Materials*, 2d ed. (Boston: Little, Brown, 1962), p. 594.

110. Barker, *Abuse of Diplomatic Privileges*, p. 156.

111. See "Terrorism Around the World," in Clifford E. Simonsen and Jeremy R. Spindlove, *Terrorism Today: The Past, the Players, the Future* (Upper Saddle River, NJ: Prentice-Hall, 2000), pp. 73–296.

112. Often because of the controversial nature of their initiatives and tendency to make enemies.

113. Including the US ambassadors to Lebanon, Cyprus, Sudan, Guatemala, and Afghanistan. Paul Wilkinson, *Terrorism and the Liberal State*, 2d ed. (New York: New York University Press, 1986), p. 263.

114. On networking, see Gabriel Weimann, *http://www.terror.net: How Modern Terrorism Uses the Internet*, Special Report no. 116 (Washington, DC: US Institute of Peace, March 2004).

115. *New York Times*, September 8, 1998, p. A6. The embassy was bombed on August 7, 1998.

116. J. Bowyer Bell, *Transnational Terrorism* (Washington, DC: American Enterprise Institute for Public Policy Research, 1975).

117. Jonathan R. White, *Terrorism*, 4th ed. (Belmont, CA: Wadsworth, 2003), pp. 291–296; Daniel Benjamin, Martha Crenshaw, and Daniel Byman, *Global Terrorism After the Iraq War*, Special Report no. 111 (Washington, DC: US Institute of Peace, October 2003).

118. Wilkinson, *Terrorism*, p. 263.

119. Article 29. See Damrosch et al., *International Law*, p. 578.

120. See J. Craig Barker, *The Protection of Diplomatic Personnel* (Burlington, VT: Ashgate, 2006).

121. The embassy in Beirut was first destroyed in April 1983 and then relocated. *New York Times*, September 21, 1984, pp. 1, 8, 9. The US embassy in Kuwait was also destroyed in a terrorist attack.

122. *New York Times*, June 26, 1985, p. 9.

123. *New York Times*, September 8, 1998, p. A6.

124. Ibid.

125. *New York Times*, July 22, 1999, p. A9. In June 1999, six US embassies in Africa were temporarily closed because of impending terrorist attacks. *New York Times*, June 26, 1999, p. A3.

126. See Herz, *Diplomats and Terrorists*.

127. Interview for the fifteen-part PBS television series *Terrorism* (1996).

128. See http://www.state.gov/s/ct.

129. *International Legal Materials* 10 (1971), p. 255. Twenty-one kidnappings of diplomatic personnel took place between 1968 and 1971, seventeen of them in Latin America. Wilkinson, *Terrorism*, p. 260.

130. Wilkinson, *Terrorism*, p. 261.

131. See the rules of international law pertaining to extradition in Damrosch et al., *International Law*, pp. 1177–1196.

132. *International Legal Materials* 13 (1974), p. 41. Emphasis added.

133. Drawn up by the Council of Europe. Covey T. Oliver, Edwin B. Firmage, Christopher L. Blakesley, Richard F. Scott, and Sharon A. Williams, *The International Legal System: Documentary Supplement* (Westbury, NY: Foundation, 1995), pp. 615–620.

134. Damrosch et al., *International Law*, pp. 544–548.

135. Ibid., pp. 549–556.

136. Ibid., pp. 556–563. Other conventions have been concluded to combat terrorism. See UN Office on Drugs and Crime, http://www.unodc.org/unodc/terrorism_conventions.

137. See Eric Rosand and Alistair Millar, "Strengthening International Law and Global Implementation," in *Uniting Against Terror: Cooperative Nonmilitary Responses to the Global Terrorist Threat*, edited by David Cortright and George A. Lopez (Cambridge: Massachusetts Institute of Technology Press, 2007), pp. 51–82.

138. See the experience of fifteen other women ambassadors as detailed in Morin, *Her Excellency*, pp. 1ff.

139. More details are provided in Morin, *Her Excellency*, pp. 211–227.

140. Morin, *Her Excellency*, p. 212.

141. In the US foreign service, junior ranks are identified by higher class numbers. See Table 6.1.

142. See F. Jeffress Ramsay, *Africa*, 7th ed. (Guilford, CT: Dushkin, 1997), "Guinea-Bissau," pp. 40–42, and "Cape Verde," pp. 28–29.

143. Normally countries with which diplomatic interaction is limited. Gore-Booth, *Satow's Guide*, pp. 74–75.

144. Morin, *Her Excellency*, p. 212.

145. Ziring, Riggs, and Plano, *United Nations*, pp. 53–55. See also Leon Gordenker, ed., *The United Nations in International Politics* (Princeton: Princeton University Press, 1971), "The United Nations and Economic and Social Change," pp. 151–183.

146. See also Seymour Maxwell Finger, *American Ambassador at the UN: People, Politics, and Bureaucracy in Making Foreign Policy*, 2d ed. (New York: Holmes and Meier, 1988).

147. Morin, *Her Excellency*, p. 213.

148. Ramsay, *Africa*, pp. 135–137. See also Tony Avirgan and Martha Honey, *War in Uganda: The Legacy of Idi Amin* (Westport: Laurence Hill, 1982).

149. This can be illustrated by the assassination in August 2003 of Sergio Vieira de Mello, special UN envoy in Iraq. *The InterDependent* 1, no. 1 (Fall 2003), pp. 19–20.

150. Morin, *Her Excellency*, pp. 217–219.

151. Ibid., p. 219.
152. See examples in ibid., pp. 219–220.
153. World Bank Survey, *1993 Britannica Book of the Year,* p. 365. See also Ramay, *Africa,* pp. 154–156.
154. World Bank Survey, *1992 Britannica Book of the Year,* p. 362.
155. Ibid., p. 371. See also Ramsay, *Africa,* pp. 83–87.
156. World Bank Survey, *1994 Britannica Book of the Year,* p. 373.
157. Morin, *Her Excellency,* p. 211.

PART 2

Modes of Diplomacy

States and other international actors have turned to new modes of interaction with the evolution of the international situation. But long-established procedures have not been simply abandoned. Diplomacy is indeed rooted in tradition and much continuity can be found in the field. Traditional methods, however, become modified to fit new circumstances and to meet new needs. The diplomatic process is thus normally in a state of flux and adaptation. But things are now moving faster.

International upheavals such as world wars invite innovation—witness the creation of the League of Nations and the United Nations. But nontraumatic change may also propel societies to do things very differently, as in the case of the European Union. Diplomatic practice may thus undergo very substantial transformation. Technology is an important factor.

For example, with easy global transportation, the risk of epidemics is magnified, hence the urgent need to bolster public health diplomacy; for example, in the World Health Organization, interdependence is pushing international actors toward more extensive multilateral work—and as a consequence, bilateral diplomacy is being used to assist multilateral ventures. We must now examine how the various modes of diplomacy are evolving to meet global challenges and prepare for the future.

7 The Resident Mission

The resident mission—the classic embassy in a national capital—is
an old tool of diplomacy dating back to the mid-1450s.[1] The transformation of
the international system (see Chapter 3), however, began to affect its role. The
unprecedented devastation and suffering caused by World War I motivated
governments to experiment with new techniques. The League of Nations was
a first major step in that direction. Later, the growth of complex interdependence pushed states toward multilateral relations.

World War II gave further impetus to the creation of new channels of
diplomatic interaction. New international organizations were created. States
now increasingly rely on international organizations and multilateral conferences to address the problems facing humankind. The embassy can no longer,
by itself, provide the diplomatic means to cope with the changing global system.[2] In fact, helped by the ease of modern transportation, foreign ministries
have expanded their use of special missions in the conduct of their foreign
relations.

The vast expansion of the subject matter of diplomacy leads to a steady
blurring of the distinction between domestic and foreign affairs.[3] More specialized government departments maintain direct communication with their
counterparts abroad in what is now called transgovernmental relations (see
Chapter 3). Have we reached a point at which embassies are becoming irrelevant?[4] A number of authors and analysts have long concluded that this is the
case.[5] International practice, however, indicates that embassies have continued
to adjust to new circumstances. States continue using them, but their role is
evolving. There are functions for which other diplomatic channels are better
suited, but embassies continue to serve purposes that are not served by the
other forms of interaction.[6] Furthermore, embassies now facilitate activities
carried out elsewhere, all of which needs to be examined.

▓ Representation

Embassies remain an important instrument of representation in foreign capitals.[7] Countries, of course, have very different needs in this respect. Many do not have to be represented in certain national capitals (perhaps because their mutual relations are limited). They have different policy interests. Many states have very limited resources and must limit the number of their foreign missions. Even the United States maintains only about 130 embassies in foreign capitals[8] (in addition to a substantial number of consulates and missions to international organizations, adding up to about 250 posts overseas). Burkina Faso, a sub-Saharan African nation, maintains embassies in five countries: Canada, the United States, China, Japan, and Taiwan. France and the United States have embassies there.[9]

By contrast, in February 2003, 189 of the 191 members of the United Nations (now 192) maintained permanent delegations in New York.[10] A number of nonmembers, or entities that are not sovereign states, have observer missions there. All of these delegations are of course important diplomatic instruments for remaining in touch with the rest of the world, and it must be conceded that, for many countries, representation at the UN (and at a number of other organizations) is a practical alternative to the opening of embassies in national capitals. In addition, the many international conferences now routinely convened on a wide variety of issues, and various forms of direct ad hoc contacts, seem to serve the needs of many nations, particularly among the less affluent. However, when two countries maintain active bilateral relations or desire to expand them, embassy representation offers serious advantages.

More effective relations and communication between two governments are usually among the benefits of embassy representation. Regular consultation can foster a sense of partnership and common purpose, particularly when there is a genuine desire to work together as the occasion arises. The vast broadening of the subject matter of diplomacy[11] has led to changes in the form of embassy representation. In the traditional model, foreign service officers (provided by the foreign ministry) carried out the task of representation. The proliferation of highly specialized issues to be approached internationally (e.g., labor issues)[12] has led departments other than the foreign ministry to engage in their own foreign relations and participate in the diplomatic process.[13] They send their own agents (i.e., non–foreign service officers) to work abroad, often as resident representatives in the embassy of their country.[14] This has long been the case with the armed services using military attachés to collect military intelligence and interact with their foreign counterparts.[15] Many departments now follow this model (although their agents are not necessarily identified as attachés) as the need arises (e.g., agriculture, treasury, and justice). The practice varies with the nature of the work and the location of the post (see Box 7.1).[16]

Box 7.1   The US Embassy in Paris in 2005

Department of State Personnel

Ambassador
Deputy chief of mission

Major Sections

Political Affairs (a minister-counselor)
Economic Affairs (a minister-counselor)
Public Affairs (a minister-counselor)
   Press Office
   Cultural Affairs Office
Consular Affairs (a minister-counselor)
Administrative Affairs (a minister-counselor)
Agricultural Affairs (a minister-counselor)
Commercial Affairs (a minister-counselor)
Scientific, Technological, and Environmental Affairs (a counselor)
Africa Regional Services (a branch of the State Department's Bureau of
   African Affairs)
Regional Security Office (a branch of the State Department's Bureau of
   Diplomatic Security; responsible for providing security services to
   all US missions, personnel, and facilities in France)

Representation of Other Departments

Defense attaché (Department of Defense)
Tax attaché (Department of the Treasury)
Customs attaché (US Customs and Border Protection, US Department
   of Homeland Security)
Space attaché (European representative, National Aeronautics and Space
   Administration, NASA)
Voice of America Finance Office for Europe and Africa
Foreign Agricultural Service (Department of Agriculture)
Commercial Service (Department of Commerce)
Internal Revenue Service (Department of the Treasury)
Office of Defense Cooperation (Department of Defense)
National Science Foundation, Europe office

continues

> **Box 7.1   Cont.**
>
> **Other Posts Under the Authority of the Embassy**
>
> Consulates-general in Marseilles and Strasbourg
> Limited consular facilities called "American Presence Posts" (APPs)—a
> new method of achieving expanded outreach—in Lyon (1998),
> Toulouse (1999), Bordeaux (2000), Rennes (2000), and Lille (2003)
> (their purpose is to support US business, to explain US policy and
> society, and to build bridges of greater understanding and friendship
> with the people of the region; they also provide limited consular ser-
> vices for US citizens, with all visa questions referred to consular
> services of the US embassy in Paris)
>
> Separate and independent from the embassy, the United States also main-
> tains in Paris its mission to the OECD (established in 1961, it has twenty-six
> member states) and its delegation to UNESCO, a specialized agency of the
> UN headquartered in Paris (missions to international organizations are not
> under the authority of the embassy).
>
> *Source:* http://www.embassyworld.com; http://www.state.gov.

This structural arrangement greatly complicates the task of the chief of
mission. All these agents are formally under his or her authority but do not receive their orders from the foreign ministry. Professionally, they remain outside the foreign service, but somehow the chief of mission must lead them to
work as a cohesive unit. In a US embassy, *the country team* is a management
device composed of the main sections of the mission, including representatives of the government agencies outside the State Department. It meets regularly under the direction of the ambassador or the deputy chief of mission, in
the attempt to achieve some coherence (or, at least, to avoid working at cross-
purposes).[17] But it is readily admitted that this contemporary embassy structure (in important embassies, some 60 percent of the diplomatic staff are
non–foreign service personnel) makes it difficult to maintain consistency.[18]
Gone are the days when the foreign ministry held sway (i.e., dominated the
conduct of foreign relations). Thus, one of the major tasks of an ambassador
these days is more likely to try to *coordinate* the efforts of very independent
people than to *direct* the implementation of the nation's foreign policy.

There is a strong element of advocacy in representation, with each sending state taking pains to explain and promote its own causes or policies in a
given situation, or to defend its programs, as the case may be. In other words,
each sending state tries to influence the receiving government,[19] not only in

the conduct of its foreign relations, but even, on occasion, in some aspects of its domestic policy insofar as these are of interest to the sending state.

Better bilateral communication can be generated by means of a resident mission. Though governments are communicating in a large variety of ways as they move away from the stilted and time-consuming formalism of earlier centuries (e.g., diplomatic notes transmitted exclusively by the embassy), cultural differences, as well as differences in respective political mind-sets, can create communication problems. Such problems can be alleviated by effective use of diplomatic representation: what a government means by what it is saying may require cultural interpretation.[20] In other words, diplomats are often needed to provide a context for what governments try to communicate; and the more disparate the cultures and the political systems, the greater the need for someone with a sophisticated knowledge of the society to convey the meaning and thrust of the message. Government officials in their own capitals are often more culture-bound than experienced diplomats. Conversely, what the host state wants to convey may require an equally sophisticated understanding of the local political system and culture if it is to be meaningful to the other state. Mere translation, even by expert linguists, may not convey the full import of what is being said. Professional, experienced diplomats are invaluable in providing this kind of service. And the importance of face-to-face interaction should not be overlooked.[21]

Some of the communication is among embassies of the same country (in different capitals), primarily to share relevant information. When an embassy comes across information pertaining to a third state, it communicates that information to its own nation's embassy in that state. This is particularly frequent in the case of neighboring countries. In a similar vein, when an embassy's message to its home government relates to a third state, it sends a copy to its own nation's embassy in that state.[22]

Technology is revolutionizing embassy communications (see Chapter 4), enabling missions to have substantial input into the policymaking process (if the national government manages to avoid information overload).[23] When the messages are sent but not read by their intended recipients, this situation tends to generate frustration and, ironically, even a sense of isolation on the part of the diplomats involved. Administrative procedures frequently lag behind technological capacity.[24] Another problem related to the communication revolution is that governments may overinstruct their diplomatic missions, resulting in serious restriction of their initiative in the field. Micromanagement of missions overseas is easily counterproductive, particularly in the day-to-day conduct of operations and approach to the host government. The embassy has the best insights for tactical decisions, which Ambassador Robert Schaetzel saw as "an element critical to the effectiveness of foreign relations."[25] Greater freedom should therefore be given to the embassy in this respect.

One Embassy or Two?

Presumably, when one country maintains an embassy in a foreign capital, that embassy can be a sufficient link between the two governments. Does the other country need to open an embassy of its own in the capital of its counterpart? To save resources,[26] some countries do not reciprocate in this matter of embassy representation.[27] One embassy in one capital or the other will be the link between the two governments. However, as embassies serve a variety of functions beyond communication, each state may prefer to maintain an embassy of its own in the other's capital.

Some governments have the same ambassador accredited to several countries (e.g., several small Caribbean island states close to one another), a practice referred to as "multiple simultaneous appointments" (see the case study on Melissa Wells's experience in Chapter 6). Officially, the sending state is equally represented in all of them. Diplomats have represented the United States to as many as eight countries simultaneously.[28] A small staff may be maintained in each capital, with the ambassador visiting as needed. In this fashion, a number of states use their diplomatic mission in Washington, D.C., or in Ottawa to represent them at the UN. Others do it the other way around. (Travel between New York and Washington, D.C., does not take long, and travel to Ottawa takes only a little longer.) Some countries have devised other ways of achieving representation. For example, on June 16, 2003, Saudi Arabia and Bahrain signed a diplomatic cooperation agreement under which the diplomatic mission of either country will represent the other in any state in which they have no permanent mission.[29]

Interestingly, despite global interdependence, more than three-fourths of the states of the world maintain only limited permanent representation in foreign capitals (see Table 7.1). Thus 95 states (just about half of the states of the world) maintain no more than 5 embassies in foreign capitals. Only 4 states maintain more than 100 embassies (Canada, France, the United States, and Japan, in descending order).[30] This distribution highlights the importance of the United Nations as a means of diplomatic interaction for much of the world's governments (the UN has 192 members and observer delegations for most of the nonmembers). Of course, states tend to desist from opening diplomatic missions abroad for financial reasons, particularly when they have limited relations with (and perhaps limited interest in) the states concerned. Contact at the UN may, for many, be amply sufficient, particularly when international conferences will bring them together on problems of common concerns, and special missions can be sent, ad hoc, to address specific issues with any nation in the world. Interestingly, the European Union, an international organization rather than a sovereign state, maintains a diplomatic mission in Washington, D.C., that serves many of the functions of a classic em-

Table 7.1   Bilateral Permanent Representation in Foreign Capitals, 2005

Number of Embassies[a]	Number of States That Send (or Fail to Send) Missions
0	23
1–5	72
6–10	30
11–15	14
16–25	18
26–50	22
51–75	8
76–100	2
101–125	1
126–150	0
151–175	2
176+	1

Source: http://www.embassyworld.com/embassy/directory.
Note: a. Consulates and other posts are excluded.

bassy.[31] The UN Development Programme maintains permanent missions of its own in the capitals of many developing nations. The purpose of these resident missions is avowedly more limited than that of normal embassies.[32]

■ Public Diplomacy

While representation is frequently used to influence the host government, it is increasingly also being used to influence the host society.[33] Public opinion in the age of mass communication plays an increasing role in the political life of a state—and this is not simply the case in democracies. Dag Hammarskjöld, during his tenure as Secretary-General of the United Nations, stressed that public opinion is "a living force in international affairs," and characterized it as perhaps the "most important new factor in diplomacy."[34] Embassies therefore become extensively involved in fostering a favorable impression of their own nation in the host state. See Box 7.2.

Diplomats are thus extensively involved with the media,[35] in interviews and on talk shows, and with opinion leaders in all walks of life.[36] Public diplomacy involves not only creating a better understanding of the political objectives of the sending state and fostering support for its policies, but also creating an appeal for all aspects of its culture. The United States, for example, maintains an extensive network of US libraries overseas and sponsors technology displays, student exchanges, art shows, recitals by its famous musicians, and lectures by its most prominent academics.[37]

Box 7.2 Embassy Building Boom in Washington

The diplomatic climate in the US capital is changing. The movers and shakers seem to be bored with the traditional dinners and receptions. The spouse of an important government official confided: "It has to be really worth it to get us to an embassy." But getting the attention of major opinion leaders and other influential people is still the name of the game on Embassy Row, and the latest stratagem is to build a bigger, more distinctive, more impressive embassy.

The District of Columbia has set aside a tract of land to create an Embassy Park in continuation of the current embassy district, and many of the new diplomatic palaces are being built in this area. The *New York Times* spoke of it as "the frenzied competition . . . to gain attention in the capital of the last remaining superpower." More than a dozen countries have built or are in the process of building embassies the size of castles. The State Department, without identifying any nation (a matter of diplomatic discretion), readily acknowledges that there is a construction boom. These embassies come adorned with towers and waterfalls—perhaps a nod to the architectural extravagance of Las Vegas. The press counselor for the Finnish embassy, a moss-green granite-and-glass showpiece, said she "had no idea a building could be such an important diplomatic tool."

Italy built an immense pale-pink palazzo in 2001 on four wood-lined acres. Cultural and social events need to be spectacular, and to do that, the Italian ambassador stresses, you need space—the space of a new, modern embassy—as well as Alexandra Rizza, the soprano, and Carla Fracci, the prima ballerina, performing in your glass-domed great room. Even China, traditionally a thrifty nation, retained the services of I. M. Pei's prestigious firm to design a new embassy.

But things are changing in another direction. Beyond social dazzle, embassies have found that embracing a cause—the national symphony or UNICEF—is a powerful way of attracting the power brokers of Washington. The Austrian embassy produced an award ceremony for Search for Common Ground, the nonprofit organization dedicated to conflict resolution. Opening their glamorous ballrooms for charities of all kinds is the new way to compete for attention—and the nonprofit organizations love it. Will it last? Probably not. And the diplomatic community will have to find new ways to eclipse the competition. In the meantime, even more spectacular embassies are being erected.

Source: Elizabeth Becker and James Dao, "A Washington Must: Embassies with Élan," *New York Times,* August 17, 2002, pp. A1, A6.

In the heart of the very society to be influenced, embassies are in an ideal position to engage in public diplomacy. However, the spread of terrorism and the resulting insecurity of diplomatic premises are affecting the fulfillment of this mission (see Chapter 6). Countries that have suffered from embassy bombing, particularly the United States, are taking steps to make their diplomatic facilities less vulnerable, in some instances relocating them away from urban traffic and within building structures capable of surviving bomb blasts. Without architectural skill, however, these embassies often project an image of embattled fortresses—massive and forbidding rather than inviting.[38] The current embassy building boom in Washington, D.C., is obviously a diplomatic vote of confidence in US homeland security.

Writing about the embassy that the United States rebuilt in Kenya after the 1998 bombing, Michael Lewis commented: "An embassy can speak to the world of America's freedom and openness, its confidence and prosperity or, as with the Kenya Embassy, its fear. As these buildings change, so will the public face that America presents to the world."[39] In 1985, the State Department set up a commission to establish guidelines for building new embassies. The "glass curtain" that was the hallmark of the 1950s, a picture of openness and flowing space, elegant and inviting, was the first casualty. Window space was limited to 15 percent of the wall surface. Buildings must be set back 100 feet from the street and built on at least fifteen acres, probably relegating them to the periphery of the capital. Public diplomacy is hurt by these developments. Nevertheless, the prestige enjoyed by diplomatic personnel (particularly the ambassador), among opinion leaders and the upper echelons of the social order, helps embassies in their public relations function.[40] Consulates in various parts of the host country are now extensively involved in public diplomacy.[41]

Some embassies go so far as to retain the services of public relations firms in the host country to conduct outreach campaigns. And this even extends to lobbying in countries in which this form of political activity on behalf of foreign interests is allowed (e.g., the United States). Jarol Manheim called it a growth industry.[42] US firms provide a variety of services to foreign governments, including communication strategy, economic image development, export, investment and tourism promotion, the production of promotional materials, media relations, and media monitoring,[43] tasks that are normally performed by embassy personnel. In 1987, 161 countries availed themselves of these services in the United States (see Table 7.2).

Many political systems do not permit, or do not lend themselves to,[44] this mode of lobbying or public relations. But when it is feasible, the use of public relations professionals adept at dealing with the local culture and political system is a practical strategy (even though by no means cheap). Embassies, of course, can continue their own efforts, but do not always have the means or the professional skills to do it extensively or effectively.[45]

Table 7.2   Countries That Spent the Most for Public Relations Services in the United States, 1987

For All Services (US$ millions)		For Political Services (US$ millions)	
Japan	36.9	Japan	26.8
Colombia	34.0	Israel	13.2
Jamaica	31.7	Canada	9.1
United Kingdom	19.8	Saudi Arabia	5.8
Israel	18.8	Indonesia	5.6
Canada	16.0	China	5.3
Australia	15.8	South Korea	3.8
Ireland	14.6	France	3.7
Mexico	14.3	Australia	3.4
Bermuda	12.4	Angola	3.2
Bahamas	11.5	South Africa	3.0
South Korea	8.6	Taiwan	2.7

Source: Jarol B. Manheim, *Strategic Public Diplomacy and American Foreign Policy: The Evolution of Influence* (New York: Oxford University Press, 1994), p. 21.

▉ Information Gathering: The Intelligence Function

One of the most important functions of an embassy is to provide an accurate picture of political conditions and trends in the host country. Diplomats must "observe and report."[46] Located in the national capital and in regular contact with government officials, embassy officers could not be in a better position to serve this purpose. This may be the most important justification to maintain an embassy in a foreign capital. There is no better vantage point from which to observe a given political system—at least so long as the diplomats do not limit themselves to reporting what their governments want to hear. Observing the whole of political reality, however distasteful, is vital if this information is to be of political value. Judging from the number of times that governments have been totally taken by surprise when revolutions occur (e.g., in Iran, 1979), it seems that there are gaps in what is reported.[47] It may also be that some decisionmakers are ideologically unprepared to accept what is reported, and that some officers in the field prefer to report what their superiors prefer to hear (see the case study on communication problems at the end of this chapter).

Embassy personnel strive to remain connected with people in the host society who are knowledgeable about the key elements defining the host state (political, military, economic, as well as sociocultural). Contact with journalists and other media people can be particularly rewarding, as well as rapport with diplomats from other embassies.[48] The intelligence function of embassies is enhanced when diplomats enlist the help of consulates in other parts of the country to obtain information away from the capital. Vital as the capital is, it is frequently an imperfect reflection of the political climate in the whole country. Paying attention to regional differences can be critical.[49]

Maintaining contact with the opposition is also an important part of trying to assess the political situation in a given country.[50] It provides a different perspective, perhaps a different sense of the political situation. It may also enable the opposition to acquire a more accurate understanding of the outlook of the sending state and of its policies (particularly useful when today's opposition becomes tomorrow's government). But establishing contact with the opposition can be a delicate matter, and it varies with the political culture of the host state and the type of relationship existing between the two countries. In the case of a democratic country that maintains good relations with the state of the embassy, contacts with opposition groups usually present no difficulty, so long as they do not amount to open support against the established government.[51] Some opposition groups, however, may present problems either because of their extremism or because they are trying to play up the diplomatic contact to advance their cause and give a misleading interpretation of the event. And certain officials, even in friendly governments, may take exception to contacts with the opposition in some circumstances.[52] Diplomats will not want to jeopardize their relations with the government in contacting the opposition.[53] As a rule, openness in these contacts (without necessarily advertising them) will be preferable.

If the relations between sending state and host state are less than cordial, contact with the opposition may complicate the relationship. Authoritarian governments may view the opposition as subversive and the embassy may have a hard time justifying any type of rapport.[54] And in some cases, the opposition may be illegal. Some contacts with the opposition have led to the expulsion of the diplomats involved.[55] In the end, contacts with the opposition may provide useful information, but the practice requires caution and must vary with the circumstances. In the practice of diplomacy, there is a duty of noninterference in the internal affairs of the host state.[56] Some governments are quick to object that embassy contact with the opposition constitutes "meddling." However, noninterference is really not a hard and fast category. A government is entitled to use its diplomatic representative to intervene with the host government to change the course of its policy, and even to apply pressure to do so. This type of intervention, government to government, using diplomatic channels, is acceptable (and common), even if threats are conveyed. But the publication of an article by the embassy that attacks how the host government is conducting its internal affairs would be a violation of international law, as would, of course, organizing and financing opposition activities or any form of subversion, and fomenting civil disturbances.

Covert intelligence, or espionage, is a different form of information gathering. Many countries have intelligence agents on their embassy staff. Embassy work is their cover.[57] When the Iranians captured the US embassy in

Tehran (which they characterized as a "nest of spies"), they identified two spies from the Central Intelligence Agency. Though someone working daily in an embassy office will make an improbable spy, that person may be a valuable recruiter and an intermediary with the real spies, collecting documents and other materials from them, at prearranged locations, and using the embassy's means of communications, such as the diplomatic bag (protected by diplomatic immunity—see Chapter 6), to send out of the country what the secret agents have collected.

Counter-espionage services in the host state spend a good deal of time identifying the covert intelligence people on embassy staffs. Once this has been achieved, many countries will not expel them, knowing that others would eventually be sent to replace them. It is easier to keep those identified under surveillance, to identify the underground agents. Nevertheless, the use of embassies for the collection of secret intelligence complicates diplomatic work. There is always the risk of public exposure when espionage involving embassy personnel is revealed, inevitably causing public embarrassment. An added measure of distrust may result from uncertainty as to whether all clandestine agents on the embassy staff have been identified.

An embassy can also become the target of the espionage efforts of the host state. The pervasive desire to expose contradictions between public positions and secret realities and, of course, the drive to obtain classified information that will give a foreign relations advantage to the state collecting this information frequently lead to efforts to penetrate embassy security arrangements: by electronic means, infiltration of embassy staff, obtaining access to embassy codes, placing diplomats under various forms of surveillance, and whatever else may give access to privileged information.[58] "Friendly" states have been found spying on their allies (as in the case of Jonathan Pollard, who was convicted of spying on the United States for Israel). Even the offices of the UN Secretary-General have been regularly bugged.[59]

Spying on embassies and embassy personnel is as old as the history of embassies. Technology has increased the risk (see the case study on the US embassy in Moscow in Chapter 4). This situation greatly contributes to the diplomatic obsession with secrecy, occasionally verging on paranoia. The Cold War exacerbated the problem. Successful diplomacy is often said to depend on the fostering of trust. It is ironic that diplomatic interaction must take place in an environment permeated with distrust and rampant insecurity.

With the spread of terrorism, insecurity has now reached a new level: *physical* insecurity (see Chapter 6), which affects embassy work more than the other forms of diplomacy (special missions, conferences, etc.). A resident mission is a visible, accessible symbol of the sending state. Terrorism adds to the pressures under which embassy diplomats must work. Taking precautions, in itself, can complicate diplomatic work. It can be time-consuming, it can become exasperating,[60] and it is expensive. Security issues affect diplomatic practice. They are part of the world in which we live, and cannot be dismissed as inconsequential. Diplomacy is adjusting to this evolving situation, but it must not be blown out of proportion, as secrecy and classification tend to be.[61]

Negotiations

Negotiations are inherent in all forms of diplomacy,[62] but in an interdependent world that increasingly resorts to multilateral modes of interaction, the embassy is left out of many international negotiations. Nevertheless, relations with host states continue to require a good deal of bilateral negotiating that embassies are well suited to handle, unless the issues are so specialized that a special mission may be judged more appropriate. Embassies, too, are becoming more involved in bilateral aspects of larger negotiations—for example, a mission coordinating joint action with its host state in a multilateral project undertaken by an international organization or conference. Embassies are thus helping the multilateral process (see Chapter 8), another transformation of their mission.

Embassies are also involved in a supporting role in negotiations undertaken by special missions (increasingly used for specialized or technical transactions, since embassy personnel may not have the needed expertise).[63] The embassy can provide local assistance and logistical support. Its knowledge of the host government can be useful to the special mission in planning its approach. It can also engage in ancillary or follow-up negotiations. On occasion, the ambassador joins the special envoy in meetings with key government officials or in devising strategy (see the case study on the Yemen crisis in Chapter 9). Some commentators note that the use of other diplomatic channels illustrates the loss of significance of the classic embassy.[64] And in a sense this is true, since the international system has found a need for new forms of diplomatic interaction. But the new services provided by the embassy can be important to the operation of the other diplomatic procedures, and often to their success. The embassy also retains its significance in functions not served by the other forms of diplomatic interaction.

The Consular Function

"So various are the functions of a consul," Satow observed, "that there can be no precise and at the same time universally acceptable definition of the term."[65] Consular work has become an integral part of a country's diplomacy, with consular officers integrated into the foreign service. Consular practices, privileges, and immunities are regulated by the 1963 Vienna Convention on Consular Relations.[66]

A consulate section is normally found at the seat of the embassy in the national capital,[67] but can be located in a different building for easier access. Additional consulates may be opened by agreement with the host state. This is particularly helpful when the host country is large or when a good deal of traffic takes place between the two countries (trade, tourism, transnational activity, and the like).[68] Consulates may be opened, again with the consent of the host state, where the sending state does not maintain an embassy. Consular representation may also be possible in unrecognized states (thus permitting limited relations) where these consulates were already established under the previous regime—for example, in Hanoi before the 1954 partition of Indochina and the creation of (unrecognized) North Vietnam. Britain retained its consulate-general there throughout the Vietnam War.[69]

The more important consulates (more extensive responsibilities, larger staffs) are given the rank of consulate-general and are headed by a consul-general. Consulates function under the authority of the embassy (when there is one, which is normally the case).[70] In very large countries, some consulates may be thousands of miles away from their embassy. One section of the embassy ensures regular contacts, but the nature of the relationship is dependent upon the management style of the chief of mission. Some ambassadors like to give their consulates a good deal of autonomy. In the hands of competent consuls, much can be gained from their local initiative. Other ambassadors prefer tight controls, and consuls must toe the line.[71]

The United States, however, has given its consulates, by act of Congress, separate authority (i.e., outside the jurisdiction of the ambassador) to issue visas.[72] In principle, according to the letter of US law, consuls issue visas under the authority of Congress, regardless of the preferences of their superior, the ambassador. But consuls still owe their promotion (by and large) to the ambassador's assessment of their performance, which can occasionally create some delicate situations (truly testing the diplomatic skills of the parties involved).[73] The reason for the occasional conflict is that the issuance of a visa at the request of an important official in the host government (e.g., the foreign minister for a cousin with a dubious past) can help the embassy in its political relationship with the government. This is politics. But it is the consul who will have to answer to US congressional investigations for visas issued by his or her staff.[74]

· Consular work also involves the welfare and protection of the citizens of the sending state in the host country,[75] and this function is not performed by the other diplomatic mechanisms used by states. But "citizen protection" is often misunderstood. Foreigners must abide by the law of the state in which they are traveling or residing. If they break the law, their embassy cannot protect them from the consequences. However, under international law, the host state must observe an international standard of decent treatment of aliens (e.g., it must not deny them access to court). If their international rights are violated, they may turn to their embassy and try to obtain redress.

A process of international claims is governed by international law,[76] but the aggrieved individual must first exhaust all local remedies before an international claim may be entertained. Furthermore, it is up to the individual's own state to decide whether to take up the case, and the process can be painfully lengthy. States have no international obligation to espouse any claim on behalf of any of their nationals.[77] Political concerns involving relations with the offending state often lead governments to place potential claims on the back burner, and years may elapse before a claim is actually pursued by the aggrieved individual's state.

Consulates will not provide funds for stranded citizens (although many kindhearted consular officers have rescued desperate people with funds from their own pockets). But consular officers will visit their nationals in jail, help them obtain legal counsel, notify next of kin in case of death in the host country, and provide assistance in obtaining medical care. Consular work provides a human element to the various functions performed by embassies.[78] Charles S. Kennedy, for instance, reported with pride that his consulate-general staff "politely extracted an elderly American woman from one of the better local hospitals [the name of the country is diplomatically omitted from this published account], when her leg was scheduled to be amputated within hours because of blood clots. They got her quickly to a US military hospital from which she walked out on both legs several weeks later."[79] The consul-general commented later: "It is occasions like this that make consular work so worthwhile."[80]

Consulates help with commercial relations and serve a variety of administrative functions, such as replacing certain lost documents, providing notary public services, and registering children born abroad. And they help their government in a variety of other ways—for instance, assisting the US Social Security and Veterans Administrations in ensuring that payments to expatriates are justified.[81] It is important to acknowledge that consulates have become an integral part of a country's diplomacy. Consulates away from the nation's capital are now political, economic, and cultural outposts, adding to the information-gathering capability of the embassy. This is particularly important in very large countries such as India and Brazil, in which some regions are very different from the national capital, thus helping the sending state achieve a more accurate understanding of the country as a whole.

Consulates can be helpful in maintaining contact with the opposition (when politically feasible). Consulates attract less attention than embassies in the national capital. Informal consular contacts with members of the opposition are less likely to be misrepresented (although they, too, can be controversial). Consulates are also expected to engage in important public diplomacy functions. The United States is now using streamlined posts called "American Presence Posts," which offer only limited consular services. They are intended to maintain a US presence in more regions and to facilitate public diplomacy. They are expected "to explain American policy and society and to build bridges of greater understanding and friendship with the people of the region."[82]

As with embassies in the national capital, consulates have their share of agents who serve other government departments, according to the significance of the regions in which the consulates are located and the nature of the workload (e.g., the Immigration and Naturalization Services, the Federal Bureau of Investigation, and US Customs and Bureau of Narcotics, in some border areas). At a large, centrally located consulate-general in Europe, there may be a dozen or more agencies represented, plus regional offices of such bodies as the General Accounting Office or the Internal Revenue Service.[83]

▓ The Administrative Function

To address the problems of complex interdependence (e.g., economic imbalance), nations conclude an increasing number of international agreements. The United States concludes more than 160 treaties and 3,500 executive agreements annually.[84] Nations also participate in a vast network of international institutions. The international system is thus much more tightly structured, and this leads to a substantial bureaucratization of international relations, in the sense that many facets of the international system are governed by international agreements and legal regulations that require the implementation of a variety of administrative procedures. Embassies are involved in the administration of treaty arrangements (e.g., ensuring compliance and doing the paperwork specified by international arrangements).[85]

Members of permanent missions to international organizations (e.g., the United Nations) have much fewer administrative duties of this kind, although this varies with the organization. The UN's specialized agencies (e.g., the World Trade Organization) create administrative concerns of their own for national missions (see Chapter 8).[86] Relations between an embassy and its government, too, entail a good deal of administrative routine such as processing of data, filing of reports, and sundry administrative tasks—deskwork performed by the diplomatic staff. And to ensure accomplishment of all these tasks, the ambassador needs to be a proficient administrator.[87]

▓ The Ceremonial and Symbolic Function

The ceremonial and symbolic function is much more developed at the embassy level than in the other forms of diplomacy, though this function is present to some degree in all diplomacy. A diplomatic representative, after all, represents the sending state. This function is more pronounced at the bilateral level. In a national capital, an embassy is a major symbol of the state it represents—a reason why embassies have been attacked by terrorist movements. Embassies are also, for the same reason, a focal point for popular demonstrations against the sending state—witness the takeover of the US embassy in Tehran by a youthful mob during the 1979 Iranian revolution.

Some countries, rich and poor, spend extravagantly to build an impressive embassy and make a statement in a given capital (see Box 7.2). The motivation varies. This can be done in a friendly capital or it can happen in a hostile country. No doubt, the intent is to impress, but often the matter is purely subjective. Ostentation is not a universal practice. Many embassies are downright modest in appearance.[88] Cost is undoubtedly a factor, but so too is the fact that countries do not attach the same importance to their relationship with specific countries. The ceremonial function of embassies remains extensive.[89] A good deal of it is rooted in tradition. Monarchs used to put on lavish celebrations, and representatives of foreign states were duly invited.

Ceremony today plays a much lesser role in national capitals, but there is still a good deal of it for state celebrations and patriotic observances, and embassy personnel must represent their governments at these functions. When the function is sufficiently important, the chief of mission, presumably the ambassador, needs to be there.[90] If the occasion is unusual (e.g., a national funeral), foreign countries are likely to be represented by their chief executives, with ambassadors most likely joining them too.[91] Embassies generate ceremonial functions of their own (e.g., for their national observances), but these tend to be more modest. Many double as public relations functions. Other embassies are of course invited. But so are people in the community, opinion leaders, and other influential individuals.

As a leftover from earlier centuries, embassies remain fairly addicted to social functions. Some diplomats defend the practice as a useful opportunity to meet colleagues and collect information, and doubtless some of this takes place. But many diplomats consider it a waste of time. It is certainly a time-consuming imposition on the members of the diplomatic profession: after a full day at the embassy, they must dash home and change clothes in preparation for spending yet another evening at yet another social event.[92] And the larger the number of embassies in a capital, the larger the number of functions to attend. Many observers of the diplomatic scene have advocated reducing this type of activity as one of the reforms needed in resident diplomacy. Governments will still have their own observances to be attended by diplomatic representatives. The ceremonial and symbolic function will not vanish. But embassies could cut back on their own social functions. This is easier said than done, however, as social functions are part of the diplomatic culture and rooted in tradition.

▥ Provisional and Stopgap Diplomatic Arrangements

When governments break diplomatic relations, the loss of regular embassy contact becomes a problem.[93] The situation may be alleviated when the sending state, with the prior consent of the host state, entrusts, even in wartime, the protection of its interests and those of its nationals to a third state acceptable to the host state. This may include the custody of the premises of the mission, together with its property and archives in the territory of the host state. This is well established in international law (the 1961 Vienna Convention on Diplomatic Relations) and widely practiced.[94] The third state is known as the "protecting power."[95]

The costs incurred by the protecting power will be defrayed by agreement with the protected state. The details of these understandings will vary with the states concerned and the scope of the interests to be protected. States with a tradition of neutrality, such as Switzerland, have long provided such services.[96] This procedure, however, can provide only limited diplomatic service. The embassy of the protecting power must continue to attend to its own diplomatic representation, which reduces the amount of time that can be devoted to the interests of the protected state.

Beginning in the mid-1960s, a modification of this procedure was tried and quickly gained widespread acceptance. This entails the establishment of an "interests section" for a nonrepresented state (again, by agreement with the host state), under the authority and protection of a third party. Under this arrangement, a number of diplomats from the embassy that was closed as a result of severance of diplomatic relations assume the duty of protecting the interests of their home state in the host country, but officially work in the embassy of the state that has accepted the role of protecting power, under its authority. The arrangement even goes so far as to allow this interests section to function in the very premises of its own embassy (officially and formally closed, but operating as a branch of the embassy of the protecting power). All diplomats of the interests section retain their diplomatic immunities as if belonging to the protecting embassy.[97]

An early example of this new procedure occurred when Egypt broke diplomatic relations with the United States upon the outbreak of war with Israel in 1967. US interests in Egypt were taken over by the Spanish embassy in Cairo as protecting power. A US official, however, remained in the US embassy in Cairo, whose formal status had become that of a US interests section of the Spanish embassy. This official, initially, was only responsible for administrative services. But in 1968, when a UN mediator began working for an Arab-Israeli settlement, it became clear that US diplomatic involvement in Cairo was necessary to achieve progress in the negotiations. As a result, US diplomatic presence in the US interests section grew to six or seven persons, led by a diplomat of counselor rank. At no time did the US officials move out of the US compound and into the Spanish embassy.

The United States eventually undertook a new peace initiative. Given the complexity and high level of the negotiations, it became necessary to send a more senior US diplomat to Cairo, in February 1972. An official with the rank of minister (not formally recognized in Cairo) arrived, assisted by a team of experts in Middle East affairs. He had access to Egyptian president Gamal Abdel Nasser, as would have been the case with a regular ambassador.[98] This procedure, of course, goes far beyond what would be feasible with the traditional institution of protecting powers. The regular staff of the embassy who provide protection could not undertake this kind of diplomatic service. However, it has its own limitations. This procedure cannot be used in time of war. The diplomatic staff of the interests section usually remains small, and given existing friction, access to the host government may be limited—the government may even boycott the mission altogether.[99]

Frequently, however, diplomatic relations are broken to show extreme displeasure, but without any desire to aggravate the situation. Continued diplomatic contact is often seen as beneficial, the breach being primarily symbolic. For example, the government of Iceland broke diplomatic relations with the United Kingdom in February 1976 and a British interests section of the French embassy was established in Reykjavik. It was composed of all the members of the former British embassy other than the ambassador, and was instructed to continue normal business as much as possible.[100] Breaking diplomatic relations may provide some satisfaction, and may even be viewed as some form of sanction, but it complicates the conduct of foreign relations: hence these efforts to mitigate the disruption.

Consulates may also be used to maintain contact. A break in diplomatic relations does not automatically terminate consular relations. The 1963 Vienna Convention on Consular Relations makes it clear that the consular officer of a sending state may, with the consent of the receiving state, be authorized to perform diplomatic acts (e.g., contacting the central government)[101] when the sending state has no diplomatic mission and is not represented by a third state as protecting power. Agreement on what type of contact may be maintained will of course depend upon the states concerned and the situation.

▨ Embassies in Disguise

Countries unable to maintain formal diplomatic relations because of current problems (e.g., nonrecognition) may nevertheless maintain extensive, but unofficial, diplomatic contact. Their intent here is not to hide their diplomatic interaction,[102] but to keep it unofficial (no presentation of credentials, no inclusion into the diplomatic corps). They can maintain liaison missions under whatever label serves their purpose. The relations remain unofficial and do not alter legal status (e.g., no recognition is implied in the relationship). When in 1973 the United States and the People's Republic of China decided to accelerate their rapprochement, the two countries exchanged liaison offices. These were perceived as virtual embassies, but without official, formal status. In fact, both countries sent senior diplomats to head these posts, who were empowered to maintain relations with the leadership of both governments.[103]

A similar procedure was used to maintain diplomatic relations with Taiwan after US recognition of the People's Republic of China on January 1, 1979. The diplomatic problem, however, was different. Until then, the United States and Taiwan had maintained full diplomatic relations. But both Taiwan and Communist China were adamantly opposed to any type of "two China" policy. Thus the United States could not exchange embassies with Beijing while continuing to maintain official diplomatic relations with Taiwan. Accordingly, it closed its embassy in Taipei and opened a liaison office there, presented as the American Institute in Taiwan (AIT). This body is described as "a non-profit, private corporation,"[104] and currently has a total staff of over 300, about the size of a large embassy. The Taiwan Relations Act of April 10, 1979, provides that "any programs, transactions, or any other relations conducted or carried out by the President or any Agency of the United States Government with respect to Taiwan shall . . . be conducted and carried out by or through the American Institute in Taiwan."[105] The Department of State, through a contract with the AIT, provides a large part of its funding. Symbolism has significant meaning to many nation-states.

The AIT has a small Washington headquarters office that acts as liaison with US government agencies and its counterpart in Taiwan. What used to be the Chinese embassy is now the Taiwan Economic and Cultural Representative Office (TECRO), which is headed by a representative (appropriately generic in title). TECRO has a total staff comparable in size to that of the AIT in Taipei (over 300 people). It includes the same sections found in a regular embassy, including a consulate in Washington. TECRO oversees twelve economic and cultural offices, headed by directors-general,[106] corresponding to the consulates that an embassy would control throughout the country. Taiwan is represented in forty-six countries by similar economic and cultural offices.[107]

Other countries not otherwise represented maintain some form of resident diplomatic representation that does not amount to a full-service embassy. These informal missions come in a variety of forms and sizes and are diversely titled (e.g., trade missions, commercial offices, information or tourist offices, scientific missions, or cultural affairs centers). They may indeed provide these specialized services, but they also provide representation. It is reported that during the war in Vietnam, two North Vietnamese journalists who resided in London in the 1960s were used by the British government as intermediaries in dealing with the Hanoi government. All of these ways of maintaining contact have been called "unconventional" modes of diplomatic representation—unconventional, no doubt, but widely used. Resident representation remains practical.[108]

■ Case Study: Communication Problems and Their Consequences

When Pakistan came into existence in August 1947,[109] it consisted of two distinct territories: West Pakistan, where the capital was located, and East Pakistan, more populous, composed of the former Indian province of East Bengal and the Sylhet district of Assam.[110] West Pakistan and East Pakistan were separated by about a thousand miles of Indian territory.[111] In language, culture, and ethnic background, these two Pakistani regions were totally disparate. The only real bond between them was their state religion, Islam. They also differed greatly in economic resources, East Pakistan being dismally poor.[112] The United States had a consulate-general in Dacca, the main city in East Pakistan; it was a post of great significance, given the distance from the capital and the stark contrast with the western region.

Pakistan was governed by General Mohammed Ayub Khan, who seized power in a military coup in 1958 and promulgated a military dictatorship in 1962.[113] The country had long-standing ties and mutually beneficial relations with the United States, and was a major recipient of US assistance. General Ayub Khan, in fact, had developed a friendship with the US president.[114] Early on, the central government had caused friction with East Pakistan over the language issue: in 1952, Urdu was declared Pakistan's official language.[115] Although Bengali, the main language of East Pakistan, was finally admitted as the joint official language in 1954, discontent continued, as East Pakistan was underrepresented in the administration and in the armed forces. In 1970, Bengali representation in the elite civil service amounted to only 16 percent, and representation in the army officer corps amounted to a mere 5 percent.

The people of East Pakistan felt excluded from major policymaking and received a disproportionately small share of Pakistan's development resources.[116] With a population of 75 million, East Pakistan had 7,600 doctors, compared to 12,400 in West Pakistan's population of 55 million. Similar disparity existed in other areas, such as education investments. Between 1947 and 1969, the number of colleges in West Pakistan had grown from 40 to 271, against a progression of 50 to 162 in East Pakistan; and 66 percent of US assistance was distributed in the west.[117] As a result of this sharp discrimination, East Pakistan made a more determined effort to organize politically and be heard. The East Bengal Muslim Awami League, the first opposition party in

Pakistan, created in 1949,[118] became an instrument of emancipation. Its leader, Shaikh Mujibur Rahman ("Mujib"), was a strong advocate of autonomy—and eventually full independence—for East Pakistan.[119]

Diplomatic Appointments

General Ayub Khan had been complaining in Washington, D.C., that the US bureaucracy was treating him unfairly in the allocation of assistance, and that he was being politically neglected—which was probably the case.[120] In 1964, President Lyndon Johnson, to improve the relationship, called in a close personal friend to take over as ambassador and reassure the general and his dictatorial regime that an effort was being made to correct the situation. The new appointee, however, had no diplomatic experience.[121] Although this appointment would signal personal attention and concern on the part of the US president, no doubt a positive move of psychological value, an absence of diplomatic experience could be considered a dangerous proposition in the midst of a delicate situation that could easily deteriorate. Indeed, East Pakistan was increasingly frustrated and restive.[122]

At about the same time, a new consul-general, a professional diplomat with previous experience in the country and in the region, was appointed to head the Dacca post. Because of the peculiar geographical situation, the consulate-general had the unusual privilege of communicating directly with Washington in its political and economic reporting, without previous clearance by the embassy—which would eventually contribute to the demise of this consul-general. Copies of consulate reports were of course sent to the embassy.[123]

About a year after the consul-general and the ambassador took their posts, the 1965 war over Kashmir aggravated the relationship between East and West Pakistan.[124] The consul-general saw the widening split between the two regions as leading toward more insistent demands for autonomy or moving toward secession. General Ayub Khan and the ruling elite, however, believed that the war had strengthened national unity and so did the US ambassador. Popular discontent mounted against the regime. The Awami League, the East Pakistan party, supported a program of reforms,[125] but negotiations with the Pakistani leadership failed.[126]

Conflicting Diplomatic Reports

The consul-general began reporting on the growing East Pakistan movement for autonomy or independence. He described it in detail, pointing out that early compromise on the part of the central government stood a good chance of preserving national unity and that the US government could exercise its considerable influence in this direction. But the current policy of the Pakistani government toward the eastern region (profound neglect and occasional repression) was likely to radicalize the masses and their leadership in East Pakistan. The US embassy, however, was taking the opposite view, and reported to Washington that the regime was strong and getting stronger. It flatly opposed any idea that compromise with the East Pakistanis was necessary to preserve Pakistan's unity.[127]

Meanwhile, the popularity of General Ayub Khan deteriorated in West Pakistan[128] and opposition escalated in the eastern region. The consul-general's fears seemed to be confirmed, encouraging him to continue reporting to Washington the worsening situation. The US embassy in the national capital continued disagreeing and began to let the consul-general know that his alarmist views were not welcome—at first, by delicate hints, then more openly, and eventually bluntly. But the consul-general would not listen. He saw the mounting danger and was becoming more and more frustrated at the ambassador's inability to perceive what was happening in East Pakistan. His reports to Washington became frantic, predicting a bloody civil war and Indian intervention, all of which would harm US interests in the region.[129]

Pakistan's own embassy in Washington informed General Ayub Khan of the source of the dissenting reports received by the State Department, and began to complain to the US ambassador in Pakistan that the consul-general was attempting to create a secessionist movement in East Pakistan. The US ambassador held out for a long time, to his credit. But as the matter had profound significance, not only for Pakistan but for the United States as well, one may wonder why the ambassador did not review the entire issue personally with the consul-general and take an interest in the evidence he was trying to communicate.

Efforts to Silence the Consul-General

The ambassador personally asked the consul-general to stop his reporting, and issued written orders to the consulate and to all operating agencies in its region (apparently he did not trust them either) to stop all contact, even the mildest social conversations, with any individual or member of any group in the region not on record as supporting the central regime. Even covert intelligence sources of many years' standing had to be dropped.[130] This was obviously intended to placate General Ayub Khan. Meanwhile, the situation was deteriorating, with serious disruptions and arrests taking place.[131]

The ambassador's action stemmed the flow of negative reports somewhat, but did not stop them. Finally, the ambassador ordered the consul-general to exchange positions with an officer in the embassy (unlikely to help his career). When this officer became consul-general, he dutifully characterized his predecessor's reports as alarmist and unjustifiable on the basis of the facts available in East Pakistan. Interestingly, during the next four years, several principal officers were assigned to the consulate-general in East Pakistan. Some of them may have had difficulty maintaining an optimistic view of the situation, and fared poorly when reporting unrest in their jurisdiction.[132]

General Ayub Khan remained inflexible and lost his support in West Pakistan as well. He was removed on March 26, 1969, by General Agha Muhammad Yahya Khan,[133] who undertook a program of reforms. General elections were held in December 1970,[134] during which the Awami League won overwhelming victory in the east and a majority in Pakistan's National Assembly. Shaikh Mujib, leader of the Awami League, should therefore have been appointed prime minister, but the general would not accept and negotiations on a constitutional compromise broke down. The convening of the new National Assembly was postponed indefinitely on March 2, 1971,[135] and the pace of events in East Pakistan, including street violence, accelerated.

Consul-General Vindicated

On March 4, 1971, Mujib called for a general strike across East Pakistan. The response was overwhelming. Violence escalated. The Pakistani military responded with enormous brutality. General Yahya Khan went to Dacca on March 15 and held an ultimate round of negotiations with Shaikh Mujib, which resulted in an impasse on March 24.[136] This was the last straw. On March 26, Shaikh Mujib proclaimed the independence of the People's Republic of Bangladesh,[137] and General Yahya Khan ordered his military to crush the rebellion. The scale of the repression against the civilian population and its sheer brutality were appalling and unparalleled in this part of the world. By mid-May, the number of refugees in India had reached an estimated 10 million.[138]

Resistance continued. The Liberation Army of East Bengal launched a major offensive in November 1971,[139] and India entered the fray. On November 22, Indian forces along the border started to provide artillery fire to protect the liberation army. On December 3, Pakistan's air force attacked India's northern air bases,[140] and on December 4, India declared war on Pakistan and routed its armed forces. Pakistan surrendered on December 16.[141]

Failure to respond to the danger signs and early warning from East Pakistan, clearly articulated as the storm gathered, was very costly. An estimated 3 million died in the uprising and subsequent war. Ironically, greater attentiveness on the part of the ambassador, and greater willingness to acknowledge and report the unpleasant truth, might not have made any difference if Washington had already made up its mind to support the generals, come what may—and it would not have been the first time that an ambassador was ignored. As things stood, the ambassador reported what the government wanted to hear, portraying as an aberration what the consul-general in the east was allowed to report directly, thus reinforcing the tragic misconceptions of the policymakers. Selective reporting (screening out unpopular information) is always detrimental to decisionmaking.

It probably would have been a better strategy for the consul-general to try to convince the ambassador instead of bypassing him. In a fight with the ambassador, a consul must normally lose. To avoid this kind of clash, professionals advocate greater interaction between the chief of mission and consuls, particularly those located in remote areas of a country. Periodic conferences and visits are desirable and may yield greater understanding of complex situations.[142]

■ Study Questions and Discussion Topics

1. Are resident missions relevant today? What are their functions?
2. Why do so many states maintain so few embassies in foreign capitals? Is it detrimental to them? How do they maintain contact?
3. Is multilateral diplomacy displacing bilateral diplomatic relations?
4. Is public diplomacy affecting the diplomatic process?
5. Are ceremonial functions dysfunctional in modern culture?
6. Why do states need foreign missions "in disguise"?
7. What is the connection between embassies and espionage?

■ Suggested Reading

Dorman, Shawn, ed. *Inside a U.S. Embassy: How the Foreign Service Works for America.* Rev. ed. Washington, DC: American Foreign Service Association, 2005.

Herz, Martin F. ed. *The Consular Dimension of Diplomacy.* Washington, DC: Institute for the Study of Diplomacy, School of Foreign Service, Georgetown University, 1983.

———. *Contacts with the Opposition: A Symposium.* Washington, DC: Institute for the Study of Diplomacy, School of Foreign Service, Georgetown University, 1979.

———. *The Modern Ambassador: The Challenge and the Search.* Washington, DC: Institute for the Study of Diplomacy, School of Foreign Service, Georgetown University, 1983.

Innis, Pauline B., Mary Jane McCaffrey, and Richard M. Sands, *Protocol: The Complete Handbook of Diplomatic, Official, and Social Usage.* Dallas: Durban, 2002.

Manheim, Jarol B. *Strategic Public Diplomacy and American Foreign Policy: The Evolution of Influence.* New York: Oxford University Press, 1994.

Miller, Robert Hopkins. *Inside an Embassy: The Political Role of Diplomats Abroad.* Washington, DC: Congressional Quarterly, 1992.

Plischke, Elmer. *U.S. Department of State: A Reference History.* Westport: Greenwood, 1999.

Schaetzel, J. Robert. "Modernizing the Role of the Ambassador." In *Modern Diplomacy: The Art and the Artisans,* edited by Elmer Plischke. Washington, DC: American Enterprise Institute for Public Policy Research, 1979.

Notes

1. Harold Nicolson, *Diplomacy,* 3d ed. (New York: Oxford University Press, 1964), p. 13. However, the Pope appointed a permanent representative at the Court of Byzantium in 453. Harold Nicolson, *The Evolution of Diplomatic Method* (London: Constable, 1954), p. 33. See discussion of the Renaissance in Chapter 2 in this volume.

2. R. P. Barston, *Modern Diplomacy,* 2d ed. (New York: Longman, 1997), "The Changing Nature of Diplomacy," pp. 1–8.

3. Robert O. Keohane and Joseph S. Nye, *Power and Interdependence,* 2d ed. (Glenview, IL: Scott Foresman, 1989), pp. 24–27, 33–37.

4. Nicolson, *Diplomacy,* pp. 1–40; Barston, *Modern Diplomacy,* pp. 1–8.

5. See discussion of Zbigniew Brzezinski and Henry Kissinger cited in G. R. Berridge, *Diplomacy: Theory and Practice,* 2d ed. (New York: Palgrave, 2002), p. 116. See also P. M. Kaiser, *Journeying Far and Wide: A Political and Diplomatic Memoir* (New York: Scribner's, 1992), p. 262; Adam Watson, *Diplomacy* (New York: Routledge, 2004), pp. 132–157; J. Robert Schaetzel, "Modernizing the Role of the Ambassador," in *Modern Diplomacy: The Art and the Artisans,* edited by Elmer Plischke (Washington, DC: American Enterprise Institute for Public Policy Research, 1979), pp. 262–276.

6. Kishan S. Rana, *Inside Diplomacy,* 2d ed. (New Delhi: Manas, 2002).

7. See Kishan S. Rana, *The 21st Century Ambassador: Plenipotentiary to Chief Executive* (New York: Oxford University Press, 2005).

8. See http://www.embassyworld.com/embassyldirectory. There are just under 200 sovereign states in the world today.

9. See http://www.embassyworld.com/embassyldirectory.

10. The two exceptions were Kiribati and Palau. Courtney B. Smith, *Politics and Process at the UN: The Global Dance* (Boulder: Lynne Rienner, 2006), p. 35.

11. A result of the growth of complex interdependence. See, for example, Keohane and Nye, *Power and Interdependence,* pp. 26–27.

12. In the full range of their complexity: wages, working conditions, social security, vacations, labor management relations, health benefits, and so much more.

13. Elmer Plischke, *U.S. Department of State: A Reference History* (Westport: Greenwood, 1999), pp. 506–509. Examining US practice, Plischke notes: "Most astonishing, the third major category of Federal agencies concerned with a broad variety of aspects of American foreign affairs since World War II encompasses approximately 125 independent government agencies" (p. 474). See also ibid., pp. 474–479.

14. See Charles S. Whitehouse, "Running an Embassy," in *The Modern Ambassador: The Challenge and the Search,* edited by Martin F. Herz (Washington, DC: Institute for the Study of Diplomacy, School of Foreign Service, Georgetown University, 1983), p. 46.

15. See, for example, Burton M. Sapin, *The Making of United States Foreign Policy* (Washington, DC: Brookings Institution, 1966), pp. 260–261.

16. Whitehouse, "Running an Embassy," p. 46.

17. Sapin, *Making of United States Foreign Policy,* pp. 134, 275–286.

18. Plischke, *U.S. Department of State,* pp. 506–509.

19. Martin Mayer, *The Diplomats* (New York: Doubleday, 1983), pp. 82–101.

20. Aside from defense and justification.

21. Raymond Cohen, *Theater of Power: The Art of Diplomatic Signalling* (London: Longman, 1987), pp. 2–3.

22. Langston Craig, "'Leisure, Gentility, and Decorum': A Typical Day of an American Ambassador," in Herz, *Modern Ambassador,* pp. 51–52.

23. Administrative structures become ill equipped to handle communication traffic on the massive scale made feasible today.

24. Wilson Dizard Jr., *Digital Diplomacy: U.S. Foreign Policy in the Information Age* (Westport: Praeger, 2001), p. 100.

25. Schaetzel, "Modernizing the Role," p. 273. He points out, however, "It must be accepted that under the best of circumstances the ambassador will be only peripherally involved in the design and direction of American foreign policy."

26. In an economic move in February 2002, Denmark decided to close ten embassies and consulates. *New York Times*, February 21, 2002, p. A6.

27. For example, the following countries maintain embassies in Botswana: Britain, China, France, Russia, and the United States. Canada and Denmark maintain consulates. Botswana maintains embassies in Belgium, Britain, China, and the United States. See http://www.embassyworld.com.

28. In the post–World War II era, more than ninety US diplomats held simultaneous assignments commissioned to some fifty nations. By the mid-1990s, however, most of these simultaneous combinations were superseded by separate appointments to individual countries, except for the continued grouping of Caribbean island states as well as some Pacific Ocean states. Plischke, *U.S. Department of State*, pp. 502–503.

29. *Gulfwire Digest* no. 202 (June 23–29, 2003).

30. See http://www.embassyworld.com. Embassies only. Other missions not included. This database specifies Canada, 176; France, 162; United States, 156; and Japan, 104. Embassies identified by some other names (e.g., British "high commissions") are included in these figures. The database does not indicate how multiple representations are counted (e.g., one ambassador accredited to several countries). When all overseas diplomatic posts are counted (including consulates and missions to various international organizations, and other continuing agencies), the 2005 count for the United States is somewhat above 250. This, of course, applies to other nations as well. For the evolution of US representation after 1945, see Plischke, *U.S. Department of State*, pp. 493–502, esp. tab. 7.6, pp. 494–498. Also, a large number of nations maintain at least one mission at the United Nations. Many maintain additional missions at UN offices in Geneva and in Vienna and other missions at the headquarters of UN specialized agencies (e.g., in Paris, Rome, Montreal, and Washington, D.C.). This chapter, however, is concerned with the traditional embassies accredited to national governments.

31. See http://www.embassyworld.com.

32. Tom Boudreau, *A New International Diplomatic Order,* Occasional Paper no. 24 (Muscatine, IA: Stanley Foundation, 1980), pp. 10–11.

33. Jan Melissen, ed., *The New Public Diplomacy: Soft Power in International Relations* (New York: Palgrave Macmillan, 2006); Eytan Gilboa, "Diplomacy in the Media Age: Three Models of Uses and Effects," in *Diplomacy,* edited by Christer Jönsson and Richard Langhorne (London: Sage, 2004), vol. 3, *Problems and Issues in Contemporary Diplomacy,* pp. 96–119.

34. Dag Hammarskjöld, "New Diplomatic Techniques in a New World," in Plischke, *Modern Diplomacy,* p. 88.

35. See Jarol B. Manheim, *Strategic Public Diplomacy and American Foreign Policy: The Evolution of Influence* (New York: Oxford University Press, 1994), pp. 126–147.

36. R. S. Zaharna, "The Soft Power Differential: Network Communication and Mass Communication in Public Diplomacy," *The Hague Journal of Diplomacy* 2, no. 3 (October 2007), pp. 213–228.

37. See, for example, Francis J. Colligan, *Two Decades of Government-Sponsored Cultural Relations* (Washington, DC: US Department of State, 1958); Robert Blum, ed.,

Cultural Affairs and Foreign Relations (Englewood Cliffs, NJ: Prentice-Hall, 1963); Manheim, *Strategic Public Diplomacy,* pp. 39–121. On the importance of public diplomacy, see Mark Leonard, "Diplomacy by Other Means," *Foreign Policy* (September–October 2002), p. 48.

38. The US embassy in Bahrain illustrates the problem: massive and austere, it displays doors reminiscent of those leading to bank vaults. To make it more forbidding, the entire structure is battleship gray, while its neighbor, an elegant private residence, is airy and sparkling white—an unfortunate contrast.

39. Michael J. Lewis, "Glass Walls to Bunkers: The New Look of U.S. Embassies," *New York Times,* July 27, 2003, p. 6.

40. Kathy R. Fitzpatrick, "Advancing the New Public Diplomacy: A Public Relations Perspective," *The Hague Journal of Diplomacy* 2, no. 3 (October 2007), pp. 187–211.

41. Smith Simpson, "The Consular Contribution to Diplomacy," in *The Consular Dimension of Diplomacy,* edited by Martin F. Herz (Washington, DC: Institute for the Study of Diplomacy, School of Foreign Service, Georgetown University, 1983), pp. 17–19. See also discussion of the consular function in this chapter.

42. Manheim, *Strategic Public Diplomacy,* pp. 14–35.

43. Ibid., pp. 26–27.

44. For example, because of the culture or political structuring.

45. Pierre C. Pahlavi, "Evaluating Public Diplomacy Programmes," *The Hague Journal of Diplomacy* 2, no. 3 (October 2007), pp. 255–281.

46. A classic way of presenting this aspect of their mission. See Article 3 of the 1961 Vienna Convention on Diplomatic Relations. See also Robert Hopkins Miller, *Inside an Embassy: The Political Role of Diplomats Abroad* (Washington, DC: Congressional Quarterly, 1992), pp. 14–37; Kingdon B. Swayne, "Reporting Function," in Plischke, *Modern Diplomacy,* pp. 350–363.

47. An interesting example concerning the secession of East Pakistan is presented in John W. Bowling, "Tale of Three Dilemmas," in Herz, *Consular Dimension,* pp. 62–66. See case study at the end of this chapter.

48. Manheim, *Strategic Public Diplomacy,* pp. 126–129. Mayer, *Diplomats,* pp. 70–71. Mayer comments: "A surprisingly high proportion of what an ambassador knows or believes comes from frequent conversations with other countries' ambassadors" (p. 70).

49. Simpson, "Consular Contribution," pp. 14–19. See case study in this chapter.

50. Martin F. Herz, ed., *Contacts with the Opposition: A Symposium* (Washington, DC: Institute for the Study of Diplomacy, School of Foreign Service, Georgetown University, 1979), pp. v–vii.

51. See Ambassador William H. Sullivan's comments in ibid., pp. 1–4.

52. Some controversies create a good deal of sensitivity in government circles. See Ambassador Parker T. Hart's comments in Herz, *Contacts with the Opposition,* pp. 33–34.

53. See Hans J. Morgenthau's comments in Herz, *Contacts with the Opposition,* pp. 4–6.

54. See Ambassador Wells Stabler's comments in Herz, *Contacts with the Opposition,* pp. 55–59.

55. See Hart's comments in Herz, *Contacts with the Opposition,* p. 34.

56. B. Sen, *A Diplomat's Handbook of International Law and Practice,* 3d ed. (Dordrecht: Nijhoff, 1988), pp. 88–91.

57. David D. Newsom, "Clandestine Collection," in Miller, *Inside an Embassy,* pp. 38–45.

58. Dean A. Minix and Sandra M. Hawley, *Global Politics* (St. Paul, MN: West Group, 1998), pp. 328–332.

59. Warren Hoge, "On Bugging News, Annan Had Low-Key Reaction to Old Practice," *New York Times,* February 28, 2004, pp. A6, A26. See also Chapter 4 in this volume.

60. One diplomat could not remember the new, multidigit elevator code number. Before pressing the floor number, he had to fumble through his coat pockets to find the card on which he had written it (probably a totally illegal way to proceed) and his company waited until he finally found it. The elevator was inside the embassy, past the entry checkpoints, and presumably a secure area. But the coded device was no doubt an added security measure. I was present in the elevator during this incident.

61. David D. Newsom, "The Diplomat's Task Versus Security," in *Diplomats and Terrorists: What Works, What Doesn't—A Symposium,* edited by Martin F. Herz (Washington, DC: Institute for the Study of Diplomacy, School of Foreign Service, Georgetown University, 1982), pp. 9–11.

62. See Miller, *Inside an Embassy,* pp. 73–75.

63. Elmer Plischke, "The New Diplomacy," in Plischke, *Modern Diplomacy,* pp. 54–72.

64. Schaetzel, "Modernizing the Role," pp. 262–276.

65. (Lord) Gore-Booth, ed., *Satow's Guide to Diplomatic Practice,* 5th ed. (New York: Longman, 1979), p. 211.

66. Covey T. Oliver, Edwin B. Firmage, Christopher L. Blakesley, Richard F. Scott, and Sharon A. Williams, *The International Legal System: Documentary Supplement,* 4th ed. (New York: Foundation Press, 1995), pp. 362–390.

67. Shawn Dorman, ed., *Inside a U.S. Embassy: How the Foreign Service Works for America,* 2d ed. (Washington, DC: American Foreign Service Association, 2003).

68. On consular functions, see R. G. Feltham, *Diplomatic Handbook,* 4th ed. (New York: Longman, 1982), pp. 48–50. See also Gore-Booth, *Satow's Guide,* pp. 216–221.

69. Berridge, *Diplomacy,* p. 140.

70. W. Wendell Blanké, "The Constituent Posts," in Herz, *Consular Dimension,* pp. 59–62; see also the other studies in ibid., "Relations Between Consulates and Embassies," pp. 62–71.

71. Victor Wolf Jr., "How to Get the Best from Constituent Posts," in Herz, *Consular Dimension,* pp. 69–71. See also Archer K. Blood, "Seen from Both Sides," in ibid., pp. 66–69; Bowling, "Tale of Three Dilemmas," pp. 62–66.

72. A visa is a formal authorization to enter the state of the consulate. Countries have created different categories of visas (e.g., tourist visas) that are valid for a limited period of time, or immigration visas to settle in the country. A passport, by contrast, is an international identity document issued by the state of nationality, usually needed to cross a border and even to buy a plane ticket for an international flight. Visas are normally stamped into a passport. Some countries issue passports to people without nationality (stateless persons) or to refugees. But these people usually still need a visa to enter a country. See A. LeRoy Bennett and James K. Oliver, *International Organizations: Principles and Issues,* 7th ed. (Upper Saddle River, NJ: Prentice-Hall, 2002), pp. 379–382. See also Ian Brownlie, *Principles of Public International Law,* 4th ed. (Oxford: Clarendon, 1990), pp. 558–559.

73. Herz, *Consular Dimension,* pp. 23–50, esp. Charles S. Kennedy, "Some Visa Cases Recalled," and Martin F. Herz, "Sparring with the Foreign Minister," in ibid., pp. 33–34 and 23–26, respectively.

74. Taylor Branch and Eugene M. Propper, "A Cautionary Tale," in Herz, *Consular Dimension,* pp. 35–39. See also David D. Newsom, "This Is Where Fraud Was Invented," in ibid., pp. 30–33.

75. Robert E. Fritts, "Consular Services and Foreign Policy," in Herz, *Consular Dimension,* pp. 5–8. See also Herz, *Consular Dimension,* pp. 51–58, esp. Charles S. Kennedy, "'Protection & Welfare' and Passports: Some Cases Remembered," pp. 51–56.

76. Brownlie, *Principles,* pp. 477–508.

77. Lori F. Damrosch, Louis Henkin, Richard Crawford Pugh, Oscar Schachter, and Hans Smit, *International Law: Cases and Materials,* 4th ed. (St. Paul, MN: West Group, 2001), pp. 742–805. An obligation to act on the claims of its nationals may of course be created by domestic legislation.

78. Giving an idea of the extent of this type of work, Ambassador Robert Fritts reports that in 1982, US consulates worldwide inquired into reports of about 172,000 Americans missing or experiencing difficulty abroad. They assisted over 5,500 arrested Americans (1,500 in jail), and handled nearly 6,000 next-of-kin death cases and about 3,500 hospital and illness cases. They were also involved in the evacuation of Americans from countries engulfed in war or revolution. Robert E. Fritts, "Consular Services and Foreign Policy," in Herz, *Consular Dimension,* p. 7.

79. Kennedy, "'Protection & Welfare,'" p. 51.

80. He gives a number of other examples of how consular personnel have so often helped people in dire need. Ibid., pp. 52–56.

81. See Gore-Booth, *Satow's Guide,* pp. 217–218. See also Feltham, *Diplomatic Handbook,* pp. 48–50.

82. See http://www.embassyworld.com and http://www.state.gov.

83. See http://www.state.gov. See also Blanké, "Constituent Posts," p. 61.

84. Barston, *Modern Diplomacy,* p. 5.

85. See Damrosch et al., *International Law,* esp. discussion of state responsibility, pp. 742–819, and discussion of international economic law, pp. 1573–1637. See also Kenneth F. Warren, *Administrative Law in the Political System,* 3d ed. (Upper Saddle River, NJ: Prentice Hall, 1996), pp. 26ff., 360–361.

86. See also Robert S. Jordan, ed., *International Administration: Its Evolution and Contemporary Applications* (New York: Oxford University Press, 1971); Chris de Cooker, ed., *International Administration: Law and Management Practices in International Organizations* (Dordrecht: Nijhoff, 1990).

87. Ambassador Robert Schaetzel stresses the importance of administrative competence. Schaetzel, "Modernizing the Role," pp. 270–271. See also Ambassador David D. Newsom, "The Tasks of an Ambassador," in Herz, *Modern Ambassador,* p. 33.

88. See http://www.embassyworld.com. See also, for example, http://www.burkina embassy-usa.org/embassy.html.

89. Feltham, *Diplomatic Handbook,* pp. 34–35.

90. See Herz, *Modern Ambassador,* pp. 31–59.

91. John R. Wood and Jean Serres, *Diplomatic Ceremonial and Protocol: Principles, Procedures, and Practices* (London: Macmillan, 1970); Pauline B. Innis, Mary Jane McCaffree, and Richard M. Sand, *Protocol: The Complete Handbook of Diplomatic, Official and Social Usage* (Dallas: Durban, 2002).

92. Herz, *Modern Ambassador,* pp. 31–59.

93. See G. R. Berridge, *Talking to the Enemy: How States Without "Diplomatic Relations" Communicate* (New York: St. Martin's, 1994).

94. Articles 45–46.

95. Gore-Booth, *Satow's Guide,* chap. 20, sec. 18, p. 166.

96. See the brief historical background in Berridge, *Diplomacy,* pp. 133–134. See also Eileen Denza, *Diplomatic Law,* 2d ed. (Oxford: Clarendon, 1998), pp. 399–402.

97. Berridge, *Diplomacy,* pp. 134–135.

98. Gore-Booth, *Satow's Guide,* chap. 11, sec. 11, p. 189.

99. Berridge, *Diplomacy,* pp. 137–138.

100. Ibid.

101. As discussed previously, consulates are now normally performing a number of diplomatic functions (e.g., public diplomacy, observing, analyzing, reporting, etc.). See also Herz, *Consular Dimension,* pp. 14–22.

102. If they wish, states can establish secret relations by means of covert missions or contact in some other national capital or in an international organization.

103. Berridge, *Diplomacy,* pp. 140–141.

104. See http://www.embassyworld.com.

105. Ibid.

106. Found in Atlanta, Boston, Chicago, Guam, Honolulu, Houston, Kansas City, Los Angeles, Miami, New York, San Francisco, and Seattle. See http://www.embassy world.com.

107. Ibid.

108. Berridge, *Diplomacy,* p. 141.

109. On August 14, in accordance with the Indian Independence Act, enacted by the British parliament. In order to separate the areas with a Muslim majority, the Indian subcontinent was divided into two states: Pakistan and India. *Worldmark Encyclopedia of the Nations,* 5th ed. (New York: Wiley, 1976), vol. 4, p. 270. See discussion on the evolution of the problem in Denis Wright, *Bangladesh: Origins and Indian Ocean Relations, 1971–75* (London: Oriental University Press, 1988), pp. 52–59.

110. Aside from problems in communication and failure to heed early warnings of crisis, this case illustrates the important role of consulates in observing the evolution of situations in regions that are very different from the embassy's locale. It also illustrates problems that may arise in the relationship between consuls and ambassadors.

111. *Europa World Year Book 2004,* 45th ed. (New York: Europa, 2004), "Bangladesh," p. 680.

112. *Worldmark,* vol. 4, pp. 28–29. See also W. Norman Brown, *The United States and India, Pakistan, Bangladesh,* 3d ed. (Cambridge: Harvard University Press, 1972), pp. 206–209.

113. Brown, *United States,* p. 211. See also Lawrence Ziring, *Politics in Pakistan: The Aub Khan Era* (Syracuse, NY: Syracuse University Press, 1971).

114. Bowling, "Tale of Three Dilemmas," p. 63.

115. *Europa,* p. 680; Wright, *Bangladesh,* pp. 64–69, 73–74.

116. Wright, *Bangladesh,* pp. 61–69.

117. Sumit Ganguly, *Conflict Unending: India-Pakistan Tensions Since 1947* (New York: Columbia University Press, 2001), pp. 52–53. Additional statistics may be found in the *Europa World Year Book* for specific years under "Pakistan" and "Bangladesh."

118. Wright, *Bangladesh,* pp. 63, 69–74.

119. *Europa,* p. 680; Wright, *Bangladesh,* pp. 74–93.

120. Bowling, "Tale of Three Dilemmas," p. 64.

121. On this issue, see Herz, *Modern Ambassador,* pp. 85–176.

122. Wright, *Bangladesh,* pp. 92–97. See also Brown, *United States,* pp. 210–211.

123. Normally, consulate reports and analyses are sent to the embassy as raw material for the embassy's own reports. Bowling, "Tale of Three Dilemmas," p. 64. See also Leonard F. Walentynowicz (administrator of the Bureau of Security and Consular

Affairs, US Department of State), "Needed: More Imagination and Flexibility," in Herz, *Consular Dimension,* pp. 20–22.

124. Bowling, "Tale of Three Dilemmas," p. 64; Ganguly, *Conflict Unending,* pp. 53–55.

125. Wright, *Bangladesh,* pp. 119–121.

126. Ganguly, *Conflict Unending,* pp. 53–55.

127. Bowling, "Tale of Three Dilemmas," p. 64. It was agreed that preserving Pakistan's unity was in the interest of the United States. See G. W. Choudhury, *India, Pakistan, Bangladesh, and the Major Powers: Politics of a Divided Subcontinent* (New York: Free Press, 1975).

128. Wright, *Bangladesh,* pp. 96–97.

129. Bowling, "Tale of Three Dilemmas," p. 65. Washington did not seem to be alarmed. Apparently, US policymakers accepted the ambassador's assessment of the situation. The fact that he was a close friend of the president may have been a factor.

130. Bowling, "Tale of Three Dilemmas," p. 65.

131. Wright, *Bangladesh,* pp. 95–96; Ganguly, *Conflict Unending,* p. 54; Brown, *United States,* p. 211.

132. Bowling, "Tale of Three Dilemmas," p. 65.

133. Wright, *Bangladesh,* pp. 96–97. General Yahya Khan replaced him as president. See also Ganguly, *Conflict Unending,* pp. 54–55, who speaks of his overthrow "in a military coup." The country was then under martial law.

134. Wright, *Bangladesh,* pp. 98–99.

135. *Europa,* p. 680.

136. Ganguly, *Conflict Unending,* pp. 59–60.

137. *Europa,* p. 680.

138. Ganguly, *Conflict Unending,* pp. 55–61.

139. *Europa,* p. 680.

140. Ganguly, *Conflict Unending,* pp. 62–68.

141. *Europa,* p. 680; Ganguly, *Conflict Unending,* pp. 68–71.

142. Bowling, "Tale of Three Dilemmas," p. 65, also p. 63. See also Blood, "Seen from Both Sides," pp. 66–69.

8 International Organization Diplomacy

International organizations have introduced remarkable changes in the practice of diplomacy. States are increasingly challenged by a variety of international problems, such as environmental degradation, that they cannot solve single-handedly. And many of these problems need continuing attention and some form of international management, as they cannot be solved once and for all. States have therefore created various types of international bodies, particularly since World War II, to deal with such problems collectively. International organizations provide forums for diplomatic interaction and decision-making. These organizations, however, also participate in the diplomatic process to carry out the mandates laid out in the documents that created them, or to implement the programs formulated by the member states. International organizations are thus international actors, engaging in extensive diplomatic activities. International organization diplomacy, however, is substantially different from the kind practiced in national capitals by embassy personnel. A variety of factors account for its special character.

▓ The Multilateral Dimension

The classic type of diplomacy practiced by embassy personnel in national capitals is bilateral. The essential task of an embassy staff is to maintain contact with the host state and defend the interests of its own nation. In an international organization, by contrast, a national delegation represents its country in the organization, defending its national interests, to be sure, as an embassy mission does, but within the organization, while seeking to fulfill the mission given to the organization by the states that created it. To do that, these diplomats need to work with the representatives of all the other member states and with organization officials—professionals employed by the organization itself rather than by any of the member states.

Some of these organization officials not only work with state representatives within the organization, but may also work directly with governments, as when UN Secretary-General Kofi Annan examined with the Sudanese government in Khartoum what needed to be done to stop the massacres in Western Sudan, or when World Bank officials negotiate with the leadership of third world governments on the financing of development projects. International organization officials also work with other organizations on joint projects—for example, when UN Children's Fund (UNICEF) professionals plan public health programs with the World Health Organization (WHO) and the UN Development Programme (UNDP). The multilateral enterprise has achieved huge proportions.

In this environment, diplomats represent a wide range of political systems, each with its own priorities and perceptions of the world and its problems. In their day-to-day activities, all of these professionals must contend with a greater range of cultural differences, work habits, and diplomatic styles. It is no longer just a matter of adjusting to the environment of the host capital (which they must still do in the foreign city that is hosting the organization's premises); they need to cope with the diversity of the whole membership and organization staff. If some organizations are small (e.g., eight members in the Nordic Council), the United Nations is nearly global (192 members plus the observers).

By definition, multilateral diplomacy is thus more complex than the traditional bilateral type. The larger the membership, the more elaborate the structure and the more complex the process. When large numbers of people need to interact, effective procedures must be devised. National parliaments have long faced this challenge, and multilateral diplomacy has quite naturally borrowed from them a variety of techniques, which in turn has led to the notion of "parliamentary diplomacy"[1] or "diplomacy by parliamentary procedures,"[2] seen by some as "open diplomacy."[3]

This development has been attacked as a corruption of diplomacy[4]—diplomacy conducted in the glare of publicity, reminiscent of President Woodrow Wilson's drive for "open covenants openly arrived at."[5] Though much of the debating function in international organizations is open to the media and affects the diplomatic process, much confidential interaction takes place in international organizations within the context of this parliamentary diplomacy. In other words, much diplomacy is shielded from the media and unwarranted publicity. Genuine negotiations, conducted with due respect for confidentiality, are indeed normally taking place, but in the context of a more complex environment.[6]

In large organizations, the membership forms coalitions or "blocs."[7] These are diverse, based on common ideology, shared interests, or regional affinity. Bloc members engage in extensive intrabloc diplomacy, which is indispensable to achieving and maintaining cohesion and acting in unison. The huge incentive in overcoming their differences is that smaller powers may thus more easily stand up to those who might be tempted to run the show. This also entails much back-and-forth communication with the governments of these coalitions, who need to be coaxed to alter their own favorite positions to permit bloc cohesion—and it often takes a good deal of convincing to achieve this objective (delegates negotiating with their *own* governments when they hear the usual retort: "Why can't the *other* governments change their position?").

Blocs seek to work with other blocs, thus generating a good deal of interbloc diplomacy in preparation for upcoming agenda issues. Blocs must organize for this sort of work, which involves, for example, selecting bloc representatives. Blocs also interact with the organization secretariat and with the leadership of subsidiary bodies of the organization—for instance, to convince a committee chair to allow more time for bloc deliberations. Individual states outside a given bloc may negotiate with bloc membership (or its representative) for bloc support—or for the purpose of influencing its course of action. Some national delegations designate one of their diplomats to act as bloc liaison. The president of the UN General Assembly usually remains in touch with voting blocs by inviting a member of each important bloc to serve in his contact group. The UN Secretary-General, too, regularly consults with bloc presidents. Bloc diplomacy is thus quite elaborate.[8]

A special characteristic of multilateral diplomacy is its "fluidity" (referring to the rapidly changing character of the diplomatic situation).[9] This phenomenon is rooted in the large amount of diplomatic interaction taking place not only in official gatherings, but also in the margin of meetings, in the corridors, and beyond organization premises. Negotiations are continuous. When agreement is reached between key players on some aspect of a question under consideration, the negotiating balance may be changed. The other delegates need to adjust to the new situation. They may have to change their negotiating stance and their approach or strategy. The next round of negotiations may thus be very different from the one that preceded it. Such fluidity is normal in this kind of environment, although each agenda item may have its own dynamics. There is a greater element of unpredictability (see Box 8.1).

This fluidity can present difficulty for strategists who are monitoring the negotiations from afar, in foreign ministries. Rapid communications, of course, enable decisionmakers, by and large, to maintain contact with diplomats in the field and remain aware of what is happening[10]—but not minute by minute, and not several time zones away. For example, when no agreement is impending and the negotiations seem to be on-course, there is no need to maintain a vigil by telephone or computer. Key policymakers in the foreign ministry can attend to other business and be inaccessible for a time. But if, at this juncture, there is an unexpected break in the negotiations and a vote is to

Box 8.1   The Rapidly Changing Diplomatic Process

I remember a negotiating session in a UN committee, during a meeting of the General Assembly in New York, that took a whole day to produce an understanding on just one point of a much larger agenda. At the end of the day, the various delegations had overcome their differences—or had at least accepted that it was time to move on. Everyone went home. When the session resumed the next morning, the presiding officer opened the meeting by reassuringly observing, "It seems we have reached agreement on this issue. Does anyone wish to add anything before we take a vote?" (chairs do not want to give the impression that they are trying to rush things). At this point, an older delegate, who had arrived late and was just reaching her desk, cleared her throat and asked—very tentatively, no sign that she intended to challenge anyone or anything—"Does this paragraph, then, mean that . . ."—whatever the clarification was. Well, as it turned out, a number of delegates let it be known (in no uncertain terms) that this was *not* the intent *at all.* And they were off and running. The negotiations had to start all over again, which goes to show that it may sometimes be unwise to seek too many clarifications.

take place in short order, how can delegates obtain new instructions? How should they vote? Is abstaining an alternative? Not everyone can secure a postponement to obtain instructions. In a fluid situation, instructions to the field may thus have to be different.

Some contingency planning is needed so that the delegations may know how to respond officially without further instructions. Greater autonomy and more substantive responsibility for heads of delegation may be necessary, at least under certain circumstances. Micromanagement from afar (always somewhat problematic) may end up becoming very costly in such a setting. Many delegates privately complain that their superiors back home have little understanding of the complex situations they face. But this has long been heard in classical (bilateral) diplomacy as well. Still, it is more pronounced in the fluid environment of a large multilateral setting.[11]

▨   Institutional Structure

The diplomacy carried out in international organizations—the mode of interaction, techniques, and strategies used—is significantly affected by the institutional framework, which of course varies from one organization to the next, although some organizations have comparable structures. What works in one organization tends to be replicated elsewhere. However, organizational structure is negotiated among states and the outcome depends in large measure on the international climate; the extent to which these states are prepared to work together; their purpose, leadership, political astuteness, and creativity; and other factors affecting the negotiation process. Great upheavals, such as World Wars I and II, led states to experiment (e.g., with the creation of the League of Nations, the United Nations, the Coal and Steel Community).

Some structural arrangements have been radically different, as in the case of the International Labour Organization (ILO),[12] in which labor and management representatives (in addition to foreign ministry diplomats) were given the right to participate and vote independently from government representatives on national delegations. People with different professional orientations (and of nondiplomatic backgrounds) were thus invited to take part in the international diplomatic process and develop global labor standards. Also, as a given organization functions, its own inner dynamics result in the development of new ways and means, and new written and unwritten rules, to meet diplomatic needs as the situation changes. To some extent, each organization creates its own diplomatic culture and process. This also happens in the component parts of a given organization. For example, the UN Security Council for a number of years was stymied by the use of the veto power in the struggles spawned by the Cold War. Eventually (while the Cold War was still in progress), Council members learned to work around the crippling use of the veto.[13]

When an issue was to be considered by the Security Council, its fifteen members began to meet informally (instead of convening in a formal session). This is known as "informal consultation." The diplomatic interaction was off-the-record. It was often acrimonious, but the representatives continued exploring the issues and looking for areas in which cooperation was possible. When a compromise was reached, then an official meeting of the Council could be called—an agreement was in place, and the meeting (often less than fifteen minutes in duration) simply formalized the decision. The debating and haggling had been done in the margin of the formal rules and the Council became much more productive. This procedure is now well established. The bulk of the Council's work now takes place in such informal consultations. A consultation room was built in 1978 for this purpose, adjacent to the Council chamber.[14] Of course, there is no guarantee that agreement can be reached. Great powers can always insist on a formal meeting so as to cast a negative vote and register their ire, but the desire to look for a cooperative approach tends to prevail.[15]

Membership

The composition of an organization makes an enormous difference in the type of diplomacy practiced there. A global organization can easily resemble the Tower of Babel. Incompatible national agendas, profound cultural and political differences, and bitter conflict among members can hinder diplomatic interaction. Sheer numbers can make the diplomatic process unwieldy, to say the least.[16] Some organizations, such as the European Union, are very selective in their admission process, which reduces conflict; but even friendly states have their differences. The addition of twelve members is now affecting interaction to the point that the European institutional framework needs to be restructured.[17] Moreover, individual members of any organization can be expected to change over time. Governments change; public sentiments fluctuate; domestic problems can drastically affect the behavior of some of the member states. These changes are often unpredictable and hard to control.[18] Consequently, membership will remain a significant factor of diversity and change in international organization diplomacy.

Membership in international organizations enables a larger number of states to participate in the diplomatic process. Quite significantly, organizations make it possible for very small or underdeveloped states to be actively involved in international affairs,[19] even when they have no strategic or other appeal to the great powers. The fact of membership makes them participants in organization deliberations, adding their voices to the international dialogue, negotiations, and decisionmaking, and thus expanding the diplomatic process. Coalitions or voting blocs give them greater influence. Great powers may bemoan this development, but great powers hold no monopoly on political wisdom. The need to win the support of the less-developed states to achieve their diplomatic objectives forces the more established states to involve them in their projects and engage in a good deal of diplomacy with them. Many small states today play a growing role in world affairs.

Another diplomatic consequence of membership in international organizations, and another facet of the expansion of the diplomatic dialogue, pertains to the substance of the interaction. Many nations, including the great powers, are impelled to participate in the discussion of issues they would prefer to ignore, such as the spread of HIV/AIDS, environmental degradation, and the plight of the destitute. They are drawn into the diplomatic interaction when these issues are placed on the agenda by other members[20]—particularly when some form of action is contemplated.

■ Function of the Organization

The purpose or mission of an international organization is another factor that defines its diplomacy. Many organizations, large or small, are highly specialized or technical in their work. Political considerations usually remain important, but the primary focus tends to go beyond political concerns for most members. International political issues will be less pronounced in the negotiation of standards of air-worthiness for passenger aircraft in the International Civil Aviation Organization (ICAO), one of the UN's specialized agencies, than in the discussion of nuclear energy in the International Atomic Energy Agency (IAEA), another UN body. The member state representatives involved in this work will require specialized training or expertise: for example, nuclear engineering in the IAEA, or medical or public health experience in the World Health Organization. The mission of the organization and the professional training of the representatives will inevitably give a special character to this kind of diplomacy. Some foreign ministry personnel will still be found in these national delegations. Their professional experience in diplomatic negotiations and the conclusion of international agreements, and their knowledge of world politics and related security concerns, are undoubtedly important, but a whole array of experts and professionals in a large variety of fields are needed in the diplomatic work of these organizations, and many of them have little diplomatic experience. Inevitably, this affects the character of the diplomatic process. Experts are constrained by the technical parameters of their field, even when they must heed the political considerations of the governments they represent (governments continue to instruct their delegations on their policy choices).

■ Parliamentary Procedure

International organization diplomacy, no matter how greatly influenced by these factors, is even more significantly defined by a process indispensable to multilateral interaction.[21] It has been compared to the political process found in national parliaments.[22] This process can be misleading, particularly when it is considered a "corruption" of diplomacy.[23]

A multilateral setting requires presentations (i.e., formulations of proposals, statements of position) before the entire membership. Many people, in and out of organizations, call this a "debate"; but in large assemblies, this is more like a series of monologues. Very often, a right of reply is given to the membership following certain procedures that seldom permit an instant reply. In general, respondents must place their names on a speakers' list and wait until all those who were previously scheduled to speak are done. Thus a long time may elapse (and many more speeches on different subjects must be heard) before a response can be given. In fact, a respondent may be wise to remind the assembled diplomats what was the original point that is now to be discussed or disputed. This seldom amounts to what one might call a "lively debate." Nevertheless, competing positions can be heard. The "debate" need not be public. Some rules of procedure permit informal discussion, back and forth, when deemed necessary. This kind of exchange is generally moderated by the chair of the meeting. It comes closer to a debate when the participants may ask to be recognized by raising their hand and some continuity can be maintained in the interaction.

The debate format may have a negative effect on diplomacy. A position taken in an open debate may complicate the give and take of subsequent negotiations. A diplomat may find it more difficult to back down after taking a stand in a debate. A public statement therefore tends to reduce flexibility in the negotiating process, unless cautiously presented and carefully qualified. On the positive side, ideas may be tested in the open forum: suggestions are tentatively presented to see how the assembled diplomats will react. In the debating process, diplomats endowed with oratorical skill have an obvious advantage, as Adlai Stevenson showed at the UN. His superb oratory was frequently capable of swaying some delegates before a vote, or of winning support in some disputed issues. Oratorical effect, however, may lead diplomats to depart from the reserve and tact that are the hallmark of professional diplomacy. By and large, debates remain civil enough, but if the atmosphere of the meeting is sufficiently charged, or the issue sufficiently ideological, intemperate or even abusive language is occasionally used by some delegates, particularly in open forums (on the issue of politicization, see Chapter 9).

The media become a more conspicuous factor when issues are debated outside closed meetings. Just as happens in national politics, some pronouncements are intended for public consumption. States are increasingly conscious of the importance of public opinion in foreign relations, and diplomats are enlisted in the effort to sway the public despite the fact that diplomatic work normally requires a good deal of quiet interaction away from the limelight and the mass media. It must be acknowledged also that some public pronouncements or leaks to the media may be resorted to for diplomatic reasons—for example, to test the reaction to ideas or propositions. They may also be used (undiplomatically) to embarrass "the other side" or otherwise put it at a disadvantage. But there is a price to be paid: distrust, which hampers subsequent diplomatic work.

Decisions in multilateral diplomacy require voting procedure. Many forms of voting are specified in the constitutions of international organizations or their bylaws.[24] Voting procedures can be somewhat elaborate, as in the weighted system of the International Monetary Fund (IMF) (see Box 8.2), or in the formula of the UN Security Council, in which a decision requires the affirmative vote of the five permanent members, with a negative vote thus amounting to a veto. Some votes are by secret ballot, voice, or show of hands; some are electronically expressed (the members press a button on their desk), recorded (a list of how each member decided is issued), or unrecorded (only the outcome is shown). Votes can also be changed (see Box 8.3).

Decision by consensus is a procedure that has become popular in some organizations, particularly UN bodies. In this case, the delegates let the officers know informally (i.e., during the negotiations or the diplomatic process) that they are not opposed to what is proposed. If it turns out that no delegates voice any opposition, this is understood as a sign of consensus. One need not be *for* the proposition. One need only refrain from opposing it. During the last meeting

Box 8.2   Weighted Voting in the International Monetary Fund

Voting power is determined by the financial commitment to the International Monetary Fund of each member state. This commitment is specified as a quota. A member's quota is determined by its economic position relative to other member states (the same formula is used in the World Bank). Various economic factors are taken into account in determining changes in quotas, including gross domestic product, current account transactions, and official reserves.

Quotas are denominated in special drawing rights (SDRs), the IMF's monetary unit for accounting purposes. The largest IMF member is the United States, with a quota of 37.1 billion SDRs (about $55.2 billion), and the smallest member is Palau, with a quota of 3.1 million SDRs (about $4.6 million).

The quota essentially determines a member's voting power in IMF decisions. Each IMF member has a basic 250 votes plus 1 additional vote for each 100,000 SDRs of quota. Accordingly, the United States has 250 + 371,493 = 371,743 votes (17.1 percent of the total), and Palau has 250 + 31 = 281 votes (0.013 percent of the total).

Source: http://www.imf.org/external/np/exr/facts/quotas.

Box 8.3   Changing One's Vote

During a meeting of one of the large main committees of the UN General Assembly that I attended, after a vote had just been completed, one of the delegates asked if he could change his vote (not an unusual occurrence). The Assembly president accepted and asked him what the change was to be. "Please change my vote from *abstain* to *absent*." He wasn't joking, but the whole membership had a good laugh.

on an issue, the chair (addressing the assembled delegates) will declare: "It is my understanding that there is a consensus on this issue. Do I hear anyone to the contrary?" (Or words to that effect.) If any delegate is opposed to making this decision by consensus (e.g., having failed to notify the chair during the informal polling of the delegates or having changed his or her mind), all this diplomat needs to do is ask that a vote be taken, in which case the meeting will resort to whatever voting method is allowed. Otherwise the chair simply announces: "Hearing no objection, the proposition is approved." This is a decision by consensus—a procedure that is expeditious and quite popular. No majority is recorded. It is a low-key procedure that can facilitate some decisions.

Another feature of the parliamentary process is the role of committees in international organization diplomacy. The main bodies of international organizations distribute their workload to committees. This enables them to accomplish more. Some are sessional committees: they meet during the annual meeting of the organization. The General Assembly of the United Nations has six main committees,[25] each composed of the entire UN membership ("committee of the whole"). The 170 (or more) items on the General Assembly agenda[26] are distributed among these specialized committees, although some items may be assigned directly to a plenary meeting of the Assembly itself. Thus seven bodies of the whole membership work more or less simultaneously during the annual session of the UN General Assembly. Other committees are ad hoc, meeting according to their own schedule until their negotiations are accomplished. Some of them end up deliberating over a number of years. Others are permanent committees. Some are of limited membership. All of these committees[27] send what they accomplish (draft resolutions, proposed work programs, etc.) to the body that created them for final decision.

One of the diplomatic consequences of this committee structure is that national delegations need additional personnel to take care of the workload, since these committees have their own independent work schedule and may often meet simultaneously. Small delegations are thus handicapped,[28] as certain diplomats may have to cover a multiplicity of committees. When their meetings overlap, these delegates have to run from one committee to another to catch the issues of interest to their state, and miss out on the interaction taking place in their absence. The committee structure also leads to a degree of specialization among members of diplomatic delegations—at least for delegations large enough to afford the division of labor. All of this entails additional staff meetings for national delegations to coordinate diplomatic work and ensure that all representatives of a given nation work in unison and present to the outside world a coherent expression of their state's foreign policy.

Committee diplomacy tends to make the work of the members of national delegations more interesting.[29] The division of labor ensures that more members of a delegation are given substantive responsibilities. Even junior officers are in charge of the interaction pertaining to their committee. An interesting by-product of this situation is a departure from a long-standing diplomatic tradition in which officers are expected to interact at equal rank. Each country selects its representative on a given committee according to its own priorities and availability of personnel. A country attaching great importance to a particular issue or subject matter is likely to be represented on the committee discussing it by its head of mission, probably a diplomat with the rank of ambassador. Another country, having different concerns or a limited staff, may send a junior officer. Thus the interaction in committees frequently takes place across a variety of diplomatic ranks.

All this multilateral diplomatic work, particularly in large organizations, will necessitate the use of rules of procedure that are often complex.[30] A skillful use of these rules is important to achieve one's diplomatic objectives: rules pertaining to precedence, placing issues on the agenda, the presentation of resolutions, closing a debate, or the order in which voting will take place. Nothing comparable is found in bilateral diplomacy (unless one includes rules of protocol and local usages). Diplomatic strategy will be significantly affected by the rules of procedure of a given organization, and diplomats need to learn how to use them in their work.

Each organ and each subsidiary body controls the handling of its own agenda. A committee, usually called a general committee or a bureau, made up of the officers of this body and a representative of the secretariat (i.e., the bureaucracy), and perhaps the heads of the main committees, will oversee the preparation of draft resolutions and the flow of documents, determine whether additional meetings are needed, and much more, particularly in regard to monitoring how the diplomatic work is progressing to respect the larger time frame of a particular session.

Timing is a huge concern of international organizations.[31] The diplomatic timetable is defined by a variety of factors, the first of which is customary practice. Annual meetings, for example, tend to start and end upon dates that become customary. There is pressure for diplomats to operate within this time frame: the pressure to accomplish all that must be done during the limited time available can be grueling[32]—for example, in the last stages of the annual session of the UN General Assembly. Extra meetings are often required to meet deadlines. Controversial issues produce deadlocks, which can destroy a meeting's work schedule; extra negotiating sessions must be squeezed in and perhaps night sessions—in times of crisis, even all-night sessions (see, for example, the case study on the Suez crisis in Chapter 3). The timetable is also defined by the agenda. The larger the organization and the more extensive its agenda, the more critical timing becomes. The officers of a particular meeting will keep pushing the delegates to make progress. Thus international organization diplomacy is extremely conscious of deadlines.

There are deadlines for everything: deadlines to get material into the hands of the secretariat to get it translated and distributed for consideration when a particular agenda item is to be considered; deadlines for the discussion of specific agenda items; deadlines set by committees to produce the resolutions and other drafts to be submitted to the main bodies; and of course, the ultimate deadline of the specified end of the session. All of this adds a considerable amount of stress to the work of these diplomats, not to mention the members of the secretariat.[33] Most sessions start slowly. Diplomats try to take care of the easy items first, but even then, they still often fall behind. As time marches on, delegates have to be threatened with the convening of night meetings to finish all agenda items. Diplomatic work becomes hectic even when there is no crisis, or the crisis is simply to address all agenda items before adjournment. Time pressures may push diplomats to reach agreement on stalled issues—or make mistakes. Legislatures in many democracies face similar time pressures.

In all this, how much diplomacy is actually conducted? Some analysts conclude that, in this parliamentary environment, diplomacy as it was known in the nineteenth century is compromised.[34] Of course, the process is different. Interdependence and the problems faced by international society have made multilateral diplomacy a necessity. And multilateral diplomacy is impossible without the paraphernalia of parliamentary procedure. But an enormous amount of diplomatic work is actually accomplished, as traditionally understood—quiet interaction, communication, consultation and negotiation, the search for common ground and alternatives to confrontation.

The "debating," speech-making, and vote-taking are all preceded by painstaking, quiet diplomacy and behind-the-scenes negotiations. Diplomacy takes place in the corridors; at lunch meetings, dinners, and receptions; in exchanges of messages; over the telephone; and even in the assembly halls and committee meetings as other representatives are making speeches. Delegates move about the meeting room, gather at a desk to confer with another diplomat, or caucus in the back of the room.[35] All of this is "diplomacy" in the full sense of the term, though the purpose may be different. It may be to obtain a more favorable outcome when a vote is taken for a particular decision or resolution. Or it may be intended to rally support for a more judicious use of funds or a more accommodating presentation in the course of the debate. Diplomatic interaction in the margin of speech-making or between committee meetings may also be intended to find terms to defuse a conflict, or lead more states to provide troops for a peacekeeping operation. As with introducing new legislation in the US Congress, diplomats intent on presenting a resolution in an international organization need to engage in a good deal of diplomacy and old-fashioned horse-trading to obtain cosponsors as an indication of support, even before the matter comes up for discussion on the floor. In fact, international organizations generate much more diplomatic negotiations than conventional representation in national capitals. Every item placed on the agenda requires some form of negotiation because of the diversity of positions held by the member states. Most of the extensive committee work entails multilateral negotiations. Negotiations precede the debates, continue during the debates, and even continue after positions have been publicly presented in the debates.[36]

As organizations address a variety of very specialized or technical matters,[37] experts and specialists in many fields, in addition to foreign service officers, participate in these negotiations. This development contributes to changes in the style of diplomatic negotiations. Change is also caused by the broad range of cultures assembled in large international organizations.[38] This can be a challenge for diplomatic officers who have never served in any inter national organization.[39] It has been suggested that diplomats ought to receive special training for multilateral work (many have to make do with training on the job). And experienced officers ought to be kept longer in this line of work instead of being rotated back to bilateral duties (as is frequently the case).

■ Other Aspects of International Organization Diplomacy

A number of peculiarities may be found in international organization diplomacy. First, in a formal sense, only member states may be *participants in the diplomatic process of international organizations*. Some organizations, however, such as the UN, agree to receive observer delegations. These cannot vote, but they may be given a variety of privileges, such as the right to attend the meetings of the main organs, address the membership in a variety of situations, and receive copies of all official documentation. And in any case, they engage in extensive diplomacy, interacting with state delegates on issues of interest to them. Observer status is occasionally granted to nonstates or revolutionary organizations, such as the Palestine Liberation Organization (PLO), further expanding the realm of diplomatic interaction.

Representatives of member states interact extensively with members of organization secretariats, who are indispensable to the functioning of international organizations. Some secretariat members—and not just the secretary-general—have diplomatic rather than administrative functions (or both). Many participate in decisionmaking, particularly in the programs they operate jointly with member states. They engage in the continuing diplomatic activity required for the implementation of projects mandated by the member states. They promote agreement among states, act as mediators, and engage in a variety of problem solving.[40] In some organizations, such as the European Union, nonmembers send liaison missions to maintain contact with the organization and its membership. This practice further highlights the importance of international organizations as actors in international affairs. Just as states need to maintain contact with other states, some need to maintain contact with organizations in which they do not participate. Many international organizations experience the same need to keep abreast of developments in certain organizations and maintain their own liaison missions. This is true particularly of the specialized agencies linked to the United Nations by international agreement. They are dispersed around the world, and need to follow the proceedings of the main organs at UN headquarters in New York.

Nongovernmental organizations (NGOs), more and more anxious to play a role in world affairs, are pushing hard to be heard and to influence the diplomatic process. Moved by the growth of global civil society and NGO activism, a number of international organizations are accepting various forms of NGO participation (see Chapter 5). The World Bank, for example, is now including NGO representatives in the planning and decisionmaking pertaining to a variety of projects. NGOs are particularly helpful in the implementation of projects at the grassroots level. International organization interaction with NGO representatives is expanding in a variety of fields, particularly in economic and social development and humanitarian pursuits. International organizations are thus instruments of interaction between state representatives and NGO leadership. They are a factor in the expansion of international activity and in the development of unconventional channels to address a growing variety of international problems, although most of these organizations were not designed to move in this direction when they were created.

Second, a form of activity called *nonagenda diplomacy* takes place in a number of organizations. It refers to transactions conducted in the margin of the agenda (the regular work program of an organization, normally drawn up by the membership). Nothing prevents member states from using their diplomatic delegates in any organizations to conduct diplomatic business of their own with other delegates, totally outside the agenda—literally bilateral diplomacy carried out in an international organization.[41] An organization can indeed be a useful point of contact for nations that maintain no diplomatic relations with each other. This may be because of their efforts to reduce costs (i.e., curtail traditional diplomatic representation), or because they do not normally need to be in regular contact, or perhaps because of enmity. In fact, in this case, the organizational setting may permit contacts that might be too politically sensitive to maintain in any official manner. This form of interaction occasionally occurs in national capitals as well, between the embassies of two states that do not maintain diplomatic relations with each other. Normally, of course, state embassies in a foreign capital conduct diplomatic business exclusively with the host state.

Third, another less conventional feature in international organization diplomacy is provided by *state representatives in non-national roles*. This is termed "less conventional" because diplomats normally act in the name of their own states and seek to protect their states' interests (more or less narrowly defined, depending upon the countries' policy orientations). Organizations are divided into a variety of subsidiary bodies, commissions, and committees composed of representatives of member states. These substructures normally elect their own officers from the ranks of their diplomatic membership. The chief officers ("presidents" or "chairs") are expected to facilitate the work of these bodies instead of acting as promoters of their own states' interests. For example, the chair of a committee cannot discriminate against the representative of a country engaged in hostile relations with his or her own country. Professional behavior demands impartiality. Failure of the committee chair to act impartially will keep this person from being chosen for such a position of leadership in the future.[42] Member states, by and large, understand the situation and do not interfere, although trying to be a state agent *and* an impartial officer can be a difficult balancing act.

Another form of non-national behavior often arises spontaneously. Some diplomats are natural facilitators, independent of their government instructions. As they work with their colleagues, they act as problem-solvers, troubleshooters, or even mediators in conflicted situations within the organization. This type of activity is usually appreciated and makes such diplomats more effective.

Fourth, international organizations invite *leadership* in the ranks of diplomatic personnel. Normally, governments take initiatives and instruct their representatives to carry them out. Member states exercise leadership. However, national diplomats still take initiatives on their own authority—not working at cross-purposes with their own state policies, but rather to solve international problems by adopting non-national roles. In a sense, this is an extension of the role of some diplomats as facilitators. But the diplomatic process in international organizations lends itself to the individual exercise of leadership.[43]

Heads of annual meetings, committees, and sub-bodies, in their non-national roles, are expected to lead in order to get the job done, work with the organization bureaucracy, push committee members to make greater effort to produce their resolutions, suspend regular proceedings and engage in informal negotiations to break a deadlock, and so much more. Their leadership can make a great deal of difference in the fulfillment of their organizational tasks. Some leadership techniques developed by diplomats have evolved into widely accepted procedures. In the UN General Assembly, the president (a member state diplomat) usually creates his own cabinet, under the name "Friends of the President," to help him in the complex task of running the four-month-long annual meeting of the Assembly (among other duties outside the meeting itself) and to process up to 200 agenda items. The president selects a number of trusted delegates whose judgment he values, and meets periodically with them to solicit advice on leading the Assembly, strategizing, and conducting various presidential tasks.

Contact groups represent another informal device by means of which the president remains in touch with the various groupings of delegates, voting blocs, and caucuses that have a significant impact on the business of the Assembly. These are made up of delegates who have the trust of their groups and can convey to the president a sense of the deliberations of each group, and even help this officer guide the groups in tackling the Assembly's agenda. The president uses his diplomatic skills to ensure the success of the annual session, a large undertaking.[44] In addition, small informal negotiating groups have long been used by the officers of multilateral gatherings to help with the difficulties that arise in the negotiating process (e.g., during the conclusion of a treaty, if a few states are blocking progress).[45] The representatives of the key countries involved in the deadlock are brought together, which generally amounts to just a few delegates, as their allies will be likely to fall in line when the leading protagonists have come to a compromise. These negotiating groups can work separately on the issues that are producing the deadlock while the regular negotiations continue simultaneously on the other aspects of a treaty or whatever else is being negotiated.

Fifth, a substantial amount of diplomacy in international organizations is focused on *running the organization* (and not just a meeting)—that is, doing what it takes to keep the organization functioning effectively: election of officers, adoption of the budget, and administrative oversight, among other tasks. These issues are of course politically important to the member states and involve a significant amount of diplomacy; in fact, some of this diplomacy may lead to a restructuring of the organization or change the ways in which international issues are resolved.[46]

▣ Diplomatic Role of the International Organization Bureaucracy

International organizations have created a new species of diplomat: diplomats who are not representing a specific nation-state or controlled by a particular foreign ministry. They receive their instructions from the international organization departments for which they work, or from the organization's chief executive officer, who is under the authority of the member states. Some of the diplomatic functions of these international public servants (i.e., secretariat personnel) may come from the documents that created the organization (e.g., the UN Charter) or from the unwritten rules flowing from practical experience. A good example is found in the diplomatic work of the Secretary-General of the United Nations. Not only is he chief UN administrator, in charge of the UN bureaucracy (the Secretariat), but the Charter specifies that "the Secretary-General may bring to the attention of the Security Council any matter which *in his opinion* may threaten the maintenance of international peace and security."[47]

Even more important, the UN membership, from the very beginning of the organization in 1945, wanted him to play an important political role. For that reason, they chose Trygve Lie, foreign minister of Norway, to be the first occupant of the post, instead of a career civil servant as was done in the League of Nations. Lie was an activist, and so was his successor, Dag Hammarskjöld. The latter's effective diplomacy came to define what was expected of future Secretaries-General. And a number of UN officials are used to carry out the diplomatic functions of the office of the Secretary-General (under the latter's authority). These, too, are diplomats in non-national roles. And there are more of them than is usually acknowledged.[48] They enjoy diplomatic immunities fully comparable to those of national delegates. Such immunities are usually specified in the documents (i.e., treaties) that created these organizations. In the case of the United Nations, the matter is governed by the General Convention on the Privileges and Immunities of the United Nations,[49] and by the Agreement Between the United States of America and the United Nations Regarding the Headquarters of the United Nations.[50] Other headquarters agreements have been negotiated between organizations and their host states.

National governments have also legislated on the matter, granting international organization officials in the diplomatic category the same immunities found in the 1961 Vienna Convention on Diplomatic Relations. The usual procedure specified in treaties and domestic legislation is for the chief administrators of international organizations to provide the foreign ministry of the host state a list of the international organization officers who are of diplomatic grade and entitled to specified immunities.

Many members of international secretariats—even some who are not officially of diplomatic rank—are instrumental in facilitating the diplomatic process within a given organization.[51] They are a link between the national representatives and the bureaucracy. Secretariat diplomats help the agency's chief executive carry out his or her mandate, and are thus sent as negotiators, mediators, observers, and troubleshooters to intervene in a vast variety of crisis situations. Some of them are needed to take care of the negotiations and other political aspects of peacekeeping operations. Their work serves as a reminder that international organizations, in addition to being a forum for diplomatic interaction, have become "international actors" in the full sense of the term: they are intended to work with other international actors. Some secretariat personnel provide a diplomatic link with other international organizations[52] and cooperate on joint projects. Equally included in this category of international organization diplomats are the directors of a large variety of technical or specialized bodies (e.g., such as the IAEA—see Box 8.4) as well as the agents of those bodies. They are the chief executive officers of their organizations, responsible for the fulfillment of their missions. But to do their job and implement their programs, they must negotiate with state representatives, raise funds with governments, and negotiate with them to secure their cooperation and to facilitate the work of their organizations. All of this is diplomatic work—program diplomacy—vastly expanding the realm of traditional diplomacy.

The diplomacy of international organization officials has a tendency to grow. Many organizations network and negotiate joint projects.[53] As organizations are given more tasks to perform in the world, some of them find it necessary to be represented abroad, so that we find diplomatic agents representing international organizations in foreign capitals, working with their host governments to facilitate interaction with the agencies concerned. An example of this phenomenon is found in the field representatives of the UN Development Programme who work in developing nations, and EU representatives in Washington.[54] The UN Environment Programme (UNEP) maintains liaison personnel with the European Union

Box 8.4   UN Atomic Agency and Chief Win 2005 Nobel Peace Prize

Mohamed ElBaradei, reelected for a third term as director-general of the
International Atomic Energy Agency (IAEA), shared the 2005 Nobel Peace
Prize with his agency for the difficult endeavor of preventing the spread of
nuclear weapons. It was the eighth time that the prize has been awarded to
the UN or one of its officials or agencies. Notably, ElBaradei had succeeded
in dismantling Iraq's nuclear program in the 1990s, and Libya's more recently. His diplomacy had been particularly significant in the midst of the international conflicts associated with his mission. The United States had been
particularly antagonistic and uncooperative with regard to his work in Iraq,
and subsequently with regard to Iran.

ElBaradei, sixty-three at the time of the award, was born in Cairo and
studied law there; he earned his doctorate in international law at New York
University, and taught there from 1981 to 1987. He joined the IAEA in 1984
as legal counsel and deputy director-general for external relations. Observers
praise him for having learned to balance the competing pressures from member states.

Source: New York Times, October 8, 2005, pp. A1, A6.

in Brussels, with the Arab League in Cairo, and with UN headquarters in New
York. It also maintains representatives in regional offices.[55] Most of these agents
do not come from the foreign service of any nation.[56] They may have some international experience in the field of the organization—for example, nuclear engineering for the IAEA; public health, medicine, social development, or even public relations for UNICEF and WHO—but they all learn their diplomacy from
practical experience.

▨ Channels of Diplomatic Activity

Diplomatic work pertaining to international organizations is conducted in a
variety of interactions, not limited to relations between the representatives of
member states in the organization, though the latter constitute the main element of this diplomatic exercise. The larger the organization, the more complex the process. Some agenda items present little difficulty and consensus is
easily reached, but many issues seriously divide national delegates. Global society is very interdependent, but its component units continue to see our common problems from very different perspectives, and it is frequently difficult to
develop common approaches. The multilateral diplomatic process is thus frequently tortuous.[57]

In light of the difficulty in achieving cooperation from other governments, delegations may try to persuade their own governments to modify their own positions and their instructions for the sake of achieving some form of agreement. Thus delegations negotiate with their own governments. A common complaint of diplomats in this multilateral environment is that policymakers back home are too often out of touch with the complex reality of the situation in the field—and there is a degree of truth to this argument. Buried under the mass of dispatches, many policymakers are not sufficiently conversant with what diplomats in the field are telling them, and this problem is not limited to multilateral diplomacy. This channel of interaction—communication with one's own government and policymakers—needs greater attention. Better bureaucratic arrangements to this effect can help the conduct of foreign relations.[58]

There is also a growing amount of bilateral diplomacy conducted (through traditional channels—embassies) in connection with multilateral activities. For example, pairs of countries attempt common efforts within a given organization, or attempt to resolve their differences in connection with an issue being dealt with in a multilateral forum. These bilateral efforts may even be requested by representatives in the multilateral forum, as when a chief of mission requests his or her government to intervene with another government in the attempt to obtain greater cooperation in a given organization. Some embassies are devoting an increasing percentage of their duties to multilateral work, another manifestation of complex interdependence.[59]

As well, diplomats from different countries frequently help one another in international organizations—and not necessarily on orders from their governments. Delegates often ask their counterparts to intercede with hostile colleagues to avoid deadlock. More systematic forms of networking take place, particularly in large organizations (i.e., bloc politics), which some call "the group system." All kinds of coalitions are possible. In fact, the memberships of some coalitions change according to the issue at hand. Joining forces and voting together gives the participants greater significance. Third world nations have long been conscious of this, particularly at the UN,[60] but great powers, too, know how to play the game.

National delegates know the importance of working with the secretariat of their organization, another channel of diplomatic activity. Secretariat members do not, as a rule, formally take part in the political interaction, but they are extremely important for the effective functioning of the complex structures found in international organizations. Having the support of secretariat personnel helps to avoid bureaucratic bottlenecks. Organization officials also facilitate contacts between national representatives, and many organizations (as international actors) now conduct their own diplomatic relations, so national delegates need to work with them. As mentioned previously, some international organizations send their own officials on special missions to negotiate with national governments (particularly in mediation efforts) and with other organizations.

Thus international organizations have created a complex network of diplomatic activity. There are now about 200 nation-states in the world, and more than 1,800 international organizations, not to mention their subsidiary bodies (see Chapter 5). As interdependence becomes more pronounced, particularly with the expansion of globalization, it is likely that more avenues of diplomatic activity will become available, which will further complicate the conduct of foreign relations.

▓ Peacekeeping Diplomacy

Peacekeeping is a fairly novel method of preventing the escalation of conflict.[61] It is rooted in the use of diplomacy to permit the peaceful deployment of an international, neutral force, in an effort to separate antagonists, provide impartial, reliable policing of a tense situation, and monitor future developments. This usually implies extremely delicate diplomatic proceedings involving conflict on the verge of escalation, high emotions, and profound reluctance to compromise. For the operation to remain peaceful, the parties involved in the confrontation must give their consent to the deployment of the force, and often to every aspect of the operation: composition of the force (i.e., what national contingents are acceptable on their territory), what the force will be allowed to do in the field, duration of the operation, who will be allowed to order its withdrawal, and many matters difficult to specify in advance need to be negotiated. It takes a great deal of diplomacy to negotiate all these issues. A further difficulty is that the bitterness of many confrontations and the legacy of brutality may necessitate a long-term peacekeeping effort, thus requiring more extensive diplomatic activity.[62]

International organizations do not have a monopoly on peacekeeping procedures, since any group of states may embark upon this kind of intervention. But international organizations offer a better guarantee of impartiality and may thus have a diplomatic advantage. Too, international organizations are more likely to undertake the difficult and expensive task. The spread of ethnic and other forms of civil conflict around the world has led to a more extensive recourse to peacekeeping. Interdependence induces nations and international organizations to be more concerned about these kinds of conflict, as they tend to spread beyond the territory in which they originate, particularly when terrorism is used.

Peacekeeping operations became recognized as an effective tool in the wake of the 1956 Suez crisis and the diplomatic efforts of UN Secretary-General Dag Hammarskjöld (see the case study in Chapter 3). The dangerous situation was brought under control and many at the UN saw great hope in the future use of this method. Though peacekeeping has indeed become an important instrument of conflict management, its success hinges on the critical role of diplomacy.[63] As of mid-2007, the UN has undertaken sixty-one peacekeeping operations, seventeen of which were deployed in trouble spots around the world, involving more than 100,000 personnel.[64]

▣ Case Study: Dag Hammarskjöld's Mission to Beijing

Fifteen US Air Force personnel who had been serving under the UN Unified Command during the Korean War were being held by Communist China. These included eleven crew members of a B-29 that had been shot down on January 12, 1953, during a leaflet-dropping mission over North Korea, and four jet pilots who had been shot down between September 1952 and April 1953 after straying over the Chinese border.[65] The war was over but the United States and the People's Republic of China remained locked in bitter enmity.[66]

In November 1954, Radio Beijing[67] announced that the eleven had been convicted of espionage by a military tribunal and sentenced to prison terms ranging from four years to life. On December 4, the United States asked the UN to secure their release. Two days later, the US government specified that the Secretary-General be personally involved in the negotiations. Dag Hammarskjöld accepted, provided he was requested to do so by the General Assembly, and the United States proceeded to draft a resolution to that effect (with appropriate cosponsors). But even before the Assembly acted, Hammarskjöld was exploring with trusted friends how to approach the problem. On such occasions, he liked to invite a few people to dinner at his apartment and conduct what amounted to an all-night seminar, exploring alternatives and developing a strategy. Hammarskjöld was remarkable for his ability to dialogue through the night and still manage to put in a full day of work at the UN.[68] His friends and close associates, too, must have been endowed with strong resilience.

On December 10, the General Assembly passed a resolution requesting the Secretary-General to seek the release of the airmen, importantly specifying "by the means most appropriate in his judgment."[69] This mission, however, looked far from promising, as the United Nations, under US leadership, had systematically excluded Communist China from membership. Moreover, it was a time of increased tension in the Far East and in the Taiwan Strait,[70] creating an angry mood among the American public and generating frequent verbal attacks between the antagonists.

Gambling to See Chou En-lai

Hammarskjöld was convinced that his only chance of success was to negotiate directly with Prime Minister Chou En-lai. The first hurdle, however, was to convince Chou to meet with him. Indeed, he ran the risk of a humiliating refusal that would harm his stature as Secretary-General. There was another difficulty: the

General Assembly resolution mandating Hammarskjöld's mission contained a strong condemnation of China—remarkably inserted at the insistence of the United States—another example of ideology undercutting diplomacy. Not surprisingly, the wording triggered profound anger in Beijing.

The Secretary-General began consulting with heads of mission in New York, seeking support for his unconventional and risky mission to Beijing. He was officially requested to do the negotiating, but ultimately he needed to retain the support of the key actors in the UN. The United States had already concluded that this effort would fail; its strategy in requesting UN intervention may have been intended simply to expose Beijing's intransigence and increase international opposition to China. In such circumstances, a negotiator could not be blamed for feeling used. But Hammarskjöld accepted the challenge. Some UN delegations thought that it might be wise for the Secretary-General to begin by contacting Chou En-lai through an intermediary, and suggested using a special envoy acting secretly. Hammarskjöld of course realized that if he were to approach Chou directly, he would risk a flat refusal. But a secret inquiry, if it failed, would remain secret, outside the public record.[71] Thus he chose the direct approach, despite the risk.

Hammarskjöld sent Chou two communications. The first one, on the same day the General Assembly acted (December 10, 1954), was sent by commercial cable, published four hours later (thus making public his attempt to meet with Chou), and was to arrive in Beijing as soon as possible after news reports of the UN decision. In it, he endeavored to present his visit as his own initiative, rather than in his capacity as representative of the General Assembly[72]— his "completely free" role, which eventually came to be known as "the Beijing formula." In the second message, sent secretly through Indian channels, Hammarskjöld stressed the extraordinary nature of his initiative: it was the first time that the UN Secretary-General would personally visit a capital for negotiations. Hammarskjöld suggested that he and Chou establish a confidential contact through the Chinese ambassador in Stockholm, Sweden, to make all necessary arrangements. He explained that he was planning to be there on December 19 and 20.[73]

Hammarskjöld's approach worked. Chou En-lai replied that he was prepared to receive him, and in a second cablegram sent the same day, Chou emphasized the distinction between Hammarskjöld's mission and the General Assembly's resolution—Hammarskjöld had indeed made a smart distinction, the very thing that is so often vital in the conduct of diplomacy: the art of diplomatic signaling.[74] Chou added that he found the Assembly resolution "absurd."[75] Before his departure, Hammarskjöld organized another all-night seminar to perfect his approach to the case:[76] he invited two prominent US jurists to dinner (including Philip Jessup),[77] and led them into a discussion of the international legal issues of the case (the status of prisoners of war in international law, their rights, and the obligations of detaining powers, among others).

The Secretary-General wanted to present his case on legally solid foundations. He recruited an interpreter from Sweden and asked the British foreign ministry to provide the best international legal adviser it could find. Humphrey Waldock, international law professor at Oxford, joined his team. He also took with him the chief of the UN Department of Public Information[78]—an interesting touch that showed his appreciation for the importance of the media in diplomatic work.[79]

On December 17, 1954, Hammarskjöld left New York for the meeting of the Swedish Academy that he had been scheduled to attend. It served as a cover for his conference with the Chinese ambassador in Stockholm, as arranged by Chou En-lai, to discuss his trip to Beijing. To ensure secrecy, they met at a private lunch at the home of a close friend of Hammarskjöld's. They agreed that the meeting in Beijing would last four or five days. The discussion would be on "pertinent questions" and there would be no agenda. Chou was undoubtedly interested in discussing China's UN membership and the issue of Taiwan, and these were probably significant factors in his decision to see Hammarskjöld.

The Mission

The Secretary-General returned from Stockholm on December 21. Once the Beijing visit had been publicly announced, he tried to downplay the mission and declined all requests to take any press correspondents with him. But there was an avalanche of speculation in the media. Leaving on December 30 for Beijing,[80] he stopped in London, Paris, and New Delhi to meet with the respective prime ministers and gain more support for his mission. He reached Beijing on January 5, 1955. After lunch with the Swedish ambassador, he paid a courtesy visit to Chou En-lai, who later gave a reception for him in the Palace of Purple Light, after which Hammarskjöld dined privately with Chou. Hammarskjöld and his personal staff stayed at the Swedish embassy and the rest of his party were accommodated at a hotel.[81]

The official conversations took place daily in the sitting room of the premier's office in the old palace called the Hall of the Western Flowers, beginning at three in the afternoon and breaking off between five and six, except on one occasion when the talks continued until after eight.[82] In between, the Chinese did everything possible to make their guests' stay enjoyable: visits to cultural sites, an opera performance, and a great deal of sightseeing. It was bitterly cold, but Hammarskjöld loved every aspect of this gracious hospitality. During the official talks, only Hammarskjöld, Chou, and the Chinese interpreter spoke. Hammarskjöld's interpreter followed and checked the translation. From the very outset, Hammarskjöld and Chou showed mutual respect and understanding, an important element in the talks, which were conducted at a high level of intellectual finesse and courtesy. At the informal dinner on the first evening, they agreed that their talks would begin with the prisoner-of-war issue. Hammarskjöld stressed that he did not speak for any one nation or even a majority of nations. He was acting in fulfillment of his constitutional responsibility under the Charter—his own independent intervention for the reduction of international tensions.[83]

In their four meetings, both men held to their respective positions on the American airmen. Hammarskjöld insisted that they were prisoners of war on a mission under UN command, not criminals, and that freeing them would contribute to a reduction of tension with the United States. Chou insisted that they were spies and that China had a sovereign right to bring them to court. They also discussed matters of concern to China, among them China's seat at the UN, currently occupied by the Nationalist regime, Communist China's right to the territory of Taiwan, as well as the US decision to send 14,000 Chinese prisoners to Taiwan without giving them the option to go to mainland China. Despite their inability to agree, both acknowledged the importance of their dialogue. Indeed, they had established an excellent rapport and made a good impression on each other. They issued a joint communiqué stating: "We feel that these talks have been useful and we hope to be able to continue the contact established in these meetings."[84] Given the highly sensitive—even explosive—nature of the issues discussed, this communiqué was in itself an accomplishment. Chou provided information on the health of the prisoners and other matters of importance to the families, as well as photos. Chou also offered to provide government assistance for the families to visit the prisoners. On Hammarskjöld's last night in Beijing, Chou hosted a magnificent dinner for Hammarskjöld and his entire staff.

Hammarskjöld returned to New York on January 13, 1955. Two aides joined his party in San Francisco and warned him that the media were already characterizing the mission as a failure, which led Hammarskjöld to issue a cautionary statement: "The door that has been opened can be kept open, *given restraint on all sides*"—which is so hard to achieve in highly emotional confrontations.[85] His first step in New York was to give the US ambassador at the UN, Henry Cabot Lodge, a preliminary account of his conversations in Beijing. The following day, at a press conference, he warned against inflammatory media accounts, which in the past had "often frozen positions in a way which has rendered the situation much more difficult."[86]

Multiple Setbacks

Unfortunately, the political climate in the United States did not encourage a calmer outlook. Immediately upon Hammarskjöld's return, the US assistant secretary of state, Walter Robertson, publicly denounced "China's gangster role."[87] And a few days later, Senator William Knowland rated the mission to

Beijing as "a failure by any standard or yardstick" and accused the United Nations of "a massive propaganda build-up . . . to silence those who would analyze the fact." He warned of a "Far Eastern Munich."[88] On January 19, Hammarskjöld went to Washington to meet with John Foster Dulles, Lodge, and Robertson. But they gave him only time enough for a condensed account of his Beijing conversations and, significantly, no opportunity to discuss a US response to Chou's offer of family visits, or future strategy. Worse yet, part of Hammarskjöld's account of his confidential discussion with Chou was leaked to the Associated Press. Four days later, Hammarskjöld wrote to Waldock at Oxford,[89] "I am afraid that their emotions have run away with their political wisdom," and he went on to quote part of a prayer that had been offered in the US Senate: "Fanatical foes whose pledged word is worthless . . . who, for their own ends, callously traffic in normal human affections and family ties."[90]

The Chinese offer of family visits to the prisoners was announced both in Beijing and at the UN on January 21. The US State Department immediately stated that it could not in good conscience encourage the family visits, expressing safety concerns, and proceeded to denounce the motives of the Chinese government. Hammarskjöld at once publicly stated that he had no doubt about the safety of the prisoners' families. In fact, some of the families showed great interest in the Chinese offer, and others visited UN headquarters to make inquiries, all of which led to a letter written by Dulles himself on January 27 to all the families stating that in light of China's belligerent attitude, no US citizens would be allowed to travel to China. The letter was released to the press the same evening.[91]

Mediators need enormous patience—and it does not necessarily shield them from deep frustration. The refusal to let the families travel to China was a serious setback. Hammarskjöld knew that Chou En-lai needed a pretext to release the prisoners and still preserve Chinese national pride and avoid the implication that he was yielding under US (or UN) pressure. There was a possibility that the prisoners could have been allowed to leave with their families as a humanitarian gesture.[92] But this door was now closed, at least for the time being.

There was another setback in the negotiation process: tension escalated suddenly in the Taiwan Strait.[93] Congress gave the president authority to use force not only to defend Taiwan but also to act against Communist forces that might be part of an attempt to invade Taiwan. The United States sent the Eighteenth Fighter Bomber Wing to Taiwan and placed the Seventh Fleet into full combat readiness, and the crisis was brought to the UN Security Council. Everything seemed to be moving against the continuation of Hammarskjöld's negotiations. The Council invited Beijing to send a representative to participate in the discussion of the issue. After formally conveying this invitation, Hammarskjöld sent a personal message to Chou through Swedish channels, stressing the opportunity that this invitation offered. However, before the message reached Beijing, Chou had responded to the formal invitation, rejecting it in a strongly worded note—another missed opportunity. Polarization and ideological disposition can hamper diplomacy. This episode demonstrates also the vital importance of faster communication, but in 1955, leaders did not pick up the telephone as readily as they do now (see Chapter 4 regarding such developments in contemporary diplomacy).

The United States took strong exception to Hammarskjöld's invitation to Chou, and it objected also to the Council's invitation—more pernicious consequences of polarization and ideology. All of this shows the importance of mediation when the disputants find it so difficult to talk. But the circumstances were not propitious to press for the release of the American prisoners. Hammarskjöld, nevertheless, did not give up.

Renewed Efforts

On February 17, 1955, he wrote to Chou, pointing out again that no charges had been brought against four of the prisoners aside from their intrusion into Chinese airspace, and that the time they had spent in jail was already far in excess of the normal pretrial detention period. He noted that freeing them, a decision in line with Beijing's professed humanitarian policies, would not be interpreted as renouncing China's sovereign rights. Chou took more than a month to reply, but told Hammarskjöld that the prisoners' case was being addressed seriously and diligently, and that he appreciated the efforts Hammarskjöld had made. Much belligerent talk kept coming from Washington, to which Beijing replied in kind. On March 28, Hammarskjöld wrote to Lodge, explaining again that Chou must be allowed to act without the semblance of pressure from the outside, and that his pride and prestige must be preserved if he were to release the prisoners. For this reason, Hammarskjöld stressed, he needed the cooperation of the United States in reducing public pressure. On the other hand, Hammarskjöld wanted India and Thailand to urge Chou to free the prisoners in the interest of reducing tension in East Asia, and asked the UN permanent representatives of these two countries to ask their chief executives, Prime Minister Jawaharlal Nehru and Prince Wan Waithayakon, to approach Chou on this issue at the forthcoming Bandung Conference of Asian and African States.[94]

Hammarskjöld also decided once again to use a meeting of the Swedish Academy to provide a cover for another meeting with the Chinese ambassador in Stockholm; a close friend arranged a luncheon at his mother's house, which was near the Chinese embassy. There, on April 23, the two men spoke for two and a half hours with only the ambassador's interpreter present. He asked the ambassador to tell Chou that he was impatient to the point of deep disappointment, and asked him to inquire of Chou if there was anything he, Hammarskjöld, could do in order to facilitate finding a solution; he also pointed out that the possibility of maintaining contact with Beijing depended on the outcome of the prisoners' issue. The ability to approach the problem in this fashion is the enormous advantage of a mediator[95]—particularly the Secretary-General of the UN.[96] In the two and a half hours of discussion, it was never a matter of whether the prisoners would be released, but only *how* it would happen.[97]

Upon his return to New York, Hammarskjöld informed the UN representatives of the United States, the Soviet Union, and Britain, in general terms, of his conversation with the Chinese ambassador—here again, Hammarskjöld was maintaining contact with key actors and keeping them aware of developments. However, there was no response to the message he had sent through the Chinese ambassador in Stockholm. So, on May 16, he asked Chou for a reply and asked also if he intended to reply to the letters that the families had written him (Hammarskjöld's strategy to maintain *private* pressure), adding that he desperately needed some evidence to support people in the United States who had advocated restraint and patience. Chou's reply was given to the Swedish ambassador in Beijing on May 29 and stated that the Chinese Supreme Court had ordered the deportation of the four jet pilots on May 24, and that they would probably reach Hong Kong on May 31. Persistence was paying off. However, the message was delayed in transmission from the Swedish embassy in Beijing and did not reach Hammarskjöld until May 30, which enabled Krishna Menon, India's ambassador to the UN,[98] to announce the release first, and later attempt to claim credit for the release of the airmen.[99]

Menon had for some time been a source of uneasiness for Hammarskjöld. He had traveled to Beijing and met with Chou, but would not reply to Hammarskjöld's inquiries, and the latter was afraid that uncoordinated initiatives on the prisoner issue might complicate his efforts. Multiple independent mediation initiatives are not unusual in certain international situations, even by a variety of international actors, including NGOs (see Chapter 5).[100] But without coordination, they can work at cross-purposes. Menon had long disliked Hammarskjöld,[101] and the latter had noticed a change of attitude in Chou after Menon's visit to Beijing in late May. Of concern also was the news that the Swedish ambassador in Moscow had taken it upon himself to visit Beijing.[102]

These complications did not deter Hammarskjöld, who continued pressing both sides—the United States, to tone down the rhetoric, and Beijing, to release the remaining prisoners. He waited about a month before his next approach, in the form of a letter to Chou delivered by the Swedish ambassador in Beijing on July 8, pressing him with regard to the remaining eleven prisoners and saying that he very much hoped he would not have to report to the UN the failure of his mission. Chou quickly replied through the Chinese consul-general in Geneva. He was clearly annoyed and told Hammarskjöld that judging from Dulles's and Lodge's speeches, the United States was not interested in reducing tension, and he added that he was not about to release the prisoners because of pressure, and he considered his threat of a report to the UN as an example of such pressure. But he concluded by indicating his intention to continue the dialogue with Hammarskjöld on the basis of the friendly attitude that had inspired their talks in Beijing.

Success

Aside from US pronouncements, two of the four jet pilots who had been released published articles in *Life* and *U.S. News and World Report* toward the end of June that "might almost have been specifically written to discourage the Chinese from releasing any more prisoners."[103] Diplomats have long complained about some of the complications created by what appears in the media. Hammarskjöld told Lodge how dangerous this sort of reporting could be for the other prisoners. But, luckily, things took a different turn. At a luncheon in Stockholm in early July, the Chinese chargé d'affaires asked a close friend of Hammarskjöld's what he would like for his fiftieth birthday, which was on July 29. The reply was, books, Chinese paintings, but most of all, the release of the eleven prisoners. Twice, subsequently, the embassy called to check the date of Hammarskjöld's birthday.[104] Mention was made also that he would be spending his vacation in southern Sweden during the last week of July and could always go to Stockholm if needed. Events followed in dramatic fashion.

On August 1, Hammarskjöld received, through the little post office in the village near his isolated summer retreat, a message from Chou transmitted through Swedish diplomatic channels, and then, fifteen minutes later, a telephone call from his close assistant in New York, telling him that Radio Beijing would be announcing the release of the eleven American airmen. Chou's message, communicated to the Swedish ambassador in Beijing, read:

> The Chinese Government has decided to release the imprisoned U.S. fliers. This release from serving their full term takes place in order to maintain friendship with Hammarskjold and has no connection with the UN resolution. Chou En-lai expresses the hope that Hammarskjold will take note of this point. The Chinese Government hopes to continue the contact established with Hammarskjold. Chou En-lai congratulates Hammarskjold on his fiftieth birthday.[105]

This was a great victory for Dag Hammarskjöld, and congratulations were received from all parts of the world. In the end, Chou did not continue relations with him, although Hammarskjöld tried to resume friendly contact on a number of occasions. It may well be that Chou had expected more substantial political benefits from his gesture. The success vastly increased Hammarskjöld's stature and helped him play a larger role in future international issues. This episode illustrates the possibilities and limitations of international organization diplomacy and demonstrates the difficulties involved in achieving effective mediation when a turn of events can threaten to destroy painfully accomplished progress.

▓ Study Questions and Discussion Topics

1. Is international organization diplomacy a corruption of the classical art? What are its drawbacks, its limitations? What are its benefits?
2. What different types of diplomacy are conducted in international organizations?
3. Why have international organizations proliferated? Why do states seek representation in these organizations (thus adding to their expenses and requiring larger diplomatic staffs)?
4. Is multilateral diplomacy comparable to bilateral diplomacy? In what ways are they different? (Give examples.)
5. What is different in peacekeeping diplomacy?

▓ Suggested Reading

Bailey, Sydney D. "The Evolution of the Practice of the Security Council." In *Paths to Peace: The UN Security Council and Its Presidency,* edited by Davidson Nicol. New York: Pergamon, 1981.

Bennett, A. LeRoy, and James K. Oliver. *International Organizations: Principles and Issues.* 7th ed. Upper Saddle River, NJ: Prentice-Hall, 2002.

Berridge, G. R., and A. Jennings, eds. *Diplomacy at the UN.* New York: St. Martin's, 1985.

Cox, Robert W., Harold K. Jacobson, et al. *The Anatomy of Influence: Decision-Making in International Organization.* New Haven: Yale University Press, 1974.

Fasulo, Linda M. *Representing America: Experiences of U.S. Diplomats at the UN.* New York: Praeger, 1984.

Finger, Seymour Maxwell. *American Ambassadors at the UN: People, Politics, and Bureaucracy in Making Foreign Policy.* 2d ed. New York: Holmes and Meier, 1988.

Nicol, Davidson. *Paths to Peace: The UN Security Council and Its Presidency.* New York: Pergamon, 1981.

Urquhart, Brian. *Hammarskjold.* New York: Norton, 1972.

———. *Ralph Bunche: An American Life.* New York: Norton, 1993.

Wood, David M., and Birol A. Yeşilada. *The Emerging European Union.* 3d ed. New York: Pearson, 2004.

▓ Notes

1. Bruce Russett, Harvey Starr, and David Kinsella, *World Politics: The Menu for Choice,* 7th ed. (Belmont, CA: Wadsworth, 2004), p. 117.
2. Hans J. Morgenthau, *Politics Among Nations: The Struggle for Power and Peace,* rev. ed. (New York: McGraw-Hill, 1993), pp. 369–370.
3. G. R. Berridge, *Diplomacy: Theory and Practice,* 2d ed. (New York: Palgrave, 2002), p. 150.
4. Morgenthau, *Politics,* pp. 368–370.

5. Elliott R. Barkan, *Diplomatic History of the United States* (New York: Monarch, 1966), p. 95. See also Morgenthau, *Politics*, p. 369.

6. See Brian Urquhart, *Hammarskjold* (New York: Norton, 1972). See also Brian Urquhart, *A Life in Peace and War* (New York: Harper and Row, 1987); Seymour Maxwell Finger, *American Ambassadors at the UN: People, Politics, and Bureaucracy in Making Foreign Policy,* 2d ed. (New York: Holmes and Meier, 1988).

7. See Peter R. Baehr and Leon Gordenker, *The United Nations in the 1990s* (New York: St. Martin's, 1992), pp. 52–55.

8. See Inis L. Claude Jr., *Swords into Plowshares: The Problems and Progress of International Organization,* 4th ed. (New York: Random House, 1971), pp. 135–136, 362–366; Richard A. Falk, "The United Nations: Various Systems of Operation," in *The United Nations in International Politics,* edited by Leon Gordenker (Princeton: Princeton University Press, 1971), pp. 218–222. Bloc formation is also interesting in multilateral conferences. See, for example, discussion of the nine-year Law of the Sea Conference in Bernard H. Oxman, David D. Caron, and Charles L. O. Buderi, eds., *Law of the Sea: U.S. Policy Dilemma* (San Francisco: Institute for Contemporary Studies, 1983).

9. See, for example, Urquhart, *Hammarskjold,* pp. 172–183.

10. George Ignatieff (permanent representative of Canada to the United Nations, 1966–1969), "Prompt and Regular Access to Political Government at Home Is Essential," in *Paths to Peace: The UN Security Council and Its Presidency,* edited by Davidson Nicol (New York: Pergamon, 1981), pp. 130–139.

11. See R. G. Feltham, *Diplomatic Handbook,* 4th ed. New York: Longman, 1982), pp. 10–11.

12. Created by the Treaty of Versailles in 1919. See Moshe Y. Sachs, *The United Nations: A Handbook on the United Nations, Its Structure, History, Purposes, Activities, and Agencies* (New York: Wiley, 1977), pp. 125–137; Hector G. Bartolomei de la Cruz, Geraldo von Potobsky, and Lee Swepston, *The International Labor Organization: The Standards System and Basic Human Rights* (Boulder: Westview, 1996), pp. 3–18, and bibliography, pp. 289ff.

13. Sydney D. Bailey and Sam Daws, *The Procedure of the UN Security Council,* 3d ed. (New York: Oxford University Press, 1998), esp. pp. 60–75. See also Sydney D. Bailey, "The Evolution of the Practice of the Security Council," in Nicol, *Paths to Peace,* pp. 37–47.

14. Bailey and Daws, *Procedure,* p. 44.

15. Lawrence Ziring, Robert E. Riggs, and Jack C. Plano, *The United Nations: International Organization and World Politics,* 4th ed. (Belmont, CA: Wadsworth, 2005), pp. 269–272. And there are occasions when more than negotiations and resolutions are called for. The Security Council, for example, can appoint a mediator or request the UN Secretary-General to address the problem.

16. See Claude Jr., *Swords into Plowshares,* pp. 83–101.

17. See David M. Wood and Birol A. Yeşilada, *The Emerging European Union,* 3d ed. (New York: Pearson, 2004), pp. 117–133, 173–190.

18. See, for example, Linda B. Miller, "International Organization and Internal Conflicts: Some Emerging Patterns of Response," in Gordenker, *United Nations,* pp. 130–150.

19. See characteristics of states involved in the international system in Russett, Starr, and Kinsella, *World Politics,* app. B. Well over 120 are developing third world countries. See also A. LeRoy Bennett and James K. Oliver, *International Organizations: Principles and Issues,* 7th ed. (Upper Saddle River, NJ: Prentice-Hall, 2002), pp. 317–322.

20. See, for example, US policy development occasioned by the UN decision to convene a conference on science and technology for development, in Jean M. Wilkowski, *Conference Diplomacy II: A Case Study—The UN Conference on Science and Technology for Development, Vienna, 1979* (Washington, DC: Institute for the Study of Diplomacy, School of Foreign Service, Georgetown University, 1982), pp. 15–32.

21. Frans W. Weisglas and Gonnie de Boer, "Parliamentary Diplomacy," *The Hague Journal of Diplomacy* 2, no. 1 (April 2007), pp. 93–99.

22. See, for example, Morgenthau, *Politics,* pp. 369ff.

23. Ibid. See also Frederick H. Hartmann, *The Relations of Nations,* 6th ed. (New York: Macmillan, 1983), pp. 105–107.

24. Voting forms include unanimity, simple majority of the membership, simple majority of those present and voting, many types of qualified majority, and so forth. See Bennett and Oliver, *International Organizations,* pp. 91–96.

25. Disarmament and security; economic and financial; social, humanitarian, and cultural; special political and decolonization; administrative and budgetary; and legal. See http://www.un.org/ga/maincommittees.shtml.

26. The agenda of the fifty-eighth session of the UN General Assembly (2003) had 173 items. See UN Doc. A/58/50, http://www.unsystem.org.

27. Aside from its six main committees, in 2001 the UN General Assembly had fifty-three committees, boards, commissions, and other subsidiary and ad hoc bodies. *Yearbook of the United Nations, 2001,* vol. 55 (New York: United Nations, 2003), pp. 1455–1458. For the European Union structure, see Wood and Yeşilada, *Emerging European Union,* pp. 91–116.

28. (Lord) Gore-Booth, ed., *Satow's Guide to Diplomatic Practice,* 5th ed. (New York: Longman, 1979), p. 314.

29. See Finger, *American Ambassadors,* esp. chap. 2, "USUN: The U.S. Mission to the United Nations and the General Assembly," pp. 12–40.

30. For example, on UN Security Council rules of procedure, see Bailey and Daws, *Procedure,* pp. 441–454.

31. See Finger, *American Ambassadors.*

32. See, for example, F. Y. Chai, "A View from the UN Secretariat," in Nicol, *Paths to Peace,* pp. 84–93, esp. p. 92.

33. Finger, *American Ambassadors,* p. 16. See also Melissa Wells's comments on her time at ECOSOC in Chapter 6's case study.

34. See, for example, Hartmann, *Relations of Nations,* pp. 104ff.; Morgenthau, *Politics,* pp. 369ff.

35. Arthur J. Goldberg (US permanent representative to the UN, 1965–1968), "The Importance of Private Negotiations," in Nicol, *Paths to Peace,* pp. 117–119.

36. E. R. Appathurai, "Permanent Missions in New York," in *Diplomacy at the UN,* edited by G. R. Berridge and A. Jennings (New York: St. Martin's, 1985), pp. 94–108. See also Baehr and Gordenker, *United Nations,* p. 59.

37. Bennett and Oliver, *International Organizations,* pp. 297–383. See also examples provided in R. P. Barston, *Modern Diplomacy,* 2d ed. (New York: Longman, 1997), pp. 185–199.

38. See Chadwick F. Alger, "Non-Resolution Consequences of the United Nations and Their Effect on International Conflict," in *Theory and Research on the Causes of War,* edited by Dean G. Pruitt and Richard C. Snyder (Englewood Cliffs, NJ: Prentice-Hall, 1969), pp. 200–201, also 198–200.

39. Gore-Booth, *Satow's Guide,* pp. 311–314. See also Finger, *American Ambassadors,* pp. 12–40.

40. Ziring, Riggs, and Plano, *United Nations,* pp. 145–150.

41. Berridge and Jennings, *Diplomacy,* pp. 173–221, esp. "'Old Diplomacy' in New York," pp. 175–190.

42. Chadwick F. Alger, "Decision-Making Theory and Human Conflict," in *The Nature of Human Conflict,* edited by Elton B. McNeil (Englewood Cliffs, NJ: Prentice-Hall, 1965), pp. 283–285.

43. Ivor Richard (UK permanent representative to the UN, 1974–1979), "The Council President as a Politician," in Nicol, *Paths to Peace,* pp. 242–254.

44. Bailey and Daws, *Procedure,* p. 72; Spyros Blavoukos, Dimitris Bourantonis, and Panayotis Tsakonas, "Parameters of the Chairmanship's Effectiveness: The Case of the UN Security Council," *The Hague Journal of Diplomacy* 1, no. 2 (September 2006), pp. 143–170; Ole Elgström, "The Presidency: The Role(s) of the Chair in European Union Negotiations," *The Hague Journal of Diplomacy* 1, no. 2 (September 2006), pp. 171–195.

45. For example, the Contact Group on Bosnia, set up in April 1994 after negotiations in London, consisting of France, Germany, Russia, the United Kingdom, and the United States. The group had a certain independence from the UN Security Council as it was attempting to broker a diplomatic solution following the relative stalemate in the Council and the failure of other diplomatic initiatives. It met at various times at the foreign minister level. The map designed by the group became the basis for the territorial settlement embodied in the Dayton Accords. Bailey and Daws, *Procedure,* p. 72.

46. See, for example, activities of the Fifth Committee, the General Assembly's Administrative and Budgetary Committee, and the work of the Secretariat. See Ziring, Riggs, and Plano, *United Nations,* pp. 145–159.

47. Article 99. Emphasis added.

48. Ziring, Riggs, and Plano, *United Nations,* pp. 145–159.

49. Adopted by the General Assembly on February 13, 1946.

50. Adopted by the General Assembly on December 14, 1946.

51. Ziring, Riggs, and Plano, *United Nations,* pp. 145–149.

52. The increasing cooperation between international organizations is creating a new order of diplomatic work. Many organizations are headquartered in different countries and need to maintain permanent representation with counterpart organizations to permit effective interaction. See *Yearbook of International Organizations, 2006–2007,* 43d ed. (Munich: Saur, 2006).

53. For example, the UNDP, UNICEF, the World Bank, and WHO cooperate on a regular basis in third world development.

54. See http://www.undp.org.

55. See http://www.unep.org.

56. Some are seconded (i.e., temporarily released) by the foreign service of a member state. See case study on Melissa Wells's UN service in Uganda in Chapter 6.

57. See, for instance, Oran R. Young, "The United Nations and the International System," in Gordenker, *United Nations,* pp. 10–59.

58. See, for example, discussion of how the problem presents itself in the recollections of Charles William Maynes (assistant secretary of state for international organization affairs, 1977–1979), in *Representing America: Experiences of U.S. Diplomats at the UN,* edited by Linda M. Fasulo (New York: Praeger, 1984), pp. 252–260.

59. A former Australian chief of mission told me that some 50–60 percent of his embassy's work had some multilateral purpose.

60. See Appathurai, "Permanent Missions," p. 102.

61. James S. Sutterlin, *The United Nations and the Maintenance of International Security: A Challenge to Be Met* (Westport: Praeger, 2003), esp. pp. 1–52, 115–166.

62. A UN peacekeeping force has been in Cyprus since 1964. United Nations, *The Blue Helmets: A Review of UN Peace-Keeping*, 2d ed. (New York: UN Department of Public Information, 1990), pp. 279–311. A UN peacekeeping force has been in the Golan Heights since 1974, and another has been in southern Lebanon since 1978.

63. Urquhart, *Hammarskjold*, pp. 195–230. See also Dag Hammarskjöld, "United Nations Emergency Force," in Lincoln P. Bloomfield et al., *International Military Forces: The Question of Peacekeeping in an Armed and Disarming World* (Boston: Little, Brown, 1964), pp. 268–280; Brian E. Urquhart, "A UN Perspective," in Bloomfield et al., *International Military Forces*, pp. 126–144.

64. "UN Peacekeeping Operations Background Notes," http://www.un.org/depts/dpko/dpko/bnote.

65. This case study is based primarily on the very detailed account given in Urquhart, *Hammarskjold*, pp. 94–131. A shorter account is given in Joseph P. Lash, *Dag Hammarskjöld: Custodian of the Brush-Fire Peace* (Garden City, NY: Doubleday, 1961), pp. 56–65.

66. Wilfrid Knapp, *A History of War and Peace, 1939–1965* (New York: Oxford University Press, 1967), pp. 235–239, 255–258, 262–264.

67. Radio Peking at the time.

68. Urquhart, *Hammarskjöld*, pp. 96–99. Urquhart chose to omit the diacritic from Hammarskjöld's name. See also Joseph P. Lash, *Dag Hammarskjöld: Custodian of the Brushfire Peace* (Garden City, NY: Doubleday, 1961), pp. 46–55.

69. Urquhart, *Hammarskjold*, p. 99.

70. Knapp, *History*, pp. 255–258, 262–264. See also Daniel S. Cheever and H. Field Haviland Jr., *Organizing for Peace: International Organization in World Affairs* (Boston: Houghton Mifflin, 1954), pp. 144, 370–372, 458, 463, 468.

71. Urquhart, *Hammarskjold*, p. 100.

72. Bennett and Oliver, *International Organizations*, pp. 424–434.

73. Urquhart, *Hammarskjold*, p. 101.

74. See Raymond Cohen, *Theater of Power: The Art of Diplomatic Signalling* (London: Longman, 1987).

75. Urquhart, *Hammarskjold*, pp. 102–103.

76. Leigh Thompson, *The Mind and Heart of the Negotiator*, 2d ed. (Upper Saddle River, NJ: Prentice-Hall, 2001), pp. 9–32.

77. A former US permanent representative to the UN and subsequently a judge at the International Court of Justice.

78. Urquhart, *Hammarskjold*, pp. 99, 103.

79. See Jarol B. Manheim, *Strategic Public Diplomacy and American Foreign Policy: The Evolution of Influence* (New York: Oxford University Press, 1994).

80. Hammarskjöld chose Ilya Tchernyshev, a Soviet undersecretary-general, to be in charge in his absence, rather than Ralph Bunche (Lash, *Dag Hammarskjöld*, p. 60), an interesting diplomatic touch. Hammarskjöld cultivated the support of the major UN members for his mission. Tchernyshev was at the airport, along with Lodge, to wish him well on his journey.

81. Urquhart, *Hammarskjold*, pp. 103–104.

82. Compare with Fred Charles Iklé, *How Nations Negotiate* (New York: Harper and Row, 1964).

83. Urquhart, *Hammarskjold*, pp. 105–107. Compare with the literature on mediation—for example, Saadia Touval and I. William Zartman, eds., *International Mediation in Theory and Practice* (Boulder: Westview, 1985); Thomas Princen, *Intermediaries in International Conflict* (Princeton: Princeton University Press, 1992). See also Chapter 9 in this volume.

84. Urquhart, *Hammarskjold*, p. 112.

85. Ibid., p. 113, emphasis in original. See case study on the Yemen crisis in Chapter 9. See also Jacob Bercovitch and Jeffrey Z. Rubin, *Mediation in International Relations: Multiple Approaches to Conflict Management* (New York: St. Martin's, 1992).

86. Urquhart, *Hammarskjold*, p. 113. He was anxious to avoid violent reactions that would close the door to future contacts with Chou En-lai.

87. Urquhart, *Hammarskjold*, p. 114.

88. Ibid. See also Lash, *Dag Hammarskjöld*, p. 58; Geir Lundestad, *East, West, North, South: Major Developments in International Politics Since 1945*, 4th ed. (New York: Oxford, 1999), pp. 60–67.

89. The international law professor who had been his legal adviser on the Beijing mission.

90. Urquhart, *Hammarskjold*, p. 115. Mediators must often cope with similar obstacles. See case study on the Yemen mission in Chapter 9. See also Bercovitch and Rubin, *Mediation*.

91. Dulles added: "We do not think it prudent to afford the Chinese Communists further opportunities to provoke our nation and strain its patience further." Urquhart quipped: "Who was increasingly belligerent[?]" and "Who was straining whose patience[?]" Urquhart, *Hammarskjold*, pp. 115–116. And Urquhart pointed to "a vivid and critical contemporary analysis of U.S. policy" in "The Hidden History of the Formosa Crisis," *I. F. Stone's Weekly*, February 7, 1955, and in "The Inner Politics of a False Alarm," *I. F. Stone's Weekly*, February 14, 1955.

92. Hammarskjöld wrote personally to Dulles on January 27, stressing this point and how the US response undermined efforts to get the prisoners released. Urquhart, *Hammarskjold*, p. 116.

93. This was rooted in China's continuing effort to gain control over Taiwan. See Alan Lawrance, *China's Foreign Relations Since 1949* (Boston: Routledge and Paul, 1975); Jerome Alan Cohen, ed., *The Dynamics of China's Foreign Relations* (Cambridge: Harvard University Press, 1970).

94. Urquhart, *Hammarskjold*, pp. 119–120. The Bandung Conference was scheduled for April 18–24, 1955. Support from the nonaligned nations was of course very desirable, and more likely to be forthcoming if sought by the UN Secretary-General. Hammarskjöld made it a practice to maintain contact with key leaders in this bloc.

95. See Jacob Bercovitch, "Mediation in International Conflict: An Overview of Theory, a Review of Practice," in *Peacemaking in International Conflict: Methods and Techniques*, edited by I. William Zartman and J. Lewis Rasmussen (Washington, DC: US Institute of Peace, 1997), pp. 125–153.

96. Chou probably saw the value of his assistance and support for his larger objective of eventually gaining China's seat in the UN, now occupied by Taiwan.

97. Urquhart, *Hammarskjold*, pp. 120–122. See also Lash, *Dag Hammarskjöld*, p. 63, who says that the ambassador agreed that the release of the prisoners was just a matter of time.

98. And a member of the Indian parliament. *Merriam-Webster's Biographical Dictionary* (Springfield, MA: Merriam-Webster, 1995).

99. Urquhart, *Hammarskjold*, pp. 122–124.

100. See also Zartman and Rasmussen, *Peacemaking*, pt. 3, "Practitioners," pp. 317ff., esp. Cameron R. Hume, "A Diplomat's View," pp. 319–336, and Andrew S. Natsios, "An NGO Perspective," pp. 337–361.

101. Lash, *Dag Hammarskjöld*, for example p. 174.

102. Urquhart, *Hammarskjold,* p. 124.
103. Ibid., p. 125.
104. Lash, *Dag Hammarskjöld,* pp. 63–64. See also Urquhart, *Hammarskjold,* pp. 125–126.
105. Urquhart, *Hammarskjold,* p. 126. This message was given to Hammarskjöld on August 2 in Geneva, where he was to attend a UN meeting. It was probably the same as the message that was transmitted to his summer retreat in Sweden the day before.

9 Special Mission and Conference Diplomacy

Both special missions and international conferences serve ad hoc and temporary diplomatic purposes Missions sent to conferences might be counted as special missions. However, conferences, particularly the very large ones, generate a diplomatic process of their own that is much more structured and elaborate. Conference diplomacy is therefore discussed separately in this chapter.

Special Mission Diplomacy

A considerable volume of diplomacy is now carried out by means of special missions. This has also been called ad hoc diplomacy or diplomacy by itinerant agents, extraordinary diplomats, special envoys, temporary delegations, and similar denominations.[1] It is a broad and flexible category serving a vast variety of purposes. The United Nations tried to draw some official boundaries for the purpose of determining who is entitled to diplomatic immunities. It ended up endorsing the Convention on Special Missions in 1969.[2] But this convention does not cover the full spectrum of special mission diplomacy. By special agreement (often informal), states agree to receive special missions that are not included in the 1969 convention and may also give them special diplomatic protection.[3] The 1969 convention therefore does not restrict the conduct of diplomacy by means of special missions.

■ Characteristics

The main distinguishing feature of these missions is their temporary nature, which does not necessarily mean short. Some missions are open-ended and may take months, or even years when issues are protracted and negotiations intermittent. The United States has sent a number of special envoys to the Middle East on missions of long duration. President Dwight Eisenhower's envoy, Eric Johnston, served there with the rank of ambassador for several years; his post was not full-time and did not carry accreditation to a single state.[4] Ambassador Dennis Ross served as special Middle East coordinator in the administration of President Bill Clinton for about eight years, dealing directly with the states involved in the peace process. He facilitated the Jordan-Israel 1994 peace treaty, assisted Israelis and Palestinians in reaching the 1995 interim agreement, worked intensively to bring Israel and Syria together in that same period, and succeeded in brokering the 1997 Hebron Accord.[5]

Usually, each mission has its own special focus or objective. Once achieved, the mission is terminated; it is thus temporary by definition, even when the process is prolonged. Special missions are properly contrasted to resident missions that are "permanent," even though the diplomatic agents serving there are normally rotated.[6] Some special agents may remain in residence in one location for the entire duration of their mission (e.g., negotiating a particular arrangement). Neither are they necessarily sent by a single national government. Several states may choose to send a joint mission.[7] As an example of diversity in the work of special envoys, Robert Murphy, personal representative of President Franklin Roosevelt, was sent secretly to gain the support of the Free French Forces in North Africa during World War II. He later became political adviser to the commandant of the US forces in Europe, then participated in the sessions of the Council of Foreign Ministers in Paris to address postwar issues.[8] Special representatives are not necessarily members of the foreign service of a particular country. US presidents have sent a wide variety of individuals as special envoys—for example, Roosevelt used his close friend Harry Hopkins throughout the war, sending him on numerous missions to the Soviet Union as his personal representative to negotiate issues of the greatest importance with Joseph Stalin.[9]

Some appointments are formal; others are completely informal. Single agents as well as entire delegations will be used as the mission warrants. Special agents may be given whatever title will serve the purpose—or no title at all, as was the case with Harry Hopkins.[10] Some US presidents are said to have appointed over twenty-five persons in a single year with the rank of ambassador, without sending any of their names to the Senate before appointment.[11] In March 1949, the rank of ambassador at large was formally established by the United States, and more than thirty persons were appointed by presidents between that time and the late 1990s. Only a few were career officers, such as Paul Bremer III, U. Alexis Johnson, and Llewellyn Thompson. Most were noncareer, including Philip Jessup, who later became a member of the International Court of Justice, Ellsworth Bunker, Arthur Goldberg, and Henry

Cabot Lodge Jr.[12] Some ambassadors at large have specialized in certain areas, such as refugee affairs.[13]

Experts are frequently sent to deal with technical issues. High officials and former presidents (e.g., Jimmy Carter)[14] may be chosen to emphasize the importance attached to the mission. Senior foreign service officers are also likely to be chosen for delicate mediation tasks. But the US Department of State has also used private individuals for some missions—for instance, Bryant Wedge, who had taught at the University of Chicago, Yale University, and the Fletcher School of Law and Diplomacy, was sent to establish contact with young revolutionaries in the Dominican Republic in 1965 and to initiate a dialogue with the US embassy in Santo Domingo.[15] Special missions are thus exceedingly diverse. Flexibility and adaptability to circumstances are essential qualities.

▓ Ancient Origins and Contemporary Relevance

Special missions are the oldest form of diplomacy. In classical antiquity, Greek city-states maintained political contact by means of special delegations. These would bring messages to neighboring governments or negotiate agreements. No permanent representation was maintained at the political level. In matters of commerce, consulates were well established in the Greek city-states by the fifth century B.C.E. Consuls were usually citizens of the states in which they served, providing commercial information and facilitating trade; but they were also used to initiate diplomatic negotiations.[16] It was not until the mid-1450s that permanent representation came into use, among Italian city-states (although, beginning in C.E. 453, the Pope had a permanent representative at the court of Byzantium).[17] After 1500, permanent embassies from the main Italian states were opened in London, in Paris, and at the court of Charles V.[18] They became the standard means of diplomatic relations, completely eclipsing special missions.

The use of special missions did not disappear, however. For example, President Woodrow Wilson received precious assistance from Colonel Edward House's missions.[19] The United States also used special missions in the 1920s and 1930s to observe international proceedings it could not attend as a full-fledged participant because of its isolationist policy. Remarkably, however, the use of special missions remained limited until World War II. At this point, such missions became a critical instrument for the coordination of war efforts among the Allies. The revolution in aircraft technology and the resulting explosion in commercial aviation were undoubtedly factors in the rapid postwar expansion of special mission diplomacy. The large increase in the volume and diversity of diplomatic relations, brought about by complex interdependence and the globalization of human activity,[20] contributed also to a larger use of special missions to accomplish what could not be done by the resident staffs for lack of expert personnel or because of simple overload.

The United States has used special missions extensively, but so have other nations.[21] Heads of state, foreign offices, and other government departments use special agents. A growing number of international organizations have tasks to perform away from their headquarters and use special missions. The UN Secretary-General carries out missions for the Security Council and the General Assembly; he also uses personal representatives for his growing diplomatic role in trouble spots around the world. (See Box 9.1.) Ralph Bunche[22] distinguished himself in that capacity. Count Folke Bernadotte,[23] assassinated in Palestine in 1948, and Sergio Vieira de Mello,[24] killed in Iraq in 2003, are examples of UN special representatives who engage in difficult missions for the world organization.

Many heads of international agencies and programs send their own special agents to carry out specific tasks related to their own international functions. In a different category, private independent experts are sent by international organizations to perform a multiplicity of diplomatic tasks. They are neither representatives of governments nor officials of the organizations concerned; rather they undertake missions for the independent exercise of their expert functions. As early as 1946, the Convention on the Privileges and Immunities of the UN and the Convention on the Privileges and Immunities of the Specialized Agencies specified that such experts performing missions for the UN would be granted special status.[25] The proliferation of international organizations has thus enormously increased the volume of special mission activity.

Box 9.1   UN Special Middle East Coordinator

In May 2005 the UN Secretary-General named Alvaro de Soto, a veteran Peruvian diplomat, as his special coordinator to the Israeli-Palestinian peace process, replacing Terje Rød Larsen, a Norwegian (of Oslo peace process fame–see Chapter 11). De Soto was a UN official for twenty-three years. He negotiated and drafted the 1990–1991 pact that ended the ten-year conflict in El Salvador, and was the major UN negotiator for the failed effort to reunify Cyprus. He was also the UN representative for the Western Sahara conflict that involved Morocco. In his new post, de Soto additionally serves as the UN Secretary-General's representative to the Palestine Liberation Organization and the Palestinian Authority.

Source: New York Times, May 6, 2005, p. 14.

Other nonstate actors make use of special missions to promote their causes in the international political process. Special missions are even more important to them, as they are usually unable to maintain permanent missions abroad. This is the case particularly with many revolutionary organizations, such as the Palestine Liberation Organization (PLO). They use special agents to seek assistance from governments and to lobby international organizations or international conferences.[26] As well, transnational actors, such as nongovernmental organizations (NGOs) and multinational corporations (MNCs), are becoming increasingly active in international politics. Because they are private sector actors, their special representatives are not given much (if any) recognition in international circles; but they have become a factor in the conduct of diplomacy. Some NGO delegations are now authorized to participate in international meetings. Some are even invited to contribute to the decisionmaking process of a number of international organizations, such as the World Bank,[27] and others are deeply involved in the diplomacy of international mediation.

Usefulness of Special Missions

The proliferating use of special missions in contemporary international relations[28] is explained by their remarkable usefulness. This diplomatic instrument is extremely flexible and therefore versatile. A single agent may be sufficient to carry out certain missions, but for other tasks, a full contingent of negotiators and experts will be used. As the subject matter of international relations has become extraordinarily diverse—no human endeavor is now excluded from the international agenda—the flexibility of special missions is an enormous asset. Virtually all international actors—whether major powers or less-developed states, international organizations or NGOs—use this instrument to participate in international affairs. One of the main functions of special missions is to engage in negotiations, particularly in technical or specialized fields—for example, to stop an epidemic—where the task requires distinctive skills or knowledge and the use of experts (especially when these are not available in resident missions). This approach is well suited to complex problems, enabling negotiators to remain focused on the matter over extended periods of time, free from other obligations. This method keeps the normal diplomatic links (e.g., embassy personnel) from being overburdened. The unusual competence or stature of a special envoy may also offer a greater chance of success.

Occasionally, it is a failure of the other channels of communication that leads to the use of special missions, such as to facilitate the release of the US airmen who were captured by Communist China in the early 1950s (see case study in Chapter 8). Governments and international organizations use special envoys for a variety of *troubleshooting missions* as the need arises in various parts of the world. Many diplomats have made names for themselves as roving problem-solvers.[29] Such missions sharpen the focus of diplomatic action, particularly helpful in *mediation missions* (see the case study on Yemen in this chapter). Indeed, mediation is carried out primarily by means of special missions. Henry Kissinger's itinerant negotiations came to be described by the media as "shuttle diplomacy."[30] He saw the contending parties one at a time, back and forth, exploring what they were prepared to accept by way of settlement, before they were ready to talk to each other face to face.

Mobility, the ability to negotiate with a variety of parties and in diverse locations, and the freedom to act on very short notice are enormous advantages. They permit diplomats to engage difficult situations before they become worse,[31] and are ideal for low-visibility transactions beyond the reach of the media—for example, Henry Kissinger, on a visit to India, became ostensibly confined to his room for a few days with the flu, but he was actually in Beijing making arrangements for President Richard Nixon's historic visit to China. Ad hoc emissaries are particularly useful in fluid, unstructured situations. They can be sent as conditions evolve.[32]

Special missions supplement embassies for *consultation work.* In preparation for the 1974 World Food Conference, Ambassador Edwin Martin, senior adviser to Secretary of State Henry Kissinger, and in charge of US preparation for the conference, traveled to more than a dozen countries, urging their governments to prepare for the event and presenting US concerns—a common strategy to avoid surprises when the negotiations get formally under way.[33] We note here national envoys preparing the ground for *multilateral* negotiations (promoting the policies of their own governments). An important emissary is often used to convey a special message or to emphasize the significance of a diplomatic initiative. For example, at a critical juncture in the Arab-Israeli peace process (after President Anwar Sadat's dramatic visit to Jerusalem), when, once again, the negotiations deteriorated, President Jimmy Carter decided to invite Prime Minister Menachem Begin and President Sadat to Camp David in an effort to salvage the negotiations. In August 1978, to elicit a favorable response by both adversaries, President Carter sent Secretary of State Cyrus Vance to Jerusalem and to Cairo to personally deliver a handwritten invitation.[34] Special messengers can indeed make an enormous difference in international communications.[35]

Special envoys are occasionally given symbolic or *ceremonial functions.* The more routine or recurring celebrations are generally left to permanent missions. But for momentous occasions, such as the fiftieth anniversary of the 1944 Allied landing in Normandy, special missions composed of important officials are de rigueur. Funerals of state leaders, coronations, and the like fall in that category. Three former US presidents represented President Carter at the funeral of Egyptian president Anwar Sadat, who was assassinated in 1981.[36] There is of course an element of public diplomacy in such functions. Some missions have an explicit public relations purpose, as when Byron Price was sent to Germany in August 1945 by President Harry Truman as his "personal representative in charge of public relations between American occupation forces and the German people." His instructions were broad: "You are hereby authorized to visit any place you deem necessary for this purpose. . . . At the end of your assignment, the duration of which you yourself will determine, I request you to submit to me your report and recommendations."[37]

Other special missions may be *observer missions,* in which the sending country (in an official or unofficial capacity) observes proceedings or meetings in which it is not participating. Some observers engage in a good deal of very real diplomacy. *Fact-finding missions* are particularly important in conflict settlement, since the disputants often have very different perceptions of the situation. Fact-finding in international politics frequently involves dealing with officials and requires genuine diplomatic skill as well as investigative talent.[38]

Related to this function is *international monitoring,* frequently referred to as "observation" (e.g., in foreign elections to guarantee authenticity and legitimacy). Former heads of state (e.g., President Jimmy Carter), or highly respected personalities, are often invited to serve on such missions.[39] Some such mission may be highly controversial or even dangerous—witness the January 2005 elections in Iraq. *"Study" missions* are occasionally dispatched to foreign theaters, as in November 1944, when President Roosevelt sent Mike Mansfield (without specification of rank or title) to study political and economic conditions in China; or in January 1947, when President Truman sent Herbert Hoover (again, no rank or title) to Britain, France, Germany (the US zone), Italy, and states of Central Europe "to study food and collateral problems."[40] Observation and monitoring have expanded in scope beyond these various diplomatic missions. International organizations, particularly the UN, have used them as a form of peacekeeping, often on a large scale involving the deployment of military units.[41] Such military observers may have fact-finding and reporting functions. There is an overlap with diplomatic missions, but there is usually a considerable difference in the nature and size of the operations involved.

Some special missions are used to conduct diplomatic business in the absence of diplomatic relations (e.g., to deal with unrecognized states or governments).[42] The same applies to nonsovereign entities, such as revolutionary groups, insurgents, and dependent territories. Thus, in 1942, the United States sent special missions to India (i.e., before independence) and Martinique (then under the Vichy regime).[43] Occasionally, special missions are sent as a preliminary step for the reopening of ruptured relations.[44] In a category related to special missions, foreign ministers increasingly travel to other countries, troubleshooting, negotiating, and meeting with other officials. Heads of other executive departments also engage in this kind of diplomacy. Special agents often travel with them on these missions. They are frequently assisted by the resident ambassador in the host country. Presidents and other important decisionmakers travel on special missions of sorts (see Box 9.2).

Box 9.2   Secretary of State Condoleezza Rice's First Mission

Immediately upon being nominated by President George W. Bush, in November 2004, to the post of secretary of state, Condoleezza Rice decided to undertake a special mission to Europe and the Middle East—her very first diplomatic initiative. Usually, a number of high foreign officials and heads of government visit Washington, D.C., shortly after inauguration to discover what may be about to change in US policy (see Chapter 10). This time, however, things worked in reverse: the new secretary of state made the rounds to important capitals.

The war in Iraq had badly fractured the Western partnership. France, Germany, and a number of European powers remained convinced that the war was a grievous blunder. Aggressive rhetoric by the United States about Iran's nuclear ambitions was widely regarded as dangerous, and the Bush administration was considered far too aloof from the Arab-Israeli conflict. Rice saw an urgent need to create a more positive image. A dramatic visit in the opening days of her new role as secretary of state was her chosen strategy: it would demonstrate her awareness (and the president's) of the concerns of these countries, and would likely be perceived as an effort to improve the situation—some old-fashioned fence-mending.

Rice was confirmed by the Senate on January 26, 2005. Eight days later, she landed in Europe to visit some ten countries in seven days—perhaps a bit rushed. But the message was clear and importantly articulated in a presentation before a specially invited group of intellectuals at the prestigious Institute of Political Studies in Paris. With considerable charm and warmth, she called for France and Europe to put aside differences with the United States and embark on a joint effort to expand freedom in the Arab world, build a new Iraq, and bring about peace in the Middle East. She sought to assure her audience that the Bush administration wanted to work in partnership with a stronger, united Europe to build a safer and better world. Such was the message for the whole visit. That same evening, she was received by President Jacques Chirac at the Elysée Palace. Her mission also took her to London, Berlin, Warsaw, Turkey (a Russian special envoy came to see her there as well), Jerusalem, Ramallah, Rome, the European Union in Luxembourg, and NATO in Brussels.

Rapprochement must of course depend upon how the states concerned will act in response to unfolding events. But this was a positive first step, and it was accepted as an important initiative.

Sources: Steven R. Weisman's articles in the *New York Times:* February 5, 2005, p. A3; February 6, 2005, p. 4; February 7, 2005, pp. A1, A10; February 8, 2005, pp. A1, A12; February 9, 2005, p. A11; February 10, 2005, p. A6.

For all their usefulness and versatility, special missions have their limitations. They cannot replace permanent missions. As seen in Chapter 7, embassies in national capitals serve a variety of purposes that are beyond the means of temporary missions. And although it is useful to be able to focus exclusively on a particular matter or problem, addressing the entire relationship between two nations or dealing with the membership and bureaucracy of an international organization requires a resident mission.[45] Special missions, because of their temporary character and their narrower focus, frequently need to rely on other diplomatic channels in their work. The resident mission in a given capital provides all the background information needed to approach local officials. It is frequently used to make the necessary appointments (preceding the arrival of the special envoy), and takes care of all logistical support (hotel arrangements, clerical assistance, communications with the sending state during the mission, etc.). Some special envoys involve the local ambassador in developing their strategy to approach local decisionmakers. This ambassador may even be invited to participate in the work of the special envoy—all of this, of course, depending upon the nature of the mission and circumstances.

▓ Modus Operandi

The flexibility of special missions and the ad hoc nature of this mode of diplomacy permit unconventional diplomatic procedures and different diplomatic styles, though all the skills of diplomacy remain indispensable, particularly as special missions are often involved in negotiations. The greater absence of structure, frequent need for rapid action, and pressure to adapt to changing circumstances lead to greater spontaneity and inventiveness. Also, the purposes served are so diverse that a great deal of diversity in method must be anticipated.[46]

Some special missions are sent as a result of prior agreement between the governments concerned. Their duties are often defined·in advance, including specification of their diplomatic status and issuance of appropriate credentials—in other words, some missions are highly structured. Others are given more freedom to deal with the situation as best they can. A mission normally needs to be acceptable to the visited state,[47] but arrangements for its arrival may be ambiguous, perhaps hastily made over the phone. A state's relationship with a resident mission can be problematic. Many special missions welcome the help of embassies. But there are times when resident officers are simply bypassed, or kept uninformed, thus creating resentment and perhaps leading them to work at cross-purposes. Much depends on what the people who decide to send special missions choose to do, and on the nature of the mission, the problem at hand, and the circumstances.

Diplomats embarking upon a special mission may not have to operate single-handedly. For example, UN Secretary-General Dag Hammarskjöld, during his 1955 mission to Beijing, took with him an interpreter, a special international legal expert, his assistant, his secretary, the chief of the UN Department of Public Information, and his personal aide.[48] When two governments reach agreement on a special mission, the rank and diplomatic status of the person may be specified. When the UN sends one of its officials on a mission, even an independent expert to work as a consultant on a development project, the person is protected under the Convention on the Privileges and Immunities of the UN or the Convention on the Privileges and Immunities of Specialized Agencies.[49] Nations that want to ensure the protected status of an envoy on a special mission can simply add the person (temporarily) to the staff of its embassy in the host country, with appropriate rank and due notification to the foreign ministry. The person will thus enjoy the same diplomatic privileges and immunities as the diplomatic personnel of the embassy. Otherwise, the immunities of special agents have remained controversial.[50]

When the UN International Law Commission had completed its draft convention on diplomatic relations, it decided to add provisions for the protection of special envoys. The Vienna Conference, however, refused to include any article on special missions in the 1961 convention. The UN General Assembly requested the drafting of a new treaty exclusively devoted to special missions.[51] After several years of consultation and negotiations, a new convention, on special missions, was submitted in December 1969 for ratification.[52] But most states, including the major powers, refused any involvement with it. As of 2006, only thirty-eight states were parties to the convention.[53] The State Department specifies that "in the absence of a treaty or other international agreement, the United States has no general expectation that a foreign government will accord diplomatic privileges and immunities to a person who may be denominated a 'special agent of the President.'"[54] In practice, special consideration is often given to special envoys as a matter of courtesy, and to facilitate their missions.

▓ International Mediation

Characteristics of International Mediation

One of the major functions of special mission diplomacy is to engage in international mediation. This is a procedure by which a third party helps states settle their differences. It is a brokering function that may involve as little as bringing the disputants together to negotiate, or as much as formulating the terms of settlement. Either way, the goal is to help the disputants come to an understanding. What the mediator formulates is nonbinding and may be the object of negotiations between the parties to the dispute. Mediation is a widely used form of diplomacy: 255 of 310 conflicts between 1945 and 1974 involved some form of official mediation by a regional or international organization, and so did 49 of 77 major conflicts between 1919 and 1965.[55] Between 1945 and the end of the Cold War in 1989, the United States mediated approximately 87 international conflicts worldwide (about 30 of these in Latin America and 38 in the Middle East). In the same period, the Soviet Union mediated 17 international conflicts (excluding Eastern Europe).[56]

Mediation can be of critical importance in extremely bitter disputes between parties that refuse to communicate or distrust each other. This is often the case when ideology or matters of principle are involved. The situation may be so polarized that the parties cannot politically afford to meet. Profound cultural differences may also prevent the initiation of negotiations. The mediator is then the only link between the contestants. Mediation may also be indispensable when the opponents, after lengthy negotiations, remain completely deadlocked, or when one of the parties decides that resort to armed force is a better alternative. The adversaries may also be so focused on what divides them that they are unable to see alternatives to their predicament (see Box 9.3).[57]

Mediation may be initiated in a large variety of ways.[58] The disputants themselves, realizing their difficulty, may agree to invite a third party of their choice, or may turn to an international organization for help. However, when the dispute is serious enough, they may not be able to agree to this sensible measure. Others must then intervene without invitation: states having an interest in solving the conflict, or international organizations, have taken this initiative, and so has the UN Secretary General on his own authority.[59] Transnational actors have intervened, such as the World Council of Churches and the All-African Council of Churches in the civil war in Sudan (1971),[60] and so have NGOs, such as the International Committee of the Red Cross in the 1967–1970 Nigerian civil war.[61] Occasionally, private citizens become mediators, as in the 1992–1993 Oslo peace process.[62] (See Chapter 11.)

Several states may cooperate in offering mediation, perhaps jointly selecting a common mediator. If they all want to take an active part in the process, they must maintain contact to avoid working at cross-purposes. Several states may try to mediate in succession if efforts fail. On occasion, several states will try to mediate a conflict separately, even competing with each other in the pursuit of different agendas. Between 1925 and 1945, in ten disputes taking place in Latin America, thirty-five countries served as intermediaries; after 1945, in just thirteen disputes, there were sixty-three mediation attempts.[63] This easily complicates the negotiations and is often less than helpful. Dag Hammarskjöld complained that his 1955 negotiations with China (over the capture of US airmen) became more difficult when Krishna Menon of India intervened in Beijing without consulting him.[64] Although a head of state may be officially designated as mediator in a conflict, a special agent will usually conduct the negotiations and

---

Box 9.3   Head-of-State Mediation in a Hostage Situation, 2007

The Revolutionary Armed Forces of Colombia (FARC), a leftist movement, has been engaged in guerrilla warfare for the past four decades and has been holding about forty-five hostages in jungle camps in Colombia for a number of years (in some cases for almost a decade). FARC has sought the release of about 500 imprisoned guerrillas in exchange for its captives.

In August 2007, President Hugo Chávez of Venezuela offered to negotiate the release of the hostages. President Alvaro Uribe of Colombia accepted. A Colombian lawmaker assisted Chávez, who met with a representative of FARC in Caracas, Venezuela. The Venezelan president also met with French president Nicolas Sarkozy in Paris (one of the hostages is a French citizen), but in more than two months of negotiations, no agreement was reached, and President Uribe lost interest. On November 21, Uribe withdrew his support for the mediation, claiming a breach of protocol when learning that Chávez had phoned General Montoya of Colombia for information about the hostages, despite a request from Uribe not to have any direct contact with high-ranking military officials. President Sarkozy quickly urged President Uribe to reconsider—but to no avail. Antagonists can be less than accommodating, and mediation can be immensely frustrating. In fact, a few days later, Uribe and Chávez exchanged insults over the matter and Venezuela recalled its ambassador. In January 2008, however, the revolutionaries informed Chávez that they were prepared to release two of the hostages. Uribe approved the transaction and suspended military operations in the area while Venezuelan representatives received the two hostages in the thick Colombian jungle. This was hailed as a breakthrough in Venezuela—and negotiations will probably continue. Relations between the two presidents might even improve.

Sources: Articles in the *New York Times:* November 23, 2007, p. A6; November 28, 2007, p. A16; January 10, 2008, p. A6; January 11, 2008, p. A6.

---

do the actual mediating. However, President Jimmy Carter personally worked with Anwar Sadat and Menachem Begin in the Camp David mediation in 1978.

In the work of international organizations and multilateral conferences, informal unofficial mediation of a different kind is a frequent occurrence—for example, when delegations disagree in the formulation of a resolution, other representatives will intervene, often on their own authority, to help them overcome their differences and prevent deadlock.[65] Committee chairs know that it is one of their duties to facilitate the interaction and intervene as necessary to move things along, or designate colleagues to do so in their names. Some diplomats acquire a reputation for their skill as facilitators or problem-solvers.[66]

Mediation Strategy

The choice of method in mediation is of course influenced by such factors as the nature of the conflict, the parties, what is at stake, as well as the styles of the special agents and the interests of the international actors who decide to serve as mediators. Neutrality on the part of such international actors is not a requirement, but a serious interest in bringing about a workable settlement *is*, and so is a degree of trust in the negotiator. A state that is aligned with one of the parties may still be effective, if it is committed to facilitating an arrangement that will be acceptable to both sides. In fact, closeness to one party may be seen as an advantage if it can use its influence (or wield pressure) to induce its friend to compromise, as in the case of US participation in Israeli-Palestinian negotiations.[67]

Actual mediator participation in the negotiations can vary enormously. It can be minimal,[68] as in the 1992–1993 Oslo peace process, during which Norway's participation was very low-key, but real. The Norwegian foreign minister attended all sessions and helped the negotiators remain focused on their important task. He facilitated the interaction. Too, any form of assistance may increase (or decrease) as the need arises. The main goal is to keep the parties talking and guide them to reach some form of agreement. In protracted conflicts, even a modest kind of settlement, such as the one reached at Oslo in 1993 in the Israeli-Palestinian negotiations, can be viewed as a breakthrough. One important task of mediation is to overcome setbacks.[69] Often, an incremental approach (i.e., a step-by-step progression) is the most practical, particularly in a deep-rooted conflict: it is a matter of negotiating what can be negotiated.[70] Each step forward improves confidence in the process.

Some forms of mediation are primarily procedural: persuading the antagonists to communicate, perhaps at a distance, as in the case of *shuttle diplomacy*, during which the mediator travels back and forth, negotiating with the adversaries in their respective capitals. A variant of this procedure is found when it is possible to bring representatives of the conflicting states to the same location, even though they refuse to talk to each other. Here again, the mediator goes back and forth, conveying messages, proposals, and responses, as when UN Undersecretary-General Ralph Bunche mediated a suspension of hostilities between Egypt and Israel on the Island of Rhodes in 1949. Such mediations have been called "proximity talks."[71] The UN Secretary-General does a good deal of this routinely in his New York office, talking to the permanent representatives of states that want no association with each other. Such mediations have also been called "indirect talks," particularly when the participants are not continuously present at the same location, but periodically take turns meeting individually with the mediator.

The hope is always that the mediation will have a catalytic effect, leading the opponents to resume direct contact. Some analysts call it the "relationship-oriented" approach. But in the process of trying to bring the parties together, the mediator often makes suggestions, especially when the parties fail to see available alternatives to their conflicting positions. The mediator may even be able to produce terms of settlement (more or less elaborate, more or less comprehensive) so that the parties may find something concrete to discuss and negotiate among themselves—unless, of course, they accept the mediator's terms as presented. Some analysts call it the "resolution-oriented" approach.[72] But it is easy to see that the process should not be rigid and that mediators should probably not limit themselves to one approach. Some have spoken of "exploratory mediation" when a special agent is sent to the parties in conflict to explore the possibility of negotiations.[73] The first phase of ambassador Bunker's mission in the Yemen crisis, before he was officially named mediator and sent back to the Middle East, could be called exploratory, particularly as the United States was still urging the UN Secretary-General to use his own special envoy to mediate.[74]

Mediators are helpful in contributing to a change in perception (more feasible when the mediator enjoys the trust of the disputants). In this respect, providing assurances that the concessions are reciprocal and balanced is important, as the antagonists are often convinced that they are making greater concessions than the other side. Changing the parties' expectations, too, can be a step forward, and so can making them aware of the cost of failing to reach agreement.

Mediators are occasionally in a better position to lead the conflicting parties to make concessions when these concessions are seen as granted, however implausibly, to the mediator rather than to the other party. This is more likely to happen in proximity talks or in shuttle diplomacy exercises. In a similar vein, proposals are more acceptable when they are seen as coming from the mediator rather than from the other side. An arrangement settling the dispute may be more acceptable if presented in a declaration by the mediator rather than as an agreement between the disputants. For example, the final agreement in the Iran hostage negotiations took the form of a declaration by the Algerian government (the mediator).[75] A prestigious mediator (actual negotiator or international actor in whose name the mediation is carried out) who enjoys an aura of authority, influence, and widespread respect is more likely to achieve such results.

Concessions will be more easily granted when the mediator can offer positive inducements. Arrangements for the verification of compliance may help, but are not always feasible. Agreement may also be facilitated when guarantees can be provided, such as by the UN Security Council or by individual states. Other positive inducements have taken the form of financial arrangements, debt cancellation, or offers of development assistance. Much depends upon what the parties find appealing and how much the sponsors are willing to offer to reward concessions. Negative inducements are also used: pressure from the international community, curtailment of assistance, and the like. But these need to be wielded with caution, as they can also have the opposite effect—hardening positions or breaking up the negotiations.[76]

Special missions are thus a very significant tool of diplomatic inter-action.[77] Their flexibility and versatility guarantee their continued usefulness. As international society becomes more complex, international actors will find new ways of using them and may therefore want to train more agents for this purpose. Negotiating skills, no doubt, are critical.[78] As specialized or technical skills are increasingly needed to address certain international problems (e.g., environmental and health issues), the needed experts are often recruited outside the foreign service (e.g., from research institutions) for temporary diplomatic missions. Periodic training should be provided for greater diplomatic proficiency.

▓ Case Study: The Yemen Crisis

The Yemen crisis offers a good example of the use of special missions for the purpose of preventing an escalation of the conflict between Egypt (then known as the United Arab Republic [UAR]) and Saudi Arabia over a revolution in Yemen. This case demonstrates how mediation may lead enemies to reach agreement, however reluctantly. It shows also, in the realm of diplomatic method, how a mediator may work with the local ambassadors in trying to ne-gotiate with the conflicting sovereigns, as well as parallel interaction with the United Nations.

The Problem

In September 1962, a military coup overthrew the traditional monarchy in Sana‘a, the capital of Yemen, and a republic was proclaimed. The head of the toppled regime fled and organized guerrilla operations in northern Yemen.[79] The new republican regime asked UAR president Gamal Abdel Nasser to pro-vide assistance to crush the royalists. Soon, more than 20,000 Soviet-equipped UAR combat troops were in Yemen.[80] Saudi Arabia felt threatened by this UAR intervention, as Nasser had vowed to free the Middle East from reac-tionary monarchies. Moreover, Yemen had negotiated a loose association with the UAR, formally presented as a "union."[81] Washington saw these events as a threat to the stability of the region, particularly because of Soviet willingness to support Nasser's ventures.[82]

Saudi Arabia responded by sending arms and money to the Yemeni royal-ists. Nasser thereupon ordered air strikes against Saudi border towns from which war supplies flowed to the royalists, and the United States began to fear an escalation of the conflict. Washington had a clear interest in maintaining a

moderate pro-US regime in Saudi Arabia, an oil-rich and strategically important country, and it feared that the Soviets might gain a foothold in the Middle
East through their increasing cooperation with the UAR. Making the situation
more delicate, the United States had been trying to improve relations with
Nasser in order to reduce Soviet influence in the UAR. It was therefore reluctant to accede to Saudi requests for a full show of support in resisting UAR attacks. It was equally reluctant to press Nasser too hard, for the same reason. A
diplomatic solution to the confrontation over Yemen was therefore essential.[83]

President John F. Kennedy sent a personal letter to Crown Prince Faisal,
acting chief executive in Saudi Arabia, while King Saud was convalescing in
Europe, assuring him of US support for Saudi integrity and sovereignty. However, Faisal's confidence in the United States was shaken in December 1962
when the US government recognized the Yemeni republic (the royalists were
unlikely to succeed in their struggle).[84] Furthermore, Faisal wanted Nasser to
make the first move toward disengagement. In fact, both sides saw the conflict
as a matter of honor and neither one wanted to be the first to disengage.

During the winter of 1962–1963, the United States used its embassies in
the UAR and Saudi Arabia to coax the two governments to discontinue their
intervention. This was the beginning of (unacknowledged) mediation, interestingly using the US ambassador in each capital to show Nasser and Faisal what
each had to gain from being the first to disengage, but this led nowhere. The
military situation in Yemen reached a stalemate.[85] At the beginning of 1963,
the United States urged UN Secretary-General U Thant to appoint a mediator
to deal with the crisis. However, he was sensitive to the charge that he was too
closely aligned with US interests and did not want to act without the explicit
prior consent of all parties involved in the conflict, and this took time.

At the end of January 1963, the United States decided to send a special
envoy to Faisal on an unofficial basis to urge him to suspend, at least temporarily, his support of the royalists, so that Nasser could fulfill his public
pledge of December 1962 to withdraw UAR troops from Yemen. The mission
failed; Faisal continued to insist that Nasser take the first disengagement
step.[86] In the meantime, the UN Secretary-General decided to send to the Middle East a special envoy, Ralph Bunche, on a fact-finding rather than a mediation mission.[87] Washington complained again that U Thant was not acting
with sufficient urgency,[88] and decided to send its own mediator, selecting
Ellsworth Bunker, a seasoned diplomat.[89] This did not help to improve relations with the Secretary-General.[90]

The Bunker Mission: Preliminary Phase

In late February 1963, President Kennedy and the National Security Council
outlined the US plan for a Nasser-Faisal disengagement. It was thus a mediation effort that involved strong direction from the highest level of the govern-

ment, showing the importance attached to the crisis (some mediation efforts leave much more latitude to the mediator in finding a settlement). On March 1, President Kennedy himself met with Ambassador Bunker to review the situation. Bunker was to deliver to Faisal a personal letter from the president emphasizing US support for Saudi Arabia, in an attempt to reassure Faisal that the US interest in disengagement was not hostile. The letter concluded: "[Ambassador Bunker has my] complete confidence. . . . [He] is authorized to speak frankly on my behalf. I . . . hope that you will talk with him on the same basis as you would with me."[91] This, of course, enhanced the stature of the mediator. Bunker was authorized to offer, if it could facilitate the disengagement, the temporary stationing of US fighter aircraft in Saudi Arabia, as a token of US commitment to Saudi security.[92] Bunker was not yet officially identified as a mediator.

Bunker left for the Middle East on March 6, the same day that the UN special envoy completed his fact-finding mission on behalf of the Secretary-General. The UN envoy thought that the Yemen situation could easily deteriorate, with far-reaching repercussions: "I do not exclude the possibility that Yemen could become a Cuba in the Near East."[93] On February 8, a military coup had taken place in Baghdad, led by an officer dedicated to Nasser's doctrine of pan-Arabism and the overthrow of royalist governments. This event underscored the increasingly precarious positions of monarchies such as Saudi Arabia and Jordan.

Faisal had refused to meet with the UN mission on the grounds that it was not impartial, since it had visited Sana'a and Cairo but had not met with the Yemeni royalists.[94] The United States, on its part, was anxious to reassure U Thant that it was not trying to undercut the UN effort. Accordingly, the State Department informed the UN Secretary-General that Bunker was being sent to improve US-Saudi relations. No mention was made of a US decision to undertake its own mediation mission. U Thant was told also that Bunker would support UN efforts in that he would attempt to secure from Faisal an unconditional invitation to see the UN envoy, Ralph Bunche. To facilitate Bunker's mission, John Badeau, the US ambassador in Cairo, met with Nasser on March 4 and requested a suspension of UAR bombing of Saudi targets during the Bunker-Bunche efforts. Nasser accepted.[95]

Upon arriving in Saudi Arabia on March 6, Bunker was met by Parker Hart, US ambassador in Saudi Arabia, who briefed the special envoy on Faisal's proud and sensitive personality.[96] Bunker had a meeting with the crown prince the same evening, at 9:30 P.M. (after the long flight from the United States, this kind of schedule tests a diplomat's resilience). Bunker presented Faisal with a disengagement plan to be discussed at a second meeting, the next day. Talcott W. Seelye, a career foreign service officer who served as Bunker's aide during the mission, also attended these meetings, along with their interpreter.[97]

Faisal showed profound distrust of Nasser,[98] but accepted tentatively the idea of a simultaneous disengagement (a step forward), and showed interest in the US offer of military assistance. Faisal took advantage of the second meeting to request US assistance to set up two powerful television stations in Saudi Arabia. The following day (March 8), Ambassadors Bunker and Hart cabled the State Department that they considered it essential that the UN representative proceed to Saudi Arabia as soon as possible, to carry forward with the momentum of the US initiative and progress made in softening Faisal's position.

Bunker worked with Hart, the US ambassador, throughout the course of his initial negotiations, consulting him, keeping him abreast of developments, and approaching the State Department jointly on the recommended next step.[99] Throughout the mission, too, the department was kept informed and consulted. Interestingly, it is clear from the cable that they assumed the UN Secretary-General was involved in a process of mediation with his own special envoy.[100] Bunker and Hart therefore proceeded to recommend that the UN special envoy be warned (through UN channels) that he had been extensively quoted on Middle East radio and in press reports and was seen as pro-UAR by the Saudis. Nevertheless, if Nasser could be convinced to end his attacks on Saudi Arabia, including radio propaganda, Faisal was ready to resume harmonious relations. They also stressed that the UN diplomat should realize that Faisal was extremely sensitive to any appearance of caving to either UAR or US pressure.[101]

Upon returning to the United States, Bunker met with the UN Secretary-General and Bunche on March 10, reviewed the situation, and stressed the importance of Bunche returning to Saudi Arabia immediately while Faisal was in a receptive state of mind. But U Thant remained cautious: he would send his representative on this mission only if the Saudi representative to the UN ascertained that Faisal would receive him without requiring that he also visit the Yemeni royalists,[102] and only after he received the reactions of Cairo and Sana'a to the disengagement plan that Bunker proposed to Faisal (only the idea of simultaneous disengagement was tentatively accepted at this time). U Thant was seen by Washington as reluctant to cooperate with the United States in solving the UAR-Saudi conflict, and still fearful of being accused by the Soviet Union of serving US interests.[103]

On March 11, Bunker conferred with President Kennedy, reviewing US strategy. Both agreed that the preferred choice was to have the UN special envoy proceed to Saudi Arabia within the week with full authority to mediate, but it seemed to them that U Thant would not support this proposal. Bunker returned to New York and again met with U Thant and his envoy, on March 12 and 13. From these conversations, Bunker thought that the UN Secretary-General remained unwilling to act with the speed needed to maintain the momentum in the disengagement negotiations. The United States, therefore, decided to continue acting on its own initiative. The State Department sent Bunker back to the Middle East to mediate.[104]

The Bunker Mission: Second Phase

Ambassador Bunker's initial visit to Saudi Arabia had been officially presented as a mission to discuss US-Saudi relations and accessorily to coax Faisal to see the UN representative. This time, Bunker was to negotiate with both Faisal and Nasser. But he was not officially designated as the US mediator for the sake of easing relations with U Thant, as the United States wanted the disengagement to take place under the auspices of the UN. The State Department's official position vis-à-vis U Thant was that Bunker's mission was in support of, and ancillary to, the United Nations effort (mediation is often complex and roundabout).

Bunker started this part of his mission in Riyadh, the Saudi capital, but his meeting with Faisal was delayed until March 17 because of a bad sandstorm. He conveyed orally to Faisal a personal message from President Kennedy stressing the importance of quickly adopting the US disengagement plan. He also conveyed the president's keen interest in the television stations project (Faisal knew Kennedy could not refuse). Preparations were under way for US experts to come to Saudi Arabia to work out the details. In the course of this three-hour meeting, Bunker discussed the US disengagement formula in the most favorable light *from the Saudi point of view* so as to preserve the honor of the crown prince. Bunker artfully suggested that *suspension* of aid to the royalists would be understood as discontinuation.

After this meeting, Bunker reported to the State Department that if he could secure from Nasser a pledge of troop withdrawal from Yemen, he believed that Faisal would be willing to cooperate with a United Nations–sponsored disengagement. A serious snag, however, soon developed: on March 18, the next day, Ambassador Badeau, in Cairo, sent an urgent cable to Bunker that Nasser would not meet with him. This rebuff placed the entire mediation effort in jeopardy and prompted a sharp debate within the State Department (many mediators remain much more independent). Bunker cabled from Saudi Arabia that he believed he should meet with Badeau in Beirut, Lebanon. Remaining in Saudi Arabia would arouse Faisal's suspicion. The department approved.[105]

On March 20, after their meeting in Beirut, Bunker and Badeau cabled the State Department, indicating that, in consultation with Badeau, Bunker had drawn up a list of conditions for disengagement that he believed would be acceptable to Faisal and not unreasonable to Nasser. Badeau, upon returning to Cairo, would present these proposals to Nasser and urge a direct meeting with Bunker. The cable also suggested that the State Department should urge U Thant to send a message to Nasser urging him to receive Bunker. The State Department, however, did not want to seek the help of the UN Secretary-General. Instead, it instructed Badeau to tell Nasser of the awkward situation created by his refusal to receive the US president's envoy. But no pressure was to be applied. The department directed Badeau to indicate his understanding of

Nasser's current preoccupation (Nasser had invoked complex unity talks in Cairo with a number of Arab states), but to express the hope he could soon meet with Bunker. The department also instructed Badeau to emphasize that Bunker's proposals were intended to facilitate a future UN mission—again, using the UN as an umbrella, hoping that it would be a more acceptable sponsor for the disengagement.[106]

On March 23, Badeau succeeded in meeting with Nasser and stressed that meeting with Bunker would pave the way for a UN mediator to work out the modalities of a disengagement agreement. But Nasser was not convinced. Badeau persisted and Nasser finally agreed to see Bunker on April 1. Reporting this concession to Washington, Badeau emphasized the importance of keeping this agreement secret, as Nasser was extremely sensitive to any appearance of his bowing to US pressure, particularly after the *New York Times* reported on March 9 that Nasser had agreed to suspend its air attacks on Saudi Arabia in response to "stern American warnings." This kind of statement can be fatal to the mediation process, another example of the media becoming an unintended factor in diplomatic negotiations (see the case study on Beijing negotiations in Chapter 8, and the case study on the Suez negotiations in Chapter 3).

On March 24, Bunker cabled Washington from Beirut that he could not return to see Faisal without some report on Nasser's reactions to the disengagement proposals. He recommended Ambassador Hart in Riyadh be instructed to tell Faisal that Nasser could not see Bunker until April 1 because of the unity talks taking place in Cairo, and that the serious illness of Bunker's wife[107] forced him to return to the United States. Either Bunker or the UN special envoy would meet with Nasser to hear his reaction to the proposals and then proceed to Riyadh. The State Department accepted this approach, but wanted Badeau to obtain Nasser's reaction to the disengagement proposals *before* the meeting of April 1. In the meantime, Bunker returned to Washington. On March 25, Badeau cabled back to say that trying to obtain Nasser's views before the April 1 meeting would not work—and he was not sure Nasser would want to discuss the matter with him instead of Bunker, the presidential emissary, ahead of the planned meeting with him—evidence of the particular importance of a special presidential envoy. The State Department accepted Badeau's objections and decided that Bunker must return to the Middle East.

Conclusion of the Negotiations

Bunker as well as Badeau met with Nasser on April 1 (Badeau was respected in Cairo and had succeeded in maintaining a dialogue with Nasser at a time of uncertain relations with the United States). Bunker opened the meeting with an oral message from President Kennedy, then reviewed the ground covered with Faisal and showed where the crown prince's position had softened. But Nasser distrusted Faisal. In a second meeting, on April 2, the details of the disengagement proposal were discussed. The negotiations were difficult, even though Bunker was prepared to accept a token withdrawal of UAR forces to begin the disengagement. Nasser maintained that no troop withdrawal could take place until Saudi aid to the royalists had stopped. The matter was critical, as Bunker needed a simultaneous token Egyptian withdrawal at the very beginning of Saudi suspension of aid. Without it, Faisal would not budge. The discussion remained inconclusive, and an impasse was reached on simultaneous disengagement.[108]

A third meeting took place on April 3. Bunker pared down the disengagement terms to what Nasser could accept *without* reference to simultaneous disengagement (which would have brought an immediate refusal). By the end of the meeting, Bunker had identified what terms Nasser could accept, and knew that Faisal could be brought around to accept the main thrust of those terms. Bunker had purposefully left out the issue of simultaneous disengagement from the negotiations—and so managed to reach agreement on the other points. Upon leaving, however, Bunker told Nasser informally that if he "really wanted to make it probable that he would not return to bother him again,"[109] then he needed to be specific about withdrawing at least a company or so on the day when Faisal would begin to interrupt his support for the royalists. Nasser agreed! This was the backdoor approach. The fact that, psychologically, they were no longer in a negotiating mode probably made a difference. They were more at ease and detached from the task at hand. It did not seem to be a concession in a bargaining session.[110] At any rate, it was a breakthrough, as it meant agreement on the element of simultaneity, to which Faisal attached such enormous importance.[111]

It is interesting that toward the end of the third day of negotiations, Nasser inquired whether the proposals discussed would be made public. If so, Nasser stated that the wording would have to be carefully considered and that he might want to make some changes. Badeau reassured him that the disengagement should be carried out with as little publicity as possible. And he noted wisely that if it were made public, it would be difficult for both sides to refrain from propagandistic statements, which might complicate the situation.[112] Bunker traveled to Saudi Arabia the next day, April 4, to meet with Faisal. He went over the terms that had been accepted by Nasser. Faisal tried to modify some and add a few, but in the end he announced suddenly that, as a gesture of confidence in President Kennedy, he was prepared to accept the revised disengagement proposal presented by Bunker. He is reported to have added: "I don't trust Nasser, but I trust you, Ambassador Bunker, and that is why I go along with this agreement."[113] Following this diplomatic success, Bunker returned to Cairo.

On April 9, Bunker met once again with Nasser and the two agreed to some rewording likely to be acceptable to Faisal. Nasser even agreed to an early date for the commencement of disengagement. In his report to Washington, Bunker emphasized the need for prompt UN action in the verification process. On April 10, the Saudi deputy foreign minister informed Ambassador Hart that Faisal had accepted all the terms of disengagement as modified the day before by Bunker and Nasser. Agreement had been achieved and it was now the task of the UN to ensure verification of the actual disengagement.[114] The mediation efforts did not resolve the conflict between Saudi Arabia and the UAR, but they averted an escalation of the conflict in the unfolding Yemen crisis.[115]

Conference Diplomacy

▓ Current Proliferation

International conferences are nothing new. They have brought leaders together to face common problems and have brought wars to an end as far back as classical antiquity. What is new is the vast increase in the use of this method of negotiating international issues. More problems need to be approached internationally. Extensive globalization of human endeavors has made international actors interdependent and forced them to work together to a larger and larger extent. This implies the convening of conferences, particularly multilateral conferences or meetings, however they may be called. Elmer Plischke provides some interesting statistics pertaining to US participation in international meetings and conferences.[116] Until 1900, the United States was involved in only 100 international conferences, averaging somewhat less than one per year. In the next quarter century, 1900 to 1925, its participation increased to nearly 180, averaging 7.2 per year. The pace increased considerably as the world moved closer to World War II. By the late 1930s, it reached 100 per year, or nearly two a week; the rate of participation increased even faster during the war.

The post–World War II era saw an explosion of multilateral activity. Between 1946 and 1955, the number of meetings attended by the United States jumped to 2,643, or about 260 per year, and this figure climbed to well over 300 a year by the 1960s (more than one new conference each working day), 650 for 1965 alone, and 900 to 1,000 a year in the 1980s.[117] And these were just the meetings attended by the United States. Many nations, of course, held conferences of their own that the United States did not attend (e.g., a vast variety of regional gatherings), and these are therefore not included in Plischke's figures. The total number of international conferences held around the world is thus far larger—a truly astounding phenomenon. Daniel Cheever and H. Field Haviland's more comprehensive statistics for the pre–World War II period are symptomatic of this remarkable escalation (see Table 9.1).

Some conferences, although not connected to any permanent institutional structures (at least not initially)[118] are recurring international meetings (see

Table 9.1   Total Number of International Conferences, 1840–1939 (by decade)

	Number of Conferences
1840–1849	5
1850–1859	22
1860–1869	75
1870–1879	149
1880–1889	284
1890–1899	469
1900–1909	1,082
1910–1919 (World War I)	974
1920–1929	2,913
1930–1939	3,655

Source: Daniel S. Cheever and H. Field Haviland Jr., *Organizing for Peace: International Organization in World Affairs* (Boston: Houghton Mifflin, 1954), p. 32.

Box 9.4). The diplomatic processes in the meetings of most international organizations and multilateral conferences have many common features. Furthermore, some special meetings of international organizations (e.g., the UN General Assembly's special sessions) are comparable to ad hoc conferences in many respects, and are convened in place of international conferences. Interestingly, international organizations convene conferences of their own on a wide range of issues, as may serve their purposes. The broadening of subjects addressed by international conferences is remarkable (see Box 9.5).[119]

Conference diplomacy is, by nature, short-term diplomacy, from a few days to two or three weeks. Keeping large numbers of delegations together for any length of time creates serious logistical complications and adds to the cost. When a conference cannot complete its work within this time frame, the normal procedure is to adjourn and reconvene at a later time. The Law of the Sea Conference took nine years to complete its work. It started with an annual session. But when the negotiations proved more difficult than anticipated, two sessions were convened annually. Conference diplomacy tends to imply a multilateral process, but it can also be bilateral, in which case it might be called a "meeting."[120] Terminology, however, is frequently inconsistent. Some multilateral gatherings are announced as meetings—and by a variety of other names (see Box 9.5).[121]

With so many international organizations now available to address any international issue, one may wonder why so many conferences are convened, tying up so many diplomats and other officials. International conferences have become a full-time, yearlong responsibility of foreign ministries and other executive departments. In the early 1960s, close to 2,800 US delegates were involved annually in conference work. Interestingly, only about 40 percent of these officials represented the Department

**Box 9.4　The Global Initiative to Combat
Nuclear Terrorism, 2006–2007**

A global initiative was started by Presidents George W. Bush and Vladimir Putin on July 15, 2006, in St. Petersburg, Russia, to create a multilateral partnership in response to the growing threat of international terrorism. On October 30–31, 2006, the representatives of thirteen governments (Australia, Canada, China, France, Germany, Japan, Italy, Kazakhstan, Morocco, Russia, Turkey, the United States, and the United Kingdom) met in Rabat, the capital of Morocco, and reached agreement on a statement of principle as well as terms of reference for implementation and assessment. The International Atomic Energy Agency, a UN agency, has been invited to serve as an observer in this project. It was also decided to open the partnership to other nations committed to combating nuclear terrorism. The members pledged to keep their own nuclear materials under control and to combat trafficking in nuclear materials that might fall into the hands of terrorists.

A second conference meeting was held in February 2007 in Ankara, Turkey, and a third in June 2007 in Astana, Kazakhstan, bringing together nineteen states (Afghanistan, Armenia, Cambodia, Cape Verde, Cyprus, Czech Republic, Denmark, Georgia, Greece, Israel, Macedonia, Montenegro, Netherlands, Pakistan, Palau, Romania, Spain, Sri Lanka, and Ukraine) to join the original thirteen. More states will undoubtedly be enlisted into this cooperative venture as more conferences are convened to address the problem.

Sources: http://www.state.gov/t/isn/c; http://www.whitehouse.gov/news/releases/20006/07.

most of the others were agents of other federal departments and agencies,[122] and even members of Congress, all serviced by the State Department.[123] The simplest answer is that conferences are found useful. An international conference is a flexible diplomatic medium that enables the participants to remain focused on a limited or specialized agenda.[124]

Some issues are best approached between a select number and kind of participants (e.g., close allies, or states sharing a particular outlook toward a problem), in the expectation that cooperation will be easier. Detractors among the membership of given organizations may thus be avoided. Ad hoc gatherings are easy enough to arrange between a limited number of states that are interested in working together. Or conferences may be organized to involve participants at a specific level of expertise or authority (e.g., ministerial meetings). In other words, conferences permit selection of the diplomatic participants best suited to the kind of interaction desired.

The choice of venue may in some instances be an important consideration—for example, a neutral environment when the parties are concerned about the im-

Box 9.5   Select List of Conferences and Meetings, 2004–2005

2004

International Conference on the Reconstruction of Liberia, New York, February 5–6.

Convention on Biological Diversity, Kuala Lumpur, Malaysia, February 9–20.

Global Forum on Internet Governance, New York, March 25–27.

General Assembly Plenary Meeting and Expert Consultations on the Global Road Safety Crisis, New York, April 14–15.

Third Session of the Permanent Forum on Indigenous Issues, New York, May 10–21.

UN Conference on Trade and Development XI (UNCTAD XI), São Paulo, Brazil, June 13–18.

Unlearning Intolerance: Confronting Islamophobia—Education for Tolerance and Understanding, New York, December 7.

2005

International Meeting for the Ten-Year Review of the Barbados Program of Action for Sustainable Development in Small Island Developing States, Port-Louis, Mauritius, January 10–14.

World Conference on Disaster Reduction, Kobe, Japan, January 18–22.

Twenty-Eighth Special Session of the General Assembly for the Commemoration of the Sixtieth Anniversary of the Liberation of the Concentration Camps, New York, January 24.

Conference on Biodiversity: Science and Governance, Paris, France, January 24–28.

continues

pression created by certain negotiations. Saving face is often a critical concern. In the same vein, the format and structure as well as the modus operandi of a conference can be adjusted to fit the purpose of the diplomatic exercise—for example, exchange of information, exploration of avenues of cooperation, settlement of a difference, or drafting of a treaty, each requiring different preparation, approaches, or type of work. Rules of procedure can be designed accordingly. The agenda of a conference can be tailored to the needs of the conferring states, precisely focused on what they want to accomplish, thus enabling conference participants to pay more attention to the problem at hand.[125] This is particularly important at a time when the agendas of international organizations are becoming more crowded. An international conference may also be a more expeditious way

---

Box 9.5   Cont.

Ten-Year Review of the Implementation of the Copenhagen Declaration
and Program of Action and the Outcome of the Twenty-Fourth Spe-
cial Session of the General Assembly, New York, February 9–18.
Beijing + 10 Conference: Forty-Ninth Session of the Commission on
the Status of Women, New York, February 28–March 11.
Eleventh UN Congress on Crime Prevention and Criminal Justice,
Bangkok, Thailand, April 18–25.
2005 Review Conference of the Parties to the Treaty on the Non-
Proliferation of Nuclear Weapons, New York, May 2–27.
Fifth Session of the UN Forum on Forests, New York, May 16–27.
Fourth Session of the Permanent Forum on Indigenous Issues: Millen-
nium Development Goals and Indigenous People, New York, May
16–27.
Twenty-Second Session of the Subsidiary Bodies of the UN Framework
Convention on Climate Change, Bonn, Germany, May 16–27.
Caribbean Regional Seminar on Decolonization, Canouan, St. Vincent
and the Grenadines, May 17–19.

Source: http://www.un.org/events/conferences.htm.

---

of addressing certain issues: many organizations meet only once a year with no
provisions for special meetings.[126]

All of these considerations say something about the variety of conferences
encountered. Various typologies can be devised—for example, contrasting an
exploratory consultation to a treaty-making gathering or to a dispute-settlement
exercise. But the substance of international relations is too diverse to hope for
a comprehensive classification. New forms of conference will be devised when
new needs are found. And all of this says something about the utility of conference diplomacy. Naturally, conference diplomacy is not a panacea; other forms
of diplomacy serve their purpose. But as international affairs become more diverse and more complex, it is easy to see how this flexible mode can be extensively used despite the fact that the increasing number of meetings creates a serious burden for even the best-equipped governments.

Conference diplomacy, however, is not free from problems, in addition to
the issue of numbers. "Politicization" can greatly reduce the productivity of
some international meetings.[127] But this term is a misnomer. Politics normally
plays a legitimate role even in the most technical subject matter. State interests
are always affected, and the participants are expected to have different agendas. It is the role of diplomacy to facilitate political accommodation. "Politicization" is meant to refer to the misuse of a conference to bring up issues that

are not germane to what the conference is trying to accomplish (e.g., bringing up the issue of the Arab-Israeli conflict, or any other controversial issue, in a conference on a totally different subject). Some delegations take advantage of even the most technical negotiations to bring up highly divisive but mostly irrelevant, ideological issues, literally hijacking the conference. This happened with great regularity during the Cold War as bitter confrontations kept the delegates from addressing the main items on the agenda. The more emotional the issue, the more likely it is to derail the diplomatic process. This is more likely to happen in world conferences.

Large conferences have also been hampered by massive public demonstrations, the most notorious being the World Trade negotiations in Seattle in 1999, which triggered chaotic rioting against the effects of globalization.[128] Extensive precautions have since been taken to protect a number of conferences from international protesters. The publicity generated by some very large conferences has also led to the charge that these gatherings have become mere media events—too large, too much in the limelight to be able to accomplish any substantive results. Convening a world conference on some of the difficult problems facing global society gives the impression of action. The broad action programs approved in these gatherings, however, remain mostly unimplemented. Still, these conferences have kept important issues, such as women's rights, environmental protection, and third world poverty, on the public agenda, an important matter if more efforts are to be made to address them.

■ Preparatory Work

Diplomatic conferences may be convened by a state, a group of states, or, increasingly today, international organizations. The success of a conference is dependent upon a good deal of preparation, which of course varies with the size of the conference and its subject matter.[129] The convener decides who will participate and usually shoulders responsibility for appropriate preparation. A *secretariat* needs to be assembled as soon as possible. It will be of critical importance when the conference is meeting, but it has a great deal to do to ensure adequate preparation for the conference. If the conference is convened by a single state, that state's own bureaucracy will staff the secretariat. The person heading the secretariat is of special significance, as his or her leadership in the preparatory phase as well as during the conference is a significant element in the success of the proceedings.[130] If several states are responsible for the conference, they will have to agree among themselves on the composition and structure of the secretariat. They will also have to agree on the site of the conference and how to share the cost.

An international organization is likely to draw on its own secretariat to service the conference. The membership of the organization will make all necessary decisions. It will usually create a preparatory committee for this purpose.[131] The secretariat can provide important technical expertise in preparing for the conference and during the actual proceedings.[132] The secretariat is also entrusted with the preparation of documents: background papers, statistical surveys, and, most importantly when a conference is to draft a treaty, the preparation of a working text after surveying the membership, which helps to determine the items on which there is broad consensus, and the various positions held on different aspects of the treaty, giving an initial sense of the scope of the forthcoming negotiations.[133]

Draft rules of procedure may be provided by the agency that is sponsoring the conference, or they may be prepared by the secretariat. They cover the way the agenda is approved, official languages, whether meetings are public or closed, powers of the conference president, rights of delegates, methods of making motions, debate procedure, submission of proposals and amendments, rules on elections, voting methods, and the like. Some conferences barely refer to them, but when a conference is large and the agenda is controversial, rules of procedure are indispensable. Past experience, and standing rules of organizations, provide helpful guidance.[134] The secretariat assembles proposals submitted by the conference membership. The secretariat may also prepare some resolutions for the conference (in addition to those proposed by the conference participants). It can thus be seen that secretariats can play an important role in the preparation for a conference, but this is not always recognized, resulting in an occasional lack of care in selecting staff members or inadequate funding for their activities.[135]

The parties convening a conference will usually establish a *preparatory committee* ("PrepCom" in international organization jargon), or convene preparatory meetings. A world conference usually requires three or four years of preparatory work—negotiations that can be just as intense as the negotiations during the conference itself. It is indeed useful to achieve as much agreement as possible before the conference begins, and a great deal of diplomatic activity is devoted to it, not only in the preparatory committee but also between national capitals, or between national delegations within the organization sponsoring the conference, if such is the case. Organization bureaucracies may also have a leading role in the preparatory process. Interagency rivalry can be a factor. The future of agencies working in the area covered by the conference may be affected by conference negotiations—for example, new agencies may be created, taking away some of their current functions, all of which is likely to generate turf battles.[136]

The preparatory committee or preparatory meetings may be open to all organization members (or invited states), or they may be more selectively constituted. In a large organization, such as the UN or one of its specialized agencies, even if all members are invited to participate, many will abstain. However, 90 to 100 of them may decide to play a role, which means that preparatory sessions will amount to very substantial international conferences themselves, normally convened in a number of sessions, depending upon the magnitude of the task, perhaps one or two per year.[137] Meetings of the preparatory committee may also be attended by other international organizations (many UN specialized agencies have a stake in UN-sponsored conferences) and by NGO observers. Some NGOs may be invited as participants in the preparatory work, but this is still somewhat uncommon. Many NGOs are trying to play a larger role and undoubtedly will achieve greater participation in the future. The head of the preparatory committee plays an important role in guiding the negotiations. For this reason, and for the sake of continuity, it is better to avoid rotating this position, even when it is politically tempting, to satisfy a diversity of participants.

When the conference is convened by an international organization, the organ making this decision (e.g., the UN General Assembly) is likely to have specified a number of elements (location, dates, budget). The preparatory committee may be asked to put together a detailed conference agenda, a matter of critical importance with serious political implications that is often hotly debated. But the resolution calling for the conference usually spells out the purpose of the conference, and may specify some of the issues requiring discussion. On the other hand, when a conference is convened by a state or a small group of states, some kind of agenda (or at least provisional agenda) will have to be sent along with the invitations to attend. Decisions to attend or not will be significantly influenced by what the conveners propose to do.

Related to the agenda is the structure of the conference. It is often important to break up the conference into committees that will be given portions of the agenda to negotiate.[138] Having these committees meet simultaneously imposes a burden on the smaller delegations, but it enables the conference to get more accomplished. The conference plenary can vote on committee resolutions as they are drafted (i.e., without having to wait until the end of the proceedings). Often, when an item is decided in committee, it does not have to be debated again in plenary, unless the item is particularly controversial, in which case the battle is likely to resume. If the conference is to produce a treaty, a drafting committee will be needed to write what the conference approves, using appropriate legal terminology, filling gaps, identifying contradictions in the details, and otherwise drafting a document that will reflect what was accepted in the course of the political interaction. A poorly crafted treaty creates implementation difficulties.

Some multilateral conferences (e.g., on women's rights, the environment, or population) attract an enormous amount of NGO and media attention, and this must be taken into account in preparing for a conference, particularly in selecting a site. Some cities simply do not have the communication facilities and hotel accommodations needed for such large assemblies. For example, the UN Conference on the Environment and Development (UNCED), held in Rio de Janeiro in 1992, brought together representatives of 170 countries, 1,500 accredited observers, and 30,000 other interested persons and NGO representatives.[139] To meet the needs of NGOs and other interested persons from the private sector and keep them from getting in the way of the diplomatic proceedings, organizers of high-visibility world conferences make provision for *parallel forums:* conferences (near the site of the official meetings) in the course of which public affairs officers provide daily briefings on conference proceedings and NGOs may present their views.[140]

An important part of preparing for a conference needs to be done at the national level by each invited state. This may involve, depending upon the subject of the conference, putting together a diplomatic delegation with the needed technical competence and expertise. Foreign ministries frequently must depend upon personnel from other ministries. A government may find it advantageous to appoint an officer with the responsibility of coordinating national preparation for participation in the conference.[141] Often, conference participation requires a certain amount of policy development for the purpose of giving members of the delegation the instructions needed to guide their work.[142] In technical conferences, this may require cooperation among several government agencies beyond the foreign ministry. Preparing proposals for the national delegation to present in the course of the conference is another task, and it may entail consulting or negotiating with other governments to develop common positions. Coalition building need not wait until the conference is in session. This type of work is likely to enlist the support of embassies in select capitals, to pave the way for joint initiatives, and may also involve special missions for the same purpose.

In democracies, preparing the public for what is to be accomplished in international conferences may be a necessity, depending upon the nature of what is to be negotiated. Public meetings for special interest groups and NGO representatives are often organized. Hearings may be conducted by government agencies and parliamentary bodies. Special attention may also be given to the media. Some of these public information efforts can be continued during the negotiation phase.

▓ Conference Proceedings: Structure and Process

Conference proceedings are very similar to what takes place in international organization meetings of the same size.[143] They involve, among other things, parliamentary diplomacy, decisionmaking procedures, and various bloc arrangements.[144] (See Chapter 8.) One difference, however, is that the representatives of conference participants are chosen separately for each conference. They do not have the advantage of knowing one another as the permanent representatives do in international organizations. Still, many foreign offices draw on a certain pool of diplomats to serve in international conferences and eventually, many delegates end up meeting again here and there, in subsequent conferences. In the case of technical international conferences, the selection of national representatives skilled in the specialized subject matter of the conference is an asset for the proceedings.

The presidency needs to provide leadership in the proceedings.[145] A difference, however, is in the practice of inviting the chief executive of the host state to preside over the conference. Few will have the time to be that involved in the proceedings, and provision will have to be made for actual leadership, perhaps among the vice presidents. An important element of leadership in international conferences usually comes from the director-general (heading the conference secretariat, an appointive office).

NGOs tend to find a greater role in large conferences than in the proceedings of international organizations. The bulk of international conferences will not be of interest to NGOs, but large conferences of human interest (e.g., food or population) are now more likely to provide limited opportunity for civil society participation in the diplomatic process, with many NGOs fighting for greater input and organizing for increased participation. For example, following the International Conference on Financing for Development (Monterrey, Mexico, 2002), three constituencies created specialized bodies to coordinate postconference engagement with the intergovernmental process of financing for development: a number of civil society organizations established an International Facilitating Group on Financing for Development; business sector organizations transformed their Conference Coordinating Group into the Coordinating Committee of Business Interlocutors on Financing for Development; and the International Parliamentary Union formally established an interparliamentary task force to examine issues related to financing for development.[146]

Many large or high-visibility conferences need to prepare a final communiqué to provide an account of what was accomplished. This tends to be a carefully negotiated document. Some conferences make extensive provisions for follow-up diplomatic proceedings. For example, the 2002 Monterrey conference laid out a program of action for several bodies of the United Nations.[147] Every two years, the UN General Assembly was to host a two-day "High-Level Dialogue on Financing and Development" at UN headquarters in New York;[148] every two years also, the UN Economic and Social Council (ECOSOC) was to hold a special high-level meeting. On April 18, 2005, this meeting brought together the leadership of the World Bank, the International Monetary Fund (IMF), the World Trade Organization (WTO), and the UN Conference on Trade and Development (UNCTAD) to follow up on the Monterrey conference. In addition, the Financing for Development Office, a division of the UN Secretariat, was to organize three sets of multistakeholder consultations, including experts from the official and private sectors as well as the academic community and civil society, to examine issues related to the mobilization of resources for financing development and poverty eradication.[149]

In the final analysis, international conferences have provided another opportunity for small states, and occasionally for other international actors, to participate in the diplomatic process. Granted, many conferences are restricted to carefully chosen participants. But international organizations have been rather open in extending invitations to their conferences, and this has led to the active involvement of a variety of states that would not have otherwise participated in the global public policy process (e.g., on environmental issues). Diplomatic conferences have thus contributed to the expansion of the public dialogue. And despite the cost and the trouble to prepare for all these conferences, international actors find this mode of interaction useful. The world of diplomacy, for better or worse, is far from having seen the end of this mode of interaction.

▓ **Study Questions and Discussion Topics**

1. What explains the modern popularity of special missions? Shouldn't permanent missions and international organization representation suffice?

2. What is needed for successful mediation?

3. What international actors engage in mediation today? Who is better equipped to succeed?

4. What is the difference between "good offices" and "mediation"? Is this an immutable difference?

5. Why are international conferences proliferating today? What do they accomplish?

6. Are NGOs likely to influence the course of events during international conferences? What is their effect on the diplomatic process?

7. Is the massive presence of the media an impediment to diplomatic effectiveness in large conferences?

▓ **Suggested Reading**

Aurisch, Klaus L. "The Art of Preparing a Multilateral Conference." *Negotiation Journal* 5, no. 3 (1989), pp. 279–288.

Bercovitch, Jacob, and Jeffrey Z. Rubin, eds. *Mediation in International Relations: Multiple Approaches to Conflict Management.* New York: St. Martin's, 1992.

Ilan, Amitzur. *Bernadotte in Palestine, 1948: A Study in Contemporary Humanitarian Knight-Errantry.* New York: St. Martin's, 1989.

Kaufman, Johan. *Conference Diplomacy: An Introductory Analysis.* 2d ed. Dordrecht: Nijhoff, 1988.

Kissinger, Henry. *Diplomacy.* New York: Simon and Schuster, 1994.

Martin, Edwin McC. *Conference Diplomacy: A Case Study—The World Food Conference, Rome, 1974.* Washington, DC: Institute for the Study of Diplomacy, School of Foreign Service, Georgetown University, n.d.

Princen, Thomas. *Intermediaries in International Conflict.* Princeton: Princeton University Press, 1992.

Rubin, Jeffrey Z., ed. *Dynamics of Third Party Intervention: Kissinger in the Middle East.* New York: Praeger, 1981.

Stoessinger, John G. *Henry Kissinger: The Anguish of Power.* New York: Norton, 1976.

Walker, Ronald A. *Multilateral Conferences: Purposeful International Negotiation.* New York: Palgrave Macmillan, 2004.

▓ Notes

1. Elmer Plischke adds: executive agents, presidential envoys, extraordinary personal emissaries, and special representatives. Elmer Plischke, *U.S. Department of State: A Reference History* (Westport: Greenwood, 1999), p. 405.

2. UN General Assembly Resolution 2530 (XXIV), December 8, 1969. The convention entered into force on June 21, 1985. Louis Henkin, Richard Crawford Pugh, Oscar Schachter, and Hans Smit, *International Law: Cases and Materials,* 3d ed. (St. Paul, MN: West Group, 1993), p. 1211. Article 1 specifies: "A 'special mission' is a temporary mission, representing the State which is sent by one State to another State with the consent of the latter for the purpose of dealing with it on specific questions or of performing in relation to it a specific task." M. Paszkowski, "The Law of Special Missions," *Polish Yearbook of International Law* 6 (1974), pp. 267–288.

3. See following discussion on special missions.

4. Henry M. Wriston, "The Special Envoy," *Foreign Affairs* 38, no. 2 (January 1960), pp. 221–222. Ian J. Bickerton and Carla L. Klausner, *A Concise History of the Arab-Israeli Conflict,* 4th ed. (Upper Saddle River, NJ: Prentice-Hall, 2002), pp. 138–139.

5. See http://www.washingtoninstitute.org. See also Dennis Ross, *The Missing Peace: The Inside Story of the Fight for Middle East Peace* (New York: Farrar, Straus and Giroux, 2004); Dennis Ross, *Statecraft: And How to Restore America's Standing in the World* (New York: Farrar, Straus and Giroux, 2007).

6. Franciszek Przetacznik, "Diplomacy by Special Mission," *Revue de Droit International et de Sciences Diplomatiques et Politiques* 59, nos. 2 and 3 (1981), pp. 109–176.

7. The receiving state needs to give its consent to such an arrangement, according to Article 5 of the 1969 Convention on Special Missions.

8. He became ambassador to Belgium in 1949 and to Japan in 1952, and eventually served as assistant secretary of state and undersecretary of state. Plischke, *U.S. Department of State,* p. 519.

9. See Robert E. Sherwood, *Roosevelt and Hopkins: An Intimate History,* rev. ed. (New York: Grosset and Dunlap, 1950).

10. See, for example, list of special agents sent by US presidents on foreign missions in Maurice Waters, *The Ad Hoc Diplomat: A Study in Municipal and International Law* (The Hague: Nijhoff, 1963), pp. 175–181.

11. Wriston, "Special Envoy," p. 219.

12. Many held other prestigious diplomatic appointments (as seen in the case studies in this volume).

13. Plischke, *U.S. Department of State*, p. 522.

14. In the wake of the devastating December 26, 2004, tsunami in Southeast Asia, former presidents George H. W. Bush and Bill Clinton were sent to the region by President George W. Bush, in February 2005, to stress US concern and emphasize the need for more donations for the overwhelming task of reconstruction. *New York Times*, February 20, 2005, p. 3.

15. Bryant Wedge, "Mediating Intergroup Conflict in the Dominican Republic," in *Conflict Resolution: Track Two Diplomacy* (Washington, DC: Center for the Study of Foreign Policy, Foreign Service Institute, US Department of State, 1987), pp. 35–39. See Chapter 1's case study in this volume.

16. Harold Nicolson, *The Evolution of Diplomatic Method* (London: Constable, 1954), p. 8.

17. Ibid., p. 33. See also Garrett Mattingly, *Renaissance Diplomacy* (Boston: Houghton Mifflin, 1955), chap. 6, "Precedents for Resident Embassies," pp. 64–70. See also Chapter 2 in this volume.

18. Harold Nicolson, *Diplomacy*, 3d ed. (New York: Oxford University Press, 1964), p. 13.

19. See Richard W. Leopold, *The Growth of American Foreign Policy: A History* (New York: Knopf, 1962), esp. pp. 244–245, 294–295.

20. See, for instance, Marvin S. Soroos, *Beyond Sovereignty: The Global Challenge of Global Policy* (Columbia: University of South Carolina Press, 1986); James N. Rosenau, *Turbulence in World Politics: A Theory of Change and Continuity* (Princeton: Princeton University Press, 1990).

21. Many developing nations maintain few embassies in foreign capitals.

22. Benjamin Rivlin, ed., *Ralph Bunche: The Man and His Time* (New York: Holmes and Meier, 1990); Peggy Mann, *Ralph Bunche: UN Peacekeeper* (New York: Coward, McCann, and Geoghegan, 1975); Brian Urquhart, *Ralph Bunche: An American Life* (New York: Norton, 1993).

23. Amitzur Ilan, *Bernadotte in Palestine, 1948: A Study in Contemporary Humanitarian Knight-Errantry* (New York: St. Martin's, 1989).

24. *The InterDependent* 1, no. 1 (Fall 2003), pp. 19–21.

25. Ludwik Dembinski, *The Modern Law of Diplomacy: External Missions of States and International Organizations* (Dordrecht: Nijhoff, 1988), pp. 124–125.

26. Some of these special agents end up being resident representatives or permanent observers rather than working in temporary missions.

27. See http://www.worldbank.org. See, for example, Richard W. Stevenson, "The Chief Banker for the Nations at the Bottom of the Heap," *New York Times*, September 14, 1997, sec. 3, pp. 1, 13. See also World Bank, *World Bank–Civil Society Collaboration: Progress Report for Fiscal Years 2000 and 2001* (Washington, DC, 2002).

28. Milan Bartoš, "Le Statut des Missions Spéciales de la Diplomatie Ad Hoc," *Recueil des Cours de l'Académie de Droit International* 108 (1963), pp. 470–488.

29. Plischke lists many of them in his reference history, *U.S. Department of State*, pp. 521–522.

30. John G. Stoessinger, *Henry Kissinger: The Anguish of Power* (New York: Norton, 1976), esp. pp. 175–204; Henry A. Kissinger, *Diplomacy* (New York: Simon and Schuster, 1994).

31. See "Approaches to Conflict Management: Preventive Diplomacy, Mediation, and Multi-Track Initiatives," in *Managing Global Chaos: Sources of, and Responses to, International Conflict*, edited by Chester A. Crocker and Fen Osler Hampson, with Pamela Aall (Washington, DC: US Institute of Peace, 1996), pp. 377–529.

32. See the case study on the Yemen crisis in this chapter.

33. Edwin McC. Martin, *Conference Diplomacy: A Case Study—The World Food Conference, Rome, 1974* (Washington, DC: Institute for the Study of Diplomacy, School of Foreign Service, Georgetown University, n.d.).

34. Both Begin and Sadat immediately accepted, without prior conditions. See, for example, Bickerton and Klausner, *Concise History,* pp. 193–198.

35. See the special role of President Roosevelt's friend Harry Hopkins in working with Stalin during World War II, in Sherwood, *Roosevelt and Hopkins.*

36. Dembinski, *Modern Law,* p. 60.

37. Quoted in Waters, *Ad Hoc Diplomat,* pp. 117–118.

38. International organizations, the UN in particular, have had frequent occasion to use missions for that purpose. See A. LeRoy Bennett and James K. Oliver, *International Organizations: Principles and Issues,* 7th ed. (Upper Saddle River, NJ: Prentice-Hall, 2002), pp. 109, 127.

39. See, for example, Hilaire McCoubrey and Nigel D. White, *International Organizations and Civil Wars* (Brookfield, VT: Dartmouth, 1995), pp. 207–218.

40. Waters, *Ad Hoc Diplomat,* pp. 117–118, 177.

41. See McCoubrey and White, *International Organizations,* pp. 79, 85–92.

42. As was shown in Chapter 7. Some missions become embassies in disguise, as large and important as permanent missions.

43. Following the armistice agreement with Germany. Wriston, "Special Envoy," p. 236.

44. Henry M. Wriston, *Executive Agents in American Foreign Relations* (Gloucester, MA: Peter Smith, 1967), pp. 368–405, esp. p. 405.

45. George C. McGhee, ed., *Diplomacy for the Future* (Washington, DC: Institute for the Study of Diplomacy, School of Foreign Service, Georgetown University, 1987); Robert Hopkins Miller, *Inside an Embassy: The Political Role of Diplomats Abroad* (Washington, DC: Congressional Quarterly, 1992); James P. Muldoon Jr., JoAnn Fagot Aviel, Richard Reitano, and Earl Sullivan, eds., *Multilateral Diplomacy and the United Nations Today* (Boulder: Westview, 1999).

46. Przetacznik, "Diplomacy by Special Mission," pp. 109–176; Wriston, "Special Envoy," pp. 219–237; Plischke, *U.S. Department of State,* pp. 331–333, 517–525.

47. Article 1 of the 1969 Convention on Special Missions.

48. Brian Urquhart, *Hammarskjold* (New York: Norton, 1972), p. 103. See Chapter 8's case study in this volume.

49. Dembinski, *Modern Law,* p. 125. See also Linda S. Frey and Marsha L. Frey, *The History of Diplomatic Immunity* (Columbus: Ohio State University Press, 1999).

50. B. Sen, *A Diplomat's Handbook of International Law and Practice,* 3d ed. (Dordrecht: Nijhoff, 1988), pp. 40–45.

51. Dembinski, *Modern Law,* p. 10; Waters, *Ad Hoc Diplomat,* p. 114.

52. General Assembly Resolution 2530 (XXIV), December 8, 1969, carries as an annex the text of the Convention on Special Missions. See Lori F. Damrosch, Louis Henkin, Richard Crawford Pugh, Oscar Schachter, and Hans Smit, *International Law: Cases and Materials,* 4th ed. (St. Paul, MN: West Group, 2001), p. 1291.

53. The United States has not ratified it. Damrosch et al., *International Law,* p. 1291. See also Dembinski, *Modern Law,* esp. p. 273; UN, *Multilateral Treaties.*

54. Waters, *Ad Hoc Diplomat,* p. 124.

55. Thomas Princen, *Intermediaries in International Conflicts* (Princeton: Princeton University Press, 1992), p. 5.

56. Saadia Touval, "The Superpowers as Mediators," in *Mediation in International Relations: Multiple Approaches to Conflict Management,* edited by Jacob

Bercovitch and Jeffrey Z. Rubin (New York: St. Martin's, 1992), pp. 235–236. See also Ross, *Statecraft*, pp. 216–236.

57. Jacob Bercovitch, "The Structure and Diversity of Mediation in International Relations," in Bercovitch and Rubin, *Mediation*, pp. 1–29.

58. Arthur S. Lall, ed., *Multilateral Negotiation and Mediation: Instruments and Methods* (New York: Pergamon, 1985); I. William Zartman and J. Lewis Rasmussen, eds., *Peacemaking in International Conflict: Methods and Techniques* (Washington, DC: US Institute of Peace, 1997).

59. See Ross, *Missing Peace*.

60. Or mediation by the Vatican as in the Beagle Channel dispute, 1978–1984. I. William Zartman and Saadia Touval, "International Mediation in the Post–Cold War Era," in Crocker, Hampson, and Aall, *Managing Global Chaos*, p. 450. See Thomas Princen, "Mediation by a Transnational Organization: The Case of the Vatican," in Bercovitch and Rubin, *Mediation*, pp. 149–175.

61. David P. Forsythe, "Humanitarian Mediation by the International Committee of the Red Cross," in *International Mediation in Theory and Practice*, edited by Saadia Touval and I. William Zartman (Boulder: Westview, 1985), pp. 243–244.

62. Terje Rød Larsen, director of the Norwegian Institute for Applied Social Science, and Yair Hirschfeld, professor of Middle East history at Haifa University. *New York Times*, September 5, 1993, p. 6. See Chapter 11 in this volume. See also A. Paul Hare, "Informal Mediation by Private Individuals," in Bercovitch and Rubin, *Mediation*, pp. 52–63; Herbert C. Kelman, "Informal Mediation by the Scholar/Practitioner," in Bercovitch and Rubin, *Mediation*, pp. 64–96.

63. Princen, *Intermediaries*, p. 5.

64. Urquhart, *Hammarskjold*, pp. 124–125. See Chapter 8's case study in this volume. See also case studies of multiparty mediation in *Herding Cats: Multiparty Mediation in a Complex World*, edited by Chester A. Crocker and Fen Osler Hampson, with Pamela Aall (Washington, DC: US Institute of Peace, 1999).

65. See also A. Paul Hare, "Private Individuals," in Bercovitch and Rubin, *Mediation*, pp. 52–63; Herbert C. Kelman, "Informal Mediation by the Scholar/Practitioner," in Bercovitch and Rubin, *Mediation*, pp. 64–96.

66. Ambassador Tommy Koh of Singapore was one of them. See Lance N. Antrim and James K. Sebenius, "Formal Individual Mediation and the Negotiators' Dilemma: Tommy Koh at the Law of the Sea Conference," in Bercovitch and Rubin, *Mediation*, pp. 97–130.

67. Bercovitch, "Structure and Diversity," pp. 8–14.

68. "Good offices," traditionally distinguished from "mediation," implies no participation in the negotiations. It may involve simply making facilities available where negotiations will take place (i.e., a neutral setting).

69. Dennis Ross, *Statecraft*, "Eleven Rules for Mediation," pp. 237–258, and "Negotiations: Twelve Rules to Follow," pp. 187–215.

70. Edward R. F. Sheehan, "How Kissinger Did It: Step by Step in the Middle East," in *Dynamics of Third Party Intervention: Kissinger in the Middle East*, edited by Jeffrey Z. Rubin (New York: Praeger, 1981), pp. 44–91.

71. Johan Kaufmann, *Conference Diplomacy: An Introductory Analysis*, 2d ed. (Dordrecht: Nijhoff, 1988), pp. 5–6.

72. Jeffrey Rubin makes this distinction between relationship-oriented and resolution-oriented approaches. D. M. Kolb speaks of orchestration strategies (managing the interaction) and deal-making strategies (affecting the substance of a conflict). Cited in Jacob Bercovitch, "Mediation in International Conflict: An Overview of Theory, a Review of Practice," in Zartman and Rasmussen, *Peacemaking*, p. 136.

73. Kaufmann, *Conference Diplomacy,* p. 99.

74. Christopher J. McMullen, *Resolution of the Yemen Crisis, 1963: A Case Study in Mediation* (Washington, DC: Institute for the Study of Diplomacy, School of Foreign Service, Georgetown University, 1980), pp. 7–20. See this chapter's case study.

75. G. R. Berridge, *Diplomacy: Theory and Practice,* 2d ed. (New York: Palgrave, 2002), p. 190. See also Randa M. Slim, "Small-State Mediation in International Relations: The Algerian Mediation of the Iranian Hostage Crisis," in Bercovitch and Rubin, *Mediation,* pp. 206–231.

76. See Saadia Touval, "The Superpowers as Mediators," in Bercovitch and Rubin, *Mediation,* pp. 240–244. See also Lawrence Susskind and Eileen Babbitt, "Overcoming the Obstacles to Effective Mediation of International Disputes," in Bercovitch and Rubin, *Mediation,* pp. 30–51.

77. See Jeffrey Z. Rubin, "Conclusion: International Mediation in Context," in Bercovitch and Rubin, *Mediation,* pp. 249–272.

78. I. William Zartman, and Maureen R. Berman, *The Practical Negotiator* (New Haven: Yale University Press, 1982), pp. 16–41.

79. Saeed M. Badeeb, *The Saudi-Egyptian Conflict over North Yemen, 1962–1970* (Boulder: Westview, 1986), pp. 3–6; Manfred W. Wenner, *Modern Yemen, 1918–1966* (Baltimore: Johns Hopkins University Press, 1967), pp. 193–197; Edgar O'Ballance, *The War in Yemen* (London: Faber and Faber, 1971).

80. *The Middle East,* 9th ed. (Washington, DC: Congressional Quarterly, 2000), pp. 223–225, 396; William L. Cleveland, *A History of the Modern Middle East* (Boulder: Westview, 1999), pp. 304–307, 437–439.

81. Wenner, *Modern Yemen,* pp. 184–187; James Jankowski, *Nasser's Egypt, Arab Nationalism, and the United Arab Republic* (Boulder: Lynne Rienner, 2002), p. 140.

82. Roy R. Andersen, Robert E. Seibert, and Jon G. Wagner, *Politics and Change in the Middle East: Sources of Conflict and Accommodation,* 7th ed. (Upper Saddle River, NJ: Prentice-Hall, 2004), pp. 240–249; H. W. Brands, *Into the Labyrinth: The United States and the Middle East, 1945–1993* (New York: McGraw-Hill, 1994), pp. 83–85.

83. McMullen, *Resolution,* pp. 1–6, 9.

84. Gerald de Gaury, *Faisal, King of Saudi Arabia* (London: Arthur Barker, 1966), pp. 110–112; Wenner, *Modern Yemen,* pp. 199–209.

85. McMullen, *Resolution,* pp. 4–5. Badeeb, *Saudi-Egyptian Conflict,* pp. 61–64.

86. McMullen, *Resolution,* pp. 7–8.

87. U Thant made this decision after consultations with Saudi Arabia, Egypt, the new Republic of Yemen, as well as the US State Department. He did not consult the Yemeni royalists. Dana Adams Schmidt, "The Civil War in Yemen," in *The International Regulation of Civil Wars,* edited by Evan Luard (New York: New York University Press, 1972), pp. 131–132.

88. As the United States saw it, fact-finding amounted to further delaying the necessary mediation.

89. His mission was based on a National Security Council policy decision, reported to be a product of McGeorge Bundy's "Little State Department" at the White House. Schmidt, "Civil War in Yemen," p. 132.

90. Some of the differences between Washington and U Thant can be seen in Seymour Maxwell Finger, *Your Man at the UN: People, Politics, and Bureaucracy in the Making of Foreign Policy* (New York: New York University Press, 1980), pp. 109–159.

91. McMullen, *Resolution,* p. 10.

92. The president's letter was followed up with military demonstrations: flights of aircraft over Jeddah and Riyadh, and a courtesy call by a US destroyer at Jeddah, probably intended as further assurances of support. Schmidt, "Civil War in Yemen," p. 130.

93. Ralph Bunche, quoted in Urquhart, *Ralph Bunche*, p. 365. Upon his arrival in Yemen, a mob almost overturned his car in a demonstration against Saudi Arabia, Jordan, and Britain. (Aden was a British colonial possession. Yemen had made a claim to it.)

94. Manfred W. Wenner, "The Civil War in Yemen, 1962–1970," in *Stopping the Killing: How Civil Wars End*, edited by Roy Licklider (New York: New York University Press, 1993), p. 113.

95. McMullen, *Resolution*, p. 11.

96. See de Gaury, *Faisal*, pp. 89–109.

97. McMullen, *Resolution*, p. 13.

98. de Gaury, *Faisal*, pp. 110–112.

99. McMullen, *Resolution*, pp. 13–17.

100. Compare with Bercovitch, "Mediation," pp. 125–153.

101. McMullen, *Resolution*, p. 17. See also Wenner, *Modern Yemen*, pp. 193–194.

102. Neither was the United States interested in visiting the royalists. See Wenner, *Modern Yemen*, p. 206.

103. McMullen, *Resolution*, pp. 17–18; Badeeb, *Saudi-Egyptian Conflict*, pp. 61–69; Wenner, *Modern Yemen*, pp. 206–207; Wenner, "Civil War in Yemen," pp. 112–113. See also C. V. Narasimhan, *The United Nations: An Inside View* (New Delhi: Viskas, 1988), "U Thant," pp. 284–289.

104. McMullen, *Resolution*, pp. 19–20. Compare with J. Lewis Rasmussen, "Peacemaking in the Twenty-First Century: New Rules, New Roles, New Actors," in Zartman and Rasmussen, *Peacemaking*, pp. 23–50.

105. McMullen, *Resolution*, pp. 21–25. Nasser's problems with the defection of Syria, which led to the breakup of the United Arab Republic, probably strengthened his desire to maintain support of the republican forces in Yemen. See Wenner, *Modern Yemen*, pp. 204–205. See discussion of the Syrian episode in Jankowski, *Nasser's Egypt*, pp. 166–178.

106. An internal debate was taking place in the State Department over the best way to deal with the contestants, but they were aware of the importance of making quick progress. Indeed, Washington received a report that the French government had made an offer to provide the Saudis with all the military assistance it desired for dealing with the situation in Yemen. Faisal was reported to have directed his representative in Paris not to turn down the offer, but to wait until he could see what US efforts would accomplish. Faisal trusted Kennedy's commitment. McMullen, *Resolution*, pp. 26–27.

107. Specifics of her illness are unknown.

108. McMullen, *Resolution*, pp. 31–33.

109. Quoted in ibid., p. 35.

110. Negotiators must be wary of moments of relaxation. Leigh L. Thompson, *The Mind and Heart of the Negotiator*, 2d ed. (Upper Saddle River, NJ: Prentice Hall, 2001), "Distributive Negotiation: Slicing the Pie," pp. 33–60.

111. McMullen, *Resolution*, p. 37.

112. Ibid., p. 35. This is an important matter in many negotiations. See Zartman and Berman, *Practical Negotiator*, pp. 215–219; Fred Charles Iklé, *How Nations Negotiate* (New York: Harper and Row, 1964), pp. 131–136.

113. McMullen, *Resolution*, p. 42. This is not an unusual element in such negotiations, highlighting again the importance of mediation. See the mediation studies cited previously, especially Touval and Zartman, *International Mediation;* Bercovitch and Rubin, *Mediation;* and Zartman and Rasmussen, *Peacemaking*. See also I. William Zartman, ed., *Elusive Peace: Negotiating an End to Civil Wars* (Washington, DC: Brookings Institution, 1995), which provides additional case studies in this area, and

Roy Licklider, "Negotiating an End in Civil Wars: General Findings," in *New Approaches to International Negotiation and Mediation: Findings from USIP-Sponsored Research,* Peaceworks no. 30, edited by Timothy D. Sisk (Washington, DC: US Institute of Peace, 1999), pp. 24–27.

114. McMullen, *Resolution,* p. 46; Schmidt, "Civil War in Yemen," p. 132.

115. See McMullen, *Resolution,* pp. 48–51. On the weaknesses of third-party negotiation efforts, see Bruce Michael Bagley and Juan Gabriel Tokatlian, *Contadora: The Limits of Negotiation* (Washington, DC: Foreign Policy Institute, School of Advanced International Studies, Johns Hopkins University, 1987).

116. Plischke, *U.S. Department of State,* pp. 567–568; also "Table of International Conferences and Meetings, 1913–1945," pp. 364–365, and a twelve-page list of some 500 conferences of various types in the post-1945 period, pp. 569–580.

117. Plischke, *U.S. Department of State,* pp. 567–568.

118. Some conferences are eventually given an institutional structure, such as the UN Conference on Trade and Development (UNCTAD)—still called a conference, but for many years a subsidiary organ of the UN. The Group of Eight (G8) summit has remained a recurring conference.

119. See also Plischke, *U.S. Department of State,* tab. 7.11, pp. 569–580. Note how official conference names vary. Some are recurring sessions of international forums with single-item agendas.

120. Bilateral meetings can be elaborate when the parties bring large delegations to negotiate a variety of issues.

121. For example, global forum, world assembly, international congress. See, for example, Box 9.5.

122. In this respect, see R. P. Barston, *Modern Diplomacy,* 2d ed. (New York: Longman, 1997), pp. 1–3; Kaufmann, *Conference Diplomacy,* pp. 118–122.

123. Plischke, *U.S. Department of State,* p. 568.

124. See Norman A. Graham, Richard L. Kauffman, and Michael F. Oppenheimer, *The United States and Multilateral Diplomacy: A Handbook* (New York: Oceana, 1984), pp. 1–12.

125. Berridge, *Diplomacy,* pp. 33–43.

126. See Bertram I. Spector, Gunnar Sjöstedt, and I. William Zartman, eds., *Negotiating International Regimes: Lessons Learned from the United Nations Conference on Environment and Development (UNCED)* (London: Graham and Trotman, 1994).

127. Robert O. Keohane and Joseph S. Nye, *Power and Interdependence,* 2d ed. (Glenview, IL: Scott Foresman, 1989), p. 33.

128. See discussion of the "Battle of Seattle" in John Baylis and Steve Smith, *The Globalization of World Politics* (New York: Oxford University Press, 2001), pp. 194–195.

129. Klaus L. Aurisch, "The Art of Preparing a Multilateral Conference," *Negotiation Journal* 5, no. 3 (1989), pp. 279–288.

130. Kaufmann, *Conference Diplomacy,* pp. 41–45, 100–113, 126–127. See also Johan Kaufmann, ed., *Effective Negotiation: Case Studies in Conference Diplomacy* (Dordrecht: Nijhoff, 1989), pp. 125 127.

131. Some preparatory committees can comprise the whole membership, and the diplomacy of their meetings can be just as intense as what will take place at the conference itself.

132. See, for instance, the World Employment Conference, convened by the International Labour Organization, and the Conference on Technical Cooperation, convened

by the UN Development Programme, in Norman Graham and Stephan Haggard, "Diplomacy in Global Conferences," *UNITAR News* 11 (1979), pp. 18–19.

133. Kaufmann, *Effective Negotiation,* pp. 125–127.

134. See Kaufmann, *Conference Diplomacy,* pp. 38–41.

135. Martin, *Conference Diplomacy,* p. 5.

136. Wilkowski, *Conference Diplomacy II,* pp. 9–12; Martin, *Conference Diplomacy,* pp. 9–15. See also James K. Sebenius, *Negotiating the Law of the Sea* (Cambridge: Harvard University Press, 1984).

137. Ibid. See also Kaufmann, *Conference Diplomacy,* pp. 33–35; Kaufmann, *Effective Negotiation,* pp. 114–118.

138. Berridge, *Diplomacy,* pp. 35–38; Kaufmann, *Conference Diplomacy,* pp. 36–38.

139. Bennett and Oliver, *International Organizations,* p. 348.

140. This became a significant feature of large international conferences after the 1972 Stockholm Conference on the Environment. See Dan Tarlock, "The Role of Non-Governmental Organizations in the Development of International Environmental Law," in Lakshman D. Guruswamy, Burns H. Weston, Geoffrey W. R. Palmer, and Jonathan C. Carlson, *International Environmental Law and World Order* (St. Paul, MN: West Group, 1999), pp. 1195–1200.

141. See discussion on how the United States prepared for the 1974 World Food Conference in Martin, *Conference Diplomacy,* pp. 17–33.

142. See Wilkowski, *Conference Diplomacy II,* pp. 15ff.

143. Ronald A. Walker, *Multilateral Conferences: Purposeful International Negotiation* (New York: Palgrave Macmillan, 2004), esp. pp. 106–227. See also Saadia Touval, "Multilateral Negotiation: An Analytic Approach," *Negotiation Journal* 5, no. 2 (1989), pp. 159–173.

144. Robbie Sabel, *Procedure at International Conferences: A Study of the Rules of Procedure at the UN and at Inter-Governmental Conferences* (New York: Cambridge University Press, 2006).

145. W. Lang, *Multilateral Negotiations: The Role of the Presiding Officers* (Laxenburg, Austria: International Institute of Applied System Analysis, 1987).

146. See http://www.un.org/esa/ffd.

147. This conference was convened by the United Nations.

148. The first one was held on October 29–30, 2003, and the second on June 27–28, 2005.

149. See http://www.un.org/esa/ffd.

10 Summit and Ministerial Diplomacy

Current international practice reveals a trend toward more diplomatic interaction taking place among chief decisionmakers—another group of nonprofessional diplomats who are changing the boundaries of diplomacy. This is occurring not only among heads of state but also among heads of executive departments (ministries), and the volume of their transactions is increasing. The main job of these people is of course to lead, to make policy rather than carry it out at the international level. Heads of state have always visited one another from time to time, plotting together, negotiating alliances, and otherwise trying to find support from other potentates. This form of summit interaction was invented long ago, even if it was not perceived as "diplomacy." But today, with the ease of communication and transportation, high-level interaction has become almost routine, and there is so much of it. What does it add to diplomacy?

The term "head of state" is used for convenience in the sense of chief executive. In some countries, for example the United Kingdom, the chief executive is the prime minister, rather than the head of state (the queen). Also, international organizations now play an important role in world affairs, and their chief executive officers, whatever their official titles (secretary-general, director-general, or anything else), must be included in the relationship.[1] Some of them are more influential than their state counterparts.

In some respects, the diplomatic work done at the ministerial level is comparable to summit diplomacy. Ministers of state are substantially chief executives in their own fields, although their actual powers will vary with the political system. In some governments, the foreign minister is more important in the conduct of foreign relations than the prime minister. Other ministers are concerned with a more limited dimension of their state's foreign relations, but the trend is for many of these executives to engage in diplomacy. There are similarities between summit diplomacy and ministerial diplomacy, but there are significant differences as well. Thus the two are discussed separately in this chapter.

Summit Diplomacy

Some of the diplomatic work of chief executives is comparable to special mission diplomacy (see Chapter 9). Their foreign visits are special missions of sorts—except for the fact that they are chief executives, meaning that they generally enjoy greater latitude, although many of them are subject to other constraints. Some of their diplomatic work, too, falls into the category of conference diplomacy. Running a government cannot be done without regard to what is happening elsewhere in the world. Things are increasingly interconnected beyond national boundaries. What used to be exclusively domestic now has international ramifications, beyond their boundaries. The distinction between domestic and international affairs is harder to maintain, and chief executives increasingly must deal with what happens internationally.[2] They do that first in making foreign policy. Granted, policymaking is not "diplomacy," properly speaking, and foreign policy is not made exclusively (or even primarily) by chief executives, but they are involved in it. They are affected by its consequences, and sometimes heads of government have a hand in carrying it out by diplomatic means.[3]

The primary advantage of diplomatic interaction at the summit level is that it involves major decisionmakers, leaders most directly responsible for governmental action.[4] Some object that these people are not diplomats by profession, although some of them could have distinguished themselves in this field if their careers had taken a different turn. But they are politicians, and we cannot forget that diplomacy is a special form of politics. Heads of government cannot feel completely out of their element when dealing with their foreign counterparts, except for an important intercultural element.

Besides, they have plenty of professional and diplomatic assistance when venturing into the international arena. Summit diplomacy is now commonplace, but it has not displaced the other modes of diplomatic interaction in importance or volume.

▓ Diverse Types of Summit Contact

Chief executives are involved in the conduct of foreign relations in many ways.[5] They find it important to contact some of their counterparts in other countries, seeking to influence them, encourage them, woo them, warn them, or even threaten them. A lot of this is of course done through regular diplomatic channels, but chief executives sometimes do not mind reinforcing the process with a personal message of their own, or even a phone call. Zbigniew Brzezinski, who was President Jimmy Carter's national security adviser, recalled: "I was many times in the Oval Office when the President would reach for the telephone and phone the Prime Minister of the United Kingdom or the Chancellor of Germany. The chances were that we probably wouldn't even bother to tell our ambassador that such a conversation took place *because it was so frequent.*"[6] Some interactions are very personal, and advances in communication technology are making it even easier to maintain direct contact. This undoubtedly changes the way things are done internationally, and technology will likely change things even more in the near future (see Chapter 4). Heads of state are still not normally expected to converse over the phone. Direct contact of this sort is maintained only with a limited number of chief executives. But when circumstances (and personal affinities) permit, this kind of interaction can facilitate political relations.

And then there are the personal envoys (see Chapter 9). This is not exactly summit diplomacy, but it can come close. Some special envoys are known to have the total trust of their chief executive, as was the case with Harry Hopkins and President Franklin Roosevelt during World War II. Hopkins could talk to Joseph Stalin or receive confidential messages from him, amounting to personal interaction between the two heads of state—or not too far from it.[7] Special envoys extend the capacity of chief executives to affect the course of events, even consciously bypassing or ignoring other diplomatic agents, as Roosevelt often did (even with his own secretary of state).

Visits by chief executives are a common form of face-to-face bilateral interaction; they are growing in number and serve a vast variety of purposes. They operate in two different ways: meetings in which the head of state is host to the foreign visitor, and in reverse direction, when that head of state visits a colleague (or a series of them, as in a regional foray). Traffic varies with the circumstances and the importance of the states concerned. Important heads of state are of course more frequently solicited and visited.[8] The less important are more likely to be the ones doing the visiting, seeking recognition, support, assistance, or whatever else they need. However, today, small states have acquired greater significance, and it is not unusual to find leaders of great powers doing the visiting, as in July 2003 when President George W. Bush made a five-day whirlwind visit to five African states (Senegal, South Africa, Botswana, Uganda, and Nigeria), staying just a few hours in some of them.[9] Summer is a popular time for such multicapital visits. UN Secretary-General Dag Hammarskjöld made it a practice to do so, commenting that he valued knowing leaders personally and that it made it easier to get in touch with them later when there were problems to address.[10]

Different types of visits can be identified.[11] State visits, with all their fanfare, pomp, and solemnity, elaborate advance preparations, and glittering mass media events, are very formal. At the other end of the spectrum, unofficial visits are very simple (even though it is hard to find a truly *simple* head-of-state visit), unheralded, and quick, perhaps on the occasion of something else, such as a simple stopover on the way back from some gathering, or a strictly business, short visit to discuss some important issue. Unofficial visits entail less advance preparation, less formality. Some take place on fairly short notice (depending upon the circumstances and purpose). The UN Secretary-General can confer with heads of state (in his office, one-on-one) when they come to New York to make their policy statements in the "General Debate," shortly after the annual opening of the UN General Assembly session in the fall.

Some heads of state or government like traveling. Others need to be pushed by necessity. President Harry Truman was not fond of visiting other capitals. He undertook only four trips abroad, involving six visits. President Dwight Eisenhower made sixteen trips, entailing thirty-seven visits; Presidents Richard Nixon and Gerald Ford made twenty foreign trips and sixty-one visits during their combined eight years.[12] From 1945 to 1990, US presidents took 105 trips involving 225 separate visits, averaging approximately 5 visits per year. These, however, were unevenly distributed during their terms of office.[13] The annual average number of presidential visits abroad, however, is significantly increasing (see Table 10.1). It is interesting that from January 2001 to November 2006, President George W. Bush, who was initially reported not to be fond of foreign travel, traveled at almost the same accelerated rate as his two predecessors. Foreign travel is increasingly an expected function of the presidency.[14]

Traffic has been heavy in the other direction as well. From 1945 to the mid-1980s, there were more than 900 visits to Washington, D.C., by foreign leaders, with the largest numbers of visits occurring during the Lyndon Johnson, Richard Nixon, and Ronald Reagan administrations.[15] In peak months there may have been as many as five to ten such visits, and sometimes more than twenty. Overall, visits averaged approximately twenty-three per year, and during President Reagan's first term, more than forty-five heads of state came to the White House annually, or nearly four per month, although in some weeks there were eight to ten. These figures do not include private or personal visits or transit through the United States, nor do they include those of former political leaders, presidents-elect, vice presidents, or leaders of international organizations.[16] Thus, Washington sees a good deal of executive traffic.[17] Prime Minister Ariel Sharon of Israel visited President George W. Bush eight times from February 2001 to July 2003.[18]

Some summit meetings are incidental to other events (e.g., the annual UN General Assembly meeting). Many chief executives take advantage of the occasion to confer with some of their counterparts. Some occasions are fortuitous (e.g., a state funeral).[19] British foreign secretary Geoffrey Howe once observed that the state funeral of Soviet secretary Yuri Andropov gave him and Prime Minister Margaret Thatcher the opportunity to meet foreign leaders with

Table 10.1 Visits Abroad by Presidents of the United States, 1901–2006

President (office term)	Time in Office	Number of Visits	Average Number of Visits per Year
Theodore Roosevelt (September 1901–March 1909)	7 years, 5 months	1	0.1
William H. Taft (March 1909–March 1913)	4 years	2	0.5
Woodrow Wilson (March 1913–March 1921)	8 years	10	1.3
Warren G. Harding (March 1921–August 1923)	2 years, 5 months	3	1.2
Calvin Coolidge (August 1923–March 1929)	5 years, 7 months	1	0.2
Herbert C. Hoover (March 1929–March 1933)	4 years	10	2.5
Franklin D. Roosevelt (March 1933–April 1945)	12 years, 1 month	52	4.3
Harry S Truman (April 1945–January 1953)	7 years, 9 months	6	0.8
Dwight D. Eisenhower (January 1953–January 1961)	8 years	37	4.6
John F. Kennedy (January 1961–November 1963)	2 years, 10 months	16	5.7
Lyndon B. Johnson (November 1963–January 1969)	5 years, 2 months	27	5.2
Richard M. Nixon (January 1969–August 1974)	5 years, 6 months	42	7.6
Gerard R. Ford (August 1974–January 1977)	2 years, 5 months	19	7.8
Jimmy Carter (January 1977–January 1981)	4 years	31	7.8
Ronald Reagan (January 1981–January 1989)	8 years	49	6.1
George H. W. Bush (January 1989–January 1993)	4 years	60	15.0
William J. Clinton III (January 1993–January 2001)	8 years	133	16.6
George W. Bush (January 2001–November 2006)	5 years, 10 months[a]	93	15.7

Source: US Department of State, Bureau of Public Affairs, Office of the Historian, http://www.state.gov/r/pa/ho/trvl/pres.

Notes: Entries cover all official visits to foreign countries made by US presidents during their tenure as president or president-elect. They also include instances of unofficial travel to foreign countries by a president or president-elect for vacation purposes, when information concerning such visits is available. Visits to dependent territories are included under the country having sovereignty over the territory at the time of the visit.

a. Visits by President George W. Bush are calculated only through November 2006.

Table 10.2   Summit Meetings Attended by US Presidents, 1990 and 2000

President George H. W. Bush (1990)

	Meeting	Location
February	Four-power inter-American drug summit	Cartagena
April	Prime minister of Canada	Toronto
	Prime minister of United Kingdom	Bermuda
July	NATO summit	London
	Economic summit	Houston
	Summit to help children	New York
September	President of Russia and president of Finland	Helsinki
November	Revolution anniversary ceremonies and Czech Federal Assembly	Prague
	Chancellor of Germany	Speyer, Ludwigshafen
	CSCE summit (to sign the Treaty on Conventional Forces)	Paris
	King of Saudi Arabia and emir of Kuwait	Jeddah, Dhahran
	President of Egypt	Cairo
	President of Syria	Geneva
	State visit to Mexico	Monterrey, Agualeguas
December	President of Brazil	Brasilia
	President of Uruguay	Montevideo
	President of Argentina	Buenos Aires
	President of Chile	Santiago
	President of Venezuela	Caracas

continues

whom bilateral meetings had not been easy to arrange, such as Spain's prime minister Felipe Gonzalez and President Zia of Pakistan.[20]

Some of the most important summit meetings occur during conferences of heads of state and heads of government.[21] Many are ad hoc—that is, convened to address a specific issue. Some are bilateral, particularly in efforts to reduce conflict—for example, President Bill Clinton's meeting with Syria's president Hafez al-Assad in Geneva in January 1994, to lend the prestige of his office to an effort to broaden the Middle East peace process.[22] Many are multilateral. The UN General Assembly convenes global summit conferences to discuss some international problem—for example, the UN Conference on Environment and Development in Rio de Janeiro (June 1992), referred to as the Earth Summit, or the World Food Summit, convened by the Food and Agriculture Organization in Rome (November 1996). These are usually large conferences in the course of which heads of state make formal presentations and perhaps sign a declaration developed in the course of several preparatory meetings. The chief executives do not usually play a large part in the negotiation process. Their presence tends to be symbolic, emphasizing the importance of the subject matter and of the conference. The diversity of summit meetings is shown in Table 10.2.

Table 10.2 Cont.

President Bill Clinton (2000)

	Meeting	Location
January	World Economic Forum	Davos, Switzerland
March	President of India	New Delhi
	President and prime minister of Bangladesh	Dhaka
	President of Pakistan	Islamabad
	Sultan of Oman	Muscat
	President of Syria	Geneva
May	US-EU summit; prime minister of Israel	Lisbon
June	Chancellor of Germany	Berlin
	President of Russia	Moscow
	President of Ukraine	Kiev
	Funeral of former prime minister of Japan	Tokyo
July	Economic summit	Nago, Okinawa
August	President of Nigeria	Abuja
	Former president of South Africa (to promote a peace agreement for Burundi); president of Tanzania	Arush, Tanzania
	President of Egypt (on the Middle East peace process)	Cairo
	President of Colombia	Cartagena
October	Israeli-Palestinian summit meeting	Sharm al-Shaikh
November	APEC summit	Bandar Seri Begawan
	President of Vietnam	Hanoi
December	Prime minister of Ireland	Dublin
	Prime minister of United Kingdom and political leaders from Northern Ireland	Belfast

Sources: http://www.state.gov/r/pa/ho/trvl/pres; Elmer Plischke, *U.S. Department of State: A Reference History* (Westport: Greenwood, 1999), pp. 569–571.

Some summit meetings (bilateral and multilateral) are recurring events.[23] For example, the Cold War summits between the US and Soviet leaderships started as ad hoc bilateral conferences (they brought summit meetings to the attention of the world).[24] However, as the superpowers tried to reduce their enmity and foster coexistence, more frequent meetings took place at irregular intervals. Other leaders meet frequently—for example, Chancellor Helmut Kohl of Germany noted that he had met with President François Mitterrand of France in excess of eighty times.[25] Certain meetings become somewhat institutionalized and lose their ad hoc character—for example, the annual meeting of the seven (eventually eight) major industrialized powers (the Group of Seven [G7] and Group of Eight [G8]).[26] The agenda changes, but the meetings take place on schedule.

Many international organizations have incorporated summit meetings into their regular operations, such as the European Union and the Gulf Cooperation

Council (see Box 10.1),[27] Many organizations also convene ad hoc summits, such as the Arab League summit of March 2002 in Beirut, which discussed an Arab peace plan for the Israeli-Palestinian conflict.[28] In January 2002, the UN Security Council held its first-ever Security Council meeting at the level of heads of state or government.[29] It is evident that international organizations contribute significantly to the increasing volume of summit diplomacy. More summit meetings are now programmed into the international system, which leaders find hard to avoid. They vary in importance and in size, but they are part of the diplomatic mainstream rather than an occasional oddity in the conduct of foreign relations.

▦ Shortcomings of Summit Diplomacy

Despite the increasing popularity of high-level meetings, summit diplomacy has its own shortcomings.[30] Time constraints remain a problem. Heads of government normally find it difficult to be away from their capitals for extended periods of time. Consequently, chief executives have less time to interact in international conferences, which can limit engagement in serious international problem solving. However, if the issues are important enough, they will take the time needed to address them: President Harry Truman's participation in the 1945 Potsdam Conference lasted eighteen days; a number of other summits took seven to nine days; the 1978 Camp David negotiations took thirteen days. Nevertheless, time remains a concern. Chief executives have a government to run and an entire political process to be concerned about. Being away for extended periods of time can be a problem.[31]

However, modern means of communication now enable leaders to remain in contact with their national capital and to continue working on domestic issues; many leaders take key officials with them (e.g., their foreign ministers), all of which to some extent alleviates the problem of being away. Furthermore, if problems develop at home, urgently requiring their presence, in most instances they can be back in a matter of a few hours. At any rate, leaders are adjusting—indeed they now participate in more international meetings than ever. Jet lag and fatigue may have an effect on the diplomatic process, although hard to document. Chief executives, given the nature of their work, may be people endowed with greater stamina. Nevertheless, time constraints and tight scheduling of summit functions may create additional burdens that affect human performance—such as loss of flexibility, irritability, flawed perception, or less imaginative responses.[32]

Less is heard about heads of state failing to be good diplomats.[33] The world is becoming accustomed to a large amount of international transactions being done by officials without diplomatic background. Enough professionals

---

Box 10.1   The Gulf Cooperation Council's 2007 Summit

The heads of the six Persian Gulf countries (Bahrain, Kuwait, Oman, Qatar, Saudi Arabia, and the United Arab Emirates [UAE]) met on December 3–4, 2007, in Doha, Qatar's capital. In addition to their usual objective of increasing solidarity among the profoundly different members of the Gulf Cooperation Council (GCC) and encouraging cooperation among their competitive governments (they frequently have divergent views on oil issues), the summit, for the first time in the GCC's twenty-six-year existence, had invited President Mahmoud Ahmadinejad of the Islamic Republic of Iran for conversations—an invitation that he was quick to accept.

Iran has often been perceived as a threat in the Persian Gulf. A number of small UAE islands near the Strait of Hormuz have been occupied by Iran for four decades, and in the days following the Islamic revolution, the Iranian leadership was fond of inviting other Muslims to topple their governments. But for all that still separated them, the GCC invited President Ahmadinejad, who lost no time proposing practical and tangible cooperation in nearly a dozen fields, ranging from education to science and technology to trade and investment. It may take a long time to establish trust, but the visit created a media "buzz." Undoubtedly, greater cooperation in areas of common interest is to the mutual benefit of the Gulf countries.

Source: John Duke Anthony, *Economic Dynamism Amidst Regional Uncertainties: GCC Summitry in Qatar* (Washington, DC: National Council on US-Arab Relations, December 2007).

---

are hovering over those chief executives during their summits that they are bound to get some help. They are rarely without expert advice. Maybe that is what makes it work. Some criticism is heard concerning heads of state circumventing their foreign ministry or making decisions without consulting their key officials or specialists, but it is more a matter of personal style than anything inherent in summit diplomacy. Some US presidents routinely ignore the State Department.[34]

Summit diplomacy is still occasionally viewed as unwarranted meddling in the diplomatic process,[35] but active participation in the conduct of foreign affairs by a chief executive is commonplace and even expanding as the political process changes around the world. Some of it is now seen as necessary. In certain international issues, it is important that the matter be taken up at the highest level. Many international organizations actively seek summit diplomacy. During the Cold War, the criticism was heard that summit meetings created unwarranted expectations, and as late as 1989 the White House went out of its way to stress the "theme of minimalism" in a meeting between Presidents

George H. W. Bush and Mikhail Gorbachev on naval units in the Mediterranean, near Malta.[36] But media hype is not limited to summit meetings. The increased frequency of summit gatherings, and their diversity, tend to make them much more normal if not routine, with considerably less media attention being paid to this mode of interaction.

Another fear going back to the Cold War, when the two superpowers engaged in dangerous confrontations, concerned the possibility that a chief executive would unwittingly send the wrong signals and prompt unwarranted expectations or dangerous decisions. In 1961, during the Vienna Conference, President John F. Kennedy gave the impression to Nikita Khrushchev that he was inexperienced and weak, encouraging the Kremlin to be more aggressive.[37] An earlier incident is frequently cited as illustrating the dangers of summit conversations. President Dwight Eisenhower, in a meeting with Nikita Khrushchev at Camp David in September 1959, innocently agreed with the Soviet leader that the situation in divided Berlin, a Western political island inside East Germany, was "abnormal." Khrushchev left Camp David convinced that the United States was ready to make concessions on the status of the divided city.[38] But misperceptions of this kind may arise in any kind of diplomatic interaction. It has been said that in 1990, Saddam Hussein was encouraged to invade Kuwait when the US ambassador in Baghdad remained conciliatory when Iraq became hostile toward Kuwait and deployed its forces along the border. The United States, as with other states in the region, firmly believed that Iraq was simply applying pressure to its neighbor, but was going to negotiate its differences with Kuwait. Saddam gave assurances to this effect to the Saudi government—and managed to fool everybody.

With regard to summit conversations, subsequent government pronouncements or actions are generally sufficient to avoid misunderstandings. In the case of Eisenhower's remark on Berlin, the State Department quickly corrected Khrushchev's false impression. Seasoned politicians are usually wary when it comes to the pronouncements of their counterparts, particularly when relationships are less than friendly. It is therefore important not to exaggerate the risks of summit interaction. Nevertheless, when a chief executive makes a commitment out of turn, or is perceived as making a commitment when none was intended, the mistake is harder to correct because it came from the highest authority.[39]

Clashes of personality may complicate summit interaction, but cultural misperceptions are a more likely occurrence, as chief executives have less experience in cross-cultural communication. Thus, in the course of Japanese prime minister Eisaku Sato's visit to Washington, President Richard Nixon was seeking a commitment, which his counterpart was unwilling to give. Sato's answer was translated as "I will do my best," a literal translation, which Nixon understood as a positive reply, whereas Sato was using a classic Japanese expression indicating that what was proposed could not be done—another way of saying no. Only later was it realized in Washington that there was no agreement. But Nixon is reported to have been outraged, believing that he had been duped. This caused distrust in their subsequent relations.[40] There is a limit also as to what chief executives can negotiate: essentially, as German chancellor Helmut Kohl said after the 1991 London G7 summit, the details must be left to the experts.[41] See Box 10.2 for an example of what can happen when this wise admonition is left unheeded.

Summit meetings are therefore not without pitfalls. One must of course consider how often such incidents occur. And even if professional diplomats make fewer mistakes, we remain faced with the fact that chief decisionmakers still believe there is merit in summit interaction: awareness of potential dangers should be an invitation to caution. The continued frequency of meetings between chief executives shows that they are not deterred.[42]

Box 10.2   Confusion at the 1982 Reagan-Thatcher Meeting

British prime minister Margaret Thatcher came to Washington, D.C., to meet with President Ronald Reagan in June 1982. At the White House, President Reagan took the initiative of mentioning the decision, reached a few days earlier, to extend a US ban on the export to the Soviet Union of energy equipment, regardless of existing contracts—particularly with the British company John Brown, which was involved in the construction of the trans-Siberian pipeline. The president added that he had learned that the people at John Brown were quite happy with his decision and did not think that they would suffer a great deal on account of it.

Thatcher's eyes blazed and she launched into a fierce attack on the president's decision, pointing out that contrary to the alleged intent of applying economic pressure on the Soviets, US exports to the Soviet Union would actually increase that year because of the lifting of the grain embargo. The president said something about not making any new grain agreement with the Soviets—which led to a muddled discussion in which neither side knew the facts about whether this would or would not in practice curtail US grain shipments to the Soviet Union.

Heads of government cannot be conversant with the details of the policy issues they must deal with. When arguing these issues, it is easy to slip into areas that are best left to their professionals. It is not easy for the advisers who are present at the conversations to "rescue" the principals, particularly when the exchange becomes heated.

Source: Nicholas Henderson, *Mandarin: The Diaries of an Ambassador, 1969–1982* (London: Weidenfeld and Nicolson, 1994), pp. 478–480.

▓ Functions of Summit Diplomacy

The object of summit meetings varies enormously.[43] Some things are better done one-on-one in visits to national capitals; others lend themselves better to multilateral gatherings. Goodwill visits are numerous (e.g., getting acquainted, courtesy visits, and promotion of cordial relations). Some are symbolic in the choice of places visited—for example, President George W. Bush's six-hour stop in Senegal and visit to the Island of Gorée (from which slaves were shipped to the Americas), and his speech deploring slavery and espousing the US sense of responsibility to Africa.[44] Some visits have a ceremonial purpose (e.g., attendance at weddings, coronations). Interestingly, the presence of many chief executives at such events leads some of them to engage in diplomatic conversations and even to arrange side meetings with some of their counterparts.

During a crisis, chief executives may want to strategize,[45] or at least discuss and explore possible alternatives,[46] or try to get a sense of how the other parties view the situation. This can be done bilaterally, in small groups, or even in international conferences, depending upon the issues or the circumstances. For example, as mentioned previously, the Arab League met at the summit level in Beirut, in March 2002, to discuss a peace plan for the Israeli-Palestinian conflict.[47] Top-level consultation, in fact, need not be restricted to crisis situations. The G8 now find it useful to meet annually. These meetings have been categorized as "serial summits."[48]

Chief executive participation in ad hoc world conferences often called by the UN marks their efforts to contribute to the public debate on important issues and shape global public policy.[49] Their involvement is often more symbolic than substantive. The presence of heads of state or government tends to confer an aura of greater importance to the proceedings, which are then publicized as summit meetings, such as the World Summit on Children (a UNICEF conference in New York, 1990), the World Summit for Social Development (Copenhagen, 1995), or the City Summit (the UN Conference on Human Settlements,[50] Istanbul, Turkey, 1996). The presence of chief executives helps raise global consciousness, usually an important objective in convening these conferences. Much more involved in actual diplomatic negotiations, heads of state or government sometimes intervene with other leaders as mediators to resolve international disputes or conflicts. President Jimmy Carter's negotiations with President Anwar Sadat of Egypt and Prime Minister Menachem Begin of Israel, at Camp David in September 1978, are a remarkable example of this type of diplomatic work. Normally, however, mediation (formally in the name of a head of state) is conducted by a professional diplomat, perhaps as a special presidential envoy.[51]

Another function of summit diplomacy pertains to the conclusion of important international agreements—important enough to warrant a meeting of chief executives. But what is involved here is usually at the tail end of the negotiation process. The treaty is normally put together by other diplomatic means. Leaders do not have the time for extended negotiations, and they do not need to be involved in the minutiae of international arrangements.[52] When agreement is reached, chief executives meet to formalize this accomplishment and sign the document, really a ceremonial or symbolic function.[53] Some delicate negotiations, however, may require the intervention of heads of state to negotiate the last remaining differences, especially when the last points are bitterly contested. It takes the authority of the chief executives to settle the matter.[54] In this case, the leaders engage in genuine negotiations, but the chances of success must nevertheless be good enough to reach that stage. Summit meetings impose deadlines on the negotiating process; the parties cannot agonize over what separates them. Failure at the summit has serious consequences, often because of the greater visibility of these proceedings. And leaders often sense that they can ill afford to be seen as failing in their endeavors, since it may diminish their stature and authority.

A different role is played by summit interaction in certain international organizations when the highest level of decisionmaking formally resides in a summit meeting.[55] Here, summit diplomacy is institutionalized, although there are many structural differences between international organizations. In the North Atlantic Treaty Organization (NATO), for example, the summit function is found in the NATO Council, which meets regularly at the ministerial level, and occasionally, on an ad hoc basis, at the level of heads of state or government (popularly referred to as "NATO summits"), to consider particularly important issues. By the mid-1990s, thirteen of these meetings had been held.[56] In the European Union, the most important political decisions have required a formal summit meeting.[57] In 1974, the European Council was created for the participation of European chief executives, who eventually met twice a year.[58] From its inception, the European organization has been an evolving institution, and the leaders have played a critical role in its growth and transformation. This is probably the most extensive and continuous summit function in existence today, unusual because it is taking place within an unprecedented process of international integration. With its expansion, the European Union will likely need to restructure this summit function.[59]

The other forms of chief executive interaction (personal letters, cables, phone calls, special presidential envoys) serve their own, if very diverse, purposes. Their use depends upon many factors—personality, affinity, style, and level of familiarity. Some leaders are more able to maintain a personal type of relationship than others, but this can no longer be viewed as unconventional. Some leaders make a conscious effort to cultivate deeply personal connections with other leaders. UN Secretary-General Dag Hammarskjöld used this approach with Chinese leader Chou En-lai to facilitate his difficult negotiations over the US airmen held in China (see case study in Chapter 8). The relationship was somewhat bumpy. Ultimately, though, the prisoners were released, together with a personal greeting from the Chinese leader to the Secretary-General, on Hammarskjöld's birthday.

▓ Preparation for Summit Diplomacy

Adequate preparation is of course important for any kind of diplomatic work, but it is even more important in summit diplomacy. Because heads of state or government are very sensitive to the appearance of failure, their diplomatic work needs to seem productive—and a great deal of diplomacy normally takes place prior to (and often long in advance of) summit interaction. Given the enormous diversity of summit diplomacy, preparatory work is equally diverse.[60]

Informal or routine summit contact will usually be at the low end of summit preparation. Low visibility makes it safe enough. Furthermore, informal or routine contact implies a certain amount of familiarity or intimacy among the leaders concerned. They know each other, and there is enough affinity between them, perhaps even enough unity in their policies, to avoid the need for elaborate advance preparation. They are fairly confident that their conversation will not be misunderstood and will remain confidential. Thus there can be a certain amount of spontaneity as one leader calls the other on the phone, or as they meet on the occasion of some international function. But this situation probably applies only to a small number of leaders, each knowing only a fairly limited number of chief executives in other countries who can be treated with this kind of intimacy. Language can be a serious barrier for this kind of informal, relaxed contact.

In incidental summit contacts, such as during the course of a ceremonial meeting or a recurring international function, a certain amount of preparation will be in order: Who needs to be seen? What issues can be discussed under the circumstances? And so on.[61] Some leaders will be contacted ahead of time: an exchange of notes, or conversations between ambassadors, or some other form of advance contact will take place. If the subject matter of the contemplated summit contact is important enough, the chief executives may arrange to have a separate meeting in the margin of the other proceedings, or they may even stay a day longer for this purpose. This kind of summit approach on the occasion of some other function can be useful for speaking with leaders who are too controversial to meet officially (e.g., enemies seeking some rapprochement).[62] In this case, precautions will be needed to avoid public visibility—hence, more careful preparation, with perhaps some discreet initial contact between UN delegations or other diplomatic agents. The possibilities are quite extensive.

Some of these ceremonial functions to be attended by heads of state are often tightly programmed—another reason why advance preparation is needed for "incidental" summit contacts. British prime minister Margaret Thatcher's schedule at one of those UN General Assembly meetings gives an idea of the kind of advance scheduling that is required to accomplish some diplomatic work on the side (see Box 10.3).

Box 10.3   Margaret Thatcher's Incidental Summit Meetings

With fifty heads of state or government converging on the United Nations in New York in 1985 for its fortieth-anniversary commemorative session, many tried to compress several days' worth of diplomacy into a single day. "It was a typical day in the Prime Minister's life," said Margaret Thatcher's assistant press secretary. "Why walk when you can run?" True or not, she liked to project the image of an engine all revved up. And certainly, her schedule was tight—but not unusually so in the course of those annual New York gatherings.

Thatcher began her day early. She read some briefings and newspapers while she ate a light breakfast in her suite at the United Nations Plaza Hotel, across the street from UN headquarters. After meeting with senior advisers, she met with Prime Minister Zhao Ziyang of China.

By 10:00 A.M., she was hurrying across the street to hear President Ronald Reagan address the General Assembly. After Ziyang and Prime Minister Rajiv Gandhi of India addressed the distinguished audience, Thatcher took her turn at the podium to speak on the problems of the world. After one more speech, by the prime minister of New Zealand, it was time for a quick photo session with a newsmagazine. Then she went across the street to the US mission, where President Reagan was hosting a working lunch for allied leaders.

After lunch, she went back across the street to hear more speeches. When this was done, she hurried to the Grand Hyatt Hotel, nearby, where she faced the world press for forty minutes. Then she granted four separate interviews with British radio and television to tell the people in her country about her day in New York.

By then, it was time for dinner—a state dinner at the Waldorf-Astoria given by President Reagan for visiting allied leaders. After dinner, she was off to Kennedy International Airport to board a Royal Air Force plane for London. It would enable her to arrive in time to preside over an early-morning cabinet meeting. Even if her air force flight enabled her to get more rest than possible on a commercial plane, this kind of schedule would likely put her stamina to the test.

Source: New York Times, October 25, 1985, p. 12.

When the summit meeting is a formal state visit, ceremonial arrangements (often elaborate) need to be made, in consultation with an executive office of the visiting official, such as program of activities, schedule, time with the chief executive of the host state, state dinners, menus, and usually some function at the foreign leader's own embassy. In addition, some activities need to be planned for the visitor's spouse, as well as appropriate (and usually glittering) entertainment—perhaps even some sightseeing. Even if no serious diplomatic exchanges are contemplated, host and guest leaders need to be briefed on the cultural oddities of the two countries. Protocol officers on both sides help to ensure that everything goes smoothly—but all of this involves much preparatory work.[63]

When substantive conversations are envisioned, a great deal of extra preparation is necessary, not only in the form of policy briefings for the heads of state involved, but perhaps also in the form of advance negotiations involving embassies or special missions, to produce an agenda and to permit a more effective outcome. But a great deal depends on the object of the visit and the nature of the relations between the two states concerned. For President Richard Nixon's historic 1972 visit to Beijing, National Security Adviser Henry Kissinger flew secretly to China to make the necessary arrangements. UN Secretary-General Dag Hammarskjöld, in preparation for his 1955 negotiations with Premier Chou En-lai in Beijing, met secretly with the Chinese ambassador in Stockholm.

For the purpose of bilateral consultations or exchanges of views, it may be more a matter of anticipating what needs to be said or avoided, and what requires firmness or conciliation when the time comes to converse. In the planning process, too, matters of format need to be agreed upon between the parties who intend to meet. This may even require an advance visiting party (from the embassy or perhaps a special mission) to work out the details: How many formal presentations? How many aides need to be present in the course of the discussion? Will there be a need for technical experts? Will there be private sessions exclusively between the leaders? The degree of cordiality or enmity between the states involved will make a great deal of difference.

In the case of a state visit (or a summit conference) a communiqué will be needed (normally, a brief overview of what the meeting accomplished). It is usually helpful to draft it in advance, if possible, to satisfy the political needs of the parties concerned. Even in informal visits, when the parties do not believe they need a communiqué, what to tell the media may have to be discussed. This can be decided during the meeting itself, along with the question of whether to appear at a joint press conference. Some leaders are touchy about taking questions from the media. At one of the stops during President George W. Bush's rapid visit to Africa in July 2003, when the two leaders appeared before a roomful of reporters, President Festus G. Mogae of Botswana opened the proceedings with a good-natured "Does anyone want to ask . . . ?"

President Bush cut him off, interjecting, "That's not the way we do it," then took the two questions he intended to answer from the American reporters, and that was the end of it (and it all happened on camera). He was smiling as he said it, but it did not sound very gracious.[64] A good deal of planning can avoid embarrassing moments, but not always. Fatigue is also a factor; visiting leaders need time to rest, and this time must be planned in advance.

Although it may seem elemental, making advance provision for keeping track of what is said or promised in the course of any summit meeting is occasionally a difficult matter. Incredibly, when Ambassador Charles E. Bohlen accompanied President Franklin Roosevelt to Tehran, Iran, in 1943, to serve as chief interpreter for the president during the wartime meeting with Winston Churchill and Joseph Stalin, he recalled that he was "startled to discover that no provision had been made by the American Government for taking minutes of the conference proceedings." Bohlen complained that, in fact, "no one was in charge of organizing meetings, setting up schedules or handling any of the numerous technical preparations for the conference."[65] Recordkeeping in summit meetings remains a problem. Understandably, in negotiations of any kind (not just summit interaction), the proceedings cannot be recorded. In the give and take of any negotiations, some offers are made only to get a counteroffer—nothing is to be entered into the official record. Instead, provision must be made for taking *notes,* since the parties need to keep track of what was said during the meeting. Ambassador Bohlen remedied the situation by finding four army secretaries to whom he could dictate his own extensive notes after each session.

President Richard Nixon secretly taped conversations that took place in his office, including a session with Russian leader Leonid Brezhnev in 1973.[66] At the 1986 summit in Reykjavik, Iceland, between Presidents Ronald Reagan and Mikhail Gorbachev, both sides relied on the traditional diplomatic method of recordkeeping: taking their own notes. But they did not exchange their versions of what took place, and President Gorbachev accused President Reagan of distorting what happened in the meeting. Normally, the responsibility falls on two or three interpreters who take notes and interpret, and on two or three foreign service officers who understand the language of the other leader and are rotated as note-takers. Having foreign service officers as note-takers is important, since knowledge of the issues discussed helps in summarizing the proceedings. The interpreters can add details and check the statements for accuracy from their own notes.

In his three meetings with President Brezhnev in 1972, 1973, and 1974, President Nixon insisted on not having any American interpreter in the room. He relied on Brezhnev's interpreter. His argument was that Brezhnev would speak more freely if both heads of state relied on the Soviet interpreter. Henry Kissinger, Nixon's national security adviser (and, by the 1974 summit, secretary of state), was Nixon's only note-taker, when he had one (perhaps a sign that he *did* rely on some form of secret tape recording).[67]

Physical security, more than ever in today's environment of international terrorism, needs to be ensured. This is usually complicated by the pageantry of state visits, which requires a good deal of public exposure. As terrorism grows around the world, protecting heads of state will become more complex. Extensive international cooperation, particularly in the collection and exchange of intelligence, can be critical for the protection of chief executives on foreign missions. Since the "Battle of Seattle" on the occasion of the 1999 World Trade Organization meeting, and other severe disruptions, as in Washington, D.C., Genoa, and Quebec City, negotiators have needed protection from mob violence, to the point that one of the G8 meetings (June 2002) was held at the remote resort village of Kananaskis, in western Canada, in the shadow of Mount Kidd, sixty miles from Calgary, Alberta, accessible by only one road running through the region. The village has three small hotels, a post office, and a general store. This made it easier to keep away uninvited guests. Nevertheless, Canada deployed 4,500 police officers and 6,000 soldiers equipped with assault rifles, who guarded access to the one road and established a fifteen-mile perimeter around the village. Cougars, wolves, and grizzly bears were said to be abundant away from the road. A 330-mile-radius no-flight zone was declared over the village, patrolled by fighter aircraft and protected also by ground-to-air missiles. Journalists were kept in Calgary at a media center, around which a barrier was erected. The city government rented two armored vehicles for riot control. The estimated cost was in excess of $200 million, which might well lead other hosts to hesitate taking this as a model for the protection of future summit meetings.[68]

Politically important summit conferences see a great deal of preconference diplomacy. The bilateral Cold War summits had a special character because of the profound enmity dividing the superpowers. Media pronouncements (on both sides), months in advance of the meetings, set the stage for these summits; positions were formulated in advance, framing the agenda and even running the risk of foreclosing some options. Diplomats, including the US secretary of state and the Soviet foreign minister, negotiated back and forth (in advance) what the summits could accomplish.

If a treaty is to be signed at a summit meeting, its terms are likely to have been put together by diplomats beforehand, although occasionally, more problematic issues may be left to the heads of state to work out in their summit. World conferences, advertised as summits, are handled like other large international conferences, with elaborate proceedings taking place during meetings of preparatory committees. Given the number of heads of state to attend such conferences, advance work, although similar to what is done at the bilateral level for state visits, is naturally more complicated and likely to include provision for large numbers of nongovernmental organizations (NGOs). A great deal of the preparatory work will be left to the secretariat, particularly the huge issue of logistics (getting some 150 delegations to work together is a daunting task). The secretariat is likely to be asked to work out the mechanics of media relations and press conferences (see Chapter 9's discussion of conference diplomacy).[69]

■ Diplomacy During a Summit Meeting

The diplomatic process during a summit meeting will vary enormously, from expression of goodwill to extremely sensitive negotiations. Formal presentations of position may alternate with open-ended conversations, with a good deal of give and take. The more serious or delicate the object of the meeting, the larger the group of officials involved (foreign ministers, other cabinet ministers, diplomats, experts, etc.). The heads of state may have several of these professionals at their side while interacting or negotiating. But they may also want, at some point, to confer privately, without anyone else present (with the exception of interpreters).

The proceedings may well be subdivided into a number of "sessions," either because it was planned that way to facilitate the negotiations or as a result of the interaction itself. Some ceremonial functions or state dinners may take place between rounds of negotiation, but pomp and ceremony will vary.[70] If the visits are frequent (e.g., the Israeli prime minister coming to the White House), the summit meeting is likely to be very businesslike and streamlined (a "working summit").

The process of negotiation will of course vary with the relations maintained by the states, the circumstances, personalities involved, and whatever was negotiated in preparation for the summit.[71] The 1990 Houston economic summit met two days early to enable state leaders to hold bilateral talks before their regular meeting.[72] The other state officials and diplomats in attendance are likely to engage in separate negotiations of their own, away from the limelight, between meetings of the heads of state, particularly to handle the technical issues or the details (parallel negotiations).[73] Incidental summit contacts ("funeral summits") seldom provide much time for diplomatic interaction, although separate meetings may be arranged on the margin of the official functions between some of the leaders in attendance.[74]

■ Post-Summit Diplomacy

Often, summit meetings open the way for additional diplomacy. Many provide for follow-up action. The diplomats who are to prepare for the next G8 summit usually hold a meeting shortly after the annual gathering to review what was accomplished. Later summits may continue the dialogue on certain agenda items.[75] Summit meetings that are an integral part of the decisionmaking process of international organizations (e.g., in the European Union) are particularly important in generating follow-up diplomacy. This is also true of the world summits called by the United Nations. One of their purposes is to lead states to address major international problems. Most of these conferences produce recommendations to be taken up by the UN General Assembly for implementation, including the launching of new programs or plans of action to be carried out over a number of years, for example Agenda 21, brought forth by the Earth Summit (Rio, 1992).[76] The follow-up diplomacy occasionally includes the negotiation of new international agreements, for example the UN Convention on Desertification, for which negotiations started immediately after the summit.[77] The 1978 Camp David summit (Carter, Begin, Sadat) is a good example of an ad hoc summit that generates a critical amount of additional diplomacy, which in this case led to the peace treaty between Egypt and Israel.[78]

Summit interaction is now a common diplomatic tool. State leaders routinely use it—another sign of change in the international system. But this method is not changing the relevance of other instruments of diplomacy. The negotiations that lead to a summit are significant, as the participants are conscious of the risks involved in summit failure. And follow-up diplomacy by other means completes the procedure. Summit diplomacy has become an integral part of the larger diplomatic process,[79] and will likely see increasing use in the future.

■ Case Study: The Nassau Summit and the Skybolt Crisis

Toward the end of 1962, in the depth of the Cold War, defense needs were changing.[80] The Cuban missile crisis had just ended, and had taught the world just how dangerous the global environment could become overnight.[81] Britain and the United States, despite their special relationship and their profound interest in close defense coordination, had experienced occasional difficulties in harmonizing their policies. In 1960, the United States was planning to develop a new air-launched nuclear missile, the Skybolt, and had agreed to sell it to Britain.[82] By 1962, however, Skybolt showed serious technical flaws and proved to be an excessively expensive project. On the other hand, the Polaris, a submarine-launched nuclear missile, was making excellent progress, and together with the Minuteman missile was making Skybolt redundant.[83] George Ball, undersecretary of state at the time, observed that both President John F. Kennedy and US secretary of state Dean Rusk considered Skybolt to be primarily a military matter to be handled by Secretary of Defense Robert McNamara. Ball noted further that "none of us regarded a forthcoming meeting [mid-December 1962] between [British prime minister Harold Macmillan] and Kennedy at Nassau as more than a routine affair—merely the sixth in a series."[84] Skybolt was not on the agenda and McNamara did not plan to attend.[85] It is interesting, though, how the British and US leaderships were routinely holding summit meetings. This one, however, turned out to be very different.

On November 8, 1962, McNamara briefed British ambassador David Ormsby-Gore on the problems faced by the US government with the Skybolt project and, the next day, informed British defense minister Peter Thorneycroft by telephone that Skybolt was in trouble.[86] It is noteworthy that a telephone call by the defense secretary was considered sufficient (rather than flying to London to discuss the situation or having the president take up the matter with the prime minister). No crisis was foreseen by the Kennedy administration as a result of a forthcoming Skybolt cancellation.[87] The US leadership did not seem to sense that Macmillan was in serious political trouble at home. A series of setbacks throughout 1962 had undermined his position. The success of his independent nuclear deterrent (based on the acquisition of Skybolt) was thus of critical importance for the survival of his government.[88] Both Ormsby-Gore and Thorneycroft tried to warn McNamara that the cancellation of Skybolt would have drastic political consequences for the British government and would provoke a backlash against the United States.[89]

The British leadership, alarmed, requested that Skybolt be placed on the Nassau agenda. McNamara phoned George Ball on December 7 that he had now decided to attend the summit meeting.[90] Skybolt would undoubtedly loom large in the summit discussion, and he wanted to be there. In the meantime, things followed their course in Washington and, at a budget meeting in late November, Skybolt cancellation was decided. The British government would be consulted to explore what compensation would satisfy them. As McNamara was scheduled to be in Paris on December 12 for a long-scheduled NATO ministerial meeting, he decided to stop in London the day before and meet with Thorneycroft. However, as often happens in Washington, on December 7, news of the Skybolt cancellation was leaked to the press. This caused uproar in Britain.[91] Many saw it as a breach of faith, a devious attempt on the part of the United States to deny Britain its own nuclear strike force.

The December 11 meeting with Thorneycroft went poorly. McNamara was unable to offer Polaris as a substitute: the State Department had ruled it out, as it was trying to foster European and NATO collective defense and, consequently, opposed independent nuclear deterrence (which was Macmillan's goal in the acquisition of Skybolt—or Polaris as a substitute). The Holy Loch submarine base arrangement in Scotland, offered to the United States by Macmillan when the Skybolt agreement was concluded with the Eisenhower administration, was now called into question.[92] The Anglo-American partnership was unraveling; animosity was becoming as pronounced as during the 1956 Suez crisis.

The Bahamas summit (December 18–21) was thus confronted with a deteriorating situation. Kennedy genuinely liked Macmillan and was eager to do something for him; he was also anxious to preserve the special relationship with Britain, but he shared the State Department's desire to keep Europe working together and to integrate the nuclear response (against Macmillan's drive for nuclear independence).[93] A few days before the summit, on December 16, Kennedy convened a meeting with McNamara, McGeorge Bundy, George Ball, and David Bruce, US ambassador to Britain. All were to attend the summit meeting. What could the United States offer?

The president wanted to help Macmillan. The problem was to determine what would meet the prime minister's need for this hour, but Ambassador Bruce thought that only the prime minister could decide that question.[94] (It may well be that Macmillan could not make up his mind.) The dilemma was summarized as a grave political risk for Macmillan if the United States did not help him, and a serious risk for US policy in Europe if it helped him too much.[95] They concluded that they must let Macmillan have Polaris, but with an important condition: the missile could only be used as decided collectively by NATO.[96] Macmillan was going to have a hard time accepting this restriction.

Kennedy invited Ambassador Ormsby-Gore, a close friend for many years, to fly with him to the summit. The two of them attempted to draft an alternative proposal according to which the Skybolt project would not be terminated, but the costs would be shared fifty-fifty with the British, although only Britain would deploy the missile (one may wonder whether this would have been acceptable in the United States).

In the Bahamas, Ball reported the British mood as grim.[97] Although the summit was not initially convened to address the Skybolt crisis, it naturally became the main concern.[98] When the president's plane landed, Prime Minister Macmillan was waiting at the Nassau airport, and during the usual ceremonies the local police band struck up an old English song, "Early One Morning," which Ball suspected was no coincidence. It went:

> Oh, don't deceive me,
> Don't ever leave me
> How could you use
> A poor maiden so?[99]

The British delegation, like its US counterpart, did not include any top military personnel.[100] The matter was political. Along with Macmillan were Lord Home, foreign secretary; Peter Thorneycroft, defense secretary; and Duncan Sandys, colonial secretary. A large press delegation swarmed around them.[101] Many summits have this effect (and have been criticized on this account)—the strong emotions evoked by the Skybolt issue made it even more pronounced.

When the conference opened formally on December 19, Macmillan, in his introductory remarks, showed an excellent grasp of the primary obstacles to a resolution of the problem and requested "a switch from the lame horse, Skybolt, to what was now the Polaris."[102] He also demonstrated goodwill in stating that the United States could keep the Holy Loch submarine facilities even if the Skybolt issue remained unresolved (thus moving away from the veiled threat wielded by Thorneycroft at his December 11 meeting with McNamara).[103]

Kennedy first tried his fifty-fifty proposal, but Macmillan was not interested. He then tried a late improvisation from the State Department, a joint study on next steps in British weaponry—but Macmillan wanted the matter resolved now. At this point, Kennedy turned to Polaris as a substitute, but under the control of NATO—and this became the main stumbling block. After two days of negotiations, agreement was reached.[104] Britain would be sold Polaris missiles; it would build the needed submarines and the nuclear warheads, with US technical assistance under previous agreements.[105] The missiles would be pledged to NATO, in a multinational force (the original US condition) to which the United States would also contribute, under integrated command. However, the pledge contained an escape clause: in times of supreme emergency (undefined), submarines and Polaris missiles could be withdrawn for independent British use[106]—so that they were not totally and irrevocably integrated into the NATO structure. Some British independence was preserved. Kennedy could stress the NATO integration feature and Macmillan Britain's independence.

This formula did not please everyone. This much could be expected. But the crisis was defused and the Anglo-American partnership was back on track. Macmillan was given Polaris as a substitute for Skybolt—a proposition the United States initially refused to consider. All things considered, this summit meeting was given greater significance by the fact that both countries mismanaged their diplomacy at the outset of the Skybolt affair. A major element was the failure of the Kennedy administration to perceive how explosive the matter was in Britain. It is hard to believe that the US embassy in London could not see what was happening. Somebody was not doing his job properly. Or else, somebody in Washington was not getting the message, or not listening. US decisionmakers approached the termination of the project strictly in terms of US domestic politics, without regard to British concerns or Anglo-American relations. As the Kennedy administration became disenchanted with Skybolt, US diplomacy needed to prepare the British government for what was coming.[107] Active consultation would have permitted greater efforts to create political alternatives.

The British government, on its part, when it became aware that Skybolt was in trouble, did not take any significant diplomatic initiative, or advance any proposal with Washington in the attempt to find a less damaging alternative. The matter should have been negotiated earlier, when enough time could have been devoted to the development of new positions. The two countries had close ties; Kennedy and Macmillan enjoyed mutual friendship. Greater diplomatic interaction should not have been difficult before the summit.[108] Better communication between the governments could have reduced the bitterness and sense of betrayal experienced in Britain.[109] It may well be that Macmillan himself could not decide what was his best alternative or what to propose.

It has been suggested that the tightness of the Nassau schedule, which had already been arranged, gave no time for reflection on deeper issues, such as the continuing British dependence upon US cooperation.[110] By that time, however, the situation had reached crisis proportions. The summit was the catalyst that permitted fast action. Kennedy's eagerness to help his ally and Macmillan's grasp of his predicament led them, face to face, to produce a viable compromise,[111] perhaps limping, but a way to cope with the crisis. It is probable that only a summit meeting could do it within this difficult time frame (although the tension and distrust experienced at the outset of the Nassau meeting made it initially rather unpromising). The personal attributes of the two leaders and their past relationship were undoubtedly significant factors in finding a way out.

Ministerial Diplomacy

▒ Characteristics

A related form of diplomacy is now extensively carried out by high-level government officials, often of ministerial rank, first and foremost among them the foreign minister (secretary of state).[112] This method may also be called near-summit diplomacy. It is extensive and growing in importance, particularly as serious international problems proliferate, requiring the attention of top decisionmakers (see Box 10.4). The degree of ministerial involvement will of course be conditioned by the nature of a country's political system and the extent of its participation in international affairs. However, some department heads are more inclined to be personally involved in the conduct of diplomacy than others.

An illustration of the diplomatic involvement of ministers of foreign affairs is provided by US State Department statistics on the foreign visits by the secretary of state (see Table 10.3). But a comparison of the total number of foreign visits by individual secretaries is misleading, since their years of service vary. Overall, however, secretaries of state travel extensively (as is easily confirmed by news reports).

The pace of foreign travel has thus accelerated.[113] During the early post–World War II years, the number of annual foreign visits averaged only six or seven. In the 1950s and 1960s they rarely exceeded twenty per year. They climbed to around thirty-eight a year in the 1970s, to forty-five in the 1980s, and to sixty in the 1990s and early 2000s. It is interesting to compare these figures with pre-1945 travel statistics (see Table 10.4).

Box 10.4   US-China Trade Talks, 2007

In December 2007, the United States and China conducted three days of intense economic talks, reaching agreements on food safety, energy, and environmental cooperation. The US negotiating team was led by Secretary of the Treasury Henry M. Paulson Jr. and included several cabinet members. They were met in China by the Chinese prime minister and his own team of high government officials, headed by Vice Premier Wu Yi. The talks were part of a "strategic economic dialogue" initiated a year earlier by Paulson, a former investment banker for Goldman Sachs with many years of experience doing business in China. He has emphasized that broad exchanges on long-term issues could improve the climate for agreements in specific areas.

Commerce secretary Carlos T. Gutierrez, as well as Susan C. Schwab, the US trade representative, stressed the desire of the United States to address specific issues pragmatically. In this round of negotiations, Secretary Paulson's strategic dialogue yielded agreements to ensure the safety of toys, chemicals, and other products, to combat counterfeit pharmaceuticals, to promote Chinese tourism in the United States, and to embark on a ten-year effort to cooperate on energy resources and the environment.

Source: New York Times, December 14, 2007, p. C6.

However, foreign visits vary in duration. Many are very short, lasting one day or even part of a day. For example, in 1988, Secretary George Shultz visited seventeen countries in thirteen days; and early in the following year, Secretary James Baker stopped in fourteen countries in seven days. On the other hand, some foreign visits have been lengthy; for instance, Secretary George Marshall spent sixty-four days abroad in 1948, attending the third session of the UN General Assembly in Paris, and visiting Athens, London, and Rome. Henry Kissinger spent thirty-four days on his mission to the Middle East in the spring of 1974, negotiating in Geneva and in nine Middle East nations.[114] As the tempo of foreign negotiations increases, foreign ministers may find themselves undertaking hectic schedules of foreign travel, with perhaps only thirty to forty-eight hours back home between trips; but they keep traveling. This form of diplomacy is now so commonplace that it is barely attracting public attention. It is part of the job.

There are many reasons why an increasing amount of diplomacy is conducted at this level. Foreign ministers of course have greater authority and wider discretion than other members of the foreign service; their participation in the diplomatic process can expedite some types of international proceedings or negotiations. And some problems *require* the authority of high-level decisionmakers for a solution. Ultimately, initiative is easier at the ministerial

Table 10.3   Foreign Visits by US Secretaries of State, 1945–2005

	Time in Office	Number of Visits	Average Number of Visits per Year
James Byrnes	18 months	9	6.0
George Marshall	2 years	14	7.0
Dean Acheson	4 years	22	5.5
John Foster Dulles	6 years, 3 months	117	18.7
Christian Herter	9 months	22	29.3
Dean Rusk	6 years	116	19.3
William Rogers	4 years, 7 months	119	26.4
Henry Kissinger	3 years, 4 months	216	65.5
Cyrus Vance	3 years, 3 months	113	33.2
Edmund Muskie	8 months	10	15.0
Alexander Haig	1 year, 5 months	53	35.4
George Shultz	6 years, 6 months	270	41.5
James Baker	3 years, 7 months	217	62.0
Warren Christopher	4 years	237	59.3
Madeleine Albright	4 years	269	67.3
Colin Powell	4 years	213	53.3

Sources: Elmer Plischke, *U.S. Department of State: A Reference History* (Westport: Green-wood, 1999), p. 410; US Department of State, Office of the Historian, *Foreign Travels of the Secretaries of State, 1866–1990* (Washington, DC: US Government Printing Office, 1990); http://www.state.gov/r/pa/ho/trvl/ls/8515.

Table 10.4   Pre-1945 Foreign Visits of US Secretaries of State

	Office Term	Average Number of Foreign Trips per Year
Edward Stettinius	1944–1945	20.0
Cordell Hull	1933–1944	2.5
Henry Stimson	1929–1933	2.3
Frank Kellogg	1925–1929	1.5
Charles Hughes	1921–1925	1.8

Source: http://www.state.gov/r/pa/ho/trvl/ls.

level. In the conduct of foreign relations and diplomatic proceedings, the participation of foreign ministers indicates greater importance attached to the matter at hand. Also, decisions at this level offer greater promise of effective implementation.[115] Foreign ministers thus spend an increasing amount of time traveling. George Shultz spent 440 days away from Washington during his tenure as secretary of state; John Foster Dulles, 360 days; Henry Kissinger, 348; Dean Rusk, 335; William Rogers, 252; and Cyrus Vance, 223.[116] James Baker, Warren Christopher, and Madeleine Albright probably set new records in this category.[117] The US State Department reports that Secretary Dulles traveled 560,000 miles; Rusk, 600,000; Kissinger, 555,000 (not including his earlier extensive travel as national security adviser); and Baker, more than 700,000 miles.[118]

▓ Functions

The missions, of course, vary a great deal with the international situation. Immediately after World War II came the exceptional task of negotiating a new international order. Secretary James Byrnes, for example, between April 25 and October 15, 1946, spent 135 days (or almost twenty weeks) in Paris attending the sessions of the Council of Foreign Ministers and the peace conference.[119] In less exceptional times, foreign ministers are involved in a variety of tasks during their frequent travels (bilateral as well as multilateral in their type of interaction). As well, when home, foreign ministers themselves receive many of their counterparts from other countries and engage in more diplomatic interaction. Moreover, the diplomacy of these officials is also conducted by means of other forms of direct contact (such as phone calls, personal letters, and other direct messages), depending upon such factors as the situation, personal rapport between the people involved, and management styles.

Foreign ministers often travel with their chief executives to summit meetings,[120] participating in the diplomatic process at their side or engaging in parallel negotiations on related issues taken up at the summit.[121] These are important missions, as chief executives may have to rely on the far more intimate knowledge of international affairs of their foreign ministers in the course of the proceedings. Foreign ministers also work with foreign leaders on their own in a vast variety of ways, seeking support, exploring ways to cooperate, discussing strategy, consulting, negotiating given issues, providing information, and occasionally mediating. Some of the meetings may be less than conventional, as when Secretary George Shultz met Yassir Arafat, head of the Palestine Liberation Organization (PLO). Some of the meetings may be in preparation for a forthcoming summit. Foreign ministers may also travel to convey a special message or even an invitation to a foreign ruler, their important position in their government adding to the significance of the invitation. After a long absence of diplomatic relations or even enmity, a foreign minister's visit may signal an effort toward the normalization of relations—a sign of rapprochement (see Box 10.5).

Some negotiations may be important enough (or may have reached a critical juncture) to warrant the direct involvement of the foreign minister. Troubleshooting might be included under the negotiation category, for example, the urgent visit to Pakistan and India in 2002, when the two countries were on the brink of war over the problem of Kashmir.[122]

Box 10.5   Libyan Foreign Minister Visits Washington, Early 2008

On January 3, 2008, Libyan foreign minister Abdel-Rahman Shalqam met for an hour with US secretary of state Condoleezza Rice at her State Department offices. It was the highest-level visit to Washington by a Libyan official in thirty-five years. The State Department specified that Rice pressed him on the need for Libya—if it was to continue enjoying the benefits of US friendship—to finish compensating families of the victims in the 1988 Pam Am flight 103 bombing and the 1986 Berlin discothèque attack, and to improve its human rights performance. Rice stated that she intended to visit Libya before the end of President George W. Bush's term.

Source: New York Times, January 4, 2008, p. A9.

Foreign ministers are increasingly called upon to participate in international meetings and conferences. Meetings of foreign ministers are popular on a variety of issues, such as to harmonize foreign relations, particularly between allies, or to address a particular problem.[123] They may even be called to attend large international conferences, often to emphasize the importance attached to the proceedings.[124] The bulk of the diplomatic work will often be done by the other members of the national delegation. Some organs of international organizations are mandated by their constituent instruments or their membership to meet periodically at the ministerial level (e.g., the NATO Council and the Southeast Asia Treaty Organization [SEATO] Council). The annual meeting of the UN General Assembly attracts a large number of foreign ministers, who participate (as heads of their delegations) in some of the proceedings. The proliferation of international organizations has increased the fieldwork of foreign ministers.

A number of foreign visits have a symbolic or ceremonial purpose (see Box 10.6).[125] Foreign ministers represent their chief executives, or their nations, at certain anniversary celebrations, inaugurations, funerals, and dedications of memorials. The signing of a treaty upon the conclusion of negotiations may well have a ceremonial function (see Table 10.5). As in the case of summit meetings, such occasions may be used by foreign ministers to engage in serious diplomacy with other government officials, by advance arrangement or spontaneously as they happen to have a chance to talk in the course of the ceremony.

Included under the "other" category in Table 10.5 are foreign travel for vacation purposes (seven), and a number of talks to a variety of institutions, such as an address by Secretary Baker before the International Affairs Committee of the Supreme Soviet in Moscow (February 1990). A number of special visits are also included, such as when Secretary Rogers traveled to Sana'a in 1972 to announce the restoration of US diplomatic relations with Yemen, or

---

Box 10.6 Diplomatic Visits, Symbolism, and Related Hazards

As US secretary of state Condoleezza Rice traveled to Southeast Asia in mid-July 2005, she flew into a storm of criticism because of her decision not to attend the annual summit meeting of the Association of Southeast Asian Nations (ASEAN) in Laos later that month. She was the first US secretary of state to refuse to attend in more than twenty years. In her stead, Rice sent her deputy secretary of state.

A senior Asian diplomat reported that many people were offended by the decision, charging that it reflected on her priorities. Rice defended her decision: "We have other vital travel in roughly the same time period." She planned to visit Africa during the week before the ASEAN meeting, but was due back in Washington, D.C., a day or two before her deputy would leave, although an aide said that her plans remained fluid. She could also fly to the summit from Africa. The Malaysian foreign minister voiced his concern: "I hope it is not an indication that the United States is giving less importance or showing less interest in ASEAN while focusing on the Middle East."

Some diplomats speculated that she refused to attend because Myanmar (formerly Burma) was to preside over ASEAN for the next year. The United States is highly critical of that country's military government. Asked about this point at a press conference, she did not respond directly: "There never seems to be any progress [in Myanmar's repression of political dissidents]. I asked our Thai friends who have relations with Burma and dialogue with Burma to continue to press the cases of those who are held."

Realizing the problems her decision caused, Rice arranged for a quick visit to Phuket in Thailand, which had been devastated by a tsunami some six months earlier—a symbolic gesture. She flew there on Sunday, July 10, from China, where she was discussing the North Korean nuclear program. In Thailand she said, "I am here to show that I care about Southeast Asia." But her critics remained unhappy about her refusal to attend the Laos summit. On Monday, she took a seven-hour flight to Tokyo, the next stop on her East Asian diplomatic agenda.

Source: Joel Brinkley, "Rice, in Southeast Asia, Draws Fire for Plan to Avoid Forum," *New York Times,* July 12, 2005, p. A5.

---

when Secretary Marshall met with Pope Pius XII in 1948, which set a precedent for other secretaries (who had eleven formal audiences with the Pope in Vatican City).[126]

Foreign ministers are of course the most involved at this level of diplomacy. But globalization has expanded the ministerial level of transaction. The diplomatic agenda is now much broader. More and more activities that used to

Table 10.5   US Secretaries of State: Types of Mission Abroad, 1945–1990

Mission Type	Number of Missions
Visits with foreign leaders	613
International organization sessions	173
Traveling with the president	161
Ceremonial functions	63
International conferences	26
Stopover visits	24
Meetings with foreign ministers	21
Signing of treaties	21
Negotiations (outside preceding categories)	17
Other	47
Total	1,166

Source: Adapted from Elmer Plischke, *U.S. Department of State: A Reference History* (Westport: Greenwood, 1999), p. 413.

be exclusively domestic now have an international dimension.[127] As a result, more and more governmental departments (i.e., ministries), aside from foreign affairs ministries, are involved in foreign relations, and they often prefer to take care of their own international issues themselves rather than leave their handling to the foreign ministry. Thus, department heads communicate directly with some of their counterparts in other countries, but they also meet in ad hoc conferences pertaining to their own area of specialization (healthcare, energy, agriculture—virtually all areas of governmental activity may bring heads of departments together internationally).[128]

International organizations, particularly the UN and its large number of specialized agencies, are an important factor in bringing together heads of specialized departments from their member states on the expectation that top officials in these fields will be able to accomplish more and take more initiatives than the regular diplomats working for their foreign ministries could.[129] This objective is not always reached, as some department heads, having other things to do, may not relish the thought of spending all that time away from their desks. Thus, many end up sending their deputies or special representatives to attend these sessions—never quite the same thing as having the chief decisionmakers in the field interacting with their counterparts.

Ministerial diplomacy, for all its increasing use, is far from eclipsing the other modes of diplomacy in importance, but it does constitute an alternative— more diplomacy by nonprofessional diplomats (who, like other nonprofessional officials, learn on the job). And in any case, the international community is making increasing use of diplomatic contact at this level. As more ministries (other than foreign affairs) take part, the conduct of foreign relations becomes more complex for the states concerned (at least in open political systems and democracies). Governments face the task of maintaining consistency in the foreign relations of their various departments and need to maintain more effective communication among them.

Related to this communication issue is that of keeping resident diplomats informed of what itinerant agents and ministers are doing insofar as it may concern their posts in national capitals or international organizations. Some of the specialized ministries (e.g., the US Department of Agriculture) maintain their own agents in a number of their own nation's embassies.[130] As the diplomatic process evolves, adjustments become necessary. Some states are of course quicker to adjust than others. Each system is differently organized to meet different needs. Globally, diplomacy is thus more diversified than ever before.

▓ Study Questions and Discussion Topics

1. Why is summit diplomacy often resorted to? Is it an exercise in public relations? How much diplomacy do heads of state really engage in?

2. What is the downside of these meetings? Any particular benefits that could not be obtained by other diplomatic means?

3. What are the different kinds of summit encounters?

4. What are the diplomatic differences between meetings of heads of state and ministerial interaction?

5. Why do foreign ministers travel so much today instead of leaving the diplomacy to their diplomats? And why are other heads of executive departments (i.e., specialized ministries) holding their own diplomatic conferences?

▓ Suggested Reading

Bayne, Nicholas. *Hanging in There: The G-7 and G-8 Summits in Maturity and Renewal.* Aldershot: Ashgate, 2000.

Clift, A. Denis. *With Presidents to the Summit.* Fairfax, VA: George Mason University Press, 1993.

Dunn, David H., ed. *Diplomacy at the Highest Level: The Evolution of International Summitry.* New York: St. Martin's, 1996.

Eubank, Keith. *The Summit Conferences, 1919–1960.* Norman: University of Oklahoma Press, 1966.

Fairbanks, Charles H., Jr. *The Allure of Summits.* Washington, DC: Foreign Policy Institute, School of Advanced International Studies, Johns Hopkins University, 1988.

Hodges, Michael R., John J. Kirton, and Joseph P. Daniels, eds. *The G8's Role in the New Millennium.* Brooksfield, VT: Ashgate, 1999.

Johnston, Mary Troy. *The European Council: Gatekeeper of the European Community.* Boulder: Westview, 1994.

Telhami, Shibley. *The Camp David Accords: A Case of International Bargaining.* Pittsburgh: Pew Charitable Trust, 1992.

Weihmiller, Gordon R., and Dusko Doder. *U.S.-Soviet Summits: An Account of East-West Diplomacy at the Top, 1955–1985*. Lanham: University Press of America, 1986.

▓ Notes

1. Robert W. Cox, Harold K. Jacobson, et al., *The Anatomy of Influence: Decision Making in International Organization* (New Haven: Yale University Press, 1974).

2. Robert O. Keohane and Joseph S. Nye, *Power and Interdependence*, 2d ed. (Glenview, IL: Scott Foresman, 1989), pp. 24–37.

3. Jan Melissen, "Summit Diplomacy Coming of Age," in *Diplomacy*, edited by Christer Jönsson and Richard Langhorne (London: Sage, 2004), vol. 3, *Problems and Issues in Contemporary Diplomacy*, pp. 185–202.

4. See Elmer Plischke, "Summit Diplomacy: Diplomat in Chief," in *Modern Diplomacy: The Art and the Artisans*, edited by Elmer Plischke (Washington, DC: American Enterprise Institute for Public Policy Research, 1979), pp. 169–187; Charles H. Fairbanks Jr., *The Allure of Summits* (Washington, DC: Foreign Policy Institute, School of Advanced International Studies, Johns Hopkins University, 1988).

5. R. P. Barston, *Modern Diplomacy*, 2d ed. (New York: Longman, 1997), pp. 108–109; Elmer Plischke, *U.S. Department of State: A Reference History* (Westport: Greenwood, 1999), pp. 402–409; Erik Goldstein, "The Politics of the State Visit," in Jönsson and Langhorne, *Diplomacy*, vol. 2, pp. 362–371.

6. Quoted in David H. Dunn, "What Is Summitry?" in *Diplomacy at the Highest Level: The Evolution of International Summitry*, edited by David H. Dunn (New York: St. Martin's, 1996), p. 7, emphasis added. See also Zbigniew Brzezinski, *Power and Principle: Memoirs of the National Security Advisor, 1977–1981* (New York: Farrar, Straus and Giroux, 1983).

7. Robert E. Sherwood, *Roosevelt and Hopkins: An Intimate History*, rev. ed. (New York: Grosset and Dunlap, 1950).

8. President Bill Clinton took office in mid-January 1993. Toward the end of February, British prime minister John Major visited the White House. Two weeks later (March 9), President François Mitterrand of France arrived. Three days later (March 12), Prime Minister Yitzhak Rabin of Israel arrived, followed by the Irish prime minister, appropriately on St. Patrick's Day. And in early April, President Boris Yeltsin came over. See *New York Times*, March 9, 10, and 12, 1993. More visitors followed.

9. See *New York Times*, July 9–13, 2003, for country-by-country reports.

10. Brian Urquhart, *Hammarskjold* (New York: Norton, 1972).

11. Plischke, *U.S. Department of State*, pp. 402–409; Barston, *Modern Diplomacy*, pp. 106–109.

12. Plischke, *U.S. Department of State*, p. 407; supplemented by US Department of State, Bureau of Public Affairs, Office of the Historian, "Presidential Visits Abroad," http://www.state.gov/r/pa/ho/trvl/pres.

13. Plischke, *U.S. Department of State*, p. 407. See also Plischke, *Presidential Diplomacy: A Chronology of Summit Visits, Trips, and Meetings* (Dobbs Ferry, NY: Oceana, 1986).

14. Elmer Plischke, *Summit Diplomacy: Personal Diplomacy of the U.S. Presidents* (New York: Greenwood, 1974). '

15. As reported by Plischke in the late 1990s in *U.S. Department of State*, pp. 405–406, thus leaving out the more recent presidents.

16. Plischke, *U.S. Department of State,* pp. 405–406.

17. And, obviously, leaders do not limit their foreign travel to Washington, D.C.

18. "Road to Peace," http://www.cnn.com.

19. G. R. Berridge, "Funeral Summits," in Dunn, *Diplomacy,* pp. 106–117. See also G. R. Berridge, "Diplomacy After Death: The Rise of the Working Funeral," in Jönsson and Langhorne, *Diplomacy,* vol. 3, pp. 170–184.

20. Dunn, "What Is Summitry?" p. 7.

21. Keith Eubank, *The Summit Conferences, 1919–1960* (Norman: University of Oklahoma Press, 1966).

22. *The Middle East,* 9th ed. (Washington, DC: Congressional Quarterly, 2000), p. 119.

23. See examples in Dunn, *Diplomacy,* pp. 39–162.

24. Gordon Weihmiller and Dusko Doder, *U.S.-Soviet Summits: An Account of East-West Diplomacy at the Top, 1955–1985* (Lanham: University Press of-America, 1986).

25. G. R. Berridge, *Diplomacy: Theory and Practice,* 2d ed. (New York: Palgrave, 2002), p. 176.

26. John J. Kirton, "The Significance of the Seven Power Summit," in *The Seven Power Summit: Documents from the Summits of the Industrialized Countries, 1975–1989,* edited by Peter Hajnal II (Millwood: Kraus, 1991). See also R. Putnam and N. Bayne, *Hanging Together: Cooperation and Conflict in the Seven Power Summits,* 2d ed. (New York: Sage, 1988).

27. The European Council meets twice a year. See Mary Troy Johnston, *The European Council: Gatekeeper of the European Community* (Boulder: Westview, 1994). The Gulf Cooperation Council (GCC) summit brings together the leaders of the six Gulf states (Saudi Arabia, Kuwait, Bahrain, Qatar, the United Arab Emirates, and Oman). Its twenty-second summit meeting was held in Muscat, Oman, December 30–31, 2001. *GulfWire Digest* no. 124 (December 2–8, 2001). The Association of Southeast Asian Nations (ASEAN) summit meets formally every three years and, since 1995, informally in each intervening year. The South Asian Association for Regional Cooperation (SAARC) summit meets annually. The Commonwealth Heads of Government Meeting (CHOGM) summit convenes every two years. Berridge, *Diplomacy: Theory and Practice,* p. 175.

28. James Bennett, "Two-Edged Diplomacy," *New York Times,* March 29, 2002, pp. A1, A11.

29. Boutros Boutros-Ghali, "Challenges of Preventive Diplomacy," in *Preventive Diplomacy: Stopping Wars Before They Start,* edited by Kevin M. Cahill (New York: Basic, 1996), p. 18.

30. Berridge, *Diplomacy: Theory and Practice,* pp. 169–173; David H. Dunn, "How Useful Is Summitry?" in Dunn, *Diplomacy,* pp. 252–264.

31. Things will of course vary with the political system, the circumstances, and a variety of other factors.

32. All of them impediments in the diplomatic process. Dunn, "How Useful Is Summitry?" pp. 260–261. See Box 10.3, which details Margaret Thatcher's timetable for one of her UN visits.

33. However, see Berridge, *Diplomacy: Theory and Practice,* pp. 169–173.

34. Roosevelt was notorious in this respect, as discussed previously.

35. See Eubank, *Summit Conferences,* for example p. vii. See also George Ball's critical outlook in his book *Diplomacy for a Crowded World: An American Foreign Policy* (Boston: Little, Brown, 1976).

36. Maureen Dowd, "Presidents to Meet off Malta; Bush Asks Minimum of Fuss," *New York Times,* November 2, 1989, p. 7.

37. Dunn, "How Useful Is Summitry?" p. 253.

38. Daniel Schorr, "Beware 'Summit Syndrome,'" *New York Times,* November 5, 1985, p. 23.

39. Dunn, "How Useful Is Summitry?" pp. 254–255. Dean Rusk noted that "the direct confrontation of the chiefs of government of the great powers involves an extra tension because the court of last resort is in session." Quoted in Dunn, "How Useful Is Summitry?" p. 257.

40. See Dunn, "How Useful Is Summitry?" pp. 258–259. See also Raymond Cohen, *Negotiating Across Cultures: International Communication in an Interdependent World,* 2d ed. (Washington, DC: US Institute of Peace, 1997), Raymond Cohen, *Theater of Power: The Art of Diplomatic Signalling* (New York: Longman, 1987). See also research done by the US Institute of Peace for its series on negotiating styles: for example, Scott Snyder, *Negotiating on the Edge: North Korean Negotiating Behavior* (Washington, DC: US Institute of Peace, 1999), http://www.usip.org.

41. Dunn, "How Useful Is Summitry?" p. 255, who points out that President John F. Kennedy said as much in 1961.

42. Berridge, *Diplomacy: Theory and Practice,* pp. 173–174.

43. Barston, *Modern Diplomacy,* pp. 108–109.

44. Richard W. Stevenson, "Bush, in Africa, Promises Aid but Offers No Troops for Liberia," *New York Times,* July 9, 2003, p. A8.

45. World War II grand strategy was worked out at a number of meetings between Franklin Roosevelt, Winston Churchill, and Joseph Stalin. See, for example, Keith Eubank, *Summit at Teheran* (New York: Morrow, 1985).

46. Cold War summits were recurring efforts to defuse an exceedingly dangerous competition and foster coexistence. See Gordon Weihmiller and Dusko Doder, *U.S.-Soviet Summits: An Account of East-West Diplomacy at the Top* (Lanham: University Press of America, 1986).

47. See *New York Times,* March 27–29, 2002. See especially Neil MacFarquhar, "Acceptance of Plan Signals Progress, Though Formidable Hurdles Remain," *New York Times,* March 29, 2002, pp. A1, A10.

48. Berridge, *Diplomacy: Theory and Practice,* pp. 174–178.

49. Attendance at the 1992 Earth Summit in Rio counted 102 heads of state or government, out of a total of 178 delegations; and 117 came to the 1995 World Summit for Social Development, which 186 states attended. Attendance at the 1990 World Summit on Children in New York counted 71 presidents and prime ministers. Jacques Fomerand, "UN Conferences: Media Events or Genuine Diplomacy?" in *Multilateral Diplomacy and the United Nations Today,* edited by James P. Muldoon Jr., JoAnn Fagot Aviel, Richard Reitano, and Earl Sullivan (Boulder: Westview, 1999), p. 123.

50. This conference addressed urban development.

51. Thomas Princen, *Intermediaries in International Conflict* (Princeton: Princeton University Press, 1992), "Camp David: Jimmy Carter Mediates Between Israel and Egypt, 1977–1979," pp. 69–106, and "Portsmouth: Theodore Roosevelt Mediates Between Russia and Japan, 1904–1905," pp. 107–130.

52. Often, they do not have the expertise to address technical details. See Box 10.2.

53. Elmer Plischke, "Summit Diplomacy," in Plischke, *Modern Diplomacy,* p. 185.

54. For example, many of the World War II summits, on critical matters of grand strategy or postwar order.

55. As mandated by the constituent treaty.

56. Bill Park, "NATO Summits," in Dunn, *Diplomacy,* p. 90. The first meeting at the level of heads of state or government did not occur until 1957. The second did not take place until 1974, after which meetings were held in 1975, 1977, 1978, 1982, 1985, 1988, 1989 (twice), 1990, 1991, and 1994. Ibid., p. 91.

57. This was also the case when it was the European Community.

58. Mary Troy Johnston, *The European Council: Gatekeeper of the European Community* (Boulder: Westview, 1994). "Summitry and Legitimacy," pp. 1ff. See also Jan Werts, *The European Council* (Amsterdam: North-Holland, 1992). The European Council was eventually specified in Article 2 of the Single European Act of 1987.

59. David M. Wood and Birol A. Yeşilada, *The Emerging European Union,* 3d ed. (New York: Pearson, 2004), pp. 237–241.

60. Plischke, "Summit Diplomacy," pp. 169–187.

61. Lawrence Ziring, Robert Riggs, and Jack Plano, *The United Nations,* 3d ed. (Orlando, FL: Harcourt Brace, 2000), pp. 39, 48.

62. Or leaders who are simply hard to meet, as acknowledged by British foreign secretary Geoffrey Howe.

63. To some extent, this applies also to visits by heads of prestigious international organizations. See Urquhart, *Hammarskjold,* pp. 101–113.

64. Richard W. Stevenson, "Reporter's Notebook: In and Out of Africa, Bush Is His Usual Brisk Self," *New York Times,* July 13, 2003, p. 6.

65. Bernard Gwertzman, quoting from Bohlen's *Memoirs,* in "Keeping Track of What Is Said at the Summit," *New York Times,* October 30, 1986, p. 12.

66. Ibid.

67. Ibid.

68. Clifford Krauss, "Security Tight for G-8 Talks at Idyllic Spot in Canada," *New York Times,* June 26, 2002, p. A6.

69. See also Norman A. Graham, Richard L. Kauffman, and Michael F. Oppenheimer, *The United States and Multilateral Diplomacy: A Handbook* (New York: Oceana, 1984), pp. 51ff.; Johan Kaufmann, *Conference Diplomacy: An Introductory Analysis,* 2d ed. (Dordrecht: Nijhoff, 1988), pp. 31–56.

70. Urquhart, *Hammarskjold,* pp. 104–113. See also Chapter 8's case study in this volume.

71. Lance N. Antrim, "Dynamics of Leadership in UNCED," in *Negotiating International Regimes: Lessons Learned from the United Nations Conference on Environment and Development (UNCED),* edited by Bertram I. Spector, Gunnar Sjöstedt, and I. William Zartman (London: Graham and Trotman, 1994), pp. 149–164. Also in Spector, Sjöstedt, and Zartman, *Negotiating International Regimes,* see Tommy T. B. Koh, "UNCED Leadership: A Personal Perspective," pp. 165–170, and Pamela Chasek, "The Negotiating System of Environment and Development," pp. 21–44. See also John Lanchberry, "The Rio Earth Summit," in Dunn, *Diplomacy,* pp. 220–243.

72. Berridge, *Diplomacy: Theory and Practice,* p. 182.

73. Plischke, "Summit Diplomacy," pp. 186–187.

74. See Berridge, "Funeral Summits," pp. 106–117.

75. See J. D. Armstrong, "The Group of Seven Summits," in Dunn, *Diplomacy,* pp. 41–52. See also Putnam and Bayne, *Hanging Together;* Nicholas Bayne, "The Course of Summitry," *World Today* 48, no. 2 (February 1992), pp. 27–30.

76. A. LeRoy Bennett and James K. Oliver, *International Organizations: Principles and Issues,* 7th ed. (Upper Saddle River, NJ: Prentice-Hall, 2002), pp. 348–349.

77. The convention was opened for signature in October 1994. Lanchberry, "Rio Earth Summit," p. 239. See also Spector, Sjöstedt, and Zartman, *Negotiating International Regimes.*

78. *The Middle East,* 6th ed., pp. 49–55.

79. Plischke, "Summit Diplomacy," pp. 186–187.

80. See detailed presentation of the episode in Mark Smith, "'Oh Don't Deceive Me': The Nassau Summit," in Dunn, *Diplomacy,* pp. 182–199.

81. Graham Allison and Philip Zelikow, *Essence of Decision: Explaining the Cuban Missile Crisis,* 2d ed. (New York: Longman, 1999).

82. John Baylis, *Anglo-American Defence Relations, 1939–1980: The Special Relationship* (New York: St. Martin's, 1981), pp. 66–68. This took place at the tail end of the Eisenhower administration. It was a sale agreement without any conditions attached. Britain would have control over the missiles.

83. George W. Ball, *The Past Has Another Pattern: Memoirs* (New York: Norton, 1982), pp. 262–263. There was disagreement within the Kennedy administration as to whether or not the Skybolt project should be terminated.

84. Ball, *The Past,* p. 263. No special reason is given for calling this summit meeting in Nassau for December 1962. It does seem that, as George Ball indicated, this meeting was initially perceived as peripheral.

85. Ball, *The Past,* p. 263.

86. Ian Clark, *Nuclear Diplomacy and the Special Relationship: Britain's Deterrent and America, 1957–1962* (New York: Oxford University Press, 1994), p. 351.

87. The president did not personally try to v᎒ .n Macmillan on Skybolt problems.

88. Macmillan had made nuclear independence (i.e., Britain's own nuclear deterrent, independent from NATO's) a central element of his defense policy, and he had presented Skybolt as a symbol of its fulfillment. Richard E. Neustadt, *Alliance Politics* (New York: Columbia University Press, 1970), p. 36. Neustadt, a Harvard professor, was able (like George Ball) to provide an inside view of the Skybolt crisis. President Kennedy, after the Nassau summit, concerned about the rift with Britain, set up a high-level inquiry under Neustadt.

89. Clark, *Nuclear Diplomacy,* pp. 351–352.

90. Ball, *The Past,* p. 263.

91. Neustadt, *Alliance Politics,* pp. 47, 49, who reports that the British press grew more indignant day by day.

92. Smith, "'Oh Don't Deceive Me,'" pp. 183–187. See also Neustadt, *Alliance Politics,* pp. 46–49.

93. Skybolt in British hands could have been used at the discretion of the British government.

94. Clark, *Nuclear Diplomacy,* p. 411.

95. As presented by McGeorge Bundy. Smith, "'Oh Don't Deceive Me,'" p. 188.

96. Smith, "'Oh Don't Deceive Me,'" p. 188.

97. Ball, *The Past,* p 266. Neustadt calls the British at Nassau "a tense and angry lot," *Alliance Politics,* p. 52. Henry Brandon, of the *Sunday Times* wrote that the mood was one of "nagging exasperation and bitter indignation . . . such as I have never experienced in all the Anglo-American conferences I have covered over the past twenty years."

98. The meeting opened with a brief discussion of the Congo, India, and the Test Ban Treaty, but very quickly, the Skybolt issue took center stage. Baylis, *Anglo-American Defence,* p. 72.

99. Ball, *The Past,* p. 266.

100. In both countries, the armed services were divided over the matter.

101. Neustadt, *Alliance Politics,* p. 52.

102. Quoted in Smith, "'Oh Don't Deceive Me,'" p. 190.

103. Smith, "'Oh Don't Deceive Me,'" pp. 190–191. This was also an understated reminder that Britain had pledged access to Holy Loch when it was offered Skybolt, and the British government saw the two as related.

104. Ball, *The Past,* p. 268.

105. Neustadt, *Alliance Politics,* p. 53.

106. Clark, *Nuclear Diplomacy,* pp. 416–417; Ball, *The Past,* p. 268.

107. Neustadt, *Alliance Politics,* pp. 56ff.

108. Smith, "'Oh Don't Deceive Me,'" pp. 186, 193.

109. Clark, *Nuclear Diplomacy,* pp. 357–359. See also Baylis, *Anglo-American Defence,* pp. 71–72.

110. Clark, *Nuclear Diplomacy,* pp. 412–413.

111. Smith, "'Oh Don't Deceive Me,'" pp. 193–194.

112. Henry M. Wriston, "Ministerial Diplomacy: Secretary of State Abroad," in Plischke, *Modern Diplomacy,* pp. 153–168.

113. During his first two years as secretary of state, John Foster Dulles is reported to have met Anthony Eden, then–British foreign secretary, no less than seventeen times. Wriston, "Ministerial Diplomacy," p. 157.

114. Plischke, *U.S. Department of State,* p. 412.

115. See also Wriston, "Ministerial Diplomacy," pp. 155–158.

116. Plischke, *U.S. Department of State,* p. 418.

117. See http://www.state.gov/r/pa/ho/trvl/ls.

118. Plischke, *U.S. Department of State,* p. 418. Christopher and Albright probably covered even more territory than Baker.

119. Plischke, *U.S. Department of State,* p. 412.

120. See http://www.state.gov/r/pa/ho/trvl/ls.

121. G8 foreign ministers may have a meeting of their own prior to the summit meeting. In 2001, the G8 foreign ministers met in Rome (July 17–19); the summit meeting took place in Genoa (July 21–24). In 2002, the G8 foreign ministers met in Whistler, British Columbia, Canada (June 12–13); the economic summit took place in Kananaskis, Alberta, Canada (June 25–27). See http://www.state.gov/r/pa/ho/trvl/ls.

122. The two countries have nuclear weapons. See Celia W. Dugger, "Behind India's Brinkmanship: Ominous Preparations to Follow Through," *New York Times,* January 12, 2002, p. A6; Todd S. Purdum and Erik Eckholm, "Powell Embarks on Mission to South Asian Powder Keg," *New York Times,* January 16, 2002, p. A8.

123. See http://www.state.gov/r/pa/ho/trvl/ls.

124. For example, US secretary of state Colin L. Powell, attending the World Economic Forum, Amman, Jordan (May 15–16, 2004), or the International Conference on Afghanistan, Berlin (March 31–April 1, 2004). See http://www.state.gov/r/pa/ho/trvl/ls.

125. For example, US secretary of state Colin Powell went to Colombo and Galle, Sri Lanka, on January 7, 2005, to assess tsunami damage and relief efforts. See http://www.state.gov/r/pa/ho/trvl/ls.

126. Plischke, *U.S. Department of State,* p. 416.

127. See Keohane and Nye, *Power and Interdependence,* pp. 26–27.

128. For example, the G7 finance ministers' group was created at the Tokyo economic summit in 1986. Nicholas Bayne, *World Today* 48, no. 2 (February 1992), p. 27.

129. See, for example, discussion on the creation of the World Food Council, proposed by the 1974 World Food Conference "to meet at the ministerial level" (and established by the UN General Assembly the same year), in Edwin McC. Martin, *Conference Diplomacy: A Case Study—The World Food Conference, Rome, 1974* (Washington, DC: Institute for the Study of Diplomacy, School of Foreign Service, Georgetown University, n.d.), pp. 44–49. See also Moshe Y. Sachs, ed., *The United Nations: A Handbook on the United Nations, Its Structure, History, Purposes, Activities and Agencies* (New York: Wiley, 1977), pp. 73–74.

130. As may serve their purpose. See http://www.embassyworld.com. See also Chapter 3 and Chapter 7 in this volume.

11 Track II Diplomacy

Track II diplomacy has also been called "citizen diplomacy" and "private diplomacy." It remains ill defined; political analysts use these labels to identify very different types of activity, some of which have very little to do with diplomacy.[1] The growth of transnational relations and the emergence of a global civil society (see Chapter 5)[2] may generate a greater amount of Track II diplomacy, but it is likely to remain small when compared with the other kinds of diplomacy.[3]

In one of its forms, Track II diplomacy is essentially the intervention of private individuals in the international political process—informally, unofficially, speaking for themselves rather than for a political authority. The lines become blurred when governmental authorities respond to these private initiatives and start taking part, infusing their authority, influence, and power into the process. Occasionally, too, the original initiative behind a private person's intervention is that of a state or government official. The intervention is still informal and unofficial, but it is really a form of dissimulation, an attempt to hide the government's action (perhaps because of the controversial nature of the initiative—e.g., opening conversations with a nonrecognized political entity or an unpopular group of revolutionaries). The purposes and means of intervention can vary drastically.[4]

■ Private Individual Initiatives

Some Track II initiatives are taken by private individuals, usually of sufficient stature to be received and heard in the political circles they are trying to influence. The motivation varies with each individual: a desire to make a difference, often in the pursuit of some cause (e.g., the protection of human rights or the promotion of international peace),[5] but in some instances self-promotion, the desire to achieve visibility or material gain. In any case, human motivation is often complex and hard to identify with any certainty.

Armand Hammer has often been used as an example. A very wealthy businessman, the chairman of Occidental Petroleum Corporation, educated as a physician who never set up a medical practice but succeeded remarkably in business ventures ranging from art to bourbon whisky, Hammer was the son of a Russian-born father who was a Marxist steelworker in Connecticut. Upon graduating from Columbia University Medical School, Armand Hammer went to the Soviet Union in the wake of the revolution planning to practice medicine, but instead became involved in a number of business ventures from which he profited spectacularly, catching the attention of Lenin, who ironically helped Hammer establish himself as a businessman. Hammer eventually returned to the United States, where he became even richer, was fond of associating with prominent people, and maintained contact with the Soviet leadership for more than sixty years. He saw himself as a catalyst, bringing people together, and he endeavored to foster peace between the Soviet Union and the United States, personally approaching Soviet leaders and US presidents and making the headlines. He boasted of having been instrumental in arranging the 1985 Geneva summit between Mikhail Gorbachev and Ronald Reagan, but really seems to have been a very minor figure in US-Soviet relations.[6]

Former president Jimmy Carter provides a more extensive example of this type of diplomacy—certainly more assiduously pursued—in his attempts to wield moral authority in addressing international issues. Carter's integrity, political impartiality, and absence of posturing have contributed to his effectiveness. His international stature as former US president is of course an asset. Carter has created an organization, the Carter Center, to facilitate his international activities and humanitarian work. One might thus argue that we are talking about an NGO operation, but Carter is of course the critical element.[7]

■ Case Study: Carter's International Work

When the Reagan administration was funding the Contra guerrillas in an attempt to overthrow the Sandinista government, Carter was concerned with reconciliation among the Nicaraguan people, and between Nicaraguans and Americans. Carter first visited Nicaragua in 1986 for talks with the government and the opposition while participating in a Habitat for Humanity project that was building houses for the destitute.[8] The following year, when President Daniel Ortega visited the United States, Carter invited him to visit the Habitat project on Manhattan's Lower East Side. Following the 1989 elections in Panama (in which Carter and Gerald Ford led a team of monitors), Ortega invited Carter to monitor the next Nicaraguan elections. Carter asked him: "If the count is fair, will you accept the results?"[9] Ortega agreed. Over the next several months, Carter and associates made six trips to Nicaragua to help prepare for the elections.[10]

On election day, a random sample of precincts showed that the Sandinistas were headed for defeat. Between 11 P.M. and midnight, Carter went to Ortega to give him the bad news. Ortega could not believe it. "I can tell you from my own experience that losing is not the end of the world," Carter told him. "Your greatest accomplishment as president will be if you lead a peaceful transition of power."[11] Ortega told Carter he needed time to deal with his zealous supporters, who were preparing a victory celebration. Jimmy and Rosalyn Carter went to the headquarters of Ortega's opponent, Violetta Chamorro. They asked her not to make a triumphal victory speech, and instead delay until the morning any formal statement. She agreed. Carter also persuaded her to call for national reconciliation, provided Ortega officially conceded his loss.

Throughout the night, shuttling back and forth between campaign headquarters, the Carters negotiated and arranged for delayed release of the voting results so that the Sandinista loss would not be announced until dawn. Ortega managed to convince his followers to accept defeat and go home. At 4 A.M., Carter called US secretary of state James Baker and asked him to issue a statement later that day in which there would be no Ortega-bashing. Moreover, the statement was to call for the disbanding of the Contras. At 6:30 A.M. Ortega conceded defeat. The election results were honored. A Nicaraguan diplomat at the United Nations would later say, "Jimmy Carter saved my country from civil war."[12] Eileen Babbit pointed out Carter's power of moral suasion.[13] In Togo, in August 1993,[14] Carter left the country before the voting, announcing to the international media that there was no way a fair election could be held. The vote was cancelled. Carter has continued to be involved in election monitoring.[15] He is respected and effective. He is accepted in countries that refuse to receive official US monitors.

Carter's greatest involvement in Track II diplomacy, and what he considers the most important mission of the Carter Center, is in conflict resolution and mediation.[16] Carter has intervened in international conflicts and in civil wars, some of his missions taking a number of years to complete. Occasionally, his intervention is in response to the appeal of one of the embattled leaders, as in Somalia with General Mohammed Farah Aideed. He has brought leaders of warring parties or their representatives to the Carter Center, as in the case of the conflict between Ethiopia and Eritrea, and has often visited leaders in their capitals, holding long meetings with Hafez al-Assad in Syria, Kim Il-sung in North Korea, Kim Young-sam in South Korea, and Sali Berisha in Albania, among others.

On occasion, his contacts have received the endorsement of the US administration. Ronald Reagan used every opportunity to undercut and discredit Carter, particularly in his rapport with the president of Syria,[17] and Bill Clinton always exploded in anger when Carter tried to work with Fidel Castro.[18]

Carter's personal efforts in conflict resolution and mediation were formalized under the International Negotiation Network, which he cochaired with former UN Secretary-General Javier Perez de Cuellar. This body brought world leaders to the Carter Center on a regular basis, generating relationships that enabled Carter to play a significant role in international affairs,[19] even in very difficult and complex situations such as Liberia in 2004–2005.[20]

* * *

A substantial number of people who achieved positions of leadership and prominence have engaged in Track II diplomacy and influenced the course of international events. The mass media are a factor in developing larger-than-life images and enabling certain individuals to make an impact on the world scene. Unusual personal accomplishments are a factor in the media's special attention. People like Willy Brandt,[21] Jesse Jackson,[22] and Jody Williams[23] participated in their own ways in the international political process. Mother Teresa reached out to political leaders to help those abandoned by society.[24] The Nobel Peace Prize gave some of them an even greater measure of influence. But others, like Joseph Elder, more obscure, still achieved success in their international missions.[25]

▣ Occasional Track II Diplomacy: The Result of Special Circumstances

Citizen diplomacy in this category is fortuitous, generally the result of unusual situations. The private negotiators are not ordinarily involved in diplomacy or trying to change the course of international affairs, but they happen to see an opportunity to solve a specific problem. People affiliated with religious organizations are occasionally thrust into this role because of their concern for others (e.g., in a revolutionary situation, to save lives).[26]

An example is provided by the initiative of A. Paul Hare in mediating between the Greeks and the Turks on Cyprus between 1972 and the Turkish invasion of 1974.[27] A professor emeritus at Ben-Gurion University in the Negev, Israel, Hare had a research interest in the area of group dynamics. He was involved in the resettlement of Turkish refugees on Cyprus, working with teams of volunteers composed of people of diverse ages and backgrounds he recruited from a number of countries (England, South Africa, India, and the United States). The resettlement of Turkish refugees was a delicate issue that the UN peacekeepers had not succeeded in solving in their eight years on the island. The members of the project interacted with Greek and Turkish officials as well as UN personnel. The ups and downs of the island intercommunal talks complicated their resettlement negotiations. In January 1974, they managed to persuade officials of the Greek and Turkish sides to meet face to face with members of the project, and a UN representative, to discuss subsequent steps in resettlement. But they could not even publish a statement on the meeting, as they could not find wording acceptable to both Greeks and Turks—a delicate project indeed. As it turned out, on July 15, 1974, a coup brought a change in the Greek government, and on July 20 the Turkish army invaded the area, creating even more refugees and bringing the project to an end.[28]

▓ Case Study: Track II Diplomacy in the Oslo Mediation

Fortuitous circumstances permitted the Oslo peace process to begin. However, imagination, foresight, and initiative were needed to seize the opportunity. Governments eventually became involved, but without a Norwegian researcher's initial step and persistence, nothing would have happened. In 1992, Terje Rød Larsen, director of a Norwegian nongovernmental research organization, the Institute for Applied Social Science, was doing research in the Israeli-occupied West Bank and Gaza on Palestinian living conditions, which required a good deal of interaction with Israelis and their Palestinian counterparts and led to friendly professional contacts over an extended period of time. One of the people Larsen came to know was Yossi Beilin, a member of parliament in the opposition Labor Party and a close associate of Shimon Peres, former labor prime minister and a peace advocate. At the time, the official negotiations in Washington, D.C. (started in 1991 by President George H. W. Bush), were getting nowhere.[29]

In April 1992, in the course of a meeting in Tel Aviv, Larsen offered to put Beilin in touch with important leaders of the Palestine Liberation Organization (PLO). Beilin did not exactly leap at the opportunity. He had pressing matters to deal with, such as the national election in June. Moreover, it was a criminal offense in Israel to have direct contact with any member of the PLO, and it would have been politically damaging if word had leaked out of any such meetings. But he was interested enough to ask his friend Yair Hirschfeld, a professor at Haifa University, to stay in touch with Larsen. In June, the situation changed dramatically. The Labor Party won the election and Yossi Beilin became Israel's new deputy foreign minister. Shimon Peres became foreign minister in the Yitzhak Rabin government.[30] In mid-July, Larsen was back in Tel Aviv renewing his offer to Beilin, who asked him to work with Hirschfeld. The professor would keep him informed of developments. In Oslo, Larsen was well connected. His wife, Mona Juul, worked for the Norwegian foreign office as assistant to Jan Egeland, the state secretary (i.e., second only to the foreign minister). Interestingly, too, the author of the Norwegian research project that initially brought Larsen to Israel and the West Bank was Marianne Heiberg, the wife of Johan Jorgen Holst, the Norwegian defense minister.

By September 1992, Egeland received permission from the Norwegian government to facilitate whatever contact could be arranged between the Israeli government and the PLO leadership. On September 10, Terje Larsen returned to Tel Aviv, bringing with him State Secretary Egeland, and they sat down at the Tel Aviv Hilton with Yossi Beilin, his new counterpart in the Israeli foreign ministry, and Hirschfeld.[31] Egeland made a straightforward offer: Norway was prepared to be a bridge between Israel and the PLO, not as a mediator but as a facilitator and provider of diplomatic resources, such as secure meeting places in Norway to maintain total secrecy in any negotiations that could be arranged.[32] Beilin was interested but because of the political situation in Israel could not participate. Hirschfeld would negotiate with the PLO.[33] In December, the Israeli professor met Larsen again in a London hotel for breakfast. After a brief conversation, Larsen left the room, and in his place sat Abu Alaa, a senior PLO official and a businessman, highly educated, elegant and polished, and close to Arafat. Professor Hirschfeld was violating Israeli law in meeting with Abu Alaa—but the law was repealed a month later.[34]

On January 20, the Haifa professor and Abu Alaa met again in Norway, in a private mansion some 100 miles from Oslo. But this time, they were joined by Johan Jorgen Holst, the former Swedish defense minister, who had just become foreign minister. His role: facilitate the conversation and help where needed.[35] Professor Hirschfeld was helped by a colleague from Tel Aviv University. Abu Alaa had two expert advisers. The conversations—and there was a long series of them—were informal and very relaxed, often continuing well into the night in front of the large fireplace, and made easier by the fact that they all shared a sense of humor.[36]

To the surprise of everyone, a draft agreement was soon produced. It was time to raise the level of the negotiations. Although Beilin was kept informed of all developments thus far, the two academics were the only ones speaking for Israel. Foreign Minister Peres informed Prime Minister Yitzhak Rabin of what had taken place. He was more skeptical than Peres about what could be expected from this interaction, but he was losing patience with the official negotiations in Washington,[37] and decided to proceed with the back-channel talks in Norway. He sent Uri Savir, the director-general of the Israeli foreign ministry, as well as Joel Singer to join the two unofficial Israeli negotiators. Singer was an Israeli lawyer working in a Washington, D.C., law firm, who had the trust of Rabin (the latter was always suspicious of the peace enthusiasts who worked with Peres in the Labor Party). Abu Alaa was joined by a PLO legal adviser.

They were still a long way from having a treaty. The devil is always in the details. And there were setbacks when the whole process was in doubt.[38] Formulating an official working text for the agreement was not easy. Holst was a useful facilitator. Total secrecy was maintained. Many meetings were held in the foreign minister's home, his wife providing home-cooked meals (she quipped: "We ate a lot of lamb"). Between May and August, many difficulties had to be overcome. The Norwegian team (Foreign Minister Holst, Larsen's wife, Juul, State Secretary Egeland, and Larsen himself) traveled back and forth between Norway, Tunis,[39] and Jerusalem to reassure Arafat and Rabin, and to overcome their doubts. Egeland, Juul, and Larsen, moreover, stayed permanently by the phone to answer questions and serve as a link whenever the negotiators needed them. [40]

On August 19, 1993, Foreign Minister Shimon Peres was attending a formal dinner to honor him at the start of his official visit to Norway. Shortly after midnight, after the guests had taken their leave, the Norwegian security service escorted the Palestinian and Israeli negotiating teams through a back entrance. At 1:00 A.M., Peres joined the small group of Norwegian facilitators and witnessed the initialing of the historic document by the heads of the two negotiating groups, Abu Alaa and Uri Savir—a document that took the world by surprise when the official negotiations taking place in Washington remained ineffective.[41] A Track II initiative with back-channel conversations and Norwegian facilitation had led to a diplomatic breakthrough: the Oslo Accords. International politics can have astounding twists and turns, and unconventional approaches can produce unexpected results.[42]

▨ Private Intervention with Unofficial Governmental Sponsorship

A variant in this form of Track II diplomacy involves a governmental initiative in the participation of a private individual in some form of diplomatic process. In this case it is a matter of informal or disguised governmental intervention—for example, when a state of enmity or alienation would preclude diplomatic contact if attempted by a government agent or diplomat. A person acting in his or her own name, although at the secret invitation of a government, may be able to open channels of communications.

Another reason for this indirect approach is to avoid political embarrassment or opposition. When the overture is likely to be extremely controversial (e.g., with an unrecognized government or an outlawed revolutionary movement), a government may not want to take the risk of a first move. A Track II initiative avoids this difficulty. Government authorities can deny any involvement. In the preceding Track II category, in which an initiative is genuinely private and undertaken without government sponsorship, success is often dependent upon a government eventually capitalizing on the accomplishments of a private actor (particularly when it seems that the initial move is likely to succeed); official agents then join the negotiations.[43] In the present type of diplomatic intervention (i.e., with unofficial government sponsorship), several approaches are possible. First, a government may invite the cooperation of a person already involved in Track II diplomacy (e.g., former president Jimmy Carter; see Box 11.1).

Box 11.1　Haiti Track II Mediation, 1994–1995

In the 1990s, after President Jean-Bertrand Aristide of Haiti was overthrown in a military coup, Jimmy Carter became involved in efforts to restore constitutional government on the island. In September 1994, he was asked by Haitian general Raoul Cédras to help avoid a US military intervention. Carter relayed this information to President Bill Clinton, who asked him to undertake a mission to Haiti with Senator Sam Nunn (Democrat, Georgia) and former Joint Chiefs of Staff chairman Colin Powell. The team successfully negotiated the departure of Haiti's military leaders, paving the way for the restoration of Aristide as president.

Source: Carter Center, http://www.cartercenter.org/countries/haiti.

Second, governments may choose a person who enjoys credibility under the circumstances, such as a university professor, who may be able to approach the contesting factions by using a research project as a cover, as was done in the Dominican Republic.

■ Case Study: Track II Mediation in the Dominican Crisis

In April 1965 an attempt was made in Santo Domingo to overthrow the military junta that had toppled the constitutional government in 1963. The insurgents ("constitutionalists") had the widespread support of students and other young people in the country. In their midst and among their leaders were some communists. Within four days of the beginning of the insurrection, the US Marines landed for the official purpose of restoring order and separating the warring parties. This was perceived as an intent to protect the reactionary military rulers. A stalemate ensued.[44] It was the first US military intervention in a Latin American country in nearly forty years, and it brought a storm of protest from almost every Latin American nation and from other governments outside the hemisphere.[45]

Two mediation efforts, by the Organization of American States (OAS) and by the United States, were attempted and failed. The OAS then agreed to create a three-person ad hoc committee (Brazil, El Salvador, and the United States) to undertake a new round of negotiations and attempt to stabilize the political situation. The main negotiator was Ellsworth Bunker, an effective American mediator (see case study in Chapter 9). The ad hoc committee arrived in Santo Domingo on June 3, 1965, but the chances of success were dim.[46] In the margin of this effort, the US State Department was anxious to open communication with the young insurgents to explore the possibility of cooperation in building democratic institutions. Most of the potential youth leaders in the country were associated with the revolution. They were totally hostile to the US embassy in Santo Domingo and profoundly resented US official statements that characterized the revolution as communist. A neutral party was needed to begin some form of dialogue. The State Department asked Bryant Wedge whether he would be willing to travel to the Dominican Republic for this purpose. He was associated with the Center for Conflict Resolution at George Mason University, near Washington, D.C. He had taught psychiatry at the University of Chicago and at Yale University, and had been a frequent consultant on communication and negotiation projects of the State Department. He accepted the invitation, provided he would be able to act as a totally independent consultant. His travel would be paid by the US Agency for International Development (USAID), but he would not act as a representative of the United States.[47]

Wedge arrived in Santo Domingo on September 25, 1965, five months after the beginning of the insurrection,[48] and established himself in a hotel near the demarcation line between the contesting parties. He entered the constitutionalists' zone, and walked for several hours among the tense crowds, armed patrols of young men visible everywhere. He was dressed as a US scholar, and obviously looked totally out of place. He was going to let them make the first move. Juan Bosch, the deposed president, had just returned from exile and addressed the crowd; at some high point in the speech, Wedge joined the crowd in raising their arms in the clenched fists of the revolutionaries. Within minutes, three young men approached Wedge and asked him who he was. This was the beginning of the interaction he was seeking.[49] He explained that he was doing research on the political psychology of revolution, had come to study what was happening there, and would stay for three weeks. Of course, they did not believe him, thinking he was an agent for the Central Intelligence Agency. But he listened to their vigorous criticism of the US intervention. They wanted their point of view heard. And they proceeded to elaborate, then began a critique of Juan Bosch's speech and asked for Wedge's thoughts. He found them a thinking audience willing to reexamine their own ideas—and many more conversations took place over the next three weeks as they jointly diagnosed the sociopolitical realities of the nation.

Having established contact with the revolutionaries, he needed to dialogue with the US diplomatic mission. The embassy had consented to Wedge's intervention, but his venture was unsettling to these officials. He was formal and respectful of bureaucratic structures, showing that he understood the rigors of the foreign service. He called on the ambassador and introduced himself to every section of the embassy that was in any way concerned with youth affairs, and found that considerable stereotyping had taken place. Both groups showed considerable hostility.[50] But challenging the stereotypes would damage his credibility. The objective was to communicate in order to try to understand viewpoints rather than to challenge them. As it turned out, embassy officials were very interested in his findings about the young revolutionaries. And he could relate these findings without defending or condemning the revolutionaries.

Embassy officials and young revolutionaries understood that cooperation would be beneficial. The US mission was vitally interested in reestablishing political stability, but the leadership and active elements needed to rebuild the country would have to be drawn from the young revolutionaries and the universities (which were themselves supporting the revolutionary movement). Furthermore, the United States did not want to see the youth pushed into the arms of the communists. Conversely, the young revolutionaries wanted assistance to strengthen their country and its institutions, and the US had much to offer. But the two sides viewed each other as enemies.[51]

Bryant Wedge saw that if the opponents could work together pragmatically on some concrete project, leaving politics aside, they would slowly overcome their enmity.[52] He suggested bringing in nonpolitical experts to work with the local reformists to strengthen the university in Santo Domingo. These experts were to work as technical consultants in various academic fields (e.g., pharmacy, engineering, and university administration). They were to develop recommendations in joint consultation with their Dominican counterparts. The reformists did not reject the proposal. Washington accepted it and a competent research organization was asked to administer the project.

In May 1966, Wedge returned to the Dominican Republic with a project director and the support of USAID. Wedge and the project director offered to recruit any experts the university designated. The consultation began in July and Wedge accompanied the first three experts, some of them non-US citizens. A genuine working relationship soon developed; the university administration and students both recognized the complete seriousness of the project.[53]

The experts were eventually invited to have lunch with the US ambassador, who expressed an interest in the consultation project. After some deliberation on all sides, the rector of the university invited to his home twenty leading members of the embassy to join twenty leading members of the university administration and faculty, including members of the important Reform Commission, in honoring the expert consultant group. To the guest list were added the Mexican ambassador (one of the experts was Mexican), the papal nuncio, and two bishops, who, along with the expert consultants and Wedge, were expected to act as neutral buffers. For over fifteen months the two groups (pro-revolution university people and US embassy personnel) had been watching each other without direct contact.[54]

During the reception, much discussion took place in small groups. The next day, Wedge met with a sizable sample of the participants from each group. There was no change whatsoever in basic beliefs, nor would any participant from either side admit to having learned anything new. But the members of each group now recognized their counterparts as serious professionals who were sincere in their commitments to the development of a better society, no matter how much they might differ in social philosophy and method. They now perceived each other as people they could work with in limited ways.

Two days later, the US ambassador invited the university rector for lunch. Five days after this event, Wedge reciprocated the rector's earlier hospitality with a party. This time, however, the guest list was different: persons from the university and the US embassy who were less concerned with policy and more involved in program administration. Except for the expert consultants, no neutral buffers were present. While the dialogue was in some respects similar to what happ;ned in the first reception, with a good deal of assertiveness on both sides, the process was reduced in intensity and the focus of the discussion was quite practical: how to put the joint recommendations resulting from the consultants' visit into practice.[55]

‘ Contact had been reestablished and endured. The university administration had to proceed carefully and justify any cooperation with US programs in order to maintain good relations with the students. The US mission itself had to take great care in allocating technical assistance funds in the face of overwhelming demands from other sectors of the society. But contact and communication continued. Undoubtedly the intervention of a person without official ties with the United States was critical in the resumption of local contact between hostile camps. To be sure, this episode can only be characterized as a footnote in the larger task of restoring political stability in the Dominican Republic,[56] but it illustrates a process that can produce useful results in a variety of situations—not a substitute for the other diplomatic channels,[57] but a tool that, under some circumstances, may achieve what regular diplomatic interaction cannot.[58]

▨ NGO Initiatives

A good deal of Track II diplomacy is conducted by nongovernmental organizations (NGOs) and their agents, many of them highly professional and talented.[59] These participants are fully comparable to private individuals engaged in international negotiations. Their work is nonofficial and their initiatives are private. Given the proliferation of these organizations, much more Track II diplomacy of this kind is likely to be conducted than of the types examined previously. NGOs mobilize volunteers in support of given causes. They also generate extensive resources,[60] and more and more NGOs want to influence decisionmakers and affect the course of international negotiations.[61] To do that, a large number of NGO representatives target international organizations and conferences. A number of diplomats and international organization officials find NGO representatives to be worthwhile allies, and NGO agents become participants in at least some parts of the diplomatic process. Some state delegations to international organizations or diplomatic conferences have even included (on an ad hoc basis) NGO representatives.[62]

The pioneer in NGO diplomacy is the International Committee of the Red Cross (ICRC). Its humanitarian mission has led it to negotiate with belligerents for the protection of victims of war. It is involved in the development of new laws of war, for which it convenes diplomatic conferences. It also negotiates with the people and states that are fighting civil wars or revolutions, to induce them to observe norms of humane conduct.[63] A growing number of NGOs practice Track II mediation in a large variety of conflicts, particularly in the post–Cold War era, with the proliferation of civil and ethnic insurrections. The Quakers' American Friends Service Committee, the Mennonite Central Committee, the World Council of Churches, and other volunteer groups have undertaken mediation of conflicts where official representatives of states and international organizations did not succeed in opening a dialogue between the conflicting parties.[64]

▣ Track II Diplomacy with Problem-Solving Workshops

In the field of conflict resolution, a number of initiatives focus on seminars or workshops to bring enemies together. Under the guidance of trained practitioners (often academic conflict resolution experts) the participants learn to dialogue, and they are invited to devise a practical plan to bring their conflict to an end. The experts do not offer any suggestions. They are not mediators; they are facilitators. The members of the workshops (i.e., the parties to the conflict) must learn to interact (under the guidance of the workshop leaders) and engage in problem solving. Herbert C. Kelman, of Harvard University, has been actively engaged for a number of years in developing this method, which he calls "interactive problem solving."[65]

This is widely discussed as another form of Track II diplomacy, but it very quickly leaves the realm of diplomacy when the participants, although belonging to groups in conflict, have no contact with, no influence on, the decision-makers who are orchestrating the struggle in the field. The participants may learn reconciliation; they may discover how to transcend their enmity to engage in problem solving; they may find imaginative solutions for the ongoing conflict that others may eventually learn from;[66] but the parties to the conflict—the communities or political factions and their leaders—are not immediately touched by the interaction taking place in the workshops. As pointed out at the start of this chapter, "Track II diplomacy" as a label is frequently used very loosely. Some of these workshops, however, are a genuine diplomatic exercise in conflict resolution, when the leaders of the conflicting parties are involved in one way or another in the workshop process and when their decisions are affected by it.

■ Case Study: The Georgian-Ossetian Dialogue

In the 1990s, South Ossetia was trying to break away from the Republic of Georgia. After years of civil war, the two sides agreed to a cease-fire in 1992. South Ossetia had de facto independence but suffered from isolation and economic stagnation; tens of thousands of refugees were unable or unwilling to return to their homes. The newly independent former Soviet Republic of Georgia, on the other hand, was trying to recover from its own war of independence, and build a new nation while facing separatist movements in South Ossetia and Abkhazia.[67] Enmity between Georgia and Ossetia was profound and there was no communication between their governments.

In April 1995, Roger Fisher, founder of the Conflict Management Group (CMG), and Keith Fitzgerald, his associate, traveled to the region to meet with the Georgian and Ossetian leaderships—a private, unofficial Track II initiative, but what they offered was somewhat different.[68] It was not mediation. The CMG team suggested an informal, unofficial discussion in which a few knowledgeable and influential people from each side would generate options that might later be recommended to the leaders. CMG professionals would facilitate the discussions (which CMG called "facilitated joint brainstorming"). The participants would meet as private persons rather than as officials, which would enable them to speak more candidly. An effort would be made to develop personal relationships, enabling them to listen to one another. Any ideas developed during the interaction would be those of the participants. The facilitators would not propose terms of settlement. Confidentiality and nonattribution would be enforced. No credit could be claimed for any ideas generated, nor could blame be assigned.

Rather than focusing on the issues separating them, the participants were to consider the process by which they might deal with them. The facilitators would explain negotiation theory and guide participants to improve their ability of dealing with one another. The participants could only speak for themselves, and were not allowed to seek or make any commitments.[69] On this basis, Georgian president Eduard Shevardnadze and South Ossetian leader Ludwig Chibirov asked the CMG to proceed with the project. The Norwegian foreign ministry agreed to provide the funding for the venture (the CMG had earlier conducted a seminar on international mediation for these Norwegian officials, which apparently motivated the Norwegian government to help with the South Ossetia project).

The CMG also formed a partnership with the Norwegian Refugee Council's regional office for the Transcaucasus (an NGO) in Tbilisi, the capital of Georgia, and with members of the Norwegian Red Cross. This allowed the project team to maintain a permanent presence in the region, an important element because of the logistical difficulties in the Caucasus and the near-total isolation of Tskhinvali, the capital of South Ossetia. It was decided that the first brainstorming session would address practical problems, such as repairing roads and railways and restoring telecommunications, without reference to the issue of South Ossetia's constitutional status.[70] This is remarkably reminiscent of the way Bryant Wedge interested the young revolutionaries in the Dominican Republic in cooperating to strengthen the university—a practical endeavor that bypasses ideological considerations (see previous case study).

The first facilitated joint brainstorming session took place in Norway in January 1996, and was seen as a breakthrough by the participants and the leaders on both sides. The influential people who participated conceived a number of joint projects and ideas for moving forward. At the end of the session, the participants requested a follow-up meeting expressly to address the difficult issue of South Ossetia's constitutional status. This took place in May 1996, also in Norway, and again facilitated by the CMG and the Norwegian Red Cross. The participants generated many ideas concerning constitutional issues, such as the division of executive, legislative, and judicial powers, human rights politics, border and security arrangements, and many other highly sensitive issues. They also designed a possible framework for an official bilateral negotiation process and expressed the desire that their respective leaders meet for the first time.

A year later, a meeting between Shevardnadze and Chibirov took place and an official Georgian-Ossetian negotiation process was established. Some project activity also took place, but a number of political events in the region (Russian presidential elections, the war in Chechnya, the meeting between Shevardnadze and Chibirov, and the establishment of the official negotiation process) delayed the next facilitated joint brainstorming session until June 1997. This new session was funded by the US Institute of Peace and the Norwegian foreign ministry, and was focused on possibilities for economic cooperation, refugees and their repatriation, what people on each side could do to increase public confidence in a process of reconciliation, and the possibility of a political settlement of the status question.[71]

Ultimately, the main accomplishment of this effort was that the unofficial, informal interaction helped to establish an official bilateral process where it did not exist. And it helped to prepare key individuals to take part in the negotiations (as many of the participants in the informal process became participants in the official negotiations). A serious challenge was not having the needed human and financial resources to bring the parties together more frequently, as was the desire expressed by virtually all the participants. And there was a limitation inherent in the procedure: the joint brainstorming process generated new ideas, but decisions had to be left to those with official authority. This is what makes the brainstorming possible.[72]

However, the parties in conflict must reckon with those who, on both sides, benefit politically and financially from chaos and conflict (e.g., smuggling operations and other organized criminal enterprises), who sometimes attempt to frustrate normalization efforts through intimidation or political manipulations. The political status of the breakaway province of South Ossetia remains unsolved. About 300,000 people displaced by the conflict have yet to return home.[73] At the same time, other regional actors, particularly the Russian Federation and the Organization for Security and Cooperation in Europe (OSCE), found themselves engaged in official efforts to settle the conflict. The NGO team—the CMG and the Norwegian Red Cross—maintained a good working relationship with the OSCE mission in Georgia, and the participants routinely informed official representatives about the usefulness of the work done at the unofficial level. In addition, the NGO team received valuable assistance from the Norwegian foreign ministry, the Norwegian embassy in Moscow, as well as the US embassy in Tbilisi and the State Department in Washington, D.C. The NGO effort was never isolated from the official channels. Indeed, the team remained in contact with senior Georgian and Ossetian officials in an unofficial, informal capacity.[74]

*   *   *

Many other groups have created similar interactive problem-solving workshops in connection with a variety of conflicts, although some of them have resulted in negative outcomes. The Community of Sant'Egidio, an independent Catholic lay organization headquartered in Italy, and increasingly involved in international peacemaking, brought together in 1994–1995 leaders of political groups and parties involved in Algeria's civil war. After two colloquia, a declaration of principles for the settlement of the crisis was signed by leaders representing parties that received more than 80 percent of the vote in the 1991 elections and began their civil war in the wake of the military coup. But the Algerian government rejected this document from the outset as interference in Algeria's internal affairs and an attempt to manipulate the Algerian political debate. The Sant'Egidio leadership received death threats from Algerian sources and had to solicit police protection from the Italian government.[75]

An increase in transnational relations facilitated by spectacular advances in communication technologies is likely to foster greater private involvement in diplomacy, particularly under the sponsorship of NGOs. The magnitude of these efforts will remain small when compared with the official diplomatic process of states and international organizations. But past experience indicates that private initiatives have accomplished important diplomatic results. Global civil society is an expanding reality. The private sector will not be deterred by the power of national states—if anything, that very power, and the glaring mistakes made by these actors (or their lack of concern for the global common good), will energize more individuals and their NGOs to become involved and attempt to change the course of events. And private, unofficial initiatives may permit some degree of interaction that is not possible at the official level.[76]

▓ Study Questions and Discussion Topics

1. What is Track II diplomacy? How many varieties are there? Do they really involve diplomacy?
2. Is Track II diplomacy truly useful or merely peripheral? How does it affect the normal diplomatic process?
3. What factors may give Track II diplomacy a measure of effectiveness?
4. How is Track II mediation initiated? Are we likely to see more of it?
5. What circumstances invite resort to Track II diplomacy?

▓ Suggested Reading

Berman, Maureen R., and Joseph E. Johnson, eds. *Unofficial Diplomats.* New York: Columbia University Press, 1977.

Brinkley, Douglas. *The Unfinished Presidency: Jimmy Carter's Journey Beyond the White House.* New York: Viking, 1998.

Cooper, Andrew F., and Brian Hocking. "Governments, Non-Governmental Organizations, and the Re-calibration of Diplomacy." In *Diplomacy,* vol. 3, edited by Christer Jönsson and Richard Langhorne. London: Sage, 2004.

Corbin, Jane. *Gaza First: The Secret Norway Channel to Peace Between Israel and the PLO.* London: Bloomsbury, 1994.

Davies, John, and Edward Kaufman, eds. *Second Track/Citizen's Diplomacy: Concepts and Techniques for Conflict Transformation.* New York: Rowman and Littlefield, 2002.

Edwards, Michael, and John Gaventa, eds. *Global Citizen Action.* Boulder: Lynne Rienner, 2001.

Forsythe, David P. "Humanitarian Mediation by the International Committee of the Red Cross." In *International Mediation in Theory and Practice,* edited by Saadia Touval and I. William Zartman. Boulder: Westview, 1985.

Fox, Annette Baker, Alfred O. Hero Jr., and Joseph S. Nye Jr., eds. *Canada and the United States: Transnational and Transgovernmental Relations.* New York: Columbia University Press, 1976.

Hare, A. Paul. "Informal Mediation by Private Individuals." In *Mediation in International Relations: Multiple Approaches to Conflict Management,* edited by Jacob Bercovitch and Jeffrey Z. Rubin. New York: St. Martin's, 1992.

Kelman, Herbert C. "Informal Mediation by the Scholar/Practitioner." In *Mediation in International Relations: Multiple Approaches to Conflict Management,* edited by Jacob Bercovitch and Jeffrey Z. Rubin. New York: St. Martin's, 1992.

McDonald, John W., Jr., and Diana B. Bendahmane, eds. *Conflict Resolution: Track-Two Diplomacy.* Washington, DC: US Department of State, Foreign Service Institute, Center for the Study of Foreign Affairs, 1987.

Rees, Elfan. "Exercises in Private Diplomacy: Selected Activities of the Commission of the Churches on International Affairs." In *Unofficial Diplomats,* edited by Maureen R. Berman and Joseph E. Johnson. New York: Columbia University Press, 1977, pp. 111–129.

Saunders, Harold H. *Politics Is About Relationship: A Blueprint for the Citizens' Century.* New York: Palgrave Macmillan, 2005.

Warner, Gale, and Michael Shuman. *Citizen Diplomats: Pathfinders in Soviet-American Relations and How You Can Join Them.* New York: Continuum, 1987.

▨ Notes

1. See John W. McDonald Jr. and Diane B. Bendahmane, eds., *Conflict Resolution: Track Two Diplomacy* (Washington, DC: US Department of State, Foreign Service Institute, Center for the Study of Foreign Affairs, 1987). See also Louise Diamond and John McDonald, *Multi-Track Diplomacy: A Systems Approach to Peace,* 3d ed. (West Hartford, CT: Kumerian, 1996).

2. See also Ann M. Florini, ed., *The Third Force: The Rise of Transnational Civil Society* (Washington, DC: Carnegie Endowment for International Peace, 2000); Michael Edwards and John Gaventa, eds., *Global Citizen Action* (Boulder: Lynne Rienner, 2001).

3. John Davies and Edy Kaufman point out: "Second track diplomacy is not an alternative but a complementary system that takes advantage of resources and opportunities unavailable at the official level." "Second Track/Citizens' Diplomacy: An Overview," in *Second Track/Citizens' Diplomacy: Concepts and Techniques for Conflict Transformation,* edited by John Davies and Edward (Edy) Kaufman (New York: Rowman and Littlefield, 2002), p. 5. See also John W. McDonald, "The Need for Multi-Track Diplomacy," in Davies and Kaufman, *Second Track/Citizens' Diplomacy,* pp. 49–60.

4. Maureen R. Berman and Joseph E. Johnson, eds., *Unofficial Diplomats* (New York: Columbia University Press, 1977).

5. See studies in Davies and Kaufman, *Second Track/Citizens' Diplomacy.*

6. Eric Pace, "Armand Hammer Dies at 92; Industrialist and Philanthropist Forged Soviet Links," *New York Times,* December 12, 1990, p. A14. See also Steve Weinberg, *Armand Hammer: The Untold Story* (Boston: Little, Brown, 1989). Hammer elicited some very negative appraisals. Anthony Sampson, in his review of Carl Blumay's *The Dark Side of Power: The Real Armand Hammer* (New York: Simon and Schuster, 1992), stated, "But behind the glory, he was a bleak and isolated buccaneer who was apparently only really interested in fame and profit." "Agent of Influence," *New York Times,* December 12, 1992, p. 23; Gale Warner and Michael Shuman, *Citizen Diplomats: Pathfinders in Soviet-American Relations and How You Can Join Them* (New York: Continuum, 1987).

7. The Carter Center was officially opened on October 1, 1986, but had been actually functioning for a number of years. Its first conference on the topic of the Middle East had been held in November 1983. See Peter G. Bourne, *Jimmy Carter: A Comprehensive Biography from Plains to Postpresidency* (New York: Scribner, 1997), pp. 482–486. Carter enlisted the support of twelve political leaders—current or former chief executives—and established a very successful group of "freely elected heads of government" to promote democracy through the independent monitoring of elections.

8. A project, continuing today, in which volunteers build homes for the impoverished in many countries, including the United States. The Carters became increasingly involved in this organization after they left Washington, D.C. Bourne, *Jimmy Carter,* pp. 482–484, 493–495.

9. Bourne, *Jimmy Carter,* p. 494.

10. See Douglas Brinkley, *The Unfinished Presidency: Jimmy Carter's Journey Beyond the White House* (New York: Viking, 1998), pp. 296–305.

11. Bourne, *Jimmy Carter*, p. 494.

12. This episode is reported in Bourne, *Jimmy Carter*, pp. 493–494, and also in Brinkley, *Unfinished Presidency*, pp. 305–308.

13. Eileen F. Babbitt, "Jimmy Carter: The Power of Moral Suasion in International Mediation," in *When Talk Works: Profiles of Mediators*, edited by Deborah M. Kolb et al. (San Francisco: Jossey-Bass, 1994), pp. 375–393.

14. Brinkley, *Unfinished Presidency*, p. 375.

15. The Carter Center sent election monitoring teams to Haiti (1987, 1990), the Dominican Republic (1990), Surinam (1991), Guyana (1990–1992), Zambia (1993), Paraguay (1993), Mexico (1992–1994), and Palestine (1996). Bourne, *Jimmy Carter*, p. 494.

16. Babbitt, "Jimmy Carter," pp. 374–393.

17. Bourne, *Jimmy Carter*, pp. 491–492, 496–497, 500–505.

18. He even sent Al Gore to get Carter to stop meddling in Cuban policy. Brinkley, *Unfinished Presidency*, p. 457.

19. Bourne, *Jimmy Carter*, p. 500. See also Babbitt, "Jimmy Carter," pp. 380–381.

20. The African Governance Program is another division of the Carter Center. Bourne, *Jimmy Carter*, pp. 490–491. See http://www.cartercenter.org/countries/liberia.

21. Former German chancellor and a voice for reconciliation and peaceful change. See Willy Brandt, *My Life in Politics* (New York: Viking, 1992), esp. chap. 6, pp. 340–415.

22. Karin L. Stanford, *Beyond the Boundaries: Rev. Jesse Jackson in International Affairs* (Albany: State University of New York Press, 1997).

23. Architect of the movement to ban landmines and the treaty embodying this effort (see Chapter 5).

24. See Anne Sebba, *Mother Teresa: Beyond the Image* (New York: Doubleday, 1997), "Politics," pp. 210–241.

25. Joseph Elder, a Quaker, was engaged in mediation work. See Thomas Princen, "Joseph Elder: Quiet Peacemaking in a Civil War," in Kolb et al., *When Talk Works*, pp. 427–458; Princen discusses his work with the Tamils and the Sri Lankan government.

26. See C. H. "Mike" Yarrow, "Quaker Efforts Toward Reconciliation in the India-Pakistan War of 1965," in Berman and Johnson, *Unofficial Diplomats*, pp. 89–110. See also Elfan Rees, "Exercises in Private Diplomacy: Selected Activities of the Commission of the Churches on International Affairs," in Berman and Johnson, *Unofficial Diplomats*, pp. 111–129. See also the section on NGO initiatives in this chapter.

27. A. Paul Hare, "Informal Mediation by Private Individuals," in *Mediation in International Relations: Multiple Approaches to Conflict Management*, edited by Jacob Bercovitch and Jeffrey Z. Rubin (New York: St. Martin's, 1992), pp. 52–63.

28. Ibid., pp. 59–60.

29. Three accounts provide details on this unusual diplomatic episode: Clyde Haberman, "How the Oslo Connection Led to the Mideast Pact," *New York Times*, September 5, 1993, pp. 1, 6 (remarkably put together by means of interview for publication on Sunday, before the final signing ceremonies); Jane Corbin, *Gaza First: The Secret Norway Channel to Peace Between Israel and the PLO* (London: Bloomsbury, 1994); and Jan Egeland, "The Oslo Accord: Multiparty Facilitation Through the Norwegian Channel," in *Herding Cats: Multiparty Mediation in a Complex World*, edited by Chester A. Crocker, Fen Osler Hampson, and Pamela Aall (Washington, DC: US Institute of Peace, 1999), pp. 529–546 (Jan Egeland was second only to the Norwegian foreign minister, and intimately associated with the facilitation of the negotiations). See also Karin Aggestam, "Two-Track Diplomacy: Negotiations Between Israel and the PLO Through Open and Secret Channels," in *Diplomacy*, edited by Christer Jönsson

and Richard Langhorne (London: Sage, 2004), vol. 3, *Problems and Issues in Contemporary Diplomacy,* pp. 203–227.

30. Ian J. Bickerton and Carla L. Klausner, *A Concise History of the Arab-Israeli Conflict,* 4th ed. (Upper Saddle River, NJ: Prentice-Hall, 2002), p. 255.

31. Haberman, "How the Oslo Connection Led to the Mideast Pact," p. 8; Corbin, *Gaza First,* pp. 23–24.

32. Functions well-known as "good offices." However, in diplomatic practice, providing good offices often evolves into greater involvement in the negotiation process, a form of mediation.

33. Haberman, "Oslo Connection," p. 8.

34. Corbin, *Gaza First,* pp. 29ff.

35. This is where Norway offered more than good offices.

36. Haberman, "Oslo Connection," p. 8.

37. Bickerton and Klausner, *Concise History,* pp. 253–262.

38. Egeland, "Oslo Accord," pp. 535–537.

39. Arafat ran the PLO from Tunis.

40. Haberman, "Oslo Connection," p. 8. See also Egeland, "Oslo Accord," pp. 537–538.

41. Haberman, "Oslo Connection," p. 8.

42. See Aggestam, "Two-Track Diplomacy," pp. 221–222. See also Egeland's own perception of the advantages of the Oslo back channel: Egeland, "Oslo Accord," pp. 538–539.

43. See example in Jesse Jackson's negotiations in Syria in 1983–1984, in Stanford. *Beyond the Boundaries,* pp. 94–106.

44. Abraham F. Lowenthal, *The Dominican Intervention* (Cambridge: Harvard University Press, 1972). See also Piero Gleijeses, *The Dominican Crisis: The 1965 Constitutionalist Revolt and American Intervention* (Baltimore: Johns Hopkins University Press, 1978).

45. Bryant Wedge, "Mediating Intergroup Conflict in the Dominican Republic," in McDonald and Bendahmane, *Conflict Resolution,* pp. 35, 38–40.

46. Audrey Bracey, *Resolution of the Dominican Crisis, 1965: A Study in Mediation* (Washington, DC: Institute for the Study of Diplomacy, School of Foreign Service, Georgetown University, 1980), pp. v–xviii, 1–29.

47. Wedge, "Mediating Intergroup Conflict," pp. 35–37.

48. On the political climate in Santo Domingo at the time, see Gleijeses, *Dominican Crisis,* pp. 262–281.

49. Wedge, "Mediating Intergroup Conflict," pp. 40–41.

50. On the tensions found in the Dominican Republic, see José A. Moreno, *Barrios in Arms: Revolution in Santo Domingo* (Pittsburgh: University of Pittsburgh Press, 1970), esp. pp. 98–113.

51. Lowenthal, *Dominican Intervention,* pp. 132ff.

52. Also, some progress was being made in stabilizing the political situation and the installation of a provisional president (Hector Garcia Godoy). See Bracey, *Resolution of the Dominican Crisis,* pp. 31ff. See also discussion of problems that remained unsolved, in Gleijeses, *Dominican Crisis,* pp. 277–281.

53. Wedge, "Mediating Intergroup Conflict," pp. 46–48.

54. Suspicion would of course endure for a long time. To make progress in such a situation, proceeding slowly and cautiously was indispensable. See Wedge, "Mediating Intergroup Conflict," pp. 46–50.

55. Wedge, "Mediating Intergroup Conflict," pp. 48–49.

56. See Bracey, *Resolution of the Dominican Crisis,* pp. 31–41.

57. Other diplomatic efforts to resolve the Dominican crisis are discussed in Bracey, *Resolution of the Dominican Crisis.*

58. See Landrum Bolling, "Strengths and Weaknesses of Track Two: A Personal Account," in McDonald and Bendahmane, *Conflict Resolution,* pp. 53–64.

59. Andrew F. Cooper and Brian Hocking, "Governments, Non-Governmental Organizations, and the Re-calibration of Diplomacy," in Jönsson and Langhorne, *Diplomacy,* pp. 79–95. See also Chapter 5.

60. Their skill in using the new communication technologies has made some of them very powerful.

61. Some NGOs have been particularly successful at building effective coalitions. See Lloyd Axworthy, "Toward a New Multilateralism," in *To Walk Without Fear: The Global Movement to Ban Landmines,* edited by M. Cameron et al. (New York: Oxford University Press, 1998); Lloyd Axworthy, "Lessons from the Ottawa Process," *Canadian Foreign Policy* 5, no. 3 (1998), pp. 1–2.

62. Former Canadian foreign minister Lloyd Axworthy points out that the Canadian government negotiating team at the 1996 Geneva landmine meeting included Valerie Warmington, chair of the Canadian campaign to ban landmines. Matthew J. O. Scott, a member of the Canadian Steering Committee of Mines Action, also accompanied the Canadian government delegation to Sydney, Australia, in July 1997, for a regional meeting of states interested in the same question. Matthew J. O. Scott, "Danger—Landmines! NGO-Government Collaboration in the Ottawa Process," in Edwards and Gaventa, *Global Citizen Action,* p. 133, n. 11. As one commentator in the journal of the Canadian professional association of foreign service officers observed in 1998: "Diplomats will have to work constructively with non-traditional partners. . . . There is much that we need to learn about the new issues; but there are also some specialized skills and knowledge that we have that the special interest groups need." Ibid., p. 125.

63. David P. Forsythe, "Humanitarian Mediation by the International Committee of the Red Cross," in *International Mediation in Theory and Practice,* edited by Saadia Touval and I. William Zartman (Boulder: Westview, 1985), pp. 233–249. See also Jacques Freymond, "The International Committee of the Red Cross," in Berman and Johnson, *Unofficial Diplomats,* pp. 142–151.

64. "Kosovo May Need Track-Two Negotiations," *Peace Watch* 4, no. 5 (August 1998), pp. 1–2.

65. See Herbert C. Kelman, "Informal Mediation by the Scholar/Practitioner," in Bercovitch and Rubin, *Mediation in International Relations,* pp. 64–96. Kelman cautions, however, that use of the term "mediation" in this connection is inaccurate, as the scholar-practitioner is only a facilitator. The line between facilitation and some forms of mediation can be thin.

66. These people-to-people unofficial contacts have been called "Track II diplomacy" by Joseph V. Montville, a foreign service officer in the US Department of State. Gale Warner and Michael Shuman, *Citizen Diplomats: Pathfinders in Soviet-American Relations and How You Can Join Them* (New York: Continuum, 1987), p. 5. The off-the-record Dartmouth conferences brought together influential Soviet and American citizens. Ibid., p. 6.

67. See Bruno Coppieters, ed., *Contested Borders in the Caucasus* (Brussels: Vub Press, 1996).

68. See Keith Fitzgerald's own account, "Georgian-Ossetian Joint Brainstorming," from which this summary is drawn, in *Private Peacemaking: USIP-Assisted Peacemaking Projects of Nonprofit Organizations,* edited by David Smock (Washington, DC: US Institute of Peace, 1998), pp. 6–9.

69. See Herbert C. Kelman, "The Interactive Problem-Solving Approach," in *Managing Global Chaos: Sources of, and Responses to, International Conflict,* edited by Chester A. Crocker and Fen Osler Hampson, with Pamela Aall (Washington, DC: US Institute of Peace, 1996), pp. 501–519.

70. Fitzgerald, "Georgian-Ossetian Joint Brainstorming," p. 7.

71. Ibid., p. 8.

72. See Pat K. Chew, ed., *The Conflict and Culture Reader* (New York: New York University Press, 2004); Nigel Biggar, ed., *Burying the Past: Making Peace and Doing Justice After Civil Conflict* (Washington, DC: Georgetown University Press, 2003). See also Roland Paris, *At War's End: Building Peace After Civil Conflict* (New York: Cambridge University Press, 2004); Stella Ting-Toomey and John G. Oetzel, *Managing Intercultural Conflict Effectively* (Thousand Oaks, CA: Sage, 2001).

73. US Department of State, "Background Notes on Countries of the World: Georgia," http://www.state.gov/r/pa/ei/bgn/5253.

74. Fitzgerald, "Georgian-Ossetian Joint Brainstorming," pp. 8–9.

75. Marco Impagliazzo, "The St. Egidio Platform for a Peaceful Solution of the Algerian Crisis," in Smock, *Private Peacemaking,* pp. 10–12.

76. Harold H. Saunders, *Politics Is About Relationship: A Blueprint for the Citizens' Century* (New York: Palgrave Macmillan, 2005).

PART 3

Conclusion

12 The Future of Diplomacy

The tempo of international relations will increase—spectacularly, no doubt—propelled by technology and interdependence. Technology provides the means for extensive international activity; interdependence makes interconnection inevitable. This can of course be a formula for confrontation and conflict. Diplomacy provides an alternative. It can help very different societies build bridges and work together. Some political leaders and their ruling elites, however, are impatient. They are ambitious and want more than diplomacy can provide. Violence seems to produce faster results. Others are angry and reject diplomatic dialogue. Still more are guided by ideology and self-righteousness. In their limited universe (all black and white, with no shades of gray), one does not negotiate with detractors, often perceived as evil—witness President George W. Bush's mention of the "Axis of Evil" in his State of the Union Address on January 29, 2002, referring to Iraq, Iran, and North Korea, to which John Bolton, undersecretary of state at that time, added Libya, Syria, and Cuba in a speech on May 6, 2002.[1]

Under these conditions, diplomacy does not fare well. Another limitation is found in incompetent governance—not really rejecting diplomacy, but unequal to the task, disorganized, failing to bring professional talent to the international dialogue, or unable to recognize diplomatic opportunity. Outstanding examples are found in French, British, and US diplomacy of the 1930s. But the twenty-first century provides an ample number of cases as well, with Myanmar under its military junta, Afghanistan with the Taliban, Sudan under Omar al-Bashir, and many more.[2] Despite all these impediments, an increasing amount of diplomacy is helping international society. Diplomacy has remarkably adjusted to its changing global environment and promises to continue adapting. New ways of interacting will be tried, some of them radically different.[3] This is already happening to meet the special needs of the European Union.[4] Imagination, leadership, circumstances, and the pressure of necessity, as usual, will play a role in diplomatic evolution. Interestingly, some of the novel practices eventually become accepted as new dimensions of diplomacy, such as public relations ("public diplomacy"), now seen as an indispensable part of foreign service work. But well-established diplomatic forms, rooted in the practice of earlier centuries, will endure.[5] Diplomacy will remain a blend of novelty and continuity. Even in the new modes, such as international organization diplomacy, many of the classic forms of diplomatic behavior retain their relevance.[6] Tradition and inertia keep many procedures in use, even when some updating would be desirable.[7]

Diversity among international actors is likely to become more pronounced, challenging established diplomatic methods. Given current unrest in so many parts of the world, new political systems will inevitably come into existence. In a clash of civilizations, common norms of diplomatic dialogue are harder to maintain.[8] However, the past half century permits a degree of optimism. The number of independent states more than doubled,[9] bringing to the table people with no diplomatic experience, some of them anxious to reject current diplomatic norms. Bitter clashes took place—witness UN General Assembly meetings. But in the end, the diplomatic framework endured, with some adjustments.[10] Decorum was an early casualty, but new rules of protocol were drafted. And with the participants intent on continuing their dialogue (if frequently angry), more issues could be negotiated between larger and larger numbers of participants. A new diplomatic culture is emerging, just as it did in earlier centuries, even though the challenge may be greater today. The process of acculturation will continue, and with it, easier relationships will result.

The creation of a large number of international organizations led to profound changes in diplomatic method, made necessary by the multilateral nature of the work as well as the fact that these organizations became international actors. Remarkably, the new practices were taken in stride. The participation of international agencies in the diplomatic process was not challenged.[11] A substantial number of international organization officials (secretaries-general, their representatives, heads of agencies, and some members of international secretariats) became accepted as a matter of course as a new category of diplomats entitled to diplomatic immunities, although belonging to none of the foreign services of member states (they are international civil servants). They negotiate in the name of their organizations and serve in a variety of diplomatic functions, such as special envoys, agents in the creation of development programs, or mediators in international disputes.

The process of *adaptation and innovation* will continue as international relations evolve. The most dramatic example is currently provided by the European Union, a diplomatic system facilitating the integration of its twenty-seven members and the advent of supranational institutions, long believed impossible in modern international affairs. Wherever this may lead, the procedural innovation is remarkable[12]—a clear demonstration of the versatility of diplomacy when international actors are willing to go beyond established boundaries.

Interdependence is fostering international integration—witness the multiplicity of economic unions and common markets.[13] Integration is likely to permit—require—new diplomatic procedures, some borrowed from existing unions, others crafted for the special needs of the region. The general practice of diplomacy is likely to be affected by such regional developments. Procedures seen to be effective among specific associations of states may eventually be tried elsewhere. The creation of regional structures is also inviting new relationships.[14] Outside states (i.e., states that are not members of these arrangements) have shown keen interest in developments (political, economic, etc.) taking place within the regional structures. Some of them now send diplomatic representatives, accredited to specific organizations, to maintain contact, perhaps reminiscent of the observers formally accepted by other organizations such as the UN. The exact nature of the relationship is defined by the organization concerned. The counterpart of this function is now established: the European Union sends diplomatic representatives of its own to the capitals of non-EU members. Thus new links are in the process of development—a novelty, but taken in stride.

The vast *expansion of transnational relations* is opening up new forms of interaction that, in many respects, remain uncharted—but no less real. Some governments are still uncomfortable with most transnational agents. Many are reluctant to accept them in the diplomatic process and resent what they perceive as unwarranted interference. But international civil society is becoming more important (see Chapters 3, 5, and 11). Transnational movements are often a manifestation of a grassroots conviction that their concerns are not being heard by the public authorities and a distrust of those in power. The communication revolution has increased the influence of nongovernmental organizations (NGOs). There are more of them; many are well organized and intent on making a difference in some areas of the international agenda such as humanitarian and social justice causes. Large-scale networking and use of the media to mobilize public opinion make it difficult to ignore them. With increasing frequency, NGOs force states to address neglected problems, such as genocide in Darfur.[15]

International organizations and international conferences have given NGOs greater opportunity to be heard.[16] Some governments—still a small minority—have included them in their policymaking process, even placing some of their representatives on their diplomatic delegations (see Chapter 5).[17] The boards of directors of some international organizations (e.g., the World Bank) invite NGO representatives to participate in their decisionmaking.[18] Undoubtedly, the impact of civil society on the diplomatic process will remain limited when compared with the role of nation-states and intergovernmental organizations, but their influence will grow.[19]

Multinational corporations (MNCs) are a very different segment of civil society. They, too, are undergoing massive growth. They are a power to reckon with (see Chapter 5).[20] Diplomacy is one of the tools they are using to protect their narrow economic interests—although there is reluctance to call it diplomacy. On the other hand, many MNCs are perceived as a threat by the less-developed nations, and they are condemned by the many critics of capitalism. The UN is trying to persuade these corporations to be more socially responsible by means of self-regulation. Their political and diplomatic skills, combined with their economic power and huge resources, have contributed to their success in escaping international control.[21] Very diplomatically, they profess to support the UN's conciliatory approach. It will probably take some monumental corporate scandal to achieve effective regulation and international accountability. In the meantime, they will continue to wield enormous power[22] and use it in their negotiations with other international actors.

Revolutionary movements and terrorist organizations have become permanent fixtures in the international system. They operate transnationally. Given widespread ethnic, nationalist, and sectarian unrest around the world, civil conflict will undoubtedly spread. The leaderships of revolutionary groups usually seek support from other revolutionary movements and from friendly governments, building networks. All of this implies resort to a good deal of diplomacy and negotiation, even as violence spreads.[23] Some movements even maintain permanent diplomatic representation abroad, where feasible. Yassir Arafat was among the most successful in this respect. A number of international organizations provide some form of official status to the more established revolutionary groups, thus facilitating their diplomatic work. Friendly governments go so far as to give full diplomatic status to their protégés. None of this will change in the future, although the revolutionary groups will come and go. The diplomatic process will thus grow even more complex, even more diverse and challenging: indeed, some revolutionary groups make difficult negotiation partners—witness the long-drawn-out process in Somalia or in Sudan. This will test the patience and pragmatism of the diplomatic profession.

Diversity will also increase in the subject matter of *the diplomatic agenda.* More issues, once exclusively domestic, will have international ramifications and will require diplomatic attention. This trend is very visible today.[24] The distinction between domestic and international issues will become even more blurred. Interdependence and globalization are significant factors in this phenomenon. Economic integration in some regions will require the harmonization of legal systems, as is the case on a continuing basis in the European Union, and even more diplomatic negotiations will be needed to make it happen. More diplomats will thus have to address issues that used to be the exclusive concern of the domestic order, such as healthcare, education, and unemployment. Good generalists can undoubtedly negotiate a great many of these issues. Some problems, however, reach a level of technical specificity, as in the spread of disease, that requires expert knowledge not usually available in the foreign service.

International organizations, particularly the UN's specialized agencies, have accelerated this trend by placing more technical issues on their agenda,[25] to be discussed or negotiated by the diplomatic representation of their member states and organization officials. International conferences, organized in increasing numbers, do the same.[26] Inevitably, national delegations need to include non–foreign service experts.[27] In some cases, delegations are almost entirely composed of specialized, non–foreign service officials[28]—another sign of change in the diplomatic process. States respond to new needs according to available means. If it works well enough, the practice endures. In the future, more experts and specialized personnel will be found participating in the diplomatic process. Some foreign offices, however, may endeavor to train their own people differently. In 2000, the US State Department became concerned about the need to acquire greater foreign service proficiency in science, and long-term plans to this effect were introduced. This will become even more imperative in the future (see Chapter 3). But, given current trends in the makeup of the diplomatic agenda, it is doubtful that foreign offices will be able to do without any outside specialists.

The internationalization of domestic public policy has expanded *transgovernmental relations*. Executive departments other than foreign affairs (e.g., agriculture, justice, and labor) need to address the growing international dimensions of their fields. As a result, in many governments, these departments have opened international affairs divisions. They maintain direct contact with their foreign counterparts abroad (e.g., interior department to interior department to track down terrorists). They also send their own officials to participate in specialized international conferences as representatives of their departments,[29] at which time they may be recognized as diplomatic personnel since they are documented as official delegates. The transactions they engage in are indistinguishable from diplomatic work.[30] Transgovernmental relations have proliferated without making the headlines (see Chapter 3).[31] It is of course up to each government to devise its own procedures for the coordination of the foreign activities of its executive departments to ensure foreign relations coherence, not the easiest of tasks.

Another consequence of the involvement of many executive departments in foreign relations is *ministerial diplomacy*.[32] International organizations, particularly the UN's specialized agencies, have fostered this development. For the purpose of promoting international cooperation in certain areas (e.g., energy conservation), these UN agencies convene international conferences "at the ministerial level," in the course of which new policies or agreements are negotiated. Bringing major decisionmakers to the conference table is intended to simplify the bureaucratic process, cut red tape, and induce faster action. Whether it does or not deserves to be examined (some ministers send a representative).

Here again, this is diplomacy by officials whose primary functions are not diplomatic. But foreign service officers normally join them in the course of the proceedings, particularly from the national representation at agency headquarters (e.g., Rome for the Food and Agriculture Organization).[33] This practice is likely to continue in the future given the trend toward diplomatic interaction in highly specialized fields.

The European Union has institutionalized this ministerial procedure in its Council of Ministers (the frequency of the meetings varies with the importance of the subject matter)[34]—which amounts to more diplomacy being conducted outside the regular channels, although when the procedure is used routinely, it becomes a part of the "regular channels." Such meetings are likely to foster more transgovernmental contacts. Just as the multinational corporate world has learned to be proficient in the political arena to protect its interests, heads of executive departments are learning to use the tools of diplomacy. Doubtless, new procedures will be devised to facilitate this process, just as they were in the European Union. The procedure will keep changing: it is how nation-states and other international actors are rewriting the rules of diplomacy. Ministers of foreign affairs, too, are spending more and more time in international meetings—after all, they are major architects of their nations' foreign relations. Diplomacy used to be left to the members of the foreign service, the professional diplomats. But foreign ministers are now expected to participate in high-level meetings, and they spend inordinate amounts of time on the road (see Chapter 10).

Heads of state are themselves more extensively involved in foreign relations, another manifestation of the chief executive syndrome, in which major decisionmakers are expected personally to take part in the diplomatic dialogue. It may be unorthodox in nineteenth-century terms, but international actors have now made it commonplace. As chief executives, they are conversant with the foreign issues of concern to their countries. Better means of transportation and communication facilitate their participation in international meetings. A number of international organizations have institutionalized summit interaction—indispensable for the European Union, but widely used elsewhere, as in the Arab League and the Gulf Cooperation Council. Summit meetings must now be seen as an integral part of the diplomatic process, of course different from the other diplomatic modes, but productive enough to occur with increasing frequency (see Chapter 10). Certain forms of partnership are created by these meetings—a positive element. Many leaders remain in personal contact by means of private messages, and frequently consult even by telephone. Even heads of international organizations now participate in both formal and informal summit dialogues—a new dimension of international politics.[35]

With all this transformation in the diplomatic process, what will happen to the more *traditional modes* of diplomatic relations, particularly the embassy? Affluent states, heavily involved in international affairs, find permanent missions in foreign capitals useful. Even though multilateral diplomacy is becoming more important, the embassy remains significant, and not just as a bilateral instrument. It is frequently used to coordinate joint action in a multilateral forum.[36] And states are still doing a great deal of bilateral work. The embassy is well suited for it. It is indispensable for monitoring the unfolding of politics in a foreign capital, as well as an instrument of communication and of public relations. Consular services, too, are increasing in importance as civil society becomes more internationally mobile.[37]

To be sure, the work of the embassy has changed and will continue to evolve, thus keeping it capable of meeting new diplomatic needs. The composition of embassy staff is now very different, with so many government departments beside the foreign ministry having representatives working at post—in some cases 60–70 percent of the professional staff (see Chapter 7). More administrative work is being done at this level, to the point that diplomats are now recommending that more management training be provided particularly for chiefs of mission.[38] And public relations ("public diplomacy") is being given greater emphasis in the work of permanent missions. Nevertheless, many developing countries maintain few embassies of their own. They are vitally interested in world affairs and anxious to play a role. But these nations do the bulk of their diplomacy in multilateral forums—international organizations and conferences. They have embassies only in a limited number of states of special interest to them. Most of them do not have the means for a more extensive network of embassies. The other channels serve their purpose better.

Special missions have grown in popularity. This is hardly surprising given their flexibility and versatility. They supplement other forms of diplomatic relations and are used as the need arises. Global interdependence and the fast-moving pace of so many international situations increase their usefulness and future relevance. For example, they permit fast intervention in a deteriorating situation (see Chapter 9), provide an effective diplomatic instrument to build international networks, and make it possible to approach a government in the absence of diplomatic ties. Special envoys can be chosen to capitalize on their special status, skills, and competence.[39] This mode of diplomatic interaction is thus unlikely to fall into disuse.

In the final analysis, the increasingly complex web of interaction among international actors reveals a remarkably large number of people actually doing diplomatic work and participating in the diplomatic process (whether officially acknowledged or not). This should not come as any surprise. Diplomacy grew out of a need to maintain relations across cultural and political boundaries. This need has vastly increased, and diplomacy keeps evolving as the world continues to change. The process is not about to stop. The world will become more interdependent and international actors will endeavor to remain effectively connected. They will turn to diplomacy to do so, and new methods will be devised to address new situations. A changing global environment invites experimentation. The pressure and urgency of new problems will lead (as they did before) to a transformation of diplomacy.

Nevertheless, some of the old procedures will undoubtedly remain in use. Tradition is not about to disappear from diplomacy; besides, some of the old diplomatic institutions (such as special missions) are versatile and adapt to different circumstances. But new procedures will be found useful or necessary. The basic skills that make diplomacy what it is will remain indispensable, regardless of what new instruments or techniques may be invented: these skills are personal attributes, however acquired, enabling people of different races, cultures, and political affiliations to communicate and work together. Among them are tact, understanding of other people's ways, respect, honesty, integrity, patience, and of course linguistic ability and common sense. These are the elements that will remain critical in any mode of interaction. They permit us to bridge differences, making diplomacy an essential and enduring element in international relations.[40]

▣ Study Questions and Discussion Topics

1. What is the future of diplomacy? Will it retain its importance?

2. What procedural or structural changes may displace diplomacy? Will technology change its character and course? How?

3. Are new diplomatic techniques in the offing? Are they likely to improve the diplomatic process or will they make any difference?

4. What is the most striking thing you learned in this study of diplomacy? What caught your imagination?

5. What would you suggest to improve the way diplomacy is carried out?

▣ Suggested Reading

Coolsaet, Rik. "The Transformation of Diplomacy at the Threshold of the New Millennium." In *Diplomacy,* vol. 3, edited by Christer Jönsson and Richard Langhorne. London: Sage, 2004.

Crabb, Cecil V., Jr., Leila E. Sarieddine, and Glenn J. Antizzo. *Charting a New Diplomatic Course. Alternative Approaches to America's Post–Cold War Foreign Policy.* Baton Rouge: Louisiana State University Press, 2001.

Finger, Seymour Maxwell. *Inside the World of Diplomacy: The United States Foreign Service in a Changing World.* Westport: Praeger, 2002.

Henrikson, Alan K. "Diplomacy's Possible Futures." *The Hague Journal of Diplomacy* 1, no. 1 (March 2006), pp. 3–27.

Hocking, Brian, and David Spence, eds. *Foreign Ministries in the European Union: Integrating Diplomats.* New York: Palgrave Macmillan, 2006.

Keukeleire, Stephen. "The European Union as a Diplomatic Actor: Internal, Traditional, and Structural Diplomacy." *Diplomacy and Statecraft* 14, no. 3 (September 2003), pp. 31–56.

Langhorne, Richard. "Current Developments in Diplomacy: Who Are the Diplomats Now?" In *Diplomacy,* vol. 3, edited by Christer Jönsson and Richard Langhorne. London: Sage, 2004.

Leonard, Mark. "Diplomacy by Other Means." In *Diplomacy,* vol. 3, edited by Christer Jönsson and Richard Langhorne. London: Sage, 2004.

Melissen, Jan, ed. *Innovation in Diplomatic Practice.* New York: St. Martin's, 1999.

Ronfeldt, David, and John Arquilla. *What If There Is a Revolution in Diplomatic Affairs?* Virtual Diplomacy Report. Washington, DC: US Institute of Peace, 1999.

Ross, Dennis. *Statecraft: And How to Restore America's Standing in the World.* New York: Farrar, Straus and Giroux, 2007.

Sharp, Paul. "Who Needs Diplomats? The Problem of Diplomatic Representation." In *Diplomacy,* vol. 3, edited by Christer Jönsson and Richard Langhorne. London: Sage, 2004.

Warkentin, Craig, and Karen Mingst. "International Institutions, the State, and Global Civil Society in the Age of the World Wide Web." *Global Governance* 6, no. 2 (April–June 2000), pp. 237–257.

Wiseman, Geoffrey. "'Polylateralism' and New Modes of Global Dialogue." In *Diplomacy,* vol. 3, edited by Christer Jönsson and Richard Langhorne. London: Sage, 2004.

■ Notes

1. See Noam Chomsky, *Rogue States: The Use of Force in World Affairs* (Cambridge, MA: South End, 2000).

2. See Cecil V. Crabb Jr., Leila E. Sarieddine, and Glenn J. Antizzo, *Charting a New Diplomatic Course: Alternative Approaches to America's Post–Cold War Foreign Policy* (Baton Rouge: Louisiana State University Press, 2001).

3. See Brian Hocking, "Catalytic Diplomacy: Beyond 'Newness' and 'Decline,'" in *Innovation in Diplomatic Practice,* edited by Jan Melissen (New York: St. Martin's, 1999), p. 21.

4. Its diplomatic process keeps evolving. The European Union now attends the annual Group of Eight (G8) summit, represented by the president of the European Commission and by the leader of the country currently holding the presidency of the European Council (changes every six months). See http://www.state.gov/e/eeb/ecosum.

5. See (Lord) Gore-Booth, ed., *Satow's Guide to Diplomatic Practice,* 5th ed. (New York: Longman, 1979).

6. For example, in cross-cultural communication and negotiation, the importance of the basic elements of trustworthiness, tact, and courtesy, among others.

7. In some cases long overdue—for example, in the case of certain diplomatic immunities. See Chapter 6. The diplomatic profession is notorious for the survival of archaic practices, particularly in ceremonial functions.

8. See research done by the US Institute of Peace for its series on negotiating styles: for example, Scott Snyder, *Negotiating on the Edge: North Korean Negotiating Behavior* (Washington, DC: US Institute of Peace, 1999), http://www.usip.org.

9. From about 70 in 1945 to close to 200 in 2005.

10. For example, the UN Conference on Trade and Development (UNCTAD) became a forum for North-South interaction.

11. See, for example, Dag Hammarskjöld's biography by Brian E. Urquhart, *Hammarskjold* (New York: Norton, 1972). See also Chapter 3's case study on the Suez crisis, and Chapter 8's case study on the mission to Beijing.

12. Eventually a constitution will revamp this diplomatic mechanism, probably testing new procedures. See Philip Raworth, *Introduction to the Legal System of the European Union* (Dobbs Ferry, NY: Oceana, 2001); Stephen Keukeleire, "The European Union as a Diplomatic Actor: Internal, Traditional, and Structural Diplomacy," *Diplomacy and Statecraft* 14, no. 3 (September 2003), pp. 31–56; Dominic McGoldrick, *International Relations Law of the European Union* (London: Longman, 1997). See also http://europa.eu.int/abc/history/index and http://europa.eu.int/comm/external_relations.

13. Many of them of a limited character.

14. These associations need not be "regional," although most are.

15. See David Ronfeldt and John Arquilla, "What If There Is a Revolution in Diplomatic Affairs?" Virtual Diplomacy Report (Washington, DC: US Institute of Peace, February 1999), p. 1, http://www.usip.org/virtualdiplomacy/publications/reports/ronarqisa99.

16. Peter Willetts, "From 'Consultative Arrangements' to 'Partnership': The Changing Status of NGOs in Diplomacy at the UN," *Global Governance* 6, no. 2 (April–June 2000), pp. 191–212.

17. See also Craig Warkentin and Karen Mingst, "International Institutions, the State, and Global Civil Society in the Age of the World Wide Web," *Global Governance* 6, no. 2 (April–June 2000), pp. 237–257.

18. See also Diana Tussie, ed., *Civil Society and Multilateral Development Banks: Global Governance* (special issue) 6 (October–December 2000), pp. 399–517; Diana Tussie and Maria Fernanda Tuozzo, "Opportunities and Constraints for Civil Society Participation in Multilateral Lending Operations: Lessons from Latin America," in *Global Citizen Action,* edited by Michael Edwards and John Gaventa (Boulder: Lynne Rienner, 2001), pp. 105–117.

19. Their contributions to the diplomatic process are already noticeable not only in their signature efforts on women's issues, but also in mediation and peacemaking. Nadim N. Rouhana, "Unofficial Intervention: Potential Contributions to Resolving Ethno-National Conflicts," in *Innovation in Diplomatic Practice,* edited by Jan Melissen (New York: St. Martin's, 1999), pp. 111–132; Andrew S. Natsios, "An NGO Perspective," in *Peacemaking in International Conflict: Methods and Techniques,* edited by I. William Zartman and J. Lewis Rasmussen (Washington, DC: US Institute of Peace, 1997), pp. 337–364; and J. Lewis Rasmussen, "Peacemaking in the Twenty-First Century: New Rules, New Roles, New Actors," in Zartman and Rasmussen, *Peacemaking,* pp. 23–50. See also Jackie Smith, Charles Chatfield, and Ron Pagnucco, eds., *Transnational Social Movements and Global Politics: Solidarity Beyond the State* (Syracuse, NY: Syracuse University Press, 1997).

20. A. Claire Cutler, Virginia Haufler, and Tony Porter, eds., *Private Authority and International Affairs* (Albany: State University of New York Press, 1999).

21. Usha C. V. Haley, *Multilateral Corporations in Political Environments: Ethics, Values, and Strategies* (River Edge, NJ: World Scientific, 2001).

22. Richard A. Higgott, Geoffrey R. D. Underhill, and Andreas Bieler, eds., *Non-State Actors and Authority in the Global System* (New York: Routledge, 2000).

23. It is acknowledged that many see revolutionary activity and diplomacy as incompatible. David Armstrong, "The Diplomacy of Revolutionary States," in *Innovation*

in Diplomatic Practice, edited by Jan Melissen (New York: St. Martin's, 1999), pp. 43ff. The reality, however, is that revolutionaries are using diplomacy in order to prevail.

24. For example, a cartoon of the Prophet Mohammed in the Danish press (February 2006) caused extensive demonstrations and even violence in many parts of the world.

25. See the regular agenda of the annual meeting of the World Health Organization, or the questions discussed by its executive board, at http://www.who.int.

26. For example, the Conference on Biodiversity, Paris, January 24–28, 2005, or the UN Forum on Forests, New York, May 16–27, 2005. See http://www.un.org/events/conferences. See also Chapter 9 in this volume.

27. See J. Robert Schaetzel, "Modernizing the Role of the Ambassador," in *Modern Diplomacy: The Art and the Artisans,* edited by Elmer Plischke (Washington, DC: American Enterprise Institute for Public Policy Research, 1979), pp. 265–266.

28. This is particularly the case in gatherings pertaining to medical or public health issues. See World Health Organization proceedings at http://www.who.org.

29. For example, US Labor Department officers representing the United States at the annual assembly of the International Labour Organization in Geneva.

30. See an example involving the US Drug Enforcement Administration in a statement by Steven W. Casteel, assistant administrator for intelligence, before the Senate Committee on the Judiciary, May 20, 2003, at http://www.dea.gov/pubs/cngrtest.

31. Robert O. Keohane and Joseph S. Nye, *Power and Interdependence,* 2d ed. (Glenview, IL: Scott Foresman, 1989), pp. 24ff.

32. For example, ministers of justice from several countries discussing issues of law enforcement. See Chapter 10.

33. The headquarters of these organizations are scattered around the world. Each member state is represented there by a permanent diplomatic mission.

34. Other organizations have done the same—for instance, the Organization of Petroleum Exporting Countries (OPEC) convenes periodic meetings of its oil ministers.

35. For example, the leadership of the European Union in the G8 Summits.

36. Some ambassadors say that a good 60 percent of the work of their missions is related to multilateral diplomacy. Even if this is not an accurate measurement, it can be taken as an indication of significance.

37. The bulk of the foreign service personnel of industrialized nations are posted in permanent missions of the traditional type (see Chapter 7).

38. Seymour M. Finger, *Inside the World of Diplomacy: The U.S. Foreign Service in a Changing World* (Westport: Praeger, 2002), chap. 8, "A Foreign Service for the 21st Century," p. 156.

39. As with the quick US response to the 2005 tsunami disaster in Southeast Asia. *New York Times,* February 20, 2005, p. 3.

40. Alan K. Henrikson, "Diplomacy's Possible Futures," *The Hague Journal of Diplomacy* 1, no. 1 (March 2006), pp. 3–27.

Acronyms

AIT	American Institute in Taiwan
APPs	American Presence Posts (limited service consular facilities)
ASEAN	·Association of Southeast Asian Nations
CGIAR	Consultative Group on International Agricultural Research
CHOGM	Commonwealth Heads of Government Meeting
CMG	Conflict Management Group
CSCE	Conference on Security and Cooperation in Europe
CSIS	Center for Strategic and International Studies
DEA	Drug Enforcement Administration (United States)
ECOSOC	Economic and Social Council (United Nations)
FAO	Food and Agriculture Organization
FARC	Revolutionary Armed Forces of Colombia
G7	Group of Seven
G8	Group of Eight
G-77	Group of 77
GNI	gross national income
GNP	gross national product
FAO	Food and Agriculture Organization
IAEA	International Atomic Energy Agency
ICAO	International Civil Aviation Organization
ICBL	International Campaign to Ban Landmines
ICC	International Criminal Court
ICRC	International Committee of the Red Cross
ICSID	International Center for the Settlement of Investment Disputes
IFAD	International Fund for Agriculture and Development
ILO	International Labour Organization
IMF·	International Monetary Fund
MIGA	Multilateral Investment Guarantee Agency

MNC	multinational corporation
NAFTA	North American Free Trade Agreement
NATO	North Atlantic Treaty Organization
NGO	nongovernmental organization
OAS	Organization of American States
OCHA	Office for the Coordination of Humanitarian Affairs
OECD	Organization for Economic Cooperation and Development
OPEC	Organization of Petroleum Exporting Countries
OSCE	Organization for Security and Cooperation in Europe
PLO	Palestine Liberation Organization
SAARC	South Asian Association for Regional Cooperation
SDR	special drawing rights
SEATO	Southeast Asia Treaty Organization
SECI	Southeast European Cooperative Initiative
SIU	Sensitive Investigative Unit (of the DEA)
SRSG	Special Representative of the Secretary-General
TECRO	Taiwan Economic and Cultural Representative Office
UAE	United Arab Emirates
UAR	United Arab Republic
UNAIDS	Joint UN Programme on HIV/AIDS
UNCED	UN Conference on the Environment and Development
UNCTAD	UN Conference on Trade and Development
UNDP	UN Development Programme
UNEF	UN Emergency Force (Suez crisis)
UNEP	UN Environment Programme
UNESCO	UN Educational, Scientific, and Cultural Organization
UNFPA	UN Population Fund
UNHCR	UN High Commissioner for Refugees
UNICEF	UN Children's Fund
UNITAR	UN Institute for Training and Research
UNRRA	UN Relief and Rehabilitation Administration
USAID	US Agency for International Development
USIA	US Information Agency
WFP	World Food Program
WHO	World Health Organization
WTO	World Trade Organization

Bibliography

Aall, Pamela. "Nongovernmental Organizations and Peacemaking." In Crocker, Hampson, and Aall, *Managing Global Chaos* (1996), pp. 433–443.

Acuña, Carlos H., and M. Fernanda Tuozzo. "Civil Society Participation in World Bank and Inter-American Development Bank Programs: The Case of Argentina." *Global Governance* 6, no. 4 (October–December 2000), pp. 433–456.

Adcock, Frank, and D. J. Mosley. *Diplomacy in Ancient Greece.* London: Thames and Hudson, 1975.

Aggestam, Karin. "Two-Track Diplomacy: Negotiations Between Israel and the PLO Through Open and Secret Channels." In Jönsson and Langhorne, *Diplomacy* (2004), vol. 3, pp. 203–227.

Alger, Chadwick F. "The Emerging Roles of NGOs in the UN System: From Article 71 to a People's Millennium Assembly." *Global Governance* 8 (January–March 2002), pp. 93–117.

———, ed. *The Future of the United Nations System: Potential for the Twenty-First Century.* Tokyo: UN University Press, 1998.

———. "Non-Resolution Consequences of the United Nations and Their Effects on International Conflict." In *Theory and Research on the Causes of War,* edited by Dean G. Pruitt and Richard C. Snyder. Englewood Cliffs, NJ: Prentice-Hall, 1969, pp. 197–212.

Anderson, Malcolm. *Policing the World: INTERPOL and the Politics of International Police Co-operation.* New York: Oxford University Press, 1989.

Anderson, Matthew S. *The Rise of Modern Diplomacy, 1450–1919.* New York: Longman, 1993.

Anthony, John Duke. *Economic Dynamism Amidst Regional Uncertainties: GCC Summitry in Qatar.* Washington, DC: National Council on US-Arab Relations, December 2007.

Antrim, Lance N. "Dynamics of Leadership in UNCED." In Spector et al., *Negotiating International Regimes* (1994), pp. 149–164.

Antrim, Lance N., and James K. Sebenius. "Formal Individual Mediation and the Negotiators' Dilemma: Tommy Koh and the Law of the Sea Conference." In Bercovitch and Rubin, *Mediation in International Relations* (1992), pp. 97–130.

Appathurai, E. R. "Permanent Missions in New York." In Berridge and Jennings, *Diplomacy at the UN* (1985), pp. 94–108.

Armstrong, David. "The Diplomacy of Revolutionary States." In Melissen, *Innovation in Diplomatic Practice* (1999), pp. 43–59.

———. "Revolutionary Diplomacy." In Jönsson and Langhorne, *Diplomacy* (2004), vol. 2, pp. 381–394.

Armstrong, J. D. "The Group of Seven Summits." In Dunn, *Diplomacy at the Highest Level* (1996), pp. 41–52.

Ashman, Charles B., and Pamela Trescott. *Diplomatic Crime: Drugs, Killings, Thefts, Rapes, Slavery, and Other Outrageous Crimes.* Washington, DC: Acropolis, 1987.

Aurisch, Klaus L. "The Art of Preparing a Multilateral Conference." *Negotiation Journal* 5, no. 3 (1989), pp. 279–288.

Aviel, JoAnn Fagot. "The Evolution of Multilateral Diplomacy." In Muldoon et al., *Multilateral Diplomacy and the United Nations Today* (1999), pp. 8–14.

———. "NGOs and International Affairs: A New Dimension of Diplomacy." In Muldoon et al., *Multilateral Diplomacy and the United Nations Today* (1999), pp. 156–164.

Axworthy, Lloyd. "Lessons from the Ottawa Process." *Canadian Foreign Policy* 5, no. 3 (1998), pp. 1–2.

———. "Towards a New Multilateralism," in Cameron et al., *To Walk Without Fear* (1998), pp. 448–459.

Ayoob, Mohammed. "State Making, State Breaking, and State Failure." In Crocker, Hampson, and Aall, *Managing Global Chaos* (1996), pp. 37–52.

Babbitt, Eileen F. "Jimmy Carter: The Power of Moral Suasion in International Mediation." In Kolb et al., *When Talk Works* (1994), pp. 374–393.

Bagley, Bruce Michael, and Juan Gabriel Tokatlian. *Contadora: The Limits of Negotiation.* Washington, DC: Foreign Policy Institute, School of Advanced International Studies, Johns Hopkins University, 1987.

Bailey, Sydney D. "The Evolution of the Practice of the Security Council." In Nicol, *Paths to Peace* (1981), pp. 37–47.

Bailey, Sydney D., and Sam Daws. *The Procedure of the UN Security Council.* 3d ed. New York: Oxford University Press, 1998.

Bailey, Thomas A. "Advice for Diplomats." In Plischke, *Modern Diplomacy* (1979), pp. 223–236.

Ball, George W. *Diplomacy for a Crowded World: An American Foreign Policy.* Boston: Little, Brown, 1976.

———. *The Past Has Another Pattern: Memoirs.* New York: Norton, 1982.

Barker, J. Craig. *The Abuse of Diplomatic Privileges and Immunities: A Necessary Evil?* Brookfield, VT: Dartmouth, 1996.

———. *The Protection of Diplomatic Personnel.* Burlington, VT: Ashgate, 2006.

Barnet, Richard J., and Ronald E. Müller. *Global Reach: The Power of the Multinational Corporation.* New York: Simon and Schuster, 1974.

Barston, R. P. *Modern Diplomacy.* 2d ed. New York: Longman, 1997.

Bartoli, Andrea. "Mediating Peace in Mozambique: The Role of the Community of Sant'Egidio." In Crocker, Hampson, and Aall, *Herding Cats* (1999), pp. 245–277.

Bartolomei de la Cruz, Hector G., Geraldo von Potobsky, and Lee Swepston. *The International Labor Organization: The International Standards System and Basic Human Rights.* Boulder: Westview, 1996.

Bartoš, Milan. "Le Statut des Missions Spéciales de la Diplomatie Ad Hoc." *Recueil des Cours de l'Académie de Droit International* 108 (1963), pp. 425–560.

Baylis, John, and Steve Smith. *The Globalization of World Politics.* New York: Oxford University Press, 2001.

Bayne, Nicholas. *Hanging in There: The G-7 and G-8 Summit in Maturity and Renewal.* Aldershot: Ashgate, 2000.

Ben-Asher, Dror. *Human Rights Meet Diplomatic Immunities: Problems and Possible Solutions.* Cambridge: Harvard Law School, 2000.

Bennett, A. LeRoy, and James K. Oliver. *International Organizations: Principles and Issues.* 7th ed. Upper Saddle River, NJ: Prentice-Hall, 2002.

Bercovitch, Jacob. "Mediation in International Conflict: An Overview of Theory, a Review of Practice." In Zartman and Rasmussen, *Peacemaking in International Conflict* (1997), pp. 125–153.

––––––. "The Structure and Diversity of Mediation in International Relations." In Bercovitch and Rubin, *Mediation in International Relations* (1992), pp. 1–29.

Bercovitch, Jacob, and Jeffrey Z. Rubin, eds. *Mediation in International Relations: Multiple Approaches to Conflict Management.* New York: St. Martin's, 1992.

Berman, Maureen R., and Joseph E. Johnson, eds. *Unofficial Diplomats.* New York: Columbia University Press, 1977.

Berridge, G. R. *Diplomacy: Theory and Practice.* 3d ed. New York: Palgrave, 2005.

––––––, ed. *Diplomatic Classics: Selected Texts from Commynes to Vattel.* New York: Palgrave Macmillan, 2004.

––––––. "Funeral Diplomacy," in Dunn, *Diplomacy at the Highest Level* (1996), pp. 106–117.

––––––. "'Old Diplomacy' in New York." In Berridge and Jennings, *Diplomacy at the UN* (1985), pp. 175–190.

––––––. *Return to the UN: UN Diplomacy in Regional Conflicts.* New York: Macmillan, 1991.

––––––. *Talking to the Enemy: How States Without "Diplomatic Relations" Communicate.* New York: St. Martin's, 1994.

Berridge, G. R., and A. Jennings, eds. *Diplomacy at the UN.* New York: St. Martin's, 1985.

Berridge, G. R., Maurice Keens-Soper, and T. G. Otte. *Diplomatic Theory from Machiavelli to Kissinger.* New York: Palgrave, 2001.

Biggar, Nigel, ed. *Burying the Past: Making Peace and Doing Justice After Civil Conflict.* Washington, DC: Georgetown University Press, 2003.

Binnendijk, Hans. "Tin Cup Diplomacy." In Wittkopf and Jones, *The Future of American Foreign Policy* (1999), pp. 279–282.

Bjorgo, Einar. *Space Aid: Current and Potential Uses of Satellite Imagery in Humanitarian Organizations.* Virtual Diplomacy Report no. 12. Washington, DC: US Institute of Peace, 2002.

Blanké, W. Wendell. "The Constituent Posts." In Herz, *The Consular Dimension of Diplomacy* (1983), pp. 59–62.

Blavoukos, Spyros, Dimitris Bourantonis, and Panayotis Tsakonas. "Parameters of the Chairmanship's Effectiveness: The Case of the UN Security Council." *The Hague Journal of Diplomacy* 1, no. 2 (September 2006), pp. 143–170.

Bloomfield, Lincoln P., et al. *International Military Forces: The Question of Peacekeeping in Our Armed and Disarming World.* Boston: Little, Brown, 1964.

Blum, Robert, ed. *Cultural Affairs and Foreign Relations.* Englewood Cliffs, NJ: Prentice Hall, 1963.

Boli, John, and George M. Thomas. "World Culture in the World Polity: A Century of International Non-Governmental Organizations." In Lechner and Boli, *The Globalization Reader* (2000), pp. 262–268.

Bolling, Landrum. "Strengths and Weaknesses of Track Two: A Personal Account." In
. McDonald and Bendahmane, *Conflict Resolution* (1987), pp. 53–64.

Borosage, Robert L. "Money Talks: The Implications of U.S. Budget Priorities." In Honey and Barry, *Global Focus* (2000), pp. 1–19.

Bosc, Robert, S. J. *La Société Internationale et l'Eglise*. 2 vols. Paris: Bibliothèque de la Recherche Sociale, 1968.

Boudreau, Tom. *A New International Diplomatic Order*. Muscatine, IA: Stanley Foundation, 1980.

Boulding, Elise, and Jan Oberg. "United Nations Peace-Keeping and NGO Peace-Building: Toward a Partnership." In Alger, *The Future of the United Nations System* (1998), pp. 127–154.

Boutros-Ghali, Boutros. "Challenges of Preventive Diplomacy: The Role of the United Nations and Its Secretary-General." In Cahill, *Preventive Diplomacy* (1996), pp. 16–32.

Bowling, John W. "Tales of Three Dilemmas." In Herz, *The Consular Dimension of Diplomacy* (1983), pp. 62–66.

Bracey, Audrey. *Resolution of the Dominican Crisis, 1965: A Study in Mediation*. Washington, DC: Institute for the Study of Diplomacy, School of Foreign Service, Georgetown University, 1980.

Branch, Taylor, and Eugene M. Propper. "A Cautionary Tale." In Herz, *The Consular Dimension of Diplomacy* (1983), pp. 35–39.

Bretherton, Charlotte, and John Vogler. *The European Union as a Global Actor*. New York: Routledge, 1999.

Briggs, Ellis O. "This Is a Professional Game." In Herz, *The Modern Ambassador* (1983), pp. 146–153.

Britton, Roswell. "Chinese Interstate Intercourse Before 700 B.C." In Jönsson and Langhorne, *Diplomacy* (2004), vol. 2, pp. 91–111.

Bull, Hedley. "Diplomacy and International Order." In Jönsson and Langhorne, *Diplomacy* (2004), vol. 1, pp. 74–91.

Buzan, Barry. "Negotiating by Consensus: Developments in Technique at the UN Conference on the Law of the Sea." *American Journal of International Law* 75 (1981), pp. 324–348.

Cahill, Kevin M. *Preventive Diplomacy: Stopping Wars Before They Start*. New York: Basic, 1996.

Cameron, Maxwell A., Robert J. Lawson, and Brian W. Tomlin, eds. *To Walk Without Fear: The Global Movement to Ban Landmines*. New York: Oxford University Press, 1998.

Campbell, Brian. "Diplomacy in the Roman World (c. 500 B.C.–A.D. 235)." In Jönsson and Langhorne, *Diplomacy* (2004), vol. 2, pp. 175–192.

Carter, Charles A. "The Ambassadors of Early Modern Europe: Patterns of Diplomatic Representation in the Early Seventeenth Century." In Jönsson and Langhorne, *Diplomacy* (2004), vol. 2, pp. 232–250.

Center for Strategic and International Studies, Advisory Panel on Diplomacy in the Information Age. *Reinventing Diplomacy in the Information Age*. Washington, DC, 1998.

Chabasse, Philippe. "The French Campaign." In Cameron et al., *To Walk Without Fear* (1998), pp. 60–67.

Chai, F. Y. "A View from the UN Secretariat." In Nicol, *Paths to Peace* (1981), pp. 84–93.

Chasek, Pamela. "The Negotiating System of Environment and Development." In Spector et al., *Negotiating International Regimes* (1994), pp. 21–44.

Cheever, Daniel S., and H. Field Haviland Jr. *Organizing for Peace: International Organization in World Affairs*. Boston: Houghton Mifflin, 1954.

Chew, Pat K., ed. *The Conflict and Culture Reader.* New York: New York University Press, 2001.

Chomsky, Noam. *Rogue States: The Rule of Force in World Affairs.* Cambridge, MA: South End, 2000.

Clark, A.-M. "Non-Governmental Organizations and Their Influence on International Society." *Journal of International Affairs* 48 (1995), pp. 507–525.

Clark, A.-M., E. J. Friedman, and K. Hochstetler. "The Sovereign Limits of Global Civil Society: A Comparison of NGO Participation in UN World Conferences on the Environment, Human Rights, and Women." *World Politics* 51 (1998), pp. 1ff.

Clark, Ian. *Nuclear Diplomacy and the Special Relationship: Britain's Deterrent and America, 1957–1962.* New York: Oxford University Press, 1994.

Clark, John D. "Ethical Globalization: The Dilemmas and Challenges of Internationalizing Civil Society." In Edwards and Gaventa, *Global Citizen Action* (2001), pp. 17–28.

Claude, Inis L., Jr. "Multilateralism: Diplomatic and Otherwise." In Jönsson and Langhorne, *Diplomacy* (2004), vol. 2, pp. 367–377.

———. *Swords into Plowshares: The Problems and Progress of International Organization.* 4th ed. New York: Random House, 1971.

Clift, A. Denis. *With Presidents to the Summit.* Fairfax, VA: George Mason University Press, 1993.

Cogan, Charles. *French Negotiating Behavior: Dealing with* La Grande Nation. Washington, DC: US Institute of Peace, 2003.

Cohen, Raymond. "The Great Tradition: The Spread of Diplomacy in the Ancient World." In Jönsson and Langhorne, *Diplomacy* (2004), vol. 2, pp. 44–55.

———. *Negotiating Across Cultures: International Communication in an Interdependent World.* 2d ed. Washington, DC: US Institute of Peace, 1997.

———. *Theater of Power: The Art of Diplomatic Signalling.* London: Longman, 1987.

Colligan, Francis J. *Two Decades of Government-Sponsored Cultural Relations.* Washington, DC: US Department of State, 1958.

Coolsaet, Rik. "The Transformation of Diplomacy at the Threshold of the New Millennium." In Jönsson and Langhorne, *Diplomacy* (2004), vol. 3, pp. 1–24.

Cooper, Andrew F., John English, and Ramesh Thakur, eds. *Enhancing Global Governance: Toward a New Diplomacy?* Tokyo: UN University Press, 2002.

Cooper, Andrew F., and Brian Hocking. "Governments, Non-Governmental Organizations, and the Re-calibration of Diplomacy." In Jönsson and Langhorne, *Diplomacy* (2004), vol. 3, pp. 79–95.

Corbin, Jane. *Gaza First: The Secret Norway Channel to Peace Between Israel and the PLO.* London: Bloomsbury, 1994.

Covey, Jane G. "Critical Cooperation? Influencing the World Bank Through Policy Dialogue and Operational Cooperation." In Fox and Brown, *The Struggle for Accountability* (1998), pp. 81–122.

Cox, Robert W., Harold K. Jacobson, et al. *The Anatomy of Influence: Decision Making in International Organizations.* New Haven: Yale University Press, 1974.

Crabb, Cecil V., Jr., Leila E. Sarieddine, and Glenn J. Antizzo. *Charting a New Diplomatic Course: Alternative Approaches to America's Post–Cold War Foreign Policy.* Baton Rouge: Louisiana State University, 2001.

Craig, Langston. "'Leisure, Gentility, and Decorum': A Typical Day of an American Ambassador." In Herz, *The Modern Ambassador* (1983), pp. 50–59.

Crocker, Chester A., and Fen Osler Hampson, with Pamela Aall, eds. *Herding Cats: Multiparty Mediation in a Complex World.* Washington, DC: US Institute of Peace, 1999.

————, eds. *Managing Global Chaos: Sources of, and Responses to, International Conflict.* Washington, DC: US Institute of Peace, 1996.

Cronin, Bruce. "The Two Faces of the United Nations: The Tension Between Inter-governmentalism and Transnationalism." *Global Governance* 8, no. 1 (January–March 2002), pp. 53–71.

Cutler, A. Claire, Virginia Haufler, and Tony Porter, eds. *Private Authority and International Affairs.* Albany: State University of New York Press, 1999.

Czempiel, Ernst-Otto, and James N. Rosenau, eds. *Global Changes and Theoretical Challenges: Approaches to World Politics for the 1990s.* Lexington, MA: Lexington Books, 1989.

Daniel, Donald C. F., and Bradd C. Hayes. *Coercive Inducement and the Containment of International Crises.* Washington, DC: US Institute of Peace, 1999.

Davies, John, and Edward Kaufman, eds. *Second Track/Citizens' Diplomacy: Concepts and Techniques for Conflict Transformation.* New York: Rowman and Littlefield, 2002.

Davison, W. Philips. "News Media and International Negotiation." *Public Opinion Quarterly* 38 (1974), pp. 174–193.

de Callières, François. *On the Manner of Negotiating with Princes.* Translated by A. F. Whyte. Washington, DC: University Press of America, 1963 (1716).

de Cooker, Chris, ed. *International Administration: Law and Management Practices in International Organizations.* Dordrecht: Nijhoff, 1990.

de Laboulaye, François, and Jean Laloy. "Qualifications of an Ambassador." In Herz, *The Modern Ambassador* (1983), pp. 67–71.

Dembinski, Ludwik. *The Modern Law of Diplomacy: External Missions of States and International Organizations.* Dordrecht: Nijhoff, 1988.

Denza, Eileen. *Diplomatic Law: A Commentary on the Vienna Convention on Diplomatic Relations.* 2d ed. New York: Oxford University Press, 1998.

Deshingkar, Giri. "Strategic Thinking in Ancient India and China: Kautilya and Sunzi." In Jönsson and Langhorne, *Diplomacy* (2004), vol. 2, pp. 79–90.

Diehl, Paul F. *The Politics of International Organizations: Patterns and Insights.* Chicago: Dorsey, 1989.

The Diplomacy of Counterterrorism: Lessons Learned, Ignored, and Disputed. Special Report no. 80. Washington, DC: US Institute of Peace, 2002.

Dizard, Wilson, Jr. *Digital Diplomacy: U.S. Foreign Policy in the Information Age.* Westport: Praeger, 2001.

Dodds, Felix. "From the Corridors of Power to the Global Negotiating Table: The NGO Steering Committee of the Commission on Sustainable Development." In Edwards and Gaventa, *Global Citizen Action* (2001), pp. 203–213.

Dolan, Michael, and Chris Hunt. "Negotiating in the Ottawa Process: The New Multilateralism." In Cameron et al., *To Walk Without Fear* (1998), pp. 392–423.

Dorman, Shawn, ed. *Inside a U.S. Embassy: How the Foreign Service Works for America.* Rev. ed. Washington, DC: American Foreign Service Association, 2005.

Dunn, David H., ed. *Diplomacy at the Highest Level: The Evolution of International Summitry.* New York: St. Martin's, 1996.

————. "How Useful Is Summitry?" In Dunn, *Diplomacy at the Highest Level* (1996), pp. 247–268.

Edwards, Michael, and John Gaventa, eds. *Global Citizen Action.* Boulder: Lynne Rienner, 2001.

Egeland, Jan. "The Oslo Accord: Multiparty Facilitation Through the Norwegian Channel." In Crocker, Hampson, and Aall, *Herding Cats* (1999), pp. 527–546.

Elgström, Ole. "The Presidency: The Role(s) of the Chair in European Union Negotiations." *The Hague Journal of Diplomacy* 1, no. 2 (September 2006), pp. 171–195.

Eubank, Keith. *Summit at Teheran*. New York: Morrow, 1985.

———. *The Summit Conferences, 1919–1960*. Norman: University of Oklahoma Press, 1966.

Fairbanks, Charles H., Jr. *The Allure of the Summits*. Washington, DC: Foreign Policy Institute and Johns Hopkins University, 1988.

Falk, Richard A. "The United Nations: Various Systems of Operation." In Gordenker, *The United Nations in International Politics* (1971), pp. 184–230.

Farhangi, Leslie Shirin. "Insuring Against Abuse of Diplomatic Immunity." *Stanford Law Review* 38, no. 6 (July 1986), pp. 1517–1547.

Fasulo, Linda M. *Representing America: Experiences of U.S. Diplomats at the UN*. New York: Praeger, 1984.

Fatemi, Khosrow, ed. *The New World Order: Internationalism, Regionalism, and the Multinational Corporations*. New York: Pergamon, 2000.

Feltham, R. G. *Diplomatic Handbook*. 4th ed. New York: Longman, 1982.

Fenzi, Jewell. *Married to the Foreign Service: An Oral History of the American Diplomatic Spouse*. New York: Twayne, 1994.

Ferrell, Robert H. *American Diplomacy: The Twentieth Century*. 4th ed. New York: Norton, 1988.

Finger, Matthias. "Environmental NGOs in the UNCED Process." In Princen and Finger, *Environmental NGOs in World Politics* (1994), pp. 186–216.

Finger, Seymour Maxwell. *American Ambassadors at the UN: People, Politics, and Bureaucracy in Making Foreign Policy*. 2d ed. New York: Holmes and Meier, 1988.

———. *Inside the World of Diplomacy: The U.S. Foreign Service in a Changing World*. Westport: Praeger, 2002.

Fitzpatrick, Kathy R. "Advancing the New Public Diplomacy: A Public Relations Perspective." *The Hague Journal of Diplomacy* 2, no. 3 (October 2007), pp. 187–211.

Florini, Ann M., ed. *The Third Force: The Rise of Transnational Civil Society*. Washington, DC: Carnegie Endowment for International Peace, 2000.

———. "Transnational Civil Society." In Edwards and Gaventa, *Global Citizen Action* (2001), pp. 29–40.

Fooner, Michael. *Interpol: Issues in World Crime and International Criminal Justice*. New York: Plenum, 1989.

Forsythe, David P. "Humanitarian Mediation by the International Committee of the Red Cross." In Touval and Zartman, *International Mediation in Theory and Practice* (1985), pp. 233–249.

Fox, Annette Baker, Alfred O. Hero Jr., and Joseph S. Nye Jr., eds. *Canada and the United States: Transnational and Transgovernmental Relations*. New York: Columbia University Press, 1976.

Fox, Jonathan A., and L. David Brown, eds. *The Struggle for Accountability: The World Bank, NGOs, and Grassroots Movements*. Cambridge: Massachusetts Institute of Technology Press, 1998.

Frey, Linda S., and Marsha L. Frey. *The History of Diplomatic Immunity*. Columbus: Ohio State University Press, 1999.

Freymond, Jacques. "The International Committee of the Red Cross as a Neutral Intermediary." In Berman and Johnson, *Unofficial Diplomats* (1977), pp. 142–151.

Fritts, Robert E. "Consular Services and Foreign Policy." In Herz, *The Consular Dimension of Diplomacy* (1983), pp. 5–8.

Fulton, Barry, ed. *Net Diplomacy.* Virtual Diplomacy Reports nos. 14–16. Washington, DC: US Institute of Peace, 2002.

Galbraith, John Kenneth. *Ambassador's Journal: A Personal Account of the Kennedy Years.* Boston: Houghton Mifflin, 1969.

Galtung, Fredrik. "A Global Network to Curb Corruption: The Experience of Transparency International." In Florini, *The Third Force* (2000), pp. 17–47.

Gaventa, John. "Global Citizen Action: Lessons and Challenges." In Edwards and Gaventa, *Global Citizen Action* (2001), pp. 275–287.

Gelfand, Michele J., and Jeanne M. Brett, eds. *The Handbook of Negotiation and Culture.* Stanford: Stanford Business Books, 2004.

Gilbert, Felix. "The 'New Diplomacy' of the Eighteenth Century." In Jönsson and Langhorne, *Diplomacy* (2004), vol. 2, pp. 251–279.

Gilboa, Eytan. "Diplomacy in the Media Age: Three Models of Uses and Effects." In Jönsson and Langhorne, *Diplomacy* (2004), vol. 3, pp. 96–119.

Godsey, Fred. *A Gathering at the River: Stories from a Life in the Foreign Service.* Menlo Park, CA: Markgraf, 1989.

Goldberg, Arthur J. "The Importance of Private Negotiations." In Nicol, *Paths to Peace* (1981), pp. 117–119.

Goldstein, Erik. "The Politics of the State Visit." In Jönsson and Langhorne, *Diplomacy* (2004), vol. 2, pp. 357–380.

Gordenker, Leon, ed. *The United Nations in International Politics.* Princeton: Princeton University Press, 1971.

Gordenker, Leon, and Thomas G. Weiss. "NGO Participation in the International Policy Process." In Weiss and Gordenker, *NGOs, the UN, and Global Governance* (1996), pp. 209–222.

Gore-Booth (Lord), ed. *Satow's Guide to Diplomatic Practice.* 5th ed. New York: Longman, 1979.

Graham, Norman, and Stephan Haggard. "Diplomacy in Global Conferences." *UNITAR News* 11 (1979): 14–21.

Graham, Norman, Richard L. Kauffman, and Michael F. Oppenheimer. *The United States and Multilateral Diplomacy: A Handbook.* New York: Oceana, 1984.

Gruber, Karl. "Common Denominators of Good Ambassadors." In Herz, *The Modern Ambassador* (1983), pp. 62–66.

Haas, Ernst B. *Beyond the Nation-State: Functionalism and International Organizations.* Stanford: Stanford University Press, 1964.

Hackett, Kenneth. "The Role of International NGOs in Preventing Conflicts." In Cahill, *Preventive Diplomacy* (1996), pp. 269–284.

Hajnal, Peter, II. *The G7–G8 System: Evolution, Role, and Documentation.* Aldershot: Ashgate, 1999.

———, ed. *The Seven Power Summit: Documents from the Summits of the Industrialized Countries, 1975–1989.* Millwood: Kraus, 1991.

Haley, Usha C. V. *Multinational Corporations in Political Environments: Ethics, Values, and Strategies.* River Edge, NJ: World Scientific, 2001.

Hamilton, Keith, and Richard Langhorne. *The Practice of Diplomacy: Its Evolution, Theory, and Administration.* New York: Routledge, 1995.

Hammarskjöld, Dag. "New Diplomatic Techniques in a New World." In Plischke, *Modern Diplomacy* (1979), pp. 86–91.

———. "United Nations Emergency Force." In Bloomfield et al., *International Military Forces* (1964), pp. 268–280.

Hara, Fabienne. "Burundi: A Case of Parallel Diplomacy." In Crocker, Hampson, and Aall, *Herding Cats* (1999), pp. 139–158.

Hare, A. Paul. "Informal Mediation by Private Individuals." In Bercovitch and Rubin, *Mediation in International Relations* (1992), pp. 52–63.

Haufler, Virginia. "Industry Regulation and Self-Regulation: The Case of Labor Standards." In Cooper et al., *Enhancing Global Governance* (2002), pp. 162–186.

Hayes-Renshaw, Fiona, and Helen Wallace. *The Council of Ministers.* New York: St. Martin's, 1997.

Heinrich, Waldo H., Jr. *American Ambassador: Joseph C. Grew and the Development of the United States Diplomatic Tradition.* New York: Oxford University Press, 1966.

Held, David, Anthony McGrew, David Goldblatt, and Jonathan Perraton. *Global Transformations: Politics, Economics, and Culture.* Stanford: Stanford University Press, 1999.

Henderson, Nicholas. *Mandarin: The Diaries of an Ambassador, 1969–1982.* London: Weidenfeld and Nicolson, 1994.

Henrikson, Alon K. "Diplomacy's Possible Futures." *The Hague Journal of Diplomacy* 1, no. 1 (March 2006), pp. 3–27.

Herz, Martin F., ed. *The Consular Dimension of Diplomacy.* Washington, DC: Institute for the Study of Diplomacy, School of Foreign Service, Georgetown University, 1983.

———, ed. *Contacts with the Opposition: A Symposium.* Washington, DC: Institute for the Study of Diplomacy, School of Foreign Service, Georgetown University, 1979.

———, ed. *Diplomacy: The Role of the Wife—A Symposium.* Washington, DC: Institute for the Study of Diplomacy, School of Foreign Service, Georgetown University, 1981.

———, ed. *Diplomats and Terrorists: What Works, What Doesn't—A Symposium.* Washington, DC: Institute for the Study of Diplomacy, School of Foreign Service, Georgetown University, 1982.

——— "Maxwell Gluck and All That." In Herz, *The Modern Ambassador* (1983), pp. 96–104.

———, ed. *The Modern Ambassador: The Challenge and the Search.* Washington, DC: Institute for the Study of Diplomacy, School of Foreign Service, Georgetown University, 1983.

———. "Sparring with the Foreign Minister." In Herz, *The Consular Dimension of Diplomacy* (1983), pp. 33–34.

———. "Who Should Be an American Ambassador." In Herz, *The Modern Ambassador* (1983), pp. 163–166.

Hevener, Natalie Kaufman, ed. *Diplomacy in a Dangerous World: Protection for Diplomats Under International Law.* Boulder: Westview, 1986.

Higgins, Rosalyn. "UK Foreign Affairs Committee Report on the Abuse of Diplomatic Immunities and Privileges: Government Response and Report." *American Journal of International Law* 80 (1985), pp. 135ff.

Higgott, Richard A., Geoffrey R. D. Underhill, and Andreas Bieler, eds. *Non-State Actors and Authority in the Global System.* New York: Routledge, 2000.

Hillen, John. *Blue Helmet: The Strategy of UN Military Operations.* Washington, DC: Brassey's, 1998.

Hocking, Brian. "Catalytic Diplomacy: Beyond 'Newness' and 'Decline.'" In Melissen, *Innovation in Diplomatic Practice* (1999), pp. 21–42.

Hocking, Brian, and David Spence, eds. *Foreign Ministries in the European Union: Integrating Diplomats.* New York: Palgrave Macmillan, 2006.

Hodges, Michael R., John J. Kirton, and Joseph P. Daniels, eds. *The G8's Role in the New Millennium.* Brookfield, VT: Ashgate, 1999.

Holsti, Kal J., and Thomas Allen Levy. "Bilateral Institutions and Transgovernmental Relations Between Canada and the United States." In Fox et al., *Canada and the United States* (1976), pp. 283–309.

Honey, Martha, and Tom Barry, eds. *Global Focus: U.S. Foreign Policy at the Turn of the Millennium.* New York: St. Martin's, 2000.

Hook, Steven W. *U.S. Foreign Policy: The Paradox of World Power.* Washington, DC: Congressional Quarterly, 2005.

Hopkins, Raymond. "The International Role of 'Domestic' Bureaucracy." *International Organization* 30, no. 3 (Summer 1976), pp. 405–432.

Huntington, Samuel P. "Transnational Organizations in World Politics." *World Politics* 25 (April 1973), pp. 333–368.

Hurewitz, J. C. "Ottoman Diplomacy and the European State System." In Jönsson and Langhorne, *Diplomacy* (2004), vol. 2, pp. 305–315.

Ignatieff, George. "Prompt and Regular Access to Political Government at Home Is Essential." In Nicol, *Paths to Peace* (1981), pp. 130–139.

Iklé, Fred Charles. *How Nations Negotiate.* New York: Harper and Row, 1964.

———. "Negotiating Effectively." In Plischke, *Modern Diplomacy* (1979), pp. 364–372.

Ilan, Amitzur. *Bernadotte in Palestine, 1948: A Study in Contemporary Humanitarian Knight-Errantry.* New York: St. Martin's, 1989.

Impagliazzo, Marco. "The St. Egidio Platform for a Peaceful Solution of the Algerian Crisis." In Smock, *Private Peacemaking* (1998), pp. 10–11.

Innis, Pauline B., Mary Jane McCaffrey, and Richard M. Sand. *Protocol: The Complete Handbook of Diplomatic, Official, and Social Usage.* Dallas: Durban, 2002.

International Labor Organization. *Codes of Conduct for Multinational Enterprises.* Geneva: International Labour Organization, 2002.

Johnston, Mary Troy. *The European Council: Gatekeeper of the European Community.* Boulder: Westview, 1994.

Jönsson, Christer. "Diplomatic Signaling in the Television Age." In Jönsson and Langhorne, *Diplomacy* (2004), vol. 3, pp. 120–138.

Jönsson, Christer, and Martin Hall. "Communication: An Essential Aspect of Diplomacy." In Jönsson and Langhorne, *Diplomacy* (2004), vol. 1, pp. 396–415.

———. *Essence of Diplomacy.* New York: Palgrave Macmillan, 2005.

Jönsson, Christer, and Richard Langhorne, eds. *Diplomacy.* 3 vols. (vol. 1, *Theory of Diplomacy;* vol. 2, *History of Diplomacy;* vol. 3, *Problems and Issues in Contemporary Diplomacy*). London: Sage, 2004.

Jordan, Robert S., ed. *International Administration: Its Evolution and Contemporary Applications.* New York: Oxford University Press, 1971.

Judge, Anthony. "NGOs and Civil Society. Some Realities and Distortions: The Challenge of 'Necessary-to-Governance Organizations' (NGOs)." *Transnational Associations* 47, no. 3 (1995), pp. 156–180.

Kaiser, P. M. *Journeying Far and Wide: A Political and Diplomatic Memoir.* New York: Scribner's, 1992.

Karns, Margaret P., and Karen A. Mingst. *International Organizations: The Politics and Processes of Global Governance.* Boulder: Lynne Rienner, 2004.

Kaufmann, Johan. *Conference Diplomacy: An Introductory Analysis.* 2d ed. Dordrecht: Nijhoff, 1988.

———, ed. *Effective Negotiation: Case Studies in Conference Diplomacy.* Dordrecht: Nijhoff, 1989.

———. "Summit Diplomacy: Conference Style." In Kaufmann, *Effective Negotiation* (1989), pp. 165–171.

Keens-Soper, Maurice. "François de Callières and Diplomatic Theory." In Jönsson and Langhorne, *Diplomacy* (2004), vol. 1, pp. 485–508.

Kegley, Charles W., Jr., and Eugene R. Wittkopf. *World Politics: Trend and Transformation*. 11th ed. Boston: Wadsworth, 2008.

Kelley, John Robert. "U.S. Public Diplomacy: A Cold War Success Story?" *The Hague Journal of Diplomacy* 2, no. 1 (April 2007), pp. 53–79.

Kelman, Herbert C. "Informal Mediation by the Scholar/Practitioner." In Bercovitch and Rubin, *Mediation in International Relations* (1992), pp. 64–96.

———. "The Interactive Problem-Solving Approach." In Crocker, Hampson, and Aall, *Managing Global Chaos* (1996), pp. 501–519.

Kendig, K. *Civil Society, Global Governance, and the UN*. Tokyo: UN University Press, 1999.

Kennan, George F. *American Diplomacy*. Expanded edition. Chicago: University of Chicago Press, 1984.

———. "Diplomacy Without Diplomats?" *Foreign Affairs* 76, no. 5 (September–October, 1997), pp. 198–212.

Kennedy, Charles S. "'Protection and Welfare' and Passports: Some Cases Remembered." In Herz, *The Consular Dimension of Diplomacy* ('983), pp. 51–56.

———. "Some Visa Cases Recalled." In Herz, *The Consular Dimension of Diplomacy* (1983), pp. 23–26.

Keohane, Robert O., and Joseph S. Nye. *Power and Interdependence*. 2d ed. Glenview, IL: Scott Foresman, 1989.

Keukeleire, Stephan. "The European Union as a Diplomatic Actor: Internal, Traditional, and Structural Diplomacy." *Diplomacy and Statecraft* 14, no. 3 (September 2003), pp. 31–56.

Kinney, Stephanie Smith. "Developing Diplomats for 2010: If Not Now, When?" *American Diplomacy* 5, no. 3 (2001), pp. 1–14.

Kirisci, Kemal. *The PLO and World Politics: A Study of the Mobilization of Support for the Palestinian Cause*. New York: St. Martin's, 1986.

Kissinger, Henry A. *Diplomacy*. New York: Simon and Schuster, 1994.

———. "A New National Partnership." *Department of State Bulletin* (February 17, 1975), p. 199.

Kleiner, Juergen. "Diplomacy with Fundamentalists: The United States and the Taliban." *The Hague Journal of Diplomacy* 1, no. 3 (November 2006), pp. 209–234.

Koh, Tommy T. B. "UNCED Leadership: A Personal Perspective." In Spector et al., *Negotiating International Regimes* (1994), pp. 165–170.

Kolb, Deborah M., et al., eds. *When Talk Works: Profiles of Mediators*. San Francisco: Jossey-Bass, 1994.

Korten, David C. *Getting to the 21st Century: Voluntary Action and the Global Agenda*. West Hartford, CT: Kumarian, 1990.

Lall, Arthur S., ed. *Multilateral Negotiation and Mediation: Instruments and Methods*. New York: Pergamon, 1985.

Lanchberry, John. "The Rio Earth Summit." In Dunn, *Diplomacy at the Highest Level* (1996), pp. 220–243.

Lang, W. *Multilateral Negotiation: The Role of Presiding Officers*. Laxenburg, Austria: International Institute of Applied System Analysis, 1987.

Langhorne, Richard. "Current Developments in Diplomacy: Who Are the Diplomats Now?" In Jönsson and Langhorne, *Diplomacy* (2004), vol. 3, pp. 331–342.

———. "The Development of International Conferences, 1648–1830." In Jönsson and Langhorne, *Diplomacy* (2004), vol. 2, 280–304.

————. "Establishment of International Organizations." In Jönsson and Langhorne, *Diplomacy* (2004), vol. 2, pp. 343–356.

Lash, Joseph P. *Dag Hammarskjöld: Custodian of the Brush-Fire Peace.* Garden City, NY: Doubleday, 1961.

Lawson, Robert J., Mark Gwozdecky, Jill Singlair, and Ralph Lysyshyn. "The Ottawa Process and the International Movement to Ban Anti-Personnel Mines." In Cameron et al., *To Walk Without Fear* (1998), pp. 160–184.

Lechner, Frank J., and John Boli, eds. *The Globalization Reader.* Oxford: Blackwell, 2000.

Lent, Tom. "The Search for Peace and Justice in Guatemala: NGOs, Early Warning, and Preventive Diplomacy." In Rotberg, *Vigilance and Vengeance* (1996), pp. 73–92.

Licklider, Roy. "Negotiating an End in Civil Wars: General Findings." In Sisk, *New Approaches to International Negotiation and Mediation* (1999), pp. 24–27.

————, ed. *Stopping the Killing: How Civil Wars End.* New York: New York University Press, 1993.

Litfin, Karen T. "Public Eyes: Satellite Imagery, the Globalization of Transparency and New Networks of Surveillance." In Rosenau and Singh, *Information Technologies and Global Politics* (2002), pp. 65–89.

Liverani, Mario. *International Relations in the Ancient Near East, 1600–1100 B.C.* New York: Palgrave, 2001.

————. *Three Amarna Essays.* Malibu, CA: Undena, 1979.

Love, Maryann Cusimano, et al., eds. *Beyond Sovereignty: Issues for a Global Agenda.* 2d ed. Belmont, CA: Wadsworth, 2003.

Luce, Clare Booth. "The Ambassadorial Issue: Professionals or Amateurs?" in Herz, *The Modern Ambassador* (1983), pp. 128–136.

Lund, Michael S. "Early Warning and Preventive Diplomacy." In Crocker, Hampson, and Aall, *Managing Global Chaos* (1996), pp. 379–402.

————. *Preventing Violent Conflict: A Strategy for Preventive Diplomacy.* Washington, DC: US Institute of Peace, 1996.

Madden, Thomas F. "Venice's Hostage Crisis: Diplomatic Efforts to Secure Peace with Byzantium Between 1171 and 1184." In *Medieval and Renaissance Venice,* edited by Ellen E. Kittell and Thomas F. Madden. Urbana: University of Illinois Press, 1999, pp. 96–108.

Manheim, Jarol B. *Strategic Public Diplomacy and American Foreign Policy: The Evolution of Influence.* New York: Oxford, 1994.

Mann, Peggy. *Ralph Bunche: UN Peacekeeper.* New York: Coward, McCann, and Geoghegan, 1975.

Martin, Edwin McC. *Conference Diplomacy: A Case Study—The World Food Conference, Rome, 1974.* Washington, DC: Institute for the Study of Diplomacy, School of Foreign Service, Georgetown University, n.d.

Maslen, Stuart. "The Role of the International Committee of the Red Cross." In Cameron et al., *To Walk Without Fear* (1998), pp. 80–88.

Mathews, Jessica T. "Power Shift." *Foreign Affairs* 76, no. 1 (January–February 1997), pp. 50–66.

Mattingly, Garrett. "The First Resident Embassies: Medieval Italian Origins of Modern Diplomacy." In Jönsson and Langhorne, *Diplomacy* (2004), vol. 2, pp. 214–231.

————. *Renaissance Diplomacy.* Boston: Houghton Mifflin, 1955.

Mayer, Martin. *The Diplomats.* New York: Doubleday, 1983.

Mayotte, Judy. "NGOs and Diplomacy." In Muldoon et al., *Multilateral Diplomacy and the United Nations Today* (1999), pp. 167–176.

McClanahan, Grant V. *Diplomatic Immunity: Principles, Practices, Problems.* New York: St. Martin's, 1989.

McCoubrey, Hilaire, and Nigel D. White. *International Organizations and Civil Wars.* Brookfield, VT: Dartmouth, 1995.

McDonald, John W. "The Need for Multi-Track Diplomacy." In Davies and Kaufman, *Second Track/Citizens' Diplomacy* (2002), pp. 49–60.

McDonald, John W., and Diana B. Bendahmane, eds. *Conflict Resolution: Track Two Diplomacy.* Washington, DC: US Department of State, Foreign Service Institute, Center for the Study of Foreign Affairs, 1987.

McGhee, George C., ed. *Diplomacy for the Future.* Washington, DC: Institute for the Study of Diplomacy, School of Foreign Service, Georgetown University, 1987.

McGlen, Nancy E., and Meredith Reid Sarkees. *Women in Foreign Policy.* New York: Routledge, 1993.

McGoldrick, Dominic. *International Relations Law of the European Union.* London: Longman, 1997.

McKay, Vernon, ed. *African Diplomacy: Studies in the Determinants of Foreign Policy.* New York: Praeger, 1966.

McMullen, Christopher J. *Resolution of the Yemen Crisis, 1963: A Case Study in Mediation.* Washington, DC: Institute for the Study of Diplomacy, School of Foreign Service, Georgetown University, 1980.

Mekata, Metoko. "Building Partnerships Toward a Common Goal: Experiences of the International Campaign to Ban Landmines." In Florini, *The Third Force* (2000), pp. 143–176.

Melissen, Jan, ed. *Innovation in Diplomatic Practice.* New York: St. Martin's, 1999.

———, ed. *The New Public Diplomacy: Soft Power in International Relations.* New York: Palgrave Macmillan, 2006.

———. "Summit Diplomacy Coming of Age." In Jönsson and Langhorne, *Diplomacy* (2004), vol. 3, pp. 185–202.

Mendershausen, Horst. *The Diplomat as a National and Transnational Agent: A Problem in Multiple Loyalty.* Morristown, NJ: General Learning Press, 1972.

Merlini, Cesare, ed. *Economic Summits and Western Decision-Making.* New York: St. Martin's, 1984.

Miller, Linda B. "International Organization and Internal Conflicts: Some Emerging Patterns of Response." In Gordenker, *The United Nations in International Politics* (1971), pp. 130–150.

Miller, Robert Hopkins. *Inside an Embassy: The Political Role of Diplomats Abroad.* Washington, DC: Congressional Quarterly, 1992.

Mittelman, James H. *The Globalization Syndrome: Transformation and Resistance.* Princeton: Princeton University Press, 2000.

Morin, Ann Miller. *Her Excellency: An Oral History of American Women Ambassadors.* New York: Twayne, 1995.

Muldoon, James P., Jr. *The Architecture of Global Governance.* Boulder: Westview, 2004.

———. "The Challenge of the Global Economy for Post–Cold War Diplomacy." In Muldoon et al., *Multilateral Diplomacy and the United Nations Today* (1999), pp. 80 86.

Muldoon, James P., Jr., JoAnn Fagot Aviel, Richard Reitano, and Earl Sullivan, eds. *Multilateral Diplomacy and the United Nations Today.* Boulder: Westview, 1999.

Munn-Rankin, Joan M. "Diplomacy in Western Asia in the Early Second Millennium B.C." In Jönsson and Langhorne, *Diplomacy* (2004), vol. 2, pp. 1–43.

Narasimhan, C. V. *The United Nations: An Inside View.* New Delhi: Vikas, 1988.

Natsios, Andrew S. "An NGO Perspective." In Zartman and Rasmussen, *Peacemaking in International Conflict* (1997), pp. 337–364.

Nelson, Paul. *The World Bank and NGOs: The Limits of Apolitical Development.* London: Macmillan, 1995.

Neustadt, Richard. *Alliance Politics.* New York: Columbia University Press, 1970.

Newsom, David D. "The Diplomat's Task Versus Security." In Herz, *Diplomats and Terrorists* (1982), pp. 9–11.

———. "The Tasks of an Ambassador." In Herz, *The Modern Ambassador* (1983), pp. 32–36.

———. "This Is Where Fraud Was Invented." In Herz, *The Consular Dimension of Diplomacy* (1983), pp. 30–33.

Nicol, Davidson, ed. *Paths to Peace: The UN Security Council and Its Presidency.* New York: Pergamon, 1981.

Nicolson, Harold. *Diplomacy.* 3d ed. New York: Oxford, 1964.

———. "Diplomacy Then and Now." In Jönsson and Langhorne, *Diplomacy* (2004), vol. 1, pp. 39–49.

———. *The Evolution of Diplomatic Method.* London: Constable, 1954.

Noguez, Maria Isabel Studer. "How Global Is Ford Motor Company's Global Strategy?" In Higgott et al., *Non-State Actors and Authority in the Global System* (2000), pp. 174–192.

Numelin, Ragnar. *The Beginnings of Diplomacy.* New York: Philosophical Library, 1950.

Oakley, Phyllis E. "Paving the Way for Women: Department of State 2002." In Dorman, *Inside a U.S. Embassy* (2005), pp. 129–130.

Obolensky, Dimitri. "The Principles and Methods of Byzantine Diplomacy." In Jönsson and Langhorne, *Diplomacy* (2004), vol. 2, pp. 112–129.

Pahlavi, Pierre C. "Evaluating Public Diplomacy Programmes." *The Hague Journal of Diplomacy* 2, no. 3 (October 2007), pp. 255–281.

Paris, Roland. *At War's End: Building Peace After Civil Conflict.* New York: Cambridge University Press, 2004.

Park, Bill. "NATO Summits." In Dunn, *Diplomacy at the Highest Level* (1996), pp. 88–105.

Parkhill, James. "Diplomacy in the Modern World: A Reconsideration of the Bases for Diplomatic Immunity in the Era of High-Tech Communications." *Hastings International and Comparative Law Review* 21 (1988), pp. 565–596.

Raszkowski, M. "The Law of Special Missions." *Polish Yearbook of International Law* 6 (1974), pp. 267–288.

Phelan, Edward Joseph. *Yes and Albert Thomas.* London: Cresset, 1936.

Piening, Christopher. *Global Europe: The European Union in World Affairs.* Boulder: Lynne Rienner, 1997.

Pinder, John. *The European Union: A Very Short Introduction.* New York: Oxford University Press, 2001.

Plischke, Elmer. "Career Status of United States Diplomats." In Plischke, *Modern Diplomacy* (1979), pp. 297–304.

———, ed. *Modern Diplomacy: The Art and the Artisans.* Washington, DC: American Enterprise Institute for Public Policy Research, 1979.

———. "The New Diplomacy." In Plischke, *Modern Diplomacy* (1979), pp. 54–72.

———. *Presidential Diplomacy: A Chronology of Summit Visits, Trips, and Meetings.* Dobbs Ferry, NY: Oceana, 1986.

———. "Summit Diplomacy: Diplomat in Chief." In Plischke, *Modern Diplomacy* (1979), pp. 169–187.

———. *Summit Diplomacy: Personal Diplomacy of the U.S. Presidents.* New York: Greenwood, 1974.

———. *U.S. Department of State: A Reference History.* Westport: Greenwood, 1999.

Princen, Thomas. *Intermediaries in International Conflict.* Princeton: Princeton University Press, 1992.

———. "Joseph Elder: Quiet Peacemaking in a Civil War." In Kolb et al., *When Talk Works* (1994), pp. 427–458.

———. "Mediation by a Transnational Organization: The Case of the Vatican." In Bercovitch and Rubin, *Mediation in International Relations* (1992), pp. 149–175.

Princen, Thomas, and Matthias Finger. *Environmental NGOs in World Politics: Linking the Local and the Global.* New York: Routledge, 1994.

Przetacznik, Fanciszek. "Diplomacy by Special Mission." *Revue de Droit International et de Sciences Diplomatiques et Politiques* (1981), pp. 109–176.

Putnam, R., and N. Bayne. *Hanging Together: Cooperation and Conflict in the Seven Power Summits.* 2d ed. London: Sage, 1988.

Queller, Donald E. *Early Venetian Legislation on Ambassadors.* Geneva: Librairie Droz, 1966.

———. "Medieval Diplomacy." In Jönsson and Langhorne, *Diplomacy* (2004), vol. 2, pp. 193–213.

———. *The Office of Ambassador in the Middle Ages.* Princeton: Princeton University Press, 1967.

Quinney, Nigel. *U.S. Negotiating Behavior.* Special Report no. 94. Washington, DC: US Institute of Peace, October 2002.

Ramcharan, B. G. *The International Law and Practice of Early Warning and Preventive Diplomacy: The Emerging Global Watch.* Dordrecht: Nijhoff, 1991.

Rana, Kishan S. *Inside Diplomacy.* 2d ed. New Delhi: Manas, 2002.

———. *The 21st Century Ambassador: Plenipotentiary to Chief Executive.* New York: Oxford University Press, 2005.

Rasmussen, J. Lewis. "Peacemaking in the Twenty-First Century: New Rules, New Roles, New Actors." In Zartman and Rasmussen, *Peacemaking in International Conflict* (1997), pp. 23–50.

Rees, Elfan. "Exercises in Private Diplomacy: Selected Activities of the Commission of the Churches on International Affairs." In Berman and Johnson, *Unofficial Diplomats* (1977), pp. 111–129.

Richard, Ivor. "The Council President as a Politician." In Nicol, *Paths to Peace* (1981), pp. 242–254.

Risse-Kappen, Thomas, ed. *Bringing Transnational Relations Back In: Non-State Actors, Domestic Structures, and International Institutions.* New York: Cambridge University Press, 1995.

Rittberger, Volker. "Global Conference Diplomacy and International Policy-Making: The Case of UN-Sponsored World Conferences." In Jönsson and Langhorne, *Diplomacy* (2004), vol. 1, pp. 378–395.

Rodman, Kenneth A. *Sanctions Beyond Borders: Multinational Corporations and U.S. Economic Statecraft.* Lanham, MD: Rowman and Littlefield, 2001.

Ronfeldt, David, and John Arquilla. *What If There Is a Revolution in Diplomatic Affairs?* Virtual Diplomacy Report. Washington, DC: US Institute of Peace, 1999.

Rosenau, James N. *The Study of Global Interdependence: Essays on the Transnationalisation of World Affairs.* New York: Nichols, 1980.

Rosenau, James N., and J. P. Singh, eds. *Information Technologies and Global Politics: The Changing Scope of Power and Governance.* Albany: State University of New York Press, 2002.

Ross, Dennis. *The Missing Peace: The Inside Story of the Fight for Middle East Peace.* New York: Farrar, Straus and Giroux, 2004.

————. *Statecraft: And How to Restore America's Standing in the World.* New York: Farrar, Straus and Giroux, 2007.

Rotberg, Robert I. "Conclusions: NGOs, Early Warning, Early Action, and Preventive Diplomacy." In Rotberg, *Vigilance and Vengeance* (1996), pp. 263–268.

————, ed. *Vigilance and Vengeance: NGOs Preventing Ethnic Conflict in Divided Societies.* Washington, DC: Brookings Institution, 1996.

Rouhana, Nadim N. "Unofficial Intervention: Potential Contributions to Resolving Ethno-National Conflicts." In Melissen, *Innovation in Diplomatic Practice* (1999), pp. 111–132.

Rubin, Jeffrey Z., ed. *Dynamics of Third Party Intervention: Kissinger in the Middle East.* New York: Praeger, 1981.

Sabel, Robbie. *Procedure at International Conferences: A Study of the Rules of Procedure at the UN and at Inter-Governmental Conferences.* New York: Cambridge University Press, 2006.

Saunders, Harold H. *Politics Is About Relationships: A Blueprint for the Citizens' Century.* New York: Palgrave Macmillan, 2005.

Schaetzel, J. Robert. "Modernizing the Role of the Ambassador." In Plischke, *Modern Diplomacy* (1979), pp. 262–276.

Schlesinger, Stephen C. *Act of Creation: The Founding of the United Nations—A Story of Superpowers, Secret Agents, Wartime Allies and Enemies, and Their Quest for a Peaceful World.* Boulder: Westview, 2003.

Scholte, Jan Aart. *Globalization: A Critical Introduction.* New York: St. Martin's, 2000.

Schulzinger, Robert D. *American Diplomacy in the Twentieth Century.* New York: Oxford University Press, 1984.

Scott, James M., and Elizabeth A. Rexford. "Finding a Place for Women in the World of Diplomacy: Evidence of Progress Toward Gender Equity and Speculation on Policy Outcomes." *Review of Public Personnel Administration* 17 (Spring 1997), pp. 31–56.

Scott, Matthew J. O. "Danger—Landmines! NGO-Governmental Collaboration in the Ottawa Process." In Edwards and Gaventa, *Global Citizen Action* (2001), pp. 121–133.

Scott, Noel. "The South African Campaign." In Cameron et al., *To Walk Without Fear* (1998), pp. 68–79.

Sebenius, James K. *Negotiating the Law of the Sea.* Cambridge: Harvard University Press, 1984.

Sen, Biswanath. *A Diplomat's Handbook of International Law and Practice.* 3d ed. Dordrecht: Nijhoff, 1988.

Sharp, Paul. "Who Needs Diplomats? The Problem of Diplomatic Representation." In Jönsson and Langhorne, *Diplomacy* (2004), vol. 3, pp. 58–78.

Sheehan, Edward R. F. "How Kissinger Did It: Step by Step in the Middle East." In Rubin, *Dynamics of Third Party Intervention* (1981), pp. 44–91.

Shepard, Jonathan. "Information, Disinformation, and Delay in Byzantine Diplomacy." In Jönsson and Langhorne, *Diplomacy* (2004), vol. 2, pp. 130–174.

Simmons, P. J. "Learning to Live with NGOs." *Foreign Policy* no. 112 (Fall 1998), pp. 82–96.

Simmons, P. J., and Chantal de Jonge Oudraat, eds. *Managing Global Issues: Lessons Learned.* Washington, DC: Carnegie Endowment for International Peace, 2001.

Simpson, Smith. "The Consular Contribution to Diplomacy." In Herz, *The Consular Dimension of Diplomacy* (1983), pp. 14–19.

Sinnar, S. "Mixed Blessing: The Growing Influence of NGOs." *Harvard International Review* 18 (1995–1996), pp. 54–57.

Sisk, Timothy D., ed. *New Approaches to International Negotiation and Mediation: Findings from U.S. Institute of Peace–Sponsored Research.* Washington, DC: US Institute of Peace, 1999.

Slim, Rando M. "Small-State Mediation in International Relations: The Algerian Mediation of the Iranian Hostage Crisis." In Bercovitch and Rubin, *Mediation in International Relations* (1992), pp. 206–231.

Smith, Courtney B. *Politics and Process at the UN: The Global Dance.* Boulder: Lynne Rienner, 2006.

Smith, Gaddis. *American Diplomacy During the Second World War, 1941–1945.* 2d ed. New York: Knopf, 1985.

Smith, Gerard C. *Disarming Diplomat: The Memoirs of Gerard C. Smith, Arms Control Negotiator.* New York: Madison, 1996.

———. "Non-Professional Diplomats: Do We Need Them?" In Herz, *The Modern Ambassador* (1983), pp. 168–170.

Smith, Gordon S. *Reinventing Diplomacy: A Virtual Necessity.* Washington, DC: US Institute of Peace, 1999.

Smith, Jackie, Charles Chatfield, and Ron Pagnucco, eds. *Transnational Social Movements and Global Politics: Solidarity Beyond the State.* Syracuse, NY: Syracuse University Press, 1997.

Smith, Jackie, and Hank Johnston, eds. *Globalization and Resistance: Transnational Dimensions of Social Movements.* Lanham, MD: Rowman and Littlefield, 2002.

Smith, Mark. "'Oh Don't Deceive Me': The Nassau Summit." In Dunn, *Diplomacy at the Highest Level* (1996), pp. 182–199.

Smock, David, ed. *Private Peacemaking: USIP-Assisted Peacemaking Projects of Nonprofit Organizations.* Washington, DC: US Institute of Peace, 1998.

Smyser, W. R. *How Germans Negotiate: Logical Goals, Practical Solutions.* Washington, DC: US Institute of Peace, 2003.

Smythe, Elizabeth. "State Authority and Investment Security: Non-State Actors and the Negotiation of the Multilateral Agreement on Investment at the OECD." In Higgott et al., *Non-State Actors and Authority in the Global System* (2000), pp. 74–90.

Snyder, Scott. *Negotiating on the Edge: North Korean Negotiating Behavior.* Washington, DC: US Institute of Peace, 1999.

Sofer, Sasson. "Old and New Diplomacy: A Debate Revisited." In Jönsson and Langhorne, *Diplomacy* (2004), vol. 2, pp. 395–414.

Solomon, Richard, and Sheryl J. Brown. *Creating a Common Communication Culture: Interoperability in Crisis Management.* Virtual Diplomacy Report no. 17. Washington, DC: US Institute of Peace, 2004.

Spector, Bertram, Gunnar Sjöstedt, and I. William Zartman, eds. *Negotiating International Regimes: Lessons Learned from the United Nations Conference on Environment and Development (UNCED).* London: Graham and Trotman, 1994.

Spiro, P. J. "New Global Communities: Nongovernmental Organizations in International Decision-Making Institutions." *Washington Quarterly* 18 (1995), pp. 45–56.

Stanford, Karin L. *Beyond the Boundaries: Rev. Jesse Jackson in International Affairs.* Albany: State University of New York Press, 1997.

Starr, Harvey. *Anarchy, Order, and Integration: How to Manage Interdependence.* Ann Arbor: University of Michigan Press, 1997.

Stearns, Monteagle. *Talking to Strangers: Improving American Diplomacy at Home and Abroad.* Princeton: Princeton University Press, 1996.

Strange, Susan. "States, Firms and Diplomacy." In Jönsson and Langhorne, *Diplomacy* (2004), vol. 1, pp. 352–366.

Strobel, Warren P. "The Media and U.S. Policies Towards Intervention: A Closer Look at the 'CNN Effect.'" In Crocker, Hampson, and Aall, *Managing Global Chaos* (1996), pp. 357–376.

Sullivan, Earl. "Multilateral Diplomacy in the Post–Cold War World." In Muldoon et al., *Multilateral Diplomacy and the United Nations Today* (1999), pp. 202–209.

Susskind, Lawrence E. *Environmental Diplomacy: Negotiating More Effective Global Agreements.* New York: Oxford University Press, 1994.

Susskind, Lawrence E., and Eileen Babbitt. "Overcoming the Obstacles to Effective Mediation in International Disputes." In Bercovitch and Rubin, *Mediation in International Relations* (1992), pp. 30–51.

Sutterlin, James S. *The United Nations and the Maintenance of International Security: A Challenge to Be Met.* Westport: Praeger, 2003.

Swayne, Kingdon B. "Reporting Function." In Plischke, *Modern Diplomacy* (1979), pp. 350–363.

Talbott, Strobe. *"Globalization and Diplomacy: A Practitioner's Perspective."* In Jönsson and Langhorne, *Diplomacy* (2004), vol. 3, pp. 362–374.

Tandon, R. *NGO-Government Relations: A Source of Life or the Kiss of Death?* New Delhi: Society for Participatory Research in Asia, 1989.

Tarlock, Dan. "The Role of Non-Governmental Organizations in the Development of International Environmental Law." In *International Environmental Law and World Order,* edited by Lakshman D. Guruswamy, Burns H. Weston, Geoffrey W. R. Palmer, and Jonathan C. Carlson. St. Paul, MN: West Group, 1999, pp. 1195–1200.

Taylor, Jeremy. "Private-Sector Diplomats in the Global Economy." In Muldoon et al., *Multilateral Diplomacy and the United Nations Today* (1999), pp. 102–110.

Telhami, Shibley. *The Camp David Accords: A Case of International Bargaining.* Pittsburgh: Pew Charitable Trust, 1992.

Thompson, Leigh. *The Mind and Heart of the Negotiator.* 2d ed. Upper Saddle River, NJ: Prentice-Hall, 2001.

Ting-Toomey, Stella, and John G. Oetzel. *Managing Intercultural Conflict Effectively.* Thousand Oaks, CA: Sage, 2001.

Tomlin, Brian W. "On a Fast Track to a Ban: The Canadian Policy Process." In Cameron et al., *To Walk Without Fear* (1998), pp. 185–211.

Toon, Malcolm. "In Defense of the Foreign Service." In Herz, *The Modern Ambassador* (1983), pp. 154–162.

Touval, Saadia. "Multilateral Negotiation: An Analytical Approach." *Negotiation Journal* 5 (1989), pp. 159–173.

———. "The Superpowers as Mediators." In Bercovitch and Rubin, *Mediation in International Relations* (1992), pp. 232–248.

Touval, Saadia, and I. William Zartman, eds. *International Mediation in Theory and Practice.* Boulder: Westview, 1985.

Tussie, Diana, ed. *Civil Society and Multilateral Development Banks: Global Governance* (special issue) 6 (October–December 2000), pp. 399–517.

Tussie, Diana, and Maria Fernánda Tuozzo. "Opportunities and Constraints for Civil Society Participation in Multilateral Lending Operations: Lessons from Latin America." In Edwards and Gaventa, *Global Citizen Action* (2001), pp. 105–117.

U Thant. *View from the UN.* Garden City, NY: Doubleday, 1978.

United Nations. *The Blue Helmets: A Review of UN Peace-Keeping.* 2d ed. New York: UN Department of Public Information, 1990.

Urquhart, Brian E. *Hammarskjold.* New York: Norton, 1972.

———. *A Life in Peace and War.* New York: Harper and Row, 1987.

———. *Ralph Bunche: An American Life.* New York: Norton, 1993.

———. "A UN Perspective." In Bloomfield et al., *International Military Forces* (1964), pp. 126–144.

US Advisory Commission on Public Diplomacy. *Report.* Washington, DC: US Information Agency, 1986.

US Department of Justice. *The International Criminal Police Organization (INTERPOL): US National Central Bureau, Washington, DC—Point of Contact for International Law Enforcement.* Washington, DC, 2002.

Vagts, Alfred. *The Military Attaché.* Princeton: Princeton University Press, 1967.

Walentynowicz, Leonard F. "Needed: More Imagination and Flexibility." In Herz, *The Consular Dimension of Diplomacy* (1983), pp. 20–22.

Walker, Ronald A. *Multilateral Conferences: Purposeful International Negotiation.* New York: Palgrave Macmillan, 2004.

Warkentin, Craig, and Karen Mingst. "International Institutions, the State, and Global Civil Society in the Age of the World Wide Web." *Global Governance* 6, no. 2 (April–June 2000), pp. 237–257.

Warmington, Valerie, and Celina Tuttle. "The Canadian Campaign." In Cameron et al., *To Walk Without Fear* (1998), pp. 48–59.

Warner, Gale, and Michael Shuman. *Citizen Diplomats: Pathfinders in Soviet-American Relations and How You Can Join Them.* New York: Continuum, 1987.

Waterman, P. *Globalization, Social Movements, and the New Internationalism.* London: Mansell, 1998.

Waters, Maurice. *The Ad Hoc Diplomat: A Study in Municipal and International Law.* The Hague: Nijhoff, 1963.

Watson, Adam. *Diplomacy: The Dialogue Between States.* New York: Routledge, 2004.

———. *The Evolution of International Society.* New York: Routledge, 1992.

Wedge, Bryant. "Mediating Intergroup Conflict in the Dominican Republic." In McDonald and Bendahmane, *Conflict Resolution* (1987), pp. 35–52.

Weihmiller, Gordon R., and Dusko Doder. *U.S.-Soviet Summits: An Account of East-West Diplomacy at the Top, 1955–1985.* Lanham, MD: University Press of America, 1986.

Weimann, Gabriel. *Cyberterrorism: How Real Is the Threat?* Special Report no. 119. Washington, DC: US Institute of Peace, 2004.

———. *http://www.terror.net: How Modern Terrorism Uses the Internet.* Special Report no. 116. Washington, DC: US Institute of Peace, 2004.

Weinfeld, Moshe. "The Common Heritage of Covenantal Traditions in the Ancient World." In *I Trattati nel Mondo Antico: Forma, Ideologia, Funzione,* edited by Luciano Canfora, Mario Liverani, and Carlo Zaccagnini. Rome: L'Erma di Bretschneider, 1990, pp. 175–191.

———. "Covenant Making in Anatolia and Mesopotamia." *Journal of the Ancient Near Eastern Society of Columbia University* 22 (1993), pp. 135–139.

———. "Covenant Terminology in the Ancient Near East and Its Influence on the West." *Journal of the American Oriental Society* 93 (1973), pp. 190–199.

Weisglas, Frans W., and Gonnie de Boer. "Parliamentary Diplomacy." *The Hague Journal of Diplomacy* 2, no. 1 (April 2007), pp. 93–99.

Weiss, Thomas G., and Jarat Chopra. *United Nations Peacekeeping.* New York: Academic Council on the United Nations System, 1992.

Weiss, Thomas G., David P. Forsythe, and Roger A. Coates. *The UN and Changing World Politics.* 2d ed. Boulder: Westview, 1997.

Weiss, Thomas G., and Leon Gordenker, eds. *NGOs, the UN, and Global Governance.* Boulder: Lynne Rienner, 1996.

Werts, Jan. *The European Council.* Amsterdam: North Holland, 1992.

Whitehouse, Charles S. "Running an Embassy." In Herz, *The Modern Ambassador* (1983), pp. 46–49.

Wilkowski, Jean M. *Conference Diplomacy II: A Case Study—The UN Conference on Science and Technology for Development, Vienna, 1979.* Washington, DC: Institute for the Study of Diplomacy, School of Foreign Service, Georgetown University, 1982.

Willetts, Peter. "From 'Consultative Arrangements' to 'Partnership': The Changing Status of NGOs in Diplomacy at the UN." *Global Governance* 6, no. 2 (April–June 2000), pp. 191–212.

———, ed. *Pressure Groups in the Global System: The Transnational Relations of Issue-Oriented Non-Governmental Organizations.* New York: St. Martin's, 1982.

Williams, Jody, and Stephen Goose. "The International Campaign to Ban Landmines." In Cameron et al., *To Walk Without Fear* (1998), pp. 20–47.

Williams, Marc. "The World Bank, the World Trade Organization, and the Environmental Social Movement." In Higgott et al., *Non-State Actors and Authority in the Global System* (2000), pp. 244ff.

Williams, Phil. "Crime, Illicit Markets, and Money Laundering." In Simmons and de Jonge Oudraat, *Managing Global Issues* (2001), pp. 106–150.

———. "Emerging Issues: Transnational Crime and International Control." In *Global Report on Crime and Justice,* edited by Graeme Newman. New York: Oxford University Press, 1999, pp. 221–242.

Wiseman, Geoffrey. "Pax Americana: Bumping into Diplomatic Culture." *International Studies Perspectives* 6, no. 4 (November 2005), pp. 409–430.

———. "'Polylateralism' and New Modes of Global Dialogue." In Jönsson and Langhorne, *Diplomacy* (2004), vol. 3, pp. 36–57.

Wittkopf, Eugene R., and Christopher M. Jones, eds. *The Future of American Foreign Policy.* 3d ed. New York: St. Martin's, 1999.

Wittkopf, Eugene R., Charles W. Kegley Jr., and James M. Scott. *American Foreign Policy: Pattern and Process.* 6th ed. Belmont, CA: Wadsworth, 2003.

Wolf, Victor, Jr. "How to Get the Best from Constituent Posts." In Herz, *The Consular Dimension of Diplomacy* (1983), pp. 69–71.

Wood, David M., and Birol A. Yeşilada. *The Emerging European Union.* 3d ed. New York: Pearson, 2004.

Wood, John R., and Jean Serres. *Diplomatic Ceremonial and Protocol: Principles, Procedures, and Practices.* London: Macmillan, 1970.

World Bank. *The Bank's Relationship with NGOs.* Washington, DC, 1998.

———. *Involving Non-Governmental Organizations in Bank Supported Activities.* Washington, DC, 1998.

———, Social Development Staff. *World Bank–Civil Society Collaboration: Progress Report for Fiscal Years 2000 and 2001.* Washington, DC, 2002.

World Health Organization. *Collaboration Within the United Nations System and with Other Intergovernmental Organizations.* Fifty-Fourth World Health Assembly, A54/32, April 18, 2001, and A54/32 add. 1. Geneva.

———. *Use of Languages in WHO.* A54/INF.DOC/2, April 2001. Geneva.

Wriston, Henry Merritt. *Executive Agents in American Foreign Relations.* Gloucester, MA: Peter Smith, 1967.

————. "Ministerial Diplomacy: Secretary of State Abroad." In Plischke, *Modern Diplomacy* (1979), pp. 153–168.

————. "The Special Envoy." *Foreign Affairs* 38, no. 2 (January 1960), pp. 219–237.

Wriston, Walter B. "Bits, Bytes, and Diplomacy." *Foreign Affairs* 76, no. 5 (September–October 1997), pp. 172–182.

Yarrow, C. H. "Mike." "Quaker Efforts Toward Reconciliation in the India-Pakistan War of 1965." In Berman and Johnson, *Unofficial Diplomats* (1977), pp. 89–110.

Zaharna, R. S. "The Soft Power Differential: Network Communication and Mass Communication in Public Diplomacy." *The Hague Journal of Diplomacy* 2, no. 3 (October 2007), pp. 213–228.

Zartman, I. William, ed. *Elusive Peace: Negotiating an End to Civil Wars.* Washington, DC: Brookings Institution, 1995.

Zartman, I. William, and Maureen R. Berman. *The Practical Negotiator.* New Haven: Yale University Press, 1982.

Zartman, I. William, and J. Lewis Rasmussen, eds. *Peacemaking in International Conflict: Methods and Techniques.* Washington, DC: US Institute of Peace, 1997.

Zartman, I. William, and Saadia Touval. "International Mediation in the Post–Cold War Era." In Crocker, Hampson, and Aall, *Managing Global Chaos* (1996), pp. 445–461.

Ziring, Lawrence, Robert Riggs, and Jack Plano. *The United Nations: International Organization and World Politics.* 4th ed. Belmont, CA: Wadsworth, 2005.

Zonova, Tatiana V. "Diplomatic Cultures: Comparing Russia and the West in Terms of a 'Modern Model of Diplomacy.'" *The Hague Journal of Diplomacy* 2, no. 1 (April 2007), pp. 1–23.

Index

About the Book

This comprehensive new text offers a fresh, up-to-date look at the evolution, politics, and practice of diplomacy. How much of traditional diplomacy remains relevant today? How is the conduct of foreign relations changing?

Leguey-Feilleux first provides a solid grounding in the history of traditional diplomacy, beginning with ancient times. He then reviews the forces of contemporary change—the dramatic developments in both international politics and the realm of technology that have affected the practice of diplomacy—and explores the full range of diplomatic modes.

Designed to be both authoritative and engaging, and with abundant in-depth case studies, *The Dynamics of Diplomacy* provides readers with a thorough understanding of all that contemporary diplomacy entails.

Jean-Robert Leguey-Feilleux is professor of political science at St. Louis University. He has published widely in the field of international affairs.